GW00870887

OXFORD JUNIOR ENCYCLOPAEDIA

INDUSTRY AND COMMERCE

OXFORD JUNIOR ENCYCLOPAEDIA

GENERAL EDITORS

LAURA E. SALT AND ROBERT SINCLAIR

ILLUSTRATIONS EDITOR: HELEN MARY PETTER

VOLUME VII

INDUSTRY AND COMMERCE

OXFORD UNIVERSITY PRESS

Oxford University Press, Ely House, London W. 1

GLASGOW NEW YORK TORONTO MELBOURNE WELLINGTON
CAPE TOWN SALISBURY IBADAN NAIROBI DAR ES SALAAM LUSAKA ADDIS ABABA
BOMBAY CALCUTTA MADRAS KARACHI LAHORE DACCA
KUALA LUMPUR SINGAPORE HONG KONG TOKYO

FIRST PUBLISHED 1951
REPRINTED WITH CORRECTIONS 1955, 1957
1964 REVISED AND RESET
REPRINTED WITH CORRECTIONS 1970

PHOTOSET AND PRINTED BY BAS PRINTERS LIMITED
WALLOP, HAMPSHIRE

PREFACE

IN authorizing the preparation of this work the Delegates of the Oxford University Press had foremost in mind the need to provide a basic book of reference for school libraries. In form it was to be a genuine encyclopaedia, in treatment and vocabulary suitable for the young reader. To many children (and indeed to many adults) reading is not a natural activity: they do not turn to books for their own sake. But they can be trained to go to books for information which they want for some particular purpose—and thus, very often, to form a habit which will be of lifelong value. Their capacity to read continuously for any length of time being limited, they can absorb knowledge better if they get it in small quantities: therefore they will often read reference books when they may reject the reading of more extended matter. Again, it is probably true to say of such readers that their approach is from the particular to the general, and from the application to the principle, rather than the reverse, that their main interest is in the modern world around them, and that since they are not very good at conceiving things outside their own experience, their capacity for grasping abstract ideas is limited. On the other hand, once their interest is aroused, they will often pursue a subject to remarkable lengths, so long as its development is logical and the treatment avoids dullness.

But such generalizations can easily be overdone: many children using the books will not be of this type. Moreover, it was evident from the first that a project involving so great an amount of work, however exactly it might meet its principal mark, would be fully justified only if it could be of service to a far wider circle of readers. Even for the age-group first in mind, anything like 'writing down to children' must plainly be taboo—but clear exposition and simple language are no bad qualities in writing for any audience. Here, then, it seemed, was the opportunity to provide a work of reference suitable for many readers to whom the large, standard encyclopaedias are too heavy and technical, and the popular alternatives for the most part neither sufficiently complete nor authoritative. The fact that the plan allowed for an exceptionally large proportion of illustrations to text (between one-quarter and one-third of the total space) is an advantage to any reader, since pictures may, in many instances, save whole paragraphs of involved explanation. With these secondary aims well in mind, therefore, the General Editors have ventured to hope that the encyclopaedia may find usefulness not only among certain younger children, but also among older students in clubs, libraries, and young people's colleges, and even to no small extent among their parents and other adults who may wish for a simple approach to some unfamiliar or forgotten subject.

SCOPE AND EMPHASIS. Within certain limits the OXFORD JUNIOR ENCYCLOPAEDIA purports to be reasonably comprehensive, though (in common with all general encyclopaedias) not exhaustive. Chief among these limits is that matter already easily available in school text-books is included only so far as its presence is necessary for the proper understanding of the subject under discussion. Thus, although an immense field of history is surveyed, it will be found mainly under headings dealing with its effects, or in the biographies of those who lived to make it. Purely technical or scientific subjects, also, are omitted except when they have some general interest. In natural history and kindred studies the immense variety of forms necessarily led at times either to their treatment by groups or to their omission on purely arbitrary decisions as to which species would, in all probability, never be looked for, or because there was nothing particularly interesting to say of them. In point of general balance the stress is laid rather on the modern world, though due space is given to the factors which have shaped it, no less than to those which are changing it.

ARRANGEMENT. The encyclopaedia consists of twelve volumes and an index. Each of the twelve main volumes is arranged alphabetically, and each deals with a particular range of related subjects (*see* PLAN OF VOLUMES, p. xii). Within its terms of reference, then, each volume is self-contained, and, owing to the great number of single-line cross-references, can well be used alone. The index covers all entries in the encyclopaedia. This arrangement, which has the incidental advantage of making the encyclopaedia easier to revise, arose mainly from one consideration. If articles were to be kept really short—and, in fact, few approach and almost none exceeds 2,000 words—many subjects could be dealt with comprehensively only by referring the reader to other relevant articles—itself a desirable thing to do. It was clearly preferable for these to be under his hand, rather than be dispersed through any of the twelve volumes at the caprice of the alphabet. This the present arrangement achieves to a great extent. If it has led to a small amount of overlapping, that again is not without its advantages.

The cross-references play an indispensable part in the make-up of the encyclopaedia. They are of two kinds: references in the text to further articles amplifying the particular point under review, and references at the end of an article to others taking the whole subject farther. Therefore, a reader looking up any wide subject, such as MONEY, and following up its cross-references either in the text or at the end of the article, can discover under what main headwords the subject is treated. These, again, will refer him to any subsidiary articles, as also, in many cases, to those of a complementary nature. Thus he may be guided either from the general to the particular or vice versa. It is believed that the titles of the twelve volumes (see

p. xii), in conjunction with their sub-titles, will usually lead the reader straight to the volume containing the information he wants. In selecting headwords, the rules generally followed have been to prefer the familiar, or even the colloquial, reserving the technical alternative for a single-line entry, and to group narrow subjects under a headword of wider scope. Thus, for ACCOUNTANCY, *see* BOOK-KEEPING, for PIECE WORK, *see* WAGES; for CHEQUE, *see* BANKING; and for JOURNEYMAN, *see* CRAFT GUILDS.

L. E. S., R. S.

Oxford, 1951

LIST OF CONTRIBUTORS

VOLUME EDITOR

H. V. R. Geary, M.C.

CONTRIBUTORS

Leslie Aitchison, D.Met., M.Sc., F.R.I.C., F.R.Ae.S., M.I.Mech.E., F.I.M., formerly Professor of Industrial Metallurgy in the University of Birmingham.

B. Alwyn Jay, Director, Timber Development Association, Ltd.

Reginald O. Baker, Editor, *The Caterer and Hotel Keeper.*

T. R. Barnard.

Dora Billington, A.R.C.A. President, The Arts and Crafts Exhibition Society.

G. M. Boumphrey.

Stanley W. Bowler, F.R.P.S., F.R.S.A., F.P.S.

T. G. W. Boxall, O.B.E., Chief Technical Officer, London Brick Company, Ltd.

David Boyce.

Asa Briggs, M.A., B.Sc. (Econ.), Fellow of Worcester College, Oxford.

Martin S. Briggs, F.R.I.B.A.

Peter Bryan.

L. J. Burke, Anglo American Corporation of South Africa, Ltd.

E. A. Carpenter, B.A., Lecturer at the City of London College.

J. C. Chaston, Ph.D., A.R.S.M., A.Inst.P., F.I.M.

Ernest J. Clyne.

Sydney M. Cockerell.

G. D. H. Cole, M.A., Professor of Social and Political Theory, Oxford.

J. G. Cook, Ph.D.

J. G. Davis, D.Sc., Ph.D. (Lond.), F.R.I.C.

D. M. Desoutter.

G. Dilley, Ph.C.

P. J. Flitton, B.Com., Economic Adviser to the National Federation of Building Trades Employers.

Helmut and Alison Gernsheim.

R. H. Glossop, F.I.M.Wood.T., Principal Lecturer in Work Study and Management, High Wycombe College of Further Education.

A. Grierson, M.Sc. (Eng.), D.I.C., C.Eng., F.I.Min.E., M.I.M.M., Senior Lecturer in Mining.

Reginald Haggar, A.R.C.A.(Lond.), R.I.

F. M. S. Harmar-Brown, M.A.

C. H. Hartwell, Trades Union Congress Press Publications Officer.

Stuart H. Hastie, O.B.E., M.C., B.Sc., F.R.I.C.

M. T. C. Hastings, M.A.

R. W. Hayman, F.Z.S.

C. H. Hayward.

Leslie Herman.

Frank Hill, Wool (and Allied) Textile Employers' Council.

G. Horner, A.R.I.C., M.Sc.

S. A. Horwood, M.B.E.

Gordon Hughes

Allen Hutt, M.A. (Cantab.), Editor, *The Journalist.*

A. S. Irvine, M.A. (Oxon.).

T. M. Jones.

C. Kisby, A.R.C.A., A.T.I.

J. Korn, F.B.S.I., A.M.I.I.A., Principal, The Cordwainers Technical College.

N. H. Leyland, Director, Oxford Centre for Management Studies.

J. S. Lindsay, F.S.A.

Gordon Logie, A.R.I.B.A., A.M.T.P.I., A.A.Dip.

John Lowe, Assistant Keeper, Department of Ceramics, Victoria and Albert Museum.

S. R. W. Martin, Ph.D., A.R.C.S., F.R.I.C., D.I.C.

C. G. McAuliffe, B.A.

G. M. McLean.

Roger Manvell, B.A., Ph.D., formerly Director of the British Film Academy.

R. H. Marriott, D.Sc., F.R.I.C.

E. C. J. Marsh, B.Sc. (Lond.), F.R.I.C., F.I.M.

T. E. Metcalfe, M.B.E.

J. H. Bernard Moore, B.Com., Lecturer in Commerce at the City of London College.

J. M. Myers, Librarian, Rowntree and Company, Ltd.

R. I. Payne, C.B.E.

Raymond Postgate.

D. Dylan Pritchard, M.A. (Wales).

J. M. Pullen.

A. B. Purbrick, A.I.C.S.

A. Hingston Quiggin.

H. Richardson, A.I.W.Sc., Timber Research and Development Association, Ltd.

Eirlys R. C. Roberts, B.A. (Cantab.), Editor and Research Director, *Which?*

R. A. Rosser, B.A., B.Sc., A.R.I.C.

P. M. Rowe, Press Officer, British Man-made Fibres Federation.

Ronald Sheppard, Editor, *Baker's Review.*

Margaret Simeon, A.R.C.A.

Wallace V. Smedley, F.R.S.A.

H. Smith, M.A., B.Litt., Vice-Principal of Ruskin College, Oxford.

Richard J. Smith, F.T.I.

Francis Spear, A.R.C.A.

Claude H. Spiers, M.A., Ph.D. (Cantab.).

S. P. E. Tilley, Dunlop Rubber Company, Ltd.

E. N. Tiratsoo, Ph.D., D.I.C., B.Sc., A.R.S.M., F.G.S., F.R.G.S., M.Inst.Pet.

W. Reay Tolfree, A.C.I.S., A.I.B., Member of the Royal Economic Society.

A.H. Vause, P.D. Leake Fellow, Oxford Centre for Management Studies.

A. L. Waddams, B.Sc., A.R.C.S., D.I.C., A.M.I.Chem.E., Commercial Development Manager, B.P. Chemicals (U.K.) Ltd.

P. A. Wells, M.A., M.Sc., F.Inst.P., formerly Director of Education to the International Wool Secretariat.

Gordon West.

T. D. Whittet, B.Sc., Ph.D. (Lond.), F.P.S., F.R.I.C., D.B.A., Group Chief Pharmacist and Lecturer in Pharmacy, University College Hospital and Medical School, London.

R. Windle, Fellow, Oxford Centre for Management Studies.

Assistant Editors—W. F. Jeffrey, Hester Burton

ACKNOWLEDGEMENTS

THE EDITORS wish to acknowledge the help given in the preparation of the text by T. K. Derry, D.Phil. (Oxon.), and by the late G. T. Hollis, Hon. M.A. (Oxon.), and in the selection of historical prints from the Constance Meade Collection by the late Dr. John Johnson, C.B.E. They also wish to thank all those who have freely contributed material for the text and have lent photographs. The illustrations of works in the British Museum, the National Gallery, the Victoria and Albert Museum, and the Wallace Collection are reproduced by permission of the Trustees of these institutions. The Hallmarks on p. 21 are reproduced by permission of the Executors of the late Frederick Bradbury, F.S.A., from his book *Guide to Marks of Origin on British and Irish Silver Plate and Old Sheffield Plate Makers' Marks*, published by J. W. Northend, Sheffield. Others who have given assistance include:

Achille Serre, Ltd.; Addis, Ltd.; Advertising Association; George Allen & Unwin, Ltd.; Association of Jute Spinners and Manufacturers; Bank of England; Batchelors Peas, Ltd.; Board of Trade; The Bowater Paper Corporation, Ltd.; The Brewers' Society; Lieut.-Colonel H. S. Bristowe; British Aluminium Company, Ltd.; British Egg Marketing Board; British Jute Trade Federal Council; British Man-made Fibres Federation; British Motor Corporation, Ltd.; British Ropes; British Travel Association; E. W. Bryan, Ltd.; Cadbury Brothers, Ltd.; The Cake and Biscuit Alliance; Cement and Concrete Association; Chartered Insurance Institute; Consumers' Association, Ltd.; The Cornish Mining Development Board; Cunard Steam-ship Company, Ltd.; De Beers Consolidated Mines, Ltd.; Department of Employment & Productivity; The Distillers' Company, Ltd.; The Dunlop Company, Ltd.; Dyers and Cleaners Research Organisation, Ltd.; Federation of British Carpet Manufacturers; Fibreglass Ltd.; Flour Advisory Bureau; The Gas Council; Goldsmiths' Company; Hawker Siddeley Group, Ltd.; Hudson's Bay Company; Imperial Chemical Industries; The Imperial Tobacco Company (of Great Britain and Ireland) Ltd.; Infab; The Institute of Quarrying; The International Nickel Company (Mond), Ltd.; The International Wool Secretariat; The Irish Linen Guild; The Linoleum Manufacturers' Association; Lloyds Bank, Ltd.; London & Cambridge Economic Service; London Chamber of Commerce; The Milk Marketing Board of England and Wales; The Mining Association of Great Britain; Ministry of Agriculture and Fisheries; Ministry of Technology; Montague Burton, Ltd.; National Coal Board; National Federation of Building Trades Employers; National Institute of Industrial Psychology; Petroleum Information Bureau; The Press Council; James Rennie; Joseph Rodgers & Sons, Ltd.; Rowntree & Company, Ltd.; Royal Exchange Assurance Co.; Royal Mint; Arthur Sanderson & Sons, Ltd.; The Scotch Whisky Association; The Shirley Institute; The Silk Centre; Smedley's Ltd.; Tate and Lyle, Ltd.; The Textile Council; Timber Research and Development Association, Ltd.; Sir Francis Towle, C.B.E.; Trades Union Congress; Unilever, Ltd.; Walpole Bros. (London), Ltd.; Whitbread & Co., Ltd.; W. D. & H. O. Wills; Wool, Jute, and Flax Industry Training Board.

COLOUR PLATES

PLAN OF VOLUMES

I. MANKIND
EVOLUTION
ANCIENT WORLD
RACES AND NATIONS
RELIGIONS
MYTHOLOGY
FOLK-LORE

II. NATURAL HISTORY
BEASTS
BIRDS
FISHES
REPTILES
INSECTS
PLANTS

III. THE UNIVERSE
PHYSICAL LAWS
ASTRONOMY
GEOLOGY
WEATHER
GEOGRAPHY
COUNTRIES AND TOWNS

IV. COMMUNICATIONS
LANGUAGE
WRITING
PRINTING
BROADCASTING
LAND TRAVEL
AIRCRAFT
SHIPS

V. GREAT LIVES
PHILOSOPHERS
ARTISTS
WRITERS
SCIENTISTS
REFORMERS
LAWGIVERS
EXPLORERS

VI. FARMING AND FISHERIES
HOME CROPS
TROPICAL CROPS
DOMESTIC ANIMALS
FORESTRY
HUNTING AND TRAPPING
FISHING
GARDENING

VII. INDUSTRY AND COMMERCE
MINING
MANUFACTURE
CRAFTS
MARKETING
MONEY
BUSINESS

VIII. ENGINEERING
POWER
MACHINERY
FUELS
MATERIALS
TOOLS
INSTRUMENTS
STRUCTURES

IX. RECREATIONS
THEATRE
CONCERT
DANCE
CLUBS AND SOCIETIES
FAIRS AND CIRCUSES
SPORTS AND GAMES
PETS

X. LAW AND SOCIETY
WORLD AFFAIRS
GOVERNMENT
JUSTICE
ARMED FORCES
PUBLIC SERVICES
LOCAL GOVERNMENT

XI. HOME AND HEALTH
HOUSES AND FURNITURE
HOUSEKEEPING
THE KITCHEN
THE NURSERY
CLOTHES
HEALTH

XII. THE ARTS
LITERATURE
DRAMA
MUSIC
PAINTING
SCULPTURE
ARCHITECTURE

INDEX AND READY REFERENCE VOLUME
Covering entries in all 12 volumes

HOW TO USE THIS BOOK

THIS VOLUME is one of twelve, each on a separate subject, the whole set forming what is called an encyclopaedia, or work from which you can find out almost anything you want to know. (The word comes originally from the Greek *enkuklios*, circular or complete, and *paideia*, education.) Each of the twelve volumes is arranged alphabetically within itself, as twelve dictionaries would be.

The difference between a dictionary and an encyclopaedia is that, while the first gives you no more than the meanings and derivations of words, the second tells you a very great deal more about their subjects. For instance, from a dictionary you could find that COPRA is the dried kernel of the coconut, from which coconut oil is obtained, and you would learn little more; but an encyclopaedia will tell you that the principal producing countries are Indonesia, the Philippine Islands, Malaya, and Ceylon; that it is an important ingredient in the manufacture of soap; that it is used for making margarine, salad oil, and cooking oils; and it will also tell you how the copra is separated from the nut and how it is dried. Then a dictionary contains nearly every word in the language; but an encyclopaedia deals only with words and subjects about which there is something interesting to be said, beyond their bare meanings. So you should not expect to find every word in an encyclopaedia—every subject is there, but not every word.

There are two ways in which you can find a subject in the OXFORD JUNIOR ENCYCLOPAEDIA. The first way is to study the Plan of Volumes on the opposite page, and then to decide in which volume the subject comes. The second way is to make use of the Index. Very often you will be able to tell from the title alone which volume contains the information you need; but if not, the list of sub-headings on the plan opposite will help to direct you. For example, if you want to read about people, the way they have lived at different times and places, and the things they have believed and worshipped, you would turn to Volume I. If, however, you want to find out about an animal or plant, you would look it up in Volume II, Natural History; but if you wanted to know how that animal or plant is used in something like farming, fishing, or trapping, you would find it in Volume VI. If your subject were something in nature that does not have life—such as the sun, or a particular country or river, or a kind of stone—you would find it in Volume III, with tides, earthquakes, the weather, and many other things. Matters connected with communication of any kind—of people, or goods, or even of ideas—are in Volume IV. So you would look there for languages and printing and broadcasting, as well as for ships and trains and roads. But if it is the engineering side of any of these things that interests you, Volume VIII, Engineering, is the place to look. Recreations are in Volume IX, which includes games and sports, entertainment, clubs, animal pets, and sporting animals. How we are governed and protected by the State, the law, and the armed forces is told in Volume X. Volume XI deals with almost everything connected with our homes, from the building and furnishing of the house to the clothes and health of those who live in it. The titles of Volumes V and XII, Great Lives and The Arts, explain themselves. A rather fuller account of the volume you are reading, on INDUSTRY AND COMMERCE, is given on page xv opposite. If you cannot find your subject readily by this means, then you must make use of the Index. An article on page xv of the Index Volume will tell you how to do this.

To find your subject in the volume, think of its ordinary name, and then look it up just as though you were using a dictionary—the As on the first page and the Zs (if there are any) on the last. If you cannot find it, try a more general word. For instance, if you want to read about Negatives, and cannot find them under that name (as you cannot), try either PHOTOGRAPHY, HISTORY OF or PROCESS REPRODUCTION—either of which will lead you to it. As you read any article, you will probably come across the titles of other articles in some way connected with what you are reading. You will know that they are titles of other articles because they will be printed in capital letters. Either they will be followed by (q.v.) in brackets (this is short for the Latin *quod vide*, and means 'which see'), or else they themselves will be in brackets, with the word *see* in front of them. You can look up these other articles at once if you want to know more about the particular point dealt with, or you can save them up until you have finished the article you are reading. At the end of any article you may find the words 'See also', followed by one or more titles in small capital letters. If you look these titles up, they will tell you still more about the subject that interests you. These last 'cross-references' are very useful if you want to look up a particularly wide subject (such as MINING or TRADE), because they show you at once the titles of all the main articles dealing with it. You can then decide for yourself which to read.

WHAT YOU WILL FIND IN THIS VOLUME

THIS VOLUME IS ABOUT THE WAY THINGS ARE MADE, AND THE ORGANIZATIONS WHICH ARE NECESSARY TO ENABLE MEN TO MAKE, TO SELL, AND TO BUY THE THINGS THEY USE

RAW MATERIALS. This volume tells how the minerals needed for manufactures are extracted from the earth. Metals and coal are obtained by MINING, stone by STONE-QUARRYING, and oil from OIL WELLS. Some raw materials have to be converted into other products before they can be used in industry. You will read how petrol and other substances are prepared from mineral oils by DISTILLATION, how chalk and clay are made into CEMENT and BRICKS AND TILES, and how use is made of BY-PRODUCTS from manufactures. The CHEMICAL INDUSTRY gets it raw materials from the air as well as the earth to make ACIDS and ALKALIS, and countless chemical substances which form the basis of many manufactures, such as PLASTICS.

MANUFACTURES. You will read how the great industries of the world, such as SHIPBUILDING and the BUILDING INDUSTRY, are organized. In many industries, such as POTTERY and GOLD AND SILVERWORK, the hand craftsman still does much of the work, while in the others, such as PRINTING, the machine has almost taken the place of the hand worker. Articles on the COTTON and WOOL INDUSTRIES explain how these materials are spun and woven into fabrics. Other articles describe how our food is made—how FLOUR-MILLING grinds the grain ready for BAKING, how SUGAR-REFINING extracts sugar from cane and beet, and how BREWING is done.

ORGANIZATION OF INDUSTRY. To make production run smoothly in modern industries, FACTORY ORGANIZATION is necessary. In the Middle Ages CRAFT GUILDS had governed masters and workmen, and controlled WAGES and APPRENTICESHIP. But since the INDUSTRIAL REVOLUTION things have changed. Businesses are controlled by LIMITED COMPANIES and PUBLIC UTILITY COMPANIES, while LABOUR is organized in TRADE UNIONS. Managers must follow the rules of BUSINESS ORGANIZATION, and must study the science of STATISTICS when calculating how best to act.

MARKETING. The history of TRADE is a long story, from the early barterings of primitive peoples, to the medieval organizations of the MERCHANT ADVENTURERS and the HANSEATIC LEAGUE, the later merchant explorers of the CHARTERED COMPANIES, and finally to the elaborate organizations of modern INTERNATIONAL TRADE. Manufacturers use the service of WHOLESALE TRADING and RETAIL TRADING to distribute their goods to the people who want them. They make know their goods by TRADE FAIRS and EXHIBITIONS and by all the many devices of ADVERTISING AND PUBLICITY; and they find out what the public want by various methods of MARKET RESEARCH.

MONEY. Trade cannot advance very far without a medium of exchange. Here you can read about the strange things used as PRIMITIVE MONEY to pay for goods, and how gradually our modern MONEY system has evolved, using not only COINS but other more convenient methods of PAYMENT. As trade developed, so did the business of BANKING, and the methods of financing trade by CAPITAL, subscribed in the form of STOCKS AND SHARES. Safeguards against misfortune in business are now provided by INSURANCE.

The words in capitals are the titles of some of the articles

A

ACCOUNTANCY, *see* Book-keeping.

ACCOUNTING, MACHINE. There are many objections to keeping the accounting records of a business in ordinary handwriting. Figures, from Invoices (q.v.) or other documents, may be copied into the books wrongly. Columns of figures may be wrongly totalled. Mistakes may be made in calculating the balances of the accounts: that is, the differences between their debit and credit sides (*see* Book-keeping). Handwritten records also require a large staff of clerks; this is wasteful as clerical labour is not directly productive.

The keeping of accounts by means of accounting machines gets over these objections; but the machines themselves are fairly expensive, and, like other machines, will not pay for themselves unless they are regularly used. Machine accounting, even by the simplest and cheapest machines, is therefore hardly possible for the very small firm; and the more expensive machines are used only by the very largest organizations, such as leading industries, public utility corporations, and important local authorities like the Greater London Council.

The earliest accounting machines were the adding machine and the cash register. The cash register, in its less elaborate forms, merely gives a duplicated list of individual sales and the total, although it can also be designed to give totals for different classes of sales. It is therefore not, in a strict sense, an accounting machine.

The adding machine was really the forerunner of the modern accounting machine. It has two forms. The first merely delivers a total of the items to be added up. The operator presses down the keys of the machine for each item, and then presses another key which causes the machine to show the total of the items. Some of these machines are small and compact enough to be used on the counters of retail stores, and they are generally useful whenever columns of figures have to be added up or checked. The other form of adding machine not only delivers a total but prints a list of all the items; this list is made on a continuous roll of narrow paper, which can be torn off as required. By using rolls of papers interleaved with carbon paper, duplicate and triplicate lists can be obtained. Most of these machines not only calculate and type a total, but also a series of sub-totals. They were first used in large numbers by the big London bankers, and the London Bankers' Clearing House, for listing and totalling immense numbers of cheques. Other firms soon discovered the value of these machines, and by the beginning of the present century they were in general use. The early machines were operated entirely by hand. About 60 years ago they were adapted for electrical power, and their working speed was greatly increased. But whether hand or electric machines were used, the keys of the machine had to be depressed by the hand of the operator for each separate item. As in all machines, a human limit was thus set to the speed at which these adding machines could be made to work.

The adding machine has rather limited uses for accounting purposes, as book-keeping involves not only addition but also subtraction. Several machines are now in regular use which perform both these operations. The ledger-posting machine has a keyboard containing not only figures but also letters; it is really a combination of a simple Typewriter (q.v. Vol. IV) and an adding and subtracting machine. These machines do not, of course, write records on to the bound pages of an ordinary ledger; loose sheets, or thin cards, are used instead. As in the adding machine, the record can be typed and calculated in duplicate or triplicate. The duplicate record can be posted to the customer as his statement of account, and thus the clerical labour of making out a separate statement is avoided.

In the simpler forms of ledger-posting machine, the balance of the customer's account, brought forward from the previous month, has to be put in by the operator, who may possibly put in the wrong balance by mistake. A more complicated and rather expensive form of ledger-posting machine automatically memorizes, for each one of a series of accounts, the balance that was last calculated. Each customer's account is given a number, and, when the keyboard is set to this number, the last balance is automatically brought forward and typed in.

Many business calculations involve multiplication and division, as well as addition and subtraction. Machines have been invented for such calculations; they perform all the normal operations of arithmetic, but do not type out the separate figures of each calculation. They add, subtract, multiply, and divide, in numbers or in money, or in weights and measures; and their keyboards can be adapted for all kinds of money systems or systems of weights and measures, decimal or other. These machines can work out interest, discount, and percentages, and also foreign-exchange calculations.

A more elaborate type of machine uses what is generally known as the 'punched card system'. These machines are comparatively expensive, and would only be found profitable by the larger firms and corporations. It is usual for the manufacturers of the machines to supply them, and maintain them in efficiency and repair, for a fixed annual rental. There are two main forms of these machines now used in Britain; although one differs slightly from the other, the principle of each is the same. Small cards, about half the size of a postcard, are used, and holes are punched in them; the firm using the cards works out a standard code, by which a hole punched in a particular place means a particular letter, or figure, or sum of money. To avoid the mistakes that all human beings are liable to make, all holes are punched twice. The first operator will punch holes in a card from, say, a pay-sheet; they are then passed on to a second operator who repeats the process on a slightly different machine called a verifier. If the second operator depresses a key not corresponding to a hole in the card the machine will lock, thus detecting an error. As it is unlikely that two operators would make the same error, the possibility of mistakes is thus reduced to a minimum, and mistakes that do occur can be put right at an early stage. Once the cards have been punched, other machines can sort them out into any conceivable groupings or arrangements. Totals and calculations are done in another machine, called the tabulator. This

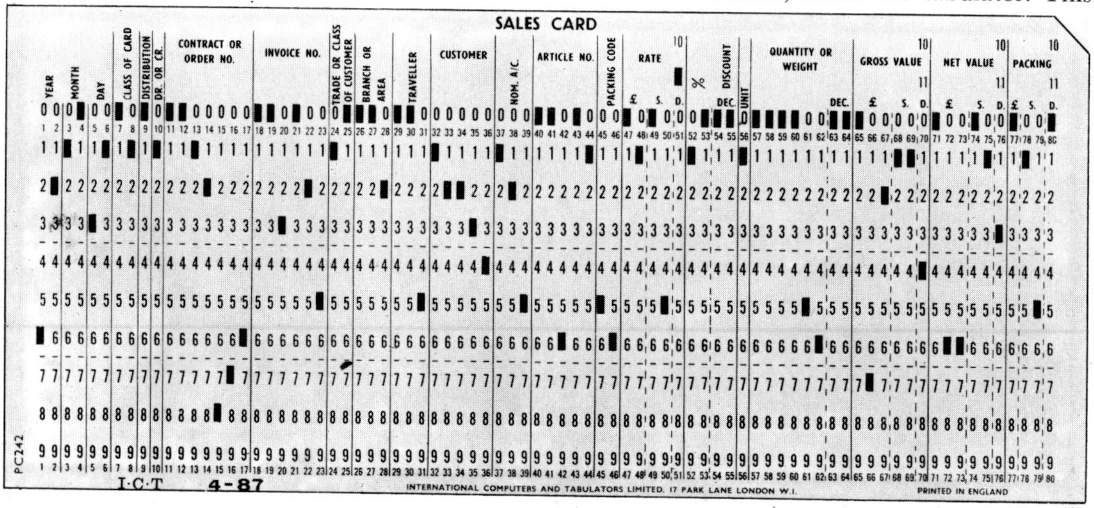

I.C.T.

AN 80-COLUMN SALES CARD PUNCHED WITH DETAILS OF A SALE

The information is recorded on the cards by means of the holes which are punched in the appropriate columns. From these sales cards are prepared the invoices for dispatch to customers, and a subsequent analysis of sales which may be required under a variety of headings

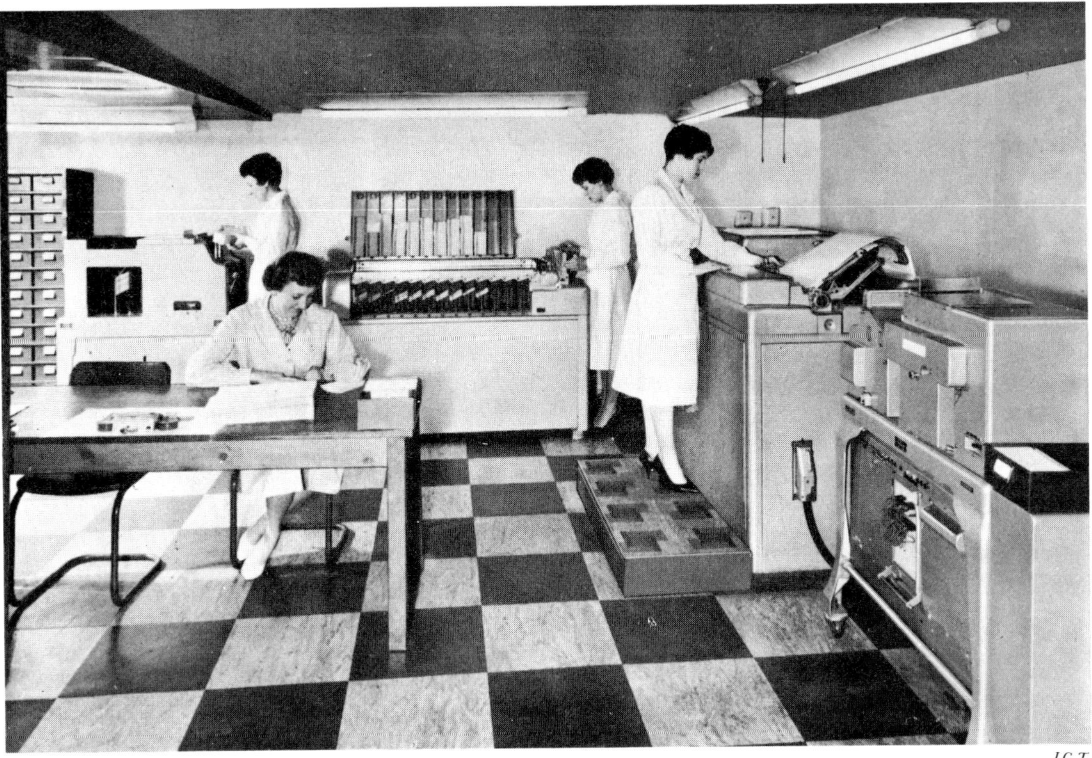

I.C.T.

A PUNCHED CARD SYSTEM INSTALLATION

At the back is the machine for sorting information, and the one on the right is the tabulator

reproduces, on a continuous roll of paper, all the details on the punched cards, translating the punched holes into typed letters and figures, and giving sub-totals and grand totals. Such tabulators are responsible for some of the electricity and gas accounts that are sent out to British householders.

The most elaborate of all CALCULATING MACHINES is the electronic COMPUTER (qq.v. Vol. VIII). Its main advantage is the great speed of its calculations, but its cost restricts its use to very large firms which can use their computers for analytical and statistical purposes as well as for accounting.

See also BOOK-KEEPING.
See also Vol. IV: COUNTING INSTRUMENTS.

ACETIC ACID, *see* ACIDS, Section 3.

ACIDS. 1. The word acid originally meant 'sour substance' and is derived from the Latin *acidus* meaning sour. Most acids have this sour property: for example, citric acid, responsible for the sourness of lemon juice, acetic acid—the principal constituent of vinegar, and lactic acid, which is found in sour milk. As our knowledge of CHEMISTRY (q.v.) progressed, it was discovered that acids had many other common properties in addition to sourness—in particular that they would all react chemically with ALKALIS (q.v.) to form compounds, known as salts, and water; and that, combined with water, they all contained hydrogen in a specially active form. To-day, it is this hydrogen activity that decides whether a compound is an acid, and how acid it is.

The best-known example of an acid reacting with an alkali to form a neutral salt and water is the combination of hydrochloric acid (HCl) and caustic soda (NaOH) to give sodium chloride or common salt (NaCl) and water (H_2O); and all acids can be 'neutralized' by alkalis in this way.

Acids containing carbon atoms are termed organic acids because most of them were originally derived from living organisms; the others are termed inorganic.

2. INORGANIC ACIDS. Sulphuric acid (oil of vitriol) was probably known to the ancients, but its first mention is generally ascribed to Geber, an Arab chemist about the 8th century A.D., who refers to the 'spirit' which can be expelled from ALUM (q.v.) and which possesses solvent powers. In early times small quantities were produced either by the distilling of ferrous sulphate (green vitriol) or by the burning of sulphur and saltpetre in moist vessels in the presence of air. Early in the 18th century an English quack doctor named Ward produced acid in Surrey by the second of these methods, using glass vessels which held 66 gallons. In 1846 Roebuck, of Birmingham, replaced the fragile glass vessels by lead chambers, and was soon supplying acid made in this way to linen bleachers in England and Scotland (*see* LINEN INDUSTRY). This early work laid the foundations of the modern sulphuric acid industry. The method at first used was a modification of this 'lead chamber' process; but now a method called the 'contact' process has almost entirely replaced it. The different stages of this process are demonstrated in the diagram below.

The first stage in the process is to produce sulphur dioxide gas by burning sulphur in air. The raw material used is normally naturally occurring sulphur, which comes principally from the U.S.A. or Mexico; or sulphur recovered from 'sour' (that is, sulphurous) natural gas; or the metal sulphide ore known as 'pyrites'.

The second stage is to oxidize the sulphur dioxide gas to convert it into sulphur trioxide gas. Sulphur dioxide and oxygen from the air are combined in the presence of the metallic element, vanadium, which acts as a catalyst (that is, it helps chemical reaction without itself being chemically altered). In the last stage the sulphur trioxide thus produced is absorbed in water and becomes sulphuric acid.

Sulphuric acid, first used in bleaching and tinning, is now used in enormous quantities for making ARTIFICIAL FERTILIZERS (q.v. Vol. VI). Other important uses are in the descaling or 'pickling' of metals in certain stages of production, and in the manufacture of explosives, dyes, drugs, metal sulphates, petroleum refining, and plating. Sulphuric acid has a very wide range of uses in many different industries.

Hydrochloric acid (muriatic acid) is a solution of hydrogen chloride gas in water. The gas is sometimes found in nature in the free state or dissolved in water—for example, in gases coming off volcanoes, in springs, and in some rivers. The Arabian alchemists were well acquainted with *aqua regia*, a mixture of hydrochloric acid and nitric acid; but pure aqueous hydrochloric *spiritus salis* (spirits of salt) is first heard of in the 15th century. Glauber, a German chemist, produced the acid in 1648 by the action of sulphuric acid on common salt. Since then there have been several improvements, but the production of hydrochloric acid from salt is still carried out on an industrial scale. Later, the method was developed of producing hydrogen chloride by burning hydrogen and chlorine together. Though the method is still

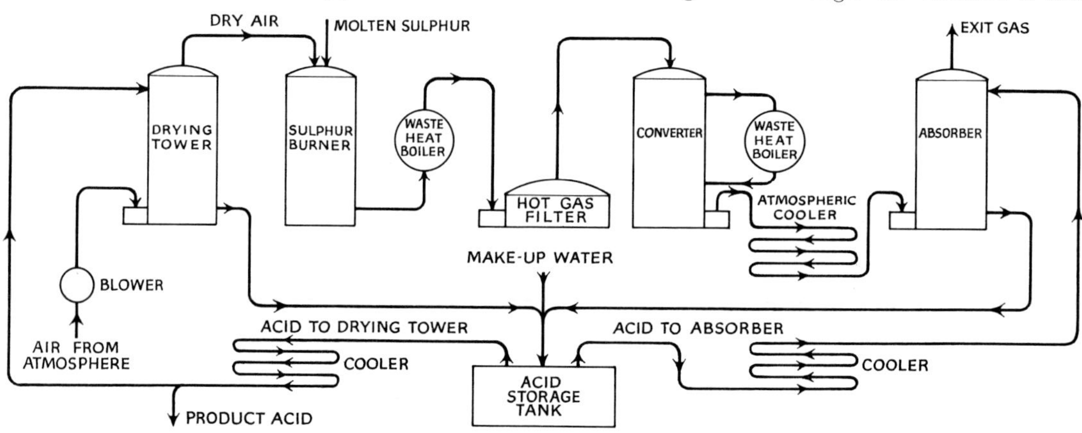

DIAGRAM OF THE CONTACT PROCESS FOR PRODUCING SULPHURIC ACID FROM SULPHUR

First stage: molten sulphur is burnt in the burner (top left) in the presence of air which has been made very dry by an acid treatment in the drying-tower. Second stage: the burning has produced sulphur dioxide gas, which is then filtered and passes to the converter; there it combines with air in contact with a catalyst (see article above) and becomes sulphur trioxide gas. Next, in the absorber (right), the gas is absorbed in water and becomes sulphuric acid. Spare heat is used to warm boilers

Imperial Chemical Industries Ltd.

THE SULPHURIC ACID PLANT AT SEVERNSIDE

The sulphuric acid is used for the production of fertilizer

used, the production pattern has greatly changed. Because a number of chlorination processes produce hydrogen chloride as a BY-PRODUCT (q.v.), what they provide is ample to meet most demands. Indeed, it is more than enough and therefore new processes are now operated: in one of these (catalytic oxidation), chlorine is recovered from hydrogen chloride; in the other (oxychlorination), a mixture of oxygen and hydrogen chloride is used instead of chlorine to effect chlorination. Hydrochloric acid has many uses in chemical manufacture: for example, in descaling metal, in textile processing, and in the production of glucose.

Nitric acid (*aqua fortis*) occurs in nature chiefly as the nitrates of potassium and sodium (Bengal saltpetre and Chile nitre) Some nitric acid is formed by electrical discharges in the atmosphere, and is washed down by rain. The ancient Egyptians are believed to have used nitric acid to dissolve silver. It was well known to the early alchemists, and in the 16th century it was used to part gold and silver (*see* CHEMISTRY, HISTORY OF). About 1658 Glauber prepared it by heating saltpetre with sulphuric acid. This process was used for many years, Chile nitre taking the place of saltpetre, and has only recently been abandoned. In 1785 Henry Cavendish showed that the acid could be produced by passing electric sparks through moist air, the oxygen and nitrogen of the air combining. More than 100 years later this method was adopted on a large scale in Norway, where air was passed through an electric arc furnace and absorbed the nitrogen oxides in water to form nitric acid. About 1788 the Rev. Isaac Milner of Cambridge discovered that AMMONIA (q.v.) could be oxidized to gases which, when absorbed in water, form nitric acid. This process is now by far the most important industrial method for manufacturing nitric acid. The essential feature is that ammonia and oxygen are passed together over a red-hot platinum gauze, which acts as a catalyst. Platinum is very expensive, and a considerable amount of gauze is needed. There are many variations on this basic technique: for instance, the oxidation or the subsequent absorption in water may be carried out under pressure. This produces a more concentrated acid, but uses up the expensive catalyst more quickly. Nitric acid is most important in the manufacture of synthetic nitrate fertilizers (*see* ARTIFICIAL FERTILIZERS, Vol. VI) but it is also used in making explosives, dyestuffs, surface coatings, and other chemical products.

3. ORGANIC ACIDS. Acetic acid is well known as the effective constituent of vinegar. It has traditionally been made by the oxidation of alcohol—which takes place, for example, when wine is allowed to go sour. Vinegar is made from wine, cider, or fermented malt.

Acetic acid as a pure chemical is still commonly made by the oxidation of pure alcohol. Acetaldehyde, however, which is the intermediate product, is now increasingly being made by the oxidation of ethylene. Alternatively, acetic acid (as well as other organic acids) can be made in one step by the controlled oxidation of a liquid petroleum fraction (*see* OIL REFINING).

The largest use for acetic acid is in the manufacture of the man-made fibre cellulose acetate (*see* TEXTILE FIBRES, MAN-MADE). Large amounts are also used for making other chemicals and solvents, in dyeing, for the pickling of food, in artificial vinegar manufacture, leather tanning and finishing, and oil refining.

Formic acid occurs in many fluids of animal origin, such as sweat (*see* SKIN, Vol. XI). It was discovered in 1760 by Rey, who obtained it from the bodies of red ants. *Formica* is the Latin for ant, and from this the acid got its name. The traditional manufacturing process is based, in principle, on the combination of carbon monoxide and water. More recently, formic acid has been made, as a co-product of acetic acid, in the process of oxidizing a suitable hydrocarbon such as a light petroleum.

Formic acid is made and used on a much smaller scale than acetic acid. It is used in certain textile dyeing and printing processes. It is also used for coagulating into rubber the milky-white fluid, called latex, that is collected from the rubber tree (*see* RUBBER, Vol. VI). The acid is used in TANNING (q.v.), in the rayon industry, and for making many inorganic and organic compounds. The latter are used as solvents in preparing varnishes and lacquers. It has also been found to have a valuable preservative effect when added to silage.

See also ALKALIS; CHEMISTRY, INDUSTRIAL; CHEMISTRY, HISTORY OF.

See also Vol. III: CHEMISTRY.

ADVERTISING AND PUBLICITY. 1. Advertising is one of the ways in which merchants and manufacturers market their goods. It has become an important and specialized branch of modern economic life. The word 'advertising' comes from a French word meaning 'to bring to notice'. Advertising does two things. It tells would-be buyers that a certain article is on sale, and where they can buy it; and, when many firms supply the same article, it tries to encourage people to buy the advertiser's own brand. In fact, brands and advertising have developed together. A manufacturer of a standard commodity, such as floor polish, would only lose business to his competitors if he did not advertise his own floor polish under some striking name, or 'brand'.

'Publicity' means much the same thing as advertising, although the word is more often used in a rather special sense. For example, if a manufacturer is about to open a new factory, he may advertise in newspapers and put up posters. But he may also give publicity to the opening of the factory by inviting a famous film star to attend as well as the mayor of the nearest town. Crowds would collect to watch their arrival, while press photographers and newsreel cameramen recorded the scene. Business men also talk of a 'publicity campaign' when, for example, the wool industry draws attention to the superiority of wool, or when the government of a country such as Switzerland encourages travellers to visit it. In the same way the Buy British and the Festival of Britain (1951) publicity campaigns were intended to draw attention to British goods.

Advertising and publicity both really date from an early stage in man's economic life. Every TRADE SIGN (q.v.) over a shop is a kind of advertisement, and trade signs certainly go back at least as far as the days of ancient Rome. An actual display of the goods is another old form of advertising. In medieval times a good deal of such advertising took place at the regular TRADE FAIRS (q.v.) held in important centres. Fairs and EXHIBITIONS (q.v.) are still held to-day.

2. ADVERTISING SPECIALISTS. Most firms spending money on advertising use advertising agencies or contractors. An advertising agency is often itself an important firm with staffs of writers and artists. The agency employed to conduct an advertising campaign must first be told for what market, that is, for what kind of people, the goods to be advertised are intended. Sometimes the seller of the goods is not himself quite clear what his market will be. In that case the advertising specialist may be asked to discover what kinds of people are likely to buy the article offered, where they live, and in what quantities they are likely to buy it. Investigations of this kind are called MARKET RESEARCH (q.v.). This is usually carried out by most advertising firms as a branch of their own business, but there are firms that specialize in this alone. When the nature of the market has been studied, it is then decided what means shall be used for the advertising campaign. This depends upon the nature and extent of the market, and the kinds of people likely to be interested in the goods. The medium, or media (*see* Section 3), must be chosen and used to attract the attention of the public. The public is not a single public, all with the same ideas and reactions, but several widely differing groups of people with minds working very differently from each other's. An advertising specialist must know what people buy and the reasons why they buy it. Some people can be convinced by exaggeration or over-statement, particularly if these are repeated long enough; other people can only be convinced by under-statement or restraint.

It is often said that it is the buyers of the goods who really pay for the advertisement. This is true, for the cost of advertising is one of the costs of producing the article, and the selling price must be fixed to cover all costs. But a successful advertising campaign may so broaden the demand for a product, and increase the quantity produced, that the cost of producing each item may fall, and the selling price may then be lowered.

3. ADVERTISING MEDIA. These are the various ways of advertising. Direct advertising includes not only circulars, booklets, and pamphlets sent through the post, but also handbills distributed in the street, or to people's homes. Advertising at trade fairs and exhibitions may include other forms of advertising than display; posters may be used on the exhibitor's stand, and pamphlets may be handed to any inquirer. Cinema advertising can be done in two ways: either short films which work up to a climax disclosing the advertiser's message, or what are really posters thrown on to the screen. Today television advertising is of great importance, and from 1969 'commercials' have been made in colour. Radio advertising is illegal in Britain, and the 'pirate' stations financed by it were closed in 1967, though it is common elsewhere.

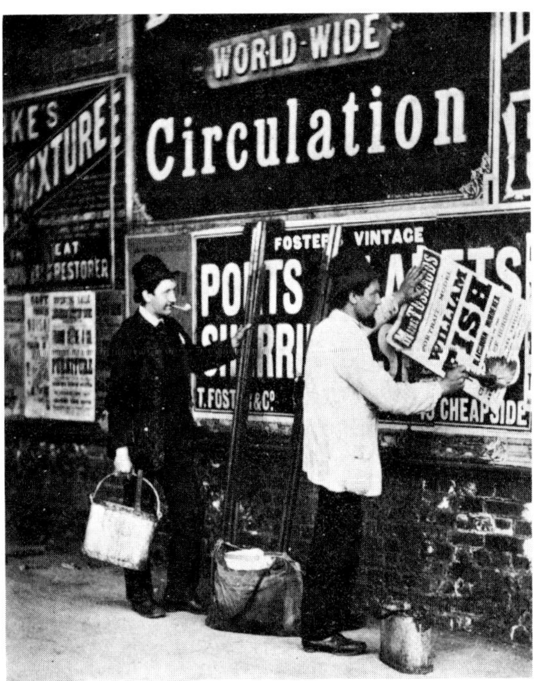

BILL-POSTERS OF THE EARLY 20TH CENTURY

4. PRESS ADVERTISING. The developments of the modern newspaper and magazine, and of press advertising, have marched in step with one another. Press advertisements are either 'classified' or 'display'. Display advertisements do not differ much from outdoor posters; they are reproduced on a small scale (in black-and-white or in colour) instead of on a large scale, and have more text. Classified advertisements are non-displayed announcements grouped under a general heading, such as 'Articles for sale and wanted' and 'Houses for sale and to let'. Measured by the money paid for them, press advertisements are the most important form of advertising. In the late 19th century newspaper proprietors, such as Alfred Harmsworth (later Lord Northcliffe), found that they could lower the price of their papers and increase circulation by developing revenue from advertisements. Circulation and advertisement revenue were closely linked; as circulation increased, there would be more readers of any given advertisement, and the advertiser could be asked to pay more; increased advertisement revenue could be used to reduce the newspaper's price, and this would increase circulation still further. Until the 1930's, the *Daily Mail* (one of

Lord Northcliffe's newspapers) often devoted the whole of its front page to an advertisement by a single firm, and at one period the price charged for one day's use of this front page was £1,000. The circulations of the popular newspapers have since been greatly increased, and sums of this kind are now obtained for a smaller allocation of space (*see* NEWSPAPER INDUSTRY).

The success of any advertisement depends on getting the public to pay attention to it. Most newspapers still use part of their front page for advertisements; it is argued that the front page will first catch the reader's eye. The publishers of the earlier magazines did not like to spoil the look of their reading matter by advertisements, and these were placed before and after the reading matter, so that the reader could avoid the advertisements, unless he wanted to read them. The Americans, who have always led the world in advertising methods, were the first to decide that there were advertising disadvantages in this separation of advertisements and reading matter, and the modern system of mixing reading matter and advertisements is now general.

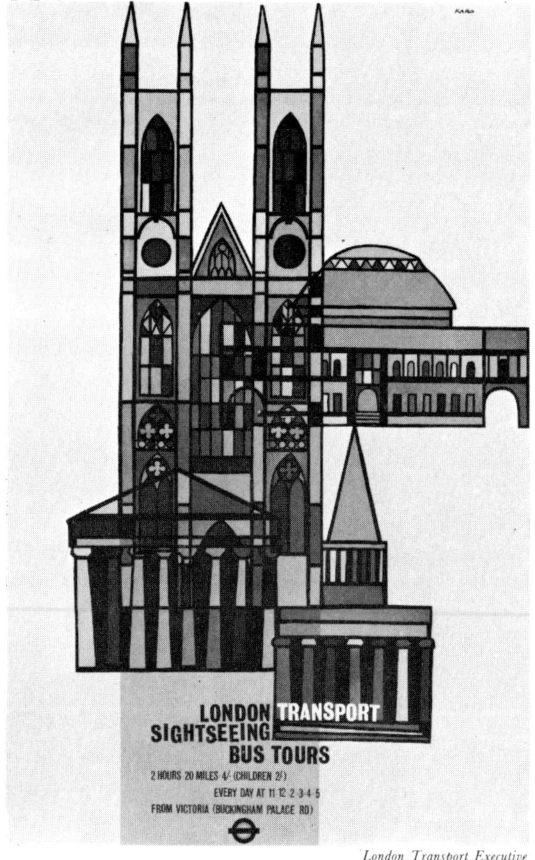

London Transport Executive

LONDON TRANSPORT POSTER

The purpose of every advertiser is to bring his message before those people who are interested in what he is trying to sell. The big, popular newspapers, which are read by all classes of people, usually carry advertisements of goods which are in general demand. The professional and trade journals generally carry more specialized advertisements. For example, an advertiser who wished to reach medical men only would advertise in the *Lancet* or the *British Medical Journal*. There are also many publications dealing with religious, ecclesiastical, intellectual, professional, sporting, or other interests, and it is rarely that an advertiser fails to find the right journal for his needs.

Firms conducting MAIL-ORDER TRADING (q.v.) often want to know which press media are the best for advertising. They can often get this information by including 'keying' devices in their advertisements. Keying can take many forms, the most usual being that advertisements in different papers give different addresses to which replies should be sent, or may ask the reader to write to a department with a special number. Thus the advertiser can see at once which newspaper was read by the person who answered the advertisement.

5. TELEVISION ADVERTISING. In Britain, this is limited to those channels controlled by the Independent Television Authority (*see* BROADCASTING, Vol. IX). The Authority licenses programme contractors to provide regional services, which are financed by selling advertising time on them. Strict control is kept over such advertising: it may only take up 7 minutes in any one hour; and all 'commercials' must first be submitted to the I.T.A.'s Advertising Control Office, without whose approval they may not be shown. £132 million was spent on television advertising in 1968, an indication of its prestige and influence.

6. OUTDOOR ADVERTISING. The POSTER (q.v. Vol. XII) is a very early form of outdoor advertising. Many examples still survive, such as the theatre play-bills of the 16th century and later. In the late 18th and early 19th centuries there were no laws controlling bill-posting. Teams of bill-posters would stick their bills on any prominent site, walls, lamp-posts, even the doors of public and private buildings, and they often took care to cover up the bills of their rivals.

Fox Photos

PICCADILLY CIRCUS AT NIGHT WITH THE BUILDINGS LIT UP BY ADVERTISEMENTS IN COLOURED LIGHTS

This was called 'fly-posting', and is now illegal if done without the permission of the owner of the site. Hoardings, walls, and other places where permission to post has been given, are now rented by large firms of bill-posting contractors, who have replaced the adventurous fly-posters of the early 19th century. Such places are given the trade name of 'sites'. Advertisement by poster has never been confined to outdoor sites; a great deal of it is done in buses, in railway carriages, and some shops (*see* colour plate opp. p. 224). Hoarding and poster advertising is not so selective as press advertising. It is, however, possible to select outdoor sites to a limited extent, and, in railway advertising, to discriminate between first-class and second-class carriages, according to the product advertised. The 'three-dimensional' poster is a recent development. Poster advertising is now restricted by law where there is danger of its spoiling the countryside.

7. DIRECT ADVERTISING. By this method the advertiser can choose the exact public he wishes to reach. It is much used in mail-order trading, lists of likely addresses being drawn up from classified directories or similar publications. Direct advertising is much used in the financial world. There is at least one firm in the City of London which specializes in the preparation of classified lists of shareholders; a prospectus for a new issue of shares in, say, a mining venture (*see* STOCKS AND SHARES) will be sent only to those who are already shareholders in mining companies. Many devices are used by direct advertisers: one is the use of the 'Births' column of a newspaper to obtain addresses of likely buyers of babies' requirements. Direct advertising can be followed up by a letter, or by a personal call from a representative.

8. OTHER PUBLICITY METHODS. Window-dressing has now become highly specialized, and for every important trade there are window-dressing specialists who can arrange much better displays than the shop-keeper himself. The larger firms and the DEPARTMENT STORES (q.v.) have window-dressing experts on their permanent staff.

AGENT. This is a person who represents individuals or firms in business. His work is generally to introduce the buyer to the manufacturer or merchant, though some agents are employed by merchants to buy goods for them from the producers or manufacturers. As the agent is buying and selling not for himself but on behalf of someone else, he does not run the same trading risks as the merchant, nor does he make the same profit. Most agents receive from their employers COMMISSION (q.v.) on the goods they sell.

Agents vary greatly in status and importance. At one extreme stands the person who happens to hear that a friend of his is going to buy a wireless set, introduces him to a shop, and then draws a COMMISSION (q.v.) on the price of the set. At the other is the firm owning a large showroom, with the exclusive district or national agency for the distribution of a certain make of car. Between these two extremes lie many classes of agent. Commercially, the most important are the manufacturers' agents: some are sole agents in a given territory for all the products of one manufacturer, and others are agents for many different lines of goods turned out by several manufacturers.

Most agents work continuously for one firm, or for a group of firms in the same industry. Firms of theatre-ticket and travel agents are excellent examples of this class (*see* ENTERTAINMENT INDUSTRY). But many firms called by the name of agent should rather be called BROKERS (q.v.): house and estate agents are examples, as are the so-called commission-agents who buy and sell produce on the various MARKETS (q.v.). The other kind of commission-agent, the bookmaker or turf accountant, is rather a speculator than an agent. Patent agents, as they are called, are hardly agents at all: they are really experts in the law and practice of patenting inventions (*see* PATENTS). But advertising agents are true agents, working mostly for the firms regularly employing them (*see* ADVERTISING AND PUBLICITY). Some agents are concerned with selling the services of an individual: a literary agent, for instance, introduces an author to a publisher, and arranges contracts, and serial and foreign publications. Similarly a theatrical agent introduces an actor to a company or a producer.

Agents are becoming increasingly important in export markets as the general economic pressure to export increases. Manufacturers who at home have their own special sales force often require some initial help in penetrating a foreign market from someone with on-the-spot knowledge of the market and its distribution arrangements. The experienced import agent can often supply such knowledge. The Government, through the Board of Trade, advises on how to find and select such agents in all parts of the world. The agent, therefore, continues to perform an important function in distributing goods and services.

AIRCRAFT INDUSTRY. There are two main things that make aircraft engineering difficult: the first is the need to make every component as reliable as possible; the second is the need to build everything as light as possible. The fact that an aeroplane is up in the air and cannot stop if something goes wrong, as a car usually can, makes it perhaps a matter of life or death that its performance is absolutely reliable.

Given a certain power of engine, and consequently a certain fuel consumption, there is a practical limit to the total weight of aircraft that can be made to fly. Out of that weight as much as possible is wanted for fuel, radio navigational instruments, passenger seats, or freight room, and, of course, the passengers or freight themselves. So the structure of the aircraft has to be as light as possible—that is, as small and as light as safety and efficiency will allow. The designer must calculate the normal load that each part of the aeroplane will have to bear. The specialist who does this is called the 'stress man'. He multiplies that load by a 'factor of safety' to take account of any abnormal stress that may be put on the part and as a precaution against errors in manufacture, accidental damage, and so on.

The stress man's final figures go to the man who designs the part, and who must make it as strong as the stress man says is necessary. One or two samples are always tested to prove that they are as strong as the designer intended them to be. Each separate part is tested; then a whole assembly—for example, a complete wing—is tested; and finally the whole aeroplane is tested. When a new type of aeroplane is being made, normally only one of the first three will actually be flown. Two will be destroyed on the ground in structural strength tests. The third one will be tested in the air.

Two kinds of strength tests have to be made on the ground. The first is to find the resistance to loading of the wings, tail, and so on until they reach the maximum and collapse. The other kind of test is for fatigue strength: in this case relatively small loads are applied thousands of times. Each may be well below what the structure could stand as a single load, but many repetitions can result in collapse. Among the

British Aircraft Corporation

BUILDING A VICKERS *VC 10*, A REAR-ENGINED LONG RANGE AIR LINER

Looking into the forward and front fuselage section

parts of the aeroplane that have to be tested for fatigue strength is the passenger cabin itself. When this is pressurized for high-altitude flying it is completely submerged in a large tank of water while the test is going on. The surrounding water has the effect of preventing the cabin from bursting like a bomb if there is a failure.

There are Government regulations which specify just how strong an aeroplane has to be, and until it has passed all the tests it cannot get a certificate of airworthiness, without which it is illegal to fly, except for test flying.

Even more difficult than making the structure strong enough is the business of making all the working parts reliable. There are the flying controls for example, the instruments, the electrical equipment, the fire precautions, and so forth. These must not only be light in weight, but must work both at high altitude where the temperature may be far below freezing and in the hot air of an aerodrome in the tropics.

To solve these problems the aircraft industry has very large staffs of research workers, with elaborate laboratories and test houses. New materials to give the best strength in relation to weight are constantly being tested. Aluminium and its alloys of metals such as titanium and beryllium, which have never before been used for engineering, are being brought into use.

A great deal of the research in aeronautical engineering is done in Government establishments, such as the Royal Aircraft Establishment at Farnborough, the National Gas Turbine Establishment, and the National Physical Laboratory. The main reason for the willingness of most governments to spend money on aeronautical research has been the importance of aircraft in the military defence of the country; and, in fact, the research work and engineering done to provide fighters and bombers has made it possible for the aircraft industries also to build airliners and freight aircraft.

Because of the country's military requirements, the aircraft industry was expanded very greatly in the First and Second World Wars, and was cut down quickly to about one tenth the size after each war. Between the two wars the Government kept a number of aircraft companies in being in various parts of the country in order to keep a nucleus of designers and technical men in practice ready to train a new staff in the event of war breaking out.

By 1960 it became obvious that the old policy was no longer wise. The devastating power of nuclear weapons makes it likely that any future war would last only a few days, and so there would be no time to expand the aircraft industry. Also, the much larger and more elaborate aircraft now being built need far bigger teams of technicians and designers to complete them quickly. A large number of small firms, therefore, are not so useful as a few very large firms. So the Government persuaded most of the companies in the British aircraft industry to amalgamate into four large groups.

Among the big tasks to be tackled by these groups is the development of supersonic aircraft—including airliners to fly at 2,000 miles an hour—and of new kinds of aircraft able to take off or land vertically. These necessitate working with new materials, and manufacturing structures that can be at a temperature of 150° C. without losing their strength. Lighter and more reliable turbine engines are needed, and new way of controlling the air flow over the wings. There must also be new ways of testing new materials and theories in the laboratories.

See also Vol. VIII: Aeronautical Engineering.

ALABASTER, *see* Marble and Alabaster.

ALCHEMY, *see* Chemistry, History of.

ALCOHOL, *see* Industrial Alcohol.

ALKALIS. 1. The word 'alkali' is the name which chemists give to a number of substances, including soda, potash, and ammonia, which in some ways can be regarded as being the opposite of Acids (q.v.). An alkali and an acid neutralize one another when brought together, and lose their chemical identity and form a salt.

More than 400 distinct trades in the United Kingdom use alkalis. They are used extensively in paper-making, glass manufacture, soap manufacture, and the production of rayon. Without alkali products we could have no glass for windows or bottles, and no aluminium for kitchenware or aircraft. There would be neither soap nor soap-powders for the laundry or the household. Not only soap, but most of the newer synthetic detergents also need alkali for their production, and many natural textile fibres could not be produced in their normal attractive form without alkali treatment. The only paper that could be made in any great quantity would be newsprint, which would be quite unsuitable for writing on; and all dyes and the non-mineral drugs would have to be boiled out of plants or animal tissues. The alkali consumption of a nation may be said to indicate its degree of industrialization, and without alkalis the complicated economic life of modern mankind would be impossible.

EARLY PRODUCTION OF POTASH

The English word 'alkali' is practically the Arabic *al-qaliy*, which means, roughly, 'the burned'; the name was probably given because wood ashes have been used as a source of alkali from very early times. Records of the use of alkali go very far back. A glass bead, well over 5,000 years old, found in Egypt was probably made from trona, an alkali which is the 'nitre' of the Bible. Trona was also used for embalming, bodies being soaked in solutions of it for long periods. On a tablet from Tello in Babylonia it is recorded that in 2800 B.C. soap was made from oil and vegetable ash. The properties and uses of alkali were well known to the Greeks and Romans. Pliny the Elder, who wrote in the 1st century A.D., gives a very full account of them in his *Natural History*. He was the first to distinguish broadly between the two commonly occurring alkalis—soda and potash. In fact, little was added to his knowledge of the subject until the 18th century.

To-day several alkaline substances are made in enormous quantities by the chemical industry. These are the sodium and potassium alkalis, and AMMONIA (q.v.) and quicklime. The three most common sodium alkalis are sodium bicarbonate (mild), sodium carbonate or soda ash (medium), and sodium hydroxide or caustic soda (strong).

2. POTASH ALKALIS. These have many specialized uses in industry. In earlier days they were extracted from wood ashes. In 1820 a more profitable vegetable source of potash was found in the residue left after distilling fermented beet-sugar molasses (*see* DISTILLATION). But already vegetable sources were being replaced by mineral sources. The Germans were mining potash mineral salts from deposits in Saxony. During the First World War, since the Allied nations could no longer get German potash, other sources were developed in the Dead Sea, in Spain, and in the U.S.A. During the Second World War, drilling for oil in Yorkshire showed the presence of beds of salt containing potash salts; and recently further sources have been developed in Canada and France. Britain's requirements of potassium are nearly all imported in the form of potassium chloride (sylvite). Most of this goes on to the land as ARTIFICIAL FERTILIZERS (q.v. Vol. VI); some is converted into potassium hydroxide, some into potassium carbonate. Hydroxide is used mainly for dyestuffs (*see* DYES) and to make special soaps such as shaving-cream; carbonate is used for special optical glasses.

3. SODA ALKALIS. Just as potash alkalis were manufactured earlier from wood ash, so soda alkalis were once made from the ashes of seaweed and sea-shore plants. Many of these plants came from the marshes along the coasts of France and Spain, but artificial salt marshes were also made for growing the plants. When the plants were burned, the ashes were fused together into blue-grey lumps. Many chemists tried to find a way of converting salt into soda, and by the end of the 18th century common salt (sodium chloride) was being treated with sulphuric acid (*see* ACIDS) to form sodium sulphate and hydrochloric acid. On heating the sodium sulphate with charcoal and limestone, and boiling the 'black ash' so formed with water, a solution of soda was obtained. This process was widely used for many years because it was a cheap method of producing bleaching-powder and chlorine as BY-PRODUCTS (q.v.). But chlorine can now be produced much more cheaply by electrolysis (*see* ELECTRIC CURRENT, Section 6, Vol. VIII), and to-day all sodium carbonate in Britain is made by the ammonia-soda process. This process causes the two components of salt (sodium chloride) and of limestone (calcium carbonate) to change places so as to produce sodium carbonate and calcium chloride. British soda alkali is manufactured by this process en-

Imperial Chemical Industries Ltd.

IMPERIAL CHEMICAL INDUSTRIES' AMMONIA SODA WORKS AT WALLERSCOTE, NORTHWICH, CHESHIRE, WHERE SODA ASH IS MANUFACTURED

The raw materials are close at hand—salt from Cheshire, limestone from Derbyshire, ammonia, coal, and coke from the Midlands. Water for cooling comes from the River Weaver and ships carry the soda ash to Liverpool, Birkenhead, and Manchester

tirely from raw materials obtained within the country. The limestone comes from Wales and Derbyshire, and brine is drawn from underground salt deposits in Cheshire and Lancashire.

Today the traditional production of caustic soda from soda ash by the lime-soda process is obsolete. Indeed the tendency is rather towards making soda ash by the carbonation of caustic soda. The combined production of chlorine and caustic soda by the electrolysis of brine (known as the Castner-Kellner process) is the chief source of both these products. As chlorine is the main requirement, the production of caustic soda tends to be more than adequate, and so there is no need for alternative methods of making it. The search today is rather to find a means of producing the chlorine without making caustic soda as well. The electrolysis of brine provides an important by-product in the manufacture of a stream of pure hydrogen. Although caustic soda in pure form is a solid, the product is normally handled in industry as a 50% solution in water.

What is called 'washing-soda' by the housewife is really crystallized soda ash. The crystals contain about one-third soda ash, the rest being water of crystallization, that is, the water which makes the soda ash take a crystalline form. Bicarbonate of soda is made by carbonating a solution of soda ash, and is one of the purest industrial chemicals made.

There are a number of silicates which vary in the proportion of caustic soda to silica. Sodium metasilicate (with a 1:1 molar ratio of caustic soda to silica) is an important component of detergents. Where there is a much higher proportion of silica to caustic soda (about 4 to 1) the type of sodium silicate known as 'waterglass' is formed. This is made by the fusion of silica (a pure sand) and soda ash. Waterglass is used domestically for preserving eggs, and can also act as an adhesive. Acidification and drying forms silica gel, which is a drying agent.

See also Acids; Chemistry, Industrial.
See also Vol. III: Chemistry.

ALUM occurs in mineral form in many parts of the world, mostly where volcanic action has taken place in the past (*see* Volcanoes, Vol. III). Its natural mineral forms are generally alunite, alumstone, or alum-rock. There are fairly extensive deposits in Italy and Hungary, in some of the Greek islands, and in various parts of North and South America. These mineral deposits are usually a mixture of aluminium and potassium sulphates.

Alum was well known to the ancients, and in his *Natural History* the Roman, Pliny the Elder, mentions it as a mordant, a fixing chemical which is used with DYES (q.v.). Although the Italian and Hungarian deposits are still mined, the uses of natural alum are now much more restricted than they were, and in recent years aluminium sulphate, manufactured from CHINA CLAY (q.v.) or bauxite (*see* ALUMINIUM INDUSTRY), has replaced the natural rock material for most industrial purposes. Alum has many uses in modern industry, principally as a mordant for the more sensitive colours, particularly the synthetic dyes, as well as in leather dressing (*see* TANNING), and for sizing the better quality papers in PAPERMAKING (q.v.).

ALUMINIUM INDUSTRY. Aluminium is the third most abundant element in the world. It accounts for some 8% of the earth's crust, a figure which is only exceeded by oxygen and silicon. It has a great affinity for oxygen, and is not therefore to be found naturally in its metallic state (*see* METAL ORES, Vol. III); most aluminium-bearing ores consist of the oxide, alumina, mixed with other compounds, mainly of iron and silicon. For the same reason, aluminium is not easily separated from its associated oxygen, and the metal cannot be obtained by direct reduction with heat in the presence of carbon, as in the smelting of iron (*see* METALLURGY, Section 2, Vol. VIII).

While most common rocks, clays, and various soils contain substantial amounts of aluminium silicate and oxides, the only material so far used on any large scale for aluminium production is bauxite, a reddish-brown, buff, or white rock, so called after Les Baux, a small town in the south of France where it was discovered. Bauxite is essentially a mixture of oxides, principally those of aluminium, silicon, and iron, in proportions varying according to locality. A workable bauxite may contain 50–60% of alumina. The biggest known deposits of bauxite in the world are to be found in Surinam in South America, in neighbouring Guyana, in Jamaica, and in the United States; large deposits also occur in the south of France, in Ghana, in Greece, in several areas of central and eastern Europe, and in Queensland, Australia.

Aluminium is made from bauxite in two stages. The first step is to produce pure alumina (aluminium oxide) from the bauxite by chemical methods. This is then converted into aluminium by electrolysis (*see* ELECTRIC CURRENT, Section

Alcan Jamaica Ltd.

KIRKVINE WORKS AND ALUMINA PLANT IN JAMAICA

6, Vol. VIII). This requires a lot of electricity—nine units for each pound of aluminium. For this reason, although bauxite is found all over the world, aluminium is produced only where the electricity is cheap—often generated by hydro-electric plants, for example the Volta river area in Ghana and the Kemano KITIMAT (q.v. Vol. VIII) districts in British Columbia, Canada. Often this means that bauxite has to be transported long distances and only in a few places, such as France and Ghana, are bauxite deposits found reasonably near the source of electrical power. Today America, Canada, and the U.S.S.R. are the biggest producers of aluminium; Norway, France, Germany, Italy, and Japan produce large quantities, and many other countries—Spain, India, New Zealand, to mention a few—produce enough for their own needs.

Aluminium has many important industrial uses. Possibly its earliest application was to the handling of food, and it is now used for pots and pans, food-processing plant, brewing equipment, milk pasteurizing plant, and other dairy equipment. It is also used to make aluminium foil for a wide range of wrapping purposes, and also kitchen and labour-saving household equipment. The present day chemical industry uses aluminium extensively, both for stationary plant and installations such as storage tanks and reaction vessels, and also for the bulk transport of liquids by large-capacity tankers.

Alcan Ltd.

ALUMINIUM INGOTS MOULDED IN CASTING WHEEL

The use of aluminium alloys is common in all forms of transport. Air transport owes its modern development almost entirely to the high-strength aluminium alloys (*see* AERONAUTICAL ENGINEERING, Vol. VIII). In road transport, both passenger and commercial vehicles make wide use of aluminium sheeting for roof and side panels; and aluminium sections, castings, and forgings are used extensively for underframes and power components. It is likely that the metal will be used to a greater extent in the development of the railways, as is happening already in America and on the Continent. Aluminium-magnesium alloys are being used more and more for marine purposes, ranging from small boats and powered craft to deck superstructures of cargo vessels and large passenger ships.

In structural work, too, aluminium alloys are rapidly increasing their scope because their lightness and durability save material, time, and labour, not only during actual erection, but also in transport and in maintenance. Bungalows, school buildings, and factory roofs can be made of aluminium. There is an all-aluminium twin-leaf bascule-type bridge at Sunderland; and travelling cranes, excavators, and huge sliding hangar doors are now made of this light, strong material.

Because it is a good conductor of electricity, aluminium is widely used for electrical equipment. Thousands of miles of steel-cored aluminium cables of the 'Grid' system take electric current over the country, whilst aluminium circuits distribute current throughout film studios and big office buildings.

Aluminium granules and powder are used in metal smelting and refining and also in the fireworks industry. For paint, aluminium paste is in general use as a basis with exceptional protective qualities and durability.

See also Vol. VIII: METALS.
See also Vol. III: MINERALS; METAL ORES.

AMMONIA is a compound of hydrogen and nitrogen and is a gas at normal temperatures. It was discovered by Joseph PRIESTLEY (q.v. Vol. V) in 1774.

From about 1850 ammonia began to be obtained in substantial quantities as ammonia 'liquor',

Imperial Chemical Industries Ltd.

COMPRESSORS FOR THE PRODUCTION OF AMMONIA BY SYNTHESIS FROM NITROGEN AND HYDROGEN

a BY-PRODUCT (q.v.) of gasworks. It was extracted with sulphuric acid, and the ammonium sulphate produced was used as a fertilizer. In the late 19th century, much research was carried out to find a method of 'fixing' the nitrogen available in the air into the soil, to increase fertility. The solution came in the early 20th century from the work of two German scientists, Haber and Bosch, who evolved a process combining nitrogen from the air with hydrogen obtained indirectly from coal, through the medium of steam. The process involves two basic reactions: the water-gas reaction, in which carbon monoxide and hydrogen are produced from carbon (coal) and steam; and the 'shift' reaction which treats the carbon monoxide with steam to produce hydrogen and carbon dioxide. Both reactions need a carefully prepared catalyst (a substance which speeds up reaction without being chemically altered itself), and the second reaction in particular also requires a high temperature and pressure. This process, operating since just before the First World War, has developed continuously. Today petroleum or natural gas has largely replaced coal, being easier to handle in a continuously operating plant, as well as providing a better source of hydrogen.

Ammonia production is one of the biggest sections of the chemical industry. More than 80% of the total production is used in fertilisers. Ammonia itself, its solutions in water, and its derivatives such as ammonium sulphate or nitrate, or urea, are all used to enrich the soil. It also has many important industrial uses.

See also CHEMISTRY, HISTORY OF; CHEMISTRY, INDUSTRIAL.
See also Vol. VI: ARTIFICIAL FERTILIZERS.

APPRENTICESHIP. The training of skilled workers has always been vital to a country's efficiency. In earlier days in England the CRAFT GUILDS (q.v.) were responsible for this training, and it took the form of a long period of apprenticeship during which a boy who wished to learn a trade was 'bound' to an employer who was a master of it. The fact that the master took the apprentice in to live as one of his own family led to this kind of apprenticeship being called 'domestic'. In former days an apprentice became a journeyman when he had finished his training (*see* CRAFT GUILDS).

Queen Elizabeth tightened up the earlier rules concerning apprenticeship, which were beginning to be disregarded in some trades as the craft guilds declined. One of the Acts of Parliament made in her reign, the Statute of Apprentices of 1563, laid down a period of seven years' training between the ages of seventeen and twenty-four as the rule for all trades, and made the local JUSTICES OF THE PEACE (q.v. Vol. X) responsible for administering the Act. As new industries arose during the INDUSTRIAL REVOLUTION (q.v.) and the guilds continued to lose their influence, the Justices applied the Act of 1563 only to crafts named in it or being practised when it was passed, and apprenticeship began to lose ground. When industry was expanding still further and becoming mechanized in the early 19th century, many of the old apprenticeship rules were thought to be a hindrance to enterprise, and in 1814 Parliament passed an Act abolishing the more important parts of the Act of 1563.

The Industrial Revolution and the Act of 1814 did not destroy apprenticeship as an institution, but changed its nature. Apprentices were still admitted to various trades, but they lived in their own homes and no longer in those of the masters responsible for them. By the beginning of the 20th century the decline of hand CRAFTSMANSHIP (q.v.) and the rise of big mechanized industries had reduced the number of trades in which employers thought apprenticeship necessary. The skilled TRADE UNIONS (q.v.), however, considered the continuance of apprenticeship to be in their own interests, as it helped them to insist on a reasonable wage-gap between the skilled and the unskilled worker. But during the First World War apprenticeship fell to a very low ebb, and in fact there was little formal training of tradesmen at all. There was far more work to be done than people to do it, and in the engineering and allied industries turning out munitions of war the 'dilution' of skilled labour with unskilled had to be accepted. The wages of unskilled workers rose considerably, and boys and young men preferred to earn immediately a full wage as an unskilled worker rather than to bind themselves for a long period of training at mere pocket-money wages. At the end of the war the Government realized that this situation was against the country's interests, and, in consultation with many of the leading trade unions, they took vigorous action. As a result, about 100,000 young unskilled workers were reclaimed as apprentices. Government training grants, supplementing the low wages of apprentices, encouraged this movement. The Second World War created much the same kind of situation, and it was met in the same way, by increasing training and maintenance grants.

The OATH to be adminiſtred to every Apprentice of the Company of APOTHECARIES, *London*, at their Binding.

YOU ſhall ſwear to be good and true to Our Sovereign Lord King GEORGE, and well and truly you ſhall ſerve your Maſter for the Term of your Apprenticehood, and in all lawful and honeſt Cauſes you ſhall be obedient unto him, and unto the Maſter, Wardens and Aſſiſtants of this Company, and have them in due Reverence. The lawful Ordinances and Secrets of the ſaid Fellowſhip you ſhall keep, and give no Information or Inſtruction thereof to any Perſon but of the ſaid Fellowſhip. In all theſe Things you ſhall well and truly behave you, and ſurely keep your Oath to your Power.

So help You, GOD.

And if it happen that you depart your Maſter's Service, you ſhall not ſerve any Perſon out of the ſaid Fellowſhip, without Licence of the Maſter and Wardens for the Time being, upon pain to forfeit and pay to the Uſe of the Company ſuch Penalty as ſhall be aſſeſſed upon you by the Maſter, Wardens and Aſſiſtants for the Time being.

God ſave King *GEORGE*.

AN 18TH-CENTURY APPRENTICE'S OATH

Apprenticeship is still an important feature of British industry, although in many branches it has become an arrangement by word of mouth, and not by a written contract. In earlier days a formal agreement in writing was invariably made between the apprentice's parent or guardian and the employer. Such agreements were called 'indentures', and had to be completed before a magistrate. Indentured apprenticeship survives nowadays mainly in trades where skill with the hands is still essential: for example, it survives in the various branches of the building industry, in bespoke tailoring, the fur trade, ship repairing, surgical and scientific instrument making, studio photography, cabinet-making, the jewellery and precious metals trades, saddlery and harness-making, printing, coopering or cask making, hairdressing, and many of the branches of engineering. Many of these trades take on 'learners' under a merely spoken agreement, as well as indentured apprentices.

AN APPRENTICE LITHOGRAPHIC PRINTER LEARNING THE FINAL ADJUSTMENTS BEFORE BEGINNING PRINTING

Today the period of apprenticeship is shorter than it was. This is largely the result of recommendations made by training boards under the Industrial Training Act of 1964, that the first year of training should be off-the-job. When the period of apprenticeship is over one is said to be 'out of one's time'. Apprentices out of their time have not yet acquired the skill of experienced tradesmen, and some of them may spend time in their trade as 'improvers'. In some trades a distinction is made between the different classes of apprentices. This is particularly true of engineering, which recognizes two distinct classes of apprentice: the 'pupil' apprentice who will eventually be a trained engineer (in the sense of a professional man who makes plans for others to carry out), and the 'trade' apprentice who will become a skilled artificer (that is, a mechanic, often highly skilled, who carries out the designs). The 'trainee' system of informal apprenticeship, for those whose educational and other qualifications are likely to fit them for executive rank in industry, is a modern form of the pupil apprentice system. Sea apprentices, or cadets, are really in the pupil apprentice class, as they are destined to be executive 'deck officers' when out of their time. Apprenticeship has always been a vigorous growth in the Merchant Navy.

A form of apprenticeship is necessary before entry into many professions, notably the law, accountancy, and the architects' and surveyors' professions, but the agreements entered into are called 'articles' and not 'indentures'.

See also DOMESTIC SYSTEM; CRAFT GUILDS.

ARTIFICIAL FERTILIZERS, *see* ARTIFICIAL FERTILIZERS, Vol. VI.

ARTIFICIAL SILK, *see* TEXTILE FIBRES, MAN-MADE.

ASBESTOS. The word 'asbestos' is Greek, and means something that will not burn. It is the general name given to a group of minerals of differing chemical compositions, but all having the same general properties. Of the different varieties, chrysolite asbestos is commercially the most important, and accounts for over nine-tenths of the present production of the world.

Although it is chemically a mineral, asbestos has many of the characteristics of a textile fibre. In fact, the French Canadians who first discovered it in Quebec called it *pierre à coton*—cotton stone. It can be spun into thread and woven into fabric in the same way as cotton, wool, hemp, rayon, and silk. It can also be felted into thin or thick masses of pliable material (*see* FELT).

Asbestos was well known to the ancients, if we can believe certain records. From it the Chinese are said to have made cloth for the cuffs or ruffles of sleeves, and when they got dirty the dirt could be burned off instead of washed. The Vestal Virgins of Rome, who had charge of the 'sacred fire' on the hearth of the temple of Vesta, were supposed to have lamps that never went out, and it is probable that these had asbestos wicks. Charlemagne, the Frankish Emperor, is said to have used an asbestos table-cloth for important banquets, and to have amused his guests after dinner by throwing it into the fire and bringing it out clean.

Asbestos occurs in nature in crystalline form, as veins running through ROCKS (q.v. Vol. III). When extracted, these veins are silky to the touch, and separate easily into individual fibres, rather like those of the cotton-plant. Asbestos is found in most parts of the world, but Canada and Rhodesia produce most of what is used today in the world's industries. The principal Canadian deposits are in Quebec and Ontario. Russia has extensive deposits in the Ural Mountains mining regions. In the early 19th century the Italians, who had local deposits of asbestos, began to work it on a large scale. But they did not foresee its many uses, perhaps because the Italian variety could not be spun on ordinary textile machinery. An invention of this period was an asbestos paper which, it

Canadian National Film Board

ASBESTOS FIBRES BEING PROCESSED AT A QUEBEC PLANT

was suggested, might be used for making bank-notes.

About 1860, important deposits of asbestos were found in Quebec. This Canadian asbestos was a great improvement on the Italian, and could be spun on the ordinary spindles used in the Lancashire cotton mills.

Wood of any kind must be kept out of asbestos mines and quarries, because the asbestos fibres are very difficult to separate from small particles and splinters of wood, which may severely damage the spinning machinery. 'Wood discipline' in asbestos mines is therefore very strict; matches are prohibited, the mine-workers being supplied with lighters. In spite of the fact that asbestos can now be spun alone, cotton is usually mixed with it to provide additional strength, but the proportion of cotton rarely exceeds one-fifth of the whole.

The industrial importance of asbestos lies in its fireproof qualities. Most people have seen it in one of its most frequent uses—the fireproof curtains which, under the theatre regulations, must be lowered and raised at least once during every public performance. In the brakes of road vehicles, the blocks which are pressed against a moving part to stop the vehicle are faced with asbestos or rubberized asbestos, since the friction causes heat. Asbestos has important uses in engineering, for the packing of various joints that have to be resistant to great heat or to corrosion by acids. The thin leaves, or gaskets, that are used to make a gas-tight joint between the cylinder block and the cylinder head of a motor engine, are made of asbestos faced with copper; similar gaskets are used to fill the joints between the car engine and the exhaust pipe (*see* INTERNAL COMBUSTION ENGINE, Vol. VIII). Asbestos is used to line filters in the manufacture of acids. Conveyor belts that have to convey hot materials are usually made with asbestos.

Mixed with rubber, it has many uses as an insulating material in electrical work. It is also greatly used for the lagging or wrapping of boilers and steam-pipes, so that heat will be retained inside the boiler or the pipe, and will not be radiated into the air surrounding it. A modern use of this kind is for heat-insulating covers for enclosing hot-water tanks in a house. These covers are not unlike a large tea-cosy in appearance, and have the same effect—that of keeping the heat in, and preventing its radiating outward.

Mixed with cement, asbestos enters into the composition of various types of fireproof board used in the building trade. Asbestos is also one of the materials used for fireproof clothing, including the fireproof gloves with which workers can lift out bodily, without injury, crucibles of molten metal from furnaces. In wartime, asbestos clothing of this sort is used by men operating flame-throwers.

Some fire brigades supply asbestos suits for firemen who have to face intense heat in chemical fires. The fire squads of airports and warships are fitted with them.

See also Vol. III: MINERALS, Section 3.
See also Vol. X: FIRE BRIGADES.

ASSAYING. 1. This was originally the testing of ores and alloys (*see* METAL ORES, Vol. III) to determine their content of gold and silver; but the term (derived from the French verb *essayer*, to test) is now used in a wider sense to denote the analysis of ores, alloys, and metallurgical products of all kinds. All trade and industry in metals and metal products, including metal smelting and refining, depends on accurate and rapid assaying.

The prospector who searches for minerals must make tests to identify those he discovers.

Later his samples are assayed independently to establish the richness of his finds. In all mining operations the value and the selling price of the ores which are shipped are settled on the basis of assay values determined from carefully selected samples. In smelting operations, such as the production of pig-iron or crude copper, the furnace charges of ore, coke, and limestone can only be calculated if assay values are already known; and for the control of steel-making and all refining processes it is necessary to rely on information provided by the assay laboratory. Assaying is used industrially to check the composition of alloys and to make certain that there are no harmful impurities in them; and in the markets of the world the prices paid for both the base and the precious metals are settled in terms of assay values. Gold, for instance, must assay more than 99·6% gold to be acceptable on the bullion market; and aluminium ingots are marketed in two grades, assaying either 98 or 99% of aluminium.

There is now no basic method of assay, and any method that will give an assay figure rapidly and with sufficient precision may be used. Most assay work involves the examination of large numbers of samples, all of similar composition.

One of the oldest methods of assay (often illustrated in 'Western' films) is the miner's concentration or 'panning' test, which is still in use for the examination of gold or tin ores (*see* GOLD-MINING). The ore is crushed, to ensure that the particles of gold or heavy tin mineral are all broken away from adhering earth and rock; and a weighed sample is stirred with water in a miner's pan—a flat-bottomed, sheet-iron pan with sloping sides. The heavier metallic concentrate settles to the bottom, and the lighter material, remaining in suspension, is carefully poured away. More water is repeatedly added and further light rock dust washed away, the pan being shaken with a jerky, circular motion. Eventually a clean residue of nearly pure gold or mineral, which can be weighed, is left in the pan.

Many of the older methods of assaying ore reproduce on a small scale the operations used in industrial SMELTING (q.v. Vol. VIII). The 'fire-assay' of gold and silver is essentially a smelting operation, and is still capable of producing accurate results. In its simplest form, as used for very rich gold concentrates or silver

HALL-MARKS

ores, the process is known as 'scorification'. It consists in heating the sample with about 200 times its weight of lead on a saucer-shaped fire-clay dish to a temperature of about 1,100° C. The heating is done in a small fire-clay chamber called a muffle furnace. This receptacle is heated by flames which pass round the sides and never come into contact with the objects inside. The molten lead dissolves the gold and silver: on

LONDON HALL MARKS

1697 TO 1719 — 1719 TO 1784

SOVEREIGN'S HEAD ADDED 1784. LEOPARD'S HEAD UNCROWNED 1822

ANNE 1702, GEORGE I 1714 | GEORGE II 1727, " " III 1760 | GEORGE IV 1820, WILLIAM IV 1830

1696	1716	1736	1756	1776	1796	1816
a	A	a	A	a	A	a
97 b	17 B	37 b	57 B	77 b	97 B	17 b
98 c	18 C	38 c	58 C	78 c	98 C	18 c
99 d	19 D	39 d d	59 D	79 d	99 D	19 d
1700 e	20 E	40 e	60 E	80 e	1800 E	20 e
1 f	21 F	41 f	61 F	81 f	1 F	21 f
2 g	22 G	42 g	62 G	82 g	2 G	22 g
3 h	23 H	43 h	63 H	83 h	3 H	23 h
4 i	24 I	44 i	64 I	84 i	4 I	24 i
5 k	25 K	45 k	65 K	85 k	5 K	25 k
6 l	26 L	46 l	66 L	86 l	6 L	26 l
7 m	27 M	47 m	67 M	87 m	7 M	27 m
8 n	28 N	48 n	68 N	88 n	8 N	28 n
9 o	29 O	49 o	69 O	89 o	9 O	29 o
10 p	30 P	50 p	70 P	90 p	10 P	30 p
11 q	31 Q	51 q	71 Q	91 q	11 Q	31 q
12 r	32 R	52 r	72 R	92 r	12 R	32 r
13 s	33 S	53 s	73 S	93 s	13 S	33 s
14 t	34 T	54 t	74 T	94 t	14 T	34 t
15 v	35 V	55 u	75 U	95 u	15 U	35 u

LONDON HALL-MARKS OF THE STUART AND GEORGIAN PERIOD

top of this molten metal there forms a slag-like layer of molten litharge (lead oxide), in which is gradually collected any rocky matter and most of any base-metal impurities. The whole lot is then poured into a mould, and the lead sinks to the bottom before cooling and solidifying. The lead is later broken away from the slag and cleaned. This lead button, which contains all the gold and silver in the original ore, is now placed on a small dish, known as a 'cupel', made of bone ash, compressed magnesia, or some similar absorbent material, and put back in a muffle furnace. The lead melts and again starts to oxidize, and as fast as the molten litharge is formed it is absorbed into the cupel. Provided that air is allowed to circulate freely through the furnace, the lead button rapidly decreases in size, until finally all the lead (together with any base metals in it) has been converted into oxide and only the gold and silver are left as a small, bright, metallic bead of alloy gleaming on the surface of the cupel. The bead, when cool, is weighed; and the proportion of gold and silver (together) in the original sample of ore can be calculated. It remains only to determine how much of each precious metal is present. The bead is flattened and dropped into boiling nitric acid; this dissolves the silver (provided that there is 4 to 10 times as much silver as gold) and so 'parts' it from the gold, which remains as a heavy powder at the bottom of the glass 'parting flask'. The pure gold is washed and weighed; and the original weight of silver— all of which has now been dissolved away—is easily calculated by subtraction.

Assays of base metal ores and alloys now usually involve 'wet' methods of analysis. The sample is first dissolved in a solution, usually by attack with ACIDS (q.v.). Sometimes a metal can then be separated by an ELECTRO-PLATING operation (q.v. Vol. VIII). Whichever method is used, the assayer must be alert to detect the presence of unsuspected impurities; and he must always be sure that the sample he is examining is a good sample of the whole.

2. HALL-MARKS. A further branch of assaying is the work of the assay offices in hall-marking gold and silver articles. The law of hall-marks dates from the time of Edward I. All gold and silver wares (with a few exceptions) must now be submitted before sale to one of the assay offices for examination and stamping. Samples are taken from each article by scraping or cutting; if the assay is satisfactory, the work is stamped with a hall-mark comprising symbols denoting the city of test (a leopard's head for London, an anchor for Birmingham, and so on), the standard of quality, and the year. Originally all hall-marking was done at Goldsmiths' Hall, London, but additional Assay Offices are now established at Birmingham, Sheffield, Dublin, Edinburgh, and Glasgow. Gold content is expressed in terms of carats or twenty-fourth parts (pure gold is 24 carats), and the standards recognized are 9, 14, 18, and 22 carats. Standard silver contains $92\cdot5\%$ of silver, the balance being usually copper. Articles which are deficient in precious metal and 'do not pass the hall' (Goldsmiths' Hall) are broken up.

See also GOLD MINING; SILVER MINING; COINING; GOLD AND SILVER WORK.
See also Vol. III: METAL ORES.

ASSETS, *see* BOOK-KEEPING.

AUCTIONS. These are public sales of goods, conducted by an auctioneer, who is required by law to have a licence for the purpose. He invites the crowd of buyers assembled in the

NOTICE OF THE SALE OF A SHIP BY AUCTION

Christie, Manson, and Woods

A PAIR OF 18TH-CENTURY DIAMOND FEATHER BROOCHES BEING AUCTIONED

auction-room to make offers, or 'bids', for the items on sale. He tries to encourage buyers to bid higher figures, and finally names the highest bidder as the buyer of the goods. This is called 'knocking down' the goods, for the bidding ends when the auctioneer bangs a small hammer on a table at which he stands. This is often set on a raised platform called a rostrum.

The ancient Romans are believed to have invented sales by auction, and the English word comes from the Latin *auctio*, meaning 'increase'. The Romans usually sold in this way the spoils taken in war; these sales were called *sub hasta*, meaning 'under the spear', a spear being stuck in the ground as a signal to collect a crowd. In England, in the 18th and 19th centuries, goods were often sold 'by the candle': a short piece of candle was lighted by the auctioneer, and bids could be made while it stayed alight. The EAST INDIA COMPANY (q.v.) sometimes used this method,and it was also used in the timber trade until quite late in the 19th century.

Practically all goods whose qualities vary from parcel to parcel, and from season to season, are sold by auction. Among these are wool, tea, coffee, cocoa, hides, skins, furs, spices, fruit and vegetables, and wines. Auction sales are also usual for land and property, antique furniture, pictures, rare books, old china and porcelain, and similar works of art. The auction-rooms at Christie's and Sotheby's, in the West End of London, are famous for such sales.

An auction is usually announced beforehand by an advertisement containing full particulars of the articles and stating where they can be seen by prospective buyers. But if the advertisement cannot give all the details, catalogues are printed, and each group of goods to be sold together, called a 'lot', is usually given a number. The auctioneer need not begin with Lot 1 and go on in numerical order; he may wait until his experienced eye sees certain people in the room whom he knows, and he will then produce the lots in which they are most likely to be interested. The auctioneer's services are paid for in the form of a percentage COMMISSION (q.v.) on the actual value obtained by the selling of the goods. The auctioneer therefore has a direct interest in pushing up the bidding as high as possible.

An auctioneer must know fairly accurately the current market values of the goods he is selling, and he should be acquainted with the regular buyers of such goods. He will not waste time by starting the bidding too low, and waiting while it climbs slowly. He will also play on the jealousies and rivalries among his buyers, and will often succeed in getting a high price because he manœuvres two business rivals into bidding against each other. It is largely on his advice that a seller will fix 'reserve' prices, that is, prices below which the goods must not be sold. But even the best auctioneers find it very difficult to stop a 'knock-out', whereby dealers illegally arrange beforehand not to bid against each other, but to nominate one of themselves as the only bidder, in the hope of buying goods at extremely low prices. If a knock-out is organized on these lines, the real auction sale takes place privately afterwards, among the dealers themselves.

See also RETAIL TRADING.

AUDITING. This means checking the accuracy of business accounts in a thorough and systematic manner. In most well-ordered businesses the accounts are ruled off and balanced at regular intervals, and they are checked by persons other than those who have written them up. Such checks are not true audits; if they are thorough, they may be called internal audits, and in many large firms internal audit is continual.

The word audit usually means external audit by an outside professional auditor. This is usually done shortly after the end of the trading year. The auditors first go through the day books and vouchers, and check the routine posting of the ledgers. They check the cash balance and ascertain the bank balance and reconcile it with the bank statements. They physically check and value other assets such as buildings, plant, inventory, and debtors. They may then prepare a trial balance, ensuring that all assets, liabilities, and ledger balances are included. Then they draw up the trading and Profit and Loss Accounts, closing off the ledgers for the year, and finally the Balance Sheet, which gives an unbiased view of the financial position of the firm at the year's end.

One-man businesses and PARTNERSHIPS (q.v.) are not obliged to employ outside auditors, although this is a wise precaution against fraud and embezzlement. But LIMITED COMPANIES (q.v.) are compelled by law to employ them, and the Balance Sheet of a limited company must bear an auditor's certificate.

There are two professional bodies recognized by law and custom in England for audit purposes: the Institute of Chartered Accountants and the Association of Certified and Corporate Accountants.

See also BOOK-KEEPING.

AUTOMATION. This is a new word, coined from 'automatic' which itself comes from two Greek words meaning 'self-moving'. Automation means the elimination of human work (office work as well as manual work) from manufacturing processes. The idea of a completely automatic factory is quite common in science fiction: for example, factories that are still in full production, although everyone has been killed by a planetary disaster years earlier. There is no doubt that full automation of many manufacturing processes is a technical possibility to-day, and a few processes such as OIL REFINING (q.v.) are very nearly completely automatic already. The engineering side of automation is discussed in PRODUCTION ENGINEERING, and a description of the machines used in the automation of office work can be found in COMPUTERS (qq.v. Vol. VIII).

Because automation is technically fascinating, it is tempting to think of it as being desirable in itself; but automation is only profitable in certain circumstances and it produces its own problems. To start with, the main reason for eliminating workers in factories is that they may cost more than machines, and so an automatic factory can produce goods more cheaply than one with the usual numbers of staff and workers. But this replacement of workers by machines will be profitable only in countries where wages are high, and only in industries where a market can be found for a greatly increased output of standardized products so that the extremely high cost of installing automatic machinery can be paid for by profits on vast sales.

Many people think that if workers are to be eliminated from production because they are too expensive, there may be unemployment, and people will consequently have less money to spend. They will then not be able to buy the products of the automatic machines, sales will fall, there will be over-production, and the change-over will eventually defeat itself. There is no doubt that in the industries going over to automation there will be at first a certain amount of UNEMPLOYMENT (q.v.). But to some extent this will be set off by an increased demand for labour in the industries producing the automatic machinery, and for machine-setters, maintenance men, and other technicians in the automatic factories themselves. Moreover, the lowering of costs and selling prices resulting from automation will leave the people who buy the products with more money to spend, and this will find its way into other industries and increase employment in those. Automation, after all, is simply one more example—though rather an extreme one—of the process that has been steadily going on ever since the beginning of the INDUSTRIAL REVOLUTION (q.v.): the unemployment temporarily caused by increased use of machinery has, in fact, been fairly quickly absorbed.

British Oxygen

CUTTING PLATES FOR NEW STANDARD SHIPS WITH A COMPUTER-CONTROLLED MACHINE

This machine, the Condor, cuts four ships' plates simultaneously. The data from the design are fed into the computer (housed in brick building on left). The computer calculates the path for the oxygen cutting nozzles to follow and records control impulses on magnetic tape. An engineer at the controls watches the machine

Like all other revolutionary changes in industrial technique, automation should in the long run be of great benefit to the human race. Goods will become cheaper and standards of living will rise, not only in the more advanced countries but also in the backward or underdeveloped countries. Much of the dirtiness and drudgery of work in factories will disappear, and the factory of the future should be a cleaner, brighter, and more spacious and airy place. Automation is also likely to speed up the tendency towards shortening the working day. A shorter working day will allow people more leisure for use in other ways—a consideration which needs to be taken into account by educationalists to-day.

At present the greatest progress in automation is being made in America and Russia, for opposite reasons. Russia wants automation because it is the quickest way of enabling her standard of living to 'catch up' with the West. There is a huge demand for standardized cars, refrigerators, washing machines, television sets, and so on, which only automation can keep up with. America wants automation because wages are so high that manufacturers cannot otherwise get their prices down to world market levels. America finds an outlet for her increased production by investing huge sums in less developed countries which can then buy her goods.

See also FACTORY ORGANIZATION; PRODUCTION.

B

BAKING INDUSTRY. 1. The professional baker has a long history. There were public bakehouses in ancient Rome from the 2nd century B.C., and in medieval England a good deal of bread was baked outside the home. From the 13th century onwards there were several laws for the 'assize' of bread, that is, for the fixing of what we should now call 'controlled' prices, which would be fair to both baker and buyer. CRAFT GUILDS (q.v.) were formed in the baking trade early in the Middle Ages, and two separate London companies of bakers received charters of incorporation in the early 14th century: the Company of White Bakers, and the Company of Brown Bakers. Nevertheless, as late as 1800, most bread eaten in Britain was home-baked or baked in communal ovens. The few commercial bakers made most of their meagre profit by moulding and baking the dough brought to them by householders. In 1804 Manchester, with a population of over 100,000, had no commercial bakers, and it long continued to be the view of country people, especially in the north, that it was extravagant to patronize a baker's shop, except on festive occasions.

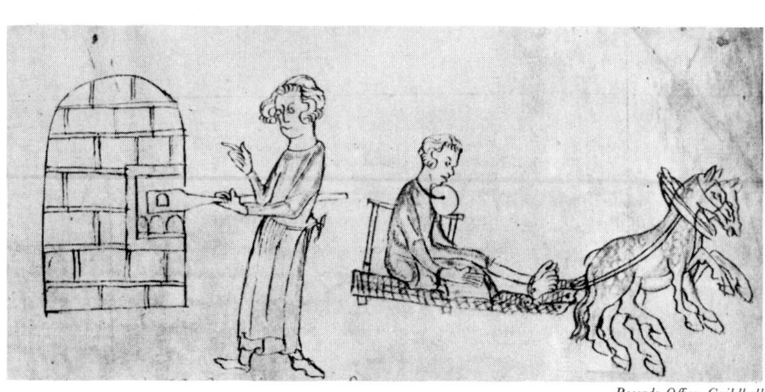

Records Office, Guildhall

A BAKER PUNISHED FOR FRAUD
14th-century manuscript (*Assisa Panis*)

It is only in the past half-century that the production of bread has taken its place as an industry; in fact until the beginning of the Second World War more than 60% of the bread in Great Britain was produced by individual family businesses, of which there were about 20,000. There are now less than half that number, and they account for little more than 20% of the total output.

To-day, two loaves in every three are made in a large bread factory controlled by one or other of the three giant bakery groups which have increased rapidly in size in the past few years. Many small bakers have either given up baking bread or have gone out of business. A high proportion of those remaining now concentrate on making fancy and speciality breads which, while total bread consumption has fallen, are becoming increasingly popular.

2. BREAD. The basic recipe for bread has changed surprisingly little since the time man learned to grind grain into flour. Bread is baked dough made from flour, moistened with water, and caused to ferment by the addition of YEAST (q.v. Vol. II). That is the principle of BREADMAKING (q.v. Vol. XI) and was the principle used by the bakers of ancient Rome. The chief processes are blending and mixing the flour, dough-mixing, loaf-making or shaping, baking, cooling, and packing.

Kneading or mixing the dough was done by hand until the middle of the 18th century, when a Frenchman invented a machine to do this. A hundred years later the Perkins steam-pipe oven was introduced, which used superheated steam and could raise oven temperatures to 260° C. At the end of the 19th century a successful machine was at last invented for shaping the bread.

In recent years the main changes in bread-making concern the improvement of machinery and ovens. Many ovens are fired either by gas, oil, or electricity, and, as a result, dust and ashes have been entirely eliminated from the modern bakehouse. In the larger factories bread is baked in huge travelling ovens through which the dough pieces pass on an endless belt.

J. Lyons and Co. Ltd.

NEARLY HALF A TON OF DOUGH—SUFFICIENT TO MAKE 450 LOAVES—BEING TRANSFERRED FROM THE MIXING MACHINE INTO THE TROUGH IN WHICH IT IS FERMENTED

Huntley and Palmers

BISCUITS EMERGING FROM A 200 FT. OVEN AT THE RATE OF ABOUT HALF A TON PER HOUR

These ovens usually form part of a completely automatic process from the preparation of the dough to the slicing and wrapping of the finished loaf.

The production of cakes has also been highly mechanized in the big bakeries, but in the smaller establishments, concentrating on high class goods, much of the work is still carried out by hand.

3. BISCUITS. In biscuit-making mechanization is even more thoroughly developed than in bread-making, and some biscuit factories now work almost entirely by automatic control based on the latest electronic devices. The consumption of biscuits in Britain has greatly increased since the war, as they are conveniently packed, keep well, and provide a ready snack. In the average home alone, each person now eats almost 6 oz. of biscuits a week. The industry's output for 1967 totalled 586,147 tons, of which 18,132 tons, valued at £8 million, were sold abroad.

See also FLOUR MILLING.

BALANCE OF TRADE, *see* INTERNATIONAL TRADE.

BALANCE SHEET, *see* BOOK-KEEPING.

BANK ACCOUNTS. Although notes and coins are needed for the small commercial transactions of everyday life, few people nowadays keep large sums of money in cash. To do so would be to run quite unnecessary risks of loss, theft, or fire. Money which is not needed for current transactions is usually invested so that it earns INTEREST (q.v.) for its owner. Money for meeting unexpected expenditure or emergencies is put into a 'deposit' account at a bank, where it earns interest at 2% below BANK RATE (q.v.). Withdrawals may be made on giving the bank 7 days' notice; reasonable amounts may be withdrawn on demand, but in this case the interest they would earn in 7 days is deducted.

The most important kind of bank account is the 'current' account, such as people keep for their day-to-day receipts and payments. Money can be paid into it in any form, and many employees now have their wages or salaries credited direct into their accounts by their employers. Withdrawals can be made, without notice, by means of cheques (*see* illustration). The most useful facility of a current account is that payments to other people can be made by cheques, and for greater safety, by 'crossed' cheques (*see* PAYMENT).

A cheque is merely a written instruction to a bank to pay money out of the account of the 'drawer' (the person signing the cheque) to the payee (the person to whom it is payable). The words 'or order' printed after the name of the payee indicate that the named payee may himself give his own orders as to payment. If, for example, he is not putting the cheque into his own bank account but wishes to pass it over to somebody else, he would have to 'endorse' the cheque by signing it on the back, whereupon it becomes payable to the 'bearer'.

No interest is allowed on current accounts, but in assessing bank charges, the bank takes into

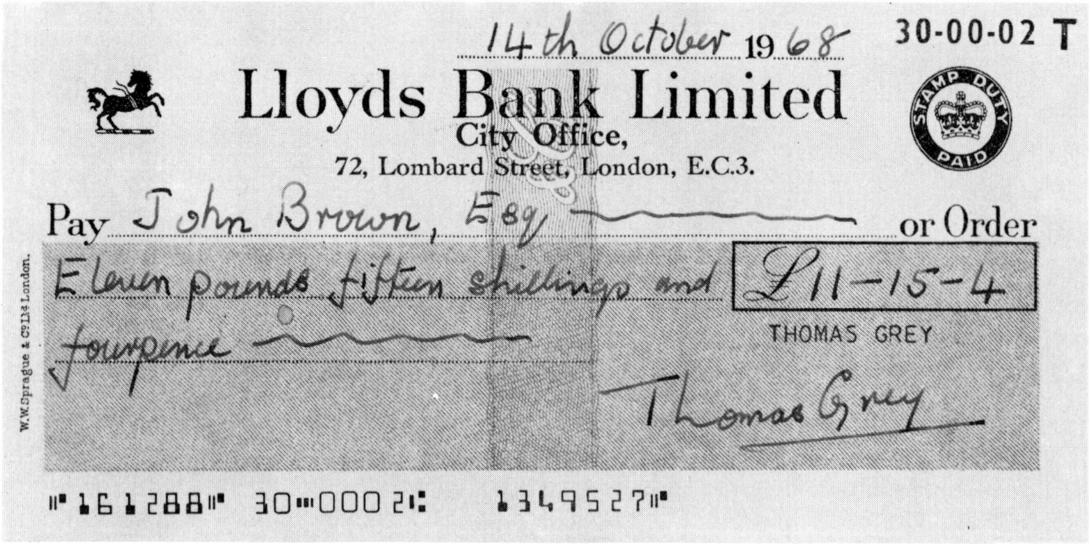

Lloyds Bank

A CROSSED CHEQUE

The numbers at the foot of the cheque provide information for automatic sorting, listing, and posting

account the value to it of the balance kept on the account. Small current accounts of employees, on which not more than 30 withdrawals take place in a half year, are usually charged a maximum of 10/–. If the average credit balance were £100, there would be no charge.

Payments can also be made to people with bank accounts through the Bank Giro System. This method, which requires only one cheque to cover any number of payments, is appropriate for paying household bills and hire-purchase instalments. For fixed amounts that fall due at regular intervals, payments can be handled automatically through Bank Giro if the customer has given his bank a 'standing order' to make them.

One of the most important functions of British Banks is making loans to business and personal customers. In judging whether a loan should be made, a bank's main criterion is confidence in the customer's ability to repay the loan in accordance with the agreement. Security (q.v.) is normally expected from a borrower but it can often be dispensed with for temporary loans to customers judged worthy of credit. When the arrangement with the bank is for the customer to draw cheques for amounts exceeding his credit balance, it is said to be by 'overdraft'. When the advance is taken on a separate account, the whole amount of the loan being debited to it and credited to the ordinary current account, it is said to be on 'loan account'. Cheques should never be drawn in excess of one's credit balance or of one's agreed 'overdraft limit'.

Banks have added considerably in recent years to their services to personal customers. Creditworthy customers may be issued with a Bankers Card, or with the particular cheque card of an individual bank. A customer with one of these is certain of having a cheque for up to £30 accepted without hesitation throughout the country, even where he is a complete stranger, for the person accepting it knows that payment is guaranteed by the bank on which the cheque is drawn.

Banks also conduct a large investment business. They obtain advice and handle the routine work for their customers in connection with every type of investment. For substantial investors they offer an Investment Management Service, and accept appointment as executor or trustee of wills and settlements. Some banks operate their own very successful unit trusts for the 'small' and 'medium-sized' investor. They also act as registrar for corporations and register companies. They issue travellers cheques, provide travellers with foreign currency and repurchase unused amounts, and offer expert advice on any matter connected with money.

Other institutions provide some but not all the services of banks. The Post Office Savings Bank accepts money on deposit, paying 2½% interest on ordinary deposits and 6½% on Investment Accounts for which longer notice of withdrawals is required. Building Societies and Hire-purchase Companies also accept deposits. None of these provides a payments transfer service.

The recently-introduced Post Office Giro does operate a payments transfer service comparable with Bank Giro, and no charge other than for the forms is made for the transfer. If money is to be paid out of the Post Office Giro, however, it can be more expensive than using a proper bank account. The P.O. Giro provides no cheque-book service, no loans or overdrafts, and no advisory service. Cash withdrawals are subject to a special charge. Today the payment transfer systems of both the banks and the Post Office are handled by large computers.

Cheques paid into banks are sent to the respective Head Offices, where they are 'cleared'; each bank exchanges them, through a CLEARING HOUSE (q.v.) for cheques from all other banks. Each day the bank settles up for the net difference between all cheques drawn on itself but collected by other banks, and all cheques drawn on other banks that its own customers have paid in. The operations of listing the cheques, sorting them into banks and branches, and totalling them up are all performed by electronic equipment. The entering of them into accounts is done by computers. The banks' increasing automation saves much time, since such information used to be recorded in ledgers by hand.

See also BANKING; PAYMENT.

BANK FAILURES. Although these are now entirely things of the past, they were a serious problem to people 100 and more years ago. They were caused because people who had deposited money in a bank were frightened that the bank would not be able to pay back their money. A 'run' on a bank is an attempt by large numbers of the bank's customers to withdraw all their deposits in cash at the same time, or change the bank's own notes for gold. But the business of banking cannot be really profitable unless customers' deposits are lent out or invested, a small amount of cash being retained as 'till money'. If, therefore, a 'run' on a bank continues until no more cash is left, the bank is forced to stop paying out. A bank which issues its own bank-notes is more likely to experience a 'run' than one that does not. Banking is an ancient practice, but English history makes little mention of banking activities until the time of the goldsmith bankers of the 17th century. They were the first English bankers to issue bank-notes. They were therefore very badly placed when in 1672 Charles II, who had borrowed heavily from them, refused to pay back his loans. This led to a run on the goldsmiths, who became unable to pay all their customers.

In the 18th century the SOUTH SEA BUBBLE (q.v.) brought down several small banks, but banking in those days was not as widely spread over the country as it was later on, and the first real outbreak of bank failures in Britain did not develop until the time of the French Revolution. It was the habit in those days, as it is now, for country bankers and merchants to keep big accounts and money reserves in London, and in 1793, when war broke out between England and France, the collapse of a big London banking house started a general panic, first in Newcastle and then all over the country. Out of about 400 country bankers then in business, 100 closed completely, and others were badly shaken. In 1797 Newcastle again led a general panic, and soon the BANK OF ENGLAND (q.v.) itself was forced to ask the Government for permission to suspend its legal obligation to give gold for its

Lloyds Bank

SAVING THE BANK IN 1825 BY BRINGING BANK-NOTES AND COIN FROM THE BANK OF ENGLAND TO TAYLORS AND LLOYDS, A PRIVATE BANK IN BIRMINGHAM

Ashmolean Museum

A BANK-NOTE OF THE NORWICH AND SWAFFHAM BANK WHICH FAILED IN 1826

It is stamped to show that the bank had failed and that two dividends were subsequently paid by the bankers

notes. In 1810, and again in 1812, the same kind of thing happened; between 1780 and 1820 nearly 1,000 banks must have closed their doors. The worst year of all for the country bankers was 1825, and a general panic followed the failure of two big London banking companies.

Such books as E. M. Craik's *John Halifax, Gentleman*, Mrs. Gaskell's *Cranford*, and especially Stanley Weyman's *Ovington's Bank*, give a vivid picture of the effect of bank failures on the life of the people in the early 19th century.

The chief reason for the many failures at this time was that every small country bank issued its own notes. When the rumour went round that a bank was in difficulties, immense queues of customers formed outside its offices, all eager to change their notes for gold or (if that could not be paid) for the notes of some other bank in which the public had not lost confidence.

When this kind of 'run' on his bank developed, a banker was put into a very difficult position. His bank would probably weather the storm if he could rapidly turn some of his investments—usually BILLS OF EXCHANGE (q.v.)—into gold or Bank of England notes; but to do this someone had to travel to London and back again by stage-coach or post-chaise, and by the time the gold or notes arrived the bank might have been forced to close its doors. In 1825 a record journey was made by post-chaise from London to Birmingham, in less than 8 hours, to bring gold and Bank of England notes to a Birmingham banking house, which thus managed to survive the crisis. At this time the fastest stage-coach took 18 hours to cover the 110 miles.

The decrease in bank failures after 1825 is generally thought to be the result of changes in the law, which deliberately encouraged large joint-stock banks, owned by many shareholders and having immense reserves which the earlier country partnerships could not build up (*see* LIMITED COMPANIES). The building of railways must also have helped bankers, for many bank failures in the early 19th century were due just as much to the difficulty of transporting stocks of gold coins quickly enough as to bad banking or bad management. Bank failures later than 1825 were of rather a different pattern, and were often quite local. The European political revolutions of 1848 brought down over 100 banks in France, Belgium, and Holland, but British concerns were not much affected. In 1857 a most spectacular failure was that of the City of Glasgow Bank; this caused so much disturbance that troops were called out to keep order. In 1866 the failure of the big London house of Overend, Gurney and Co. brought about general financial panic. In 1890 the big London merchant banking house of Baring nearly suspended payment, but with the help of the Bank of England and other City institutions it managed to survive.

By the turn of the century the new joint-stock banks in Britain had grown big, and were unlikely to be disturbed by a 'run'. But smaller private banks were not so fortunate; nor were foreign countries which had not followed the British example of the powerful bank with many branches. Abroad, one of the biggest failures of the early 20th century was that of the Knickerbocker Trust Company of New York, which caused as great a panic in that city as had the failure of Overend, Gurney and Co. in London 40 years earlier. In 1911 the Birkbeck Bank in Holborn suspended payment, and those who were present on the last afternoon before this bank closed its doors were to remember the vast crowd of tensely quiet and nervous depositors gradually edging their way towards the cashiers. The aftermath of the First World War led to many small failures, none of them of great importance. Farrow's Bank, which had built up a popular business by advertising methods which were not traditional in British banking, failed for a considerable sum. There were several failures abroad.

The last important bank failures were catastrophic in their effects. The world crisis of 1931 was ushered in by the failure, in May of that year, of the Creditanstalt of Vienna. The Darmstädter Bank in Germany—as large as one of the British 'Big Four' banks—very shortly followed suit.

Since the First World War British banking has been remarkably free from failures. Apart from the size and strength of the banks themselves, this is largely due to the disuse of gold coins as actual money, and the complete disappearance—except in Scotland and Ireland—of any form of bank-note other than those issued by the Bank of England. There is no longer any purpose in besieging the counter of a bank merely to change one's notes into other notes like them; and modern banks are so intimately linked with the life of the people that no Government would permit a 'run' upon them to be successful.

See also BANKING; BANK OF ENGLAND.

BANKING. The English word 'bank' comes from the Italian *banco* or *banca*, which meant originally a shelf or bench. The word came to be used in Italy for a tradesman's stall or counter, or a money-changer's table. The Greek word for table, *trapeza*, was used for a bank in Ancient Greece, and is still used in modern Greece. When the Italians introduced banking into other countries, the word bank came into general use. Although banks to-day are important institutions, without which business could hardly continue, the general principles of banking have changed little throughout the centuries.

In Great Britain organized banking began when the Lombards, or men from Lombardy in northern Italy, set up branch houses in London, and from them the famous street in the City of London took its name. The money of those days was of metal (*see* COINS) and the Lombards were goldsmiths and silversmiths as well as bankers. In the 16th and 17th centuries British goldsmith-bankers began to become more prominent and important.

These goldsmith-bankers began by taking in coin from private and commercial customers for safe keeping, because they could provide the

NATIONAL WESTMINSTER BANK

BARCLAYS BANK

MIDLAND BANK

LLOYDS BANK

CRESTS AND SYMBOLS OF THE 'BIG FOUR' BANKS

necessary strong-rooms, watchmen, and guards. They issued receipts for these deposits, and the owners of the coin then began to pay debts by asking the bankers to make the payments, and by handing in their receipts for alteration. This was the first step towards modern banking. The bankers soon discovered that a lot of the coin deposited with them never left their custody: they were merely asked to change its ownership from one person to another. Another move forward was made when the bankers, instead of issuing a single receipt for coin deposited with them, issued a set of receipts, in round figures, which could be handed by the holders to their creditors, in settlement of commercial transactions. Very soon these receipts, or bank-notes as they came to be called, passed from hand to hand, each holder in turn being satisfied that he could go and collect hard coin if he wanted to, and finding the passing of a piece of paper a more convenient way of doing business than cashing the paper for coin. A more advanced stage was reached when the bankers were asked to lend money, and they discovered that the borrowers would be quite content if loans were made in bank-notes instead of in actual coin.

When this stage was reached, we had the basis of modern banking. The notes simply represented claims to coin. There were more notes put in circulation by each banker than he possessed in actual coin; but he relied on two factors to enable him to meet his liabilities. First, it was unlikely that everybody to whom he owed money would ask for coin at the same time. Secondly, if such depositors did unduly press him for coin, he trusted in his ability to call in his loans fast enough to be able to satisfy those who wanted to draw coin out. Banking was seen to be a business of owing people more cash than one possessed at the moment, and of having one's assets, other than actual coin, so organized that it would be a fairly simple process to convert them.

It was obviously necessary that any LOANS (q.v.) or other investments, made with the cash originally deposited, should be well secured or have good SECURITY (q.v.) behind them, and should be made only for short periods. But some loans could be made for longer periods if some of the depositors agreed not to ask for their money within a certain fixed time. This arrangement enabled the bankers to lend money not only for longer periods but also against less perfect security, and therefore to charge higher rates of INTEREST (q.v.). But to tempt the depositor to agree to his part in the arrangement, he was offered a rate of interest by the bankers. Thus, the modern distinction arose between current accounts, which are withdrawable on demand, and deposit accounts, which earn a moderate rate of interest and are withdrawable only after proper notice has been given (*see* BANK ACCOUNTS). The PROFITS (q.v.) of a banker obviously came from the difference between the rate of interest he paid to depositors, and the rate he could charge on his loans and advances to borrowers, or could earn by investing in BILLS OF EXCHANGE, Government SECURITIES (qq.v.), or similar kinds of investment (*see* MONEY MARKET).

In the early 17th century the London goldsmith-bankers, in addition to issuing bank-notes and making loans, started the beginnings of our modern system of accounts withdrawable by cheque. A banker would open for a customer what was called a 'running cash'. This meant that he would arrange for his customer to issue orders on him in favour of other merchants up to an agreed limit; and he would either pay out notes or coin to persons presenting the orders, or would open a similar running cash for them if they so wished. It was only necessary for these written orders on bankers to be printed, in small books of perforated cheque-forms, for the running cash to develop into the modern current account as we now know it. But for many years London and country bankers not only went in for deposit-banking, as the running cash system soon came to be called, but also continued to issue bank-notes. No interest had to be paid on these, and they represented the most profitable line of operation for any banker. The business of issuing notes gradually became concentrated in the hands of the BANK OF ENGLAND itself (q.v.). In this way the ordinary business of banking took on more and more of a deposit-banking character, until it became that and nothing else.

By this time bankers had to a large extent forgotten that they had originally started up as safe deposits for their customers' coin. By issuing notes, and making loans, they were really creating a new and extra kind of money, and the only limit to this was set by the quantity of coin or Bank of England notes they thought it necessary to keep as a cash reserve. Roughly,

GEORGE GISZE, A GERMAN MERCHANT IN LONDON

Painting by Hans Holbein, 1532

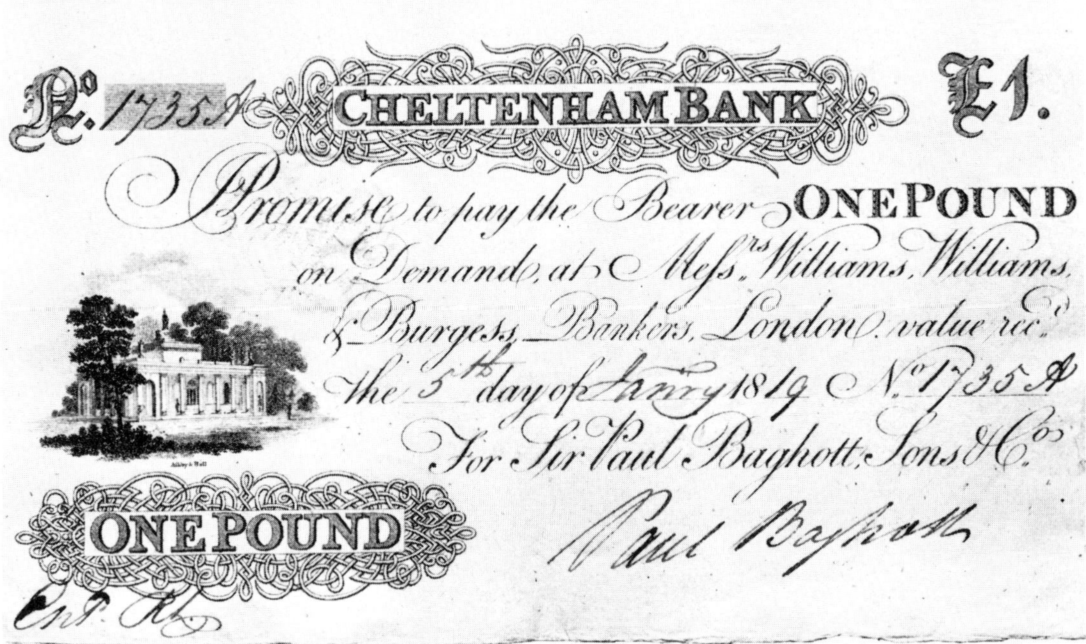

Ashmolean Museum

A BANK-NOTE OF THE CHELTENHAM BANK, DATED 1819

The date and signature were written by hand when the note was issued

the proportion of cash to their current and deposit account liabilities to customers, which experience taught them was reasonably satisfactory, was 1 to 10, or 10%. If one of his customers wanted to borrow, in order to pay the money borrowed to another customer, a banker would merely debit the account (*see* BOOK-KEEPING) of the borrower when his cheque was presented, and credit the account of the customer who paid it in. If we consider the system of banks in Great Britain as a whole, any banker lending money would debit the account of the borrower, and any banker receiving the cheque drawn would credit the account of his depositor, and so the modern saying that 'every loan creates a deposit' is seen to be true.

Two institutions have helped British banking to reach its present highly developed stage. The first are the Bankers' CLEARING HOUSES (q.v.) in London and the big provincial towns, where cheques drawn on the banks are totalled daily, taken to the head offices, and distributed to the various branches. Every evening a general balance is struck, which is settled by a mutual exchange of special cheques, or 'tickets' as they are called, on the Bank of England.

The second institution is the BANK OF ENGLAND (q.v.), where all other banks keep accounts in order to settle their clearing-house transactions. Nowadays British banks regard a balance at the Bank of England as equivalent to actual cash. To some extent the Bank of England can control the size of these balances, and thus control the use of bank credit in the whole country.

A banker must invest his customers' deposits in such a way that they can be easily turned again into money. The 'assets' side of the balance sheet of any of our big British banks shows how this is done, and how customers' deposits are invested, the rate of interest earned increasing as the investment becomes more difficult to turn rapidly into cash. First comes the item 'cash in hand and at the Bank of England', on which no interest at all is earned; then comes 'money at call and short notice', earning about $1\frac{1}{2}\%$ below BANK-RATE (q.v.); then comes 'bills discounted', on which the average rate of interest is slightly higher; then come various classes of securities, on which the return is sometimes higher still; and finally there is a large item, 'loans and advances', on which the interest-rate is often as high as 2% above Bank-rate. British banks try to restrict such loans to short-term transactions, and this custom has helped in freeing the

British banking system from the failures and crises which have so frequently affected foreign banks.

British banks also deal with other types of business. They transfer money, by their own drafts or cheques, or telegraphically, between any towns in Britain, and between London and cities overseas. This means that they are dealers in foreign CURRENCY, which is subject to RATES OF EXCHANGE (qq.v.). They issue travellers' cheques and documents called 'letters of credit', by which British tourists and travellers can obtain funds at any town in the world big enough to have a bank. They open credits in favour of exporters and importers, and thus help international trade. They open small savings accounts for depositors of modest means; they advise on, and buy and sell, government securities and other STOCKS AND SHARES (q.v.); they draw up income-tax returns and claims; and act as TRUSTEES and executors under WILLS and settlements (qq.v. Vol. X). Finally, they are in a position to obtain good information concerning the credit and standing of private individuals and merchants all over the world, and with reasonable safeguards for discretion they will let their own customers have this information (*see* CREDIT).

Including the Bank of England, there are twelve members of the London Bankers' Clearing House, of whom the most important are the 'Big Four': Barclays, Lloyds, Midland, and the National Westminster Bank. Both Scotland and Ireland have several banks, and most of them have London offices. There are several banks with London head-offices, and branches in the Dominions, Colonies, and dependencies. Likewise, many banks with head-offices in Commonwealth territories have offices in London. London is also the headquarters of many British banks operating in foreign countries, and all the important purely foreign banks have London offices. The Big Four (which were the Big Five, before the Westminster and the National Provincial were merged) control subsidiaries operating in the British Commonwealth and in certain foreign countries. No list of British banks would be complete without mention of the MERCHANT BANKERS (q.v.), specializing in international trade and finance, of which the house of Rothschild is a famous example.

See also BANK OF ENGLAND; BANK ACCOUNTS; MONEY MARKET; BANK FAILURES; SECURITIES.

BANK OF ENGLAND. In earlier days, when kings were often short of money, private business men would lend them money in exchange for some advantage for themselves. For instance, in return for a loan of £1,200,000 to William III in 1694, a London merchant named Paterson and 1,200 others obtained a Royal Charter to form themselves into a company with the name of the Governor and Company of the Bank of England. In return for the loan the Bank was also to receive £100,000 yearly from the Treasury. Since the days of Charles II bankers had found that they made more profit by issuing and making loans and advances in their own bank-notes than by lending actual gold coin (*see* BANKING). In 1697 the Bank received a limited privilege when it was decreed that no other (or rival) bank should be established by Act of Parliament. In 1797 it ran into serious difficulty because William PITT (q.v. Vol. V), the then Prime Minister, although promising to repay the Bank's loans, continually borrowed more to finance the war against Napoleon. The Bank, supported by an order of the PRIVY COUNCIL (q.v. Vol. X), had to suspend cash payments.

Many banking failures in the early 19th century led to the encouragement of the large joint-stock banks, who were permitted by an Act of 1826 to issue notes if they were situated more than 65 miles from London. Later, Government policy turned towards concentrating the note issue into the hands of the Bank of England, and the Bank Charter Act of 1844 laid down that, above an agreed limit of £14 million, the Bank of England was only to issue notes up to the value of the gold coin or gold bullion that it actually held; that no new note-issuing bank should be allowed to open in any part of Britain; and that, if any note-issuing bank should cease to issue notes, the Bank of England might increase its own 'fiduciary' issue (that is, that part of its issue covered only by SECURITIES (q.v.) and not by gold) by two-thirds of the amount that bank had issued.

During the second half of the 19th century the larger banks, organized as LIMITED COMPANIES (q.v.), gradually absorbed the smaller country banks. Under the 1844 Act banks amalgamating with joint-stock banks lost the right to issue notes, and the Bank of England took over their note issues. The London joint-stock banks, no longer having the right of note issue but able to establish branches throughout the whole country,

Bank of England

THE BANK OF ENGLAND, THREADNEEDLE STREET, LONDON E.C.2

The ground-floor wall is part of the early 19th-century building; the rest was built between 1925 and 1940

concentrated on gaining business by providing deposit banking facilities (*see* BANK ACCOUNTS), using cheques and Bank of England notes. By 1921 the last country note-issuing bank (Fox, Fowler and Co., of Wellington, Somerset) amalgamated with Lloyds Bank Limited, and the Bank of England thus became the sole note-issuing bank in England and Wales. In Scotland and Ireland the banks still retain the right to issue their own notes.

In the last years of the 19th century, the Bank of England gradually developed as banker to the state and as central reserve bank for the country rather than as a commercial bank, and to-day it does practically no private commercial business. By the 20th century it possessed the bulk of the country's stock of gold, the defence of which was a great responsibility. It was already the leader of the British banking community, and was increasingly becoming the place from which the banking system could always borrow in time of need. So, whenever its gold stock was threatened, either by the kind of commercial or political panic which causes people to exchange their bank notes for gold (*see* BANK FAILURES), or by an unbalanced state of international trade, it would put up its BANK-RATE (q.v.) in order to discourage borrowing and to bring down prices, and also to encourage foreign bankers to send funds to London because they could earn high rates of interest there.

The First World War caused London to lose to some extent its position as the world's international banking centre, and for the first time since the Napoleonic Wars it became virtually impossible to exchange Bank of England notes for gold sovereigns, although legally this was possible until the Gold Standard Act of 1925. Now that the value of the British pound was no longer fixed by its exchange value in gold (*see* CURRENCY CONTROL, Vol. X) closer co-operation between the Bank and the Treasury was essential to safeguard the internal and foreign exchange value of the pound. The Bank of England now works closely with the British Treasury and with comparable bodies overseas in a common effort to manage the world's monetary affairs. By the Bank of England Act in 1946

Bank of England

THE SENIOR GATEKEEPER AT THE BANK OF ENGLAND

He wears a scarlet and gold robe over pink, and a cocked hat. On special occasions he carries a silver-mounted staff

the Bank, then still owned by private stockholders, was brought into public ownership. There is still, however, a Governor and Company of the Bank of England under Royal Charter, with its affairs managed by the Court of Directors.

To-day the Bank of England is still the bankers' bank, linking together all commercial banking institutions of the country. An important responsibility is to check undue fluctuations in the exchange value of sterling and to conserve the country's exchange resources (*see* CURRENCY CONTROL, Vol. X). It is also the Government's banker, managing the Note Issue and the NATIONAL DEBT (q.v. Vol. X). Bank-rate is one of the instruments used to control the level of business activity. A further instrument, introduced in 1960, is the system of Special Deposits by the other banks with the Bank of England; these earn interest at approximately the same rate as Treasury Bills, and can be called for or released by the Bank in order to influence the amount of money the ordinary banks may lend. The Bank not only maintains a close liaison with other central banks overseas but has helped to establish central banks in some of the newly independent countries.

See also BANKING; MONEY MARKET.
See also Vol. X: NATIONAL FINANCE; CURRENCY CONTROL.

BANK-RATE. This is the minimum rate at which the BANK OF ENGLAND will discount approved BILLS OF EXCHANGE (qq.v.) and Treasury Bills for the members of the London Discount Market (*see* MONEY MARKET).

Movements in Bank-rate are important because all money rates throughout the country are based on it. For example, the rate of interest allowed by the ordinary commercial banks on deposit accounts (*see* BANK ACCOUNTS) is usually fixed at so much per cent. below Bank-rate, and their rates for loans usually at so much per cent. above Bank-rate. Also, these banks are regular lenders of what is called day-to-day money, or call-money, to the members of the London Money Market; and the rates for call-money tend to go up and down with Bank-rate. The Money Market is constantly engaged in discounting, or buying, Treasury Bills and bills of

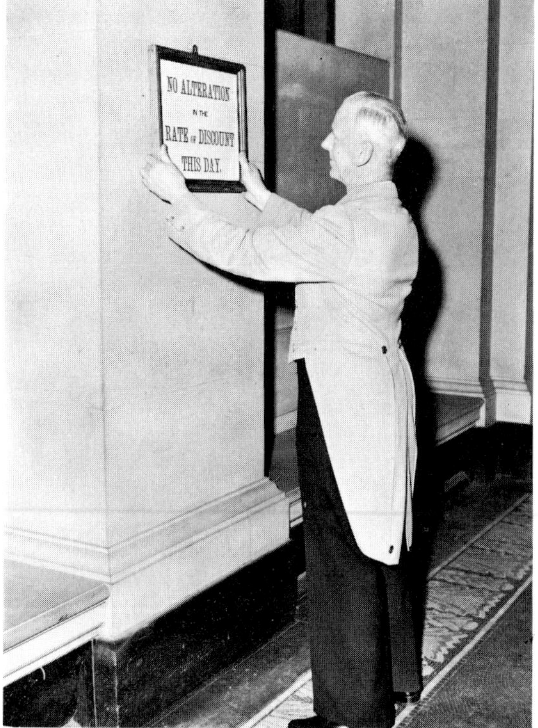

Bank of England

A MESSENGER POSTING UP THE BANK-RATE NOTICE IN THE BANK OF ENGLAND exchange; and, as the bill-discounting houses borrow call-money to do this, the price they pay for the bills will depend on the current rate for call-money. Therefore, when Bank-rate rises, all money rates, bill rates, and bank loan rates rise with it; and a fall in Bank-rate has the opposite effect.

Bank-rate is fixed with the approval of the Chancellor of the Exchequer, normally at each Thursday meeting of the Bank of England's Court of Directors. It is raised or lowered according to whether the Government wishes to encourage or discourage borrowing, for it is an important instrument of monetary control. Apart from a brief increase in 1939 at the outbreak of war, Bank-rate remained at 2% from June 1932 until November 1951. Since then it has been frequently changed, and from November 1967 to March 1968, after the devaluation of the pound, it stood as high as 8%.

See also BANKING; MONEY MARKET; CURRENCY.

BARRELS, *see* CASK-MAKING.

BARTER, *see* EXCHANGE AND TRADE.

British Travel and Holidays Assn.

MAKING A FISH TRAP

BASKET-MAKING. This is one of the oldest crafts, and one of the few which can still face the competition of machines, for the successful shaping and weaving of willow or cane has not been widely done by machinery. Baskets were made by primitive man before the art of the potter was discovered; and before the potter's wheel had been invented, POTTERY (q.v.) was made by modelling the clay on a mould of basket-work. Again, it was almost certainly the practice of intertwining grass, rushes, or canes to make baskets, which led, later, to weaving, and so to all the textile arts. In early times baskets were used more widely than now. The ancient Egyptians sometimes made their coffins of basket-work, and the American Indians used baskets in religious ceremonies. In Britain basket-work was an important craft in the Middle Ages. The records of the Company of Basket Makers in London date from the 17th century, though the Company was in existence long before that date.

Baskets vary in shape and size from the shopping basket to the huge 'skeps' used in dye-works. As new methods of transport and packing are introduced, other kinds of containers are replacing baskets; but there are many purposes for which they are still needed. The fishing industry uses baskets for traps, such as lobster-pots, as well as for packing fish.

In Britain the basket-maker generally works on his own, in a small workshop. He does not need any elaborate or expensive equipment, and he can do the whole process single-handed. It is a craft that is particularly suitable for blind people, who work either on their own or in workshops. During the First World War blind basket-makers made gun-mats and shell-baskets, and in the Second World War they made the parachute panniers used in airborne engagements. They also make all types of industrial baskets. Basket-making is a simple craft to learn, and the materials are cheap.

Until the 19th century baskets were made of locally grown materials, which in Britain were usually willows, especially osiers and hazel. Now, rattan or other cane is imported from Singapore, seagrass from China, and raffia from Madagascar. Willows need a great deal of water, and they usually grow where the beds can be flooded or irrigated in the low moors of Somerset, the Trent valley, and East Anglia, and in Belgium, Holland, Siberia, and the Argentine. The long thin shoots of the willows, 'withes' as they are often called, are harvested in the autumn and winter, when the leaf has fallen, and before the sap begins to move. If they are required to be 'buff', they are cut as early as possible and, before being peeled, are boiled in large open boilers for 6 to 8 hours. This stains them a golden-brown shade. For white willow the withes are cut later, and are left to stand in pits in at least 18 inches of water till May or June. They are peeled when they are in full leaf. Hazel has a thicker stem; it is not stripped, but is often split.

Before a basket can be made, the withes or cane must be soaked in water for from 1 to 5 hours according to size, and then laid down to mellow for a few hours. Next, they are sorted or 'cut over': that is, trimmed to the sizes needed. The basket-maker works on a slightly raised platform, and the basket he is making stands on a 'lapboard'. His tools are a 'shop knife' for cutting over the willows, a 'picking knife' for trimming long ends when finished, a 'beating-iron' for closing up the weaving as he works, shears for cutting thick sticks, and a 'commander' for straightening crooked sticks by a levering movement (*see* Fig. 1). For small work

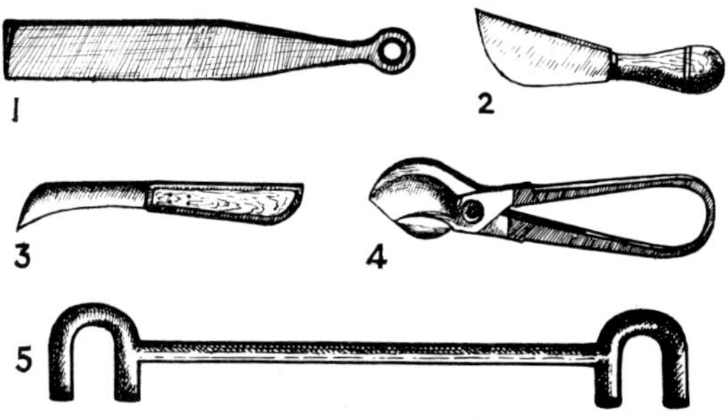

FIG. 1. THE BASKET-MAKER'S TOOLS
1. Beating-iron. 2. Picking knife. 3. Shop knife. 4. Shears. 5. Commander

lighter tools are used. Baskets are usually begun at the bottom. For a square basket the bottom is made in a screw-block (Fig. 2); round and oval bottoms are begun by forming a cross with sticks, and then opening the crossed sticks and weaving round them (Fig. 3). When the bottom is made, the uprights, or stakes, are put in, and the sides filled in by weaving until the top is reached. Various forms of plaiting or twisting are used to form a finishing border.

Different methods are used for different materials and purposes. Feeding baskets, used on farms, are made of split hazel or oak. The

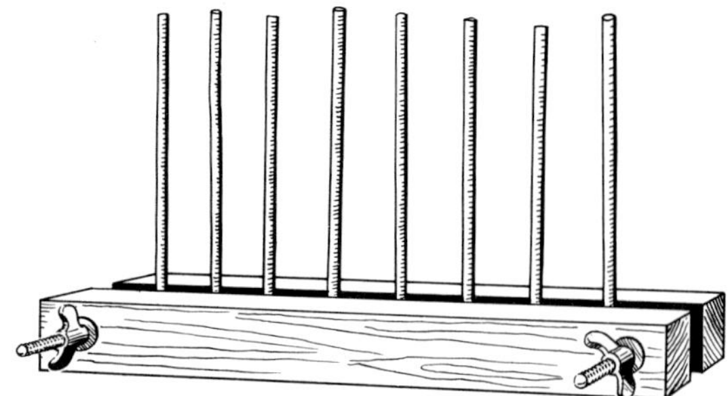

FIG. 2. SCREW-BLOCK FOR MAKING SQUARE-BOTTOMED BASKETS
Fine willows or cane are woven between the uprights

Lancashire basket-makers make light baskets in peeled buff willow. Their shopping-baskets are often called 'Southports' after the Lancashire town. The Cornish fishermen make lobster-pots

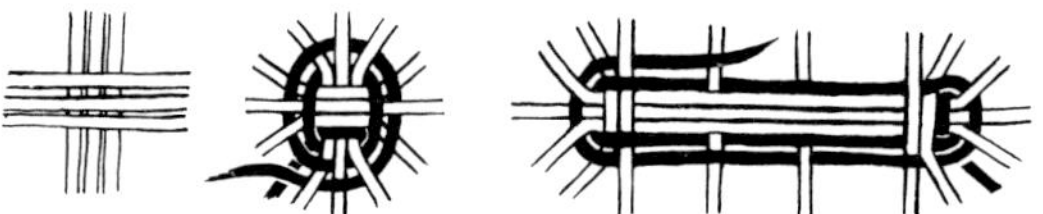

FIG. 3. THE START OF ROUND AND OVAL BASKETS

of green willows. Basket chairs are made by weaving in cane or willow and strengthening the work with wooden frames, which are often nailed together. The small boat called the Welsh coracle is a large oval basket covered with waterproofing material, made of split ash interwoven with willow twigs. It has hardly changed in form since it was used 2,000 years ago by the ancient Britons, and is still used to-day by fishermen for salmon and sea-trout in the West Wales river estuaries (*see also* CANOE, Vol. IV).

See also CRAFTSMANSHIP; WOOL WEAVING.
See also Vol. VI: RURAL CRAFTS.

BATCH PRODUCTION, *see* PRODUCTION.

BAUXITE, *see* ALUMINIUM INDUSTRY.

BEARER BOND, *see* BOND.

BEER BREWING. 1. HISTORY. The history of brewing goes back some 10,000 years to ancient Egypt—almost to the beginning of agriculture itself. The art of brewing was known to the ancient Greeks, and had established itself 2,000 years ago in Britain, for it was discovered and appreciated by the Roman invaders in 54 B.C. To the Saxons and the Danes the drinking of ale was a tradition, and they brought with them their own ideas on brewing it; but it was under the Normans that brewing was first properly organized, especially in abbeys and monasteries all over the country. The abbeys of those days looked after travellers as a duty, and the real origin of ENGLISH INNS (q.v. Vol. IV) was the guest-house attached to the abbey. Here, beer brewed by the monks was provided. Brewing was also associated with the farmhouse; the term 'brewster' (still used to-day to describe the February sessions of the Justices to deal particularly with liquor licences) no doubt derives from the activity of the medieval farmer's wife in producing beer for her family and for the farm employees. In 1881, 71,000 farmer-brewers still held home-brewing licences, but when these were abolished in 1961, very few holders were left.

Brewing on a wholesale scale began during the 16th century. Important centres were London where there were large numbers of inns and taverns, and Burton-on-Trent, where the 'hard' water was peculiarly suited to brewing pale ale. But from the Dissolution of the Monasteries in the 16th century, until quite recent times, brewing was still extensively carried on in the inn itself, although there are probably no more than 20 publican-brewers left today, among the 246 holders of brewers' licences. Beer brewing is an important industry in many other countries, especially in Germany, Czechoslovakia, and the U.S.A.

2. MATERIALS. Beer is brewed today from the same materials, and by the same principles, as have been used continuously for 5 centuries, ever since the introduction of HOPS (q.v. Vol. VI) altered the medieval 'ale' into the beer of to-day. Science has supplanted rule-of-thumb methods, as it has in many other food industries.

The chief of the materials used is malted barley (*see* MALTING), supplemented by sugar, roasted barley and malt (for colouring the dark beers), flaked barley (barley rolled out flat and partly cooked, rather like porridge oats) and flaked oats, rice, and maize. Hops are added to flavour the beer and to give it good 'keeping' qualities. YEAST is used to introduce the natural process of FERMENTATION (qq.v. Vol. II). All these materials are used under the supervision of the officers of CUSTOMS AND EXCISE (q.v. Vol. X), and everything that enters into the brewing process must be carefully entered by the brewer into the official brewing book, at least 2 hours before the process starts.

3. TECHNIQUE. The impression gained from a visit to a modern brewhouse is of a large, lofty building, containing at various levels rows of huge vessels of different shapes—mash-tuns, boiling-coppers, hop-backs, fermenting-vessels, and storage tanks—and with few employees about. There are also huge bottling plants where a single unit may automatically fill thousands of bottles in an hour. Plenty of human activity is, however, to be seen in other departments, such as the racking room where the casks are filled, and the loading stages where they are sent off to the public-houses.

The first operation in brewing occurs in the milling-room at the top of the building. Here the malt is screened or sieved to remove any particles of root, foreign seeds, and dust. The grains are then crushed into small particles called 'grist'. The grist passes down through tubes to the mash-tuns—squat-shaped cylindrical iron vessels with domed covers provided with sliding inspection doors. The function of the mash-tun is rather like that of a teapot. Here the 'liquor' is introduced, hot but well below boiling-point, and the work is begun of converting the starchy particles of malt into sugars which are soluble and fermentable. The brewer never refers to 'water', but always calls it 'liquor'; he is very particular about its absolute purity, and he generally prefers a very 'hard' liquor for pale ales and a soft liquor for stouts and brown ales. After about 2 hours in the mash-tun, this liquor, now

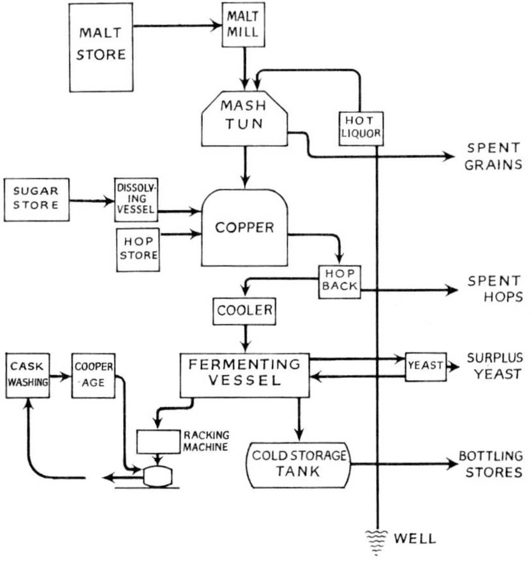

CHART SHOWING THE PROCESSES IN THE MAKING OF BEER

called 'wort', is drawn off by taps at the bottom of the vessel. At the same time, more hot liquor is spread over the grist by means of revolving arms known as 'sparges' inside the mash-tun, to get the final extract from the malt.

The wort now passes to the coppers, where the hops are added, and sugar, too, if it is to be used. Here the wort is boiled for about 2 hours, and then run off through a vessel known as the 'hop-back', an enormous strainer which removes the spent hops from the wort. This is usually the end of the first descent by gravity from the top of the building. The wort is pumped up to the top of the brewery again to pass through the refrigerators, batteries of pipes cooled by cold water passing through them. The wort passes on to the fermenting vessels, large open tanks formerly built of wood, but nowadays usually of stainless steel, copper, aluminium, or concrete with a special lining material. It is at this point that the excise officer assesses the duty on the beer by measuring its volume by the 'dip', and its strength, or 'original gravity', with a hydrometer (*see* BUOYANCY, Vol. VIII). Yeast is now introduced. Fermentation begins as the yeast grows and multiplies and throws up the familiar 'head' of foam, which at first may rise several feet high. This process lasts for some days, and as it goes on the head settles and is eventually skimmed off for further use or for sale.

The wort has now become beer, and passes to huge cylindrical storage tanks, where it is kept at a low temperature for varying periods, and sometimes for many weeks. If it is to be bottled it will be pumped through a pipe-line to the bottling depot close by, or carried by road or rail tank-wagon, or in casks, to a distant depot. Otherwise its next passage is to the racking-room, where it is run into the familiar oak casks in which it will be taken to the cellars of public-houses. In the cellars it is clarified with 'finings' made from isinglass and, after a short period in which to settle, it is ready to be drawn up through tubing, now generally made of glass or stainless steel, by the beer-engines mounted on the bar counter.

4. FINANCE AND ORGANIZATION. Of the 120 brewery companies and firms now existing, a large number are still family concerns; but most have developed into LIMITED COMPANIES (q.v.). Only a quarter of the capital of the average company is represented by the brewery and its plant; the remainder is invested in the ownership of the licensed premises in which its beers are mainly sold (*see* Section 5). Out of the price the customer pays for a glass of beer, about a half will go directly to the Treasury in beer duty. The remainder represents the cost of labour and materials in manufacture, the expenses of distribution, the profit of the brewery and the retailer, as well as the cost of maintaining, rebuilding, and improving licensed premises, which has been estimated to be £25 million a year. Over 9,000 million pints of beer are drunk in Britain annually, and in addition British beer finds its way to many other parts of the world. The beers which may be bought on draught from

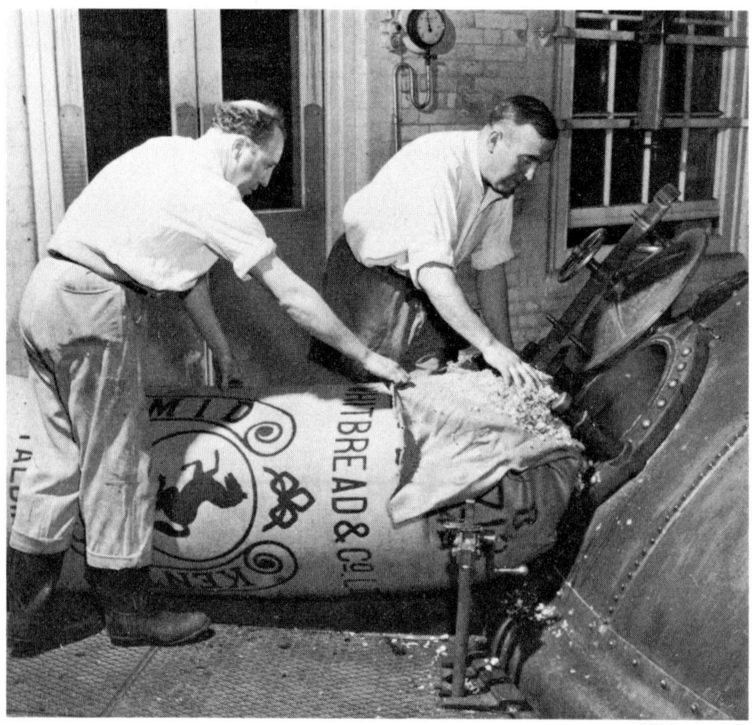

Whitbread and Co.

PUTTING HOPS INTO THE COPPER

Whitbread and Co.

PITCHING YEAST INTO THE YEAST MIXER

the cask are generally bitter beer, mild ale, and stout; other kinds are more usually bottled.

5. INNS AND TAVERNS. Under what is called the 'tied house' system, most inns and public-houses are owned by brewing companies. By the end of the 19th century they were buying inns and taverns; within 50 years they had acquired the majority of those in England and Wales. Many were rebuilt, and others renovated. The brewery owns and maintains the building, and usually also the equipment of the public rooms. It is let to a tenant at a fixed rent which is very low compared with the capital value of the house. This system allows adequate supervision of the conditions under which the brewery's beer reaches the consumer, and it facilitates long-term planning, and therefore economy of production. The well-known national brands of beer are stocked by almost every licensed house, whether 'tied' or not.

In some parts of the country the brewery retains full control of the 'tied house', which is run by a resident manager. This, too, is the practice in the State-managed houses in the Carlisle district. Of every 100 licensed premises in England and Wales, nearly 70 are let by breweries to 'tied' tenants, about 10 are directly managed by breweries, and the remainder are 'free', as are most of the houses in Scotland.

See also MALTING; WHISKY DISTILLING; CIDER-MAKING.
See also Vol. VI: HOPS.
See also Vol. II: FERMENTATION; YEAST.

BILL, *see* INVOICE.

BILLINGSGATE, *see* FISH TRADE.

BILL OF LADING. In the first place, this is a contract to convey goods from one port to another, made between a shipping company and a shipper (the person or firm which arranges for the shipping company to carry the goods). The contract states what risks will be accepted by the shipping company and what risks the shipper must insure against. Secondly, it is a receipt given by the master of a ship for the goods or cargo named in the bill of lading. The bill of lading is one of the most important documents used in international trade, and the system by which bankers lend money 'against' ships' cargoes depends entirely on it. Bills of lading are usually made out in three copies, because they are posted about the world from one banker or merchant

Shipped in good Order & Condition by Willm. Robinson Junr. & Co. of Liverpool in & upon the good Ship or Vessel called the whereof W Gibbs is Master for this present Voyage & now lying in the Port of Liverpool & bound for Oporto viz.

One Bale Merchandize
Three Parcels Patterns

marked & numbered as per Margin & are to be delivered in the like good Order & Condition at the aforesaid Port of Oporto (all & every the Dangers & Accidents of the Seas & Navigation of whatever Nature & Kind excepted) unto Mr. J. J. Cox or to Assigns Freight for the said Goods Shillings British Sterling per Ton of Forty Cubic Feet with Five per Cent for Primage Average accustomed. In Witness whereof the Master or Purser hath affirmed to four Bills of Lading all of this Tenor & Date. One of which being accomplished the rest to stand Void. Dated in Liverpool this 21 Day of February 1823.

Wm Gibbs

1 Bale 26. 3
@ 7d per foot 15. 5
Primage 10
Contribn 2. 6
£ 0. 19. 9

AN OLD BILL OF LADING

to another, and mails sometimes get damaged or destroyed.

In the third place, a bill of lading is what is called by business men a 'document of title'. The bill may be 'endorsed', like a cheque, having on its back the signature of the consignor (the person who sent the goods) or consignee (the person to whom they are sent), according to the way in which it has been drawn up. Provided that the bill is thus endorsed, the person who is in possession of it is the only one to whom the ship's AGENT (q.v.) at the port of destination will deliver the goods; without production of the endorsed bill of lading no goods will be delivered. A banker in London who is asked, say, by an exporter in London to advance money against the cargo shipped will insist upon all three copies of the endorsed bill of lading being handed to him as security. The banker then sends the bill of lading—which is usually attached to a BILL OF EXCHANGE, an insurance policy, an INVOICE (qq.v.), and other relevant documents—to his agent in the port of destination, in, say, Australia, who will arrange that the documents will only be handed to the importing merchant in Australia in exchange for the necessary cash.

Bills of lading are printed forms usually bearing the crest or coat of arms of the shipping company. They have been used for centuries, and their rather out-of-date language is left unchanged because the words and phrases used have been argued about before the law courts and have been given by judges a very definite meaning. Most bills of lading have a lengthy and picturesque list of all the risks of navigation for which the shipping line will not be responsible, such as: 'The Act of God, the King's Enemies, Pirates, Robbers, or Thieves by Land or Sea, arrests or restraints of Princes, Rulers, or People . . . barratry, jettison . . .' and so on.

See also OVERSEAS TRADE.

BILL OF EXCHANGE. This is a promise to pay a definite sum of money on a future date. A bill of exchange is a 'negotiable instrument': that is, it may be passed from one person to another; in this way VALUE (q.v.), either in goods or money, may be transferred from one person to another without the actual exchange of money. There are other documents which promise to pay money, but they are not true bills of exchange. The simplest of these is the IOU: the letters obviously representing the words 'I owe you.' An IOU is simply an acknowledgement of a debt, and cannot be bought and sold, or 'negotiated'. Between the IOU and the true bill of exchange comes the 'promissory note'. This is a negotiable promise to repay money. The difference between these three documents is seen in the examples given below of a debt of £1,000 owing to James Robinson by Thomas Perkins.

IOU

> To James Robinson
> IOU
> £1,000
> THOMAS PERKINS
> 1 Jan. 1962

Promissory Note

> £1,000 London, 1 Jan. 1962
> Three months after date I promise to pay to James Robinson or his order the sum of One Thousand Pounds.
> THOMAS PERKINS

Bill of Exchange

> £1,000 London, 1 Jan. 1962
> Three months after date pay to me or my order the sum of One Thousand Pounds value received.
> JAMES ROBINSON
> To: THOMAS PERKINS
>
> Accepted 1.1.62
> Payable at
> Midland Bank Ltd.
> Poultry, E.C.2
> THOMAS PERKINS

A special Act of Parliament, called the Bills of Exchange Act, lays down the rights and duties of persons whose names appear on bills of exchange; so in Great Britain it is more usual for promises of this kind to be drawn up in the true bill-of-exchange form. In Canada and the United States the promissory-note form is more usual, and in those countries the simple name 'note' is generally used.

A true bill of exchange is drawn up in the form of an invitation by the person claiming the money to the person owing it, and it does not become negotiable until the debtor signifies his 'acceptance' of the invitation, as in the illustration given. He is then called the 'acceptor', and the bill is called an 'acceptance'.

The interval of time between the drawing of a bill and its date of payment, or 'due date', is commonly called its 'usance'. In calculating the due dates of bills in Great Britain 3 'days of grace' are allowed by law in addition to the normal period of the bill. Thus Thomas Perkins's acceptance in the illustration is due 3 months and 3 days from 1 January 1962: that is, on 4 April 1962. Days of grace do not apply to the Treasury Bills issued by the British Government.

Money in one's pocket now, and money promised for the future, are not quite the same thing. A bill of exchange due 3 months ahead will not be worth its full face value when it is 'accepted'. The difference between the present and future value of bills is called their rate of 'discount'. It is generally stated at so much per cent. per annum. Thus, if the rate of discount were 2% per annum, a bill for £1,000 due exactly 3 months ahead would have a present value of £995. Bankers and others buy and sell bills of exchange as part of their ordinary business, and this is called 'discounting' bills. There are firms in the City of London who specialize in bill dealings and are called 'bill brokers' (*see* MONEY MARKET).

Manchester
Three Months after date pay to the order of Myself the Sum of Ninety Pounds
Value Received as advised
London

N. M. Rothschild & Sons

BILL OF EXCHANGE DRAWN BY NATHAN MAYER VON ROTHSCHILD IN 1804

Nathan Mayer opened the London house of the Rothschild banking business founded in Germany by his father

Barber Institute of Fine Arts

A DUTCH BLEACHING-GROUND

Painting by David Teniers the Younger (1610–90)

BLEACHING takes place in the making of TEXTILES (q.v.), either to give a white finish or to give a fabric a neutral colour before it is dyed. Wool and linen were the most important fabrics in the early days of the English textile industry. Wool, when well washed and scoured, was almost white, and any further bleaching was not attempted. Unbleached linen, however, had a brownish and unattractive appearance, and in the 18th century linen fabrics were regularly sent for bleaching to Holland. There were three stages in the Dutch process: steeping the fabrics for some time in alkaline liquor; repeated washings in buttermilk; and finally the spreading of the fabrics on the grass in sunshine and air for several months. This process was expensive, largely because of the long time taken. In 1756 Dr. Francis Horne of Edinburgh used a solution of weak sulphuric acid instead of buttermilk, and his process reduced the time from months to days.

Modern substances used are chlorine, hydrogen peroxide, and sulphur dioxide. The possibilities of chlorine were discovered in 1785, but it was some time before anyone invented a convenient compound. At the end of the 18th century a Glasgow chemical manufacturer introduced what is now called bleaching-powder, or chloride of lime. This is the general substance used for most modern fabrics, and particularly for cottons. Silks do not respond well to treatment by ordinary bleaching-powder, and certain kinds, particularly tussore, are usually bleached in a solution of hydrogen peroxide. Woollen fabrics may be bleached in the same way, or they may be 'stoved', that is, exposed when damp to the fumes of burning sulphur. To create a brilliant whiteness that bleaching alone cannot give, fluorescent brightening agents are now applied by a dyeing process to textiles. These agents function by absorbing ultra-violet rays and re-emitting them as a visible bluish-white light.

See also LINEN INDUSTRY; CHEMISTRY, INDUSTRIAL.

BOND. In business the word 'bond' generally means a written promise to pay money or to carry out some other undertaking. For example, importers of goods subject to Customs duty may postpone payment of duty if they sign a bond guaranteeing eventual payment. The word, however, is nowadays more specifically used for loans made by investors to governments and municipalities; in the United States it is also used for loans to industrial firms: in Britain these would be called DEBENTURES (q.v.).

In the City of London the word 'bond' generally means government and municipal loans whose ownership can be transferred from a seller to a buyer by delivery of the document which proves ownership. Such documents are called 'bearer bonds', and are given the name of 'floaters' by the members of the London MONEY MARKET (q.v.). Bearer bonds thus provide an extremely convenient type of SECURITY (q.v.) for borrowed money. As bearer bonds may change hands quite frequently, each bond has attached to it a sheet of numbered and dated coupons, about twice the size of a postage stamp, which must be cut off and handed in to the paying agent before any instalment of interest due can be claimed.

See also STOCK EXCHANGES.

BONDED WAREHOUSE, *see* WAREHOUSES.

BONUS, *see* WAGES.

BOOKBINDING. The purpose of binding a book is to hold the pages together in such a way that it can be opened for reading and closed when not being read.

1. HISTORY. Flat books replaced written rolls in the early Christian era (*see* BOOKS, HISTORY OF, Vol. IV), and the leaves of parchment were then placed between wooden boards to keep them flat. The first bound books, with the boards covered with leather, appeared in the 4th century. From that time magnificent bookbindings were made, some with decorated leather covers, some overlaid with metal set with precious stones, others with carved ivory plaques. Towards the end of the 15th century Europeans learned from the Moors to stamp patterns and letters in gold on the leather. Other materials were used too: velvet and embroidered covers were popular in Stuart England.

Until the 19th century books were seldom bound before being sold: the customer bought the printed sheets and had them bound in his favourite style, sometimes decorated with his coat of arms. Towards the end of the 18th century books began to be issued with the sheets already sewn and fastened between covers of thick cardboard. At first these were not lettered, for they were intended to be temporary cases to be replaced by leather bindings. Soon books came to be sold with the boards covered with paper, sometimes decorated with marbling, and with the title printed on stuck-on labels.

Cloth was used as a cheap substitute for leather in the early 19th century. It was often stamped to imitate leather, and stuck-on-labels persisted until a cloth was introduced which would take coloured lettering.

2. BINDING PROCESSES. Books are made of folded sheets of paper on which many pages have been printed (*see* PRINTING). The sheets are designed to be folded once or several times to

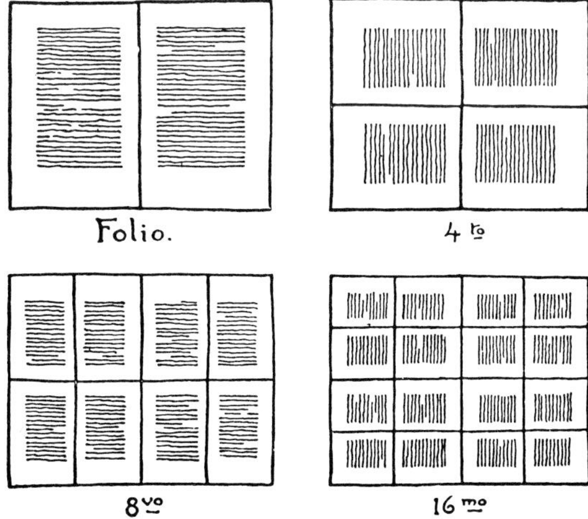

FIG. 1. HOW SHEETS OF PAPER ARE FOLDED

(Figs. 1 and 4 from Douglas Cockerell's *Bookbinding and the Care of Books*, Pitman, and Figs. 2, 3, 5 drawn by J. R. Tebbutt)

form books in Folio, Quarto, or smaller formats (*see* BOOK SIZES, Vol. IV). When folded the sheets make 'sections' of a book, each consisting of folded leaves fitting one inside another. A booklet may be made by sewing one section through the fold or 'spine'. A book is made of many sections joined together and fastened between covers. The work is done either by hand or, using quite different methods, by machine.

In hand binding the sections are held together by stitches through the back of the sections, and over tapes or round cords stretched at right angles across the spine of the book (*see* Fig. 2). An additional 'endpaper' section (generally a

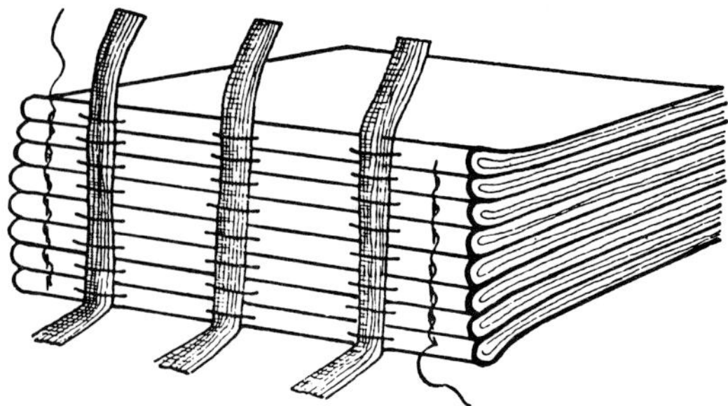

FIG. 2. THE STITCHED SECTIONS

piece of stouter paper) is sewn or stuck on at the beginning and end of the book. The ends of the tapes or 'slips' are usually pasted down on to the endpapers to make a secure fixing for the

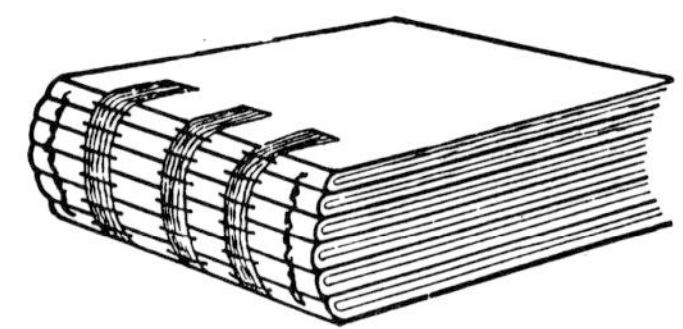

FIG. 3. THE ENDPAPERS ADDED AND THE BACK ROUNDED

boards of the book-cover. The spine of the book is brushed with thin glue and, while the glue is still soft, the book is 'rounded', either by gently tapping the spine into a convex form with a hammer or by a machine (Fig. 3). When the glue sets the book is held in shape. Rounding is followed by 'backing'; this process forms joints for the hard cover; the book is gripped between wedge-shaped backing boards in a press, and the sections are fanned out with the stroking motion of a hammer (Fig. 4).

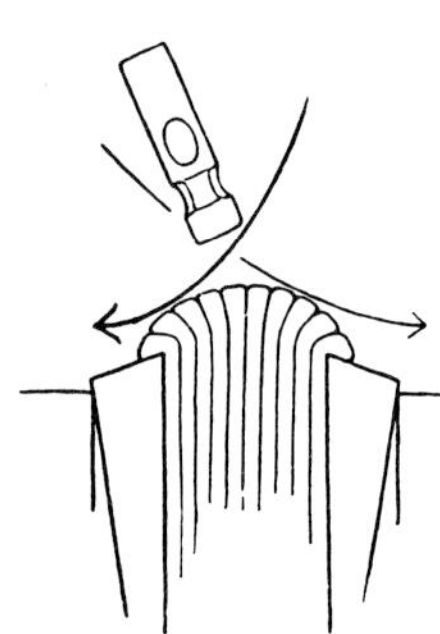

FIG. 4. BACKING THE BOOK

The book may be covered with leather, vellum, or cloth or paper. A leather cover is stuck direct to the spine. If the book is sewn on cords, the slips are laced into the boards (Fig. 5), and the book is covered with leather stuck direct to the spine, so that the cords stand out as raised bands on it. Instead of covering the whole book with the same material, it may be 'half-bound', with a piece of leather, cloth, or vellum covering the spine and part of the boards, and sometimes the corners, the rest of the boards being covered with cloth or paper.

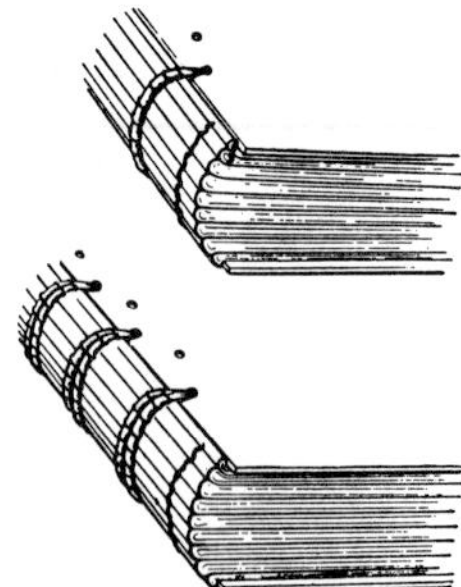

FIG. 5. CORDS LACED TO THE BOARDS

If the book is to be lettered in gold and tooled with a pattern, heated brass tools are pressed on the cover. The impression is painted with a mixture called 'glair', made of white of egg. When the glair is dry, the cover is lightly greased, and gold leaf is laid on. The hot tool is then pressed through the gold; this fires the glair, so that it holds the gold in the impression of the tool; the surplus gold round the impression is removed with a gold rubber and benzine. 'Blind tooling' is done by using the hot tools on damp leather, when they leave an impression darker than the surrounding leather. This blind tooling can be very effective, and may be satisfactorily combined with gold tooling.

3. MACHINE BINDING. Nowadays nearly all books (this encyclopaedia for instance) are bound by machinery. The sheets are first folded on machines which can be adjusted to make the required number of folds. Then the endpapers are attached by a narrow strip of glue to the first and last sections. The sections are mechanically 'gathered' together in their correct order.

An increasing number of books are now held together by what is named 'perfect' binding, that is to say simply by glue along one edge. To fit them for this, the gathered sections are put in a machine which grinds off the folded spines of the sections so that the books become collections of separate leaves. The ground edge is then sprayed with plastic glue under pressure so that it penetrates a little way between the leaves. This binding is largely used for popular 'paperback' editions.

Most books, however, are made of sections sewn together through the folds. They are then compressed in a nipping-press, and the three free sides are cut smooth. Then they go to a machine which passes the spines over a glue-roller and forces glue a little way between the sections, after which the books are mechanically rounded and backed. A strip of mull (a kind of gauze) is glued to the spine so as to overlap about half an inch on either side. The overhanging flaps of mull are afterwards pasted with the endpapers so that they stick to the covers when the books are fitted into their cases by a 'casing-in'

Thomas-Photos

HAND TOOLING A FINE LEATHER BINDING

machine. Lastly, the books are put in powerful presses until they are dry.

The cases of strawboard or millboard covered with cloth are made by successive operations on one machine.

Lettering and ornament are put on the cases by a process called 'blocking'. A block, generally of brass, on which the letters and ornament are cut in relief, is fitted in a power-driven press in which it is kept hot. A reel of film, on which vapourized gold has been deposited, is fed into the press wide enough to cover the area to be stamped in gold. The gold is coated on the back with an adhesive which fixes it in the hot impression made by the block.

Thomas-Photos

BOOKS, AFTER ASSEMBLY, HAVING THEIR CASES FITTED BY MACHINE

See also Vol. IV: Books, History of.

BOOK-KEEPING, or Accountancy, is the keeping of records of money transactions, a practice as old as the transactions themselves. Modern double-entry book-keeping dates from the merchants and bankers of the Italian Renaissance, which began in the 15th century. Until then merchants had always distinguished in their records between their assets (what they possessed and what they were owed by others) and their liablities (what they themselves owed to others). But the Italians discovered that if the difference between assets and liabilities, which was what a merchant was worth, was put on to the liabilities side of the records as a balancing item, both sides of the records added up to the same amount; and they discovered also that every transaction would cause a change in two items of the records, and that these changes would cause the total of the assets still to equal the total of the liabilities. For example, if raw materials were bought for cash, the asset 'cash' would be diminished, and the asset 'raw material' would be correspondingly increased, leaving the total of assets unchanged; while, if a liability to a merchant for goods bought on credit were paid off in cash, total liabilities and total assets would be diminished by equal amounts. As the years passed, the new accountancy became a standardized technique.

The most important rule is that records of different things must not be jumbled together. The records, or 'accounts', must aim at giving the maximum of information; and this would not be secured if a mixed collection of assets, such as raw materials, cash, plant and machinery, and what Jones owed the business, were all included in an account called Miscellaneous Assets. Another rule is that previous 'single-entry' records must be put into 'double-entry' form by totalling the assets and liabilities, subtracting the liabilities from the assets (assuming that the business is solvent), and including this difference on the liabilities side of the accounts, where it is usually called Capital in a one-man business or partnership. These opening entries

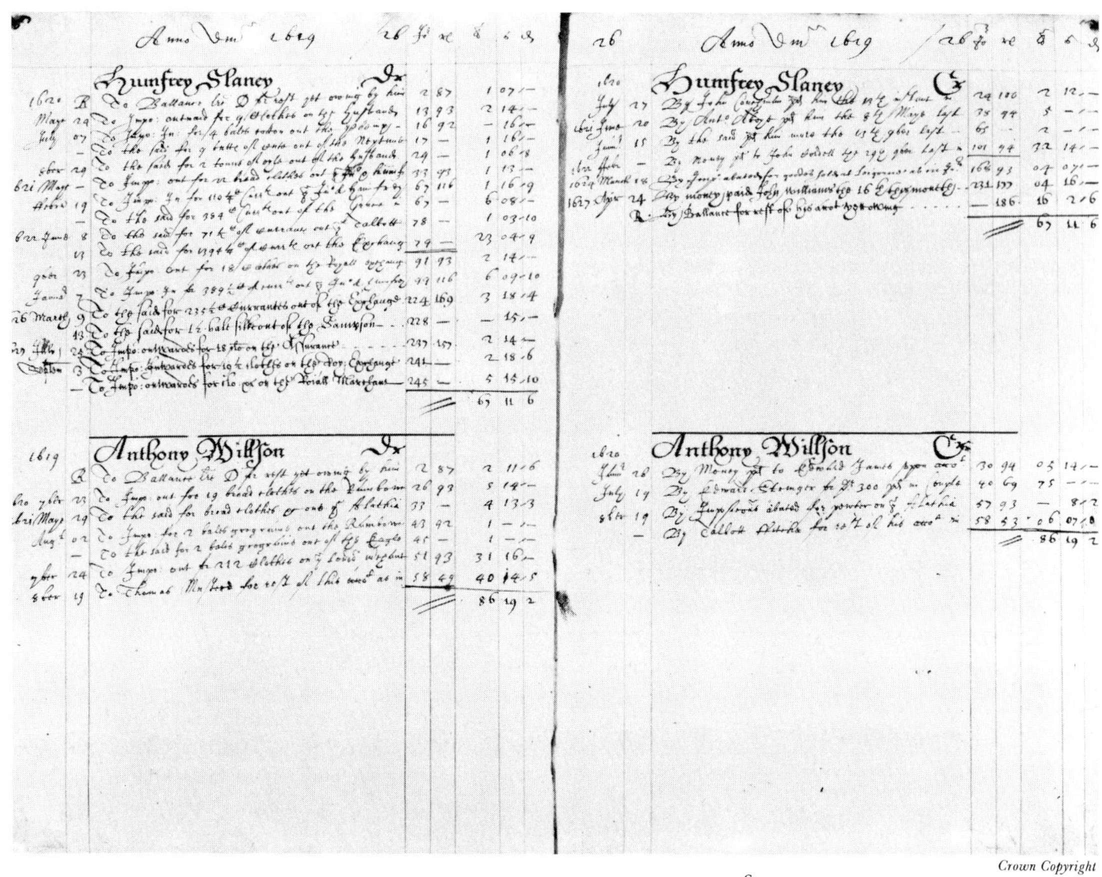
Anno Dom 1619

Humfrey Slaney Dr

Anthony Willson Dr

Anno Dom 1619

Humfrey Slaney Cr

Anthony Willson Cr

PERSONAL LEDGER OF THE LEVANT COMPANY, 1619

Debits to customers are on the left and credits on the right. At the end of the year each account is balanced.
State Papers, Foreign, Archives S.P. 105/157

are usually made through a Subsidiary Book called the Journal (which is one of the Books of Original Entry), from which the information is copied, or 'posted', into the main account-book, which is called the Ledger. If the book-keeping is done by pen and ink on old-fashioned lines, the Ledger is a bound volume with numbered pages, in which at the outset as many pages are allotted, in alphabetical order, to each separate account as may be foreseen in advance. Such Ledgers, however, soon become overcrowded, and accounts reaching the end of their allotment of pages have to be carried forward or back to any blank pages that may be found. Nowadays, loose-leaf Ledgers are more used. It is a rule of good accountancy that no entry may be made in the Ledger except on the authority of one of the Subsidiary Books. Here is an example from the Journal of J. Smith, who decides on 1 January 1960 to count up his assets and liabilities and to keep accounts on the double-entry system:

1960		*Dr.*	*Cr.*
		£	£
1 Jan.	Cash	500	
	Stock (*of goods traded in*) .	1,500	
	Sundry Debtors (*amounts owed by customers*) . . .	1,000	
	Furniture and Fittings . .	200	
	Freehold Premises . .	5,000	
	Sundry Creditors (*amounts owing to suppliers of goods*) .		1,200
	Capital, J. Smith (*balancing item: what he is worth*) .		7,000
	Being assets and liabilities at date	£8,200	£8,200

The details in brackets would not appear in the Journal; they are put in here to explain the meanings of certain conventional terms. 'Dr.' and 'Cr.' are used to signify the Assets and Liabilities sides of the Ledger respectively. To put an item on the left-hand, or Dr., side of an account is to 'debit' the item; to put it on the right-hand, or Cr., side is to 'credit' it. The 'balance' of any account is the difference between the debit and credit sides. The accuracy of the double-entry posting of the ledger can be checked by listing all these balances, when the total of debit balances should equal the total of credit balances. This is called a Trial Balance.

It is found convenient, even in the smallest of businesses, to keep the record of cash and bank transactions in a separate book, called the Cash Book. This book then becomes both a part of the Ledger and also a Subsidiary Book, from whose evidence entries are made in the Ledger itself. Thus, if W. Jones paid by cheque to Smith some money owed to him, this would appear on the Dr. side of the Bank column of Smith's Cash Book, and on this evidence and authority the account of Jones in the Ledger would be credited.

Subsidiary Books called Day Books are kept in some businesses. They record Purchases and Sales of goods on CREDIT (q.v.), and Returns and Allowances made to or by customers. They save work, because only the monthly totals for Purchases, Sales, or Returns and Allowances need be posted to those accounts. Details affecting customers' accounts must, of course, be posted daily.

Accounts in the Ledger may be Real, Personal, or Nominal. (*a*) Real Accounts are records of physical assets, such as Cash, Furniture and Fittings, Plant and Machinery, Stock, Freehold Premises, and their balances are normally debit. (*b*) Personal Accounts are naturally the accounts of persons, principally customers, although, in a partnership, the partners also may have personal accounts. The Bank column of the Cash Book is a personal account, as the Banker is normally the debtor of a business. The balances of Personal Accounts may be debit or credit. (*c*) Nominal Accounts are those which record losses or gains, expenditure or income. It is from these that the profit or loss of a business is worked out. These Nominal Accounts are the crucial part of double-entry book-keeping, and must be explained in detail.

The debit, or assets, side of the accounts records the assets of the business, whether these are physical assets, such as goods, machinery, buildings, and cash, or assets in the form of debts owed to the business by other persons. The credit, or liabilities, side records who are the owners of these assets. If the business owes as much to outside creditors as it possesses in assets, then the liabilities side will record only the amounts owing to these outside creditors. If it owes less to outside creditors than it possesses in assets, then the proprietor of the business will himself own the balance of assets not owing to outside creditors, and the amount that he owns will be recorded in his Capital Account, as explained above. From this it follows that as

STOCK AND FOIL OF A PRIVATE TALLY: A PRIMITIVE FORM OF BOOK-KEEPING

Tallies were used for receipts, the amount being indicated by notches. After these had been cut the shafts were split, the longer piece (the stock) being given to the payer, and the shorter piece (the foil) being kept for reference (compare the counterfoil of a cheque). When the accounts were audited, the two pieces were fitted together to see if they would 'tally'. This tally for £3. 13*s*. 4*d*. is dated 1361. The largest notches represent pounds (3½), the next shillings (3), and the smallest pence (4). *Exchequer, K.R., Accounts Various E. 101/678/4*

assets increase, provided that liabilities to outside creditors do not correspondingly increase, the proprietor's Capital Account will also increase. If goods, standing on the assets side of the books at £1,000, are sold for £2,000 cash, then assets are increased by £1,000 and the proprietor's Capital Account is also increased by £1,000. If it is then found that the sale of these goods has necessitated a wages payment of £50 to the salespeople who sold them, cash assets will be diminished by £50 and the proprietor's Capital Account will also be decreased by £50. The Capital Account will therefore increase by the growth of assets through profitable trading, and will decrease through the shrinkage of assets caused by the payment of wages and similar expenses. As the Capital Account is a credit balance, it follows that all increases of it will be credits and that all decreases will be debits. It is found convenient in book-keeping to open separate accounts for the various ways in which these increases or decreases of the Capital Account may come about. It is these separate accounts that are called the Nominal Accounts, and they must not be regarded as assets or liabilities. They are only detailed and temporary statements of how changes in the proprietor's Capital Account have come about, and they all eventually disappear when the financial results of the trading year are worked out.

To find the profit or loss for the trading year, the accuracy of the 'posting' must first be checked by taking out a Trial Balance. All the Nominal Account balances are then transferred to a Trading and Profit and Loss Account, in which they appear on the same side as they were on in the Ledger. The Trading Section shows gross trading profit; the Profit and Loss Section shows net profit, that is, the profit left after the expenses of distribution and administration have been deducted. Smith's Trading Account for the year 1960 might be as follows:

Dr.			*Cr.*
	£		£
Value of Stock at beginning of year	1,400	Sales	9,000
Purchases of goods	4,500	Value of Stock at end of year	900
Warehouse wages	1,500		
,, expenses	150		
Gross Profit (to Profit and Loss Section)	2,350		
	£9,900		£9,900

His Profit and Loss Account for the same year might be as follows:

	£		£
Advertising	400	Gross Profit (from Trading section)	2,350
Bad Debts	100	Rent of premises sublet	100
Delivery charges	200	Cash discounts received	200
Salaries of office staff	1,000		
Cash discounts allowed	50		
Depreciation on furniture and fittings	50		
Net Profit (to Capital Account)	850		
	£2,650		£2,650

The items 'Bad Debts' and 'Depreciation' in the Profit and Loss section arise as follows. Not only is it necessary for all the Nominal Accounts to be transferred to the Trading and Profit and Loss Account, but there must be a survey of Real and Personal assets to make sure that they are really worth their book values. If, for example, the resale value of Furniture and Fittings is less than their value as shown in the books, the difference between these values is really a loss, and must be debited to a Nominal Account called 'Depreciation', so as to state the book value accurately. Similarly, a debtor who can never be expected to pay must have his balance transferred from his Personal Account to a Nominal Account called Bad Debts, for it has ceased to be an asset and has become a loss.

The final stage is the drawing up of a Balance Sheet. The Nominal Accounts have all disappeared, and have become the single item of £850, this being net profit. This, which belongs to the proprietor, must be credited to his Capital Account. The Ledger will then contain only Real and Personal Accounts, and, if these balances are listed, the result will be:

Balance Sheet of J. Smith as at 31 December 1960

Liabilities	£	£	*Assets*	£
Sundry Creditors		500	Cash in hand	40
J. Smith, Capital:			Cash at Bank	760
on 1 Jan. 1960	7,000		Stock of goods	900
Add net profit for year 1960	850		Sundry Debtors	1,500
		7,850	Furniture and Fittings less Depreciation	150
			Freehold Premises	5,000
		£8,350		£8,350

In Britain, but in very few other countries,

Institute of Chartered Accountants

ACCOUNTANTS AT WORK

Engraving from the title-page of Waningen's *The Right Practice of Italian Bookkeeping*, 1672. Beside the ledgers are inkpots, sandbox, quills, and knives for cutting them

Balance Sheets are usually presented with the liabilities on the left-hand side and the assets on the right. No reason except tradition seems to exist for this confusing convention, which reverses the normal order of the Ledger.

These are the essentials of accountancy. Naturally, there are many refinements. Mechanical methods may be used, as in banks; Ledgers may be loose cards instead of bound books; Day Books may be merely files of duplicated invoices. Day Books may be arranged in columns, so that the Purchases and Sales of different departments of a business may be shown separately, and departmental Profit and Loss Accounts be drawn up. Expenses may be expressed as percentages of TURNOVER (q.v.) or net sales, so that the progress of the business may be constantly watched and accounts be linked up with COSTING and STATISTICS (qq.v.). Provision for DEPRECIATION (q.v.) may be arranged by rather complicated mathematical methods. The accounts of LIMITED COMPANIES (q.v.) must be presented in the form laid down by the Companies Act of 1948. Their capital being fixed, the 'balancing item' will be the undistributed profits remaining after payment of DIVIDENDS (q.v.), some of which remain undistributed for years and are called Reserves.

See also AUDITING; ACCOUNTING, MACHINE; BUDGETARY CONTROL.

BOOM, *see* TRADE CYCLE.

BOOT AND SHOE MAKING. 1. HISTORY. Boot and shoe making in Europe on modern lines dates from the 15th century when boots with heels were probably first revived in Spain. The general use of the heeled or 'European' shoe brought about great changes in the technique of boot and shoe making.

Since the introduction of the European type of shoe a device called a 'last' has been generally used. Lasts are wooden patterns of the type of foot the boots or shoes have to fit. In early days there were few lasts, and shoes were much the same shape from Elizabethan times to the early 19th century. The standard pattern, which had many small variations, was a shoe with a plain front, and a wide high tongue over the instep. The whole front was made in one piece. There was a back or 'counter', also in one piece, with two projecting portions overlapping the tongue on the instep and tied or buckled together.

2. CUTTING. Even in primitive days shoe-making involved two main tasks, cutting the materials to shape, and shoe-making proper. Egyptian pictures show this plainly, even in the days of the Pharaohs, and modern illustrations of shoe-makers at work tell the same story. Shoe-making proper is subdivided into two main processes; stitching the uppers, and 'making' the shoes. The workers who form the uppers to the lasts, and attach the bottoms to the uppers, are now called 'making-room operatives'.

Although shoes have been made of many substances, particularly for indoor use, leather is the traditional material. A piece of leather will stretch more in one direction than in another, and as some parts of a shoe must 'give' while others must not, the actual cutting of leather calls for much skill.

The cutting of sole leathers needs less varied skill than the cutting of upper leathers, as fewer kinds of hides are used. All the separate parts of the bottom of a shoe come from cattle hides only. The amount of TANNING (q.v.) depends on the purpose for which the hide is to be used. Leather for the softer parts of the shoe is mildly tanned. Parts required for the sole itself are tanned so as to produce leather of maximum 'tightness', or minimum 'stretch' or 'give'. Cutters of sole leather must see that the lines of tightness in the hide run from heel to toe. The more mildly tanned portions of sole leather are not used as outsoles, but may be used as insoles, middle-soles, or stiffenings.

The upper leather cutter, or 'clicker', has to deal with the skins of most of the animals and reptiles in the world. His trade has always

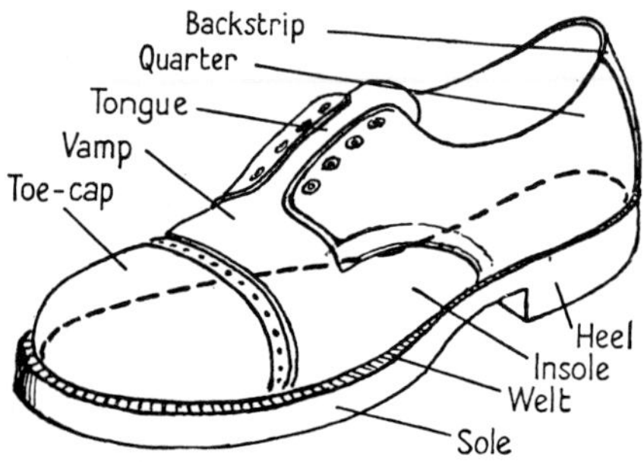

THE PARTS OF A TRADITIONAL LEATHER SHOE

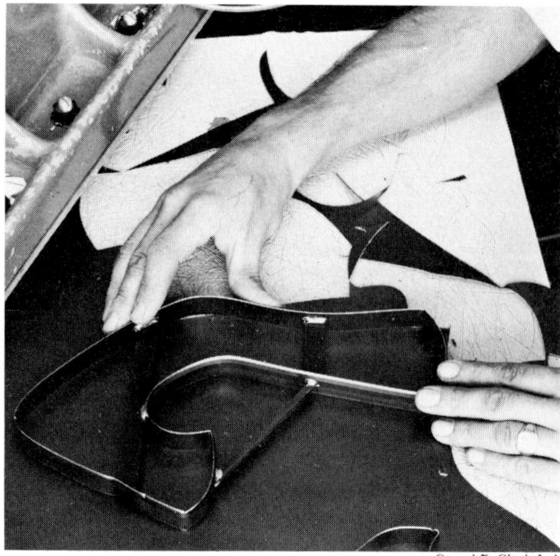

C. and J. Clark Ltd.

CUTTING LEATHER FOR THE UPPERS OF SHOES

The cutter places the knives, shaped to the patterns of the vamp and quarters, on the leather and a hydraulic press then stamps out the sections

taken a long time to learn, and as newer materials come into use, his craft becomes still more complex. His real task is to select that direction of cut in his leathers which will make the resulting shoes most likely to wear well and keep their shape, having stretch where stretch is necessary, and tightness or resistance elsewhere. In this connexion it does not matter whether the clicker cuts his leathers with a hand-knife on a board (which is the old method) or whether he uses a modern machine. The means of making the cuts is secondary to where he makes them.

3. MAKING. Boots and shoes used to be hand-sewn, and those made to measure still are, one maker completing all the processes, including finishing the bottoms of the shoes. But in recent years the shoe manufacturing industry has been largely mechanized and mass-production methods have been introduced. Modern shoe-making machines are, in the main, power-tools for doing the work carried out by hand-tools in earlier days, but in machine-production there is more DIVISION OF LABOUR (q.v.). Each operative now concentrates on a single specialized job.

High-quality precision shoe making has become largely a matter of preparing pre-fabricated sections and individual components, and then bringing them together at an assembly point. Stitching leather pieces to form the complete upper is called 'closing', an operation which is carried out by skilled girl machinists. Heels, soles, insoles, stiffeners, and other parts of a shoe are made in separate departments, and these are then mustered for assembly in the 'making' room.

Soles are often made of synthetic materials. Stitching, as in the old hand-sewn days, is still used for attaching the soles to the uppers, especially in making men's welted shoes; but the stitching is now done by machine. More commonly the sole is cemented to the upper with a very strong adhesive. The most up-to-date technique is to use high pressure vulcanizing: a complete sole and heel unit is moulded and irremovably bonded to the upper in one operation.

Although leather is still the best material for good-quality shoes, shoe uppers are now being cut from other and cheaper materials as well. PLASTICS (q.v.) are being used increasingly, and some manufacturers are already producing the all-plastic shoe. Stiletto heels are also made from plastic materials.

4. ORGANIZATION. The Worshipful Company of Cordwainers (*see* CITY COMPANIES) has always looked after and guarded the industry since it was granted a charter in 1439. 'Cordwainer' is probably an early corruption of 'cordovan', or 'cordovaner'; cordovan is an excellent soft leather originally made in the Spanish district of Cordoba. Shoe-making guilds (*see* CRAFT GUILDS) were formed in various parts of Britain at different dates, and survived until the early 19th century. The Cordwainers' Company is still an active organization to-day, and runs the Cordwainers' Technical College in London.

C. and J. Clark Ltd.

MAKING A SHOE

The toe and forepart are shaped by being pulled over the last by machine

The City and Guilds of London Institute has a long history, and has been a great help to the technical side of the shoe industry since the end of the guild and apprenticeship system. Most of the technical schools training shoe-makers to day make the Institute's syllabus the basis of their instruction. The influence of the forgotten craftsmen of the past is therefore still felt within the trade.

Until about 100 years ago the industry was principally organized on the DOMESTIC SYSTEM (q.v.); except for cutting, the storage and classification of lasts, final dressing and packing, the work was done by out-workers in their own homes. The organization of the industry on a factory basis arose from economic rather than technical causes. Until shoe lengths and widths had been standardized throughout the country, it was impossible for a single maker to have an output large enough to justify the use of machinery in a big factory. When the standardization of sizes and fittings had been achieved, the industry began to swing over to the factory system.

The boot and shoe trade is one of the earliest examples in Britain of industrial organization on the 'vertical' system. A firm so organized controls the whole sequence of processes, from purchase of the raw materials to the selling of the finished article in the retail shop.

For centuries shoe making has been the staple industry of Northampton and Stafford—Northampton shod Cromwell's Ironsides in the 17th century. Leicester, Bristol, Kettering, Wellingborough, Rushden, Leeds, and Norwich are also most important centres. In the West Country the industry has expanded greatly and to-day the largest shoe-manufacturing organization in the country is centred upon Street, Somerset, where shoes have been made for 130 years; there are also shoe factories in Plymouth, Bath, Bridgwater, Warminster, Minehead, and Weston-super-Mare. Each centre specializes in certain qualities and types. Individual factories specialize very narrowly, and firms which produce a wide variety of footwear tend to spread their production over several factories, often situated in widely separated towns. This is largely because the factory workers themselves are also specialized, and naturally prefer to stick to the work for which they have been trained.

See also TANNING; LEATHER; CLOTHING INDUSTRY.

BOTTLE-MAKING, *see* GLASS-MAKING.

Crown Copyright

17TH-CENTURY DUTCH CHANDELIER MADE OF BRASS

Victoria and Albert Museum

BRASS is the name given to a family of ALLOYS (q.v. Vol. VIII) all consisting essentially of copper and zinc. Some contain low proportions of other metals to strengthen the alloy or to increase its resistance to corrosion. Brasses containing more than 15% zinc are moderately strong and fairly resistant to corrosion; those having 38% zinc or less are ductile, that is, capable of being rolled, drawn, or spun when cold. Alloys with from 40% to 44% zinc are stronger and harder but less ductile, and can be effectively worked only when hot. From its first manufacture, at about 40 B.C., until the end of the 18th century, brass was made by heating a mixture of zinc ore and charcoal with copper; since 1800 it has generally been made by adding metallic zinc to molten copper.

The Romans used brass containing about 15% zinc for coins and artificial jewellery; they also made household utensils of soft brass. For 500 years after the fall of Rome little brass was made in Europe, but production continued in Syria and the Levant. In Persia and India brass-making began in the 6th century, the Persians later becoming famous for highly decorated brass bowls and ewers, often enriched with silver work. The Chinese first made brass in the 8th century.

In Europe, brass-making revived after 1100, and considerable industries arose in Flanders and Germany. The alloys were used for buckles, pins, brooches, ornaments, domestic pots and pans, candlesticks and, later, for harness fittings and 'horse brasses'. Many pieces were cast; others were hammered out from plates. Memorial brasses (*see* BRASSES, Vol. XII) were made of 'latten', the medieval name for brass sheets made of 60 parts copper, 30 of zinc, and 10 of lead and tin.

Machines were first used for manufacturing brass goods in the middle of the 18th century; boxes, trays, and ornaments were mechanically stamped from rolled sheets, and pins and brooches were fashioned from drawn wire. Birmingham became famous as the world-centre of this industry.

To-day, brass is widely used for components in engineering and shipbuilding, and also for domestic appliances. When strength is essential up to 44% zinc is used, and very small proportions of iron, tin, manganese, and lead are often added. Methods of manufacture vary. Rods, bars, and sections are extruded (*see* FORGING AND PRESSING, Vol. VIII); plates are hot-rolled; sheets and strips are cold-rolled. These various forms are converted by forging, hot-pressing, cold-pressing, or spinning into the components required. Brass tubes containing about 30% zinc are cold-drawn and used as vital parts of engines and condensers. Many domestic fittings and engineering components are cast.

BREAD-MAKING, *see* BAKING INDUSTRY. *See also* VOL. XI: BREAD-MAKING.

BREWERIES, *see* BEER BREWING.

BRICKS AND TILES. 1. Most building bricks and many roofing tiles used in England are made of burnt clay. Bricks form part of a wall or arch and must therefore be strong enough to carry the weight of floors and roofs and to make a stable structure. While most bricks are about the standard size much larger bricks, usually called blocks, are becoming popular; these are either perforated or made hollow to reduce their weight. Bricks are made oblong so that they can be 'bonded' together, that is interlocked with each other (*see* BRICKWORK, Vol. VIII). By contrast, roofing tiles have no weight to carry; in fact, their own weight is carried by the roofing timbers. They are therefore made as thin and as light as possible, but must be able to keep out the rain and snow.

2. HISTORY. The word 'brick' is only about 500 years old, but 'tile' is derived from the Latin *tegula*. Both bricks and tiles were used

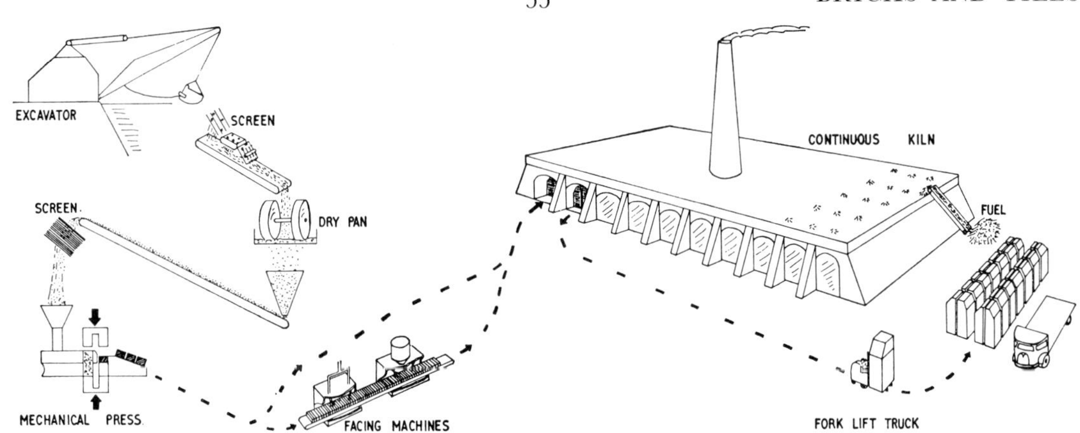

FIG. 1. DIAGRAM OF BRICK-MAKING BY THE SEMI-DRY PRESSED PROCESS

very early in architectural history. Well-burnt bricks were made in Mesopotamia at least 6,000 years ago, and there are still great heaps of them in the ruins of the city of Babylon. This was probably where the brick-making industry began. In Egypt bricks made of Nile mud mixed with sand and straw, and dried in the sun, were used from prehistoric times. In the Bible we are told how the captive Israelites had to make bricks for their Egyptian masters. To oppress them, the Egyptians made them collect their own straw and make the same number of bricks as if they had been given the straw to start with. Egyptian peasants still make bricks of mud mixed with chopped straw, and then laid out to dry in the blazing sun; and most of the houses of the villagers in the Nile Valley are built of this primitive material. Ancient Egyptian mud bricks were far larger than modern bricks, and were heavy to handle, often needing two men to lift them. Many brick buildings were erected in the countries governed by the Romans. We find bricks and tiles in England in the ruins of the chief Roman cities. Roman burnt bricks were also large (about 2 feet square), but they were only about 2 inches thick.

The arts of brick-making and brick building were lost in Britain after the Romans left about A.D. 400, and it was not until the late Middle Ages that bricks were used again in Britain. Houses and some churches, such as that of St. Osyth in Essex, were then built of brick in many parts of East Anglia. Flemish weavers had settled there, and at first the bricks used were imported from Flanders and Holland. From Tudor times onwards brick buildings became common. In 1625 the present standard size of approximately 9 by $4\frac{1}{2}$ in. by 3 in. was enforced by law, although the thickness was often less than the standard 3 inches. Centuries of experience have proved this size of brick to be the most convenient for handling, and therefore the most economical of labour.

In medieval times most houses in London were built of timber and roofed with thatch

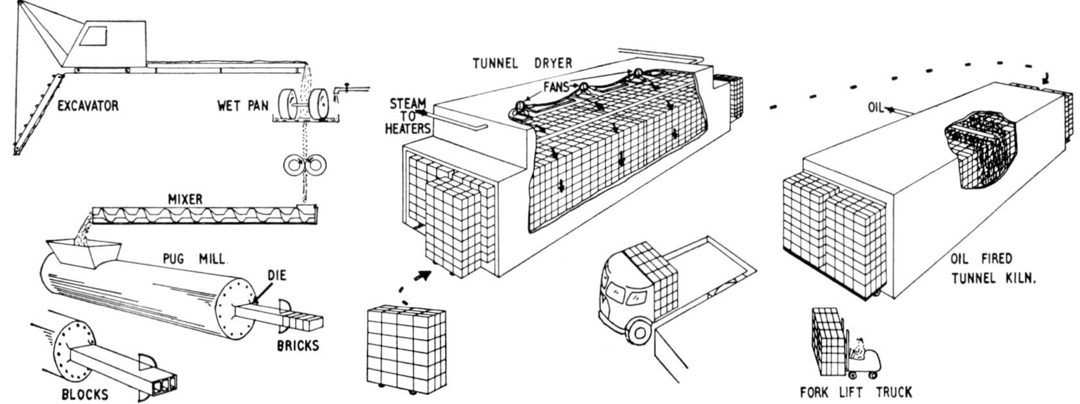

FIG. 2. DIAGRAM OF BRICK AND BLOCK MAKING BY THE WIRE-CUT PROCESS

(*see* HOUSES, HISTORY OF, Vol. XI). Serious fires occurred in 1135 and 1212, resulting in a mayoral order of 1245 that, in future, all houses in the principal streets should be roofed with tiles or slates. Nevertheless, timber houses (for example, Staple Inn, 1586) continued to be built up to the time of the Great Fire of 1666. Then wooden houses were forbidden, and this naturally gave a fillip to the brick-making trade and to the bricklayer's craft. Since then brick has been the standard material in England for walls and chimneys, except in certain districts where stone is easily obtainable; but even in those districts stone has been largely replaced by brick in modern times. Attempts have recently been made to find substitutes for brick, and many alternative systems of construction, mostly involving the use of concrete, have been evolved, but in several respects brick continues to hold its own. Brick should never be regarded as an inferior building material. If properly treated architecturally, it can be as beautiful in its way as stone, and it keeps its warmth of colour in all but the sootiest atmospheres. As the Roman work found at Verulamium (St. Albans) and elsewhere proves, brick is also extremely lasting, but this depends on the quality of the clay used and the efficiency of manufacture. All these remarks apply equally to tiles. One of the best examples of fine old brickwork in England is Hampton Court Palace. The earlier part, Wolsey's building (1515–23), is typical of Tudor work; the later part, Wren's building (1689–1702), shows English brickwork at its finest, and the bricks used have preserved their brilliant colour for nearly three centuries.

Rural Industries Bureau

MAKING BRICKS BY HAND

The surplus clay is being removed from the mould

The Worshipful Company of Tylers and Bricklayers was founded in the City of London at some unknown date in the Middle Ages, and obtained its first charter in 1568. It is still in existence. It is one of the smaller CITY COMPANIES (q.v.) and has no hall of its own; but in various ways it fosters technical education in the crafts of bricklaying and tiling.

3. BRICK-MAKING. Suitable clay or 'brick earth' for brick-making is found in most countries. It occurs in layers which were originally formed by the gradual disintegration of various rocks, then washed off by currents of water and deposited in the beds of rivers, lakes, or seas which have long since disappeared (*see* CLAYS AND SHALES, Vol. III). England is rich in clay deposits, almost all of which are used for the production of bricks. The clays range from Devonian shale, laid down over 300 million years ago, to the brick earth of south-eastern England, laid down not more than one million years ago. The type of clay has a marked bearing not only on the strength, texture, and colour of bricks, but also on the processes by which they are made.

Five distinct methods—hand-moulded, soft mud, wire-cut, stiff-plastic, and semi-dry pressed—are employed in England for making building bricks. Typical of hand-moulded and soft-mud bricks are the yellow 'London Stocks', made from a mixture of brick earth, chalk, and rubbish. Their yellow colour comes from the lime in the chalk. Wire-cut bricks are made in all parts of the country from all the clays that are sufficiently plastic for this method of brick-making, and so their properties and appearance vary widely. Blocks are always made by the wire-cut method. The stiff-plastic method is used where exceptionally strong and dense bricks are required; 'Staffordshire Blue Engineering bricks' in which the iron is reduced to give the blue colour, and the hard, dense bricks of the North of England, in which the iron is oxidized to give the bright-red colour, are typical stiff-plastic products. 'Fletton' bricks, which were first made at the

London Brick Co. Ltd.

MAKING HOLLOW BLOCKS BY THE WIRE-CUT PROCESS

The clay in the pug mill on the left is forced through a die which forms it into a continuous column. This is cut by a wire cutter on the right

village of that name near Peterborough, now account for about one-third of all the bricks used in England; they are made by the semi-dry pressed method from the Oxford Clay which, because of its shaly nature and constant moisture content, is excellently suited for breaking up and grinding in a dry grinding pan. Iron in the clay makes the Fletton brick pink, but today, a variety of colour facings are made from Oxford clay by sandblasting sand and other granular matter on to the undried brick, before burning.

Whichever method is used, the clay must first be dug, usually with some form of mechanical excavator, and then transported to the factory for processing. For each of the first four methods mentioned above (the wet processes), the raw clay is prepared by being ground and mixed with water in order to make it sufficiently plastic so that it can be moulded or formed into the shape of a brick, and to break down any impurities. For the fifth method (semi-dry pressed), the raw clay is ground in a dry pan without the addition of water, and the powder so formed is screened to remove over-size particles.

In the wet processes, the prepared clay is extruded through a die in a pug mill in a column, rather in the manner in which sausage meat is forced through a sausage-making machine. For the hand-moulded method and its mechanical counterpart, the soft-mud method, a 'clot' of clay, cut off from the column, is thrown into a wooden mould or stock (hence the name 'Stock' bricks). In the wire-cut process, for which slightly less water is used, the column of clay emerging from the die of the pug mill is cut off with a wire to the size of a brick—rather as a grocer cuts cheese. For the extrusion of perforated bricks or hollow blocks a more complicated die has to be used. For the stiff-plastic method, for which still less water is used, a clot is cut off from the extruded column and is then pressed into a brick shape in a mechanical press. In the semi-dry pressed method, for which no water is added, the powdered clay particles are pressed together in a mechanical press to form a strong, hard, 'green' brick.

Whichever method of forming the brick is adopted, the green bricks must be dried to remove nearly all the moisture they contain before they can be burnt, and since during drying the wet clay shrinks, this process must be carefully controlled. In days gone by, the bricks were dried for 3 to 6 weeks in the open air, protected by small roofs or 'hacks', but nowadays nearly all bricks are dried under cover, on hot floors, or in specially heated chambers, or in tunnels; in some cases they can be dried in as short a time as 30 hours. Semi-dry pressed green bricks of the Fletton type are strong enough to be placed directly, and before drying, into the same kiln chambers in which they are subsequently to be fired.

Burning, or firing, is a highly technical process. In the past, bricks were fired in 'clamps' or large stacks, but nowadays, specially designed permanent kiln structures of the 'periodic', the 'continuous chamber', or the 'tunnel' type are used. A periodic kiln consists of a single chamber in which the bricks are fired by heat generated in grates set in the walls of the chamber; it is loaded with dry bricks, fired, allowed to cool off, and emptied or 'drawn', ready to be set again. A continuous kiln contains a series of compartments or 'chambers' in which all the successive stages of burning are carried out, the fire being regulated to travel round the kiln from one adjacent chamber to the next. In a tunnel kiln the bricks, set on kiln cars, are made to pass continuously through a long tunnel. The temperature inside the tunnel gradually increases as the bricks advance until it reaches a maximum of about 1000° C. (for most bricks) about halfway along the tunnel. It then cools until, at the exit end, the bricks are at about air temperature. The fundamental difference between a continuous kiln and a tunnel kiln is that in the former the fire moves and the goods are stationary, and in the latter the goods move and the fire is stationary.

4. TILE-MAKING. Clay roofing-tiles are made in much the same way, and their size is governed by British Standard Specifications. A plain tile is $10\frac{1}{2}$ in. long, $6\frac{1}{2}$ in. wide, and $\frac{3}{8}$ to $\frac{7}{8}$ in. thick. The tiles are made slightly convex on the outside so that each 'course' (or row) of tiles presses firmly down on to the course beneath, and thus keeps out rain. Each has two nail-holes near the top, and two projecting 'nibs', so that the tiles may be either nailed or hung to the wooden battens beneath. The specially-shaped tiles needed for the eaves, hips, valleys, and ridge of the roof are also made of the same materials. Tiles, as well as bricks, may be manufactured with glazed faces (*see* TILES, ORNAMENTAL).

See also BUILDING INDUSTRY, HISTORY OF.
See also Vol. XI: HOUSES, HISTORY OF.

BRISTLES, *see* BRUSHES.

BROKER. This is a person whose work, like that of an AGENT (q.v.), is to bring together a buyer and a seller. Legally there is no difference between a broker and an agent; both are regarded as the legal representatives of their 'principals' (the people employing them) and the principals are bound by any engagements into which their agents enter on their behalf. A broker, however, differs from an agent in the way in which he carries out his duties. This function is generally to introduce a buyer to a seller, leaving them to arrange and settle their business themselves. Payment may be transmitted through him, but he does not actually handle his principal's goods. An agent, on the other hand, acts practically as though he were part of his principal's organization; he may hold a stock of the goods; he signs contracts of sale for his principal, collects the money, and accounts for it to his principal.

In the commercial world, therefore, the word 'agent' is usually reserved for a person or firm dealing in a physical sense with actual goods, and 'broker' for one who deals with contracts on paper, such as transactions in foreign exchange, rates of freight on cargoes, insurance, and in STOCKS AND SHARES (q.v.). The word 'broker' is also applied to firms who arrange for the buying and selling of large quantities of commodities or produce, for this is done by means of a paper contract to accept or deliver goods at some future date. The actual physical delivery of the goods is handled by shipping and forwarding agents.

The words 'broker' and 'agent' are often loosely applied, and it is rather unsafe to suppose that all persons or firms using these names really merit them in the strict commercial sense.

See also AGENT.

BRUSHES can be classified as personal, household, trade, and industrial. Personal brushes include tooth-brushes, hair-brushes, shaving-brushes, nail-brushes, and brushes for cosmetics. Household brushes include scrubbing-brushes and brooms, vacuum-cleaner brushes, shoe brushes, and clothes-brushes. Trade brushes are made for tradesmen or craftsmen, such as house-painters, artists, draughtsmen, and bill-posters. Some industrial processes require special-purpose brushes such as flour and textile mills, breweries, and papermaking works.

The backs or handles of brushes are made of various materials: of metal, wood, bone, ivory, celluloid, rubber, vulcanized fibre, and different forms of plastic material. Metal backs or holders are usual for industrial brushes. Bone handles are usually made by machinery from the shinbones of cattle. Brush fibres must be stiff and resistant without being brittle, and they must also be reasonably flexible. There is much variety in the fibres used for brush-making, vegetable, animal, or synthetic. Of the synthetic fibres, nylon is the one most frequently used, not only for tooth-brushes, but also for personal, household, and industrial brushes. The most important vegetable fibres are coir and bass. Coir is the fibre that grows on the outside shell of the coconut. Most of the world's coir comes from Ceylon. It is a very popular brush material in Europe, although little of it is used in the U.S.A. Bass is a palm-leaf fibre, and the best comes from Brazil. It is used for making good-quality clothes-brushes. A coarser bass, called kittul, used for domestic scrubbing-brushes, comes principally from Indian, Malaysia, and Indonesia (*see also* Fibre Crops, Section 8, Vol. VI).

Kleen-e-ze Brush Co.

A BRUSH-MAKING MACHINE

Holes are being drilled in the brush-holder on the right; on the left the machine fills the holders with knots of material at the rate of 80 knots a minute

Brush fibres of animal origin are either pigs' bristles or the hair of other animals. The pigs' bristles used in the trade come from the top middle part of the back and are removed after the animals have been slaughtered. China is the largest supplier, but her own growing brush industry is curtailing her export of bristles.

Hair taken from the bodies of cattle is not used in brush-making, but the tufts of hair inside the ears are much used. This hair is known in the trade as 'ox hair'. Cheap cosmetic and shaving brushes are often made from the face hair of goats. Real camel hair is not used for brush-making; the 'camel hair' brushes sold are generally made from the tail hair of squirrels. The hair of the badger is much prized in brush-making, and the best shaving-brushes are made from it. The finest quality of badger hair is known as 'silver tip'; it is dark in colour, with a white tip, and comes from Turkey or Persia.

In the brush-making trade the various fibres are called 'material'. Material is first subjected to various processes, such as grading, sizing, oiling, drying, combing, and bundling. The individual bundles of material that fit into the holes in the holders are called 'knots'. The first process in brush-making proper is to drill or bore the backs or handles to receive the material. The material is fixed into the handles by one of three different methods, 'drawn work', 'trepanning', and 'pan-setting'. In drawn work, which is used for most household and personal brushes such as tooth-brushes and nail-brushes, the material is passed through the hole in a loop of wire, which is then pulled tight. In the trepanning method, which is used for the best hair-brushes, channels are cut along the lines of the drilled holes, and wires are drawn tightly to connect the separate knots of material together.

Pan-setting is the method used for household brooms and similar large articles. Each knot of material is dipped into heated tar or pitch, tied with cord dressed with tar, and twisted into its hole. All these three processes have now been fully mechanized. The brushes used by house-painters and artists have tin containers at the brush end of the handle and into these the material is inserted and cemented or vulcanized. The final or finishing processes in brush-making are glueing on the backs, to hide the fixing of the material, and, if the backs are decorative, covering them with such material as gold, silver, ivory, leather, or highly polished veneers.

BUDGETARY CONTROL. This is the name given to a system of financial management in modern business, rather like the nation's annual Budget, or estimate of revenue and expenditure (*see* NATIONAL FINANCE, Vol. X). Before the adoption of budgetary control, financial management in business was not so precise. No exact estimates of income and expenditure were made in advance; money might run short at the most inconvenient times, and promising trading activities consequently have to be curtailed.

If a firm adopts budgetary control, its managing director and his managers prepare a budgetary statement at the beginning of the trading year. The basis for budgetary control is usually an estimate of the goods to be sold in the coming year. Past STATISTICS (q.v.) and the trends they show play an important part in framing this. Factors that may cause during the year any changes in selling prices, in the prices of raw materials, and in wages and other costs, are taken into account. In a business whose activities are organized into departments, the estimates may be drawn up departmentally.

This forecast of future business is then expanded into detailed estimates of expenditure and income, month by month, for the firm's plans must not be checked at any point through lack of money. There may be special reasons why money may be likely to run short at different times of the year—seasonal buying programmes, for instance. Steps must be taken to guard against this by selling INVESTMENTS or obtaining bank LOANS (qq.v.). If the coming year's programme involves building extensions, replacing machinery, or buying new plant to expand the production of some particularly promising line, new CAPITAL (q.v.) may be necessary, and the budget should state its amount and the way in which it will be raised.

In a manufacturing business 'standard' costs and outputs, representing objectives to be attained by the various departments, are circulated to those in charge. In a merchanting or distributing business, weekly or monthly 'targets' are framed for each department. In department stores or big retail establishments the budgetary forecast takes account of periodical bargain sales or other 'events', and what these should produce in terms of actual money. Throughout the year the detailed budget enables the head of the business to keep a continuous check on the performance of the various functions. His attention will be called to any areas where the budget and the actual performance are at variance, and this will prompt him to study such problem areas.

See also BOOK-KEEPING; BUSINESS ORGANIZATION; STATISTICS.

BUILDING INDUSTRY, HISTORY OF. The building industry still retains many traditional features and practices that have grown up through 60 centuries or more. Some of the processes of bricklaying, carpentry, plastering, and painting, known to the ancient Egyptians and Babylonians in the earliest times, are still in use to-day.

The history of the industry in Britain really begins with the Roman occupation. The excavated remains of Roman towns and villas (country houses) disclose brick or stone walls, tiled roofs, lead water-pipes, central heating by hot air carried up from furnaces through flues under the floors and up the walls, and beautiful mosaic pavements. Naturally, little is left of simpler buildings made of wood or other perishable materials. Many examples of Roman craftsmanship in all the separate trades of the industry are also to be seen in the museums at York, Verulamium (St. Albans), and the London Guildhall. Methods of building in Rome itself are set out in a book written by the architect Vitruvius some 2,000 years ago. It tells of the ways of building and the municipal by-laws, although all these practices would not have been followed exactly in the remote province of Britain.

After the Romans left in the 5th century, there was very little building in stone in Britain until the 10th century. Some building was done,

Bibl. de la Ville, Geneva

BUILDING IN THE 15TH CENTURY

In the foreground a mason is carving a stone, and a carpenter is smoothing a joist with an adze. Men are laying tiles on roofs and, behind, others are mixing and using mortar

BUILDING IN THE EARLY 19TH CENTURY

The methods had changed little since the Middle Ages

certainly, during those 5 centuries but nearly always in wood, and when stone churches were built they were mostly small and inferior to the buildings of the Romans. The period from 1066 to the time of Elizabeth, a matter of 5 centuries, may be treated as a whole; for although architecture advanced from the stern castles and the massive round-arched cathedrals of Norman days to the graceful structures of late Gothic times, methods of building remained much the same.

At first the most important patrons of building were the king and barons who built castles to protect their lands, and the monks whose large monasteries included many of the cathedrals still in use, as well as other buildings on their vast estates. It was long thought that the monks themselves designed and erected all such buildings, but it is now generally believed that the monasteries depended almost entirely upon hired laymen for all building work.

In any medieval building of substantial scale there were two leading people in charge of the work. One controlled the financial and administrative side; the other was the technically qualified 'master'. The first looked after estimates, wages, and bills for materials, and he sometimes provided transport. Sometimes he also furnished the materials. His title was usually *custos fabricae*, 'keeper of the works'. One official of this kind was William of Wykeham, the founder of Winchester College, who acted as 'Surveyor of the Works' at Windsor Castle in his early days. Another was Geoffrey CHAUCER (q.v. Vol. V). Although he was styled 'Clerk of the Works', or 'Devisor', he had no technical training, and was a civil servant in administrative charge of building operations at the Palace of Westminster.

Building stone was quarried as near the site as possible, and the different local stones gave variety to local building styles. In Devon, where hard granite was used for grander buildings, small houses were built of cob—clay beaten down to form a solid wall. Wattle and daub was used to fill in the spaces between the posts and beams in wooden houses. Although most of the timber used was home-grown oak, the importation of softwoods from Scandinavia began in the 13th century, and Henry III ordered a chamber at Windsor Castle to be specially panelled in Norway pine.

All this imported material was shipped to the nearest harbour, or to a point on a navigable river nearest to the site of the building. No good roads then existed, the only alternative to water-carriage being packhorse transport, a slow and costly business. In some parts of England, notably the south-eastern and eastern counties, where no suitable stone was available locally, all English stone as well as foreign stone had to be water-borne; it was easier to bring stone from Caen in Normandy to build churches in and near London, such as Old St. Paul's and St. Albans Abbey, than from English quarries. The stone for Eton College Chapel came from as far away as Haddleston in Yorkshire; the fine churches of Norfolk and Suffolk were mostly built of limestone from quarries in Lincolnshire, Northamptonshire, and Rutland; but many of them had walls and towers of local flint, with only the dressings, columns, and carved details in limestone. The expense of transport thus formed a substantial item in the cost of any large building, and for Vale Royal Abbey, in Cheshire, built by 1280 (where accurate accounts have been preserved) it amounted to three times the cost of the materials, although the distance to be covered was only 4 or 5 miles. The roofs of castles and churches in medieval days were mostly covered with English lead. The use of tiles began in the 13th century, when kilns for baking bricks are known to have been in operation; and in 1212 the roofs of all London houses, which until then had been covered with thatch or wood 'shingles', were ordered to be tiled after a disastrous fire. Slates, for roofing at Abingdon Abbey, are mentioned in 1404 (*see* SLATE INDUSTRY).

Building contracts in the Middle Ages were arranged between the employer and the various separate building trades. At that time, and indeed for centuries afterwards, there was no such person as the 'building contractor', undertaking work in all the crafts. The important material in most large medieval buildings was stone, and the most important craftsman on any building was the mason. Thus the person who carried out the functions of the modern architect, designing and superintending the erection of the building, was normally drawn from the ranks of the master-masons. The names of hundreds of such men are known, and the title most commonly applied to them was 'master' (*magister*, if in Latin documents), not 'master-mason'. They were mainly trained by a period of apprenticeship at the mason's bench; they used plans and models, and they were treated as professional men, sometimes taking on several commissions at the same time, just as a modern architect conducts his 'practice'. Their services were competed for by rival patrons.

Various medieval contracts with building trades have been preserved and published, as well as a large number of complete accounts for royal and church buildings. Sometimes the master-mason or master-carpenter would estimate for labour and plant only, the employer providing materials and transport; sometimes the contractor might include transport too, or even transport and materials. The number of men employed on a single contract was often very large; for example, at Beaumaris Castle in the 14th century there were 1,630 men at work; and at Windsor Castle in 1361 no fewer than 1,360 masons were forcibly recruited from all over Britain.

The enormous amount and high quality of the building carried out in Britain during the Middle Ages, when the population was relatively small, suggests that a pious enthusiasm must have led to high output; but we now know that actual conditions of labour were not ideal. Hours of work were certainly long, usually from sunrise to sunset. Thus at York Minster, in the 14th century, 20 minutes was allowed for breakfast, an hour for dinner—followed by an extra hour for a rest in the summer—and a few minutes for a drink in the late afternoon. There were numerous saints' days which were observed as HOLIDAYS (q.v. Vol. IX), generally without pay. 'Wet-time', when the weather prevented certain building operations, was seldom paid for. In spite of research, it is almost impossible to estimate the real value of the WAGES (q.v.) paid in those remote times—only a few pence a day—or to compare them with modern rates, but it is fairly clear that modern wages are higher. There was a wide difference of pay between the grades of skilled and unskilled labour. Freedom for building workers was limited. There were fines for being late or drunk, for quarrelling, idling, losing tools, bad language, and obstruction of other workmen—usually 'foreigners', as workers from any other town were called. There were also frequent disputes between the members of the various craft guilds as to the precise tasks that each should do.

The CRAFT GUILDS with their elaborate system of APPRENTICESHIP (q.v.) and the guilds connected with building follow the same pattern. The Livery Companies of the City of London still exist to promote the interests of the various trades or crafts, and they include the building crafts of Carpenters, Glaziers, Masons, Joiners, Painter Stainers, Plasterers, Plumbers, Tylers and Bricklayers (*see* CITY COMPANIES). The elaborate organization of the FREEMASONS (q.v. Vol. X) began in the 17th century, with the admission of amateur members to the masons' guilds, on the ground of their special interest in the craft as antiquaries or patrons.

It must not be forgotten that only the more ambitious of builders could afford to engage numbers of professional workers. The homes of farmers, small craftsmen, small merchants, let alone poorer people, were much more simply made and largely by what we should to-day call amateur labour. Few, if any, written accounts were kept of such work, and the structures themselves did not last many generations.

The sweeping social changes that followed the Renaissance and the Reformation affected the building industry in the 16th century. The Church lost its leading position as a patron of building. Wealthy merchants and noblemen built large mansions, and many colleges and schools were founded. Men called architects began to be employed, as learned persons who could apply the fashionable rules of Roman and Italian architecture. But medieval conditions with regard to transport and the supply of materials persisted with little change, except that more timber was imported. The various crafts continued to be separate.

The speculative builder first appeared in London towards the end of the 17th century. One famous speculator in building sites was a doctor, Nicholas Barbon, M.P., who died in 1698. He bought large mansions with their gardens, and then sold off small lots to builders who erected dwelling-houses on them. He was followed by many enterprising speculators who laid out the fine squares of Bloomsbury and the West End.

Towards the end of the 18th century the development of ROADS, CANALS, and BRIDGES (qq.v. Vol. IV), closely followed by the use of structural ironwork and the invention of the steam-engine, led to the rise of CIVIL ENGINEERING (q.v. Vol. VIII) as an industry allied to building. Possibly the appearance of the master-builder and general contractor about the same time may have been caused indirectly by these changes. Shortly afterwards quantity-surveying came into existence as an independent profession. TRADE UNIONS (q.v.) in the various building crafts began with the foundation in 1800 of the Friendly Society of Carpenters and Joiners, and developed rapidly during the 19th century into the enormous federated unions of to-day. With the increasing use of structural steelwork and concrete for large buildings, many parts of the buildings, such as windows and door frames, as well as the structural units such as steel girders, are made in factories.

See also Vol. XI: HOUSES, HISTORY OF.
See also Vol. XII: ARCHITECTURE.

BUILDING INDUSTRY, ORGANIZATION.

1. The building industry plays a very important part in Britain's economy, for it not only builds the many new houses, schools, and Government offices needed by a growing population, but it also constructs the up-to-date shops, warehouses, factories, and power-stations required by other industries. Moreover, it carries out repairs and alterations in older buildings throughout the country. It is little wonder, therefore, that in 1960 the industry employed over 1,500,000 men and used vast quantities of bricks, steel, cement, and glass.

2. MATERIALS. Many of the basic materials used in building are found in Britain, so that, except for timber, relatively little has to be imported from abroad. The clay for making bricks, tiles, and cement is quarried in this country, as are the lime needed for cement and plaster, and the gravel and sand used in the making of concrete. Building stone, slate, and flints are all home-produced, and so are small quantities of ironstone and some of the components of glass. Timber, however, has to be imported in large quantities: SOFTWOODS from Canada and the Baltic, HARDWOODS from the Commonwealth (qq.v.). Asbestos, lead, asphalt, and much of the iron ore required for making iron and steel are also imported.

3. ORGANIZATION. The building industry has a long history (*see* BUILDING, HISTORY OF) and a tradition of manual work carried out on the site or at benches in the master-builder's own workshops. Mechanization, however, is very rapidly changing the character of the industry, and PREFABRICATION (q.v. Vol. VIII), together with standardization, has certainly come to stay. Yet, in spite of these changes, conditions of work in a building firm remain very different from those in a modern manufacturing firm. Most building still takes place on sites at some distance from the builder's office and, being carried on out of doors, is affected by weather and hours of daylight, whereas work in a factory can normally be carried on continuously.

The building industry is made up of thousands of separate firms. A few are large general contractors who carry out major works throughout the British Isles and often fulfil contracts overseas as well. Their undertakings are sometimes so large—the building of an airport or the construction of harbour installations—that it is not always easy to say what part of their work belongs to CIVIL ENGINEERING (q.v.) and what to building. There are a few hundred firms which employ 500 men or more, but a great many much smaller firms employ less than ten men, and may build a small number of houses at a time, and carry out repairs in a single neighbourhood. Then there are firms that specialize in one particular branch of building, such as plastering, joinery, or electrical contracting.

Richard Costain Ltd.

MULTI-STOREY OFFICE BLOCK AT HOLBORN VIADUCT, LONDON, UNDER CONSTRUCTION

Before a building can begin, an architect has to draw up the plans, which must be approved by the local authority. The architect often consults engineers, for example about heating and electricity. If the building is at all large, a quantity surveyor normally draws up a bill of quantities, which sets out the amount of labour and materials required to complete the job. The builder himself usually has to give the owner of the property an estimate of how much money the work will cost, and sometimes an owner will ask for estimates from several builders so that he can make a choice. When the building is actually going up, a 'clerk-of-works' watches over the work to see that it is being done according to the architect's plan, and inspectors of the municipal authorities have to see that the building regulations are observed, as required by law.

Large general contractors and very large building firms employ a number of highly trained technical experts. Among these are estimators who work out in advance what the firm should charge for constructing a building; buyers, who order materials and arrange sub-contracts; contract managers; departmental managers for workshops, plant, and transport depots; and surveyors, who measure the work and check costs. The monthly payments to the contractor are based on the surveyor's measurements.

In small firms, such as those of a jobbing builder or of a private house-builder, these jobs are often done by the builder himself.

A jobbing builder's business is often run by one man, who rarely employs more than five or six men. A jobbing builder may himself practise all the crafts from bricklaying to plumbing, though he has probably been trained originally in only one of them. Sometimes he practises a single craft, carpentry for example, and employs a bricklayer, a plumber, and a painter as his assistants, and is then very like the building contractor. Although he does not fit easily into the usual industrial division between employer and trained

Holland & Hannen and Cubitts

BRICKLAYING

operative, he is a most useful member of the community. He is ready to help the householder in all emergencies, whereas a large and well-organized building firm is often too busy to risk slowing down carefully prepared timetables on large contracts merely to adjust a flushing-cistern or replace a few roof-tiles.

The private house-builder erects buildings at his own risk in the hope of finding a purchaser. The work of house-builders has sometimes been inartistic or structurally unsound, or both; but this need not be so, and often it is above reproach. The houses they build may be as good in every way as a house erected by a contractor, to the designs of a competent architect, under strict conditions. The house-builder himself may employ an architect to prepare the design, and for the sake of his own reputation and profit may observe as high standards of materials and workmanship as if he were bound by the terms of a strict contract.

Realizing the need, however, for some recognized standard of quality in privately built houses, the building industry itself set up in 1937 the National House-Builders Registration Council. This maintains a National Register of House-Builders and operates a scheme for the inspection of those houses built privately which are not otherwise subject to independent professional supervision. If, on inspection, they are found to comply with standards laid down in an agreed General Specification of Constructional Standards, the houses receive certification. The Registration Council is composed of representatives of all housing interests including architects, surveyors, building societies, building employers, and operatives; and its work has the approval and support of the Ministry of Housing and Local Government.

4. CRAFTSMEN. In 1968, the building industry employed about 600,000 craftsmen. Among these were carpenters and joiners, woodcutting machinists, bricklayers, plumbers, plasterers, roofers, and painters and decorators. The men work singly or in gangs on the building sites or in factories, stoneyards, and workshops producing components.

As well as the craftsmen, the industry employs a great many labourers, who assist the craftsmen, work in concreting gangs, and do innumerable other important but less skilled jobs on building sites. Then there is a large number of semi-skilled men, who operate the wide range of machines and plant which is found on building sites; they also do such jobs as erecting scaffolding and fixing the steelwork for reinforced concrete. Lastly, there are the transport drivers and plant and vehicle mechanics.

5. TRAINING. Those entering the industry to learn a building craft are trained under a national scheme supervised by the National Joint Apprenticeship Board. Apprenticeship comprises practical training at the employers' workshops and building sites and technical education at the local technical college. At least until the end of the year in which he reaches the age of 18, the apprentice is released by his employer for one day a week so that he can attend the college; normal wages are paid for the day. In addition he attends evening classes throughout his period of apprenticeship. He is expected to work for the craft certificates of the City and Guilds of London Institute.

Those entering the industry on the administrative side to train for positions as estimators, surveyors, contract managers, etc., are articled for training for 4 or 5 years. During that time they are given comprehensive practical training on the site and in the office in the business of building. They are given one day off a week to attend technical college to obtain the Higher National Certificate in Building or spend alternate periods of 6 months with their employer and 6 months at a university or college to obtain a degree or diploma in building. Ambitious young men will continue their studies to qualify for membership of the Institute of Building, the professional institution for those in building practice.

See also BRICKS AND TILES; SLATE INDUSTRY; STONE QUARRYING; TIMBER INDUSTRY.
See also Vol. VIII: PREFABRICATION.
See also Vol. XI: HOUSES, HISTORY OF.
See also Vol. XII: ARCHITECTURE.

BUILDING SOCIETIES. Many people wishing to own houses cannot usually put up, in a lump sum, the rather large amount of money necessary. They aim to borrow the money, and to pay it back with interest over a long term of years, sometimes 20 or 25, at a yearly charge not much greater than the equivalent rent. British banks restrict themselves to lending money for comparatively short periods. It would therefore be outside banking business to lend money to people whose aim is ultimately to own a house. Building societies, therefore, have grown up in order to help people build or buy a house of their own.

The building society is essentially a British growth, because on the Continent, and in most overseas countries, houses and flats are either rented from owners who make property investment their business, or are bought and sold outright. Foreign banks, also, are less insistent than British banks on confining themselves to short-term transactions. Except in a few capital cities, therefore, there is no exact equivalent of the British building society.

When it receives an application for an advance, the society first proceeds to value the property which the applicant proposes to buy, or land on which he proposes to build a house. Having agreed on a valuation of the property, the building society will usually consent to advance up to four-fifths of the valuation, and sometimes up to nine-tenths of it. The prospective buyer then signs a mortgage deed (*see* PROPERTY LAW, Section 4, Vol. X) in favour of the society, and the financial details are arranged between the buyer's solicitor and the society.

The rate of interest on building society advances varies with changes in general economic conditions. Each successive payment consists of increasing portions of repayment of the capital sum borrowed, and decreasing portions of INTEREST (q.v.) on the remainder still unpaid. At the end of the 20 or 25 years of the contract, when the last instalment of capital and interest has been paid over, the mortgage deed is no longer operative, and the buyer becomes the unencumbered owner of the property.

Building societies are mostly registered under the FRIENDLY SOCIETIES Acts (q.v. Vol. X), and are not organized as ordinary limited companies under the Companies Acts: they therefore stand midway between public utilities and private enterprise. This means that their capital is not a fixed amount, and that fresh SHARES (q.v.) may be issued as business expands. In addition to raising CAPITAL (q.v.) by obtaining share subscriptions, the societies also accept large sums of money on deposit for fixed periods, and the funds they have to lend thus come from both sources. The societies have the duty of ensuring that their advances are regularly repaid and that they are not made against over-generous valuations of property. A borrower who fails to keep up his repayments will often receive consideration. Many societies arrange for a temporary cessation of instalments during sickness or unemployment; in certain circumstances, a new and extended contract is entered into.

Most of the houses financed by building societies in Britain are small houses in suburbs and the country. The same methods have been adopted elsewhere, but chiefly to help people to buy land for farming. 'Land and Mortgage Banks' have this use in America and the chief British Dominions.

BULK PURCHASE is the system by which the government of a country makes contracts for the import of food and raw materials, instead of allowing the country's merchants to import as much as they can profitably sell. In modern times bulk purchase was first organized by Russia after the revolution of 1917, although 2,000 years earlier the Roman Government made similar arrangements for the imports of corn to feed the population of Rome. Bulk purchase was instituted in Britain as a wartime measure during the Second World War, not only for foodstuffs but also for war stores and military equipment. The Ministry of Food was responsible for the importation of foodstuffs, and the Ministry of Supply for other goods. These Ministries no longer function.

Since the war ended, bulk purchase has been almost entirely given up, although a few long-term contracts made earlier, and covering requirements for some years ahead, are still in force. The Defence Ministry still remains responsible for the bulk purchase of certain important defence requirements.

BUSINESS ORGANIZATION. 1. This means the detailed arrangements made in any business for taking decisions and converting them into action. There is little need for organization in a business where the owner is the only person employed in it—a small retail shop, for example. The owner of such a business both makes decisions and carries them into effect, and he can modify his policy as he carries it out. But in a large business there must be a division between the management who takes decisions, and the staff who carry them out. Decisions reached by the heads of the firm must reach those who have to carry them out. Reports must also travel in the reverse direction, from the bottom to the top: for managerial policy, like tactics in a battle, must be continuously modified as circumstances change.

There is no standard pattern of organization for all firms, or even for firms engaged in the same line of trade. Much depends on how the business has grown up. Old forms of organization, adopted many years earlier when the business was young, may still work well, because everybody is accustomed to them, and they have become part of the tradition of the business. But there are two general principles of organization that should be followed by all concerns. The first is that the duties and responsibilities of everyone, down to the most junior employee, must be very carefully defined. Everybody should know precisely what his job is, and duties should neither be left undone because nobody has been made responsible for them, nor be overlapped by more than one person or department. Secondly, responsibility should descend from top to bottom in a straight line. Each individual should have a single superior only, from whom alone he receives his orders, and to whom alone he renders his reports.

2. POLICY AND MANAGEMENT. All businesses in Britain, with a few exceptions, are one-man firms, PARTNERSHIPS, or LIMITED COMPANIES (qq.v.). The exceptions are mostly of a large and important nature, including State-owned businesses, such as the POST OFFICE and British RAILWAYS (qq.v. Vol. IV); certain non-profit-making enterprises governed by Act of Parliament, such as the B.B.C. and the Port of London Authority (*see* PORTS, HISTORY OF, Vol. IV); and some municipal businesses run by BOROUGH COUNCILS (q.v. Vol. X), such as markets or bus services. Other special kinds of business organization are those of the CO-OPERATIVE SOCIETIES and certain PUBLIC UTILITY COMPANIES (qq.v.).

Many ordinary limited companies are no bigger than partnerships, and in their organization they follow the same pattern. Neither one-man firms nor partnerships can be of any great size, for their CAPITAL (q.v.) is limited to what the owner or partners can subscribe. In a one-man business of fair size the owner will decide policy and his subordinates will carry it out. Each department has a head who receives his instructions from the proprietor and makes his reports to him direct. In a partnership business the partners usually have different qualifications and interests. In such firms each partner is often the active head of the department whose duties suit him best, and there are frequent meetings among the partners to compare notes and adjust policy. Such a form of organization comes very close to the ideal, as those who carry out policy are also those who decide what it is to be.

In large companies the problems of organization become complex. A company is owned by shareholders, but they do not decide on its policy or constitute its management; and they therefore entrust the management to a small body of directors, seldom more than a dozen and often not more than five or six, who are called the Board. The head of the Board is the Chairman, but in many companies his position is not strictly executive, and a managing director is appointed for the general day-to-day management of the firm. In most companies, the majority of the directors will be in full-time service. As in partnerships, they will often be given executive responsibility for a particular department. The role of the non-executive, part-time directors is to bring their specialized knowledge to the company, and to help plan the company's strategy, rather than to be involved in administration. They are also responsible for ensuring that a balance is kept between the executives.

3. ORGANIZATION OF DEPARTMENTS. There can be no set pattern. The departmental organization for a trading firm engaged solely in buying and selling goods must differ from that which would suit a manufacturing business. But there are certain general principles that most businesses follow. A division is usually

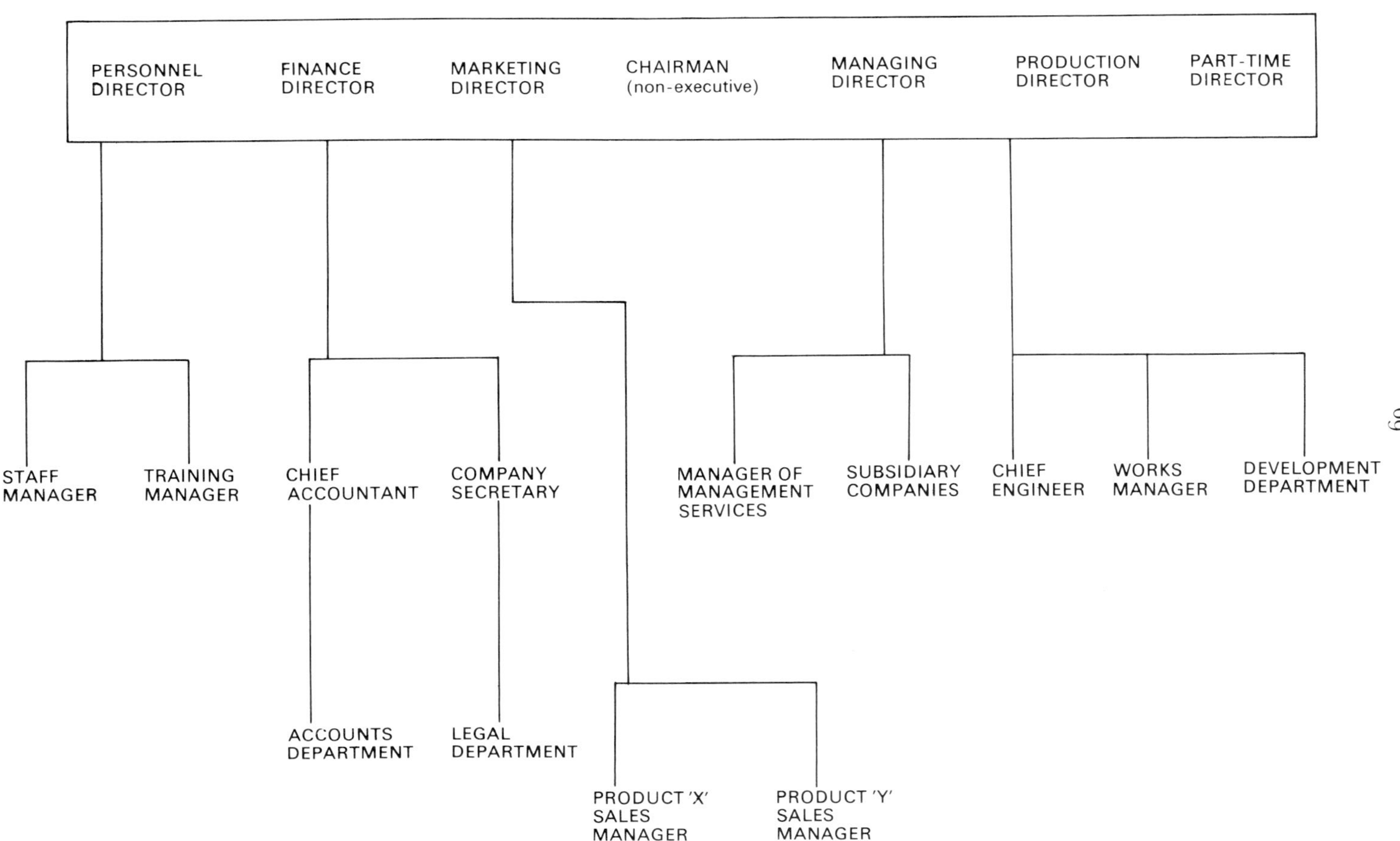

A TYPICAL ORGANIZATION CHART OF A MEDIUM-SIZED COMPANY

This company is engaged in manufacturing two products, X and Y, and has its own subsidiary companies

made between finance and accounts (*see* BOOKKEEPING), production, buying, selling, secretarial and legal matters, ADVERTISING AND PUBLICITY (q.v.), research, and staff control and recruitment. The finance officer or accountant handles the financial records and accounts, and records of stocks and supplies of goods. Usually he also supervises the collection and assembly of STATISTICS (q.v.), and if the firm is run on scientific lines and adopts any form of BUDGETARY CONTROL (q.v.) it will be his business to see that the programme laid down in advance for each department is kept to as closely as possible. In a large business the responsibility for buying goods is usually given to a purchasing manager, merchandise manager, or chief buyer, although in a business dealing in several types of goods, as in a DEPARTMENT STORE (q.v.), a certain amount of discretion may be left to the departmental buyers themselves. The sales manager is responsible for sales, for the control of salesmen and travellers, and for testing the market in new lines of goods (*see* MARKET RESEARCH). The secretary's office keeps the registers of shareholders and attends to the transfer of shares from one person to another, and deals usually with legal matters and INSURANCE (q.v.), as well as the general routine administration and correspondence of the firm. The advertising or publicity manager is responsible for all sales literature in the form of booklets and pamphlets, window-dressing and other forms of display, the 'house magazine' of the firm, if it has one, and TRADE FAIRS and EXHIBITIONS (qq.v.). If the firm has a staff or personnel manager, he is usually responsible not only for engaging the staff throughout the business but also for watching their progress and transferring from one department to another people who are not in suitable positions. Unless there is a separate welfare officer, whose job it is to look after the general well-being of the workers, such duties generally fall to the staff manager. Staff managers, welfare officers, and others outside the main channels of organization work through the appropriate department head, with the permission and knowledge of the managing director.

See also FACTORY ORGANIZATION; DIVISION OF LABOUR; STATISTICS; LIMITED COMPANIES.

BUTCHERY, *see* MEAT TRADE.

BUTTER-MAKING, *see* DAIRY INDUSTRY.

BUYING DEPARTMENT, *see* FACTORY ORGANIZATION, Section 5.

BY-PRODUCTS. When a factory is engaged in making its main product, it sometimes cannot help producing other things as well. For instance, a furniture factory cannot help producing wood shavings, and a gas-works based on coal produces tar and ammonia when making gas. These minor products are known as by-products, and many of the most useful and profitable by-products of modern industry have been discovered accidentally.

At first, by-products were often allowed to run to waste, or were dumped as refuse. In the early stages of the development of modern industry competition was not particularly keen, but, as industry expanded, many firms were forced to discover ways of adding to the income they received from selling their main product. One obvious way was to consider the by-products of manufacture, and to see whether they also could be sold to the public. To find a market for them it might be necessary to advertise and thus to place their advantages before the public (*see* ADVERTISING AND PUBLICITY); or it might even be necessary to convert such by-products, by a separate manufacturing process, into something closer to what the public wanted.

Some by-products occur naturally, and are not manufactured. Many mineral ores such as lead and silver are often found together. Fire-clay is generally found under the coal seams. The main aim of the FISHING INDUSTRY (q.v.) is fish for cooking, but such products as cod-liver oil become available at the same time. In the TIMBER INDUSTRY (q.v.) various kinds of resins are produced. Whale oil is the main objective of whaling (*see* WHALING INDUSTRY, Vol. VI), but spermaceti, ambergris, and whalebone are also produced. COPRA (q.v.), the valuable solidified white kernel of the coconut, and the fibre that covers the hard outer shell and which is used in brush-making, are inseparable products of the coconut palm. In industry and commerce it is just as important to make full use of natural by-products as of those that have been manufactured.

The number of natural and manufactured by-products is very large indeed, and there are few manufacturing processes without at least one by-product. What we call the 'services' industries, which render services to the consuming public instead of making goods for them, also have their by-products. Pig swill, for instance, is a by-product of the CATERING INDUSTRY (q.v.). Soot, a by-product of chimney-sweeping, is valuable not only as a manure but also in industry.

Some of the best examples of by-products come from our major industries. The history of the mineral oil industry is very largely the story of its development from a stage when all by-products were neglected to one in which a use is found for almost every one. Before the use of fuel-oil for raising steam, and before the invention of the INTERNAL COMBUSTION ENGINE (q.v. Vol. VIII), oil was mainly sought in order that it might be converted into paraffin or kerosene for lamps, and the residues were largely left to waste. But, nowadays, nearly all the products of mineral oil are utilized, and converted into various kinds of fuel oils such as crude oil and diesel oil, refined petrol products, solvent spirits, wax for candles, 'vaseline' or petroleum jelly, powdered carbon, and many other useful products (*see* OIL REFINING).

There are many by-products of the IRON AND STEEL INDUSTRY (q.v.). Carbon monoxide, for instance, an inflammable gas which is the main constituent of ordinary household gas, is a by-product of the smelting of the iron ore in the BLAST FURNACE (q.v. Vol. VIII). In the earlier days of the industry the hot gas was allowed to escape at the top of the furnace and to waste itself as a tall flame on coming into contact with the oxygen of the air. Later on, it was cleansed, and used for heating the steel furnaces and for firing the boilers in the power-house. The resultant saving in coal made it possible to sell pig iron or steel at a lower price than formerly. The Gilchrist-Thomas method of making steel, which was perfected just before 1880, delivers as a by-product basic slag which is an ARTIFICIAL FERTILIZER (q.v. Vol. VI) for farm and gardens.

The work of the coal GAS INDUSTRY (q.v.) created many by-products, of which the most important were tar and AMMONIA (q.v.). Tar is a useful by-product itself, but if it is further treated, many additional by-products can be obtained, some of which are extremely valuable. Many synthetic DYES (q.v.) are by-products of coal tar and so are many drugs and medicines.

Tate and Lyle

BAGASSE, A BY-PRODUCT OF SUGAR MANUFACTURE WHICH IS USED AS FUEL AND TO MAKE PAPER

Bagasse is what remains of the cane when the sugar has been extracted

There are still many by-products that cannot be fully utilized. At some steel-works slag from blast furnaces is ground into small pieces and tarred for road-making, but generally it has been found that this product cannot compete with road-metal quarried in the usual way and tarred on the spot while being laid. But modern science is continuously alert to utilize hitherto useless material. Fly ash, a waste product of power stations burning pulverized coal, can now be turned into light-weight aggregate for making cement. Iron can also be profitably recovered by magnetic separation from fly ash and similar refuse; and, as the immense slag-heaps in our mining districts have a considerable content of iron, this process may in future save much importation of iron ore from abroad.

C

CABINET-MAKING. A cabinet-maker is a craftsman who specializes in fine joinery and particularly in the making of cabinets, bureaux, tables, chairs, and other furniture of quality. Cabinet-making did not emerge as a specialized craft until just after the Restoration of 1660, when people of fashion demanded furniture that should be in keeping with the luxury of the age. In 1667 Samuel Pepys, the diarist, recorded that he found his friend Mr. Povey 'at work with a cabinet-maker making a new inlaid table'.

Up to about this time the medieval CRAFT GUILDS (q.v.) had continued to dominate the English woodwork and furniture-making trades, and separate branches of the craft worked independently of one another (*see* WOODWORK, HISTORY OF). But with the demand for more furniture during the 17th century, chair-makers and turners began to work together, and the old restrictions of the guilds were ignored. Cabinet-makers differed from these earlier furniture-makers because they worked in walnut and practised veneering, a craft which had been introduced to England from France and Holland by foreign workmen.

A veneer is a thin sheet of wood, usually about an eighth of an inch thick, which is cut from the log in such a way that it shows off the timber's figure or grain to the best advantage. In furniture-making the veneer is glued on to the carcase of a piece of furniture, which is usually of pine or some cheaper wood, and gives the effect that the whole piece is made of the veneer wood. The veneer is pressed into place with a veneering hammer, or on a curved surface with sandbags. 'Oyster' and 'burr' veneers are obtained by cutting thin pieces at a certain angle from smaller branches, burrs, boles, or the roots of trees. At first, cabinet-makers used veneer cut from walnut logs; later, mahogany, rosewood, satinwood, and many other handsome woods were used.

As the making of fine furniture became a specialized and very profitable industry, the cabinet-maker absorbed in his workshop the allied trades of the chair-maker, joiner, carver, gilder, japanner, and, eventually, even upholsterer. By the middle of the 18th century, the larger cabinet-making firms in London and the provinces not only make every type of furniture, but also had their own showrooms, undertook all kinds of upholstery and related work of interior decoration, and repaired old furniture. Throughout this period, however, and right on into the 19th century, there remained a large number of smaller firms, especially chair-makers, who continued to specialize in one particular craft, either supplying the larger general firms or selling direct to the public.

The high standard of workmanship found in 18th-century furniture was the result of an intense degree of specialization. While the cabinet-maker had brought together the different branches of the trade, workmen continued to specialize in their particular craft, and frequently one piece of furniture, a carved chair or a gilt mirror, would combine the work of three or four different men. These craftsmen worked long hours, their wages were low, and the discipline in the workshop was severe. Their tools were strong and well-made and were of the same variety as those used by cabinet-makers to-day, but there was no machinery and everything was done by hand. The lay-out of the workshops in the larger firms followed the pattern of specialization, and, apart from the general workshops, rooms were set aside for lacquer work, gilding, and upholstery. Seddon's, one of the largest London firms of the second half of the 18th century, employed over 400 craftsmen in its workshops, including upholsterers, carvers, gilders, mirror-makers, workers in ormulu, and locksmiths.

Once a successful cabinet-maker had established a large firm employing many specialized craftsmen, he seldom returned to work at the bench himself. His time was taken up with administration, purchasing timber, finding new designs, and personally attending on his more important clients. His contemporaries did not consider him a man of great importance. It is for this reason that we know so little about the lives of the great 18th-century cabinet-makers

Crown Copyright

ENGLISH SECRETAIRE BOOKCASE, PAINTED AND INLAID SATINWOOD, *c.* 1790

Victoria and Albert Museum

Crown Copyright

EARLY 18TH-CENTURY WRITING CABINET WITH WALNUT VENEER

Victoria and Albert Museum

and can point to so little work that was actually made by their own hands. For instance, Thomas Chippendale (1718–79), the son of a Yorkshire joiner, is chiefly known to us for his book of designs, *The Gentleman and Cabinet-Maker's Director* (1754). Chippendale chairs were probably not made by Chippendale himself but by a number of anonymous craftsmen using his designs.

Though a large number of 18th-century cabinet-making firms are known by name, English furniture is seldom marked, and the work of a particular firm can be identified only occasionally from existing bills or other documentary evidence. It is sometimes possible to attribute a piece to a certain maker on stylistic grounds. A number of other pieces are found which closely follow a design in Chippendale's *Director* or other pattern books of the period, but since these pattern books circulated freely in the trade, and the designs could be used by any firm, it is not possible to be certain which firm made them. French furniture is more frequently marked with the maker's name or initials, for in France the rigorous control of the guild system persisted up to the time of the French Revolution, and the stamping of furniture was insisted on in many cases by the authorities. Craftsmen commissioned by the Crown, however, were exempt, and therefore many of the finest pieces remained unmarked.

George Hepplewhite (d. 1786) and Thomas Sheraton (1751–1806) are the two best-known figures in English cabinet-making of the second half of the 18th century. Their fame, like Chippendale's, rests on the publication of important books on furniture designs rather than

Crown Copyright

ARMCHAIR OF CARVED MAHOGANY, ABOUT 1755

The back corresponds with an illustration in Chippendale's *Director*, a book of furniture designs which was used by cabinet-makers in his day. Victoria and Albert Museum

Crown Copyright

ENGLISH ARMCHAIR OF CARVED AND INLAID MAHOGANY *c.* 1775

Victoria and Albert Museum

on any particular work of their own. Indeed, no piece has ever been attributed to either of them, and in Sheraton's case it is doubtful if he ever actually practised as a cabinet-maker. He appears to have made a meagre living as a designer and drawing-master. Hepplewhite's *The Cabinet-Makers' and Upholsterers' Guide*, published 2 years after his death in 1788, translated the grander furniture style of Robert ADAM (q.v. Vol. V) into simpler and more popular terms, and represents the style prevalent between about 1775 and 1790. Sheraton's *Cabinet-Makers' and Upholsterers' Drawing Book*, published in 1794, summarized the most fashionable style of furniture of the last 10 years of the 18th century, a graceful and elegant style of which delicately inlaid satinwood and painted furniture were characteristic.

With the coming of the 19th century and the Industrial Revolution, furniture-making, like all other trades, moved towards mass-production in large factories. The general introduction of powered WOODWORKING MACHINERY (q.v. Vol. VIII) in the second half of the 19th century finally removed the major part of the furniture-making trade from the hands of the independent cabinet-maker. Today, in such centres as High Wycombe, large factories produce hundreds of pieces of furniture every day made entirely by machine. Industrial furniture-makers have developed new methods of construction and means of decoration suitable for machine cabinet-making (*see* FURNITURE INDUSTRY). Despite this, a small number of handworking cabinet-makers have continued to survive. Some of them are also designers and make high-quality furniture to modern designs, while others merely make reproductions of old furniture.

See also FURNITURE INDUSTRY; TIMBER INDUSTRY.

CAMEL HAIR, *see* HAIR TRADE.

CANNING. 1. If foods are kept for a few days in the air, they decay through attack by YEASTS, MOULDS, BACTERIA, and other types of micro-organisms (qq.v. Vol. II). By the canning process, however, the product is enclosed in a sealed container so that no infection can reach it, and the contents of the container are then sterilized by heat. This heat-sterilization destroys any initial infection which may have been present on the food or on the interior of the can. Canning avoids the necessity of using chemical preservatives, and products thus treated may be stored for many months or years without serious deterioration.

The process was discovered in 1809 by a Frenchman called François Appert. He put food in wide-necked glass bottles, which he corked lightly and then immersed in a bath of hot water, after which he hammered down the corks and sealed them hermetically. This crude method won him a prize offered by the French Government, who were keenly interested in discovering means of preserving food so that Napoleon's armies could be better supplied when on campaign. In 1810 Peter Durand, an Englishman, patented a tin plate canister to replace Appert's glass bottles, and 4 years later an English firm was supplying tinned vegetable soups and preserved meat to the Royal Navy. Although canning increased during the next 35 years, it was not till 1860, when Louis PASTEUR (q.v. Vol. V) demonstrated that the air is full of microbes and that these microbes could be killed by the application of sufficient heat, that the canning industry was put on a scientific basis.

Today, vegetables, fish, meat, fruit, and beer are canned in enormous quantities, the foremost canning countries being the U.S.A., Japan, Russia, Great Britain, and Canada. The industry has within three generations revolutionized the eating habits of a large part of the world. Strawberries and asparagus are now available in December, and Canadian salmon may be eaten by families in Europe and by explorers on the slopes of Mount Everest. The canning industry has also affected agriculture, for farmers often sell their produce straight to the canning factories. For this reason, the growing of green peas, for example, a crop which is readily harvested and prepared for canning by machinery, has now become an important factor to the English farmer in his crop rotation.

1. PREPARATION. The first stage in the canning process consists of preparing the raw material by removing diseased fruit and throwing away the waste portions such as stalks from plums, cherries, or blackcurrants, or plugs (hulls) from strawberries; after this the fruit is washed and graded for size. Vegetables such as carrots, potatoes, and other root crops are picked, washed, and trimmed largely by machine, green peas on the vine being fed into a machine which strips off the leafy stems and shells 7 or 8 tons of peas a day. Meat and fish are cleaned and trimmed by machine.

2. FILLING. Fruit is fed mechanically into cans, though with tender fruits, such as raspberries and strawberries, this is done by hand. Vegetables are first blanched, that is, immersed in hot or boiling water for a few minutes, a process that softens the vegetables and so makes it possible for machines to fill them into cans quickly—at speeds ranging from sixty to 400 cans a minute. Blanching also removes air which might otherwise cause abnormal pressure in the cans during sterilization. Fruits are not blanched because, being already soft, this treatment might make them pulpy. Meat and fish are also not blanched and, like fruit, are packed into tins cold; no liquid is added to them.

3. EXHAUSTING. To remove the air trapped between the individual berries, or slices of fruit, cans containing these goods are passed through a pre-heating process known as 'exhausting', during which the temperature of the contents is raised to about 76°C. This 'exhausting' process, through expansion by heat of the liquid contents of the can, results in the formation of a partial vacuum equivalent to a pressure of from 12 to 16 inches of mercury—that is, the pressure inside the can will be only about half the pressure of the outside air (*see* PRESSURE GAUGES, Vol. VIII). Vegetables are not usually 'exhausted' after being filled into the can because they have already been subjected to blanching, which has removed some of the air, and they are in any case filled into the cans while hot. Cans containing meat and fish are passed through a machine which withdraws all the air inside them and immediately seals the lids, a process known as 'vacuum packing'.

4. CLOSING AND STERILIZING. With fruit and vegetables, the lid is immediately seamed on to the body of the can by high-speed machines using rollers which interlock the flange of the body of the can with the flange on the lid. It is then ready for sterilizing. Cans of vegetables are sterilized in steam or water under pressure at temperatures ranging from 115°C. to 126°C. and for periods of time ranging from 12 to 35 minutes according to the type of vegetable being canned. Cans of fruit are immersed in boiling water for from 5 to 10 minutes. Because of their high natural acidity, fruits do not require the high temperatures and length of time for sterilization that are necessary for vegetables, which have little natural acid. Meat and fish are cooked at temperatures well above boiling

Batchelor's Peas Ltd. (photo by Fox Photos)

CANNING PEAS

The containers in the foreground are filled with cans and then placed three deep in retorts and sterilized. In the background filled cans are seamed and taken on a conveyor belt to continuous cookers

point, for periods of time which vary with the kinds of products being sterilized.

After sterilization, the cans are cooled rapidly to 32°C. to prevent the contents of the cans from becoming soft. The process of sterilization and cooking is usually carried out by high-speed automatic machinery.

5. LABELLING AND PACKING. Before dispatch to the retailer, the cans are labelled and packed into fibreboard cases. Many cans to-day are printed by the can maker and therefore require no paper labels.

CANTEENS, *see* CATERING INDUSTRY.

CAPITAL. In finance and business this word has many meanings. To the economist it means tools and machines which make it possible for a workman to increase his output. The expression 'national capital' means the total quantity of buildings, railways, docks, factories, plant and machinery, and tools existing in a country at any given time. There is also a further definition of capital as industrial property or INVESTMENTS, a capitalist being an owner of such property and earning PROFITS (qq.v.) from his control of industrial enterprises.

Another meaning of 'capital' emerges in the relation of capital to finance. The capital of a commercial or industrial firm is, in a broad sense, the total of shares issued by it (*see* STOCKS AND SHARES). But businesses may often use capital which is more than the total shares or stock issued: for example, they may issue DEBENTURES, or may obtain LOANS (qq.v.) from their banks or extended credit from the merchants who supply them: all these methods will increase the amount of capital which the business actually uses.

In the financial sense capital is practically the same thing as savings. A firm engaged in 'company finance' is principally concerned with obtaining the savings of private investors, in order that the money may be put at the disposal of firms needing capital.

The expressions 'fixed' and 'circulating' capital are used by directors of companies, financiers, and accountants. By 'fixed' capital they mean the amount of capital which has been more or less permanently turned into land, buildings, plant, and machinery, and so cannot easily be turned again into money. By 'circulating' capital they mean that part of capital which is continuously changing the form in which it is invested, being sometimes invested in one way and sometimes in another. For example, in times of poor trade the circulating capital of a merchant may consist of money only, or possibly of investments on which he draws INTEREST (q.v.), because he cannot employ his capital more profitably in actual trade; but when trade is good his capital may become transformed into stocks of goods, into debts owed to him by his customers, and so on.

That part of circulating capital which is available for the day-by-day working purposes of a business is called 'working' capital. The accountant usually defines working capital as the difference between current assets (such as cash, bank balance, stock-in-trade, and book debts) and current liabilities to creditors.

Fixed capital, being savings locked up in the buildings and equipment of a particular concern, cannot be withdrawn at will; and so bankers, whose investments must always be easily convertible into cash, are clearly not the proper persons to provide such capital. Fixed capital for the larger concerns is usually arranged through ISSUING HOUSES (q.v.). Finding capital for the small firm has always been difficult, and for many years there was no organization for this. In 1945 the Industrial and Commercial Finance Corporation, whose shareholders are the large British banks, was set up to fill this gap; it has since invested over £50 millions in small companies.

A firm is 'under-capitalized', or short of capital, if the total amount of capital raised is not enough to prevent its continually asking banks and similar institutions for loans. A concern is 'over-capitalized' when it has received, from shareholders or partners, so much money capital that it cannot profitably use all of it in trading or manufacturing, with the result that much of it has to be left idle in the bank, or invested in securities giving a lower rate of interest than the profits of merchanting or manufacturing.

A slight measure of over-capitalization is necessary to a growing business. Wisely run businesses provide for extension and development by what is called 'ploughing back profits'. This means that the whole of the profits are never distributed to shareholders, but a considerable amount is used to buy machinery and buildings. This practice has exactly the same effect on a firm's finances as a regular annual increase of capital.

In a national sense, a community's real capital, such as factories, railways, ships, plant, and machinery, must be continuously growing, to enable it to keep pace with advances in world technology and to secure a steady rise in the STANDARD OF LIVING (q.v.). During a war its stock of real capital will not only be damaged and partly destroyed, but will also have suffered from lack of maintenance and repair. This was the state of affairs in Britain after the Second World War.

See also EXCHANGE AND TRADE; LIMITED COMPANIES; INVESTMENT; INTEREST; PROFITS.
See also Vol. X: CAPITALISM.

CARAT, *see* ASSAYING.

CARDING, *see* WOOL-SPINNING, Section 2.

CARPET MAKING. 1. Like many other TEXTILES (q.v.), carpets can be made in various ways; they are hand knotted as Persian, Turkish, and Indian carpets are, woven, stitched, or tufted into a pre-formed backing, bonded (that is, the pile is glued to a backing fabric), and so on.

The term 'carpet' is generally used to describe material with a pile, that is, loops or tufts of yarn rising more or less at right angles to the backing, and taking the wear, as well as making the carpet soft, warm, and sound-absorbent. But flat woven multi-ply fabrics used to be woven for floor coverings, and felts and felt-like materials may also be used.

Tapestry-woven carpets and rugs have no pile and are woven simply with a warp and weft (*see* WOOL WEAVING). But, to give extra strength and thickness, the weft is put in loosely, and beaten down to cover the warp. Patterns are woven in the same way as in TAPESTRY (q.v.); coloured weft threads form the design, and the warp is usually undyed. Some primitive peoples make rugs in this way, and the method is also used in Central Asia, Turkey, and at Aubusson in France (*see* Fig. 1).

2. MANUFACTURE. In making woven carpets, the backing is woven at the same time as the pile is formed. By using different coloured yarns for the pile, patterns of many colours can be produced.

Wilton and Axminster are the two main types of mechanically-woven carpet.

(a) *The Wilton process* has a number of variations. In making Brussels carpets, the pile yarns are alternately woven into the backing, then lifted over flat metal strips or 'wires' placed on edge across the width of the material, so that raised loops are left when the wire is withdrawn sideways. Wilton carpets are made by using wires with a small blade attached at one end; the loops are sheared through to form a cut pile, when the wire is withdrawn. For cord carpets a low loop is produced by using a wire with a round cross-section. In 'face-to-face' Wilton, two carpets are woven together at the same time, and a knife blade cuts through the pile which joins the two backings.

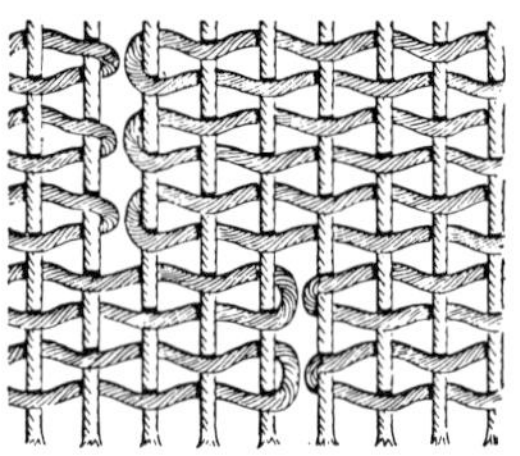

FIG. 1. TAPESTRY WEAVE
The pattern is made by different coloured weft threads

(b) *The Axminster process* has two common variations, spool-Axminster and gripper Axminster. In both, tufts are cut from differently-coloured pile yarns and inserted into the backing round successive weft threads during weaving.

(c) *Tufting* is carried out on a multi-needle version of the sewing machine, in which the yarns carried through the foundation cloth by the needles are caught by hooks or 'loopers' to form loops on the underside of the cloth when the needles are withdrawn. Knives interacting with loopers shear the loops to give a cut pile. Patterning mechanisms can produce a high or low pile.

Carpet pile is made from wool, cotton, jute, viscose rayon, nylon, acrylic, polyester, or polypropylene (*see* TEXTILE FIBRES, MAN-MADE), or any blends of these. The backing is usually made from JUTE (q.v.) or cotton yarns, sometimes flax. Artificial fibres may also be used.

3. HAND KNOTTING. The loom, the wooden frame on which a carpet is woven, may be a very crude structure. Among the nomadic tribes of Asia, it is made so simply that it can be taken to pieces when travelling. Most looms consist mainly of a framework, usually vertical, to which the warp threads are attached (sometimes to rollers) at the top and bottom. One or more rows of the foundation weft threads are woven alternately with each row of loops or pile knotted across the warp. One way of knotting is to thread a ball of wool through the warp, tie a knot, and then cut the wool to leave the length of pile required; another is to make the knot, and at the same time to take the wool round a short iron rod, making a loop which is then cut to length by drawing the knife-like edge of the rod through it. Two kinds of knot are used: the Persian, in which each of the two ends protrudes between separate weft threads, and the Turkish, in which two outstanding ends alternate with two weft threads. The Persian knot produces a closer and finer surface; but it takes more time, and has been largely replaced, even in Persia, by the Turkish knot (*see* Fig. 2).

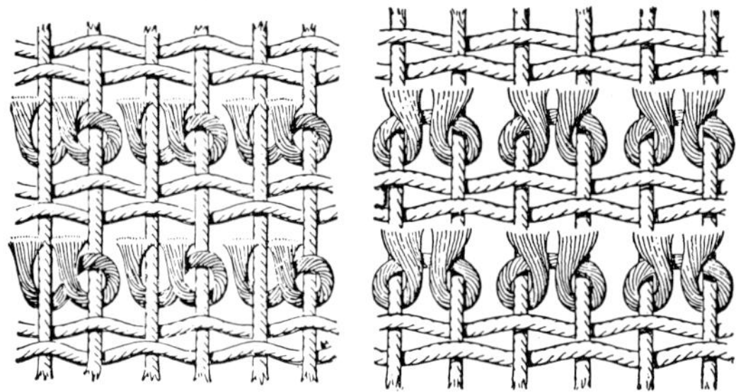

FIG. 2. PERSIAN AND TURKISH KNOTS
(Figs. 1 and 2 from A. F. Kendrick and C. E. C. Tattersall, *Handwoven Carpets*, Benn Bros.)

After knotting and cutting, the work is beaten close together with a weighted wooden or metal comb, to make a firm structure. Finally, the projecting tufts are carefully clipped to an even surface. The fineness of the carpet depends on how much care is taken over these various processes, and also on the original closeness of the warp threads. Cheap carpets may have no more than 12 tufts of pile to the square inch, while in carpets of the finest quality there may be as many as 400. The weaver usually follows the design by placing it behind the loom, so that he can see it through the warp.

4. PERSIAN CARPETS. The earliest Persian carpets still in existence date from the 16th century. They are as fine as anything that has been made since; travellers to Persia in the 17th century told of the royal workshops where the carpets were made. They were used not only in palaces and houses but in the mosques or temples as well. The designs of the early carpets were usually floral, with curving lines (as in the Chinese carpets) rather than angular lines, although the Persians are famous also for their hunting, vase, and garden designs. The colours used are very rich. In the 17th century

Persian designs were woven in India, and it is difficult to distinguish the Indian from the Persian. For the most sumptuous carpets—probably woven as royal gifts to foreign courts—silk was used.

5. Chinese Carpets. These are difficult to date, because the same designs have been used for long periods. They have certainly been woven from early times. Silk is often used, and the weaving and finishing are comparatively coarse. The designs, though partly floral, also include human figures and animals, and much symbolism in lines and curves. Yellow is the favourite colour, and the other colours used are rather delicate in tone.

6. Turkey Carpets. Very few old examples of these remain; but it is known that Turkey exported carpets to Europe, especially to Italy, in the 15th century, because they appear in pictures of the period, usually as table covers. The designs of the Turks are much more conventional and angular than the Persian, and geometrical motifs and arabesques are chiefly used, red being the favourite predominating colour. Ushak, near Smyrna, in Asia Minor, is the centre of manufacture to-day.

7. Central Asian Carpets. In this region rugs have been woven for many hundreds of years. The people are chiefly nomadic, a whole tribe moving from one pasture to another, and the rugs were used for decorating their tents and for covering the entrances. They are usually woven in the tapestry manner, with rather bold geometrical designs. The rugs from the Turkestan regions show marked Chinese influence.

Crown Copyright

A PERSIAN CARPET LOOM WITH A PARTLY FINISHED RUG ON IT

Victoria and Albert Museum

8. French Carpets. The French imported carpets from the East for some time before they began their manufacture themselves. The Savonnerie and Aubusson carpets are the most famous, the former being very fine pile carpets, the latter tapestry-woven.

9. English Carpets. Hand-knotted carpets were first made in England in about the mid-17th century. Earlier than this floors were generally strewn with rushes—even in palaces (*see* Carpets and Floor Coverings, Vol. XI). By the 18th century important carpet weaving centres were established at Wilton, near Salisbury, and at Axminster, in Devon; these names are still used for the types of carpet which were made then. Today the main centres of the carpet-weaving industry are at Kidderminster (Worcestershire), in Lancashire and Yorkshire, and the Scottish industrial belt.

See also Vol. XI: Carpets and Floor Coverings.

CARTEL, *see* Combines.

CASHMERE (HAIR), *see* Hair Trade.

CASH REGISTER, *see* Accounting, Machine; *see also* Vol. VIII: Calculating Machines.

CASK-MAKING. The making and repairing of casks is called 'coopering', and is a craft that can be traced back to the 13th century, although it is probably much older than that. Oak 'staves', some 4 inches wide and $1\frac{1}{4}$ inches or more thick, are the traditional materials, rather wider pieces of oak being used for the ends or 'headings'. Oak from around Memel, on the Baltic, has long been considered best for the purpose, but since the Second World War difficulties of trade with eastern Europe have cut off this source of supply. American oak has been widely used, but has been found to give an unpleasant taste to beer, and casks made of it have therefore to be given a lining of brewer's pitch after they are made. Oak from various other countries has been tried, and Persian oak among others has been found satisfactory. Only selected 'butts', or trunks, of oak can be used; knots must at all costs be avoided. The timber must also be cleft, that is, split, and not sawn, otherwise it will not stand up to the strains imposed by bending it to shape, although sawn boards will do for heading the ends of casks. 'Cask' is the word used by brewers and coopers; the more popular word 'barrel' is really a unit of measurement. The term 'barrel' means to a brewer a cask holding 36 gallons, just as a 'hogshead' holds 54, a 'kilderkin' 18, a 'firkin' 9, and a 'pin' $4\frac{1}{2}$ gallons.

Nowadays most casks are made for the BEER-BREWING trade, although they are much used also in the WINE TRADE and in the CIDER industry (qq.v.). The methods used by the cooper prevail wherever wooden casks are made.

To make a cask by hand, the cooper takes some twenty straight staves. He shapes them to a curving taper from the centre towards each end; and in the middle, where most of the bending is to take place, he hollows them out on the inner side, and makes the groove at either end which is to take the edge of the heading. To make them pliable, the staves are stood on end in a circle, with a hoop around to hold them, and a fire of shavings is kindled inside. A great wooden hoop is now drawn round the top of the staves. This is driven down with heavy hammers until the staves are sufficiently drawn together to enable a smaller hoop to be slipped over. So the process continues, until six hoops are on; then they are slackened back in order that the two headings may be fitted.

In these days casks are generally made by machine. In the cooperage will be found machines to shape the staves, cut the grooves, 'chamfer' or trim the ends of the staves to form the characteristic shape of the 'chime' or rim at the end of the cask, and shape up the headings. There are even machines that make the staves pliable by heating them in steam, and others that drive on the hoops. But the craftsman cooper is still to be found in almost every brewery, where he is indispensable for the constant repair of casks—fitting a new stave, or reshaping a joint, for there are more than 70 feet of joints in a cask, and none must leak. Rushes are placed between the edges of one stave and its neighbour to assist in making a good joint, but in the main the cask relies on perfect fitting

Whitbread and Co.

MAKING A CASK

The heading is being shaped to fit the cask which has two of its hoops in place

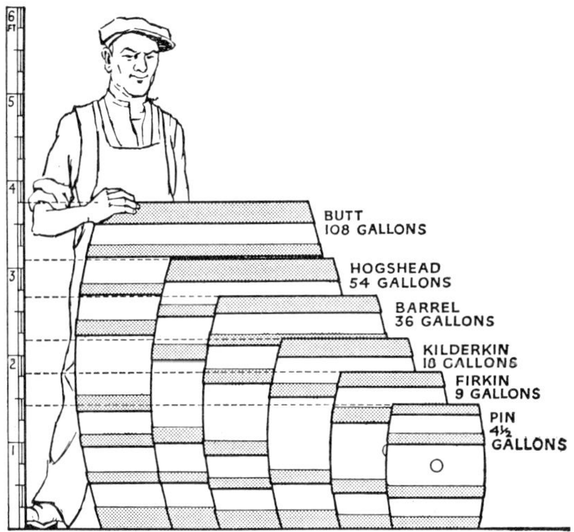

THE SIZES OF BREWERS' CASKS

and the enormous pressure applied by the hoops to make it quite tight.

Casks made of layers of timber, made on the principle of PLYWOOD (q.v.), have been used as well with some success, the advantage being that only the inner and outer faces need necessarily be of oak. Containers of stainless steel have also been used for beer.

To fill the cask, a bung-hole is provided midway down one of the staves, which is often made a bit wider than the rest to make up for the strength lost through boring the hole. In one of the headings, near the rim, will be found the tap-hole. This is a smaller aperture which takes the draw-off tap to which, with beer casks, the piping is connected in the public-house cellar. The tap-hole is closed at the brewery with a plug. After the cask has been filled, the bung-hole is closed by driving into it a wooden disk with tapered edge known as a 'shive', in the centre of which a small hole is bored partly through. When the cask has been set up in the public-house cellar, this hole receives a 'spile', or small peg of porous wood, which affords an adjustable means of letting air into the cask as the level of beer goes down.

See also BEER BREWING; WINE TRADE.

CATALOGUES, *see* WHOLESALE TRADING; AUCTION.

CATERING INDUSTRY. This includes all enterprises providing food outside people's homes. Those that provide accommodation as well as meals belong properly to the HOTEL INDUSTRY (q.v.). The catering industry in any country is specially interesting for the way in which it reflects social and economic changes.

Until the 18th century eating outside the home was not practised nearly so widely as it is to-day. In the country the traveller had to rely largely upon the coaching INNS (q.v. Vol. IV), highly efficient places which were ready to serve some sort of meal at any time of the day or night. In the towns light refreshments, such as cakes, pastries, and sweet or savoury jellies, were served in the back parlour or upper rooms of the pastry-cook's shop, but, apart from this, the taverns were the only public eating-houses. These were quite distinct from the ale-houses, which did not serve meals, and they catered for all classes. From the 16th century the custom of eating out became more popular when the 'ordinary' was established: a meal served at a fixed price and a fixed time, like the modern *table d'hôte*. The hour of serving it varied from century to century as the fashionable dinner hour varied. One of the most popular 16th-century 'ordinaries' was at the tavern opened by Richard Tarleton, the comedian of Shakespeare's day, off Newgate Street, and many other London taverns, such as the Mermaid, the Devil, and the Mitre, adopted the same practice. During Stuart times many French taverns were opened in London, serving elaborate and expensive meals, but still following the practice of the ordinary.

From the 17th century onwards, the introduction into Europe of the new beverages, coffee, cocoa, and later tea, caused a new type of catering establishment to become popular: the coffee-house. This idea came to Europe from Turkey: the first in London was established by a Turk in 1652, the first in France at Marseilles in 1671. During the remainder of the 17th century coffee-houses were opened all over Europe. They were frequented by the literary men of the 18th century, such as Addison, Steele, Swift, and Dr. Johnson, and many of these houses became celebrated CLUBS (q.v. Vol. IX).

The ordinary restaurant, as we know it to-day, is directly descended from the tavern. The word is French, and meant originally a special kind of restorative soup, being applied to a French tavern where this was served. It later came to mean an eating-house with separate tables for the diners. The first place of this kind was opened in France in 1780, and as France then led the world of fashion, eating-houses on the same model were opened shortly afterwards in other continental countries, and also in the West End of London. During the first years of the 19th century the restaurant had almost replaced the tavern as the most favoured type of eating-house. In some places, such as the City of London, the traditions of the tavern remained to some extent, notably in the 'chop-houses', with their high-backed wooden pews, where the customer picked out his own chop or steak for the grill.

With the coming of the railway in the 19th century the coaching inns lost a good deal of trade, but the demand for the town restaurant increased. French, Austrian, and Italian immigrants, escaping from political repression in their own countries after the revolutions of 1848, set up in British cities the many restaurants which still bear their names. Numbers of the refugees settled in the Soho district of London and the cheap, yet good, restaurants opened for them also became popular with British people. The restaurant habit in London dates from this time, although it never became as widespread as on the Continent.

The early railway companies found that travellers on long journeys needed meals. At important junctions there were station restaurants before the restaurant-car was invented (*see* RAILWAY COACHES, Section 5, Vol. IV). At stations such as Swindon even the express trains used to stop long enough for the travellers to get out and have a hearty meal.

One of the results of the INDUSTRIAL REVOLUTION (q.v.) was that young men began to come to the towns and cities, particularly to London, in growing numbers, as shop assistants, clerks, and apprentices, and to enter the professions. From the end of the 19th century, when the use of the typewriter became more widespread, many young women followed their example. There were not enough restaurants for all these people until multiple-branch cafés began to open. The pioneer firm opened its first London branch in 1884, and its competitor and successor 10 years later. As London grew, new branches were opened, and the movement spread to the larger provincial towns.

Both firms opened large 'popular' restaurants, on many floors, in the West End and other parts of London, and had factory premises fairly close to the centre of London, where food supplies for their branches were prepared and distributed. Other and smaller firms followed their example.

Until the Second World War began in 1939, service in these new popular restaurants was by waiters or waitresses at the larger restaurants, and by waitresses alone at the smaller cafés. In the U.S.A. popular restaurants had grown up in another way, for habits were different and wages higher, so that restaurant-owners found it cheaper to run snack-bars, and cafeterias or self-service restaurants. Between the First and Second World Wars the snack-bar spread to

THE RAMPONAUX TAVERN
A popular 18th-century tavern in the suburbs of Paris

Cardiff College

CATERING STUDENTS TRAINING IN THE PASTRY KITCHEN AT THE CARDIFF COLLEGE OF FOOD TECHNOLOGY

Britain, and chains of milk-bars were opened by milk and dairy firms. Owing to a shortage of waitresses in Britain during the Second World War, when women were needed for war work, many of the popular cafés adopted the American cafeteria system, which continued when peace came.

When food rationing finally ended in 1954, substantial meat dishes, especially steaks, began to be in great demand in restaurants; this led to the opening of many so-called 'steak houses', which provided short, simple menus, consisting mainly of steaks, chops, and similar items, cooked to order. Other types of 'speciality' restaurant followed, serving one particular food in a variety of ways; the foods included fish, chicken, egg and bacon, cheese, and even baked potatoes and doughnuts. Many Chinese and Indian restaurants were also opened by immigrants from Hong Kong, India, and Pakistan.

The rapid development of pre-cooked, quick-frozen, and air-dried foods has revolutionized kitchen methods, especially in the medium-price restaurants. By the use of these pre-prepared 'convenience' foods, labour and equipment are saved, and meals can be ready in minutes which previously took hours to prepare, using fresh materials. Today a restaurant can offer a menu of ten to twenty dishes from a kitchen which contains only a deep freeze (to store the prepared foods) and a microwave, or air-convection oven (to heat them up in a matter of seconds). Convenience foods are also used by the high-price luxury restaurants, where the chef, taking them as his basic raw material, can still exercise skill and imagination by seasoning, garnishing, and adapting them, either alone, or in combination with fresh foods. The economic importance of this development can be shown from the fact that Liverpool Corporation, with 400 schools, hospitals, police stations, etc., serving 19 million meals a year, decided in 1969 to switch entirely to frozen, pre-cooked meals, cancelling all kitchen building programmes and saving a capital outlay of £2½ million over 5 years.

Another modern feature of the catering industry is the adoption of the franchise system, already widely practised in America. Under this system, the 'operator' is franchised by a parent company to run a restaurant serving a specific range of foods. He is provided with premises, already equipped, for which he pays an 'ingoing' fee, and he is instructed in the use and preparation of the foods he will sell. Their ingredients are supplied on a regular basis. The outstanding example of catering franchise in Britain is the Wimpy Bar operation of J. Lyons, which in 1969 had 611 restaurants in operation, 150 of them being overseas.

One important branch of the industry is the factory and office canteen. This idea was started many years ago by progressive employers, at a time when poorer workmen could not afford to buy meals, and usually took to work a can of cold tea and some bread and butter tied up in a handkerchief. This they would eat in the street, or sitting, unwashed, among the machines in factories. The modern works or office canteen is a well-run, hygienic department, with a good choice of tasty foods, and is considered an important part of industrial welfare (*see* FACTORY ORGANIZATION, Section 4). It may be run by an outside firm of caterers, or by the employers themselves, or by a committee of employees.

Many small firms employing too few people to make it worth while to run a canteen have been obliged to offer a similar attraction in order to secure workers; they give their employers free luncheon vouchers, tickets which enable a meal to be bought at a reasonable price at selected public restaurants.

See also HOTEL INDUSTRY.
See also Vol. IV: INNS.
See also Vol. XI: COOKING, HISTORY OF.

CEMENT. Strictly speaking, any powdered substance is cement if, when mixed with water, it is able to be moulded and then to set hard as it dries. It is used in building, either as a mortar to bind together bricks, stones, or concrete blocks in walls and other structures, or as one of the components of concrete (*see* CONCRETE CONSTRUCTION, Vol. VIII). No other material, except perhaps steel, has had such an influence on modern architecture and modern civil engineering. The Romans called this material *caementum* or *cementum*. Nearly 2,000 years ago Vitruvius, a Roman architect, wrote a famous manual of architecture and building construction. In it he mentioned that 'there is a kind of powder which, by nature, produces wonderful results. It is found . . . round Mount Vesuvius. This, being mixed with lime and rubble, not only furnishes strength in other buildings, but also, when piers are built in the sea, they set under water.' By 'setting' he means hardening under water, which is one of the most valuable properties of cement; but the same property of 'setting' is useful in all forms of building.

The Romans discovered that certain substances could be ground and mixed with lime and water so that they combined slowly to form a 'hydraulic' cement, that is, one which resisted water. Their secret was lost for centuries, but when the English engineer, Smeaton, was commissioned in 1756 to build the first Eddystone lighthouse, he succeeded in making natural cement from Welsh limestone, which served his purpose, because it set hard under water. For some time afterwards, 'natural cement' was used, and the term 'Roman' was applied to one variety obtained from Sheppey. Modern cement, however, is an entirely artificial product. It was invented by a bricklayer from Leeds, Joseph Aspdin, who patented it in 1824, although he is said to have made the discovery in 1811. He added suitable clay to finely ground limestone, burned the mixture, and ground the resulting product. He named it 'Portland cement' because of its supposed resemblance to Portland stone, although there is little real resemblance between the two. When we speak of 'cement' today, we generally mean Portland cement, which is far stronger and more lasting than any of its 'natural'

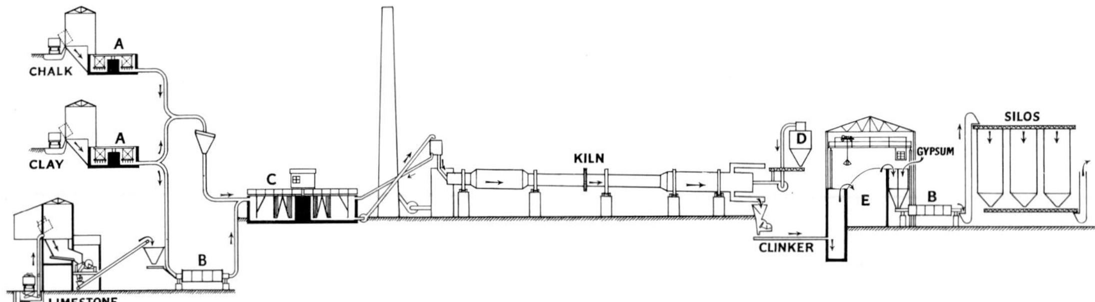

THE MAKING OF CEMENT *Cement and Concrete Assn.*

Cement slurry is made of chalk or limestone and clay. The chalk is broken up with water in a wash mill (A); clay is also mixed with water in another wash mill and limestone is crushed in a ball mill (B) with clay slurry. The slurry is stored in tanks (C) and fed from them to the kiln which is heated with powdered coal from (D). Clinker is formed which is stored in E. This is ground in a ball mill with gypsum to form Portland cement which is stored in silos until it is bagged and dispatched

predecessors, particularly as the basis of reinforced concrete.

Like brick, cement is especially valuable in British building because all its ingredients are found within the country (*see* BRICKS AND TILES). Its preparation also involves the use of large quantities of coal. It is a component of concrete, which is made by mixing it with water and bulky material ('aggregate'), such as gravel, broken bricks, or clinker. Although cement works are found in many parts of Britain where limestone or chalk is available, the chief concentration of the industry is in north Kent, along the banks of the Thames estuary and the Medway. Here suitable alluvial clay from the rivers, and chalk for burning and mixing with it, are found close together, and coal can be shipped right up to the quays beside the various works. As a result, the landscape is studded with tall, grey factory chimneys. Enormous quarries, or excavations, have been dug into the chalk hills, and sometimes houses and vegetation are covered with the grey-white dust from the works.

The two essential raw materials for cement are calcareous (chalky) substances containing lime, and argillaceous (clayey) substances containing silica and alumina. About two-thirds of the finished product consists of lime. After the ingredients have been mixed in the right proportions, and water has been added, the mixture is ground wet in a 'wash-mill'. This produces a liquid mass known as 'slurry', with the consistency of thick cream. The slurry is then burned at a very high temperature—1,400° to 1,450° C. Formerly the burning was done in a brick or stone kiln shaped like an ordinary lime-kiln. Today cement is burned in a rotary kiln, a huge steel cylinder 10–12 feet in diameter and 150 to 500 feet long, which revolves very slowly on its axis. The wet slurry is fed into the top end, and slides slowly down to the lower end where the injected fuel burns. During this process, the powdered limestone or chalk is decomposed into lime and carbon dioxide, the lime combining with the clay to form white-hot clinker. After cooling, the clinker is ground with a small proportion (about 4%) of gypsum to an extreme fineness in 'ball-mills' containing steel balls. The powder that comes out of the mill is cement, ready for packing and dispatch.

For use in building, whether as an ingredient of mortar or of concrete, the cement must be kept dry until it is actually needed. Cement for

Cement and Concrete Assn.

CEMENT SLURRY IN STORAGE TANKS (C IN DIAGRAM, p. 84)

The slurry is stirred by a revolving harrow and agitated by compressed air. The pipe on the right takes the slurry to the kiln

Cement and Concrete Assn.

ROTARY CEMENT KILN SEEN FROM THE FIRING END

Kilns may be 10–14 ft. in diameter and 300–500 ft. long, producing 3,500 tons of cement, or even more, in 24 hours. In the foreground are coolers to cool the clinker

mortar is mixed with sand and with a carefully graded amount of water. Cement for concrete has an 'aggregate' added as well. It then 'sets'—that is, dries and hardens—slowly or quickly according to the addition of accelerators or retarders. Its ultimate strength depends on the proportions of the ingredients. It may become as hard as rock; indeed, if it is used as mortar, it often becomes harder than the bricks or stone blocks that it joins together.

There are several varieties of Portland cement, including rapid-hardening, white, and coloured cements, as well as two varieties of hydraulic (water-resistant) cement which are not Portland.

See also BUILDING INDUSTRY, HISTORY OF.

CERTIFICATE OF ORIGIN, *see* OVERSEAS TRADE.

CHAIN STORE, *see* MULTIPLE SHOPS.

CHALK MINING. Chalk has many industrial uses. It is a limestone of rather loose texture occurring in many parts of eastern, south-eastern, and southern England. Most chalk contains FLINT (q.v. Vol. III), which has been formed from the fossils of tiny organisms living in the sea in remote ages (*see* LIMESTONE, Vol. III).

In the New Stone Age, which began about 2500 to 2000 B.C., men wanted flints to make axes to cut down trees. Forests had to be cleared so that the early farmers could have fields for flocks and herds to graze in as well as land for corn-growing. To get the flints, New Stone Age man began mining in the chalk. This developed into a regular industry in south-eastern and southern England, as for instance at Grimes Graves in Norfolk, at Brandon on the borders of Norfolk and Suffolk, and on the Sussex Downs, as well as in the chalk regions of France and Belgium across the Channel. The mines were dug down as circular shafts, 10 or 15 feet across and up to 20 feet deep; and, when the best flint layer was reached, galleries were dug sideways into the chalk to get out the flint lumps. A mine, therefore, had a central shaft leading from the surface of the ground, with galleries at the bottom, radiating out like the roots of a tree.

When the galleries had been dug as far as was safe, other shafts were dug near one another and the excavated chalk would be thrown back into a disused shaft. In time, therefore, there would be a group of shafts, some filled in, some open, and all with galleries underground branching out and sometimes connecting with one another. The tipping back of excavated chalk from new shafts into the old ones meant, however, that the galleries did not get filled up, except at their mouths, so that when modern archaeologists came to dig out the filling from the shafts of these flint-mines, they found the galleries just as they were left 4,000 years ago, and they could crawl along in the tracks of the original miners. All the digging in New Stone Age times was done by wedging out chalk blocks with deer-antlers and shovelling them up with the shoulder-blades of oxen, so the task must have been enormous. In the open galleries these antler picks have been found as they were dropped by the last miners out of the shaft, and some even show the imprint of the fingers and thumbs on the chalk coating on the handles. On the roofs of the galleries stains of smoke from torches or primitive lamps (a wick in a dish of fat) can also still be seen.

All around the mines have been found the waste flakes and bits of flint left over from the manufacture of axes. There is evidence of much specialization, or DIVISION OF LABOUR (q.v.); in fact, the industry seems to have been organized almost like a modern factory, on continuous-production lines. The different types of flint waste show that one worker did the first roughing-out, and passed it on to another near by who did the finer flaking, and so on (*see* PREHISTORIC TOOLS AND WEAPONS, Vol. I).

In modern days British chalk deposits are still mined for their flints. These are greatly used in the POTTERY industry (q.v.) and in road-making; from the Middle Ages onwards they have also been a favourite building material, although this use is slowly dying out.

But the main purpose in chalk mining nowadays is to get the chalk itself. Chemically, chalk is calcium carbonate; when burned it becomes lime, which is calcium oxide—sometimes called quicklime to distinguish it from the slaked lime or calcium hydrate formed when quicklime is mixed with water. Chalk in its natural form is also used as a fertilizer, and it is one of the raw materials of the CEMENT industry (q.v.). It is used in the manufacture of rubber articles and in the preparation of wallpaper, and some of the harder and more rocky kinds are used as building-stone. In the mineral-water industry chalk is the material from which the carbon dioxide is

A.C.L. Brussels

PREHISTORIC FLINT MINE AT SPIENNES, BELGIUM

Galleries have been tunnelled into the chalk, leaving columns to support the roof

made which produces the gassiness in the drinks. Whiting, which is an important constituent of putty and is also much used for polishing jewellery and plate, is made out of ground chalk mixed with water and later evaporated.

See also Vol. I: PREHISTORIC MAN.
See also Vol. III: LIMESTONE.
See also Vol. VI: LIME.

CHAMBERS OF COMMERCE. These are organizations set up to represent the views of a business community in a particular area —usually for a city or a state but, in some cases, for a whole country. In addition, Chambers of Commerce provide a range of information services, promote trade through missions and exhibitions, and provide certain internationally recognized commercial documents. In some countries they supervise commercial education.

The Guild Merchant of the Middle Ages, which was an association of all merchants in a city or town, was the forerunner of the modern Chamber of Commerce (*see* CRAFT GUILDS). Our modern term is a literal translation from the French, and it was the French who took the lead in the modern revival of the old medieval Guild. In Britain, Chambers of Commerce appeared at the end of the 18th century and became more numerous during the 19th, the London Chamber of Commerce being founded in 1881. The members of these Chambers were commercial and industrial firms. The Association of British Chambers of Commerce was formed in 1860, to act as a general clearing-house for their activities.

National Chambers of Commerce are linked through the International Chamber of Commerce, or through such regional groupings as the Permanent Conference of the Chambers of Commerce of the European Economic Community, or the Federation of Commonwealth Chambers of Commerce. These larger groupings exist to bring the businessman's views to the attention of international agencies or supra-national authorities.

See also COMMERCE.

CHARCOAL is wood that has undergone the same treatment as coal receives when it is made into coke. This treatment is technically called 'destructive DISTILLATION' (q.v.), and nowadays takes place in closed vessels from which air is excluded; these are heated, and the gassy constituents of the wood are driven off, leaving a black, brittle, and porous substance behind. This is the charcoal. It can be made by piling pieces of wood in the form of a rough pyramid, with plenty of room between the pieces for air to circulate, and covering the pile with earth and setting fire to it. This method is still used in Ashdown Forest. Sometimes portable kilns are used, which can be moved near to the available supplies of wood. Worksop, in the Midlands, is the leading British centre of the industry; here the method employed is similar to that of the Coke Oven (q.v. Vol. VIII), and makes possible the recovery of By-products (q.v.).

Charcoal has had many uses, though for some it has now been replaced by the powdery carbon or lampblack obtained as a by-product of certain processes in oil refining. One of its important properties is its capacity to absorb odours and colours; some chemicals that are not colourless in their manufactured state may be made so by being agitated in water containing powdered charcoal, or by being filtered through granulated charcoal: this is also the material used in filters for drinking-water.

As charcoal is a very pure form of carbon (although not as pure as the diamond, which is the purest form known to science), it is often used by metallurgists for smelting (*see* Iron and Steel, Vol. VIII) small quantities of metallic ores into metal that is required in its purest form. The British iron industry, before the discovery and use of coke, smelted its ores with the aid of charcoal. It is one of the constituents of gunpowder (*see* Explosives, Vol. VIII). It used to be the basis of black paints and printing inks before it was replaced by the modern products of the oil refineries. It is still used for the preparation of the finest types of Indian Ink (q.v. Vol. IV). Animal charcoal, made from calcined bones, is used in Sugar Refining (q.v.).

CHARTERED ACCOUNTANT, *see* Auditing.

CHARTERED COMPANIES are formed by Royal Charter or by Act of Parliament. Many trading companies have been formed in this way, among them the Bank of England, the Gas Light and Coke Company, the P. & O. Steam Navigation Company, and the Royal Mail Steam Packet Company (*see* Companies). The earliest was the Company of Merchant Adventurers (q.v.). This was formed at the end of the 13th century, to develop the cloth trade in that part of north-west Europe then known as Flanders, and now including north-east France, Belgium, and the Netherlands.

The next big chartered company was the Russia Company, formed in 1555. Sebastian Cabot (q.v. Vol. V), the famous navigator and explorer, was its first governor. Queen Elizabeth encouraged further companies. The East-land Company was given a charter in 1579, to trade in the Baltic lands and Scandinavia and to challenge the influence of the Hanseatic League (q.v.). In 1581 the Levant Company was formed to capture from the Venetians and the Genoese some of the trade of the Near East. In 1588 the first of a series of African Companies was founded, and in 1600 the most famous of all the chartered companies, the East India Company (q.v.).

The Stuart kings continued the Elizabethan tradition. Another company operating on the west coast of Africa was given a charter in 1618. The two earlier African Companies were merged in a new Company of Royal Adventurers into Africa in 1663. This was a more ambitious project than the others, and took in the whole of Africa as far as the Cape of Good Hope. The Royal African Company of England, founded in 1672, became its successor. In 1670 Charles II gave the Hudson's Bay Company (q.v.) its first charter. The 18th century was not noteworthy for the formation of new companies. The South Sea Company was, however, founded in 1711, but did not conduct any serious business of exploration or colonization. Its activities were almost brought to an end by the financial disaster known as the South Sea Bubble (q.v.), although it lingered on for many years before it was finally liquidated.

The chartered companies were very prominent in the earlier years of Britain's overseas development, and at that time served a useful purpose. They gave to associations of traders the prestige and power that came from operating under Royal Charter. Most of the enterprises meant adventuring into more or less unknown lands. War was then very frequent, and British lines of communication lay mainly across the seas; trading and exploring adventures were almost bound to lead to the use of troops and warships, and a single unfortunate encounter on the high seas or abroad might, for the sake of prestige, drag the country into war. Yet the Government could hardly manage such trading enterprises direct, however much it might have been interested in their success. To make it easy, therefore, for the Government to control what went on in one part of the world, a single trading company

Fox Photos

CHARCOAL BURNING IN KENT

In the foreground a pile of wood is being prepared for burning, and behind are burning piles

CHARTER OF INCORPORATION OF THE LEVANT COMPANY

Granted in 1661 by Charles II, confirming letters patent giving trading rights to the company by James I. The company was first chartered in 1581. *State Papers, Foreign Archives (S.P. 105) 108 (M.P.M. 1)*

would be given exclusive rights there. Control could be exercised in other ways. The charters were not granted for indefinite periods, but were subject to periodical renewal. When the time for renewal came, the Government could change the original conditions, if it thought fit. The right of appointment of the governors of these companies, and in many cases of their directors, was also reserved by the Government. Many governors were either members of the royal family itself, like Prince Rupert, cousin of Charles II, who was the first governor of the Hudson's Bay Company, or they were leading statesmen. Moreover, at a time when taxes were few, and hard to collect, and the Treasury was always short of money, the Government could arrange for a share in profits as part of the price to be paid for renewing a charter. Apart from all these reasons, the chartered company was an obvious form of organization in an age when strict Government control of overseas trade was regarded as the normal thing (*see* MERCANTILE SYSTEM).

The 16th and 17th centuries were the heyday of the chartered companies. During the 18th century opinion began to harden against trading privileges in any part of the world being reserved for a single concern. Agitation against the companies increased, and the competition of free-traders, whom the companies called interlopers, was allowed to grow. Although some of the companies remained in being longer than others, by the beginning of the 19th century nearly all of them had ceased to exist in their original form.

The free-trade temper of most of the 19th century did not encourage chartered companies (*see* INTERNATIONAL TRADE, Section 4), but towards the end of the century the leading European powers began to compete for colonies in Africa (the 'scramble for Africa' as it was called) and elsewhere overseas. The chartered companies were then revived. The British North Borneo Company was formed in 1882, and, like the East India Company, not only traded in its territory but governed it. After the Second World War its administration was taken over by the British Government.

One of the most famous of the late-19th-century companies was the British South Africa Company, formed in 1889 to develop Bechuanaland and the lands north of it. It owed its existence to the enterprise of Cecil RHODES (q.v. Vol. V), and it ruled Rhodesia from 1905 until 1923, when it was deprived of its administrative powers. This company and the Hudson's Bay Company still survive as commercial corporations, the British South Africa Company now being mainly interested in mining and prospecting.

See also COMPANIES; TRADE, HISTORY OF.

CHEESE-MAKING, *see* DAIRY INDUSTRY, Section 4.

CHEMICAL INDUSTRY, *see* CHEMISTRY, INDUSTRIAL.

CHEMISTRY, HISTORY OF. The study of the nature and composition of the different forms of matter, and of the interactions which can take place between them, is the science of CHEMISTRY (q.v. Vol. III). In early ages, primitive man had found out by trial and error how to carry out a number of chemical processes. By the time of the ancient EGYPTIAN CIVILIZATION (q.v. Vol. I) the more civilized men knew how to extract and work copper, tin, iron, and the precious metals, how to make pottery, glass, soap, and pigments, and how to bleach and dye textile fabrics. These arts were the beginnings of the chemical industries.

The early scientific study of chemistry, known as alchemy, grew up in the first few centuries A.D. at Alexandria in Egypt. There two important things came together: one was the practical knowledge of the men who worked in metals, pottery, and dyes; the other was the learning of the earlier Greek philosophers. These included Heraclitus, Empedocles, Democritus, Hippocrates, and Aristotle, who had long debated the nature of MATTER (q.v. Vol. III). At the same time alchemy was much influenced by

AN EARLY 19TH-CENTURY CHEMIST'S LABORATORY

ideas from the East about MAGIC and ASTROLOGY, or foretelling the future from the stars (qq.v. Vol. I).

Greek philosophers regarded speculation as superior to experiment, and some held that all matter was made up of the same four 'elements' —earth, fire, air, and water. Many people, therefore, thought that, if those elements could be rearranged, one substance could be changed into another. For instance, a base metal such as lead could perhaps be turned into gold. The chief aim of the alchemists was to find a way of doing this.

Alchemy came under Arab influence when the armies of ISLAM (q.v. Vol. I) conquered Egypt during the 7th century. They carried its study into western Europe when they advanced into Spain. Many Arabic words are still used in chemistry, for example, 'alkali', 'alcohol', 'borax', and even 'alchemy' itself, which means 'the art of Egypt'.

The greatest of the Arabic alchemists was Jabir ibn Hayyan, possibly the same person as Geber, the author of two important books on alchemy known from Latin translations dating from the 13th century. Jabir claimed that mercury and sulphur should be reckoned as 'elements', like the air, fire, earth, and water of the Greeks. He said that all metals were composed of mercury and sulphur in different proportions. To transmute a base metal to gold would require a change in these proportions, and this change was to be brought about by the action of some mysterious substance which came to be called 'the philosopher's stone'. Alchemists searched in vain for this substance for several hundred years.

Alchemy was studied widely in Europe during the 12th and following centuries and attracted the attention of many learned men, including the 13th-century alchemist, Roger BACON (q.v. Vol. V). Bacon's writings show that he was familiar with the work of the early Arabic alchemists and he also describes the manufacture of gunpowder.

Though the alchemists were doomed to failure in their efforts to make gold, they were none the less learned men engaged in a perfectly serious study. Their work led to the growth of a great deal of new chemical knowledge and of methods of making experiments. Many of the later European alchemists, however, were complete frauds who preyed upon trusting people by all sorts of tricks, and the subject fell into disrepute. By the time of Paracelsus (1493–1541) the aim of the alchemists had changed from the making of gold to the making of medicines. In particular they sought a fanciful substance called the 'elixir of life', which was to cure all ills, and which some people thought would turn out to be the same as the philosopher's stone (*see* MEDICINE, Vol. XI). This phase of chemistry lasted till about 1700.

In this period an increasing number of workers made and recorded chemical experiments in what we should regard as a scientific way. Agricola (1495–1555) studied and wrote of metallic ores and the methods of making pure metals and metallic compounds from them. He also laid the foundations of chemical analysis. The transition from alchemy to chemistry was further advanced by van Helmont (1577–1644) who studied carbon dioxide and other gases.

It was the 17th-century Irishman, Robert BOYLE (q.v. Vol. V), who finally overthrew the traditions of alchemy and began the era of modern science. In his book *The Sceptical Chymist* (1661) he insisted on the use of the scientific method of experiment, observation, and deduction. He gravely questioned the old theories of the composition of matter based on the Greek and Arabic 'elements'. He defined an element—as we still do to-day—as a substance that cannot be split up into simpler substances. Boyle made many careful experiments on the properties of gases, and established the law relating to pressure and volume which bears his name (*see* PRESSURE, Vol. III).

During the next 100 years chemical investigations were mainly directed towards the preparation of gases and the study of the composition of the air and of the process of 'combustion' or burning. Almost all men of learning at that time accepted a theory of combustion which is now known to be false—the theory of 'phlogiston'. It was thought that everything which would burn, such as coal, paper, wood, and so on, was composed of its own ash together with phlogiston; the phlogiston was believed to be lost during burning, leaving only the ash. Later came the preparation of oxygen by Scheele and Joseph PRIESTLEY in 1774, and this was followed by the brilliant researches of the French scientist LAVOISIER (qq.v. Vol. V), which finally overthrew the phlogiston theory. The fact was proved that burning is the interaction of oxygen (which forms one-fifth of the air) with whatever substance is being burnt.

The atomic theory of John Dalton (1766–1844) was the foundation-stone on which the rapidly growing science of chemistry in the 19th century was built. Of the many elements of which the earth is composed (*see* MATTER, Vol. III) only about 28 had been truly identified in 1800. By 1850 this number had risen to 54, and by the end of the century to 80. The elements were arranged in a 'periodic table', according to their atomic weight, by Mendeleyev in 1869 (*see* table, pages 278–9, Vol. III).

Until the early 1800's, practical chemistry and speculative chemistry had followed more or less separate paths. For example, while Aristotle was speculating on the nature of matter, plenty of practical Greeks were fermenting wine, refining metals, extracting natural dyestuffs such as Tyrian purple, tanning leather, and carrying out many other operations that we should today regard as chemical. But with the INDUSTRIAL REVOLUTION (q.v.), which could almost be defined as the application of science to craft, the

Alinari-Mansell

THE ALCHEMIST

Painted by Giovanni Stradano in 1570. Now in the Palazzo Vecchio, Florence

chemists, so to speak, moved into industry. Since 1850, an increasing proportion of fundamental chemical discoveries have been made in industrial firms, as opposed to university or government laboratories. For this reason, much of the history of chemistry after 1850 is in fact covered by the next article: CHEMISTRY, INDUSTRIAL.

For the last hundred years scientists both in industry and at the universities have been studying the structure of the elements themselves, a vast research, which has led to two whole new sciences, Physical Chemistry, which is concerned with the actual mechanism of chemical reactions, and Nuclear Physics (*see* NUCLEAR ENERGY, Vol. VIII).

Finally, since the 1850's chemistry 'proper' has become so complex that it is today broken down into many different branches. The three most important are probably organic chemistry, or the study of carbon compounds, silicon chemistry, and the chemistry of the living cell, which has stemmed from the analysis and later the synthesis of the important group of natural products called VITAMINS (q.v. Vol. XI).

To-day chemists are speculating about the nature of life itself, and the science-fiction dream of creating a living organism from its basic elements seems no longer such an impossibility as was at one time supposed.

See also Vol. III: CHEMISTRY; MATTER; ATOM.

CHEMISTRY, INDUSTRIAL. Although certain chemical processes such as those relating to soap, glass, and alcoholic liquors are quite ancient in origin, the development of chemical production as we know it today had to await a more mature industrial society.

Many of the early chemical developments depended on the availability of iron and steel, metallic ores, coal, and salt. The increasing sophistication of the textile industry during the course of the 19th century was one of the main forces, creating new chemical demands. In this respect,

HOW THE WORLD USES CHEMICALS

The pattern of principal consumer use

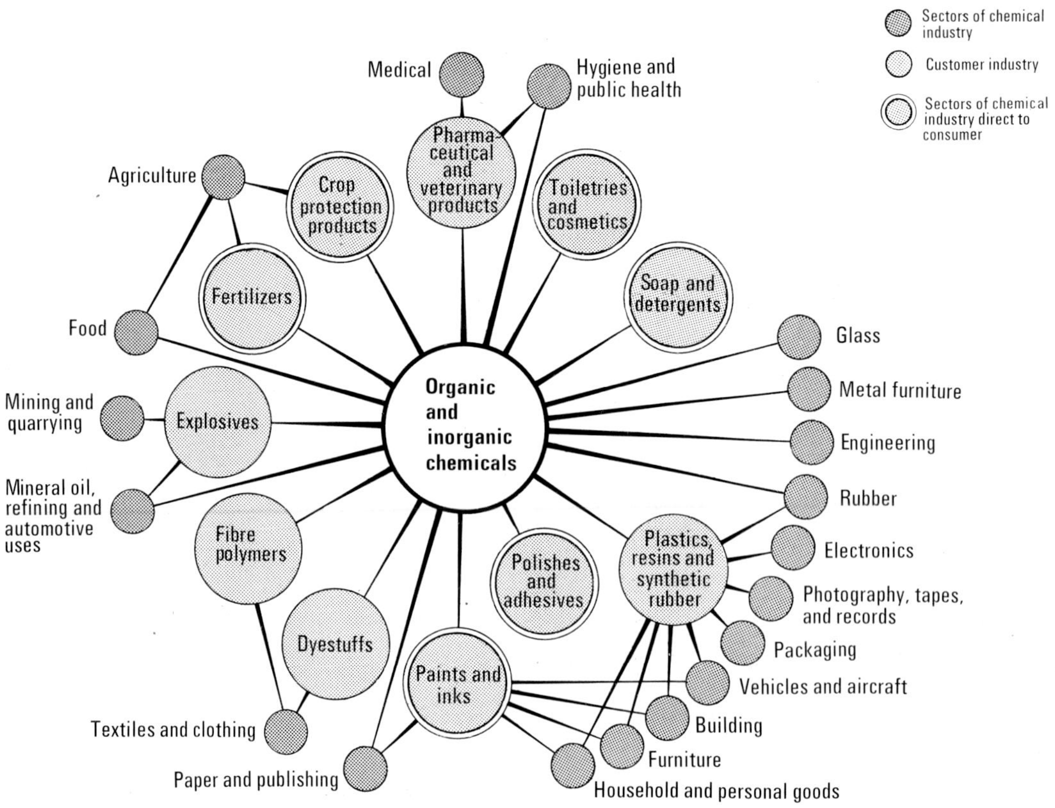

Imperial Chemical Industries Ltd.

NYLON FIBRE IS PRODUCED AT THE INDUSTRIAL CHEMICAL INDUSTRIES' TEESSIDE PLANTS

Nylon fibre has a wide variety of uses, including clothes, soft furnishings, and industrial products

one of the major breakthroughs was Perkin's discovery of mauveine in 1856. This led directly to the development of a wide range of synthetic dyestuffs (*see* DYES), and represented the first step towards the establishment of industries based on synthetic organic chemistry.

With the increase in complexity of both science and industry, it becomes more difficult to make simple definitions, such as what the chemical industry consists of, though it is clearly concerned with making the chemicals used by other industries in preparing a multitude of products. Perhaps this broad concept, sometimes termed the 'chemical process' industries is the right one for today. Whilst it obviously embraces the production of chemicals, as before, this new classification can be expanded to include the production of fertilisers to enrich the soil, pharmaceuticals for curing the sick, SOAP AND DETERGENT manufacture, PAINTS AND VARNISHES (qq.v.) and other surface coatings, cosmetics and toilet products, agricultural insecticides and pesticides, chemicals for photographic work, adhesives and disinfectants, the production of PLASTICS (q.v.), of synthetic rubbers and synthetic fibres, (*see* TEXTILE FIBRES, MAN-MADE), and perhaps even OIL-REFINING (q.v.) itself.

The traditional foundations of the chemical industry in the first half of this century were quite few in number. Chlorine and caustic soda were fundamental (*see* ALKALIS); in the earlier years caustic soda was in greater demand, but as the uses for chlorine increased, the Castner-Kellner process for the electrolysis of brine, which produced both these chemicals, assumed greater and greater importance. Sulphuric acid (*see* ACIDS) was another measure of industrial development. The raw materials for this had included spent oxide from gas-making processes, but as demand increased, pyrites and elemental sulphur were more often used. As these materials were not universally available, they began to become trading commodities on a large scale. AMMONIA (q.v.), which in 1950 was still mainly made from coal, was another cornerstone of the chemical industry.

Major industrial developments tended to be concentrated in areas that were favourable because of natural environment or industrial climate. For example, the production of calcium carbide for acetylene manufacture involved a huge consumption of electrical energy, so it was obviously sensible to locate the plants in an area offering cheap power, such as Norway. The availability of products made from coal tar depended upon the continuing carbonization of coal (*see* GAS INDUSTRY), that is, the production of coal-gas as a domestic and industrial fuel, and the production of coke for metallurgical purposes. Although these processes were widespread, they were of particular importance in countries with long established coal-based industries, such as Great Britain, the United States, and Germany. Industries using the major coal-tar products, such as benzene, toluene, naphthalene, and the cresols, were therefore to be found in all these countries.

The chemical industry is a growing one, expanding faster than the industrial economy as a whole. But this overall growth conceals wide variations within the whole range of chemical process industries. Some areas, such as soap and detergent manufacture or dyestuffs, appear to have reached a mature state of development and are now expanding relatively slowly. Other areas, such as pharmaceuticals and plastics, are still growing very rapidly. An important stimulus to growth in the chemical industry has been the increasing dependence of a large section of it on petroleum as a raw material.

The production of organic chemicals from petroleum on an industrial scale started in 1919, and the production of ammonia from a petroleum source (natural gas, in the first instance) began in 1929. Progress was relatively slow up to about 1950. At that time there was a significant but still quite small production of 'petroleum chemicals' in North America, which was fortunate enough to have both raw materials and chemical markets in the same country. Elsewhere there were only the beginnings of an industry. Yet today 80% of all organic chemicals in the world are made from petroleum, as is a similar proportion of the world's synthetic ammonia. The expansion has now spread to every continent, though, like the chemical industry itself, it is still mainly concentrated in the U.S.A., Europe, and Japan.

The great growth of organic chemicals in the past two decades has largely resulted from development in 'high polymer' products, such as PLASTICS (q.v.), synthetic rubbers, and synthetic fibres, such as nylon.

See also ACIDS; ALKALIS; DYES; PHARMACY; PAPER-MAKING; CHEMISTRY, HISTORY OF.
See also Vol. III: CHEMISTRY.

CHEMIST'S SHOP, *see* PHARMACY.

CHEQUE, *see* BANKING.

CHINA, *see* PORCELAIN.

CHINA CLAY. This is a fine, soft, white clay used in the making of pottery, paper, and other articles, and formed by the natural decomposition of feldspar, one of the chief components of granite. In the U.S.A. and other countries it is known as 'kaolin', from the place in China where it was first used.

Feldspar turns into clay by a slow geological process, either by the weathering effect of surface water on the granite (*see* DENUDATION, Section 1, Vol. III) or by the action of hot solutions coming up from deep down in the earth. The first leads to shallow deposits, and the second to deep ones; the deeper the clay, the greater the quantity and the better the quality and colour.

The most easily developed of the world's important deposits of china clay are in Britain, in the granite areas of Cornwall and Devon, such as St. Austell, Bodmin Moor, and Dartmoor. At St. Austell there are about 100 pits, and some of the most famous have a working depth of over 340 feet. These still have great untapped reserves, which it is estimated will last for at least 100 years, on the basis of a production of 1 million tons a year. Large reserves of this good clay in Cornwall and Devon are on high ground, from 700 to 1,000 feet above sea level, where there is also plenty of clear water. These two natural conditions, height of ground and abundant water, are important to the extraction of the clay, and largely determine the cost of mining.

Although the term 'mining' is used, in this industry the clay is actually washed down from

A MOULDER REMOVING A PAIR OF MELAWARE CUPS FROM THE TOOL IN WHICH THEY HAVE BEEN MOULDED

Fox Photos

CHINA CLAY PITS AT ST. AUSTELL, CORNWALL

In the foreground are tanks filled with slurry and behind them are white waste tips

the open sides of the pit by means of a high-pressure hose called a 'monitor', mounted on a movable stand and handled much as a fireman directs water on a burning building. There may be as many as four or five monitors in a large pit.

The clay-laden water, called 'slurry', flows into special pits, where the coarse grains of sand (quartz) and other impurities settle. The clay-water is then pumped to the surface of the pit, and the process of refining is repeated through a series of channels until the smallest particles of sand have gone. The liquid clay, now free of grit, is allowed to settle in tanks, to the consistency of cream; it then flows through pipe-lines to other tanks, where it remains for about 8 weeks so that the solid particles may settle to the bottom and the surplus water evaporate. In some pits this process is shortened by the use of filter-presses.

The clay, when dry enough to be handled, is taken to the drying-kiln, a long, low shed with a floor of fire-brick slabs covering flues which conduct heated air under the clay. The same shed provides storage room, called a 'linhay', where the clay is kept until shipment.

From the linhays, which are usually near a railway siding or a deep-sea port such as Plymouth and Falmouth, the clay is distributed by lorry, rail, or coastwise shipping and canal to various destinations in Britain, such as the Potteries of Staffordshire. During the present century nearly three-quarters of the output has been exported by sea direct to the U.S.A. and Canada, the largest consumers, and to many European countries.

When the industry was first set up in the 18th century, after William Cookworthy found suitable clay near Porthleven (Cornwall) in 1755, the main use of china clay was for making POTTERY (q.v.). Since then the clay has been increasingly used as a filling and coating substance which greatly improves the quality of paper. Mixed with a pulp consisting of rags, wood, or esparto grass, the clay gives paper a finer texture for printing ink, and also makes photographic paper glossy. Good printing paper has about 16% of clay, and paper with a high gloss has 25% (*see* PAPER-MAKING).

Although china clay is still mainly used for pottery and paper, it also plays an important part in the making of rubber, paint, asbestos products, fire-bricks, cement, linoleum, oil-cloth, insecticides, leather, chemicals, and medicinal preparations. It is used to stiffen textiles, and is used in cosmetics as a basis for face-powder. During the First World War a number of new uses were discovered for china clay as a substitute for certain chemicals that come from abroad and could no longer be obtained.

Even the waste from the clay-pits provides valuable BY-PRODUCTS (q.v.). The spectacular white pyramids, which are so conspicuous a feature of the Devon and Cornwall landscape, yield the sand from which concrete blocks for housing have been made for over 50 years. These dumps, sometimes containing a million tons of waste, provide a special quartz sand useful for making cement, and also flake-mica, used as a substitute for glass in furnaces and stoves because of its great resistance to heat.

Before the Second World War the china-clay industry ranked second only to coal in tonnage and value of raw materials exported from the United Kingdom. Since the beginning of the century the annual British output has risen from 500,000 to 1,000,000 tons, and over half of this is exported. The output of the industry is not due solely to the favourable natural conditions in which the clay is found, nor to mechanical power, which has progressed from the famous Cornish beam steam-engine of the 18th century to gas, to oil, and finally to electricity. It is due just as much to the skill and judgement of the individual clay-worker, using age-old methods of refining and drying, in pits where the post of 'pit-captain' is often passed from father to son.

See also CLAY; PAPER-MAKING; POTTERY.
See also Vol. III: ROCKS.

CHOCOLATE, *see* COCOA AND CHOCOLATE.

CIDER-MAKING. Cider is the fermented juice of apples, and is an apple wine of the same kind as wine made from grapes, although it contains less alcohol. Spain was the first country in Europe to make cider, and it has been for a long time a popular drink in France, particularly in Normandy. In the Middle Ages it was popular in many parts of England, and especially in East Anglia, but there is no record of its having been made before the 17th century in the west of England, which is now a great cider country. The drink went out of favour in England at the end of the 18th century, but the taste for it has since revived.

As happens with wine, fruit grown in certain districts and on certain soils makes better cider than other fruit, and it is in Devon, Hereford, and Somerset that the best cider apples are grown in England. English cider has hitherto been made from pressed and pulped apples by a process of natural FERMENTATION (q.v. Vol. II)—the same process as that by which wine is made. Fermentation must not be allowed to advance too far, or the wine will have too much acidity. Cider, like grape wine, can be either still or sparkling (*see* WINE TRADE). The best sparkling ciders are made, like champagne, by being put into bottles before fermentation is fully complete, but the sparkle is given to the cheaper ciders by the artificial introduction of carbon dioxide gas.

There is an annual cider-sampling ceremony in Somerset in May; at this ceremony a modern cider artificially fermented from a champagne yeast was first introduced.

Perry, made from pears instead of apples, is made by the same methods as cider.

H. P. Bulmer and Co.

PUTTING APPLES INTO A CIDER PRESS

CIGARETTES, *see* Tobacco Industry.

CINEMA, *see* Entertainment Industry; *see also* Vol. IX: Cinema, History of.

CITY COMPANIES. The Livery Companies of the City of London are the successors of the earlier Craft Guilds (q.v.). There are twelve principal companies: the Clothworkers, Drapers, Fishmongers, Goldsmiths, Grocers, Haberdashers, Ironmongers, Mercers, Merchant Taylors, Salters, Skinners, and Vintners. There are also about sixty minor companies. Some of these, the Carpenters and Leathersellers for instance, are wealthy and important.

The City Companies began as craft guilds in the late Middle Ages. Many of the craft guilds in time split up because the interests of the master members came into conflict with the interests of the worker or apprentice members. Such guilds became guilds of masters only, or 'liverymen', entitled to wear the 'livery' or the ceremonial uniform of the guild. Some of the more influential of these masters' guilds obtained Royal Charters forming them into corporations or companies; and so they developed into the City Companies of London.

Until the 16th century the companies retained a direct connexion with their trades, training apprentices and newcomers, regulating wages and other payments, watching over the standard and quality of work done, and controlling conditions of entrance to the trade or craft. But by the 18th century most of the companies had given up these duties, for guild control over industry and commerce had disappeared in favour of the small, independent master or the big company. They still carried on their charitable and benevolent work, looking after their old or infirm members and often pensioning their widows; they remained interested, as always, in education; and, as their charters had often conferred such privileges on them, they played an important and influential part in the civic government of the City of London, and in nominations for the office of Lord Mayor.

They also retained their wealth, and had even added to it in spite of various attempts to take it from them. Their riches had often made them the targets of jealous or moneyless kings, or of their finance ministers. After the Reformation and the dissolution of the monasteries, ministers such as Thomas Cromwell turned to the City Companies for money, and they lost a lot of their wealth and property during this period of plundering. Charles I and Charles II, who were always short of money, also took money from the companies, sometimes openly and blatantly as forced levies or loans, sometimes more politely in the guise of subscriptions to various objects. They had just begun to recover from these losses when the Great Fire raged across the City of London in 1666, and their magnificent halls and treasures and many of their records were largely swept away. Their recovery from this blow was a very slow and painful process.

By that time their functional position in English trade and industry had disappeared. They had become close corporations of influential City merchants and manufacturers, and many of their members followed trades very different from those which their companies had once so carefully supervised and controlled. For there had always been two ways in which would-be entrants to the companies could qualify as members. The practice of the trade concerned was, of course, one way. The other was to be the son of an existing member, even though he followed a different trade. Thus, the son of a Vintner was eligible to become a Vintner too, even though he practised as a lawyer, for instance. By the 18th century a City Company had therefore become a kind of club, where members of varied interests could dine and discuss business together, and where influential strangers could be hospitably entertained. As London became a larger and more populated city, and property in it owned by the companies rose in value, their wealth accumulated, until at the beginning of the 20th century it had become very considerable indeed.

There are, however, a few companies that are still occupied with details of their original trades. Of these the most noteworthy is the Goldsmiths' Company. The annual 'trial of the pyx', or approval of new coins turned out by the Royal Mint, is still their responsibility; and it is at Goldsmiths' Hall that the Assay office is located, where the hall-marking of gold and silver is carried out (*see* Assaying). The Apothecaries' Company still looks after the soundness and purity of medicines.

Many of their names now mean something different from what they meant hundreds of years ago. 'Grocer' nowadays means someone who keeps a retail shop and deals in provisions;

the name originally came from the French word for 'wholesaler', and meant a merchant on a large scale. The first whale-oil from Greenland was handled by the Grocers' Company. They founded Oundle, the public school in Northamptonshire.

'Mercer' now means a merchant in silks and satins. The word originally came from the Latin *mercator*, meaning merchant. The early Mercers dealt not only in silk, woollen, and cotton textiles, but also in oils, wines, spirits, and some metals. Richard (Dick) Whittington and Sir Thomas Gresham, the great financier of Queen Elizabeth's reign, were both Mercers. Dean Colet, the founder of St. Paul's School, was a great benefactor of the Company, and his portrait hangs in their hall. The Company runs a school in London.

The Drapers got their name from the French word for cloth—*drap*—and made and dealt in woollen cloth. Their records mention their having fitted out a ship for John Cabot's voyage to explore Newfoundland at the end of the 15th century. The Merchant Taylors originally made armour and camp equipment as well as clothes, in what is now Threadneedle Street. Their Company founded the public school of that name. The Skinners also founded one: Tonbridge, in Kent. As their name suggests, they dealt with skins and furs. The Haberdashers, who also run a school in London, absorbed several minor guilds, including the hatmakers or Milliners, so called because their craftsmen came originally from Milan, in northern Italy. The work of the Ironmongers was formerly much closer to that of the wholesale iron and steel merchant than to the retail dealings in hardware of the ironmongers of today. To the Vintners' Company, who dealt in wines, belonged not only the importers of wine but the keepers of inns and taverns where wine was sold. The Clothworkers' Company included members of the guilds of the shearmen, fullers, dyers, and weavers. The Fishmongers' records contain two names of interest: Sir John Gresham, who founded Gresham's School, at Holt in Norfolk; and Doggett, the original promoter of the annual race by the Thames watermen for Doggett's Coat and Badge (*see* Boat Races, Vol. IX).

Many of the trades carried on by some of the lesser companies are now things of the past. This is particularly true of the companies dealing with the making of bows and arrows: the Bowyers, Stringers, and Fletchers—this last from the French *flèche*. The Barber Chirurgeons originally did the work of doctors and dentists, as well as shaving and trimming hair. The Cordwainers dealt with leather, including the tanning process and the making of boots and shoes; the French word for one who keeps a boot and shoe shop is still *cordonnier*. The Founders cast vessels out of metals other than iron, principally brass and pewter. The Horners made drinking vessels and musical instruments out of horn. The Loriners, or Lorimers, made the metal parts of horse equipment, such as bits and spurs, both now forgotten trades. The craft of the Pattenmakers goes back to the days when it was impossible to walk the foul, slushy streets of London without the rough wooden clogs, or pattens, which the members of this Company turned out. The Plaisterers' Company still survives, and was originally known as the Pargetters. The Scriveners used once to carry out the duties now performed by solicitors. They had a great deal of trouble with illiterate apprentices, who lacked

S I R,

BY Virtue of a Precept from the Right Honourable the LORD MAYOR, you are deſired by the MASTER and WARDENS of the Worſhipful Company of STATIONERS, to meet at *Guildhall*, on *Monday* the 29th Day of *September*, 1777, at Nine of the Clock in the Morning, in your Livery Gown and Hood: From thence to attend the preſent LORD MAYOR to St. *Laurence*'s Church to hear a Sermon: And then to return to *Guildhall* to elect a LORD MAYOR for the Year enſuing.

Marſhall Sheepey, Beadle.

INVITATION TO MEMBERS OF THE LIVERY COMPANIES TO ELECT A LORD MAYOR OF LONDON

The invitation bears the arms of the Stationers Company

Parker Gallery

GOLDSMITHS' HALL IN THE 19TH CENTURY

The hall-marking of gold and silver articles was carried out at the Assay Office in Goldsmiths' Hall. Coloured engraving after T. H. Shepherd

the perfection of grammar and style that their masters thought necessary; a bad apprentice was ordered to a grammar school until he should be 'erudited in the books'. The Turners made parts of household furniture; and the Upholders—who were the forerunners of our modern upholsterers—assembled them. One of the most famous of the minor City Companies was the Woolmen's Company; this has now lost the important place it held in the great days of the English wool trade (*see* WOOL TRADE, MEDIEVAL). A new Company, the Launderers, was formed in 1960.

It seems to be the fate of the companies that they should be involved in national disasters. The Second World War did not injure the Companies as much as the Great Fire, although several halls were damaged and some entirely destroyed: the gaunt ruins of Salters' Hall, for instance, were for many years visible from St. Swithin's Lane. But the economic consequences of the war have to some extent hampered their ancient tradition of hospitality, and compelled them to adopt an austerity very different from the days before the war, when it was a memorable experience to dine in one of their magnificent halls, and to be served from their beautiful plate and silver. They still live on, however, as a picturesque part of the traditional splendour of the City of London. Their names survive throughout the Commonwealth and the United States as the surnames of countless families of English stock, some of whom do not know, perhaps, that their names are those of the trades followed by their forefathers.

CLAY PRODUCTS, *see* BRICKS AND TILES; POTTERY; CHINA CLAY.

CLEARING HOUSES. These are organizations which economize time and labour in settling what business men owe each other. If each of six business firms, for example, had one buying and one selling deal with each other in a day, the daily total of transactions would be thirty. If all these transactions were settled separately, thirty separate cheques would have to be made out, paid into the various banks, and dealt with by the bankers (*see* BANK ACCOUNTS); and a good deal of clerical labour would be wasted on all these details. But if the six firms formed a clearing-house for the 'clearance', or settlement, of what they owed each other, all transactions during the day would be reported to the clearing-house, which would strike a balance at the close of business. Some firms would owe money and others would be owed money; the total owed would equal the total to be received. It would then only be necessary for each firm

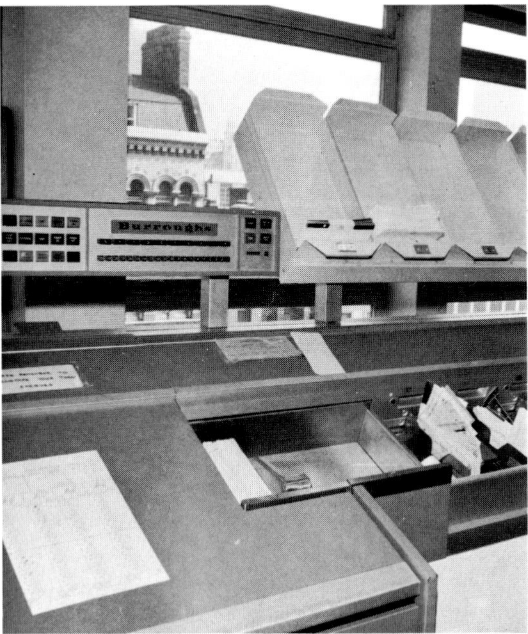

Lloyds Bank

AUTOMATIC CHEQUE SORTER IN BANK CLEARING DEPARTMENT

owing money to draw a cheque in favour of the clearing house, and for the clearing house to draw cheques in favour of the firms that were owed. All firms belonging to the clearing house could, in turn, provide the necessary clerical labour, or each firm could pay a subscription that would cover expenses: a subscription that would be much less than the expenses if no clearing house existed.

The first clearing house in Britain was the London Bankers' Clearing House, started at the end of the 18th century. By the turn of the 19th century it occupied a large building in Post Office Court, off Lombard Street, in the City of London. It was started originally by the London private bankers, to do away with an excessive number of inter-bank journeys, or 'walks', by an army of walk-clerks. The joint-stock banks were admitted in 1854.

The present members are: Bank of England, Barclays, Coutts, Lloyds, Midland, National Westminster, Glyn Mills, National and Williams Deacons. The numbers, already reduced by bank amalgamations, will be further reduced when the last three listed merge as Williams & Glyn's. The BANK OF ENGLAND (q.v.) acts as banker to the others, and adjusts their accounts at the end of the day for what they are due to pay or to receive. This settlement is, of course, in respect of the large number of cheques that are paid in daily to each member bank, and which represent claims against the banks on which they are drawn. More than two million cheques are dealt with at the Bankers' Clearing House every day of the week.

The Railway Clearing House was another institution of this kind, although it has now lost its former importance. It was started in a very small way in 1842, with less than half a dozen clerks, but grew later into a large concern. It used to share out among the various railway companies the money received for passengers or goods booked on 'through' journeys over several different lines. In the earlier days of railways the booking office at, say, King's Cross might sell a ticket to Edinburgh, involving journeys over the Great Northern, the North Eastern, and the North British Railways, then separate lines. Each line would have to receive its share of the fare, and these shares were calculated by the Railway Clearing House. Since nationalization (*see* RAILWAYS, HISTORY OF, Vol. IV), the clearing-house staff deals with accountancy and other work for British Railways. The clearing-house system is becoming increasingly used in other branches of industry and commerce. The produce and commodity exchanges (*see* MARKETS) and the London Stock Exchange have used it for many years, and it has recently been adopted in the wholesale textile trade.

See also BANKING; BANK ACCOUNTS; STOCK EXCHANGES.

CLOTHING INDUSTRY. Until the middle of the 19th century men's outer clothes were hand-made to order, by the same methods which are still used in the (hand) 'bespoke' tailoring trade. The Americans were the real pioneers of the ready-made clothing industry. It was an American, Singer, who invented the first practical sewing-machine, which led to the large-scale production of clothes in the U.S.A. Singer's machine was introduced into Britain in 1851, and a ready-made clothing industry became established in the West Riding of Yorkshire, principally in Leeds, and in London. To start with, each piece of cloth in a garment had to be cut out singly by hand; but in a few years a Leeds firm invented a mechanical cloth-cutting knife, which worked on much the same principle as a band-saw. This made it possible to cut several thicknesses of cloth at a time, to the same original pattern.

The early manufacturers made garments in a few stock sizes only. The real foundation of the wholesale ready-made clothing industry was a scientific study of human measurements made by an American firm in the second half of the 19th century. It became possible then to plan such a range of sizes and fittings that nearly everyone would find a garment to fit him, but in this, Britain lagged behind the U.S.A., because of prejudice against ready-made clothes.

The British industry was greatly helped by the big demand for uniforms in the First World War. The war also broke down many old conventions, and increased the demand for ready-made clothes. After the Second World War there was still less formality in dress; the tight and accurate fit of former days no longer interested the average man so much as the colour and design. The British section of the industry is now very efficient, and has even successfully invaded the American market. It is still located principally in Leeds and London. Mechanical knives have been improved, and can deal rapidly with as many as fifty thicknesses of cloth at a time. Portable electrical knives have also been invented, for use where the industry is not organized on factory lines. There are no operations still done by hand in the tailoring trade that cannot be done mechanically in the ready-made industry.

Wallis and Linnell

CUTTING OUT SUITS

The mechanical knife cuts through a number of thicknesses of cloth

Even the making and stitching of buttonholes, and the stitching on of buttons, are done mechanically at great speed. Mechanization is continually extended. The machine for making pocket jetts is now successfully used for trouser hip pockets, jacket inside breast pockets, and bottom pockets. Profile stitching jigs are used for such standard parts as flaps, patch pockets, snaps, tabs, welts, and sometimes collars. The introduction of fusible materials has accelerated the making of fully fused fronts in jackets, vests and overcoats, and these fusible materials are also widely used now for such parts as pocket stays and vents. In Leeds ready-made clothing manufacture is a factory industry on continuous production lines, the cloth passing from machine to machine until the finished garment is ready. Although Leeds remains the centre of the clothing industry, many factories have been set up in London and other parts of the country.

See also Wool Industry, Medieval, Section 2.
See also Vol. XI: Costume, History of.

COAL-GAS, *see* Gas Industry.

COAL-MINING. 1. Most British coals belong to the Carboniferous age (*see* Earth, History of, Vol. III). The commonest types, known as bituminous, are used in domestic grates, for gas and coke making, electricity generation, and manufacturing processes. The highest class of coal is the type known as anthracite. Between the two come the semi-smokeless steam coals. Bituminous coals are characterized by their banded structure, dull hard layers of 'durain' alternating with bright shiny layers of 'clarain'. They ignite easily, usually contain a good deal of gas and tarry matter, and burn with a smoky flame. Steam coals burn less easily, almost without smoke, and give out great heat; they were in great demand for steam shipping until Oil (q.v.) came into wide use as a fuel. Anthracites are smokeless and hard to ignite; they will not burn without a strong draught, but they contain little ash. Anthracite and steam coals are found chiefly in South Wales and Scotland.

Coal occurs in seams varying in thickness from an inch or less to as much as 30 feet, but the seams generally worked are from 18 inches to 8 feet. If the seams 'crop out' at the surface they can be worked by opencast methods (*see* Mining). Mechanical shovels are then used to remove the overlying soil and to dig out the coal. Other seams may be hundreds of yards underground, and it is then necessary to sink shafts to reach them. There are a number of collieries to-day whose deepest workings are over 1,000 yards below the surface. The seams may lie horizontally in the earth's crust, but often they are folded and tilted, and also 'faulted' or broken (*see* ROCK FORMATION, Vol. III). No two collieries will therefore have the same natural conditions to contend with.

2. SHAFT-SINKING. Most collieries to-day are served by two or more shafts; it is rarely the case that the seams can be reached by adits (*see* MINING) or tunnels driven from the surface. The choice of site for these shafts calls for great care and judgement on the part of the mining engineer. They must be convenient to railways, so that the coal raised may easily be sent away. They should also be near the centre of the area of coal to be extracted, to prevent the underground haulage roads becoming too long. The shafts are sunk by boring a large number of blasting holes or 'shot-holes' in concentric circles, charging them with explosive, firing them, and then loading out the broken rock (*see* BLASTING, Vol. VIII). As the shaft deepens, it is lined with brickwork or concrete to support the sides and keep out water. When the seam is reached, roads are driven out in the coal for some distance before the faces are opened out, leaving a pillar of coal to protect the shafts from possible damage from subsidence caused by extracting the coal around them. This is necessary not only for the

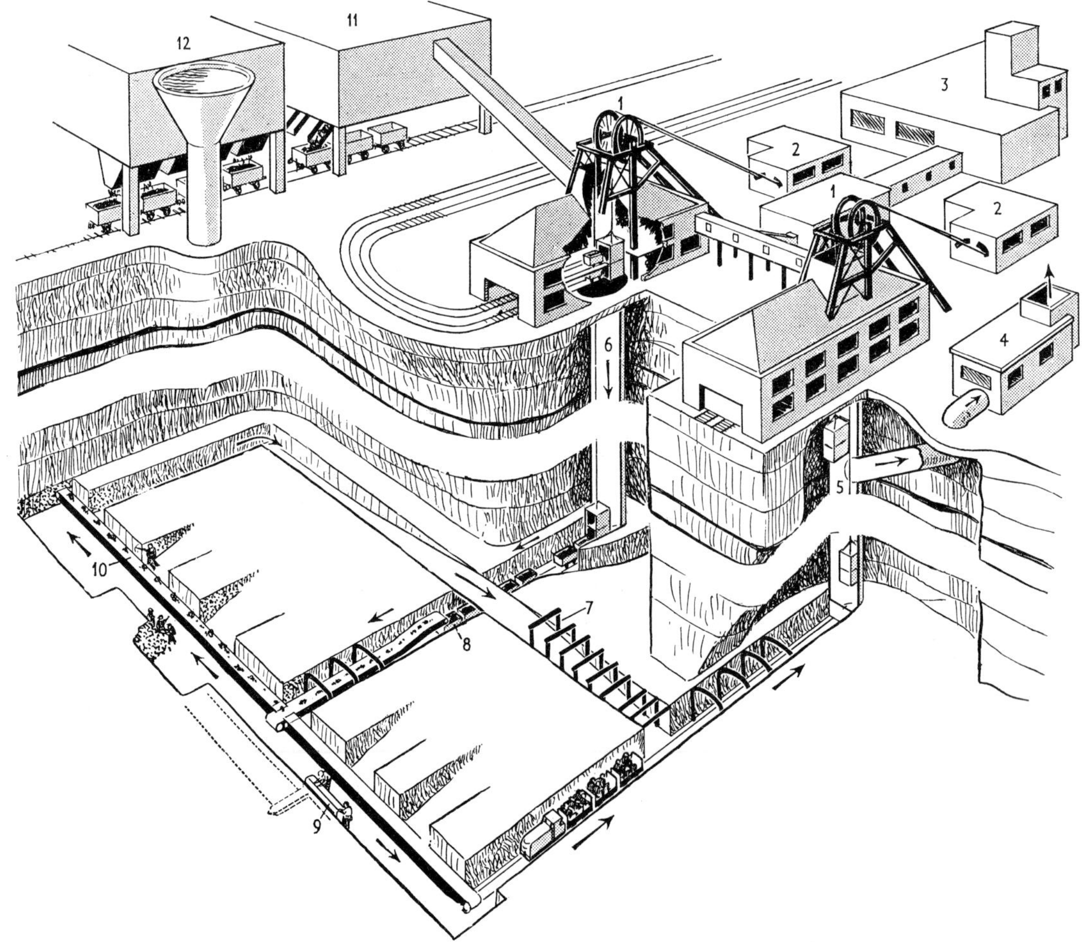

DIAGRAM OF A COAL-MINE

1. Head-gear. 2. Winding-engine house. 3. Pit-head baths and canteen. 4. Fan house. 5. Upcast air-shaft. 6. Downcast air-shaft. 7. Pit props. 8. Mine-cars ready to be loaded into cage. 9. Cutting machine at coal face. 10. Conveyor. 11. Screens. 12. Washery

National Coal Board

A COAL-CUTTING MACHINE CALLED A TREPANNER

A wheel armed with picks cuts a passage in the coal, rather like coring an apple, and the coal in the 'core' is broken and thrown on to an armoured conveyor alongside

safety of the men underground but also for reasons of cost, since a pair of deep shafts may cost one and a half million pounds to sink and equip, and they have to last the full life of the colliery—perhaps 100 years.

3. COAL GETTING. Coal was originally 'hand-got' by the miner with his pick, aided at a later stage by gunpowder; but to-day most of the output is obtained from 'faces' where the seam is worked by an electric cutter-loader (*see* MINING MACHINERY, Vol. VIII). The coal is broken from the seam by a rotating drum with hard steel teeth, and automatically loaded on to a steel conveyor belt that runs the length of the coal face (which may be 100 or 200 yards long). Coal moves from one conveyor to another on its way to the pit bottom. At the main road, conveyors discharge the coal into mine cars, or tubs, which are drawn to the pit bottom by an 'endless' rope. When the full tubs reach the pit bottom they are loaded into cages and taken up the shaft to be weighed, sorted, and cleaned.

More than nine-tenths of our coal is obtained from this method of coal-mining, which is known as the 'Longwall' system. The faces, in effect, are long walls of coal which are stripped or loaded out daily. Each face advances from 10 to 20 feet a day, usually in a direction away from the shafts. To protect himself, the miner sets up steel props to support the roof as he removes the coal. After the cut coal has been loaded out, these props are moved forward, and the conveyor belt is moved on as well. Then the electric cutter-loader is made ready for the next cut. The back row of roof supports is withdrawn, allowing the roof to collapse; and from the broken fragments 'packs' or walls are built to protect the roads and prevent the roofs from breaking down too near the coal face. Meanwhile other men are engaged in 'ripping', which is the operation of blowing down the roof in the roads to make them high enough. This is particularly necessary where the seam is thin. The rock thus blown down is also put in the packs, so far as is possible. Where there is more rock than can be dealt with in this way, it has to be loaded and sent out of the pit, forming the 'tip' that is a conspicuous feature at most collieries. More than 90% of the mines' output is machine-cut and mechanically conveyed, but hardly any of it was machine-loaded until about 1950.

Another system is known as the 'bord-and-pillar', or 'stoop-and-room' system. It is best adapted to seams lying at shallow or moderate depths. The plan is to drive a large number of roads in the seam in two directions, roughly at right angles. These are the 'bords', and thus the seam is split up into a large number of 'pillars', each from 20 to 60 yards square. These pillars of coal are afterwards extracted, starting often from the colliery boundary and working back towards the shafts. In mechanized bord-and-pillar working, each bord is cut by machine; the coal is blasted down, and then loaded by a mechanical shovel—which can load 3 to 4 tons a minute—into rubber-tired 'shuttle' cars which transport it to the main conveyor. Similar methods are employed to extract the pillars.

4. HAULAGE. Some collieries use belt conveyors to transport the coal right to the shaft, but rails still have to be laid along the underground roads to take in the supplies of props and other materials needed at the face. New mines are laid out for locomotive haulage. The locomotives transport the coal in large mine cars holding 3 or 4 tons apiece, from a main loading-point in the seam to the shaft. They are powered by diesel engines, or less commonly by electric motors and batteries. Locomotive haulage, besides being economical in manpower, is useful in taking the colliers to their work. The system requires large straight roads to be maintained, and is most easily adopted where the seams are flat, or where level roadways can be driven.

National Coal Board

A DIESEL LOCOMOTIVE HAULING COAL TUBS

Pit ponies still carry out some haulage in the collieries of South Wales, Northumberland, and Durham, but by the early 1970's, there will be none left in the mines.

5. VENTILATION. Ventilation is one of the most important problems in coal-mining. Every colliery to-day has at least one fan at work, night and day, sending fresh air round the underground workings. It is rather a surprising fact that for every ton of coal wound up the shafts, as much as 5 tons of air may have to be circulated. Nearly all coal seams contain poisonous or inflammable gases which, if allowed to accumulate, would make the air unfit to breathe, or dangerous because of the risk of explosion. The chief danger comes from 'black damp', a gas which consists of nitrogen and carbon dioxide and is noxious because it displaces the oxygen necessary to maintain life (*see* RESPIRATION, Vol. XI). The chief inflammable gas is 'firedamp' or methane, which forms with air an explosive mixture when there is between 5% and 15% present. It is because of this risk of explosion that SAFETY LAMPS (q.v. Vol. VIII) are used, either developed from the original Davy lamp or of the modern electric pattern. Electricity for power purposes is also strictly controlled, and so is blasting to bring down the coal or rip the roof. These restrictions remove the possible causes of ignition of firedamp, but the first line of defence is ventilation, which sweeps away the gas as it is given off, and prevents it from accumulating sufficiently to form an explosive mixture.

In deep mines a second reason for circulating large quantities of air is to keep the working-places cool. The temperature of the rocks of the earth's crust may increase by over 1°F. for every 100 feet we descend, and at a depth of 800 yards may approach blood heat (*see* EARTH, Vol. III). Men could not work efficiently under these conditions unless the air current kept working faces relatively cool. An elaborate system of roads has to be maintained underground to convey to the faces the fresh air descending the 'downcast' shaft, and to bring back the return air by a different route to the 'upcast'.

6. WINDING. In the past, the engines for winding the coal out of the shafts were driven by steam, which was generated at the colliery from small coal and washery refuse. Today, how-

National Coal Board

CONVEYOR CARRYING CLEAN, SPRAYED COAL FROM THE BATH TO THE SCREEN WHERE IT IS SORTED INTO DIFFERENT SIZES

ever, all pits in Britain are equipped with electric winders. Usually the tubs are raised in cages (or large lifts) and emptied at the surface, but 'skip' winding is a system now sometimes practised: the tubs or mine cars are emptied in the pit bottom into bunkers, which feed the coal into large steel boxes or skips, each holding 7 to 10 tons. The skips are drawn up the shaft, and at the top they are emptied automatically on to a belt which takes the coal to the screens or the washery.

7. Coal Preparation. Originally coal was sold unscreened, just as it came from the pit. To-day it is not only separated into different sizes—best house lumps, cobbles, nuts, beans, peas, and so on—but the larger sizes may be also picked over by hand to remove 'dirt' or rock that may have become mixed with the coal. Small coal cannot be hand picked, but is treated in a washery. It is immersed in a liquid with a density greater than that of coal, but less than that of the dirt. The coal, therefore, floats, and is skimmed off, dried, and sold; dirt sinks, and is removed from the bottom of the wash-box and sent to the tip. There are various other ingenious ways of separating clean coal from dirt.

8. The Future of Coal-mining. In 1968 the production of coal in Britain amounted to about 170 million tons, over 90% of which was mechanically cut and over 95% mechanically conveyed. The National Coal Board estimated that at this annual rate of extraction there were sufficient reserves of coal underground in Britain to last 400 years. The Coal Board's Mining Research and Development Establishment collects technical and scientific information in order to improve and increase the use of machinery. A machine is being developed, for instance, for cutting coal by remote electronic control, so that seams too narrow for men to reach can be worked.

See also Mining; Coal-mining, History of; Transport.
See also Vol. VIII: Fuels; Mining Machinery.

COAL-MINING, HISTORY OF.

1. Early History. Coal has been used by man for many more years than is generally believed, but written records of its use in very early times are scanty. The hard coal called anthracite, which is almost pure carbon, is named after a Greek word; coal was mentioned in the 4th century B.C. as being used by blacksmiths. Coal was used during the Roman occupation of Britain, for unburnt coal and cinders have been found in excavations made by archaeologists on the sites of the old Roman settlements. Most of these discoveries were made in Northumberland, which is still a famous English coalfield. But it is not until A.D. 852, long after the Romans had left, that we find any written record of its use in Britain. The *Saxon Chronicle* of the time states that the Abbot of Peterborough let the lands of Sempringham to Wulfred, one of the conditions of the lease being that Wulfred was to send to the Abbey every year a quantity of fuel, to include '12 loads of coal'. In the early 13th century Henry III granted a licence to dig for coal at Newcastle-on-Tyne. The Rolls of Parliament refer to shipments of coal from Newcastle to London in 1306. Scotland, particularly parts of Fife, was also a coal-producing area in those early days. It is recorded that, in the 13th century, the monks of Newbattle were working the 'sulphurous stone that burns', but it was not much used except in the local salt-making industry.

'Carrying coals to Newcastle' has long been an English saying, meaning the doing of some quite unnecessary task. In early days, although coal was being mined in other parts of the country, the Newcastle coalfield had the largest output, and local mining and trading were under the control of the Hostmen, a CRAFT GUILD (q.v.) or trade brotherhood which received a charter from Queen Elizabeth in 1601. Later, in the 17th and 18th centuries, the output of Newcastle and north-east England increased. This was mentioned by Daniel Defoe, the author of *Robinson Crusoe*. In his *Tour thro' the Whole Island of Great Britain*, published between 1724 and 1726, he wrote of the growing shipments of 'sea-cole' into London: the name was given because the coal was carried by sea. The trade was growing because, at that time, wood was becoming scarce all over the country, and Londoners were being forced to use coal instead of wood, although they did not take very readily to the new fuel at first. Newcastle and Whitby were the main ports for the shipment of coal to London, and a well-known riverside tavern at Wapping in East London—'The Prospect of Whitby'—was so named because the Whitby sailing colliers used to anchor in a reach of the river just offshore.

By the end of the 17th century the coal-mining industry had become well established in various parts of Britain. Between 1700 and 1750 the British output of coal rose from 2,612,000 tons to 4,774,000 tons, and by the end of the 18th century it was over 6,000,000 tons. Mining was done by very primitive methods, most of the workings being reached by cutting through hillsides, to avoid deep mining for which there was neither engineering knowledge nor equipment. No coal-mine was more than 1,000 ft. below the surface. By the end of the 18th century steam power was being used for winding engines and for pumps to suck water out of the pits (*see* COAL-MINING). Apart from other obstacles, deep mining in most districts was impossible until steam-driven pumps could be used.

2. THE MINEWORKER. The lives of the mining population have always been full of hardship. Miners' families today often talk about 'the bad old days'. Women, and boys and girls sometimes as young as 7 years, were employed underground at one time during a working day of anything from 10 to 12 hours; women were harnessed to 'tubs' or 'trams' filled with coal, and did the work done later by the pit ponies. Their menfolk, although stronger physically, were in many parts of the country little better than slaves; in the North, and in Scotland, they were often fettered with chains, working in gangs. They were tied to a particular colliery, in much the same way as the villeins were tied to their manors in the time of the FEUDAL SYSTEM (q.v. Vol. X). If a colliery owner sold his interest in a colliery to someone else, his workers were also transferred to the new owner. It was not until 1775 that the bondmen colliers of the North were freed by Act of Parliament, and another 3 years passed before another Act brought to an end the life-slavery of the Scottish colliers. But even this freedom was not complete, and it was not until 1799 that these mineworkers became as free as workers in other industries.

When the 19th century opened, the British coal-miner was no longer a slave in the eyes of the law, but women and children were still employed underground. Hours were long, and the work was very dangerous, for few safety precautions were taken. Falls of rock caused many accidents, but the greatest danger was from 'fiery' coal, which gave off a gas that formed an explosive mixture with air. This was chiefly 'firedamp' (carburetted hydrogen). The only

AN 18TH-CENTURY COAL PIT NEAR BROSELEY IN SHROPSHIRE

Horses turn the wheel which works the hoists and pack-mules carry the coal. Engraving after G. Robertson, 1788

lights then used underground were naked candles or oil lamps, both of which were dangerous. The miners themselves became concerned over the frequency of accidents and explosions, and in 1813 the local miners formed at Sunderland a Society for the Prevention of Accidents in Coal Mines. The Society employed Sir Humphry Davy to make suggestions for lowering the number of accidents, and in 1815 he invented a successful safety lamp. It was based on the principle that wire gauze will not allow a flame to pass through it, and the safety lamp originally devised by Davy was an ordinary oil lamp with the burner and flame completely encased in wire gauze. The first of Davy's new lamps was used at Hetton Colliery in 1816.

Meanwhile Parliament became interested in the problems of work and welfare in British coal-mines, and from 1800 onwards many Committees were set up to make inquiries. But changes in the law came slowly. Until the middle of the 19th century conditions remained extremely bad, and women and children still hauled trucks. It was not until 1842 that Lord Shaftesbury got a Bill through Parliament which forbade the underground employment of women and girls, and of boys less than 10 years old. The Coal Mines Regulation Act of 1850 made rules for the safer running of coal-mines, and appointed Government inspectors to visit them and see that the law was being carried out. Shaftesbury's Act of 1842 had also brought to an end the 'tied' labour that still survived in the Staffordshire coalfield, much on the lines of the old Scottish bondman system.

Further laws were passed, and by the opening of the 20th century coal-mining in Britain had become safer. But the miner's life remained hard. In 1908 an Act was passed restricting the working day to 8 hours only, but during and after the First World War British coal-miners became increasingly restive over wages and conditions. The work of coal-mining has always had a great influence on the character of those who carry it on, and this is true of other countries as well as of Britain. Usually they live in ugly and gloomy surroundings, and they work either alone or in small groups, and not in large groups

GIRL PULLING A COAL CART IN A THIN SEAM
From the Report of the Royal Commission, 1842

fact, in many parts of Britain, some of these leaders have become almost a religious legend; this is particularly true of William Abraham, still affectionately remembered as 'Mabon', the Welsh leader of the early 20th century.

By the end of the First World War it was obvious to the Government that there was grave discontent in the British coal industry, and a Royal Commission of Inquiry was set up under the chairmanship of Mr. Justice Sankey. The Commission's Report was not unanimous, but all recommended that the State should buy out the surface landowners who were paid ROYALTIES (q.v.) on every ton of coal raised. No important legislation followed this Report. In 1925 the price of coal fell seriously, through foreign competition and a world-wide depression in coal-mining; the depression was probably brought on by the increasing use of oil fuel afloat and ashore. The colliery owners wished to reduce costs by cutting wages, but the miners resisted and threatened to strike. The Government then promised to pay out a SUBSIDY (q.v.) that would make a cut in wages unnecessary. This subsidy was to end on 30 April 1926. Another Commission of Inquiry was also appointed, under the chairmanship of Sir Herbert (later Lord) Samuel, which issued its Report on 6 March 1926. Its recommendations did not please either the Government or the miners; and, as the Government would not renew the subsidy, a nation-wide strike began on 29 April. All the other important British TRADE UNIONS (q.v.) came out in a General Strike in

like factory workers. Their loneliness at work breeds great independence of character, and has sometimes tended to make them broody and ruminative in times of trouble. The records of the past history of their industry, and of the ways in which the early miners were treated, make them suspicious of those in control over them; by contrast, their trusted leaders have often fought hard on their behalf against employers and governments, and the miners have developed a tremendous sense of loyalty to such leaders. In

Radio Times Hulton Picture Library

A MINER AT WORK ON THE COAL FACE IN A NARROW SEAM

support of the miners. The actual General Strike was (in the phrase of the time) 'a nine-days' wonder', but the strike in the coalfields lingered on for many months. It was not until the Second World War that statesmen generally agreed on the desirability of NATIONALIZATION (q.v. Vol. X) as soon as the war ended. So, on 1 January 1947, the mines were transferred to national ownership, and the National Coal Board became the controllers and managers of the entire British coal-mining industry.

3. WORLD GROWTH. During the second half of the 19th century coal production increased in several countries, but chiefly in the United States and in Germany. After the American Civil War and the successful war of the Germans against the French (1870–1), America and Germany began to expand their industries, and soon became important rivals of Britain. As their coal-mining grew, so did their steel works which depended on coal. So, by the end of the century, America, Britain, and Germany were three gigantic industrial powers. One consequence of this was the building of a large German Navy to compete with the British Navy.

The figures given by various countries for the amount of their coal reserves, lying unmined in the earth, are not always reliable, but it seems that America has the greatest reserves. China comes second, the U.S.S.R. third, Germany fourth, and Britain fifth.

China and, to a lesser extent, the U.S.S.R. are going through the stage of industrial expansion experienced in this country a century or more ago; between 1957 and 1958 alone, China more than doubled her output of coal. In 1963 her output was estimated at 348 million tons, but accurate figures are not known. In 1967 the U.S.S.R. produced 595 million metric tons of bituminous coal and anthracite; America produced 551 million tons of coal and lignite (a brown coal resembling wood), but a decreasing amount of anthracite. Britain, with no lignite, produced 173 million tons; West Germany 249 million tons of lignite, but only 2 million tons of coal.

See also Vol. X: INDUSTRIAL WELFARE.

COAL-TAR DYES, *see* DYES.

COCOA AND CHOCOLATE. These are made from the beans of the CACAO tree (q.v. Vol. VI) which is grown in the tropics. The cacao bean originally came to Europe from Mexico, where it had been found by CORTES, the conqueror of that country (q.v. Vol. V), to be a valued article, not only of diet but also of trade. The beans were used as CURRENCY (q.v.) as well as the foundation of a beverage known as *chocolatl*, from which the word 'chocolate' is derived. Chocolate in the early days was always prepared as a drink, and the secret of making it was held by the Spanish Court for nearly 100 years. It then spread to England through Italy, Germany, and France, and in the 17th century a Frenchman opened a 'chocolate house' in Queen's Head Alley, Bishopsgate, in the City of London, for the sale of the drink. The new beverage became fashionable, although at that time chocolate was most unpalatable by comparison with the modern product. No sugar was used in its preparation, and the drink frequently included maize and spices. Sugar was introduced into chocolate in the later part of the 18th century by Joseph Fry of Bristol. He was the first person in this country to make chocolate more or less in the modern way, and he founded the famous Bristol firm of J. S. Fry and Sons.

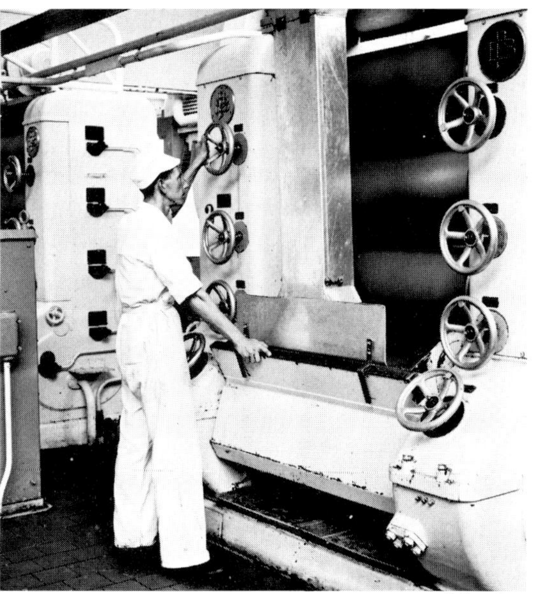

Cadbury Bros.

REFINING CHOCOLATE BY GRINDING

The cacao beans come from the plant's pods. The ripened pods are broken open with wooden billets on the plantations, and the beans are extracted, with the pulp in which they are embedded. The beans are left to ferment in heaps or boxes, and are then dried in the sun. When dried, they are packed into bags and dispatched

Cadbury Bros.

ADDING CONDENSED MILK TO CHOCOLATE

to the countries of manufacture. It is more economical to make chocolate in countries with a temperate climate, both because of manufacturing problems, and also because the demand is much heavier in cooler countries.

Five operations are necessary before the final product is ready. The beans are first cleaned and then roasted, a process which develops the chocolate flavour and also loosens the husk, which has an unpleasant taste. When the beans have been broken in a special machine, the shell or husk can be easily separated from the pieces of bean by an air blast. After roasting, some manufacturers blend the beans by mixing together different varieties, each of which has its own individual aroma. Then the beans are ground in a machine known as a 'mélangeur'; sugar is added, together with vanilla, or whatever special flavouring is desired, and cocoa butter, which is extracted from fresh cacao beans under pressure. The third operation is to refine this paste by a machine called a 'refiner', which has three or more rollers which not only grind but tear the fibres which constitute about half the volume of the bean. This combination of movements is achieved by varying the speeds of the rollers.

The fourth operation is known as 'conching'. More cocoa butter is added and the mixture is pummelled backwards and forwards by a heavy roller in a trough or 'conche'. The length of time the mixture is worked in the machine depends on the manufacturer and the type of chocolate being made, and can vary from a few hours to several days. The process helps to develop the full chocolate flavour.

The final process is tempering, when the chocolate is brought gradually to the temperature and consistency necessary for moulding. At this stage any nut or fruit fillings are added to the chocolate, which is then poured into the moulds and allowed to set. Milk chocolate is made by adding freshly condensed milk, or occasionally dried milk, to the mixture of ground beans and sugar before refining.

In making chocolate confectionery, which consists of other sweetmeats covered with chocolate, the 'centres', as the sweets in the chocolate are called, are fed on to a conveyor-belt, which carries them through a curtain of liquid chocolate and deposits them on another belt (often imprinted with the name of the maker), where they set until they are ready for packing. The machine responsible for this process is called an 'enrober'.

Cocoa as a product distinct from chocolate came into use in the mid-19th century. The discovery of how to extract the fat, or cocoa butter, from the beans was important to the development of both chocolate and cocoa. After part of the butter has been pressed out, the residue is in the form of a hard cake. This is

Cadbury Bros.

CENTRES FOR CHOCOLATES PASSING THROUGH THE 'ENROBER' TO BE COATED ground to a powder, sieved through very close-meshed screens, and it is then what is known familiarly as 'cocoa'. Cadbury Bros. first made a 'cocoa essence' in England in 1866, and they were followed by Fry's in 1868. The heads of both these firms were Quakers; in fact, all the oldest chocolate manufacturing houses in England were started by Quakers, who are also notable as having been among the first to introduce social welfare schemes for their workers.

Chocolate is carefully packed in aluminium foil to keep it clean and to protect it against damp. In tropical climates the distributor must take special precautions to keep chocolate cool because it softens at temperatures higher than 26° C., and melts at still higher temperatures. British chocolate is sold in almost every country in the world.

See also SUGAR CONFECTIONERY.
See also Vol. VI: CACAO.

COINING. This is one of the earliest nationalized industries, for since 1850 the making of our coinage has been a State monopoly. There is now only one State coining plant in Britain, at the Royal Mint in London, not far from Tower Bridge. There are, however, two companies in Birmingham which turn out coins and medals for foreign governments and public bodies.

The first process in coining is the melting of the metal in oil-fired or high-frequency electric furnaces, which melt about 8 cwt. of metal at a time. When the required temperature has been reached, the whole furnace is tilted to pour the molten metal into moulds about 2 feet long and 4 inches by 1 inch thick. After each melting, samples of the cooled metal are tested by the Mint's assay office to see that the correct composition has been produced.

Rolls of different sizes then squeeze the metal into long thin strips of the thickness of the

THE PRESS-ROOM AT THE ROYAL MINT, 1809

The blanks are put in the press by the kneeling man and stamped on both sides by turning the lever above. Coloured aquatint by Rowlandson and Pugin from Ackermann's *Microcosm of London*

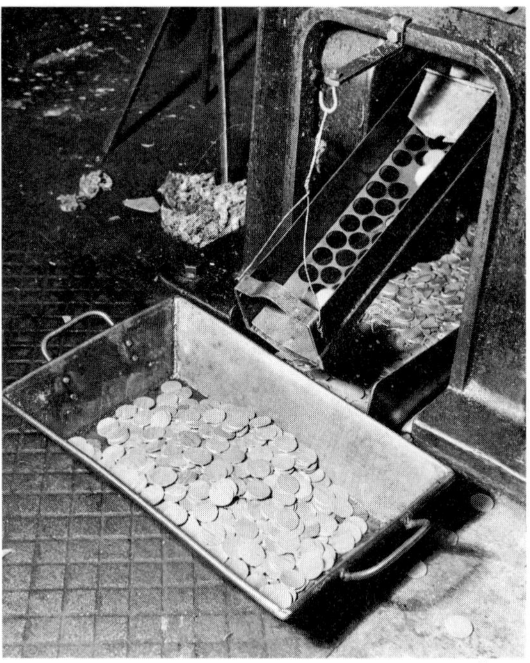

Keystone

IN THE CUTTING ROOM AT THE ROYAL MINT

As they are cut the blanks pass over a sieve through which imperfect ones drop

particular coin to be made, with intermediate annealing in special furnaces at a temperature high enough to soften the strips for further rolling. To obtain the benefits of a rapid run of production of coins made from the same sized strip, the Mint makes the same type of coin for several days on end. Thus not all coins can be seen in process of manufacture at the same time.

From the rolls the strips are passed through machines which punch out from them shaped pieces of the size and weight of the coins that they will eventually become. As yet, these pieces have no impress of a coin on them, and are called 'blanks'. When they come out from the punching machines they are annealed, and are then washed in a weak sulphuric acid solution and dried in revolving automatic driers. The scrap metal goes back to the melting furnaces.

After examination on moving belts the blanks are sent to the coining presses. Each press is fitted with two hard steel dies, one bearing the head (obverse) design, and the other the tail (reverse). These dies squeeze the blank while it is encircled by a steel collar whose inner surface is either plain or 'milled'.

Until the introduction of the reducing machine in the time of George IV, all coins were produced from dies cut by hand. As no two dies were alike, there was considerable variation in any issue of coinage. The reducing machine, however, accurately reduces to any desired size a metal copy of the model made by the artist. This model is usually four or more times the size of the coin. The steel reduction, to the size of the coin, is called a punch. After hardening, a steel impression is made from it, known as a matrix. From this a number of impressions are made: these are the working punches. From these working punches are made the working dies. This method ensures that a tremendous number of pieces can be struck, all identical.

The working dies are put in every press, and cold blanks fed into the machine at the rate of up to 300 a minute. The striking pressure is about 120 tons. Mass production on this scale became possible only with the invention of special steels. Automatic counting mechanism is incorporated in these presses, and the number of blanks that have passed through any machine and have become coins can easily be checked.

From the coining presses the completed coins go through some very careful processes of inspection. The coins are examined by eye while they travel on canvas belts which turn them over so that both sides may be seen. Pieces which have not the complete impression from the dies, or are faulty in any other way, are rejected. Samples are taken to see that the weights of the coins are correct. For some denominations each individual coin is weighed on extremely sensitive machines which automatically reject any which is lighter or heavier than the margin allowed from the standard. They are then counted mechanically into bags and sealed, with a label indicating the contents, and the counting is checked by weighing the full bag on a balance.

In the United Kingdom, gold, silver, and cupro-nickel coins are subjected every March to an inspection for good workmanship called the 'trial of the pyx', by a jury of at least six persons chosen by the Goldsmiths' Company.

See also Coins.
See also Vol. X: Mint.

COINS. From the study of the coins of different nations we can learn not only about the religion and mythology of ancient civilizations, but also about the places where they traded and the routes they took (*see* TRADE ROUTES, Vol. IV). Metals, such as gold and silver, were used as CURRENCY (q.v.) in very early times; we read in the Bible that Abraham was 'very rich in cattle, in silver, and in gold'. The value of these metals was judged by their weight. They were not coins in the sense that they were 'struck' or engraved with a device which guaranteed their weight and purity.

Coins were first struck on the coast of Asia Minor in the 8th century B.C. The first coins were of *electrum* or pale gold, and were a mixture of gold and silver. Croesus, the King of Lydia, famed for his wealth, was the first to introduce pure gold coins. The Persian coins, known as *darics* (so called after the Persian King Darius), were also made of gold. The right of making coins belonged to the king alone, though the governors of his provinces were sometimes allowed to strike silver coins of their own for special reasons.

The earliest coins of the Greek cities carried the device of the city that issued them. The coins of Aegina had a sea-tortoise, and those of Phocoea a seal. The famous coins of Athens had on one side the head of Athena, the patron goddess of the city, and on the other an owl, which was the bird sacred to the goddess. After their victory over the Persians at Marathon, the Athenians added an olive branch. Athenian 'owls' were made of silver which was mined in large quantities in the silver mines at Laurium. When Alexander the Great conquered many lands, his gold and silver coins replaced most of the local currencies. When he died, his successors put a portrait of his head on his coins.

The early coinage of Rome was a cumbrous coinage of bronze only (we read of farmers taking their money to the market in their carts). This was replaced in the 2nd century B.C. by the silver *denarius*, a coin rather smaller than a shilling. When Julius Caesar was at the height of his power, the Senate granted him the right to put his head on the coins. The claimants to power on his death usurped this right, so that by the time Augustus had consolidated the empire, portraits were common on Roman coins. Augustus put his head on one side, and some aspect of his sovereignty was depicted on the other. The Roman imperial coinage was extensive in gold, silver, and copper, and the general type remained unchanged till the end of the empire. The various invaders, Franks, Vandals, and others,

Ashmolean Museum

GREEK AND ROMAN COINS, HEADS AND TAILS

1. Aegina. Silver didrachm. 2. Athens. Silver tetradrachm. 3. Macedon. Philip II gold stater. 4. Rome. Julius Caesar silver denarius. 5. Rome. Augustus silver denarius

who destroyed the Western Empire, issued rough copies of Roman coins, and it was not until Charlemagne's reforms about A.D. 800 that the West had a good currency again. A predecessor of Charlemagne introduced the silver penny, which was the only silver coin of Europe till the end of the 13th century. It was copied everywhere in the West.

The first important coin of European commerce was the *bezant*, which was the successor of a gold coin called the *solidus* struck by the Emperor Constantine. The *bezant* got its name from Byzantium (later Constantinople, now Istanbul), and remained the standard gold coin of Europe until the florin and ducat were coined in the 13th century. The word 'florin' is derived from Florence, where the first was struck in 1252. The Venetian *ducat*, later known as the *sequin*, remained an important international coin until the beginning of the 19th century.

The British gold sovereign and half-sovereign have been of international importance since the 19th century (the sovereign is still of importance throughout the Middle East). But many centuries of coinage history passed before they appeared. During most of this time silver was the metal generally used. There were a few native British coins before the Roman occupation, but they were not of original design, being mostly imitations of the 'stater', a coin struck by Philip II of Macedon, the father of Alexander the Great. During the occupation of Britain the Romans introduced their own coins, many of which have been dug up and are now in the museums. After the Romans left, it was some time before native-made coins re-appeared.

The history of English currency begins in the 7th century with a large number of silver pieces, known to modern writers as *sceattas*, which show a great variety of designs but rarely bear the name of the king or moneyer who caused them to be issued. Soon after 750, the needs of traders between England and France gave rise to a coinage in which the name of the king who authorized its issue appears on each piece. The first names to be thus recorded are those of certain obscure kings who were reigning in Kent 760–70, but when Offa King of Mercia (757–98) had added Kent to his own kingdom he issued, apparently from Canterbury, a large currency, in which his name and that of the moneyer responsible for the quality of the coin appear on every piece. These coins, as probably the *sceattas* of an earlier time, were known as pennies, and it is with them that the continuous record of the English coinage begins. The coins of Offa, of which many bear his portrait or that of his wife Queen Cynethryth, show a beauty of design and a delicacy of workmanship which were not equalled in any later reign. These silver pennies were often cut into halves and quarters for convenience in business. To avoid this necessity Edward I coined silver halfpennies and farthings. He also tried to introduce the 'groat' or silver fourpenny piece, but it was unpopular and was dropped. Edward III successfully reissued the groat, and in 1344 he coined the gold 'noble'. Edward IV introduced the gold 'angel', and Henry VII the first 'sovereign'.

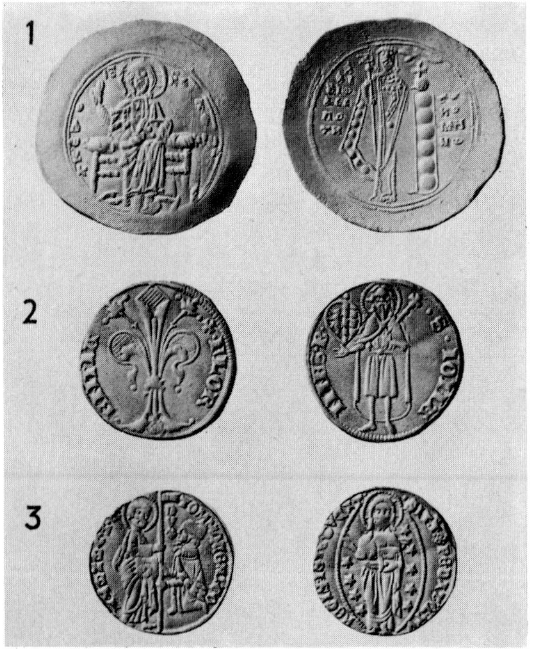

Ashmolean Museum

EARLY EUROPEAN COINS, HEADS AND TAILS

1. Gold bezant of the late Byzantine Empire. 2. Florin of Florence. 3. Sequin (ducat) of Venice

The foundations of modern British coinage were really laid in the 16th and 17th centuries. Edward VI introduced silver shillings and Elizabeth introduced silver sixpenny and threepenny pieces, which gradually replaced the groat and the half-groat (or twopenny piece). The first 'guinea' or sovereign was coined by Charles II in 1662. It was worth 20*s.* until 1717 when its value was altered to 21*s.*, and was called a guinea because it was made of gold from the Guinea Coast. Charles II also introduced the crown, the half-crown, and the shilling. In 1816 sovereigns and half-sovereigns which continued to circulate until 1914 were made with St. George and the Dragon on the 'tail'. The British florin or two-shilling piece was issued in 1849 and the double florin or four-shilling piece in 1887. The double florin and the crown or five-shilling piece were unpopular and their coining for general use was dropped, except to commemorate special events such as coronation jubilees. The brass threepenny piece was introduced in 1937, and an additional shilling design in honour of the Scottish ancestry of Queen Elizabeth, now the Queen Mother. Queen Elizabeth II shillings also have English and Scottish reverse designs. Farthings ceased to be legal tender on 1 January 1961.

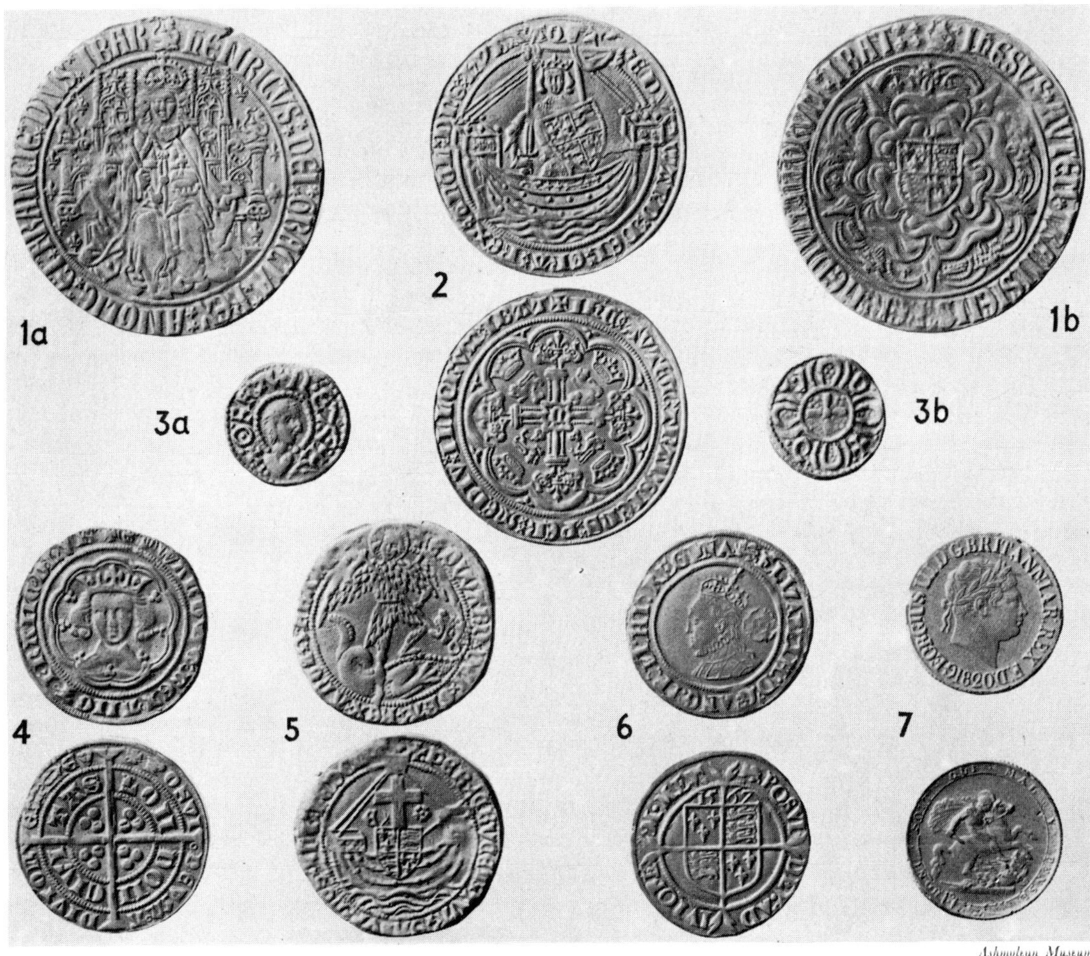

Ashmolean Museum

BRITISH COINS, HEADS AND TAILS

1. Henry VII gold sovereign. 2. Edward III gold noble. 3. Offa of Mercia silver penny. 4. Edward III silver groat. 5. Edward IV gold angel. 6. Elizabeth I silver sixpence. 7. George III gold sovereign

In 1966, the British Government adopted a decimal currency system, to be implemented by 1971. The pound remains the major currency unit, now divided into 100 new pennies, each worth 2.4 old ones. Five and ten new penny pieces, replacing the shillings and florin, were introduced in 1968. (The new coins are shown on page 266 of Vol. X.)

See also Currency; Money; Primitive Money; Coining.
See also Vol. IX: Coin Collection.

COKE, *see* Vol. VIII: Coke Oven; Fuels.

COLD STORAGE. The cooling of food and wine receptacles, particularly for long journeys, by snow, ice, or freezing mixtures has been known to man for thousands of years, but Refrigeration (q.v. Vol. VIII) by mechanical means was not invented until 1861. Many years passed before the mechanism was sufficiently reliable to be trusted. The first cargo of frozen meat came to Britain from South America in 1878, and in 1879 another frozen cargo was brought over from Australia. By the following year all steamship lines across the Atlantic were equipped with cold-storage plants, and now there is hardly a large ship on the world's deep-sea routes that is not so equipped.

Refrigeration, both afloat and ashore, has changed the trade in perishable food-stuffs. The development of refrigeration at sea has been accompanied by the erection of cold-storage

Warehouses (q.v.) at the docks and in large cities. Refrigeration has revolutionized the Meat Trade, Greengrocery, and the Egg and Grocery trades. It has greatly helped the Hotel and Catering industries (qq.v.). It has made it possible for all kinds of new services to be offered to people: for example, many department stores have large underground refrigerated chambers for the moth-proof storage of customers' furs.

The most important development in the preservation of food by freezing was the discovery of quick-freezing, which established itself commercially in the 1930's. Up to that time the preservation of food by freezing had been mainly limited to carcases of meat, such as New Zealand lamb and Argentine beef. Whole carcases of meat were slowly frozen, but the slowness of the process caused large ice crystals to form in the cells of the meat, which fractured the cell walls as the meat thawed, causing some of the juice contained in the meat to be lost and its general quality impaired. For this reason frozen imported meat was considered inferior to fresh meat.

The principle underlying quick-freezing is the rapid freezing of the product, particularly during the crucial moments when the water contained in the product forms ice crystals. The speed of the freezing encourages the formation of smaller ice crystals, which cause less damage to the product's cellular structure.

The mechanical application of the principle of quick freezing is generally achieved by one of three main methods. The first is plate freezing, the placing of the product between two hollow plates through which gas is pumped at a very low temperature; the two plates exert a pressure and extract the heat from the product. The second method is by blast freezing in which the product is placed on a tray, to a shallow depth, and draughts of cold air (at about minus 40° F.) circulate around the tray. The third method is to move the product over a bed of jets of refrigerated air; here the product enters through one end of a conveyor system consisting of obliquely-angled jets of air.

The first method named is particularly suitable for fairly bulky products such as whole fish, while the latter two methods are most suitable for granular products such as peas, sliced green beans, and chip potatoes. Frozen food is stored in bulk in large containers weighing as much as a ton or more, at a temperature of 0° F. for most fruits and vegetables, and at minus 20° F. for fish. After each product's harvesting season, the bulk packs are repacked in small packages, suitable for domestic use.

The frozen food is then transported from the quick-freezing factory to the retailer's refrigerated cabinet in an insulated refrigerated container, carried by road or rail. This container is in effect a cold store on wheels; its contents are kept frozen either by inbuilt refrigeration machinery, or by the use of dry ice (solid carbon dioxide), or liquid nitrogen.

Today all kinds of fruits, vegetables, fish, meat, poultry, and prepared dishes are quick-frozen, sold, and consumed in Britain. A very much wider range of foods is now available to the whole population than there ever was before the introduction of the quick-freezing process; the increasing number of deep freezers in shops and homes has encouraged this trend.

See also Vol. IV: Ship.
See also Vol. XI: Refrigerator.

COMBINES. Competition in industry or commerce may sometimes develop into 'cut-throat' competition. This means that the various firms engaged may repeatedly cut their prices lower and lower, in order to increase their individual sales and make more Profits (q.v.). A healthy amount of normal competition keeps a business on the alert; but cut-throat competition may upset a long-term plan, and even cause such disturbance that in the end a whole industry becomes inefficient or unprofitable.

To avoid this all the firms in an industry may decide to act in combination instead of individually. When they do this they are said to form a 'combine'. There are many ways of doing this. One method is to form a trade association, which maintains an office and a small staff out of subscriptions by individual firms belonging to it, and from time to time sends out instructions concerning the minimum prices at which their goods may be sold, maximum discounts allowed to customers, conditions of delivery, and so on.

A form of combine which interferes much more with individual freedom of action is that known as a 'cartel'. This word is of German origin, and the idea is German. The cartel is a more highly developed type of association which 'fixes' prices—keeps them up artificially. The firms belonging to it are given instructions, not only in regard to selling-prices, but also as to what they manufacture, and where they sell.

The most fully developed type of combine is the 'trust'. This is an amalgamation of several smaller subsidiary companies into one master company, sometimes called the 'holding company'. This company either takes over all the share CAPITAL of the subsidiary LIMITED COMPANIES, or else it acquires enough SHARES (qq.v.) which carry powers to vote at meetings to enable it to control their policy. Sometimes the management of affairs is entrusted to the holding company's own board of directors; but sometimes the smaller companies are allowed to carry on their own management without more interference from the holding company than would be expected in a cartel.

See also MONOPOLY.

COMMERCE. The finance of production and the movement and marketing of goods are the concern of commerce. The normal function of commerce is to help industry with the supply of capital and credit and to arrange the shifting of both raw materials and goods in process of manufacture from stage to stage until the completed goods are in the hands of the consumer.

Most writers consider that commerce includes finance; but some separate the two, saying that commerce is concerned with the movement of goods, and finance with providing the money necessary for such movement. On the whole commerce is concerned with movement: the movement of products from the mines and fields, from one country to another, from one merchant or manufacturer to another, and from stage to stage until the completed goods are finally in the hands of the consumer. But each movement requires money. Primary producers have to be paid; shipping and other transport services have to be paid for; goods have to be stored and warehoused—very often they have to be stocked for long periods, until the industries using them are ready to take them. A large amount of money is also necessary to finance the business of distributing the completed goods from factory to wholesale house, from wholesale house to shop, and from the shopkeeper to the consumer. So it is really much simpler to consider commerce as including finance.

Commercial activities might therefore be summarized as follows: the organization of MONEY and BANKING, and of CREDIT for short and long periods; TRANSPORT in all its forms; WHOLESALING, WAREHOUSES, and distribution by RETAIL TRADING; the provision of CAPITAL by investors and its collection by finance and ISSUING HOUSES; the organization of STOCK EXCHANGES (qq.v.), through which capital in commercial and industrial enterprises may change hands; the organization of the various produce and commodity markets where goods are bought and sold; and finally, the organization of ADVERTISING AND PUBLICITY (q.v.), and all the methods that exist to tell the consumer what there is for him to buy and where he can buy it.

Even this is not quite a complete list of all the specialized branches of the commercial world, and the student of commerce is always coming up against something new. There are company lawyers and chartered secretaries, skilled in company law and procedure; accountants and auditors; all kinds of agents and brokers; and specialists in more limited subjects, such as average adjusters in marine insurance, assessors in fire and accident insurance, chartered agents for PATENTS (q.v.) and inquiry agents. These branches exist because it pays other members of the commercial world to employ them for their own particular jobs.

See also TRADE, HISTORY OF.

COMMERCIAL TRAVELLERS, *see* REPRESENTATIVES.

COMMISSION. This is the usual form in which AGENTS and BROKERS (qq.v.) are paid by the firms and individuals who employ them to buy and sell goods on their behalf. It consists of a percentage on the value of goods sold or bought.

Usually commission on sales is quite easily arranged. Obviously the selling merchant wishes to obtain the highest possible price, and, if he pays his agent or broker a straight percentage on that price, the total commission will rise as the selling-price of the article rises, and both parties will be satisfied. It is not quite so easy to fix commission arrangements for brokers and agents who act as buyers. In some trades the buying services are paid for by a straightforward percentage commission; but it may sometimes be necessary for the firms employing the agents or brokers to arrange a sliding scale commission, which will go up as the price at which goods are bought goes down.

Commission, in addition to being paid to agents and brokers, is often paid to sales assistants, and to travelling REPRESENTATIVES (q.v.). Formerly many such people were paid almost entirely by commission; but nowadays the tendency is to pay more in the form of fixed salary and less in commission.

COMMODITY MARKETS, *see* MARKETS.

COMPANIES. These are associations of many people, formed to carry on business with a CAPITAL (q.v.) subscribed by all of them. The old word for 'capital' in English was 'stock', and the money put up by those subscribing the capital of a company was called the 'joint stock'; from this came the name 'joint-stock company', although nowadays this name is only used in Great Britain for LIMITED COMPANIES (q.v.).

Companies existed in ancient Rome; but we know little about how they were formed, or how they were controlled by the State. Our first definite knowledge dates from the late 14th century, when large companies began to be formed to take part in INTERNATIONAL TRADE (q.v.), and later in the exploration and development of foreign lands. In those days the State kept a firm control over business of all kinds, and companies could only be formed if their members obtained a charter from the king or ruling prince, laying down strict regulations as to what they could and could not do. Hence such companies were called 'CHARTERED' COMPANIES (q.v.). The first of these chartered companies in Great Britain was the Company of MERCHANT ADVENTURERS. Others were formed later, among them being the EAST INDIA COM-

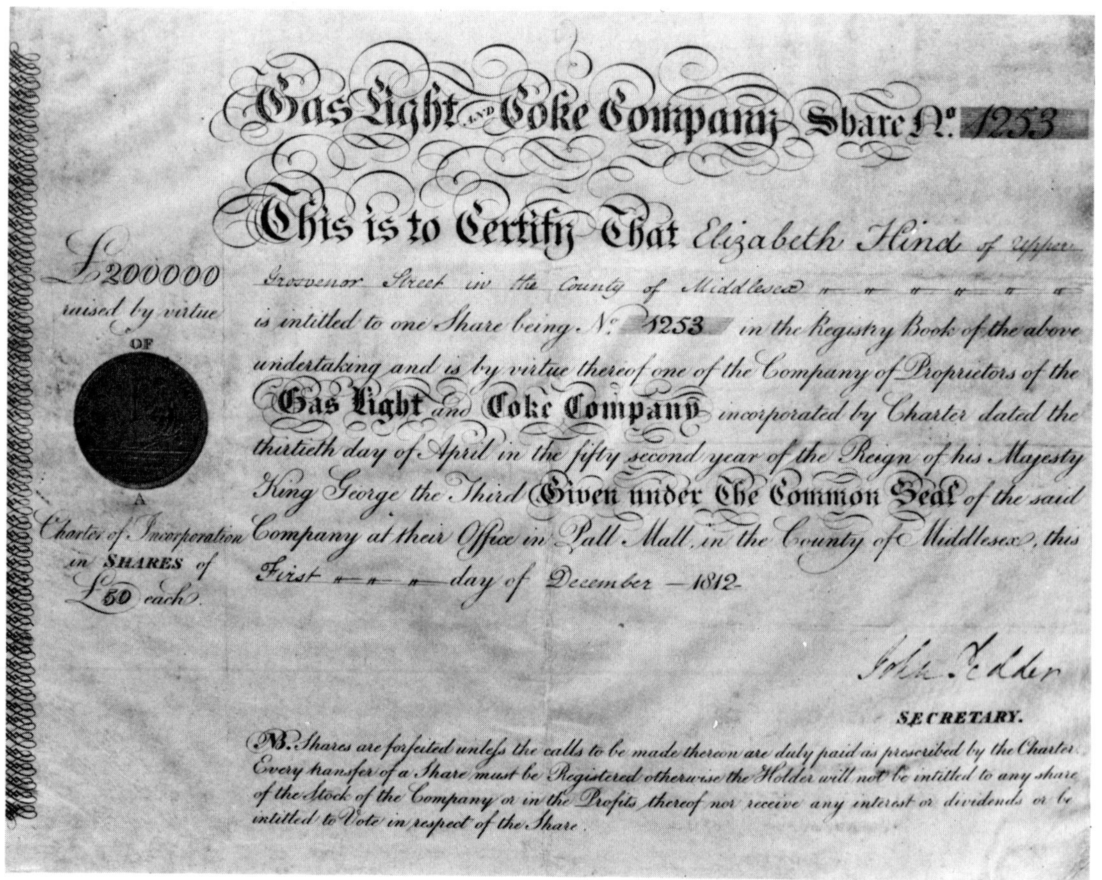

Gas Light and Coke Company Share No. 1253

£200000 raised by virtue of A Charter of Incorporation in SHARES of £50 each.

This is to Certify That Elizabeth Hind of Upper Grosvenor Street in the County of Middlesex is intitled to one Share being No. 1253 in the Registry Book of the above undertaking and is by virtue thereof one of the Company of Proprietors of the Gas Light and Coke Company incorporated by Charter dated the thirtieth day of April in the fifty second year of the Reign of his Majesty King George the Third Given under The Common Seal of the said Company at their Office in Pall Mall, in the County of Middlesex, this First day of December — 1812.

SECRETARY.

N.B. Shares are forfeited unless the calls to be made thereon are duly paid as prescribed by the Charter. Every transfer of a Share must be Registered otherwise the Holder will not be intitled to any share of the Stock of the Company or in the Profits thereof nor receive any interest or dividends or be intitled to Vote in respect of the Share.

ONE OF THE FIRST SHARE CERTIFICATES OF THE GAS LIGHT AND COKE COMPANY, ISSUED IN 1812

The company was incorporated by charter

PANY, and the HUDSON'S BAY COMPANY (qq.v.).

When the English Revolution of 1688 gave Parliament more control over financial and commercial matters than it had possessed in the days of kings ruling by 'divine right', companies were usually formed (or 'incorporated') by Act of Parliament. The first important company to be formed in this way was the BANK OF ENGLAND (q.v.) in 1694. This way of forming companies still exists today, although it is only used when the proposed companies seek special privileges for themselves which Parliament must carefully consider beforehand. The majority of modern companies are formed in the much simpler way described in the article on Limited Companies.

See also PUBLIC UTILITY COMPANIES; STOCKS AND SHARES.

Co-operative Union

THE ORIGINAL STORE OF THE ROCHDALE PIONEERS OPENED IN 1844 IN TOAD LANE, ROCHDALE

CONCRETE, *see* CEMENT; *see also* Vol. VIII: CONCRETE CONSTRUCTION.

CONDENSED MILK, *see* DAIRY INDUSTRY.

CONFECTIONERY, *see* SUGAR CONFECTIONERY; BAKING INDUSTRY, Section 3.

CONSUMER, *see* PROTECTION OF CONSUMER.

CO-OPERATIVE SOCIETIES. 1. The Co-operative movement began in the first half of the 19th century. In Britain the INDUSTRIAL REVOLUTION (q.v.) had by then enormously affected the lives and conditions of the ordinary working people. The old DOMESTIC SYSTEM (q.v.), by which goods were manufactured by the workers in their own homes, had almost been replaced by the factory system. Profits were rising and the workers felt that wages were not rising correspondingly, and that their interests were being neglected. In such conditions reformers such as Robert OWEN (q.v. Vol. V) felt that the best course for the workers would be to produce and distribute goods for themselves, and among themselves. If this was to be done, the necessary money would have to be put up by the working classes themselves. It was suggested that the CAPITAL (q.v.) for manufacturing enterprises should be subscribed by those who were going to work in them, and that the capital for marketing and retailing the goods made should come from the consumers who would buy them. The movement therefore aimed at encouraging 'producers' societies', which would provide goods and services, and 'consumers' societies', which would look after their distribution.

2. PRODUCERS' SOCIETIES. These were not at first very successful, and have never applied to more than a tiny sector of industry; by 1967 their number had been reduced to thirty-two, and their sales were declining. Because most industry requires expensive equipment, there are only a very few trades in which the wage-earners can command sufficient capital to set themselves up in co-operative production. Producers' co-operation was, however, extremely successful in agriculture, where such heavy capital expenditure was not necessary—particularly in Denmark and north-west Germany (*see* CO-OPERATION IN FARMING, Vol. VI). It was also successful in industry in Russia before the Revolution, when the stage of using a great deal of machinery had not been reached. The Russian *artel*, or co-operative producers' society, is still a feature of modern Russia.

3. CONSUMERS' SOCIETIES. These have been

very successful, and compete strongly with privately owned firms. The first retail shop on the modern model was opened in 1844 in Toad Lane, Rochdale, by a body of weavers called the Rochdale Pioneers. The method of finance they adopted has lasted to the present day. It had the advantage that, as business developed and increased, the amount of capital available for development and expansion increased also. To form a consumers' society, a sufficient number of persons were asked to promise support, and were then asked to take SHARES in it (q.v.). The minimum holding was generally only £1, and an absolute maximum of £200 was fixed by law in 1878, to prevent wealthy people from obtaining control. Owing to changes in the value of money, the maximum is now £1,000. Shares could be paid for by small regular instalments, or out of the dividend or rebate on purchases. General policy was in the hands of a committee elected by the members; but day-to-day work was carried on by managers and staff, appointed on the same conditions as in private firms. The trading policy was to sell goods at about the prices charged by private firms, and then, at the end of the trading year, to calculate what profits had been earned. These, after enough had been kept back for reserves and expansion, were shared out among all the members. This share-out was not in proportion to the number of shares held, as it is in an ordinary LIMITED COMPANY (q.v.), but in proportion to the amount of money spent on his purchases during the year by each member of the Society. This rebate, or dividend, on goods bought is generally called the 'divy'. Many co-operative societies now give dividend stamps to all who buy from them, whether members or not, rather than any other form of dividend. As many multiple firms give trading stamps with purchases, the difference between private and co-operative trading is decreasing.

The consumers' co-operative movement met with great opposition from ordinary private firms, and after a very promising start it seemed in danger of declining and even dying out. The great difficulty was the buying of wholesale supplies in markets controlled by merchants hostile to the movement. For this reason the Co-operative Wholesale Society was formed in 1862. Its object was to buy goods in large quantitites for the local retail societies to sell, and also to buy raw materials overseas and distribute them to the retail societies. The C.W.S., as the English Wholesale Society is called, was successful from the very start, and a Scottish Society was founded a few years later. The capital of the wholesale societies is provided by the retail societies, who receive the same kind of dividend on their purchases as their own customers receive from them. The wholesale societies do not set out to make profits, but to balance incomings and outgoings and to leave a small surplus for reserves and emergencies. They now have a vast business, and to finance all their operations, there is also a C.W.S. Bank.

Recently the range of products sold by the retail societies, and bought or produced by the wholesale societies, has widened. Beginning originally as grocery stores, some of the shops of the big retail societies are now more like DEPARTMENT STORES (q.v.), handling men's and women's clothing, furniture, household hardware and ironmongery, china and glass, boots and shoes, cigarettes and tobacco, and practically all the lines catered for by an ordinary department store owned by a private firm. The self-service system is becoming increasingly used (*see* SELF-SERVICE STORES). Recently, however, the co-operative societies' share in retail trade has begun to decline, while that of their rivals, the multiple stores, has been increasing. The quality of management has been criticized, and many small societies have been taken over by larger ones with the aim of improving it.

The movement has always paid considerable attention to education and political activities.

See also CO-PARTNERSHIP.

COOPERING, *see* CASK-MAKING.

CO-PARTNERSHIP. This means sharing the ownership, and to some extent the management, of industry between owners or shareholders, on the one hand, and workers on the other. The idea behind co-partnership is that it is likely to increase the loyalty of workers to their firm and to increase efficiency by removing to some degree the causes of industrial discontent. Many so-called partnership schemes have been launched at different times, but most of them have been closer to profit-sharing than to true co-partnership, and profit-sharing does not differ essentially from the system of paying bonuses in addition to WAGES (q.v.).

Like many other aspects of the workers'

movement, co-partnership was first preached as a useful industrial doctrine just before the middle of the 19th century. Among its early advocates were the economist, John Stuart MILL, and the philosopher Herbert SPENCER (qq.v. Vol. V). Co-operation (*see* CO-OPERATIVE SOCIETIES) was a parallel movement, and came to the fore at the same time. Robert OWEN (q.v. Vol. V) was prominent in all the movements for the betterment of workers' conditions; he was a pioneer of co-operation, and was also an enthusiast for co-partnership. He is reported to have told a business acquaintance, who was rather uncertain about adopting such a scheme, that it was well worth paying one's workers £5,000 a year to prevent them from wasting £10,000. It was a long time, however, before the idea took practical shape. The first important move towards its adoption in Britain was made in London in 1889, when the South Metropolitan Gas Company instituted a profit-sharing system. This was at first merely a system of bonuses in addition to wages; but in 1894 it was converted into co-partnership by arranging that workers' shares of PROFIT (q.v.) should be invested in the company's capital, and that worker-shareholders should have the right of nominating directors to the board. Other gas companies followed suit, and in 1908 the largest gas concern in the country, the Gas Light and Coke Company of Beckton, London, adopted the scheme. Several industrial firms in the Midlands and the North did the same, and one of the most successful schemes was that adopted by a great Yorkshire wool firm at Batley in the 1890's.

True co-partnership really means giving workers a stake in the business; for this they do not, like shareholders, pay any money, although any money profits later distributed to workers may be invested in the firm's SHARES (q.v.). Many schemes, by which workers may subscribe on preferential terms for shares in the companies they serve, are co-partnership schemes to a limited extent only. This last is the only form in which the co-partnership movement has made any headway in the U.S.A. A big American soap firm launched such a scheme in 1912. To be eligible for membership of it, an employee had to own capital stock in the company to the amount of a year's wage or salary. The company were prepared to advance, at an interest rate of 3% per annum, 97½% of the money required for such purchases, so that employees had to put up an actual cash deposit of only 2½%. This scheme included a provision by which worker-investors were guaranteed against loss through any fall on the STOCK EXCHANGE (q.v.) in the market-price of the stock they had bought. Some large British companies have recently started schemes of this kind, creating additional workers' shares which can be subscribed for at their original or nominal value. As the shares of such companies are usually quoted on the STOCK EXCHANGES (q.v.) at many times their original value, such schemes endow workers, free of charge, with some of the wealth they have themselves helped to create.

An important Bill was introduced in the French Parliament in 1913, but failed to pass. If it had, a nation-wide scheme of co-partnership might have prevented much of the labour trouble that developed in France later on. The Bill proposed that every commercial and industrial company should be compelled to endow its workers with one-fifth of its total share capital, on which they would receive the same rate of dividend as other shareholders and also exercise the same voting rights for the appointment of directors (*see* BUSINESS ORGANIZATION). A rather similar idea formed part of the election programme of the British Liberal Party in February 1950. A scheme rather on the French model was adopted in 1929 in the large London store now known as the John Lewis Partnership, when a director, Mr. John Spedan Lewis, handed over a large portion of his own shareholding to a trust for the benefit of the employees of the firm. Similar schemes have recently been adopted by two large British industrial firms.

COPPER-MINING. Copper was probably the first metal used by man. When copper combines with tin in an ALLOY (q.v. Vol. VIII) it forms bronze, and during the Bronze Age about 4,000 years ago (*see* PREHISTORIC MAN, Section 5, Vol. I) the countries that possessed copper were the leading communities. Copper is principally found in the form of ores or compounds of the metal, although there are in the world considerable deposits of more or less pure metallic copper. Sometimes more valuable metals, such as silver, are found with the copper, and their presence makes low-yielding copper ores profitable to mine. The bulk of the world's production comes from the ores called malachite and copper pyrites. The principal modern producing countries are the U.S.A., Chile, and the Katanga province of the Congo together with the adjacent territory of Zambia (*see* colour plate, facing p. 128). The two large financial groups responsible for most of Zambia's copper production, whose output in 1967 was 645,000 long tons, were nationalized in 1969.

Copper's chief industrial use is in the electrical trades, owing to its high electrical conductivity (*see* METALS, Section 8, Vol. VIII). Nearly half the world output is absorbed in electrical generators, motors, switchboards, transmission lines, telephones, radio and television sets, and electronic instruments. Copper may be used alone or alloyed with tin or zinc to form bronze or brass, or with other metals. It resists rust and corrosion extremely well, and is much used for the vessels and plant of the BEER BREWING and CHEMICAL INDUSTRIES (qq.v.). It is used in the building industry for hot-water boilers, water piping, and sometimes as a roofing material. A recent use of copper in the building industry is for damp-courses, to prevent damp travelling upwards through walls. In modern industry the most important chemical compound of copper is the sulphate. This has a wide range of uses: dyeing, textile printing, and electroplating are some of them. It is very effective as an antiseptic, both for human beings and for animals; and it is used as an INSECTICIDE and FUNGICIDE in gardening (q.v. Vol. VI). It is also considerably used for the prevention of rot and decay in timber.

See also MINING.

U.S. Information Service

COPPER ORE AWAITING FINAL GRINDING IN BALL MILLS WHERE IT IS GROUND TO THE CONSISTENCY OF FLOUR

COPRA. This is the dried kernel or 'meat' of the COCONUT (q.v. Vol. VI), yielding a valuable edible oil. The principal producing countries are Indonesia, the Philippine Islands, Malaysia, and Ceylon. As the coconut shells have no commercial value, it is more economical to ship the dried kernels only. The fibre covering of the shell, which is called 'coir' (*see* BRUSHES), is removed and the nuts are split open for drying, which is necessary to prevent the nuts from decaying. There are several methods of drying, and a simple and primitive method, which has been used since the trade began, is to expose the split kernels to sun and air, after which the 'meat' comes easily away from the shell. This method is still used in many of the coconut-growing districts of the world, and a white copra of quite good quality is produced which goes by the name of 'sun-dried' in the trade. A copra of better quality fetching a higher price is produced by drying the split shells artificially in 'kilns', or in long tunnels through which hot air is passed. The tunnel system is operated in Samoa, and the West Indies make much use of mechanical rotary driers. In all the artificial drying processes the shells provide a cheap and convenient fuel for the furnaces.

Well-dried copra contains about 60% of coconut oil. In some of the producing countries the oil is extracted locally, and coconut oil then becomes the commodity of export. But copra itself is still exported in considerable quantities, the oil being then extracted abroad. The extraction is carried out either by mechanical pressure, or by the use of petroleum solvents (*see* OILS, VEGETABLE).

Coconut oil has many uses in modern industry. It is an important ingredient in one of the main processes of SOAP manufacture (q.v.), especially of 'marine' soap, which lathers fairly well in sea-water. The unrefined oil has a characteristic smell and taste but both of these can be eradicated by refining. The refined oil is used for making MARGARINE, vegetable fats, shortenings for use in the BAKING INDUSTRY (qq.v.), salad oil, and cooking oils. In the making of

Lever Bros.

COPRA, THE DRIED FLESH OF THE COCONUT

cheap chocolate, coconut oil is often used as a substitute for cocoa butter.

CORK is the bark of two species of evergreen oak which grow principally around the shores of the western Mediterranean. The chief sources of modern cork are Spain and Portugal, which at some periods have produced together nearly four-fifths of the total world output. Small quantities also come from southern France and North Africa, as well as from Italy and Sardinia.

The first stripping of bark, the 'virgin cork', is cut when the trees are 15 to 20 years old. It is of poor quality and cannot be used for bottle corks, and until fairly recently was looked upon as practically useless. The second cut, made after about another 10 years, is also of poor quality, but the third and later strippings produce good cork fit for use as bottle corks. The bark is cut from the trees in strips, which are flattened under weights and soaked for a few minutes in boiling water. They are then compressed in a hydraulic press (*see* HYDRAULIC POWER TRANSMISSION, Vol. VIII), baled, and sent down to the coast for export.

Cork was well known to the ancient Romans. They used it for the soles of shoes, and to support people and fishing-nets in water. There is no record of its use for bottles until the 15th century. It is now used for mats, hat-linings, and in the making of artificial limbs. Before the First World War a firm in the City of London made men's top-hats and bowler-hats out of cork, and it was widely used for making tropical helmets. Ground into fine dust and mixed with linseed oil, cork has been used for many years in the making of LINOLEUM (q.v.). A use has now been found for 'virgin cork'. It is ground and used for second quality linoleum and also for the manufacture of corkboard for insulating purposes, particularly in refrigerating machinery.

See also Vol. II: STEMS, Section 1 (*d*).

CORNISH MINING. There are many references in Greek and Roman classical literature to the Cassiterides or Tin Islands, but there is no proof that these were the Isles of Scilly or even the mainland of Cornwall. Traces of old smelting-pits, whose date can be fixed between 300 and 200 B.C., have been found during excavations on the Cornish moors, and many ancient writers mention a trade in tin as having taken place between south-west Britain and the Mediterranean about the beginning of the Christian era. All this, however, is vague, and our earliest piece of written evidence regarding Cornish tin-mining is the Tinners' Charter of 1201. There were then four Stannaries, or mining districts, Launceston, Lostwithiel, Truro, and Helston, and each was administered by a warden. 'Stannary' comes from the Latin for tin, *stannum*. Under the Charter, the 'tinner' was granted many privileges, the greatest being that of 'bounding': that is, entering and enclosing any land to search and dig for tin; for this he had to pay the lord of the manor a toll, usually about a fifteenth part, called the 'lord's dish'. The tinner's work was regarded as of national importance; he was free of taxes and TITHES (q.v. Vol. VI) and, unless summoned by his warden, he was exempt from military service. He also had the right to divert and use any stream to help his work. He was subject to no court of law but the Stannaries Court, and this privilege freed him from serfdom to the lord of the manor and gave him the sturdy independence of character which is the heritage of the Cornish miner.

In return for these freedoms the tinner had to obey 'coinage' laws. He had to carry his smelted metal by packhorse or mule—their tracks can still be seen across the lonely Cornish moors—to one of the coinage towns: Liskeard, Lostwithiel, Truro, Helston, and Penzance. In the Coinage Hall the tin was assayed and weighed, and stamped or 'coined' with the arms of the Duchy of Cornwall (*see* ASSAYING). Before the tin could be sold, the tinner had to pay a toll of

W. J. Bennetts and Sons

A 'GUNNIES' OR WORKED-OUT PORTION OF THE LODE (VEIN) 2,160 feet from the SURFACE AT THE DOLCOATH TIN MINE, CORNWALL

about 4*s.* a hundredweight. As coinage took place only four times a year, the tinner was often in great straits for money, and frequently fell into the hands of moneylenders. The Cornish men in those days were regular SMUGGLERS (q.v. Vol. X), with a boat in every creek, and some of the tin neither saw the Coinage Hall nor paid a toll. What passed the coinage in the usual way was shipped to London. The London pewterers, whose skill was world-famous, used much of it for pewter ware for rich men's tables, but a great part found its way to the Continent and the Far East. Among other uses, it was mixed with the metal from which cannon and church bells were made, and it was used for plating or lining copper pots. Coinage was not abolished until 1838. The Stannaries, of which Sir Walter Raleigh was at one time Lord Warden, lasted until the end of the 19th century.

Before the 17th century tin was mainly 'streamed' in rivers and on the moors, and the tinner lived a solitary, outdoor, independent life, often far from villages. When the rich deposits of rock, long ago washed down by rivers, were worked out, a search began for underground veins or 'lodes', which, according to some old miners, could be located by the flickering of marsh gas, called 'Jack o' Lantern'. Underground mining involved the joint production of tin and copper, as the tin lay beneath the copper. The great problem of underground mining was drainage. Waterwheels, worked by men or horses, were replaced in the early 18th century by steam pumps, such as those invented by Newcomen and Watt, and later by Oliver Evans and Trevithick. The introduction of gunpowder for blasting increased the output, but added to the many dangers of the miner's life, which was much less healthy than that of the tinner or streamer. Cornish mines became very prosperous in the 19th century, after the highly efficient Cornish beam pumping-engine had been invented by Richard Trevithick. This was the great copper period, when mines such as Dolcoath—between Camborne and Redruth—employed 1,600 men, women, and children, and Cornwall produced three-quarters of the world's annual output.

In earlier days the mines were worked under a rather curious system. The initial cost of installing machinery was borne by shareholders called 'adventurers'. The miners, called 'tributers', worked independently in parties, consisting usually of two men with one or two boys. Instead of a settled wage, the miners received a 'tribute' or percentage of the total ore they brought to the surface. They provided their own tools, candles, ventilation, and transport, and as their livelihood depended on their skill and judgement, they became good working geologists rather than mere labourers. General underground management was in the hands of a bal-captain ('bal' is the Cornish word for mine).

Tin-dressing was done on the surface, or 'grass' as it was called. This was a trade in itself, needing much skill and experience, and was carried out on contract. The tin ore was first broken down with hammers and then washed in flowing water in a sloping, square stone trough called a 'buddle'. 'Buddling' was usually done by women or girls called 'balmaidens'. When the fine, black tin sand came out, it was made into piles, assayed, and divided into three shares: for the 'lord's dish'—landowner's ROYALTIES (q.v.)—the 'adventurers', and the 'tributers'. It was then smelted down

F. E. Gibson

ST. JUST UNITED TIN MINE WHICH WAS WORKED FOR SOME DISTANCE UNDER THE SEA IN THE 19TH CENTURY

into pure tin. Much of the desolate countryside of North Cornwall is the result of the poisonous fumes of arsenic and sulphur which killed all the plant life in the neighbourhood. Now, the arsenic and sulphur are conserved as BY-PRODUCTS (q.v.).

Conditions in the mines, though very bad by modern standards, were much better than in the Midland collieries, with their abuse of child labour (*see* COAL MINING, HISTORY OF, Section 2). In Cornish mines children were kindly treated, did light jobs only, often made their own contracts, and in the early 19th century were not employed under 10 or 12 years old. Even the depression of the 1840's, the 'hungry forties', as they were called, led to no riots in Cornwall like those in the north, although the starving miners protested very forcibly about the export of Cornish wheat. The relationship of lord, adventurer, and tributer was usually friendly, although London adventurers were not popular. But as mines grew deeper, the health of the miner was impaired by the heat and dust, and many fell victims to tuberculosis.

In the early 20th century the introduction of electric power and pneumatic drills brought a renewal of prosperity, and the First World War called forth all Cornwall's resources in tin, tungsten, and arsenic for industry. The history of Cornish mining, with its great hazards, has always been one of alternating periods of prosperity and depression. The depressions were due either to outside events, such as the replacement of pewter by earthenware, the discovery of copper on the shores of Lake Superior, and tin in Malaya, or to the shortsightedness of the 'adventurers', who abandoned mines when copper gave out because they did not see that tin lay beneath. The depression of 1894–8 drained Cornwall of its mining population. A great exodus began to the gold mines of South Africa, California, and Australia (*see* GOLD-MINING), and to the silver mines of Mexico and South America. Many Cornish mines became derelict at this time, but a considerable number survived until the great slump in 1921. Mines from the Arctic Circle to the Equator reaped the benefit of the age-old skill of the 'Cousin Jacks'—as the Cornish miners were called—and people who had hardly heard of Cornwall came to use Cornish mining terms.

There was another brief period of activity in the Second World War, when tin could not be obtained from Malaya. Today, a considerable amount of prospecting is being carried out, and three new mines are projected. The Camborne School of Metaliferous Mining still trains mining engineers in the old tradition; and both at Camborne and at Redruth Cornishmen manufacture mining tools and equipment that are exported all over the world.

See also MINING; TIN.

COSMETIC INDUSTRY. Although cosmetics (from the Greek word meaning 'to adorn') have been used from earliest times, they were, until recently, not made by specialists but as part of the occupation of the pharmacist. It was only in the latter half of the 19th century that the manufacture of proprietary brands of face powder, foundation creams, brilliantine, shampoos, and perfume grew to the stature of a separate industry, and it was not until after the First World War that the industry began to expand very greatly. In 1914 Americans spent about 40 million dollars on the purchase of cosmetics; in 1954 they spent 1,150 million dollars. In 1957 it was estimated that three out of every four women in Britain used face powders, foundation creams, and lipsticks. In 1968 cosmetic sales amounted to £110 million in Britain alone. The greater part of this huge turnover is controlled by a relatively small number of large firms; many are American, with production units here.

Goya Ltd.

THE BASE FOR LIPSTICK BEING GROUND IN A MILL

A wide variety of ingredients is used in the making of cosmetics. Emulsions of oils or fatty materials, for example, lanoline and its derivatives, are used in the manufacture of cleansing, foundation, and nourishing face creams. Older emulsifiers have now been largely superseded by complex organic chemicals which give different types of texture and appearance, and have various effects upon the skin. Toothpastes contain the following ingredients: chalk or calcium phosphate (or both) to polish the teeth; detergents to clean them; glycerine to keep the paste moist; a gum, such as tragacanth dissolved in water, to give it a smooth texture; and flavouring, such as the essential oils of peppermint, clove, eucalyptus, or wintergreen. Nail varnish is made by dissolving low-viscosity nitrocellulose in a mixture of solvents, and adding a plasticiser to make the film flexible; it is coloured by dyes and finely-ground pigment. Face powders are made from a well-blended mixture of such substances as kaolin, chalk, magnesium carbonate, magnesium stearate, zinc oxide, zinc stearate, and talc, which is then tinted with pigments and perfumed. Brilliantines used to be made from vegetable oils such as olive, arachis, and almond; but today they are all made from highly refined mineral oils, such as liquid paraffin. Deodorants all contain some kind of antiseptic, for example, hexachlorophene, and many contain an astringent aluminium salt to reduce perspiration.

Great attention to hygiene is paid in factories, and advances in the bacteriological field have made today's cosmetics much purer and safer than they ever were in the past.

There is an International Federation of Cosmetic Chemists. The Society of Cosmetic Chemists of Great Britain is its representative here.

See also Vol. XI: COSMETICS, HISTORY OF.

COSTING. 1. This is the art of finding out how much it really costs to produce certain goods or services. Cost accountants are not just ordinary accountants, but belong to a special professional body of their own, the Institute of Cost and Works Accountants. The difficulty of working out the cost of production of any goods or services arises mainly because costs of production consist of two parts: 'prime cost' and 'overhead charges'. The first are fairly easy to ascertain; the second are easy enough to ascertain as a total, but difficult to distribute accurately among the various lines of production carried on.

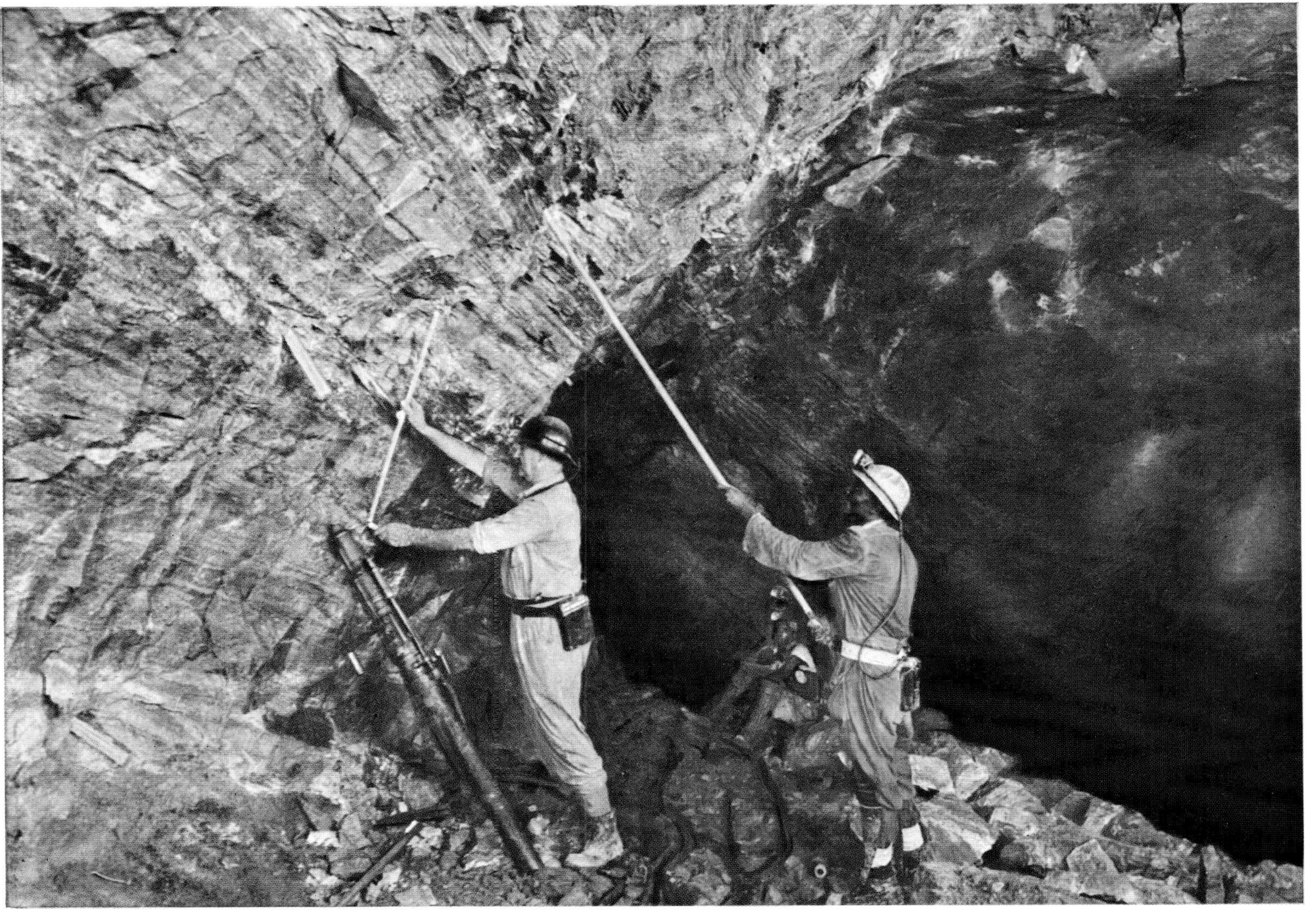

THE ROCK FACE IN A COPPER MINE 2,000 FEET BELOW GROUND

Miners are preparing holes for explosive charges

Thus, in firms making a standard article by mass production, costing is fairly simple; but in firms producing a variety of different articles it becomes much more complicated.

2. Prime Cost is the cost of the labour, the materials, and the expenses directly involved in the production of one particular article or service. To find out the labour charges for various jobs in a factory, forms called 'time sheets' are prepared for each separate job, or for each batch or 'run' of product made, and on these are filled in the hours worked by the various employees. Similar 'job' or 'batch sheets' are used for the raw materials or stores issued and used, and also for those expenses that are directly incurred on any particular job or batch. Machines called 'time-recorders', for noting the times at which workers begin and finish a particular job, are a great help in finding out exactly how much of the prime cost is taken up by labour charges.

3. Overhead Charges are all the indirect expenses of running a factory which cannot be directly related to any particular batch of goods turned out. Overhead charges can be sub-divided further into 'factory overhead' and 'general overhead'. Factory overhead includes such items as the rent, rates, taxes and insurance of the factory; motive power, fuel, lighting, and heating; wages of storekeepers, timekeepers, clerks, superintendents, and managers; freight and carriage on raw materials, and repairs, renewals, and Depreciation (q.v.) of plant and machinery (the lessening of value owing to age or wear and tear).

There are several ways in which factory overhead may be added on to prime cost in order to arrive at factory cost or production cost, and the method adopted must depend on the type of business. In small firms rule-of-thumb methods are used: the average weekly or monthly production is known, and the past year's total factory overhead can be divided by 52 or 12 and the necessary amount added on to prime cost. In larger firms more scientific methods are attempted; each separate item of factory overhead may be apportioned to prime cost in a different way. Thus any motive power expenses can be divided out between various machines according to how many hours each has run; other expenses may be split up according to the number of articles made, or according to their different values. Lighting and heating expenses can be divided up according to the sizes of the various 'shops' that are being lighted or heated, and so on.

General overhead is made up for the most part of the following items: rent and maintenance of the administrative offices; travellers' expenses and Commissions (q.v.); salaries of clerks, accountants, and managerial staff; expenses of delivering goods to customers; discounts; bad debts; and Interest on bank loans and Debentures (qq.v.). When the total has been found, the same problems of dividing it out arise as with factory overheads, and must be solved on the same lines.

When general overhead and factory overhead are added to prime cost, the result is 'total cost'. It is to this that the profit percentage or margin must be added in order that the selling price may be fixed.

See also Book-keeping; Business Organization; Factory Organization.

COST OF LIVING. This is the relationship between the money which people receive as Wages (q.v.), salaries, and other incomes, and the prices of the goods and services on which the money is spent. One might work out the cost of living at any particular date by selecting a representative family, who receive a certain income, and calculating the total cost of all the things on which they normally spend their money. But such a calculation would apply only to people in the same circumstances and with the same money income. To give a more general picture, what is usually done is to calculate the cost of living for a representative family at a chosen date, and then by a statistical device called an Index Number (*see* Statistics) to express subsequent changes as so much per cent. of the original calculation.

To do this, representative working-class families are interviewed, and a list is made of the things on which they normally spend money: different kinds of food, rail and road transport, clothing, fuel, rent, and so on. The answers given by the different families are then averaged. All the things they would normally buy are then priced on the date chosen as the standard or base for the index-number. A rough index-number could be then made by totalling up the prices of the different goods and services, but this would have the disadvantage that the price of a loaf of bread would be added, say, to the price of a hundredweight of coal, and more loaves than hundredweights of coal are usually bought by most people. So the various prices are therefore 'weighted', or multiplied by the number of times those particular things are bought in an average week or month. The money total thus arrived at is added up, and the total at the date taken as base called 100. If at the base date the goods priced cost £5, and at a later date the same bundle of things cost £6, and social habits had changed greatly since 1914. A new index was therefore constructed in July 1947, and on account of further changes in habits another was constructed in January 1956.

Some industries pay wages on a sliding scale, which moves upwards and downwards to correspond with movements of the cost of living index. TRADE UNIONS (q.v.) and other interested bodies watch the index very carefully, as the welfare of their worker members depends not so much

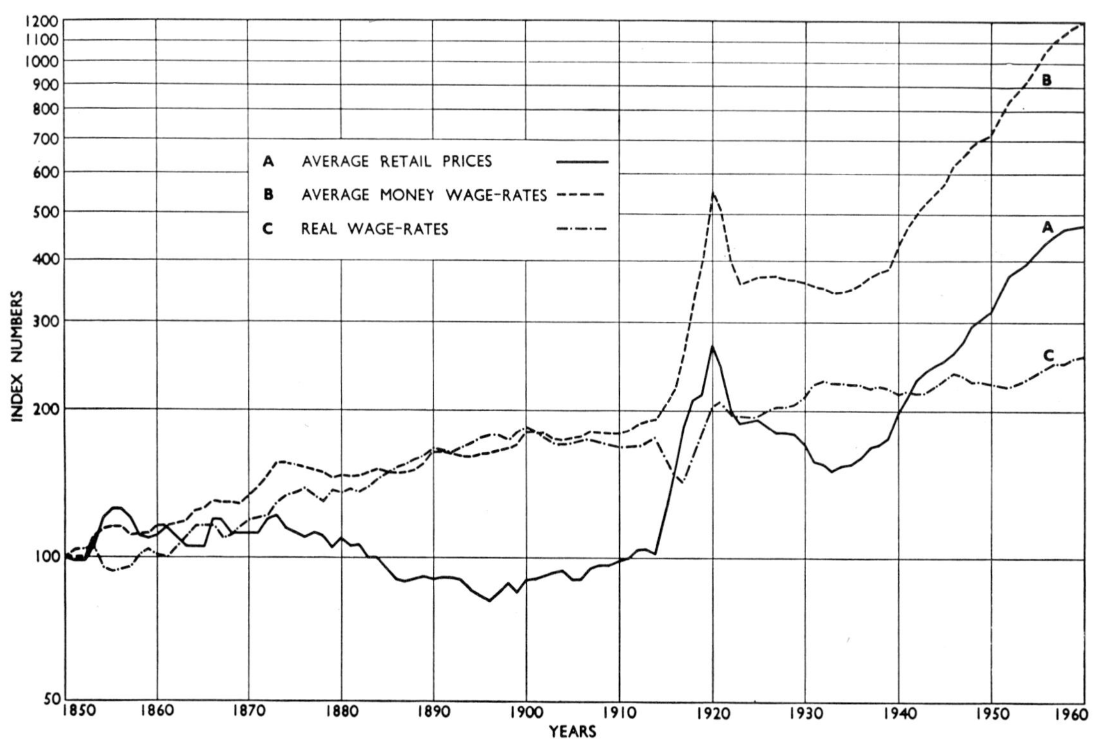

THE STANDARD OF LIVING IN BRITAIN FROM 1850 TO 1960

The curve A shows the average prices of goods, B the average money wages for each year, both starting in 1850, with the index number 100. A does not show money actually spent but the price at which goods could be bought. Money wages are not actual earnings, for these would be affected by overtime and unemployment. C shows the real value in goods of the money wage rate, allowing for the changes in money wages and in the prices of goods. It indicates, therefore, the standard of living. (Layton and Crowther, *An Introduction to the Study of Prices*, London and Cambridge Economic Service)

then the index number would be $100 \times \frac{6}{5}$ or 120. It is, of course, true that not all classes of the population spend their money in the same way, but this device provides a reasonably sound basis for measuring changes in the cost of living.

Before the First World War the base used was the average for the year 1900. Prices moved up considerably during the First World War, and, until July 1947, the average of July 1914 was used as the base. During the Second World War there was a further considerable rise in prices, upon their money wages as upon what economists call their 'real' wages, that is, the quantities of things that money wages can buy.

See also STATISTICS; STANDARD OF LIVING.

COTTAGE INDUSTRY, *see* DOMESTIC SYSTEM.

COTTON INDUSTRY, HISTORY. Cotton is a textile fibre of great antiquity, although it was not used in England for manufacturing purposes until the middle of the 17th century.

India used cotton long before it was mentioned in written records, and India was the first country to grow it on a large scale. Indeed, from about 1500 B.C. until the end of the 15th century A.D. she was the world's leading maker and exporter of cotton fabrics, and these were extremely fine and of very high quality. This was remarkable, as the cotton then grown in India was, as now, rather short in staple, that is, in the length of the fibres, and of comparatively poor quality. The fineness and quality of these fabrics owed more to painstaking craftsmanship than to the quality of the raw material, and the equipment used for their manufacture was extremely primitive.

The secrets of cotton manufacture were introduced into Europe by the Mohammedan invaders who swept westwards from the 7th century onwards. In the 14th century, when part of Spain was under Moorish rule, Granada and Barcelona were manufacturing centres.

Long before cotton manufacture started in Britain, Englishmen had known of Indian cotton goods, and had bought them from the Venetian galleys that visited the south coast every year (*see* SHIPPING). Continental Europeans, mainly Protestant refugees from Flanders, introduced the industry into England in the middle of the 17th century. East Anglia and south Lancashire, being already engaged in the wool textile industry, were the districts in which most of the refugees settled. Cloths made of cotton alone were not at first manufactured in Britain. Wool, which suited the climate of the country, was widely used for outer garments and coverings and for the undergarments of men and women, while women's dresses were chiefly made of linen or wool. There was no large overseas market for cotton goods, and until quite late in the 18th century the spinning machinery available could only spin cotton yarn strong enough to be used as weft in the weaving processes, because the warp strained the yarn more than the cotton could stand. Cotton was therefore used for weaving cloths of mixed yarns. Fustian, a mixture of cotton and linen, was one of the mixed fabrics made; and bombazine, a favourite material for the women's dresses of the 17th century, was a mixture of real silk and cotton.

There were great changes in the industry in the 18th century. This was a period of great colonial expansion, during which Britain gained political control of overseas settlements, mostly with a tropical or sub-tropical climate, where

The Textile Council

A HIGH-PRODUCTION CARDING MACHINE

The short fibres and dirt are removed, and the cotton fibres are drawn from the machine as a filmy web, which is passed through rollers to become 'sliver'

cotton goods could be sold in increasing quantities. Improvements in textile machinery made possible the spinning of stronger cotton yarns which would serve for use as warp. The southern states of America began to grow raw cotton on a big scale. Between 1780 and 1800, raw cotton imports from abroad increased ten times, and the southern states of America became Britain's greatest single supplier. By the end of the 18th century Lancashire had become the centre of the industry, with Liverpool as the port to which the raw material was brought, and Manchester as commercial and financial headquarters. The new cotton materials were cheaper than linen, and began to displace it. Districts such as Paisley and Glasgow, which had previously specialized in linen manufacture, changed to cotton spinning and weaving.

The industry made great progress during part of the 19th century, but there were occasional setbacks. During the American Civil War of 1861–5 the Union (northern) states had command of the seas, and successfully blockaded the ports of the Confederate (southern) States. And so Britain was unable to obtain imports of American cotton, and Lancashire was very hard hit for some years. There was a revival after the end of the war, but between 1873 and the end of the century there was a prolonged depression in industry, and the cotton industry was affected as much as any. There was a severe fall in the value of silver, which was then used as money by some of the countries of the East, notably India and China. The purchasing power of these countries dwindled, and they were no longer able to buy from Lancashire as many cheap cotton 'piece-goods' (cotton woven to standard length, for sale as a piece). Increased foreign competition in the cheaper varieties also hurt Lancashire, and bad trade and shortage of money on the continent of Europe led many European countries to expand their own cotton industries and to depend less on imports from Britain. Another difficulty was caused by the raising of the American TARIFF (q.v.), or customs duty, on yarns and fabrics from abroad. But by the beginning of the 20th century the British cotton industry had greatly revived; the East had once again become a fairly big buyer, and markets in the Dominions and Colonies were expanding. Foreign competition was mainly in the cheaper lines, and Lancashire began to turn out more of the finer yarns and fabrics.

This prosperity did not last, and the industry was advancing towards a crisis, which was postponed by the outbreak of the First World War.

Cotton Board

DRAWING OUT THE SLIVER INTO YARN
The yarns are wound on to bobbins

After the war there was a shortage of goods in general, cotton goods among them, and the mills were kept going feverishly until this shortage had been overcome. But in 1920 there was a world collapse of trade and of prices, and it was then generally realized that Britain was no longer supreme in the cotton industry. There were many reasons for this. Japan, taking little active part in the war, seized the opportunity to expand her own cotton industry and to develop an immense export trade. In India the political nationalist movement, seeking independence from British rule, was becoming influential and the Government encouraged the growth of an Indian cotton industry. The war had prevented many other countries from getting supplies from Britain, and these countries also started cotton industries of their own. The final blow was the increase of the import duties on British cotton goods by certain countries, particularly the U.S.A. and South America. The effect of all these influences was catastrophic for the British industry, and fell particularly hard on Lancashire, its main centre. The export of cotton piece-goods dropped from nearly 7,000 million linear yards in 1912 to under a quarter of that figure in 1938. Between 1912 and 1938 the number of people employed in the industry was nearly halved. Cotton had become one of Britain's 'depressed' industries. By 1945 not much more than one-third of those who were working in the industry in 1924 were still engaged in it. Although methods of making man-made fibres such as rayon had been perfected since the First World War, Lancashire found the same adverse world trade conditions facing her here as in the cotton market.

The end of the Second World War saw a boom in the textile industry which was not maintained. Several developing countries, notably India, Pakistan, and Hong Kong, expanded their cotton industries rapidly after 1945. As a result, the Lancashire cotton industry began to face severe competition from these countries, first in the export markets, mainly the Commonwealth, and by the mid-1950's in the home market as well, as the volume of low-priced imports increased.

In 1959 the Government took action, introducing a scheme of organized contraction and re-equipment whereby the less profitable firms were given compensation to discontinue production, while the remaining firms were given grants to install modern machinery. Before long, the major synthetic fibre producers, who were concerned to maintain a strong textile industry in Britain, played an important part in creating several large multi-fibre, multi-process textile groups. Steps have been taken to control the entry of cotton imports. In 1965 a quota was placed on all cotton goods, limiting imports from those countries whose exports had disrupted the domestic industry.

During the 1960's the cotton industry has become a more concentrated and efficient industry, processing a wide range of fibres.

See also Textile Fibres and Fabrics.
See also Vol. VI: Cotton.

COTTON MANUFACTURE. 1. Manufacturing Processes. The main processes of manufacture in the cotton industry are much the same as those in the Wool Industry (q.v.), and the machines operate on the same general principles. The raw cotton, as it comes away from the plant in the cotton fields (*see* Cotton, Vol. VI), contains a large proportion of seeds, which are removed by the process of 'ginning'. In earlier days this separation of the seeds was a lengthy process that had to be done by hand; but in 1793 Eli Whitney, an American, invented the 'gin', an apparatus with saw-like teeth that extracted the seeds mechanically. Whitney's original invention has since been considerably improved, and modified 'saw-tooth' gins are still largely used, as well as the more complicated roller-gins. The ginning process is usually performed in the actual cotton-fields, for normally two-thirds of the weight of the harvested cotton is seed, and the cost of sending away the raw cotton is reduced if the seed is removed on the spot.

The ginned cotton is closely packed in bales under great pressure, to be shipped. At this stage it looks very much like raw wool, except that it is creamy white, and does not feel greasy to the touch. It can be 'teasled' into separate fibres, which vary in length from about $\frac{1}{2}$ in. to just over 2 in., according to quality. The longer the 'staple' or length of the fibre, the higher the grade of cotton, and the finer the yarn that can be spun from it. After unbaling at the port of entry, the cotton is cleaned, and is then subjected to the 'carding' process (*see* Wool Spinning, Section 2); this removes the shorter fibres, which would not make good yarn. What is removed by the carding machines is called

The Textile Council

A MODERN HIGH-PRODUCTION RING-SPINNING FRAME

'waste', and has many uses. Sometimes it is spun into coarse yarn, either by itself, or mixed with short-stapled Indian cotton; sometimes it is mixed with wool and used for weaving the cheaper clothing fabrics of wool and cotton mixture; it also has other uses, such as the making of dusters and the wicks for oil-lamps. The cotton comes out from the carding machines as long 'slivers' or ropes, in which the individual cotton fibres lie roughly parallel to each other. For short-stapled cottons carding is the last process before actual spinning. Long-stapled cottons usually pass through a further 'combing' process, much as wool does in the making of worsted yarns. It is this combed cotton which is used for spinning the finer 'counts'. The 'count' of any particular quality of yarn is the number of 'hanks' or lengths of yarn that will turn the scale at a pound, each hank being 840 yards long. The finer the yarn, the less it will weigh, and the higher the count. Today, however, the 'Tex' system of yarn numbering is coming into use in Britain. This system is based on the weight in grammes of a kilometre of yarn, so the thicker the yarn, the higher the number.

After being combed, the slivers are passed through the 'drawing frame', which combines several slivers together, and at the same time draws them out into a single sliver in which the straight and parallel arrangement of the fibres is made more definite. When they come out of the drawing-frame, the slivers are passed through a succession of machines called 'fly-frames', which gradually reduce their thickness and prepare them for the spinning process. In this the 'rovings', as they are now called, are still further drawn out, and given the 'twist', which converts them into actual yarn.

The most common method of spinning yarn used in the cotton industry is ring-spinning. The ring-frame spins continuously and does not need very close and constant watching. Another method is mule-spinning, which at one time was universally used, but has now been generally supplanted by ring-spinning. The 'mule' combines in an improved form the original ideas of Hargreaves's spinning 'jenny' and Arkwright's roller-spinning frame. The mule needs more attention than the ring-frame, for its operation is intermittent and not continuous. Until recently the mule was regarded as the better machine; it was believed to produce a softer and better yarn, and was used for spinning the finer counts. There are now roughly ten times as many ring-spindles as there are mule-spindles being used. A new and revolutionary method of spinning called 'break spinning' is being developed but there has been little practical experience of operating this system as yet. In the method of break spinning available at present, a stream of separated fibres is drawn into and spun from a rotating 'pot'. Some of the major advantages of this system are that it can wind yarn direct on to a large package, and it requires less labour and has a higher production rate than ring-spinning.

The final process in cotton spinning is 'doubling', which means the twisting together of two or more yarns to make 2-ply, 3-ply, or multi-ply yarns. Not all yarns are 'doubled'; much depends on the purpose for which they are going to be used. Sometimes single yarn is put through the doubling process merely to put an extra twist in it. Sometimes doubling is done in order to make a yarn of mixed cotton and wool, or of mixed cotton and silk, or of a mixture of cotton and man-made fibres (*see* TEXTILE FIBRES, MAN-MADE). The doubling process gives a more even count, and also confers more strength on yarns that are to be used as warp in the weaving process (*see* WOOL WEAVING), and therefore have to stand extra strain. All yarn destined for use as sewing-thread, or for the lace and hosiery trades, is doubled as a general practice. Some of the coarser counts of yarn are also doubled, and are used for making heavy canvas. The doubling process more than doubles the strength of the combined yarn, as compared with the strength of the individual yarns that go to make it—in much the same way as a rope of three strands is more than three times as strong as any individual strand.

Cotton weaving does not differ in essentials from the methods used for the weav-

The Textile Council

A MODERN WEAVING SHED

The shed is equipped with fully automatic looms that save time and labour

ing of wool and other textile fabrics. Weaving equipment has much improved during the 1960's, the old Lancashire looms being replaced by automatic ones; however, further modernization is still needed. The woven cloths are for making up as clothes, for household and furnishing uses, and for an increasingly wide range of industrial purposes. Most of the industrial cloths are made by the weaving mills, and are bought from them by the industrial users; for example, shoe-linings are mainly made in Lancashire and sold to merchants in Leicester or Nottingham, who pass them on to the BOOT AND SHOE INDUSTRY (q.v.). Sometimes the industrial users buy yarn and weave their own cloths. For example, many makers of tires own mills for the weaving of their tire fabrics, and many of the surgical-dressing fabrics are woven in mills owned or controlled by the firms that deal in them.

After weaving, most cotton cloths pass through various finishing processes, unless they are to be sold unfinished as 'greycloth'. The main finishing processes are bleaching, sizing, dyeing, calendering, mercerizing, and printing (*see* TEXTILE PRINTING). Hypochlorite BLEACHING (q.v.) is most usual in Britain but bleaching by hydrogen peroxide, as used in the U.S.A., is increasing. Calendering is a mechanical process to give lustre and 'feel' to cotton fabrics; mercerizing gives a silky sheen or lustre, and is a combination of mechanical and chemical processes—the fabric is held under tension, and not allowed to shrink, during immersion in a bath of caustic soda.

2. ORGANIZATION. The British cotton industry is composed of many separate kinds of firms. There are the merchants in raw cotton, including the Liverpool merchants and brokers; the yarn merchants; and the piece-goods merchants who deal in woven fabrics. The producing side of the industry includes the spinners, the doublers, the weavers, and the finishers. Both merchants and producing firms tend to specialize. A spinning firm usually spins either fine or coarse yarns, but not both. Weaving firms usually weave a restricted selection of fabrics. Many yarns have to pass through intermediate processes before they are woven; sometimes these processes are undertaken by spinners, sometimes by weavers, and occasionally by specialist firms who do nothing else.

The organization of the industry changed considerably as a result of the Cotton Industry Act of 1959 which sought to reduce surplus activity and encourage firms to re-equip with modern machinery. Before then the industry was organized on a 'horizontal' basis with individual firms specializing in spinning, weaving, or finishing. During the 1960's the industry became more vertical in structure. A number of large groups have emerged, each covering the main processes in the industry, rather than specializing in one particular process. The result is that the four largest firms in the industry now control 47% of the spinning activity, 33% of the weaving activity, and 71% of the finishing activity. Yet the British industry is still predominantly horizontal, compared with the industries in many overseas countries. The producing firms work mainly to the orders of 'merchant converters' who have to keep in touch with the changing taste and fashion of the market.

The Textile Council

WEAVING A PATTERNED FABRIC ON A JACQUARD LOOM

Different coloured warp threads are controlled by a 'harness' so that they form the pattern

3. LOCATION. The cotton industry is mainly centred in Lancashire, because the damp climate was originally an advantage to this industry. A damp climate is no longer so important, as mechanical 'humidifiers' have been invented, which can increase the moisture in the air. The chemical industry of Lancashire and Cheshire has been an important influence in preventing the cotton industry from moving elsewhere.

Outside Lancashire, and the neighbouring parts of Cheshire, Yorkshire, and Derbyshire, the only big centres of the cotton industry are Glasgow, Paisley, and Belfast, although the north-west Midlands—close to the headquarters of the lace and hosiery trades—have some importance.

Towns and districts used to specialize. On the spinning side, Oldham and Rochdale were the main centres for the coarser counts, and Bolton for the finer counts. Waste spinning was done principally in Rochdale, Heywood, Stockport, and Stalybridge. Paisley was once the home of the famous Paisley shawls, made either from cotton alone or from cotton and silk. This trade collapsed between 1870 and 1880 through fashion changes, and Paisley has now become an important centre for spinning sewing-thread. A few mills in Belfast spin cotton yarns, mainly for mixture with the flax yarns that are the chief product of the district.

On the weaving side, the Blackburn and Burnley areas specialized mainly in plain cloths. Nelson and Colne made plain and coloured fabrics for clothes, including brocades, poplins, and sateens. The Preston area made fine plain cloths and sheetings. Poorer quality sheetings were made from waste yarns in the Rossendale district. Today Hebden Bridge is the centre for fustians, and Scotland still makes decorated cloths, ginghams, muslins, and poplins, but on the whole, there are fewer mills left in the industry's traditional strongholds, and those that remain have been forced to cultivate a more diverse trade.

Finishing firms are less concentrated together. Finishing processes often depend upon plenty of fresh, soft, and running water, and finishing works are often widely scattered, many being in remote valleys. Most finishing firms are in the Lancashire area, but the Vale of Leven, in Scotland, is an important centre for calico-printing.

See also COTTON INDUSTRY, HISTORY.
See also Vol. VI: COTTON.

COTTON-SEED OIL, *see* OILS. VEGETABLE.

CRAFT GUILDS. These were perhaps the most important economic organizations of the later Middle Ages. A craft guild consisted of all the skilled workers of a single trade, or 'craft', working together within a town. It was the offshoot of an earlier form of guild, the Merchant Guild, then known as 'Guild Merchant', which was a mixed association of all the qualified traders of a town, with special rights for its members to engage in WHOLESALE TRADING and RETAIL TRADING within the town (qq.v.) on market days and at other times, without having to pay either tolls or customs. There were a hundred towns in England with merchant guilds, of which the first was set up at Burford in Oxfordshire, as early as 1087.

Craft guilds were first introduced in the reign of Henry I. These guilds grew rapidly as little groups of skilled craftsmen formed organizations of their own in all the important towns of England. Eventually, in town after town, the single Merchant Guild gave way to a whole series of these new organizations.

The craft guild had three classes of members: masters, journeymen, and apprentices. The apprentices were the learners. 'Till a man grow unto the age of 23 years, he is not grown to the full knowledge of his craft.' Apprenticeship was the means of acquiring a technical education. It was based on a contract between the two parties. The master promised to keep his pupil 'as a prentice should be, that is to say meat and drink, hose and shoes, linen, wool, and his craft to be taught him, and nothing hid from him thereto'. In return the apprentice promised to be obedient, to protect his master's property, not to steal—'not even by 6*d.* in the year'—not to frequent inns or gaming-houses, nor to marry without permission. The favourite dream of the medieval apprentice was to marry his master's daughter. The length of apprenticeship varied. At first it lasted until the master declared his pupil able and well instructed. Gradually the London custom of 7 years' apprenticeship was imitated, until by the Statute of Apprentices in 1563 it became the law of the land.

When the APPRENTICE (q.v.) had completed his term, and was qualified in his craft, he could seek employment as a journeyman—a word of French origin, meaning working and paid by the day. He was usually expected to stay on for a year with his own master; and, before he himself could be admitted as a master, he was called upon to prove that 'he was full perfect in his craft' and 'of good conversation and living'. He was also at times required to provide a sample of his work, or 'masterpiece', as it was then sometimes called. These careful regulations were made to encourage a sense of responsibility, and to protect the public and the craft from unskilled workers who would discredit the trade.

Some years would pass before a journeyman gathered enough capital to set up as a master; but, during the golden age of the craft guilds, tools, skill, and a little money to buy raw materials were all that were required, and the step from workman to master could be quite easily taken. Later on, when the artisan or skilled worker found it difficult to rise to be an employer, the system of craft guilds had broken down. By the 15th century journeymen were beginning to form their own guilds to protect their special interests, and by the 16th and 17th centuries they had their own officers and regulations.

The craft guilds comprised only skilled workmen. In this way they were unlike our modern TRADE UNIONS (q.v.), for they consisted only of the qualified men of their trades, and at no time did they include the whole body of workers within a town.

Inside the guilds there was supposed to be no competition; but, as will appear, this ideal broke down. Members of the same guild were 'brothers', pledged to help each other. Any guildsman, for example, was entitled to share in a purchase another guildsman had made, at the price that had originally been paid. Men were supposed to work 'for the honour of the guild' and for the good of the community. It was thus the object of the guild to protect the consumer against bad workmanship: shoddy goods, for instance, or under-weight parcels. A craftsman who produced inferior or fraudulent wares was not only bringing disgrace upon the craft as a whole, but was also in danger of bringing down the price of the article, and therefore he was fined for his offence. Not all medieval workmen were reliable. 'A medieval craftsman', it has been said, 'was not called a man of craft for nothing'. We can still examine many of the rules that the guilds made to deal with this sort of problem. The rules at Bristol, for example, were very strict, and 'Bristol-fashion' became a phrase applied to any job well done. Bad workers were fined, and consumers had the right to complain to guild officers.

Another useful purpose of the guild was to

British Museum

MASTERS OF STONE AND WOOD GIVING EVIDENCE OF SKILL IN THEIR CRAFTS BEFORE THE CONSUL OF THE GUILD AT FLORENCE

Illumination from the Flemish manuscript *Des Proprietez des Choses*, 1482 (Roy. MS. 15, E. II, f. 265)

bring together all the workers of a particular trade, so that they could fix wages and prices. The medieval idea was that fair wages and prices could be fixed in the best interests of both producers and consumers (*see* USURY). It was easier to fix them in the Middle Ages, because craftsmen in a particular industry then usually lived together in a single quarter of the town. Some of these quarters still survive: Butchers' Row in York sees the same trade carried on, in the same buildings, as it was centuries ago.

Not all the time of the wardens or governors and craftsmen was taken up with work, and regulations concerning work. The guilds emphasized the religious and social side of life. They also acted as FRIENDLY SOCIETIES (q.v. Vol. X). They had craft guild pageants, and on holy days they performed mystery plays: the word 'mystery' meant mastery, or craftsmanship. Each guild would make itself responsible for one scene from a MIRACLE PLAY (q.v. Vol. XII). The visit of the Three Kings to the cradle of the Infant Jesus was taken by the goldsmiths, for the making of crowns and jewels was their special care. The story of the Flood was taken by the shipwrights, whose skill and traditions went back to the builders of the ark. Many of these miracle plays were in the spoken English of the day, and some have survived to this day—among them the pageant of the guild of shearmen and tailors at Coventry.

The ideals of the guilds look so attractive that it is sometimes difficult to understand why the system broke down. Some of the causes of their final decay lay within the guilds themselves; others outside them.

The first sign of the breakdown of the craft guild system was the growth of separate journeymen's guilds, which were associations of wage-earners formed inside the craft guilds, but maintaining a distinctive and independent existence. The success of the craft guilds had depended on good relations between masters and journeymen and the possibilities of journeymen becoming masters. In the 15th and 16th centuries many of the journeymen were sinking into the position of permanent wage-earners. This period of social change-over was accompanied by disputes between masters and journeymen about wages and hours. In 1441, for example, the London bakers were complaining that their servants had a brotherhood and livery, that is, a ceremonial uniform, and were demanding higher wages 'than they were wont to have of old time'; while in Coventry, in 1526, there were fierce disputes between master cappers (capmakers)—the main craft of the town—and their journeymen about an extension of working-hours. These and similar conflicts led to a clash between masters and journeymen, and to frequent attempts by the masters to crush the new journeymen's guilds.

In Elizabethan England the journeymen's guilds had completely established themselves in many crafts, and had secured recognition from the State. They were composed mainly of small masters dependent on large masters for their livelihood, and no longer dealing direct with consumers. In London, which was far ahead of the rest of the country, the rich masters were tending more and more to drop out of manufacturing. They were no longer real craftsmen, but rather dealers and merchants.

Out of the new wealthy merchant traders emerged the great London Livery Companies, such as the Mercers, Merchant Taylors, and Haberdashers; and a clear-cut distinction could be drawn between the Livery—those merchants who could afford to buy the uniforms and pay for the feasts and pageants—and the Yeomanry—consisting of small masters, who did not sell to the public or manufacture directly for them, but for the Livery. When Henry VII became king, and entered London in triumph in 1485, he was met by over 400 guildsmen riding on horseback and wearing bright mulberry-coloured gowns. The London guilds had by then become rich closed companies, with wealth and authority (*see* City Companies).

Over the country as a whole the older craft guild organizations were breaking down. In 1438, at Bristol, the cordwainers (shoemakers) were confessing that they had ceased to appoint wardens, and that no one took any more notice of the fines they imposed. As they declined—and the decline can be traced in the smaller number of miracle plays and pageants performed—the guilds began to be more and more exclusive in their organization, keeping new members out, and restricting their privileges to certain select families. This crippled their life, and compelled less wealthy craftsmen to leave the over-controlled industry in the towns, and to move towards the freedom of the countryside. This movement of industry away from the towns was quickened in Tudor England, and played a big part in the extension of the Domestic System of production (q.v.).

Some of the gaps left by the decline of the guilds were filled in by the Government. As early as 1437, an Act of Parliament claimed that 'the masters, wardens, and people of the guilds . . . make themselves many unlawful and unreasonable ordinances . . . for their singular profit and common damage to the people', and went on to order that all guild rules should be submitted to the local authorities or justices of the peace for approval. In 1504 national supervision became law, and guild rules had to be approved by the judges. In 1547, during the Reformation, the property of all religious guilds was taken over and vested in the Crown. These changes all reflected a period of guild decline. In 1563 the Government tried to preserve some of the most important features of the old system, and it drew up an elaborate code for industry, called the Statute of Apprentices. This laid down that wages were to be fixed annually by Justices of the Peace (q.v. Vol. X), that

THE GUILDHALL, LONDON, 1808
Coloured aquatint by Rowlandson and Pugin from Ackermann's *Microcosm of London*

7 years' apprenticeship for all trades and handicrafts was to be made compulsory all over the country—this had been the custom of London before—and that labour was not to be hired for periods of less than a year. There were many good intentions behind this famous statute, but the policy that it suggested was already out of tune with many of the new forces of the times. In the 17th century Charles I tried to encourage the setting-up of new craft guilds in London, but it was an impossible task; the guild system had been well suited to small towns and to local markets, and to restricted trade; but it did not fit the conditions of a new age.

See also TRADE UNIONS; DIVISION OF LABOUR; DOMESTIC SYSTEM; CITY COMPANIES.

CRAFTSMANSHIP. As the word is generally used, this means knowledge of a trade in which some form of skill with the hands is necessary. The opposite of the craftsman in modern industry is the 'machine-minder', one who merely sees that the machine he is in charge of is running properly, and perhaps performs at intervals some purely routine job, the success of which is not affected by his own judgement or skill of eye or hand. Some crafts can be assisted by machines, and do not cease to be crafts merely for that reason; other crafts or trades are handicrafts, and machines cannot assist them in any way, although, of course, tools are used. The tools, however, have to be guided by hand, and without the skill of the hand that guides them they can perform no useful services. A bricklayer or mason is a handicraftsman of this kind; he uses no machines. But many true craftsmen make much use of machines. A potter, for example, who uses the mechanical contrivance called the potter's wheel (*see* POTTERY), is truly entitled to be called a craftsman because, although it is the wheel that whirls round his lump of clay, it is the skill of his hand that fashions it.

British Travel and Holidays Assn.

CRAFTSMAN BLOWING GLASS FOR STAINED GLASS WINDOWS

Similarly, in trades that make more use of machinery than the pottery trade, skill with the hands is necessary for many purposes.

The welfare of a country depends largely on the number and skill of its craftsmen. Countries possessing few craftsmen remain economically backward. There is a tendency in highly industrialized countries for the number of craftsmen to diminish as industrial processes become more and more mechanized, until in certain trades they practically disappear. This is a fact well known to governments and to organizations such as TRADE UNIONS (q.v.) which have the welfare of workers at heart, and the institution of APPRENTICESHIP (q.v.) is encouraged both by unions and governments so that the supply of craftsmen may be maintained. This was illustrated by certain measures that were taken in Britain after the Second World War. There had been a great decline in the number of trained stonemasons, and at one period over 100 Italian stonemasons were imported to help build a waterworks dam in South Wales (*see* STONE DRESSING). In the boat and yacht building trades craftsmanship was safeguarded—even during the worst period of timber shortage—by an Admiralty 'hardship' scheme, under which yacht builders were allowed a licence for timber if they could prove that without it they would have to dismiss their craftsmen. The Royal MINT (q.v. Vol. X) still occasionally strikes gold sovereigns, although they are not needed for British currency purposes, the motive being to preserve among the Mint's craftsmen a knowledge of the craft of coining in gold.

To some extent the passing of the craftsman, or his transformation into a different kind of craftsman, is inevitable. A few examples may illustrate this. In earlier days no wood or stone could be carved unless each individual piece of carving was done from start to finish by a skilled worker. Nowadays a skilled worker is needed only to make the mould or 'masterpiece', from which a machine can make hundreds of copies of the original. Similarly, in the machine industry of earlier days, the independent skill of every worker at his bench was necessary for good performance. Nowadays the skill necessary has shifted from the worker at the bench to the machine-tool or jig-designing office; and, once the necessary machines have been designed, arranged, and set, the rest is automatic.

See also APPRENTICESHIP; CRAFT GUILDS; TRADE UNION HISTORY.

CREDIT. The word 'credit' comes from a Latin word meaning belief or trust. In commerce a person is said to receive credit when he receives goods or money on the understanding that he will pay for the goods, or repay the money, in due course. The simplest form of credit is 'personal credit', which many of us receive from time to time when we buy goods in a shop and suddenly discover that we have left our money at home. If the shopkeeper knows and trusts us sufficiently, he will allow us to take the goods at once and make payment later. When a shop allows a customer to have a regular monthly account, it is still personal credit, although of a more definite kind.

Between merchants and manufacturers this form of mutual trust is known as 'trade credit'. The terms on which it is given vary greatly. The usual credit arrangement among merchants is that payment must be made by the end of the month following the date of invoice: thus, goods dispatched on 15 January should be paid for on or before 28 February. Most firms which allow credit have their terms of business printed on their invoices or monthly statements. Merchants often find that it pays them to encourage an even quicker settlement of debts by offering a cash discount, often of $2\frac{1}{2}\%$ (or 6*d.* in the £), on all goods paid for within 7 to 10 days of the date of invoice.

A more special type of credit is 'bank credit'. The simplest form of bank credit is the 'overdraft': when the banker gives permission for a customer to draw out money in excess of the balance he has at the bank (*see* BANK ACCOUNTS). Overdrafts are occasionally granted against purely personal security: that is, against the customer's promise to repay by some pre-arranged date. More often some sort of collateral SECURITY is insisted on, such as government bonds, STOCKS AND SHARES (qq.v.), or guarantees entered into by the customer's partners or by other responsible people. The advantage of an overdraft is that the borrower has to pay INTEREST (q.v.) only on the amount actually overdrawn.

The other way of borrowing money from a bank is by a 'loan account'. This is opened for the customer at an agreed rate of interest. The full amount of the loan is charged against the customer's account, and placed to his current account for him to draw against. He pays interest on the total amount of the loan, however much or little of it he spends.

Among other forms of credit issued by bankers are circular or travellers' 'letters of credit' for use when the customer is travelling abroad. The letter of credit states the limit up to which he may draw money; it is accompanied by a booklet containing the names of the bank's agents in various towns all over the world. It is signed by the customer. The holder of a letter of credit draws as much foreign money as he needs abroad by writing ordinary cheques on his account, which are cashed up to the limit of his credit. The cheques eventually reach his own bank, and are charged to his account. Travellers' cheques are really letters of credit for round sums of money, printed on detachable forms like cheques. Another method is the 'open credit', by which a banker advises one of his own branches, or a particular banking office abroad, that it may safely cash his customer's cheques up to an arranged limit.

Some firms specialize in providing a service called 'credit rating'. They find out from the trade-connexions of the firms whose rating they are assessing, and also from their bankers and other sources of information, how reliable the firms are, and up to what sums of money they can safely be trusted in the ordinary way of business. The firms are rated A, B, or C, or on a similar basis, according to their credit-worthiness. The ratings are then printed in book form and are made available to subscribers to the service. Firms providing this kind of service also act as general commercial inquiry agents.

It is also possible to insure against losses caused by granting credit to firms or individuals who turn out to be so unworthy of it that those granting the credit lose their money (*see* INSURANCE). 'Credit insurance' is one of those branches of insurance in which the insurer himself is always asked to bear a considerable portion of the risk insured against. If this were not done, firms might be tempted to increase their business by granting credit too recklessly.

'Hire purchase' and 'payment by instalments' are special forms of credit, by which a person who buys something need not pay the whole price at once but can spread out the payment over a period of time. For these transactions a written agreement is drawn up between the seller and the buyer. Under a hire-purchase agreement the goods are delivered to the 'hirer' on payment of a small deposit of money, but they remain the legal property of the seller until the last of a series of weekly or monthly instalments has been paid. Until 1938 the law in Britain worked very much to the advantage of the seller, so that, if the hirer failed to meet even the last few instalments, the seller was entitled to take back the goods and also to keep the instalments that had already been paid. This might, and often did, cause great hardship to buyers. The Hire Purchase Act was, therefore, passed by Parliament in 1938, and this laid down (*a*) that if the hirer had already paid at least one-third of the purchase price, the seller could not obtain possession of the goods without an order from a court of law; and (*b*) that a court could order the remaining instalments to be spread over a longer period. In 1965, a new act provided further legal protection for the hirer (*see* HIRE PURCHASE, Vol. XI).

The other system of instalment selling is called 'deferred payments'. A written agreement is drawn up, as for a hire-purchase transaction, but the goods become the property of the buyer after payment of the first deposit.

Both these systems may be used not only when an ordinary customer buys something in a shop (in which case the credit is called 'consumer credit'), but also when manufacturers and merchants want to buy goods. Manufacturers may obtain new plant or machinery by paying instalments spread over a number of years; a merchant may, for example, equip himself with a new fleet of motor-vans in the same way. It is thus possible for a business firm to bring its equipment up to date by payments out of profits, without increasing its capital. There are firms that specialize in financing transactions of this kind; one of the largest is the United Dominions Trust, which works in close association with the Bank of England.

In modern days governments watch very closely the total amount of instalment credit. If it grows too large, it may lead to an increase in the demand for goods when goods are scarce, and this causes inflation (*see* NATIONAL FINANCE, Vol. X). By altering from time to time the law concerning instalment selling, governments may do much to control its total amount. Consumer credit of this kind was legally forbidden during the Second World War, and was only very gradually restored afterwards.

See also BANKING.

CREDIT NOTE, *see* INVOICE.

CURRENCY. Currency is not quite the same thing as coinage. A country's coinage is the actual metallic coins that it uses; but other kinds of money may be 'current'—or passed from hand to hand as money. All money that is current, and is reckoned by counting and not by weight, is currency. Thus guineas, sovereigns, half-sovereigns, half-crowns, shillings, pennies, and so on, are currency because they are coins, and because they pass from hand to hand without being weighed. Bank-notes are currency for the same reason, although they are not part of the coinage.

MONEY (q.v.) need not necessarily be currency. Throughout the world various things have been used as money at different times, ranging from cattle to the small shells called 'cowries', and including the precious metals, uncoined, and passing from hand to hand by weight (*see* PRIMITIVE MONEY). Primitive communities have money of this sort, but a precious metal is not usually made into coins until a later stage of development. By making it up into coins a properly organized government guarantees the weight and 'fineness' of metal used. (Fineness is the proportion of precious metal in an 'alloy' or mixture which contains also base metal for hardening purposes.)

Coinage is nearly always a State responsibility (*see* MINT, Vol. X); but currency other than coinage need not necessarily be so—although in modern times it usually is. From the 17th century onwards, in England and Wales, paper currency in the form of bank-notes was issued by private bankers on their own responsibility, and according to their own inidividual designs (*see* BANKING). But in 1921 the Treasury

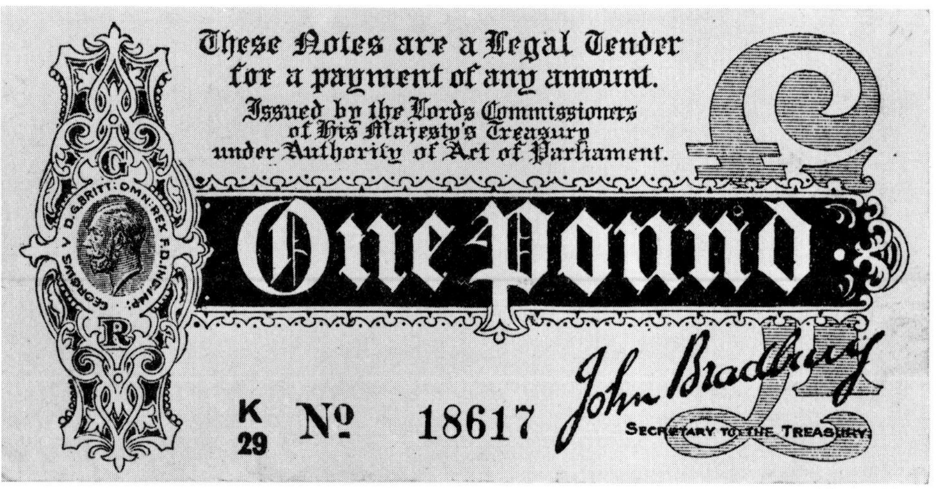

Ashmolean Museum

BRITISH TREASURY NOTE FIRST ISSUED IN 1914

Because the signature of the Secretary to the Treasury is so legible these were often called 'Bradburys'

and the Bank of England (q.v.) had become jointly responsible for all such issues. In Scotland and Ireland, however, the issue of paper currency may still be made by commercial banking firms. Such notes circulate widely but are not legal tender.

'Legal tender' means any form of currency which may legally be 'tendered', or offered, to merchants and individuals in payment for goods or debts, and in payment of taxes and other debts to the Government itself. When any coins or notes are made 'legal tender', people to whom money is due are obliged by law to accept those coins or notes in settlement of debts. In the United Kingdom since 1928 £1 and 10*s*. notes of the Bank of England have been legal tender without any limit; silver coins (including the cupro-nickel alloy which looks like silver) are legal tender up to a limit of £2; nickel-brass threepenny bits up to 2*s*. and copper coins (which are really made of bronze) up to 1*s*. for any one transaction. Bank of England notes over £1 are not legal tender in Northern Ireland or Scotland.

Pitt Rivers Museum

NOTE ISSUED IN FRANCE DURING THE FIRST WORLD WAR

Notes were issued by local Chambers of Commerce for use in their district to make up for a shortage of small coin

By an Act of 1833 Bank of England notes of £5 and upwards were made legal tender in England and Wales, in addition to gold coins. This situation lasted until August 1914 when, owing to war difficulties, Treasury notes were printed as additional legal tender without limit throughout Great Britain. These ceased to be issued in 1928 when the Bank of England took over the issue of notes of low sums.

Historically the coinage of Great Britain has consisted of guineas, half-guineas, golden sovereigns and half-sovereigns, and silver and copper coins. The gold coins were literally 'worth their weight in gold': that is, they could have been sold by weight for their face value. But if a half-crown of those days had been sold by weight, it might have fetched only a shilling, while a penny might have fetched less than a farthing. These silver and bronze coins were called 'token coins', to distinguish them from the full-value gold coins. Bank-notes are worth nothing in themselves. They are not token coins, but token currency.

Today the difference between the token and non-token currency of Great Britain is only of historical interest, since all currency is now token. By 1971, Britain will have fully adopted a decimal currency, still based on the pound, but with the ten-shilling note replaced by the 50 pence coin, and coins worth ½, 1, 2, 5, and 10 new pennies superseding the older silver and copper coins (*see* Mint, Vol. X).

See also Money; Coins; Banking.

CURRENT ACCOUNT, *see* Bank Accounts.

CURRYING is one of the finishing processes of the leather trade. In the days of the Craft Guilds (q.v.) there were two different sets of craftsmen engaged in leather manufacture: the tanners who prepared and tanned the hides, drying them out into 'crust' leather; and the curriers who 'dressed' and finished the crust leather. This separation of the two trades lasted for centuries, and in 1604 James I checked a tendency towards amalgamation by making a law that no one should be permitted to practise both crafts. This law is no longer in force, but the historical division of the leather trades still persists, and many firms today buy crust leather from tanners and specialize in currying or dressing only.

If the leather that emerges from the vegetable

Gandy Ltd.

SCOURING LEATHER AFTER IT HAS BEEN TANNED

The hide is soaked in water and cleaned by this machine which, fitted with scouring stones and brushes, moves rapidly over the table on which the hide is laid

TANNING process (q.v.) is merely dried out, it is harsh, of uneven thickness, and lacking in waterproof qualities. The currying process corrects these defects, its main purpose being to put grease into the leather to make the leather strong, supple, and waterproof. In the past the process was needed for boot and shoe uppers, harness, straps, saddlery, coach hoods and tops, and leather jerkins. Currying is carried out today on leather for footballs, driving-belts, harness and bridles, straps, hoses, cases and bags, and the uppers of heavy-duty footwear worn by farm-workers, miners, seamen, and soldiers. The process differs in detail according to the nature of the tanning and the purpose for which the leather will be used. A typical example is the treatment applied to vegetable-tanned ox-hide that is to be used as driving belting for machinery. The 'backs' of the hides, which will be used for this purpose, will have been separated from the 'bellies' by the tanner. The currier buys the backs and first soaks them in warm water or weak tan liquor to soften them. He then thoroughly cleans them, either by working over the surface of the grain with a brush and a 'slicker'—a hand tool with a broad, blunt blade—or by machinery. When the hide has been partly dried, its thickness, which varies from place to place, is evened up. This used to be done by slicing off thin films of leather with a special knife that had a sharp cutting edge at right angles to the blade. To-day this very skilled operation is done either by machine in which the hide is pressed against a rapidly revolving cylinder fitted with spiral knife blades; or by splitting off a thin layer with a machine in which the hide is pressed, edge on, against the edge of a band knife travelling at a high speed. Next comes the greasing. An old process, still much used for the best quality leathers, is called 'hand-stuffing'. The damp leather is coated on both sides with a layer of dubbin: the original dubbin was of equal parts of tallow and crude cod-liver oil, but other mixtures are now sometimes used. The leather is then hung to dry slowly in a warm room, where the water evaporates, the leather absorbs the liquid portion of the dubbin, and the more solid portions of the dubbin are left on the surface to be scraped off later.

For many purposes hand-stuffing has been replaced either by 'drum-stuffing' or 'dipping'. In drum-stuffing, the leather, when still damp, is put into a drum containing molten grease. This is absorbed into the leather. In dipping, the leather is first dried and then dipped into the grease. After greasing, there may be further treatments.

One old hand process was to soften the leather by folding it over on itself, grain to grain, and working it backwards and forwards with a wooden tool, called a 'pommel'. In the olden days this particular operation was the true currying process, although the term is applied today rather to the greasing process.

See also HIDES AND SKINS; TANNING; LEATHER; BOOT- AND SHOE-MAKING.

CUSTOMS DUTIES, *see* OVERSEAS TRADE; TARIFF.

CUTLERY INDUSTRY. Cutlery is the craft of making knives or similar cutting instruments from fine steel. The products include table and carving knives, surgical instruments, the knives used by such tradesmen as butchers and boot and shoe-makers, artists' palette knives, pocket-knives and penknives, pruning-knives, barbers' razors, scissors, carving-forks, and steels for sharpening. The industry is one of the oldest in England. It is practically confined to the Sheffield district, where the trade was already well established in the time of the 14th-century poet, Chaucer. There are some firms operating in Birmingham and other provincial towns, and a few firms specialize in tradesmen's cutlery in London.

Perhaps there is no industry in the country in which ancient traditions die harder than in cutlery. In Sheffield some of the old CRAFT GUILD (q.v.) conditions still prevail, and this is apparent in the division of the industry into three branches, forging or 'goffing', grinding, and finishing. Before the First World War methods of producing cutlery had not greatly altered from the Middle Ages, although power was used to drive grinding-wheels and to operate heavy hammers for some of the forging processes. But many types of knives and cutting-blades were still being hand-forged under the craftsman's hammer, and finished and polished by hand. Since 1918 there has been more mechanization, particularly for forging and grinding, but the production of high-class cutlery is unlikely ever to be completely mechanized.

There are three main divisions of the industry: shaping and forging the pieces of steel (*see* FORGING AND PRESSING, Vol. VIII) from which the articles will be made; tempering (*see* HEAT TREATMENT, Section 4, Vol. VIII), grinding, and polishing; and assembling and finishing. There are very few firms in the trade engaged in each of these divisions and carrying out every process from the raw steel to the finished article. The main division of labour in the trade is between firms that forge or 'goff' the blades, and firms that grind, polish, assemble, and finish. Quite a number of small firms carry out only a single process, and much work in the industry is done on the 'outworker' or DOMESTIC SYSTEM (q.v.). Grinding is a branch of the trade in which outworkers are still very numerous. In the days before steam, when a water-mill (*see* WATER POWER, Vol. VIII) was the motive power for working heavy forging hammers and driving grinding-wheels, land speculators built factories along the banks of the streams. They then let space or rooms in these 'tenement' factories to small craftsmen working on their own account, and provided them with the necessary heat, light, and power. In and around Sheffield this system still prevails to some extent, although it is on the decline since the motive power provided is now steam or electricity. Many outworkers still work in these tenement factories. Others work at piece-rates for an employer who provides them with space, light, and power, for which he charges a rent, and pays according to the amount of work done. In the cutlery industry the small craftsman is not at a disadvantage compared with the large-scale manufacturer, for many of the processes can be carried out either with quite simple machinery or entirely by hand.

Machinery is being increasingly used for the cheaper articles, but much handwork by skilled craftsmen is still necessary for those of higher quality. The blades of the best table-knives are machine-forged from short bars of good steel. Machines may be used to shape the shoulder or 'bolster' at the handle end of the blade, and the 'tang' or extension for fitting the handle.

Joseph Rodgers and Sons

THE TRADITIONAL MANUFACTURE OF A TABLE-KNIFE BLADE. THESE PROCESSES ARE NOW MECHANIZED

The blade is forged from a $\frac{3}{4}$ ft. bar of stainless steel about $\frac{1}{2}$ in. square. First the metal is drawn out in a heavy press (top left); then it is hammered to make the bolster or shoulder (top right). The tang which fits into the handle is drawn out and the blade is spread out. Next the blade is cut out (lower left). It undergoes finishing and hardening processes and is finally ground (lower right) and polished

The cheaper table-knives are made from strip steel, rolled and shaped mechanically. After being shaped, the blades are hardened, and then tempered by being re-heated to a low temperature and rapidly quenched in water. The blades of pocket-knives and penknives are tempered slightly harder than table-knives. The word 'penknife' is a title handed down from the days when the smaller blade of a pocket-knife was used for sharpening quill pens. Grinding is the next process. It is now largely mechanized, but there are still many hand-grinders in Sheffield and also in Solingen, which is the centre of the German cutlery industry. Barbers' razors are 'hollow ground': apart from the actual edge itself, the thinnest part of the blade is in the centre. Safety-razor blades, being straight, are produced and ground mechanically. Each blade of a pair of scissors is forged separately from slightly milder steel than is used for knives. High-class pocket-knives are hand-forged, and fitting the springs of such knives is a highly skilled branch of the trade.

See also Vol. VIII: IRON AND STEEL, Section 5.

D

DAIRY INDUSTRY. 1. This is one of the most important industries in many countries. Australia, New Zealand, Denmark, Holland, Canada, and parts of the U.S.A. are all notable for dairy produce, and in Britain the turnover of the industry in 1967 amounted to £700 million. Four-fifths of this sum came from the sale of fresh milk. Milk, in fact, is the most important single product produced by British farmers.

All farmers selling milk in the United Kingdom must be registered with a Milk Marketing Board. There are five of these: one covering England and Wales, three in Scotland, and one in Northern Ireland. The function of a board is to market the farmer's milk for him. It arranges for the collection of the milk from his farm and the selling of it to dairy companies, and it helps him to improve his STOCK BREEDING (q.v. Vol. VI) by providing services such as the Artificial Insemination Service.

About $5\frac{1}{2}$ million gallons of milk are collected every day from farms in England and Wales. Since milk is highly perishable and the farms often lie far distant from the towns and cities that need the milk, its transport calls for the greatest efficiency and speed. Local hauliers collect the 10-gallon churns from the farms in lorries and take them either to a local collecting depot or else straight to a dairy which pasteurizes and bottles the milk (*see* PASTEURIZATION OF MILK) and later sells it to the housewife. Relatively few farmers sell milk direct to the consumer.

Milk is carried from the country depots to the dairies in towns in huge road and rail tankers carrying anything from 1,500 to 4,200 gallons. These tankers now collect more than a quarter of the nation's milk straight from the farms. The driver tests the milk in the farmer's refrigerated vat for smell, contamination, temperature, and weight and, if satisfactory, pumps the milk through a hose into his road-tanker.

At the country depots and town dairies the milk that has been received direct from the farms is examined at the reception platform; doubtful supplies are sampled by the laboratory for testing. The sound milk is then tipped out of the churns, weighed, and passed to a receiving tank with the milk from all the neighbouring farms. This is then cooled and passed to the storage tanks. The milk may be manufactured into butter, cheese, or other milk products at the country depots, or sent to another depot for manufacture, or dispatched to a town dairy for distribution to householders.

From the milking sheds on the farms to the sealed bottles delivered at one's door, government regulations, which are strictly enforced, safeguard the quality and cleanness of milk.

2. CREAM is separated by passing milk at a temperature of about 46° C. through a separator, in which a series of conical plates revolves at high speed. The fat globules, being lighter than the rest of the liquid, collect in the central part of the separator and form the cream, which flows out through a pipe. The separated milk, being heavier, is discharged by another pipe. The cream must be separated before butter is made.

3. BUTTER is essentially the fat of milk, and should not contain more than 16% of water. There are two main types of butter: sweet cream butter for which the cream is not soured before churning, and ripened or soured cream butter. Sour cream butter has a much fuller flavour than sweet but keeps for less time. Milk is first passed through a separator to give a cream of about 38% fat. If ripened cream butter is to be made, lactic streptococci are added, and the cream is held at a temperature of about 15° C. until the required degree of souring has been obtained. The cream is cooled to 5° C. and stored for periods up to 18 hours, when it is then ready for churning.

The butter churn is a wooden or stainless steel barrel that is rotated to give the cream a series of violent shocks. This causes the membrane round the fat globules to shatter, and the fat agglomerates to produce a fat liquid stage. The liquid buttermilk is then withdrawn, and the remaining butterfat washed with chilled water to remove any residual milk solids, and firm up the fat particles. Salt may be added, after which the butterfat is 'worked' by squeezing through rollers or bars fitted in the butter churn. The moisture content is checked, and the butter packed into 56 lb. boxes, or consumer packs.

4. CHEESE is probably the most interesting milk product from the scientific point of view, as it involves physical, chemical, and bacteriological changes in the milk. Most cheese was once made only in farm-houses, but most of it is now made in creameries. The most important variety made in England is Cheddar. Milk is pasteurized, then cooled to about 22° C. and put into a vat, and a 'starter' consisting of a culture of lactic streptococci is added. As the temperature of the milk is gradually raised to about 30° C. the streptococci grow and 'ripen' the milk. When a certain acidity has been reached, a small proportion of rennet (a milk-curdling enzyme) is added. After about half an hour a fairly firm junket or curd is formed by the action of the rennet working on the milk. This is then cut into small cubes, and the temperature is gradually raised to just about 40° C. The particles of solid matter, or curd, must be stirred continuously, and, when the curd has contracted and hardened, a greenish-yellow liquid, called whey, is run off and the particles of curd are allowed to sink to the bottom, where they come together to form a sort of mattress. This is then cut into pieces, which are piled on the sides of the vat to help the drainage of the whey. During this time the acidity is continually increasing, and this helps to separate the whey from the curd. Finally, when the curd has reached the right condition, it is 'milled' or torn into small particles, mixed with salt, and packed into a hoop or mould. The moulded curd is then placed in a press for 1 or 2 days, by which time it has become a 'green' cheese. Cheddar cheese is usually graded after about a month and is considered ripe or fit for eating from 3 to 12 months later. The cheese retains practically all the fat and casein, or chief protein, in the milk, and is a very rich food.

5. MILK POWDER OR DRIED MILK. Milk is dried by two main methods, the roller and the spray process. By the roller method hot milk or pre-condensed milk is fed in between two special rollers which revolve about 15 times a minute. The rollers are hollow, and are heated by steam. The milk quickly dries and forms a film on the surface of the roller; this is carried round until it meets a knife which scrapes it off. The film then drops into a box, or into a trough, from which a screw-conveyor passes it along to the sifting, grinding, and packing departments. In the spray process hot concentrated milk is sprayed into a drying-chamber; various devices are used to produce a very fine spray, in which the tiny globules rapidly lose their moisture in a current of hot air. The finely divided powder is then collected at the bottom and packed into tins. Spray-dried milk is a fine white powder, easily reconstituted in water to form a product very like the original milk; but spray powder does not possess as good keeping qualities as roller powder, unless special care is taken. Roller powder is not easily reconstituted, and, because of the higher temperature used in its manufacture, has a distinctive flavour.

6. CONDENSED MILK. Whole or skimmed milk is first heated to about 79° C. It is held at this temperature for about 15 minutes, while cane sugar is added. The mixture is then drawn into a metal evaporator and boiled under vacuum at just over 50° C. until it has reached a concentration of about $2\frac{1}{4}$ times that of the original milk. The condensed milk is then drawn off, pumped through coolers, and filled into tins or barrels. The high concentration of cane-sugar acts as a preservative.

7. EVAPORATED MILK differs from condensed milk in not containing any added sugar. It is pre-heated, clarified, and homogenized, and then concentrated up to about twice its original content in solids. It is then sterilized in the tin, in a special pressure-heating apparatus which kills all bacteria.

8. ULTRA HIGH-TEMPERATURE PROCESSED MILK is the term for a long-keeping milk, available since 1965. The milk is heated indirectly as in a conventional PASTEURIZATION plant (q.v.). An additional final stage heats it to 135° C., after which, if packed in sterile conditions, it lasts indefinitely.

See also Vol. VI: CATTLE, CARE OF.
See also Vol. XI: MILK; BUTTER; CHEESE.

DEBENTURES are loans to LIMITED COMPANIES, usually at a fixed rate of INTEREST (qq.v.). The 'debenture holders', or persons lending the money, accept the assets of the company as security for their money.

There is a great difference between debentures and STOCKS AND SHARES (q.v.). A share

Milk Marketing Board

The milk bottles are automatically cleaned by the machine (far left), then they pass through the automatic bottle scanner to be filled with milk, capped, and placed in crates at the rate of 400 per minute

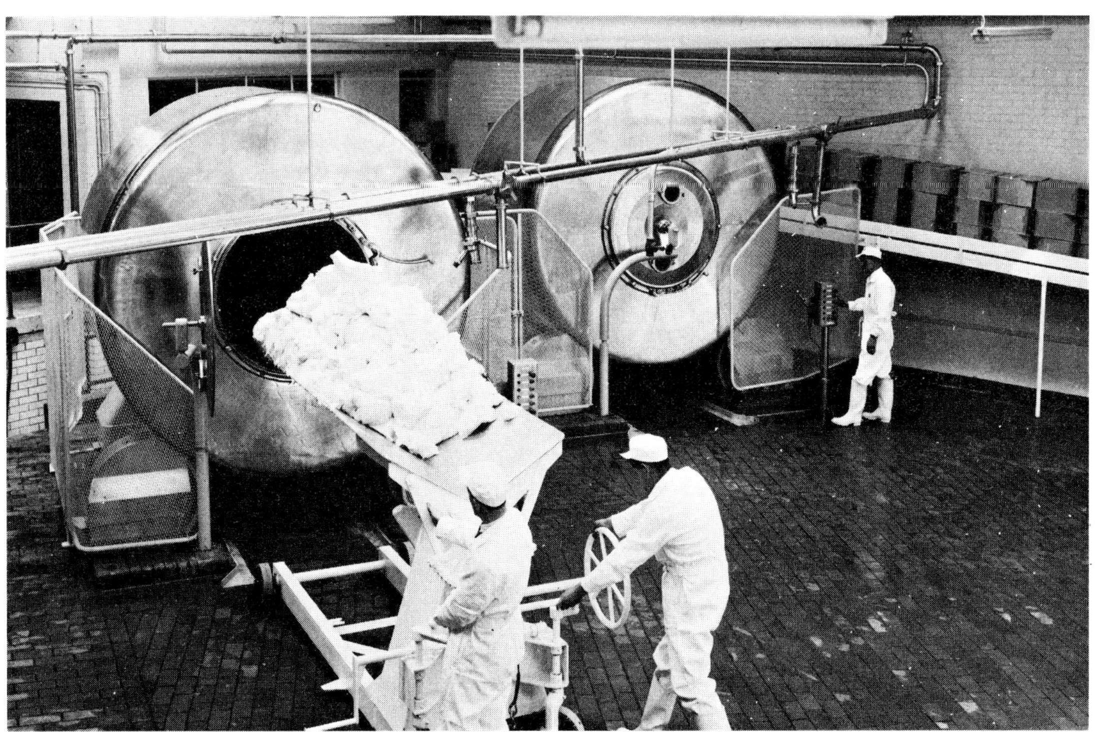

Milk Marketing Board

TWO STAINLESS STEEL BUTTER CHURNS AT KENDALL CREAMERY; EACH CAN CHURN $2\frac{1}{2}$ TONS IN $2\frac{1}{2}$ HOURS

is what its name implies: it is a share in the fortune or misfortune of the company in which it is held. If the company earns profits, the shareholders will receive a dividend; if no profits are made they will receive nothing. But the position of a debenture-holder is safer. The borrowing company must sign a trust deed, a legal contract pledging the company's land, buildings, machinery, plant, and other assets as security for the loan. The TRUST deed (q.v. Vol. X) names a body of trustees to act for the debenture-holders, and promises that the arranged rate of interest shall be regularly paid, whether profits are earned or not; it also lays down that, if the interest is not regularly paid, the trustees may be given certain rights over the business and may control its management, until either regular payment of interest can be made again, or the company's assets have been turned into cash so that the debenture-holders may be repaid.

Debentures may be 'redeemable', that is, the whole loan may be repayable to the lenders at a fixed future date; or 'irredeemable', which means that they are a permanent loan to the company. There are also 'participating' debentures, receiving a share in the company's profits as well as their fixed interest; and 'convertible' debentures, with the right of conversion into the company's 'ordinary' shares: these are very popular in times of inflation.

In spite of the severe penalties in case of default, it is an advantage for a company whose business is profitable to borrow money on debenture. It has to pay only low rates of interest for capital on which extra profits can be earned for its 'ordinary' shareholders.

See also DIVIDEND; LOAN.

DEMAND, *see* SUPPLY AND DEMAND.

DEPARTMENT STORES. There are conflicting views concerning the origin of the department store, or big retail shop which sells several different kinds of goods. It has been suggested that the department-store movement in Britain was started in the second half of the 19th century by a small group of Civil Service clerks, who bought a chest of tea at wholesale price at the London AUCTION sales (q.v.) and divided it among themselves. This group later expanded into the Civil Service Supply Association, a large department store with premises in the Strand and in the City. A more likely explanation is that Aristide Boucicaut, a Frenchman, originated the movement in 1852 by founding the Paris Bon Marché. The first department store outside Paris was opened in the U.S.A. in the late 1850's, very soon after Boucicaut opened up in Paris. In 1860 William Whiteley opened his big London store in Bayswater, and claimed to be 'the universal provider'. Other London merchants soon followed William Whiteley's example.

The provincial department store—at least on a small scale—goes back very much farther in the history of British RETAIL TRADING (q.v.). The local 'emporium', or big shop specializing mainly in drapery and household furnishing but often selling also women's wear, millinery, household hardware and ironmongery, and sometimes grocery, was a feature of Regency and Victorian England, mentioned frequently in the contemporary novel. In Mrs. Gaskell's *Cranford*, for example, Miss Matty goes into one such shop 'to buy the tea, select the silk, and then clamber up the iron corkscrew stairs that led into what was once a loft, though now a fashion showroom'. The only substantial difference between an emporium (from the Latin word for the Greek *emporion*, a shop) and the department store of the late 19th century and the present day is in scale and scope. The giant department stores of modern cities not only sell more kinds of goods, but provide more comfort for those who shop in them. In the London suburbs, as well as in the larger provincial towns, there are many small-scale department stores which from small beginnings have become large stores. Those in the Brixton, Balham, Clapham, Peckham, Holloway, and Stratford districts of London are examples of this.

The arguments in favour of the department store are that customers find it convenient to be able to do a lot of shopping under one roof, and that, as they walk through the store, they may be tempted to buy other goods besides those they have specifically come to buy. To attract the customer and display goods to advantage, department stores must have an atmosphere of spaciousness and even luxury. A great deal of what might be selling-space is devoted to passageways, corridors, and staircases, and to restaurants, cafés, lifts, escalators, and very often banking halls. These things cost much money, and the bill for lighting and heating is a large item.

To provide these facilities without charging

prices observably higher than those elsewhere, it is necessary that department stores should be able to buy on a large scale and, hence, cheaply. Indeed since the war the 'traditional' department stores have been losing ground to specialist multiple stores which could buy more cheaply. Therefore of recent years a number of previously independent department stores have come under a single ownership and management. Many of the companies control establishments both in London and in the big provincial cities. 'Chain' stores, like Woolworths, are a parallel but separate development, selling cheaper goods, providing for a different type of customer, and providing little comfort. From them, however, has developed the kind of store typified by the Marks and Spencer organization. They are mainly, but not exclusively, concerned with clothing, offering as wide a range of classes as a normal department store, but a narrower range of varieties. They enjoy much more buying power, and indeed control over manufacturers' standards, than any ordinary department store, and they sell cheaply in austere surroundings. This is the type of department store which is growing most rapidly.

See also SELF-SERVICE STORES; MULTIPLE SHOPS.

DEPOSIT ACCOUNT, *see* BANK ACCOUNTS.

DEPRECIATION. This means the decrease in the value of a business firm's property as compared with its value when first bought or constructed. The plant and machinery of a factory are particularly liable to depreciation. Wear and tear is the main reason, for even with good maintenance and repair no machine will last for ever, or work as well after years of use as it did when first bought. Machines may also lose value because they are superseded by better or more up-to-date machines; the reason for their depreciation is then called 'obsolescence'. Freehold property may depreciate as time goes on, in spite of careful maintenance and repairs; leasehold property depreciates so far as to possess no value at all when the term of the lease expires, for the owner will then lose his right to occupy and use the property (*see* PROPERTY LAW, Vol. X).

When a business firm makes up its accounts at the end of its trading year, to find out its profit or loss for the period (*see* BOOK-KEEPING), the amount of depreciation that various items of property have suffered should be allowed for in the accounts. There are several ways in which these depreciation allowances may be calculated. Some are simple and some are rather complicated, and much depends on the nature of the property concerned. It is easy to work out the amount that must be allowed for every year as the depreciation on leasehold property, for it is definitely known in advance that on a certain date such property will be of no value at all, and the problem is merely one of simple arithmetic. But many depreciation calculations must to a large extent be guesswork, although the more polite word 'estimate' is used by accountants. The total amount of depreciation for the year is one of the expenses of the business and should be subtracted from the trading profit earned in order to arrive at the true net profit.

The Companies Act of 1948 compelled most LIMITED COMPANIES (q.v.) to state clearly in their balance sheets the original cost of various items of property, and the cumulative total of depreciation allowed year by year up to the date of the accounts, so that shareholders and others studying the balance sheets could make sure that depreciation had been reasonably allowed for, and that the value of the various items of property had not been overstated.

See also BOOK-KEEPING.

DEPRESSION, *see* TRADE CYCLE.

DESIGN, *see* Vol. XII: DESIGN; INDUSTRIAL ART.

DETERGENTS, *see* SOAP AND DETERGENT MANUFACTURE.

DIAMOND INDUSTRY. The earliest diamonds known in the West came from India. In the 18th century they were found in Brazil, and in 1866 deposits were found near Kimberley, in South Africa. Though evidence of extensive deposits of diamonds has recently been found in Siberia, the continent of Africa still produces nearly all of the world's gem and industrial diamonds.

1. DIAMOND-MINING. Diamonds are found below the surface in various formations of rocks and in the gravels of river-beds (*see* DIAMONDS, Vol. III). They used to be mined or washed by the methods used in early GOLD-MINING (q.v.). The diamonds of the Kimberley area are mined by more modern methods. Below the surface layer

De Beers Consolidated Mines

DEEP IN A DIAMOND MINE AT KIMBERLEY

The conveyor belt carries the diamond-bearing blue ground which has been blasted from its place in the volcanic pipe, to the shaft in which it is hoisted to the surface

of yellow volcanic rock there lies a deep diamond-bearing layer of a distinct bluish colour. This is known as 'blue ground' and goes down to unknown depths in roughly circular deposits known as 'pipes'. These are mined from shafts put down outside the perimeter. Once the blue ground has been hoisted it is crushed, hand sorted, and screened into small particles. It is then conveyed to the washing plant where it is washed down with water into a muddy consistency from which it is easy to release the diamonds. Some 90% of this solution is known not to contain any diamonds and will be passed to the waste dumps, but the remaining 10%, or 'concentrate' as it is called, is sealed in trucks and taken to the grease tables, the final stage of the recovery operation. These are sloping and vibrating tables covered with a layer of highly refined grease. The concentrate is washed over the tables and the diamonds, because they have a strange affinity for grease, stick to the grease while the rock particles and waste solution flow off the tables. The grease is periodically scraped off the tables and the diamonds recovered. Before the grease tables were first used, all the concentrate from the washing process had to be sorted by hand.

2. Cutting and Polishing. The most valuable diamonds are blue-white stones of perfect shape and quality; the lowest category, called 'boart', consists of imperfectly crystallised diamonds of various shapes, sizes, and colours, often crushed into powder for industrial purposes. There are over 2,000 different classifications of rough diamonds. Until diamonds are cut and polished they do not sparkle like those seen in jewellers' shops. There are several varieties of diamond cuts, one of the most popular being the 'brilliant', which is a favourite for use in engagement rings. Other diamond cuts are the 'Emerald' cut (so-called because emeralds are often cut this way), which is oblong or square, with facets polished diagonally across the corners; the 'Marquise' cut, which is usually long and narrow and pointed like a boat; 'Pear-shaped', which is often used in pendants; and 'Baguettes', which are straight-sided stones used to form patterns in jewellery and which are also favourite side stones for rings.

In a rather crude form the cutting and polishing of gems was known to the ancient Egyptians, and in the Middle Ages there were gem-cutters' guilds in north-west Europe. A revolutionary change in methods of cutting and polishing was made in 1476 when Ludwig van Berquen, of Bruges, invented the use of a swiftly revolving wheel with its edge faced with diamond powder. Diamond itself is the only mineral hard enough to cut and polish diamonds. It may be necessary to split or cleave the larger stones before they are cut or polished; every diamond has a natural line of cleavage, along which it may be split by a sharp blow with a cutting edge.

A fully cut 'brilliant' diamond has 58 facets symmetrically arranged, while other cuts have fewer facets. For cutting or faceting, the stones are fixed into copper holders and held against a wheel, edged with a mixture of oil and fine diamond dust, which is revolved at about 2,500 revolutions a minute. The main cutting and polishing centres are in Belgium, Great Britain, Holland, Israel, and the U.S.A. Belgium and Holland have been famous centres of the industry since the Middle Ages.

The jewel value of brilliants depends greatly upon their colour or purity. The usual colours

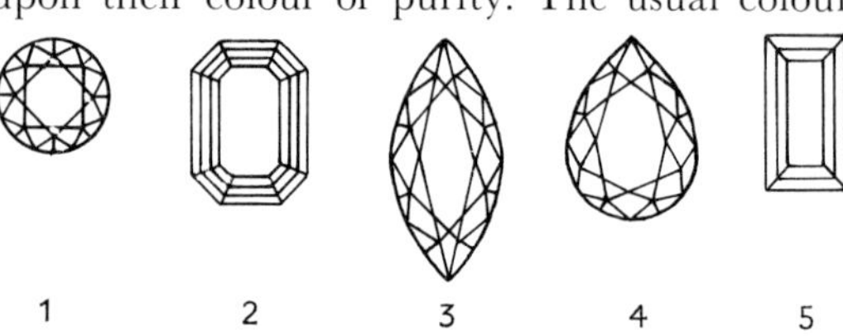

DIAMOND CUTS

1. Brilliant. 2. Emerald-cut. 3. Marquise. 4. Pear-shaped. 5. Baguette

of diamonds are white, yellow, brown, green, or blue-white; the blue-white brilliants are the stones of the finest purity and so command the highest prices. During their formation some diamonds absorb metallic oxides from the surrounding rocks and take on their colour. Thus black, red, and pink diamonds have occasionally been found.

3. THE TRADE IN DIAMONDS. Gem diamonds are a luxury, and the demand for luxuries changes much more than for necessities. If supply were not controlled in some way, changes in demand would lead to wide and disturbing movements in the price of diamonds. For these reasons the trade in diamonds has been closely controlled and illicit diamond-buying (I.D.B.) was made a punishable offence by the Government of what was then Cape Colony.

Industrial diamonds are much used in industry for cutting and grinding. The Congo produces 80% of the world's natural industrial diamonds. Such diamonds are fixed into the rock-drills used in mining and civil engineering, for driving holes into rock before blasting, and for tunnelling and sinking bore-holes (*see* MINING ENGINEERING, Vol. VIII). They are also used for edging cutting blades and tools, and band, circular, or wire saws for sawing stone. Diamond-faced tools are used for cutting and drilling glass and porcelain, for engraving delicate mathematical and scientific scales, and for dentists' drills. Diamond has also been found to be the best material for use in fine wire drawing; a tapering hole is made in a piece of diamond, through which is pulled the rod being drawn into wire. Industrial diamonds are also used as bearings or jewels in watches and electric meters. Processes have now been invented for the production of synthetic industrial diamonds, but these are of a size which only lends itself to use as an abrasive.

De Beers Consolidated Mines

DIAMOND CUTTING, OR FACETING

The diamond is set into a dop and held down on to a revolving iron disc coated with oil and diamond dust. The cutter checks the angles between facets continually

Diamonds are dealt in by weight. The unit used is the carat, and there are 5 million carats to a ton (a carat equals $\frac{1}{142}$ ounce).

See also JEWELLERY TRADE.
See also Vol. III: DIAMONDS.

DISCOUNT, *see* BANK-RATE; BILLS OF EXCHANGE.

DISPENSING, *see* PHARMACY.

DISTILLATION. Many industries use the process of distillation. The making of perfume, cosmetics, whisky, brandy and other spirits, and of industrial alcohol depends on distillation. It is an essential process in oil refining. It is also used at sea, and in countries without fresh water, for making drinkable water out of salt or brackish water.

Distillation depends on the fact that different liquids boil at different temperatures. A mixture of two liquids can therefore be separated by heating it to the temperature at which the liquid with the lower boiling-point boils. Its vapour is then condensed by cooling, and the liquid with the higher boiling-point is left behind. For example, wine, which is a mixture of water and alcohol, is distilled to produce brandy by heating it to the boiling-point of alcohol. The alcohol vapour comes off and is condensed to form brandy. Solids such as tar which vaporize at a comparatively low temperature can be distilled in the same way as liquids.

The temperature at which any liquid boils depends upon the PRESSURE of the atmosphere (q.v. Vol. III). If the pressure on its surface is lessened, the boiling-point decreases; and high-boiling substances are often conveniently distilled by combining a moderately high temperature with reduced pressure. When it is not practicable to vary the pressure, liquids not dissolvable in water can often be distilled by allowing steam to mix with their vapour. Many liquids such as crude oil consist of a mixture of several chemical compounds, each having a different boiling-point. Such liquids can be distilled in stages. The compounds with the lowest boiling-point are distilled off first; then,

Distillers Co.

MODEL OF A COFFEY STILL

The analyser is on the right, the rectifier in the middle. The distilled liquid is collected in the container on the left

as the temperature is raised, those with a higher boiling-point are distilled; and so on. The different distillates from this multiple distillation process are called 'fractions', and the process is called 'fractionation'.

'Destructive distillation' is the technical name given by chemists to the process of breaking down the chemical structure of a material by heating it without access of air. CHARCOAL (q.v.), for example, is made by the destructive distillation of wood or bones, and coke (*see* COKE OVENS, Vol. VIII) by the destructive distillation of coal. The process was originally worked to obtain the residue left in the 'retort', but now important uses have been found for the other substances (such as tar) which are formed and which vaporize, and are then condensed.

For the simplest distillations in a laboratory the liquid to be distilled is placed in a glass retort with a long tapering neck, and heat is applied (Fig. A). If the cooling effect of the air on the long glass neck is insufficient to condense the vapours, the retort is replaced by a flask to which is connected a condenser—a long central tube of glass, surrounded by a glass 'jacket' with an inlet connected to a running cold-water tap, and an outlet to a tube discharging into a sink (Fig. B). As the vapour comes away from the flask, it is condensed to liquid in the colder temperature of the central tube, and is then drawn off. Industrial and the more elaborate laboratory condensers are made on the same principle, but a spiral coil or 'worm' takes the place of the straight central tube, and condensation takes place more quickly and efficiently because a greater surface is constantly exposed to the cooling influence of the surrounding running water. The complete apparatus, consisting of retort, condenser, and receiver, is called a 'still'. In industry the still and its connexions, including the 'worm', are generally made of metal, often copper, but sometimes stainless steel or even silver is chosen, so that it is not corroded by the vapours and liquids used. The copper 'pot' still, used in the distillation of WHISKY (q.v.), is of this type.

The disadvantage of the simple laboratory still and the pot still of the type described is that they can only operate intermittently, and the retort must be freshly charged for each distillation. Another disadvantage is that they do not lend themselves to the separation of mixtures of several liquids, each with a different boiling or condensing point. A practical apparatus that would do this was invented about 1830, and this is still often called by the name of its inventor, Aeneas Coffey. In the whisky industry it is more usually called a 'patent' still. Coffey's still has since been improved, but its principle remains unchanged.

A modern Coffey still consists essentially of

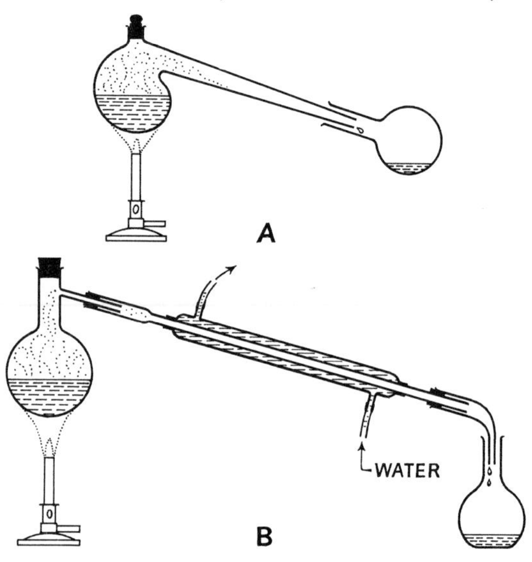

A. SIMPLE DISTILLATION. B. USING A CONDENSER

two vertical fractionating columns, called the 'analyser' and the 'rectifier'. Each is subdivided horizontally into a series of separate chambers, by means of perforated copper plates. Steam is allowed to pass into the bottom of the analyser, and to rise, at considerable pressure, through the holes in the plates. The liquid mixture to be distilled is introduced through the top of the analyser, and is prevented by the pressure of the ascending steam from falling through the holes in the plates. The hot steam, bubbling through the liquid mixture on the plates, vaporizes much of it, and carries off the vapours to the next column, the rectifier; liquid that has escaped vaporization collects on the plates, is carried away in a pipe, and pumped again to the top of the analyser. In the rectifier, liquid with the highest boiling-point tends to condense nearest to the vapour inlet; and, by using a suitable number of perforated plates, the vapour mixture can be caused to condense into the required number of liquid 'fractions', each drawn off at an appropriate level in the column.

This method of steam distillation does not suit all liquids: in the distillation of oil, for example (*see* OIL REFINING), steam is only used for a final cleansing or 'stripping' process. The liquid mixture is first vaporized, and then condensed into 'fractions' in a 'fractionating tower' subdivided into chambers and working on the same general principles as the rectifier of a patent still.

DIVIDEND. This usually means payments made to people who own STOCKS AND SHARES in LIMITED COMPANIES (qq.v.). Under British law dividends may only be paid out of earned profits, although they do not have to be paid out of the profits of the current year: they may be paid out of the accumulated profits of past years.

Dividends on CAPITAL (q.v.) may be expressed as a percentage of the capital or otherwise. Dividends on stocks are always expressed at so much per cent. For example, if a company with a capital of £100,000 in ordinary stock earns a profit of £11,000, it may decide to distribute £10,000 of this in dividend, putting £1,000 to reserve. It would then declare a dividend of 10% on the ordinary stock of the company, which means that every holder of ordinary stock would be paid a dividend at the rate of £10 for every £100 of stock he held. Dividends on shares are usually expressed as a rate per share: a company with a capital of £100,000 in £1 shares would distribute a 10% dividend by declaring a dividend of 2*s*. per share.

The word 'dividend' is also used to describe instalments paid out of the estate of a bankrupt to his creditors (*see* BANKRUPTCY, Vol. X), and also (often in its shortened form, 'divy') for the rebate on the value of purchases given by CO-OPERATIVE SOCIETIES (q.v.) to their members.

See also INTEREST; PROFITS.

DIVISION OF LABOUR. This means that workers specialize in one form of employment, instead of spending their working-day on a series of different tasks. Strength, skill, and intelligence differ very much from man to man, and those who are good at some things may be bad at others. Trying to do everything for oneself can lead to everything being done inefficiently; a jack-of-all-trades is often master of none.

The history of man's economic life, that is, of his efforts to supply himself with his material wants, such as food, clothing, and shelter, is therefore a history of increasing division of labour, or specialization at one particular job. Primitive man looked after himself; he hunted animals for food, clothed himself in their skins or furs, and either lived in caves that nature had already provided or made rough huts out of branches and animal skins. But even in the life of primitive man there was an elementary division of labour between man and woman; and at a very early stage in man's development the man hunted and fished while the woman cooked, made pots and clothes, and looked after the children. Our modern and highly complex system of division of labour has developed, step by step, from this early and primitive specialization. Each step has been taken because it has led to greater efficiency in the production of goods: either to better quality, or to a larger quantity turned out in a given time, or to both.

Division of labour may be either simple or complex. The division is simple when groups of people specialize in different trades or crafts: some people are farmers, some are blacksmiths, some are builders, some are clothworkers, some are priests, and so on. The STANDARD OF LIVING (q.v.) of the people living in a social group where simple division of labour is practised will be higher than it would be if no division of labour existed. The farmer's annual output of farm

Monotype Corporation

A MACHINIST OPERATING A VERTICAL MILLING MACHINE WHICH IS SHAPING A PIECE OF METAL TO FORM PART OF A PRINTING MACHINE

produce, the clothworker's weekly output of cloth, and so on, will be greater if each person is allowed to concentrate on the job for which he is best fitted. Skill of this kind is often handed down from father to son.

Complex division of labour exists when crafts or trades become split up into sub-crafts or sub-trades, or into a series of consecutive processes. Under simple division of labour there might be the separate trade of builder, but at different times during the day or week a builder might be a mason, a bricklayer, a carpenter or joiner, a plumber, a slater or tiler, and a labourer carrying about stone, bricks, mortar, sand, and cement. This would lead to inefficiency, as the skill of an able craftsman at one particular job would be wasted on attempts to do other jobs, or on mere unskilled labour. A system of complex division of labour, in which each general trade, such as building, has specialists in its various sub-branches, makes for greater efficiency, greater cheapness, and better quality of workmanship.

A more advanced stage is reached when labour is divided not by sub-trades but by processes. This happens in modern machine-production, when a machinist is not a general machinist, passing from one process to another, but is occupied with only one process in a series. This more advanced division of labour has generally been found to make for greater output and better work, although there is a danger that it may lead to boredom and monotony: in which case a personnel or staff manager must specialize in overcoming these tendencies, assisted perhaps by the technique of the psychologist (*see* INDUSTRIAL PSYCHOLOGY).

Differences between one country and another, or between areas of the same country; differences of soil, of climate, of mineral deposits, of physical contour, of human development lead to geographical or territorial division of labour. The damp climate of Lancashire, for instance, may make it easier to spin in that county the delicate and brittle fibres of the cotton plant. The soil and climate of Canada may be ideal for the growing of wheat. The Union of South Africa may possess deposits of diamonds or of gold-bearing quartz. The *meseta*, or high, dry table-land of Spain, may suit admirably the merino sheep.

All these forms of division of labour not only make for a great diversity between the various persons of a country, and between the populations of different countries, but they lead also to a cheaper and more bountiful production of wealth, as the economist calls the goods and services that men consume in order to satisfy their material and spiritual wants. But they also have other consequences. They create great human and social problems. These arise because there is a division of labour between the governors and the governed, the managers and the technical workers, the professions and the trades, the brain-workers and the manual workers, the economically rich nations and the economically poor ones. Such division nearly always leads to differences in the rewards and WAGES (q.v.) received by the various groups, and to the separation of people into different social classes.

Complicated division of labour of this kind usually leads to still further division. As soon as the division of labour has got beyond the family and has affected small mixed groups of workers in a village, town, or district, it is certain that the specialists in different trades or processes of manufacture will be producing a surplus of goods or services beyond their own personal or family requirements. The builder, for example, will have a house of his own already, and will not wish to live in the others he builds; the clothworker's family can perhaps consume what he makes in a tenth of his working time, but he is faced with the task of disposing of what he makes in the other nine-tenths. All these surpluses of goods must be disposed of, or sold, in some way. So must men's services, for the village schoolmaster or doctor, for instance, does not wish to consume his whole output of education or medical knowledge. All sorts of problems therefore arise connected with EXCHANGE AND TRADE, SUPPLY AND DEMAND, VALUE AND PRICE, UNEMPLOYMENT, and—if the surpluses have to be disposed of outside the country where they have been produced—RATES OF EXCHANGE (qq.v.). Finally, the amount of division of labour already existing will have to be expanded by people who specialize not in producing goods but in finding a market for them and distributing them, and in matters connected with MONEY and BANKING (qq.v.).

So in a modern community division of labour is not only extensive but complex. Not only is each separate trade or industry a part of this division, but in each of these there is a further subdivision. There arises also a vast and varied army of specialists, such as advertising agents, auctioneers, shopkeepers, agents, travellers and representatives, bankers and their clerks, financiers, stockbrokers and stockjobbers, pawnbrokers, accountants, brokers, managers, and transport workers of all kinds. These people do not directly produce goods, but the services of most are essential to our complex modern scheme of production and distribution. Those who pay for their services could not perform their specialized tasks as cheaply themselves.

See also LABOUR; UNEMPLOYMENT; SUPPLY AND DEMAND; INDUSTRIAL REVOLUTION; DOMESTIC SYSTEM.

DOCKS, *see* WAREHOUSES; *see also* Vol. IV: PORTS AND HARBOURS.

DOMESTIC SYSTEM. This means production by workers in their own houses, with comparatively simple tools or machinery. The system covered many different sorts of manufacture, and took two principal forms. In one, the small family producers would sell their wares direct to a merchant or middleman, who would then offer them on the market. In the other, the system was more complicated. A big merchant would supply the workman with materials, and then collect the manufactured goods back from him. He would pay the workman piece-rate WAGES (q.v.), so much per piece of work accomplished. In this second form, the so-called 'putting-out system', there was often considerable specialization of processes, or DIVISION OF LABOUR (q.v.). In making-up wool, the combers, carders, and spinners would carry out only one process in their houses, and the putter-out would then pass on the unfinished articles to a second set of domestic workers to improve them or finish them off.

The putting-out system was an old one, and many putters-out grew very wealthy by it. Caxton writes that the mother of St. Edmund Rich, Mabel the Rich of Abingdon, who lived in the 13th century, 'put out wool for to spin'. The system became far more important in Tudor times. The wealthy clothiers, finding their enterprise cramped by the restrictions of the guild system which laid down standards of work and rates of pay (*see* CRAFT GUILDS), moved from the towns to find workers in the peasants' cottages throughout the country villages. In such isolated surroundings, where there was no tradition of industrial employment, they could pay smaller wages and expect bigger production. The system lowered costs and prices, and increased the profits of the new leaders of industrial enterprise. Although the system was most general in the textile industries, it was to be found also in the hardware districts of the Midlands.

In the West Riding of Yorkshire the cottage manufacturer always bought his own wool, spun it for himself, and sold it to the merchants. He was no mere wage-earner, but an independent producer. In the West of England, where the woollen industry was still very important, the workman never owned the material or the goods, and was simply paid a piece-rate or 'making-wage' by the clothier who employed him. When the factory system began to spread at the beginning of the 19th century, rich clothiers, even in the West Riding of Yorkshire, began to undermine the independence of the small domestic producer. Power was becoming concentrated in the hands of the big producers.

From the worker's point of view the chief feature of the system was that he worked at home. The family, not the factory, was the working unit. The weaver sat at his loom, the wife at her spinning wheel, and the children helped as much as they could, which was often a great deal. Conditions were often extremely difficult for the workers. They had to work long hours, either for small wages or low profits, and in either case they bore the whole burden of bad trade and

Parker Gallery

A FAMILY PREPARING FLAX FOR SPINNING

Linen fibre is extracted from the stem of the flax by beetling and scutching (beating with a mallet and knife) and hackling (drawing it through wires). Coloured engraving by N. Hincks, 1791

unemployment. A ballad of the late 17th century tells of a merchant putter-out saying of himself and his workers:

> If trade goes dead, we will presently show it,
> But if it grows good, they never shall know it . . .
> Our workmen do work hard, but we live at ease;
> We go when we will and we come as we please.

Insecurity of livelihood was coupled with the necessity for hard work. Children were expected to do a good share of this. Defoe, the author of *Robinson Crusoe*, who sang the praises of the domestic system at Halifax in Yorkshire, boasted that there was 'hardly any thing above 4 years old but its hands are sufficient to itself': that is to say, busily at work. Another writer on the Halifax of those days claimed that this employment 'not only keeps their little minds from vice but . . . takes a heavy burden from their poor parents'. At Norwich, it was claimed that 'the very children, after 4 or 5 years, could everyone earn their own bread'. Far from the factory system being the start of child-labour—as it is often accused of being—it merely threw the spotlight on it, and quickened the public conscience.

Yet the domestic system had compensations. The worker could often combine industry and agriculture. There were many small clothiers' properties in Yorkshire, for example, from 3 to 15 acres of land on which the owners kept a cow or two, a pony or donkey, and perhaps a few chickens and ducks.

The workman also could take rather more holidays in his own time than he was able to do after the INDUSTRIAL REVOLUTION (q.v.) had established a new factory discipline. Indeed, this kind of worker was often taken to task for idleness. It was said that if he could earn enough to live on in 3 days' work, he would enjoy himself for the rest of the week, usually in the ale-house. This was partly a reaction against the extreme monotony of his work: for throwing a shuttle backwards and forwards was a tiring task, which only came to an end with the development of a machine—in this case the flying shuttle, invented by Kay in 1733. A London writer, Francis Place, described the lot of these workers: 'I know not how to describe the sickening aversion which at times steals over the working man and utterly disables him . . . from following his usual occupation, and compels him to indulge in idleness. I have felt it, resisted it to the utmost of my power, but have been obliged to submit and turn away from my work. This is the case with every workman I have ever known.'

The domestic system was destroyed, or reduced to very small areas of industry, by the factory system. This change-over took a long time, mainly in the 19th century. The domestic system had obvious disadvantages from the employer's point of view. Carrying and fetching raw materials and finished goods took up far too much valuable time. It left the worker with so much freedom that he could never be relied upon. The factory was a more convenient working unit, where workers could be disciplined, and extra profits secured from large-scale working.

While the new factories were being built and extended, workers on the old system were the victims of the change-over. The plight of the handloom weavers was a serious one in the early 19th century, and their complaints played a large part in such movements of social unrest as Chartism (*see* TRADE UNIONS, HISTORY OF). Their wages went steadily down. In 1799 they were earning on an average 26*s.* 8*d.* a week; during 1825–32 wages were down to 6*s.* 4*d.*; and in the 1840's, the 'hungry forties' as they were called, many workers died of starvation. The weaving of cotton cloth, like the spinning of cotton yarn, was turned into a factory industry. The transformation of the woollen industry was less quick, and that of the knitting trades even slower. But the new forces of economic expansion and concentration eventually blotted out the old method of production.

See also LABOUR; CRAFT GUILDS; FACTORY ORGANIZATION; TRADE UNIONS, HISTORY OF; DIVISION OF LABOUR.

DOUBLE ENTRY, *see* BOOK-KEEPING.

DRIED FOOD. Centuries ago man discovered that removing moisture from foods helps to preserve it and that the easiest way to do this is to expose food to sun and wind. In this way the North American Indians produce pemmican (dried meat ground into powder and made into cakes), the Scandinavians stockfish, the Tartars dried mares' milk, the Arabs dried dates and 'apricot leather'.

All foods contain water—fruit and raw vegetables contain between 75% and 90% of water, potatoes and other root vegetables 80%, lean meat from 55% to 65%, and fish anything from 65% to 80%, depending on how fatty it is. If this water is removed, the activity of the enzymes and bacteria which causes food to go bad is checked. Salting, smoking, pickling, and fermentation processes have similar effects. Methods of drying and salting foods in the home are described in the FOOD PRESERVATION article in Volume XI.

Fruit is still sun-dried in Asia Minor, Greece, Spain, and other Mediterranean countries, and also in California, South Africa, and Australia. The methods used vary, but in general the fruit is spread out on trays in a drying yard in hot sun. In order to prevent darkening, pears, peaches and apricots are exposed to the fumes of burning sulphur before drying; plums for making prunes and certain varieties of grapes for making raisins, sultanas, and currants are dipped in an alkaline solution in order to crack the skins of the fruit slightly and remove their wax coating, so increasing the rate of drying.

Today most foods can be dried mechanically. The conventional method of dehydration is to put food in chambers through which hot air is blown at a constant temperature, and a certain degree of humidity. This is the usual method for drying vegetables, which are first cut into strips, shreds, or slices, and then blanched in steam or boiling water. Whole peas and beans and minced meat and fish can also be dried in this way.

Liquids such as milk, coffee, tea, soups, and eggs may be dried by spreading over a heated horizontal steel cylinder or by spraying them into a chamber through which a current of hot air passes. In the first case the dried material is scraped off the roller as a thin film which is then broken up into relatively coarse flakes; in the second case it falls to the bottom of the chamber as a fine powder. Where individual pieces of

Food Trade Review

A DRYING PLANT FOR PREPARING SOUP MIXES

Ingredients, such as flour, are sucked up the cylinders and dried before being mixed together

meat and vegetables are required in a soup, the ingredients are dried separately and then mixed.

Accelerated freeze-drying (A.F.D.) is a newer method of dehydrating food, but it is too expensive to be widely used. The food is frozen first and then put in a vacuum chamber where it is heated gently. The ice in the food evaporates, the vapour is removed by vacuum pumps and condensers, leaving a porous material which will reabsorb water quickly. One advantage of the freeze-drying process is that meat and fish can be dried in slices up to $\frac{1}{2}$ in. thick; another is that fruit keeps its tart flavour. Liquids and vegetables can also be freeze-dried.

Air-dried foods take up less room and weigh less than the same food in cans or frozen, and they do not need to be stored in special conditions. For these reasons they are invaluable to climbers, explorers, and armies who have little storage space. They are also popular with housewives because it takes so little time to cook them.

DRUGS, *see* PHARMACY.

DRY-CLEANING. 1. HISTORY. The modern practice that we know as dry-cleaning originated in France, where as early as 1850 a cleaning process without moisture—*nettoyage à sec*—was carried out with 'camphene', an oil of turpentine distilled for burning in lamps. Dirt is mainly held in a fabric by a thin film of grease, and the advantage of using a spirit is that it removes the grease and dirt without disturbing the finish, colour, or texture, as cleaning with water often does. Dry-cleaning was unknown in the United Kingdom until 1866, when a Scottish firm in Perth brought a number of men from a Paris dyeing and cleaning works to use the French method. The new industry spread to England, mainly in centralized factories, which got their work through branch offices in various towns.

Until the First World War dry-cleaning was looked upon largely as a luxury. The need to clean thousands of uniforms during the war and the high prices of clothes after the war made dry-cleaning popular, and steam-pressing machinery shortened the time taken over pressing garments. In the 1920's 'valet' pressing shops sprang up. These did not undertake their own dry-cleaning but sent the garments to the cleaning factories, which returned them unpressed to the 'valet' shops. Later, small local dry-cleaning plants were opened, using non-inflammable solvents.

Many dry-cleaning firms also dye and moth-proof garments and household fabrics. Some firms do fireproofing and waterproofing as well. After the Second World War dyers and cleaners were twice as much in demand as before it.

2. TECHNIQUE. The main cleaning solvent in use today is perchlorethylene, although white spirit is still used. Both have their particular merits. A solvent must be chemically stable both in storage and under repeated distillation.

Each article sent to be cleaned is first examined for tears and for oddments left in the pockets. Then it is given an identification number, and sorted into the proper bin according to the colour, weight, and nature of the material. Silks and woollens, and light colours and dark, are separated from each other, as also heavy and light garments. Articles next go to the dry-cleaning machine, in which they are stirred and dipped in the cleaning solvent. The cleaning liquid is kept clear by 'clarification', the dirty liquid being passed through a filter which keeps back the particles of dirt. After the dirt has been extracted the clean solvent is returned to the machine.

When all possible dirt has been removed by the action of the solvent, articles are placed in an extractor, a spinning device which draws off most of the excess solvent by centrifugal force; the final traces are then dispersed by evaporation in a dryer through which air passes. The article goes next to the 'spotter', whose task is to take out any stains which may have resisted the cleaning solvent; this delicate work is usually done by trained girls. These marks are removed by chemicals which loosen and then dissolve the staining substances. A spotter must be familiar with all types of fabrics—wool, silk, linen, rayon, nylon, crêpe, satin, taffeta, and so on—and must know which chemical will remove a stain without damage to the fabric and its colouring. Much of the art of spotting lies in 'shading out' gradually from the centre of the mark, so that no unsightly ring will remain. Then the articles pass, often by overhead conveyor, to the finishing department. Here they are 'reshaped', and pressed by steam and hot-air machines. Each article is inspected before being sent to the customer.

The Dyers and Cleaners Research Organization conducts the industry's research and examines the reaction of new textiles to dry-cleaning.

See also Dyes.
See also Vol. XI: Clothes, Care of.

Imperial Chemical Industries Ltd.

INDIAN DYERS AT WORK

Hanks of cotton yarn are being dyed in a 'direct dye' bath containing a solution of dyestuff in water

DYES. 1. Early History. Dyed fabrics dating from 2000 B.C. or earlier have been found in Egyptian tombs, and the Roman historian Pliny refers to a well established dyeing industry in ancient Egypt. Both Plutarch and Virgil mention the rich purple now often referred to as 'Tyrian purple', and in the Bible there are several references to dyed hangings and garments, as in the story of Joseph's coat of many colours. In early British history Queen Boadicea is said to have worn a multi-coloured tunic, and the Romans are known to have had a dyeing industry at Silchester.

The dyes used in those days were not the chemical substances which we know today as 'synthetic', or sometimes as 'coal tar', dyestuffs. The ancients had to rely for their dyes on natural materials. They used plants, wood, shellfish, or sometimes simple metal salts such as Alum (q.v.), and some of the coloured iron compounds.

Many distinct colours were produced by the ancients, yet the range of actual dyes was small. The variety was probably due to the skilful use of 'mordants'. A mordant is a chemical, generally a salt of chromium, aluminium, tin, copper, or iron. Mordants themselves are not dyes and do not necessarily colour materials at all; but when they are applied before a dye they 'key' the dye on to the fabric, and the two jointly produce a coloured effect. One mordant can be used with a number of different dyes, or one dye can be used with a whole series of mordants, to give a range of different final colours.

In the early days only the wealthy could afford the rarest dyes. Tyrian purple, extracted from a shellfish, was reserved for royalty and noblemen. The ordinary people wore dull, drab shades, such as browns, buffs, and blues.

The bulk of European cloth was dyed with extracts of plants such as safflower, woad, weld, madder, and other wild growths. In the East, where indigo grew, its characteristic blue shade was the colour most widely seen in hangings, clothes, and decorations.

One method of decoration by dyeing, that of

batik printing, is still practised in Java. There the cloth, before it is dyed, is painted with wax in a decorative pattern. The part of the cloth that is covered with wax does not absorb the coloured dye, and the result is a pattern of light lines or spaces on a coloured background. More colours can be added by waxing the dyed portions and then dipping the cloth in other dyes.

2. MODERN HISTORY. The story of the modern dye industry begins in England in 1856, when a young chemistry student, W. H. Perkin, was trying to make quinine. This valuable medicine could be got only from the bark of the cinchona tree. He failed to make quinine, and produced merely a red powder. He tried again, and produced a black substance. This, on extraction with alcohol, gave a rich, violet-coloured product which, to his amazement, dyed silk. His failure was one of the most brilliant failures in the history of industrial chemistry, for his violet-coloured compound was the tiny seed from which has grown one of the world's greatest industries—the manufacture of synthetic dyes.

This new dye was called 'Aniline Purple' or 'mauveine'. Perkin discovered it at a most favourable time, for organic chemistry was then beginning to attract research workers. Meanwhile, other scientists in France, Germany, and Britain became inspired by his pioneer work and soon began their own exploration of the new field of colour chemistry.

Within 12 years a number of new synthetic dyes had been manufactured. Within 25 years great progress had been made, both in pure scientific research and in dyeing practice in industry itself. The initiative had by this time passed into the hands of German chemists. Their discoveries in theoretical chemistry and their skill in adapting them industrially made it possible to manufacture alizarine and indigo artificially, and to develop the 'azo' dyes. Old methods were given up, and the discovery of synthetic indigo eventually ruined the indigo-planters of India.

Today, water-soluble azo dyes are still the largest class of synthetic dyes in common use. Their development was due to the work of Griess (1864), a chemist employed by a brewer in Burton, who discovered the reaction between nitrous acid and primary amines. (Amines are chemical derivatives of AMMONIA (q.v.).) Perkin's work had resulted in a dye of the type known as 'basic'. Dyes of this class are extremely brilliant in shade, but on exposure to light they tend to fade. The azo dyes can be applied to a wide range of fibres and fabrics; they are moderately fast, provide a very wide range of shades, and include the groups known as 'direct cotton', 'acid wool', and 'mordant' dyes. Dyes of the first group dye cotton directly, that is, immersion of cotton in a solution of the dye in water gives dyed cotton. The acid-wool group dye wool from an acidulated dyebath, while the mordant dyes colour materials only when applied after, or along with, a suitable mordant.

Because the azo dyes are water-soluble, their fastness to wet treatments is imperfect, particularly on cellulosic materials. But in 1880 two Englishmen, Thomas and Robert Holliday, patented a method of producing insoluble azo dyes in the fibre itself. The resulting dyeings are fast to washing, bleaching, and exposure to light.

At the beginning of the 20th century a German chemist, Bohn, prepared the first of a most famous series of dyes which later became known as 'vat dyes'. These are insoluble pigments which are made soluble by chemical reaction (a process known as 'vatting'), dyed, and then made insoluble again in the fibre. This produces dyeings that are very fast.

Until then, the colour chemists had had to deal only with natural fibres, such as cotton, wool, and linen. But now man-made fibres began to be made which had very different properties (*see* TEXTILE FIBRES, MAN-MADE). Acetate rayon caused many troubles at the outset, for it could not be dyed by any of the dyes existing on the market at the time, but in 1922 the first special dyes for colouring acetate rayon were developed in Britain. These can also be applied to the newer polyamide and polyester fibres.

In 1955 an advance of tremendous importance was made with the discovery by two British chemists, W. P. Stephen and I. D. Rattee, in Manchester, of dyes that would actually react chemically with cotton and other cellulose fibres, to give extremely fast dyeings. As a result, in the following year, 1956—the centenary of Perkin's historic discovery—the first reactive dyes became available to dyers. These new reactive dyes, now available in all colours, are notable for their ease of application (being particularly suitable for modern high-speed continuous dyeing or printing), their vivid shades, and their high fastness. They are used widely on cotton, viscose

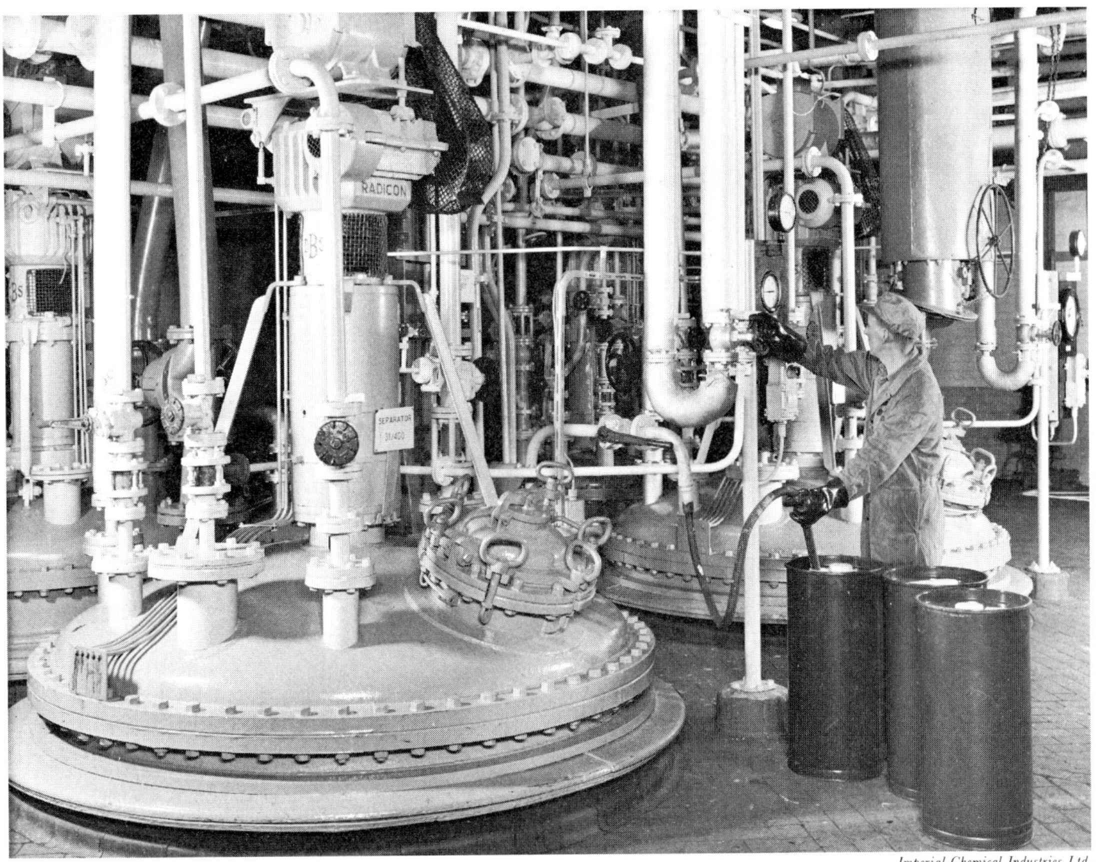

Imperial Chemical Industries Ltd.

CHEMICAL PLANT USED IN THE PREPARATION OF DYESTUFFS

rayon, and other cellulosic fibres. Different kinds of reactive dyes suitable for use on wool and nylon have also been discovered in Britain since 1955.

Dyes are used in a large number of other industries, as well as for colouring textiles. Leather, fur, paper, rubber, plastics, paint, distemper, wood, stains, buttons, and even some foodstuffs are coloured.

Thousands of different synthetic dyes are now produced, but research, both in the laboratory and in the works where dyes are used, continues in the effort to discover new and better dyes.

See also CHEMISTRY, INDUSTRIAL.

E

EARTHENWARE. This is the term used for all kinds of POTTERY (q.v.) fired at comparatively low temperatures, not exceeding 1100° C. Before it receives a glaze it is porous, may be scratched with a knife, and is granular or earthy in texture; in all these qualities it is distinct from STONEWARE (q.v.). Earthenware includes many types of pottery both glazed and unglazed: slipware, that is pottery decorated with liquid clay, lead-glazed pottery, tin-enamelled earthenware, and terracotta which is used for sculpture.

The secret of glazing earthenware with lead was discovered in Egypt, and became known to Roman and medieval potters. A special glaze, made opaque and white with tin ashes, was developed in the Near East and was brought to Spain by the Moors in the 12th century. From the 15th century knowledge of this glaze, or enamel, as it is sometimes called, spread through the rest of Europe, and earthenware glazed with it received local names: in Italy, 'maiolica' from the island of Majorca; in France, 'faience' after the pottery town of Faenza; and in Holland, 'delft'. Tin-glazed earthenware, which was made in England from 1571, is frequently called 'delftware', although the Dutch town of Delft did not become famous as a centre of manufacture until the 17th century.

Crown Copyright

MAIOLICA DISH MADE IN ITALY ABOUT 1540

It is made of tin-glazed earthenware, painted in blue with the story of Hercules and Antaeus. Victoria and Albert Museum

Coarse lead-glazed earthenware and 'delftware' are rather heavy and easily chipped. By using a new mixture of clay and other materials Staffordshire potters produced a fine cream earthenware glazed with lead suitable for everyday use. Josiah WEDGWOOD (q.v. Vol. V) developed this into his famous 'Queensware'. The discovery of kaolin or CHINA CLAY (q.v.) and china stone in Cornwall about 1768 led to further improvements, and the composition of earthenware has changed little since that time.

Earthenware was originally made in small country workshops with the potter's wheel. The first machine for making earthenware was invented in 1843. To-day most earthenware plates, cups and saucers, dishes and other vessels are mass-produced in factories by semi-automatic or completely automatic machinery, or by 'casting' in porous plaster-of-Paris moulds.

Stoke-on-Trent is the chief centre of earthenware manufacture in England. There are important manufacturers in France, Germany, Italy, Sweden, and the U.S.A.

See also POTTERY; PORCELAIN; STONEWARE.

EAST INDIA COMPANY. The Honourable East Indian Company was the greatest of the CHARTERED COMPANIES (q.v.) formed between the 14th and the 19th centuries to develop overseas trade. It was founded on 31 December 1600 by a Royal Charter granted by Queen Elizabeth to the 'Governor and Company of Merchants of London trading into the East Indies'. The first convoy, consisting of five ships under the general command of James Lancaster, left Torbay in April 1601. It reached Achin, in Sumatra, in June 1602, and returned to England with a large cargo of spices.

At the date of the first charter the world outside Europe was still not fully explored, and ideas of the exact whereabouts of the East Indies were rather vague. The term 'East Indies' in the title was originally meant to include all countries east of the Cape of Good Hope, or west of the Straits of Magellan at the southern end of South America. These extensive ideas of the lands in which the Company was to operate were soon curtailed, for the trading companies of other countries had already got a foothold in many lands.

In those days the custom was to grant exclusive rights of trading to a single company of merchants in any area. The first charter was for 15 years. The Company had, to start with, no permanent Capital (q.v.), so it bought or built ships with money lent by its members, who then used the ships to carry their own cargoes. The cargoes were sold on arrival in the East, and other cargoes were shipped home and sold in their turn; a 'voyage account' was then made out, and the proceeds were shared among the subscribers in proportion to their individual subscriptions. From the first, Profits (q.v.) were large, and on some voyages were as high as 100%.

The Company's charter was renewed in 1609 by James I. The earlier financial plan was altered, and subscribers were invited to put up money for voyages conducted by the Company as a whole, instead of voyages for their own account and profit. This decision was influenced by the disturbed state of the world. Independent ventures meant small convoys, which were much exposed to attack by Pirates (q.v. Vol. IV) or by the ships of enemy countries; a large convoy of the Company's entire fleet was stronger.

Although the main objects of the merchants founding the Company were trade and commerce, the foundation of the Company was to some extent a political move against the Dutch, who had reached the East Indies first and whom the English wished to drive out. The Dutch had been there for many years; they looked upon the East Indies, and particularly the remoter islands such as Java and Sumatra, as their own; they resented the English Company's arrival, and soon trouble began between them. The most serious incident was the Amboyna massacre of 1623, when some British settlers were tortured and killed by order of the Dutch Governor. This convinced the Company that it was hardly strong enough to claim the farther East Indies from the Dutch. It therefore confined its trading to India, Burma, and Ceylon.

This penetration into India was extremely

You do ſwear to be good and true to our Sovereign Lord the Kings Majeſty, and to his Heirs and Succeſſors, and that you will be faithful to the Governour, his Deputy and Company of Merchants of *London*, trading into the *Eaſt-Indies*, in the management of their Trade, the ſecrets of the ſaid Company which ſhall be given you in charge to conceal, by the ſaid Governour or his Deputy, you will not diſcloſe: And during the preſent joynt ſtock of this Company, you will not trade in any ſuch commodity or commodities whatſoever to or from the limits of the Companies Charter, beyond the Cape of *Good Hope*, which the Court of *Committies* have or ſhall declare from time to time, that they do or will reſerve to the ſaid Joynt Stock excluſive to any others. *So help you God.*

Meade Collection

AN OATH OF FIDELITY TO THE EAST INDIA COMPANY

successful, and was favoured by the attitude of the Mogul Emperors, who then ruled over the greater part of that country (*see* Indian Civilization, Vol. I). In 1608 Captain Hawkins sought permission to build a 'factory', or trading depot, at Surat, north of Bombay. In the south, near Madras, a factory was established at Masulipatam. In 1635 the Company was granted trading rights in Bengal and a factory was established at Hooghly, on the river of that name, north of Calcutta. In 1640 southern India headquarters were set up at Fort St. George, Madras. The charter was renewed by Oliver Cromwell in 1657. The Company now obtained the subscription of a permanent capital fund, and traded as a company, instead of merely controlling the independent trading activities of its members.

The Company had not confined its activities solely to trade and commerce. It had been forced to set up a civil administration in and around its factories; and to maintain and preserve its influence it had raised and used troops. Following the custom of the time, its ships were armed. When its charter was renewed by Charles II, the Company was given powers which gradually transformed it from a trading company into an apparatus of government. It could acquire and administer territory, fortify its possessions, issue and regulate its own coinage, engage in military and naval operations, conclude peace treaties and trading agreements with rulers of States, and generally pass the laws necessary to carry out all these duties and responsibilities. In 1662 Catherine of Braganza, the daughter of the Portuguese Royal House, married Charles II. She brought as part of her dowry some of the Portuguese possessions in western India, including the island of Bombay, with its magnificent natural harbour. In 1688 Charles II leased this prize to the East India Company at a rent of £10 a year.

To simplify and decentralize administration, the three 'presidencies', or provinces, of Bengal, Bombay, and Madras were formed. The cities of Bombay and Madras were already the Company's commercial headquarters, and they now became the administrative capitals of their respective presidencies. In 1690, after a series of local battles, Job Charnock, once an obscure clerk in the Company's Bengal service, secured Calcutta as the Company's Bengal headquarters. Calcutta became the capital of the Bengal Presidency, and later the capital of British India. From this time onwards the political history of the Company really becomes the history of British India itself. One of the greatest British statesmen in India was Robert Clive (q.v. Vol. V), who began as a clerk in the Company.

Neither in its political nor in its commercial career did the Company have an entirely smooth passage. From the late 17th century onwards its commercial interests were increasingly damaged by 'interlopers', or private traders, who voyaged in their own ships and were neither members of the Company nor bound in any way by its rules. These interlopers objected strongly to the Company's privileged position, and were determined to secure the legal right to trade on their own account. Resistance to the Company's Monopoly (q.v.) increased as the years went on. In the late 18th and early 19th centuries the disadvantages and dangers of monopoly, and the advantages of free and unrestricted trade, were pointed out by Adam Smith (q.v. Vol. V) and other economists. Their views were seized upon by the interlopers—or 'free traders'—and many statesmen and politicians became converted to their point of view. Resistance to the Company's privileges was now organized in Parliament. This movement was successful in 1813, when the Company's privileged position in Indian trade and commerce was abolished. Foreseeing that this was bound to happen, the Company had in the meantime extended its trading activities to China, and had acquired a monopoly of the China tea trade. But opposition to the Company's special position in the trade of the East as a whole was now general, and this last monopoly was taken away in 1833. The Company's trading activities diminished but its political responsibilities increased, and during the next twenty years it did much to extend the frontiers of British India and to consolidate the British hold on that country. In 1858 its organization and functions were taken over by the government of Queen Victoria as a result of the Indian Mutiny (q.v. Vol. X).

The Company's main line of communication was naturally by sea. As early as 1609 the Company constructed its own dockyard at Deptford on the south bank of the Thames, and here and elsewhere were built the famous East Indiamen. Excepting only, perhaps, the ships of the British and foreign navies, the East Indiamen were the finest and best-found ships afloat. The training and discipline of their crews were second only to those of the Royal Navy; their manning was in many respects superior, as the Company could afford good pay and conditions at a time when the Navy (q.v. Vol. X) still had to rely largely on the press-gang for recruiting. These magnificent ships were fully armed, nominally to fight pirates and rivals in self-defence, although many actions were provoked by the Company's ships. The post of master of an East Indiaman was a most profitable one, for masters were allotted a certain amount of cargo space for themselves and received also a bonus on the profits of their voyages; some masters of East Indiamen were able to retire as wealthy men after only 5 years' command.

When the trading of the Company dwindled, its administrative work grew. Addiscombe College was founded in 1809, on the same lines as Sandhurst, to train officers for the Company's army. Of the Addiscombe-trained officers, Lord

Parker Gallery

THE EAST INDIA HOUSE, LEADENHALL STREET, LONDON

Coloured engraving, 1833

Roberts, the distinguished general, was perhaps the most famous. A training college for civil administration was also needed: Haileybury, the public school just south of Hertford, began as the Honourable East India Company's College.

'Trade follows the flag' was a slogan of the 19th century. Those who used it believed that the political occupation of a country, and the setting-up of orderly government, must come before trade and commerce. The East India Company is a great example of the contrary, for in India the flag followed trade. At the summit of its power the Company touched great heights. It set out to develop trade and commerce with the East Indies. It was forced by the pressure of events gradually to drop its trading activities, to concentrate on those that were political, to administer an immense and growing territory, and finally to cede all it had built up to its parent Government.

See also CHARTERED COMPANIES; TRADE, HISTORY OF.
See also Vol. I: INDIAN CIVILIZATIONS.
See also Vol. III: INDIA.

ECONOMICS. The famous Cambridge economist, Alfred Marshall, defined economics as the study of mankind in the ordinary business of life: that is, in getting a living or in helping to satisfy the material wants of others. The word 'economics' comes from a Greek word meaning the prudent management of one's family business affairs, and has come to mean the study of business affairs in general. A study of economics should include the study of COMMERCE and INDUSTRY (qq.v.). One must know a great deal about the organization of business in one's own country and abroad before going on to study the underlying forces that control business. It is with these forces, and with what causes them to change, that the economist principally deals.

The average business man who makes or sells goods is interested in the same things as the economists; but he solves his problems very often by rough rule-of-thumb methods rather than by scientific ones, and he is more concerned with the working of his own business and less with the working of the country's or the world's business as a whole. The task of the economist is much wider than that of the business man, although many business men make use of the economist's technique without knowing it, and the best of them do this deliberately. When the business man tries to work out future changes in the market-price of his goods, or in the quantity he can profitably sell, he is doing for his own firm what the economist is continuously trying to do for the wider community. Economics is to business what MECHANICS is to ENGINEERING (qq.v. Vol. VIII). It is the theory behind the practice.

Economics is now an important science, as important as Mechanics, and quite as wide. Like other sciences, it has developed from modest and rather slow beginnings. It first began to be important in the 17th century. The early economists tried to understand the working of commerce and industry so as to advise statesmen how the general welfare of the people might be improved. The economists were able to tell the statesmen about the results likely to follow changes in the laws or customs governing trade, hours and conditions of labour, the currency, the banking system, and so on. Because of its usefulness to politicians, what is now called economics was first called Political Economy, and this title is still used at some of the universities.

'Economics' became a more popular title than 'Political Economy' towards the end of the 19th century, when most people in Britain believed that commerce and industry would flourish best without any supervision by the Government. The subject then became much more scientific. Scientists spend much of their time in trying to work out statements that are generally or universally true under all conditions, and these statements are called scientific 'laws'. Most scientific laws are also statements of cause and effect: they state that if certain circumstances change, the conditions resulting will change also. Economists try to work out the 'laws' of the business world, and on the whole they are fairly successful. Like other scientists, they have to start from certain working assumptions, and their main assumption is that everybody tries to get the greatest material satisfaction for the least cost in labour or effort or money. Economists try to work out what kinds and quantities of goods are likely to be produced and sold, and at what prices; what proportions of people's incomes will be saved and spent; how WAGES, INTEREST, rent, and PROFITS (qq.v.) will be fixed; what the value of MONEY (q.v.) will be, at home and abroad; what will be the trend of SUPPLY AND DEMAND, or the relation of VALUE AND PRICE (qq.v.); and how changes in TAXATION (q.v. Vol. X) will affect all these things. In brief, the economist tries to study what will be produced, and how this will become distributed among the various classes of the population. One of the main aids to study is the use of STATISTICS (q.v.).

As in most other sciences, there are two branches of economics: pure and applied. Pure economics is the study of a rather imaginary business world, or of a portion of it, in which people's economic behaviour is assumed to be much simpler than it actually is in the real world of everyday affairs. The applied economist tries to look at problems as they really are, with all the complications of the real world included. He applies the findings of pure economists to real situations; and his purpose is to guide the decisions of business men and politicians. Put in another way, the pure economist constructs the intellectual tools and the applied economist makes use of them. It is generally the kind of economist with a mathematical turn of mind who masters pure economics; less mathematics are needed to master applied economics. Very often the problem that an applied economist has to solve is so full of unknown quantities, which cannot be given precise values, that it is amazingly difficult for him to work out a definite answer. The applied economist must have not only a deep knowledge of his subject, but also a broad and general knowledge of human nature, combined with a flair for seizing instinctively on the real essentials of a problem. Lord KEYNES (q.v. Vol. V), one of the world's greatest economists, defined economics as a technique of thinking which assists one to the correct rather than the false conclusion. More than this cannot be claimed for economics, and the good economist is merely one less often wrong in his prophecies and conclusions than the bad one.

Economists are being increasingly used in the business world. Business men have come to realize, more and more, the necessity for planning production ahead, for only by careful planning can goods be produced cheaply, and money will be lost if a plan is carelessly embarked on and then interrupted. Business men can work out the technical details of their plans; but they want to know in what kind of business world they will have to market their goods when ready. They must try to look into the economic future, so as to find out in advance what scheme of prices, what amount of consumer demand,

Brecknell, Dolman, and Rogers Ltd.

SORTING EGGS IN A PACKING STATION

what opportunities of overseas sales, and so on will be in existence months, perhaps years, ahead when their plans have matured into actual production. Business men alone can hardly hope to solve these problems, and for their solution they are increasingly relying on the economist. The larger the typical business firm grows—and NATIONALIZATION (q.v. Vol. X) is making some firms really immense—the more need there will be in commerce and industry for the trained economist. Modern business is extremely scientific; and the more scientific it becomes the more more its planning and managerial offices resemble a laboratory of applied economics.

See also MONEY; INTERNATIONAL FINANCE.
See also Vol. X: NATIONAL FINANCE.

EGG TRADE. Through advances in the genetics, housing, nutrition, and disease control of poultry, the average number of eggs laid per hen in one year has increased from 116 in 1946/47, to over 200. Today 98% of all eggs sold in British shops are laid in the United Kingdom, compared to 50% before the Second World War.

Poultry farmers may sell their eggs either direct to the shops, at the farm gate, on retail rounds and at local markets, or to the British Egg Marketing Board. The Board is the egg-producers' own organisation, set up with the approval of Parliament, to provide a guaranteed market to all those registered with it by buying all the eggs they offer, and selling them at centrally fixed prices to the wholesalers, many of whom are packers as well. The Board collects the eggs from the farms at least once a week and sends them to packing stations. There, 10,000 eggs per hour are automatically 'candled' (i.e. a strong light is shone through them to show up any defects), and graded into first quality, as 'Large', 'Standard', 'Medium', 'Small', and 'Extra Small'. Those for retail trade are packed into cartons of 6 or 12.

The Board processes any surplus first-quality eggs at peak periods of production, as well as all second-quality and 'extra small' eggs into egg products, either whole, or separated into yolk and albumen (white). These are sold mainly to the bakery and confectionery industries.

Since the report of a Re-organisation Commission on the marketing of eggs, the Minister of Agriculture, Fisheries and Food announced in

January, 1969, that the Government intended to establish a central authority for eggs representing producer, trade, and consumer interests which would replace the British Egg Marketing Board from 1st April, 1971. All egg prices would then be determined by the conditions of the commercial market.

See also Vol. VI: POULTRY.

ENAMEL. 1. TECHNIQUE. Enamel is a glassy or vitreous substance, very similar to flint GLASS (q.v.), which is melted under great heat and then spread as a thin layer over metal objects as a decoration. Enamelling is done on gold, silver, platinum, copper, or iron. It is at its best when pure metals are used, but alloys such as brass, gold of 22 carat or less, and standard silver are also suitable.

Before the enamel is melted it has the appearance of coarse powder or tiny chips of hard material. This material, called 'flux', consists of natural stone (flint or silica) mixed with red lead, borax, and other salts. To give the enamel the colour which the artist wishes, oxides of metals are mixed with the flux. The chief oxides and the colours which result are: iron for red; lead for yellow; copper for blue or red; tin for milky white.

The flux is fused at a high temperature (700–900° C.) for a long time, until a clear, transparent glass is produced. This is ground down to a fine powder, which is laid on the metal and heated again. The temperature is such that not only will the enamel melt, but the surface of the metal will be softened enough to unite with it permanently. After this firing, the enamel can be rubbed down to make it smooth and polished. The colours must be kept separate from each other, or they would mix when heated. To ensure this there is a band of metal between each colour. This band is made in one of two ways, either by the *champlevé* or the *cloisonné* method. In *champlevé*, the enamel is laid in hollows sunk into the surface of the metal. The metal is usually cast with these hollows ready. *Cloisonné* means 'in cells': strips of metal are soldered to the surface of the object, thus producing small enclosures, which are filled with enamel. Finer designs can be produced by this method.

Another method is to cover the whole ground with translucent enamel of one colour through which are seen the metal patterns beneath. These patterns may be engine-turned (mechanically cut) or chased (*see* GOLD AND SILVERWORK).

Ashmolean Museum

CHAMPLEVÉ ENAMEL MOUNT FROM A CROSS

The figure is metal with the head in relief and the background is filled with coloured enamels. Made at Limoges, 13th century

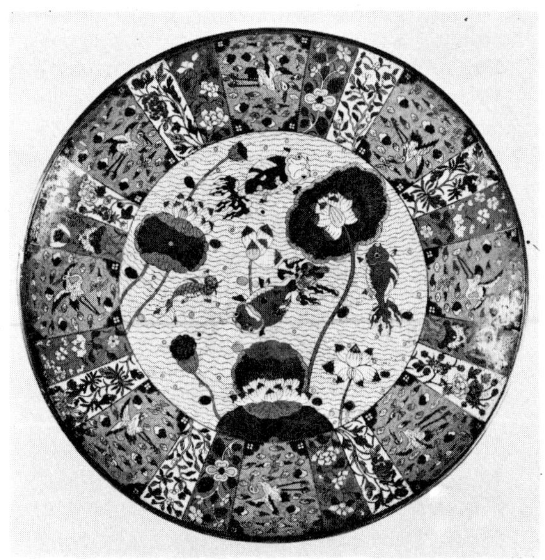

Ashmolean Museum

17TH-CENTURY CHINESE CLOISONNÉ ENAMEL DISH

Ashmolean Museum

THE BEHEADING OF JOHN THE BAPTIST

Plaque enamelled in colours, heightened with gold, on a black background. Made at Limoges, mid-16th century

Coloured enamels which have no bands separating the colours are made by painting on uncoloured enamel in oxide pigments similar to those used in making colour enamel. When heated the colours fuse with the enamel.

2. History. Enamelling has been done in Europe certainly from the time of the ancient Greeks. The craft probably came with the Romans to northern Europe, and in the East *cloisonné* enamel has a long history. The Celts, Romano-British, and Saxons decorated bowls, swords, shields, and jewellery with *cloisonné* enamel. The early enamel was thick and opaque, being only partially turned into glass, but the colours and designs were very rich.

Throughout the Middle Ages many kinds of goldsmith's work were decorated with enamel, especially the magnificent Shrines (q.v. Vol. XII) and reliquaries made for churches, and such fine objects as the Royal Gold Cup (*see* Vol. XI, p. 270). Limoges, in France, was a great centre of enamel-making from the 12th to the 17th century. At first *champlevé* on brass, with opaque enamel, was used to decorate such things as caskets, crosses, and candlesticks. The craft suffered severely when Limoges was sacked by the Black Prince in 1370, and the enamellers only recovered their fame in the 15th century. In the 16th century they produced pictures and miniatures. The subjects were painted on an enamel ground laid on copper, which was then fired. Often only black and white were used, with pale tints for the flesh. Sometimes gold or silver leaf was laid under the enamel to heighten its brilliance. Enamelled jewellery was fashionable in the 16th and 17th centuries (*see* Vol. XI, colour plate, opp. p. 224).

In the 18th century the method of enamelling over a chased ground was used for snuff-boxes, watch-cases, and other small objects. Enamelling over an engine-turned pattern was also introduced in the 18th century.

The craft of enamelling has changed little from its earliest days. Labour-saving machines can be used for some parts of the process, but the principles underlying the craft are the same as they were.

See also Jewellery Trade; Pottery.
See also Vol. XII: Romanesque Art.
See also Vol. XI: Jewellery.

ENGRAVING. This is a method of making a design on metal, either for decorative purposes or else to take prints from it on paper. For making prints the writing or design is first engraved on a metal plate, usually of copper or steel. Copper is softer to work, but the hardness of steel makes it possible to produce finer lines than would be possible on copper. A copper plate, being of soft metal, will not stand up to more than about 5,000 prints; a steel plate or steel-faced copper plate will produce many more copies. The engraver carves his design on to the metal with a short steel tool called a 'burin', with a specially sharpened cutting end. Plates for printing are engraved with the design in reverse, so that they will print the right way round when paper is brought into contact with them. To take a print, the plate is inked and all surplus ink carefully wiped off. The ink settles into the engraved portions of the plate, more ink remaining in the deeper than in the shallower cuts. The ink is transferred from the plate to the paper when the two are brought into contact in the printing press (*see* Printing).

Engraving was used in the ancient civilizations for writing or designs on precious stones and metals (*see* Gold and Silver Work), and it

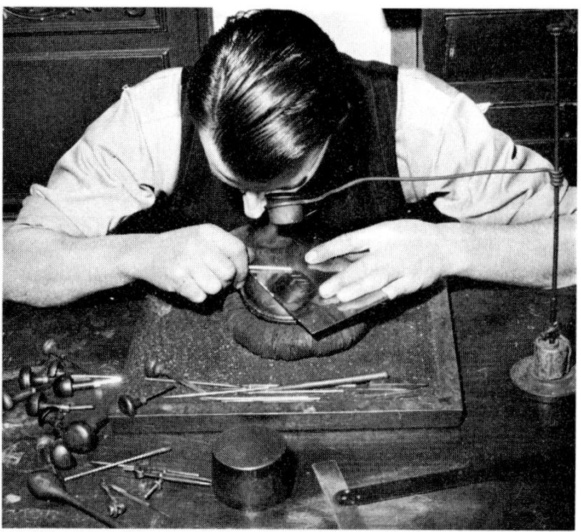

British Travel and Holidays Assn.

ENGRAVING ON COPPER

is still used for such purposes today. Prints from engraved plates or surfaces were not made in Europe before the introduction of paper in the 15th century. Some of the earliest prints on paper were taken by goldsmiths and armourers, who wished to preserve a record of the designs they used for decoration. In the 15th century playing-cards and a few maps and pictures were printed from engraved plates. Engraving only became common for book ILLUSTRATION (q.v. Vol. IV) in the 17th century; being an intaglio method of printing (the depression in the plate being inked) it could not be printed at the same time as the type, which is in relief (*see* PRINTING). The Bank of England used to engrave its bank-notes, but no longer does so. The notes or 'bills' of the U.S. Treasury, which are the paper money of the United States, have always been engraved. All British postage stamps were once engraved, and some still are. High-class visiting cards and invitation cards are engraved and so are some letterheads for business and professional stationery.

Process engraving is a relief method of printing illustrations (*see* PROCESS REPRODUCTION).

See also Vol. XII: ETCHING AND ENGRAVING; WOOD-ENGRAVING.

ENTERTAINMENT INDUSTRY. Entertainment may be organized as a public service as, for example, by the B.B.C. in its BROADCASTING PROGRAMMES (q.v. Vol. IX); or it may be presented without any regard for profit by companies which receive aid from public funds, as in the national theatres of many European countries. In Britain, the ARTS COUNCIL (q.v. Vol. IX) helps certain theatres and companies in this way. But when we speak of the entertainment industry, we are generally referring not to these semi-public bodies but to the vast network of companies which promote entertainment for profit. This industry has interests in all indoor, and occasionally certain outdoor, entertainments other than purely sporting events such as horse and dog race-meetings, athletic meetings, games, matches, and boxing tournaments. Its greatest profits are to be found in commercial television, the cinema, and the theatre.

1. COMMERCIAL TELEVISION. As a result of the Television Act of 1954 an Independent Television Authority was set up in Britain to appoint commercial television companies to provide programmes in addition to those of the B.B.C. (*see* BROADCASTING, Vol. IX). As in North America, commercial television in Britain has developed on a phenomenal scale; since 1955 the independent television companies have made the largest profits ever known in the history of British entertainment. Their programmes have proved so popular that people prefer to stay at home viewing their screens to seeking entertainment elsewhere. Cinema attendances have been cut by some 75% with the result that by 1969 over half Britain's cinemas had had to close for lack of patronage. Their threat to other branches of the entertainment industry together with their financial success has persuaded the NEWSPAPER INDUSTRY (q.v.), the film industry, and certain theatrical promoters to buy large interests in commercial television. The television companies provide entertainment, which is often costly, for a given number of hours a week; but their expenditure on their programmes is more than offset by the large fees that advertisers are willing to pay for the advertisements which are shown at recognized intervals during transmission. By 1967 British advertisers were spending as much as £124 million a year on commercial television: in America, the previous year, advertisers spent $2,600 million.

2. CINEMA. From about 1925 to 1955 the cinema was the giant in the world of entertainment (*see* CINEMA, HISTORY OF, Vol. IX). Faced with the competition of television, the U.S.A. is now producing far fewer films and concentrating its resources on those that are either sensational in subject and treatment, or that are

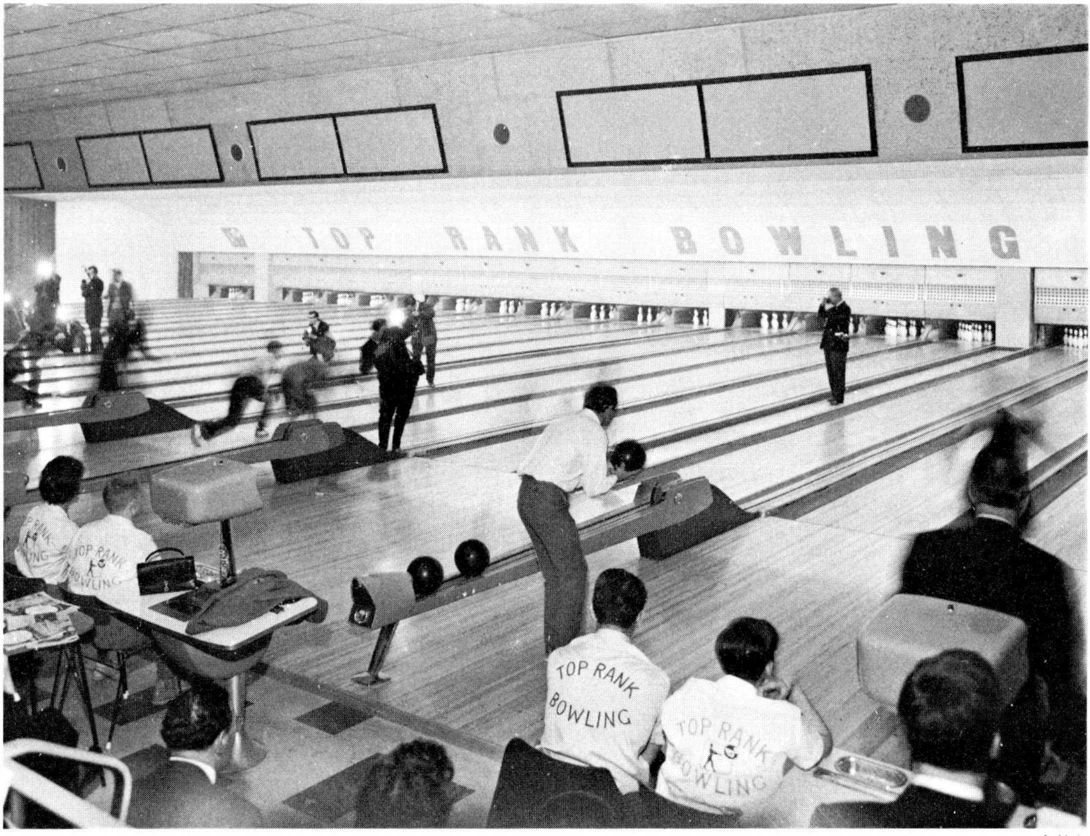

L.N.A.

A TEN-PIN BOWLING ALLEY

spectacular and lavishly produced, for example, *The Ten Commandments*, *Ben Hur*, and *Spartacus*. Many of these expensive films are designed to be shown on wide screens and are billed for long runs at individual cinemas. *Ben Hur* cost £5 million to produce. In the 1960s, American capital began to support British films. Over a fifth of a film's costs may be spent on the rent of the studio and its equipment and rather less than a fifth spent on fees to the producer, the director, the script-writer, the stars, and the supporting cast. Location costs, technicians' salaries, costumes, props, manual labour, film and laboratory costs, and such expenses as insurance and legal advice account for the remaining three-fifths. Once a film has reached the cinema, about a third of the box-office takings goes in film-rental; the rest is retained by the cinema management. Of the film-rental, the distributor takes about a third for print, publicity, and distribution charges; the balance goes to the film-makers.

3. Theatre. The theatre is historically the oldest branch of the entertainment industry (*see* Acting, History of, and Theatre, History of, Vol. IX). It, too, has suffered, especially in the provinces, from television. In 1968, London, the centre of Britain's theatrical industry, still had over forty theatres open, but in the provinces nearly a hundred theatres had closed since the end of the Second World War.

In some form or other the characteristic feature of the operatic and theatrical section of the industry has always been the promoter, the person who finances and bears the risk of production, meeting the losses if it is a failure, or taking the profits if it is a success. In earlier days the promoter was almost always one single person, although he might bring in non-working partners who were prepared to back him with money. More recently this work has generally been done by groups or syndicates, but at the head of them there is usually a single dominant personality with great knowledge and experience and, which is often more important, a real flair for gauging public taste. A still more recent development has been the merging of promoter and theatre-owner in a large company owning a chain of London and provincial theatres.

If it does not own a theatre itself, a management wanting to promote a play in London must become a tenant of a theatre, guaranteeing to pay rent for an agreed number of weeks, even if the play is not sufficiently successful to run for this period. Small theatres rent at about £600 a week, larger ones at 20% of the gross takings. The management guarantees their actors' salaries for a minimum period of 4 weeks on a provincial tour and for 2 weeks in London; most plays are 'nursed' in the provinces before being shown to the London public, and often have to 'hover' there until a theatre is ready for them in London, like aircraft waiting in the sky to land at some over-used airport.

The costs of production have mounted in recent years. For a normal play with a modest-sized cast of about a dozen actors and a single contemporary stage set, the initial production costs may amount to between £7,000 and £10,000, of which £5,000 to £8,000 may be spent on scenery, costumes, rehearsals, and publicity. The takings in a London theatre of average size, playing to good houses, may well amount to £5,000 a week, of which some £500 to £600 might represent profit. Large-scale productions, such as musicals, obviously need a very much larger outlay for cast, settings, costumes and orchestra, perhaps £50,000 or more. The production of all plays and shows represents a gamble on the tastes of the public, and most productions must run at least 2 or 3 months before their backers can hope to see a reasonable return for their investment. If the management puts on a small-cast play in a theatre it owns, the running costs (which include theatre staff, rates, repairs, insurance as well as production costs) will easily amount to about £3,300 a week.

The MUSIC-HALL (q.v. Vol. IX), so popular in Britain at the beginning of the 20th century, has been steadily declining in popularity, and over a hundred theatres specializing in this form of entertainment and the Christmas pantomime have closed since 1946. Those that remain are mostly dominated either by British and American artistes who have made their names mainly on television, or by recording stars popular with teen-agers. By 1959 only about eighty variety theatres were left in operation in the provinces.

See also Vol. IX: CIRCUSES; BALLET; OPERA.

ESTATE AGENT, *see* AGENT.

EVAPORATED MILK, *see* DAIRY INDUSTRY.

EXCHANGE AND TRADE are part of the economic life of most modern communities. Without them we should lack the variety of goods and services that most of us can now share, and in so far as this variety contributes to a higher STANDARD OF LIVING (q.v.) we should not be as well off as we are. It has taken centuries for exchange and trade to grow up to their present size, and, if we could draw a curve to represent this development, it would not be a smooth one but a series of ups and downs. For the process of development has often been interrupted by wars and invasions, and by other happenings that have caused powerful nations to decline. The history of Britain provides an example. Britain reached a high level of economic development during the Roman occupation. The departure of the legions caused the country's economic life to return to a much more primitive stage, and it is probable that 6 or 7 centuries passed before the loss was made up. Some 1,500 years have passed since the Roman legions left; during this long period the economic life of Britain has sometimes been prosperous and sometimes less so; but on the whole the record is one of continuously expanding exchange and trade.

The economic life of any community is that part of its life that is spent in satisfying material wants: for food, clothing, shelter, and so on. If these wants are satisfied within the family—as they still are in some backward or primitive communities—there are then no surplus goods to dispose of; all that is produced is needed to keep the family alive. The technical name for this type of economic system is a 'subsistence economy'.

This name would also be given to an economic system that has developed one stage further, such as a small village community of several families. In fact, this is what economists really mean when they talk or write of a subsistence economy, for human families have seldom, if ever, lived in complete isolation and been dependent solely on the labour and effort of their

THE LONDON CORN EXCHANGE, 1809
Merchants are inspecting samples of grain in small bags. Coloured aquatint by Rowlandson and Pugin from Ackermann's *Microcosm of London*

own members. The family subsistence economy is therefore difficult to track down in the records of history, and the best examples we have of it are among such primitive races as still survive, or in works of fiction such as *The Swiss Family Robinson.* Of the other and more general kind of subsistence economy, the village group, historical records are very full indeed. The English manor of the Middle Ages is a typical example. The manor was a self-contained and self-sufficient village community, having little intercourse with towns or with other communities like itself. The fields and woods produced the material for bread and meat, fuel, and beer, and the wool and skins for rough clothing and footwear. There was little left for the people of the manor to exchange for what they could not produce themselves. Some trade existed in the towns; and those towns that were ports traded not only with inland towns but with ports overseas. When we talk of the economic system of the early Middle Ages as being based on subsistence, we do not mean that there was no exchange or trade at all; we mean only that those who exchanged or traded were rather unimportant exceptions to the general rule.

When the exchanging or trading of surplus goods with other people becomes more important than the production of goods for direct consumption by the community itself, the system by which economic life is then carried on is called an 'exchange economy'. In England the change from a subsistence to an exchange economy can be said to have become fairly general by the middle of the 14th century. In 1348–9 an epidemic plague which was known as the Black Death reached England from the Continent and affected most parts of the country. Many manors lost half their population, and their land became more than was needed for the subsistence of those left alive. The lords of the manors, who had depended on the labour of their villeins, or serfs, for the farming of their own land, now found themselves short of labour; and the serfs or peasants began to realize that, being fewer in number, they had therefore become more valuable. At the same time there was an increased demand for wool by the cloth-making towns of Flanders, and many manors turned their arable land into sheep pasture and began to grow more wool. This needed fewer workers than agriculture. The peasants were also able to influence their lords to accept rent in money, or in a share of the produce raised, instead of in labour services rendered, as had been the system formerly. By the time all these influences had worked themselves out, England had developed an exchange economy, the surplus goods of the towns going to the surrounding country and villages, and these disposing of their produce to the towns. Much of the wool went abroad in the end.

This mutual exchanging benefited both town and country. Each could reap the advantages of DIVISION OF LABOUR (q.v.), or specialization in one particular branch of economic activity. The farmer was a more efficient farmer by being a farmer only; the craftsman in the town became more efficient by working at his particular craft. Both parties gained by exchanging their unwanted surplus for what they wanted more urgently. A further gain arose from the increasing use of MONEY (q.v.). If all business had been done by 'barter', or exchanging one article for another, it would have been much less satisfactory. The trouble about barter is that both parties to a transaction are obliged to take what is going instead of what they really want; such transactions are only satisfactory when there is what economists call a 'double coincidence of wants', and this happens very rarely. Money is generally acceptable to everybody; a sale for money confers on the seller the power of choosing from among many goods the particular one that he most wants, and it gives him also the chance of postponing his spending, or saving for the future, if he prefers to do so. It is therefore almost certain that a community that has developed an exchange economy will go a stage further and develop a money economy. England had reached this stage by the end of the 15th century.

The economic system of a single nation is called a 'national economy'. But this is not necessarily a final stage of development. There is the further stage of a 'world economy', in which many nations are, in an economic sense, 'members one of another'. In a world economy, exchange and trade have passed beyond the borders of a single nation, and involve the whole world. Additional advantages come from this further development. Division of labour can become extended geographically or territorially; each country that is a member of the world economy is able to exchange its surplus either for goods that it cannot produce at all or for those that it cannot produce cheaply enough.

Building up a world economy took many centuries, and was obstructed and delayed by the jealousies and rivalries of nations. It had to wait, first, for the small world of the later Middle Ages to expand into something larger. Trade at the end of the 15th century, when Cabot sailed for Newfoundland, was mainly confined to Europe, although a little trade took place on its eastern borders, particularly with Asia Minor, Central Asia, and China, and to a small extent with the East Indies. The TRADE ROUTES (q.v. Vol. IV) followed by the incense caravans of Arabia, and the Great Silk Road from China, carried traffic even in medieval times. But the enlargement of the world, from an economic point of view, really dates from the period known as the Discoveries, when Vasco da Gama, Columbus, Cabot, and others sailed southwards and eastwards and westwards and discovered lands till then merely dreamed about. The period of the Discoveries was followed by the exploration and occupation of the new lands, and by the development of trade. Individual merchants were neither strong enough nor wealthy enough for these tasks, and the work was undertaken by large companies of merchants, operating under exclusive charters granted by their governments (*see* CHARTERED COMPANIES).

There followed three centuries—the 16th, the 17th, and the 18th—of international rivalry, economic struggle, and intermittent war. But, in spite of these complications, it was a period in which trade was expanded and enlarged; and when the series of struggles ended temporarily with the long peace after Waterloo a world economy was not far off. For many years before that time the economic benefits of a widespread division of labour and unrestricted exchange and trade had been preached by the famous economist Adam SMITH (q.v. Vol. V) and his disciples.

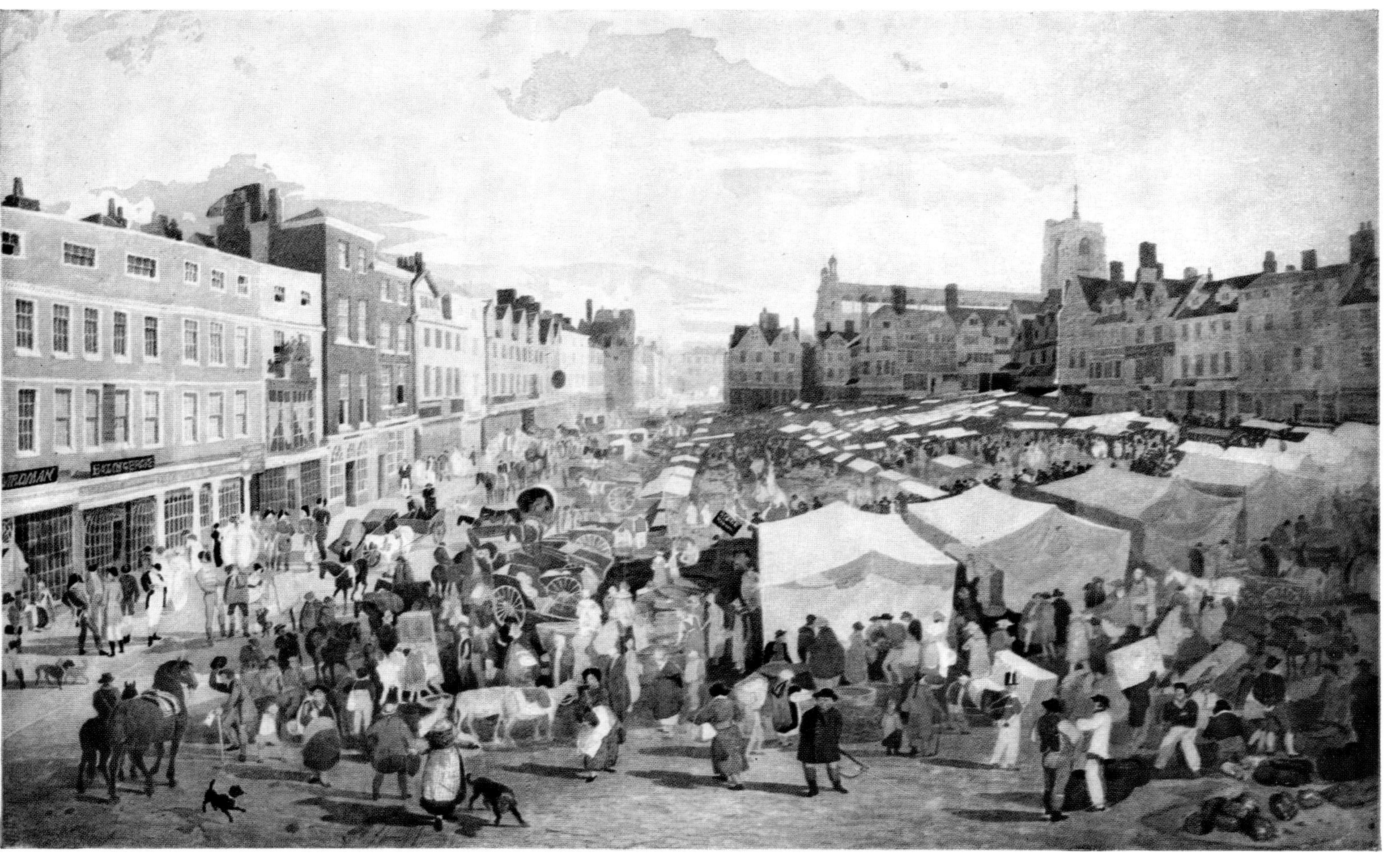

NORWICH MARKET PLACE

Painting by John Sell Cotman (1782–1842)

Smith's views gained general acceptance; although some countries, for political reasons, put up trade barriers, all were broadly agreed that a general extension of trade was in itself desirable. This extension was fostered by a great development of BANKING (q.v.), which now became an international rather than a purely national business, and these new international bankers helped merchants to spend money freely beyond their own national frontiers.

The economic history of the last 150 years is really a record of the growth of a world economy; a particularly high point was reached in 1914, just before the First World War upset the world's trading habits. Since then two world wars have been fought, and each of them caused much economic disturbance. During the depression of the late 1920's and early 1930's many countries tried to limit imports and to rely more on what they could produce for themselves; and after the Second World War many countries were forced, against their will, to do this. But most countries really believe in the advantages of exchange and trade, and the present tendency is towards the freeing of trade and the lowering of import duties when these do not conflict with a country's vital interests.

See also COMMERCE; INTERNATIONAL TRADE; MONEY; TRADE, HISTORY OF; TRADE CYCLE; FINANCE.

EXCISE, *see* TARIFFS; *see also* Vol. X: CUSTOMS AND EXCISE.

EXHIBITIONS. In industry and commerce the word 'exhibition' means a special kind of TRADE FAIR (q.v.), usually sponsored by the government of a country and organized on a national scale. The true exhibition covers all a country's industrial activities, and aims to attract universal attention. Unlike an ordinary trade fair, it has a definite political purpose, and is held at some specially significant time. The first exhibition of all, for instance, the British Great Exhibition of 1851, was held a few years after the outbreak in 1848 of revolutions all over the Continent, and its aim was to show the economic strength of Britain in a disordered world. The Festival of Britain of 1951 was timed not only to be a centenary celebration of its predecessor but also to advertise to the world Britain's recovery from the economic strain of the Second World War. In the same way the Paris Exhibition of 1878 advertised the recovery of France from the Franco-Prussian War of 1870–1. Other important exhibitions have been the British Empire Exhibition held at Wembley in 1924 and 1925, shortly after the end of the First World War, to advertise the variety of Commonwealth products, and the important

Parker Gallery

THE CRYSTAL PALACE, HYDE PARK, 1851
Coloured lithograph

Crown Copyright

A VIEW OF EXPO '67, MONTREAL, WITH THE BRITISH PAVILION TOWER IN THE BACKGROUND

exhibition held in Philadelphia, U.S.A., in 1926, to celebrate the 150th anniversary of American Independence.

In most exhibitions the architectural design of the buildings is usually well ahead of contemporary fashion. Many famous buildings have been associated with exhibitions. A great feature of the British Exhibition of 1851 was the Crystal Palace. This was first erected in Hyde Park and later removed to a site near Sydenham; it was destroyed by fire in 1936. A great new concert hall and a film theatre were erected on the south bank of the Thames for the 1951 Festival of Britain.

At the Paris Exhibition in 1878 the Palace of the Trocadéro was specially built to house the exhibits. The steel-built Eiffel Tower, a landmark of Paris, was built for the Paris Exhibition of 1889. For the Paris Exhibition of 1937 the Palais de Chaillot, which in 1948 became the meeting-place of the General Assembly of the United Nations, was built to replace the Palace of the Trocadéro.

The word 'exhibition' is also used in Britain for such annual events as the Schoolboys' and Schoolgirls' Exhibitions, which are national and in a sense universal, although they are held only for a limited section of the population. Such events as the Model Engineering Exhibition and the Ideal Home Exhibition are really trade fairs, being concerned with the products of one group of industries only.

See also TRADE FAIRS.

EXPORTS, *see* INTERNATIONAL TRADE; OVERSEAS TRADE.

F

FABRICS, *see* COTTON INDUSTRY; LINEN INDUSTRY; WOOL INDUSTRY, MODERN; TEXTILE FIBRES AND FABRICS; TEXTILE FIBRES, MAN-MADE; WOOL WEAVING; HOSIERY AND KNITWEAR.

FACTORY ORGANIZATION. 1. The aim of any manufacturing business is to produce goods as efficiently and cheaply as possible. To do this, there must be a careful arrangement of the various tasks that have to be carried out, and of the factory buildings, machines, and equipment. Manufacture introduces problems that would not have to be solved in a business engaged merely in buying and selling.

Certain general principles apply to all kinds of industries. The main problems of factory organization may be classed under four headings: the siting and layout of the factory; the type and extent of the machinery and equipment to be used; the control of employees or 'personnel', and the arrangement of their various duties; the planning and control of production, including the accurate calculation of the costs incurred in the various stages or processes of manufacture (*see* COSTING).

2. SITING AND LAYOUT. The choice of a location for the factory depends on the industry itself (*see* LOCALIZATION OF INDUSTRY), and the size and arrangement of the factory buildings themselves should be suited to the work that will be carried on in them. They must be as light and airy as possible. Fluorescent lighting is now widely used in factories for providing a light without glare, and approaches most nearly to daylight. Special shadow-proof lighting can also be installed where close or intricate work is being done. Good ventilation must be provided, and its extent will depend on the work carried on; some industrial processes give rise to poisonous gases, and the workers must not be allowed to breathe them. General working conditions must comply with the rules laid down in the Factories Act, which include special provisions for dangerous industries or processes. Large firms often have Safety Officers to supervise safety precautions for preventing accidents.

The 'ground-level' type of factory suits the small, specialized manufacturing business well, but it would not suit a brewery or a biscuit factory, or a similar large enterprise involving a sequence of many processes. Beyond a certain size, a one-floor factory becomes difficult to supervise and control. If the ground-level type suits the business, it is ideal; it has no upper storeys, and is usually constructed with 'saw-tooth' roofs, which make it possible to fit large skylights and reduce artificial lighting. Such buildings are very suitable for heavy machinery, whose foundations can be sunk into the ground. The other type of building is the 'gravity' type, which has several storeys. The top floor is generally used for the early stages of manufacture, and lower floors for later stages; the final stages, such as packing, storage, and distribution, are organized at ground-level. Modern steel and concrete building construction now makes it possible to carry out most kinds of heavy work on upper floors (*see* BUILDING CONSTRUCTION, Vol. VIII).

3. MACHINERY AND EQUIPMENT. The amount of machinery to be installed in any factory is, in the main, a question of the comparative costs of labour and machinery (*see* PRODUCTION). But there are some industrial processes for which machines are essential, as hand-labour without machinery could only turn out an inferior article (*see* CRAFTSMANSHIP). Machinery can be very expensive to buy and to keep in good repair. Its value may fall quickly, not only through age but also because it becomes out-of-date and has to be replaced by more efficient models (*see* DEPRECIATION). If there is not enough work in a factory to keep machines running, the machines become expensive to run, and the manufacturing cost of each article will rise. On the other hand, if machines are worked too much, they wear out more quickly, and the bills for repairs and maintenance become larger. It often pays best to arrange work on a double-shift system, so that the extra expense of maintaining and replacing the machines is spread over a larger volume of production. Machines

Hovis Ltd.

INSIDE A FLOUR MILL, A 'GRAVITY' TYPE FACTORY

The grain is sucked up through the pipes on the right to the top of the mill and then falls through the pipes on the left to the various milling machines on each floor

and machinists must not be left idle for lack of materials. If a continuous flow of production is aimed at, it is usual to install endless-belt CONVEYORS (q.v. Vol. VIII), which move over rollers at a set speed, so that the work moves from worker to worker without interruption. The conveyor system does not suit all forms of production, and other devices have frequently to be used, such as overhead cranes or grabs, gravity chutes, or hand-operated trucks or trolleys.

Machines must, of course, be kept in motion. The motive power used naturally varies with the industry; the processes of some industries make some forms of motive power more economical than others; for example, coke-oven and blast-furnace gas, which are by-products, are the main sources of power in the manufacture of iron and steel. The use of electrical power has now made possible great changes in factory motive power. Before electricity was introduced, motive power was usually provided by steam, gas, or oil engines, which were connected by belting with a series of overhead shafts and pulleys, from which further belts were connected to the actual machines. This had two disadvantages: a failure of the power-plant would throw all the machines out of use at the same time; and the main shafts and pulleys would have to be constantly revolving, even if only a few machines were actually operating. Electricity avoids the second of these disadvantages if each machine is provided with its own motor. The chance of a general breakdown cannot be avoided, even with electricity, although the modern 'grid' system of POWER TRANSMISSION (q.v. Vol. VIII) reduces this risk. Some factories have generating plants of their own, either for regular use with the main supply as a stand-by, or for emergency use during a failure of the main supply.

4. PERSONNEL. Since the wages of LABOUR (q.v.) are generally the largest single item in manufacturing costs, workers in a factory must be carefully selected for their suitability for the work they have to do. In a large factory there is often a Personnel Manager, trained in modern methods of staff supervision and selection (*see* INDUSTRIAL PSYCHOLOGY). Sometimes there is also an Education or Staff Training Officer, who conducts a works school for the specialized training of employees. The manager or personnel manager will keep a record card for each employee in the works, which shows the dates of his original appointment and of any promotion; the various grades through which he has passed, with their wage-rates; his holidays, other absences, and similar information. All but the senior executive staff are normally required to get a time-card stamped when they 'clock-in' and 'clock out' of the works. Except in the smallest factories, this is done by an automatic printing device attached to a clock, as only by some such method can strict time-keeping be secured. The recruitment of the 'key' workers in a factory —such as shop foremen, section managers, the designing and drawing-office staff, 'progress chasers', and inspectors—requires special care. Close contact must exist, with periodical meetings, between these employees and the higher supervisory staff and the management. Pleasant working conditions, and such things as works canteens, welfare schemes, and bonuses paid on WAGES (q.v.), all encourage good working relations, reduce an undue amount of absence from work ('absenteeism'), and prevent excessive 'labour turnover': that is, too many resignations to join other firms.

5. PLANNING. In all businesses of any size, manufacturing or other, policy is the concern of the Board of Directors. Usually a Managing Director is appointed to take day-to-day control, and to supervise the activities of the rest of the staff including the Works Manager, who is responsible for actual production (*see* BUSINESS ORGANIZATION). The output of any factory naturally depends on the orders received, and these are the concern of the Sales Manager and his outside REPRESENTATIVES (q.v.) and staff. Contact between the managing director and sales manager is close and constant, for on it depend the decisions as to what shall be produced, and in what quantity. These decisions are passed on to the Planning Department.

The job of the planning department is to arrange and combine machines, materials, and men so as to turn out the product as cheaply and efficiently as possible. It is assisted by two other specialized departments: the Drawing and Design Office, and the Buying Department. In the first of these, designs are elaborated, both for the articles to be produced and for the machines and other tools to make them with; and detailed drawings are made, from which photographic copies or 'blueprints' are taken for use in the shops where actual production will take place. It is the job of the buying department to estimate and buy the quantities of various materials that will be needed—raw materials or semi-finished goods. Assisting the buying department is the Stores Department, responsible for the actual storage of the various materials and components, and for records of their value. In a small concern the stores department reports direct to the works manager, and there is no separate buying department; in a very large factory, which may be one of a group, the buying department is usually at the head office of the whole concern.

In a large factory, turning out goods to customers' special orders, there is usually a Progress Department. This watches the progress of work through the factory; a 'chasing schedule' is drawn up, showing the various dates and times at which successive stages of manufacture should have been completed; and the 'progress chaser' makes a daily check. Priority orders are specially watched to make sure that there is no departure from the time-table originally laid down for them. A large factory would also have an Inspection or Process Control Department to ensure that manufactured articles reach the required standard. Finally, the Dispatch or Distribution Department undertakes the packing and forwarding of articles to customers.

Throughout the whole process of manufacture costs are carefully calculated and watched (*see* COSTING). Economies may be found possible by studying the comparative costs of doing the same job in different ways. A well-organized factory is not static; it is always seeking more satisfactory forms of organization and more efficient methods of production, so that its ability to trade in a competitive world may be increased.

See also BUSINESS ORGANIZATION; PRODUCTION; LOCALIZATION OF INDUSTRY.

Monotype Corporation

GROUND LEVEL FACTORY WITH 'SAW-TOOTH' ROOFS AND NORTH LIGHTS

FACTORY OVERHEADS, *see* COSTING, Section 3.

FACTORY SYSTEM, *see* INDUSTRIAL REVOLUTION.

FAIRS, *see* TRADE FAIRS.

FELLMONGERING. In a commercial sense the skins of sheep differ from those of other animals, as the wool is worth considerably more than the skin itself. Hence the special trade of fellmongering has developed. The fellmonger buys sheepskins carrying wool and separates the wool from the pelt, selling the wool to the wool merchants and the pelt to the tanner. The way in which the wool has been loosened since quite ancient days is by hanging the skins for a few days in a warm, moist atmosphere; bacteria then grow in the wool and destroy the roots, so that the wool can be easily pulled out. This method produces the best wool, uncontaminated by chemicals, and is still much used, although the pelts are liable to be damaged. A quicker and more modern method is to paint the inner surfaces of the wet skins with a strong solution of sodium sulphide, thickened with lime. The sulphide spreads through to the wool roots and destroys them, and after a few hours of treatment the wool can be pulled off. This modern process has now largely replaced the older one; it is safer for the pelt, but not so good for the wool. Fellmongered pelts can be preserved by treating or 'pickling' them with a solution of salt and sulphuric acid (*see* ACIDS). Millions of sheep skins are imported into Britain in the pickled state.

British Travel and Holidays Assn.
REMOVING THE WOOL FROM A SHEEPSKIN WHICH HAS BEEN TREATED WITH CHEMICALS

See also WOOL INDUSTRY, MODERN; TANNING.

FELT. 1. Most people have used felt, but few people know what it is. It is a fabric in which the individual fibres are closely entangled—higgledy-piggledy, like a bundle of hay—until they form a compact, substantial layer. The random arrangement of fibres is quite different from the orderly way in which the yarns or threads are arranged in woven and knitted fabrics.

Wool felts have been made from very early times. MONGOLS (q.v. Vol. I), for instance, will put layers of wool on to a large mat, sprinkle them with water, grease, and oil, and then roll up the mat. This process is repeated until the wool fibres have matted together to make a firm felt. Such felt was used for the Gilgit boots formerly worn by British soldiers serving on the North-West Frontier of India. The same type of primitive felt, spread over a framework and tied down with ropes, makes the *yurt*, or tent, in which the nomadic Mongols live.

Nobody really knows just what causes wool to felt. The simplest, and perhaps the most likely, theory is that felting is connected with the tiny scales, visible only under the microscope, with which the surface of each wool fibre is covered. If a pile of wool fibres is lubricated by oil or moisture, and is subjected to friction and pressure, the outer fibres work their way inwards into the pile, dragging other fibres with them. As a result, the whole pile tightens up and becomes more compact. In time, a firm sheet of matted fibres is made in this way, and this is what we call felt.

Two kinds of felt are made in this way: non-woven felt and woven felt. There is also needle felt, an imitation made mechanically.

Non-woven or piece-felts consist of the higgledy-piggledy arrangement of wool fibres just described. To-day these non-woven felts are usually made from wool fibres about $1\frac{1}{2}$ inches long, and from 'noil'—the short fibres of wool about $\frac{3}{4}$ to 1 inch long that are separated from the long ones in the combing process (*see* WOOL SPINNING). The wool used is obtained from merino SHEEP (q.v. Vol. VI), which are famous for felting wools of fine quality. Non-wool fibres, such as asbestos, cotton, rayon, jute, fur, and hair, may be added for cheapness or for technical reasons, according to the use for which the felt is intended.

The raw wool is first scoured to remove grease; vegetable matter such as burrs and seeds is also removed. The selected lots of wool are spread on the floor in layers, one on top of another. Vertical slices of the pile are then fed into a mixing machine, and finally agitated by a blower. This causes a very thorough blending of the wools used.

The blend is then carded (*see* WOOL SPINNING) by passing it over revolving cylinders covered with fine pins, which open out the fibres and make them roughly parallel. The web of wool which results is called a 'batt'. The batts are laid crosswise alternately, one on top of the other, sometimes to a height of 3 feet, in appearance like a pile of sheets of cotton-wool. The batts are then 'soaked' in steam, and hardened under pressure. In a later 'fulling' process the batts are rolled, lifted, pounded, and compressed by mechanical hammers; in the old days this was done by hitting the felt with wooden mallets.

2. WOVEN FELT. A woven felt is produced by 'milling' a woven wool fabric. The wool is specially selected for its felting qualities and spun and woven in the usual way. Milling is a shrinking process, in which the cloth is compressed in soapy water or acid solution to render it firmer and more compact, while the weave structure of the fabric becomes hidden by the felting of the surface fibres, giving the fabric so treated a blanket-like appearance. In fact, a blanket is merely a woven felt, with the surface fibres brushed up again to make it warm and fluffy.

Compared with other felts, woven felts have great strength and resistance to fraying, and stand up well to hard wear. They are also very efficient insulators of heat.

3. NEEDLE FELTS. Needle felts are not necessarily made of wool, the felting being imitated mechanically. A layer of fibres, which may be animal (wool and hair) or vegetable (jute), is fed into a 'needling' machine with a piece of hessian which serves as a backcloth. The needles then push the fibres through the backcloth,

Paul Popper

KIRGHIZ PEASANTS OF CENTRAL ASIA MAKING FELT

leaving them fast between the threads. This is repeated on the other side of the cloth, and the result is called a needle felt. Needle felts can be produced relatively cheaply, and so they are used when appearance does not matter: among other purposes for carpet underlays, and heat, sound, and vibration insulators.

4. FINISHING FELTS. After being dyed, the felt is 'tentered', or dried under tension, by hooks attached to its edges; this is the origin of the expression 'on tenterhooks'; most cloths were originally dried in this way. If very dense, 'rock hard' felts are required, the batts are pressed as well. Such felts are used for grinding and polishing precious stones (*see* DIAMOND INDUSTRY).

Some felts are left rough, as in felt bases for typewriters; others may be cropped to remove surface fibres—a process like mowing a lawn—and then smoothed with sandpaper, as in the making of hats, from the trilby to the 'ten gallon' hat of the Western cowboy. An ordinary wool felt hat begins as a loose cone-shaped jumble of fibres 18 inches high, 48 inches round the base, and $1\frac{1}{2}$ inches thick.

Felts may be stiffened with size, or treated with resins, to make them keep any shape to which they may be moulded. This is how bowler hats are made. Other uses of felt include footwear, washers and gaskets for machinery, and the self-sealing petrol tanks for aircraft that increase safety in flying.

The 'art and mystery of felt-making', as it used to be called, was once under the control of the Feltmakers' Company. The Worshipful Company of Feltmakers—one of the ancient guilds of Livery Companies of the City of London (*see* City Companies)—was granted a Royal Charter by James I in 1604, but it was probably in existence in the 15th century. Even in this scientific age felt-making is still very much an 'art and mystery'.

See also Textile Fabrics.

Meade Collection

MAKING FELT HATS IN THE EARLY 19TH CENTURY

FERMENTATION, *see* Beer Brewing; Wine Trade; Industrial Alcohol; Cider.

See also Vol. II: Fermentation.

FIBRE, *see* Textile Fibres and Fabrics; Textile Fibres Man-made; Wool Industry, Modern; Linen Industry; Silk; Copra; Hair Trade; Jute; Felt; Rope-making; Brushes.

See also Vol. VI: Fibre Crops.

FINANCE. This branch of commerce is concerned with providing Capital (q.v.) for business enterprises, and with dealings in the ownership of this capital after it has been raised. The financial world, therefore, includes Banks, Building Societies, Issuing Houses, Hire-purchase Companies, the various institutions forming the Money Market, and the Stock Exchanges (qq.v.). The ordinary investing public, whether private persons or commercial firms or institutions, are also part of the financial world, although they seldom realize it.

In Great Britain the banks are the main collectors of the money and savings of the general public. They use these funds for making 'short-term advances' (or lending money for short periods), principally to merchants and manufacturers who want to borrow money until their goods have been sold. The building societies finance the long-term loans required by those wishing to build or buy houses. The issuing houses arrange for the collection of long-term capital for commercial and industrial firms. As a result of all these activities, various interest-bearing or dividend-bearing securities come into existence. The Money Market deals in bills of exchange and in short-dated securities; the Stock Exchanges deal in securities of longer date.

Finance can be subdivided into private or commercial finance and public finance. The methods above described belong to commercial finance. Public finance is considered in detail in Vol. X, under the heading of National Finance. It deals with the management of Government expenditure, and with the collection of the necessary money by taxation and other means. Expenditure which cannot be covered by taxation has to be financed by borrowing. When the Government wishes to borrow, it makes use of the financial organizations in the City of London and other parts of the country, just as private individuals and business men do. Government Treasury Bills are handled on the Money Market, and Government Loans on the Stock Exchange.

See also International Finance.

FINANCE, INTERNATIONAL, *see* International Finance.

FIRECLAY, *see* Vol. VIII: Fireclays and Refractories.

FIRING, *see* Bricks and Tiles; Pottery; Earthenware.

FISH TRADE. Fish is one of the staple foods all over the world, and the fish industry is one of the most ancient and widespread (*see* Fishing Industry, Vol. VI). The industry includes the catching, marketing, and distribution of fish caught by trawlers, drifters, and smaller craft. Nearly a million tons of fish are landed by British vessels in fishing ports each year, and the fishing-boat owners and the fishermen receive about £60 million. To provide the fish that can be seen each day on the slabs of the fishmongers' shops, or which appear on the tables of hotels and restaurants, or are cooked in fried-fish shops, the industry works day and night all the year round. The fishermen do a hard job, and theirs is one of the most hazardous of callings, requiring great endurance.

The fishing industry falls into two broad divisions. The first, deep-sea fishing, is carried out in larger vessels, 80-foot or over, and includes a fleet of modern 'factory' trawlers with the facilities to freeze, and, in some cases, fillet the catch on board. The deep-sea fleet catches 'demersal' fish such as cod, haddock, and plaice ('demersal' is derived from a Latin word for 'under water', and is applied to fish that live near the sea bed).

The second type of fishing is that of the inshore fleet, which as well as demersal fish, also catches 'pelagic' fish (derived from a Greek word for the sea, and applied to surface-swimming fish). These are fish found in shoals near the coasts, such as herrings, mackerel, pilchards and sprats, and shellfish. The total landings of both fleets in Britain are sufficient to provide everyone in the population with nearly a pound of fish a week. White fish are mainly caught with trawls and seine nets. Lines are occasionally used over rocky ground.

The fish, which are bedded in broken ice in the hold, are first unloaded into huge baskets, then swung ashore and packed for auction.

The big trawlers start landing at midnight. By eight o'clock each morning hundreds of fish merchants and their workers start buying and packing fish. Ice is specially manufactured in large factories, and in it the fish is packed, ready to be dispatched on special express lorries to the inland fish-markets. Billingsgate in London was actually established as a market in 1699, although fish have been sold there since Roman times. It is now the largest inland fish-market in the world, distributing about 400 tons of fish each working day—enough to provide a fish meal for 3 million people. The fish are sold by AUCTION (q.v.); sometimes by Dutch auction, when the auctioneer offers his fish at a high figure and reduces it until a buyer is tempted to begin the bidding. The unit in the sale of herrings is the 'cran', approximately 28 stone. From the ports themselves, or from the inland markets, the fishmongers and fish-friers are supplied, and 24 hours after the fish are landed

Peter Waugh

FISH BEING TAKEN OUT OF THE FREEZER, ON BOARD A 'FACTORY' SHIP

Meade Collection

A FISHMONGER'S SHOP
An early 19th-century aquatint

they are on sale all over the kingdom. It is surprising, but true, that often fish from the ports reaches its destination faster than a railway passenger could travel the same distance. A great deal of fish is now quick-frozen and placed in COLD STORAGE (q.v.). There is therefore plenty of fish in the winter, when stormy weather makes it difficult to catch fish—especially in the far north, where there is darkness for many weeks.

Britain also imports a large quantity of sea fish, including cod, haddock, and plaice, from a number of countries, but chiefly Norway, Denmark, and Iceland. Landings by foreign vessels in British ports are reckoned as imports.

See also COLD STORAGE.
See also Vol. II: FISHES.
See also Vol. VI: FISHING INDUSTRY.

FLAX, *see* LINEN INDUSTRY; *see also* Vol. VI: FIBRE CROPS.

FLINTS, *see* CHALK.

FLOUR MILLING. Flour from wheat is eaten by more than 1,000 million people throughout the world and is the principal ingredient of bread, biscuits, cakes, confectionery, and many other foods. The grains of wheat themselves are hard and indigestible so they have to be ground or milled into a fine powder, thus producing one of the most versatile basic foods.

Millstones have been found dating from 6000 B.C. Primitive man placed the grains of wheat in the hollow of one cup-like stone and pounded them into tiny fragments with another long narrow stone. The Egyptians and later the Greeks and Romans improved upon this laborious process. They used two round stones for grinding; the upper one had a handle and could be revolved upon the lower one. Sometimes it was turned by animals, generally oxen, who were harnessed to a baulk of timber attached to the upper millstone and driven round in a wide circle. The Greeks and Romans used sieves to separate the flour particles from the coarse skins of the wheat. There is a description of a Roman water-mill in the 1st century B.C., the current of the stream driving a paddle wheel which turned the millstones, but water-mills did not come to Britain until much later; however, by A.D. 1000 there were more than 5,000 at work. By the end of the 12th century the windmill had appeared, the force of the wind turning the large blades or 'sails' which, through cogs and gears, drove the millstones.

In the 19th century three events changed the traditional pattern of 600 years. First, by using steam power to drive the stones the miller no longer had to rely on the vagaries of wind or water. Next, the North American prairies began to produce excellent wheat in abundance, and the surplus was sent across the Atlantic in three- and four-masted sailing ships to help feed Britain's fast-growing population. Finally, a Swiss miller invented a method of breaking open and grinding wheat between a series of metal rollers, which produced a much finer and whiter flour, and which was gradually taken up by millers everywhere.

To-day wheat is grown in all the continents of the world. There are many varieties, ranging

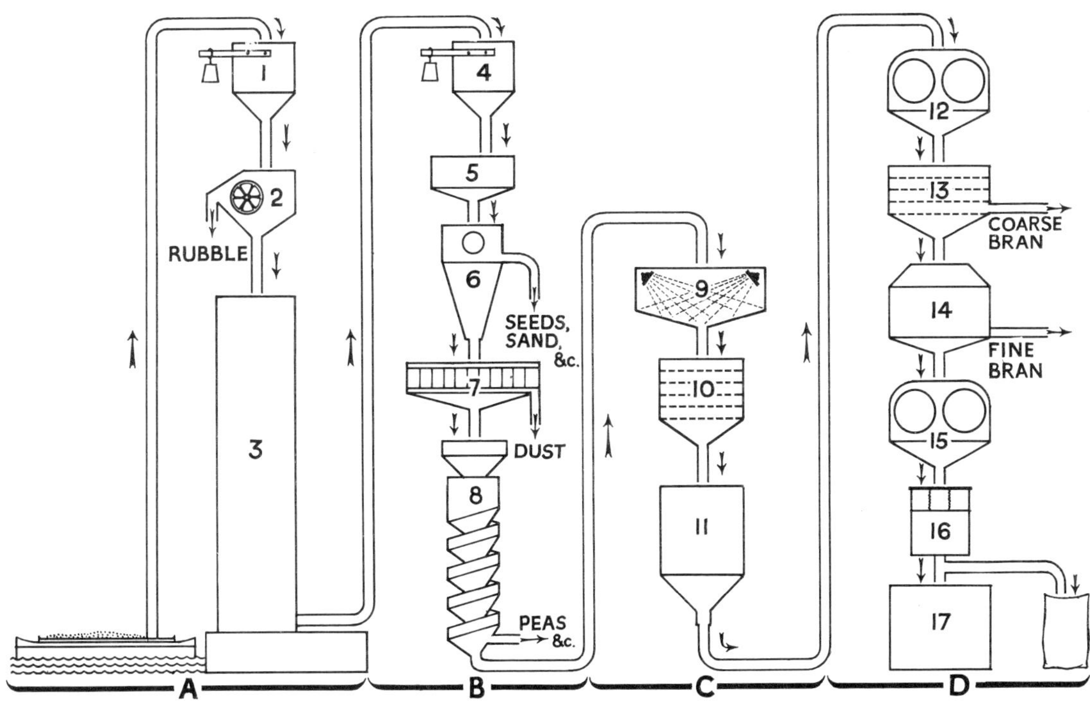

DIAGRAM OF FLOUR MILLING

A. The wheat is taken from barges by suction and weighed (1), coarse stones and rubbish are removed (2), and it is stored in silos (3)

B. Dry-cleaning plant where wheat is weighed (4), scoured (5), seeds and sand removed by rotary separator (6), dust sucked out (7), and peas, &c., spun off in spiral separators (8)

C. Washing with water (9), conditioning (10), and storing (11). It is now ready for milling

D. Break-rollers (12) remove the husk which is separated into coarse and fine bran (13 and 14) by sifting. Reduction rollers (15) grind the flour, which is sieved (16) and stored in bins (17) or sacks

from the 'hard' or 'strong' wheats of Canada, for instance, to the 'soft' or 'weak' wheats of such countries as Australia, France, and Britain. Four-fifths of the wheat for British loaves comes from overseas, mostly from Canada, the rest from the U.S.A., Australia, the Argentine, and sometimes from the continent of Europe. Britain has to import wheat because she has not enough land to grow sufficient wheat for her large population, and also because home-grown wheats are not

Flour Advisory Bureau

A FLOUR MILL AT AVONMOUTH

A ship is discharging its cargo of wheat into the mill silo

Radio Times Hulton Picture Library

WHEAT BEING STONE-GROUND IN A WATER MILL

The wheat comes through the pipe into the hopper and then into the centre of the grindstones inside the wooden casing

suitable on their own for making bread. Ocean-going ships bring the grain across the seas direct to the deep-water berths of the largest mills situated at the ports, where the wheat can be sucked straight from the holds into the mill silos. Wheat from British farms arrives at the mills by road, rail, and barge.

While the large mills are sited at the principal ports, there are many small mills in country districts, and these take rather more of their wheat from local farms. Many of these mills specialize in biscuit flour for which English wheat is ideally suited. Some of them also retain a pair of stones for grinding wholemeal flour, for which there is a small demand.

The wheat is thoroughly cleaned and 'conditioned' for milling-operations which require a quarter of all the machinery in the mill. The next stage is for the miller to mix his 'grist', selecting and blending from his store those wheats most suitable for the type of flour he wishes to produce. The wheat grain itself is a highly complex seed consisting of three main parts—the embryo (often called the germ) at the base; the brown outer skins or husks; and the white floury core (or endosperm) inside the husks. The skins stick firmly to each other and in turn to the floury endosperm. The miller's aim is to separate the white floury portion from the brown

Flour Advisory Bureau

WHEAT BLENDING MACHINERY IN A FLOUR MILL

Flour Advisory Bureau

THE SIFTER FLOOR OF A FLOUR MILL

outer skins (bran) gently and efficiently. This is achieved first through a succession of 'break rollers' which consist of two fluted metal rollers running closely together at slightly different speeds. Then, after each set of rollers, the various particles of endosperm and bran go through a series of sieving machines until the separation of floury portion and bran is complete. Finally the floury portion is reduced to a fine texture on smooth 'reduction rollers'.

Most of the flour is packed in sacks or discharged into large road 'tankers' for delivery to bakeries. Flour for use in the home and in the catering industry is weighed into packets.

The husks or bran of the wheat separated in the milling process are known as 'wheatfeed'; they are a valuable food for pigs, poultry, and cattle and help the farmer to provide eggs and bacon, meat, and milk. Some of the bran is also mixed back with the white flour for brown or wheatmeal flour.

The whole process is completely automatic from the moment the wheat is drawn from the ship to the time flour leaves the mill. So efficient are modern techniques that it would take only a dozen men in one of the large mills to produce sufficient flour to provide all the bread, cakes, biscuits, pies, puddings, and pastries for half a million people for every day of the year.

See also Baking Industry.
See also Vol. VI: Wheat.

FLOWER TRADE. The flower trade of Britain is conducted principally by specialist shops and by street hawkers and barrowmen, although many greengrocers run a flower department. The variety of flowers and foliage dealt in by an up-to-date florist is considerable, and there are nearly 200 different kinds in many florists' catalogues. There is much scope for original artistry in many branches of the trade, particularly in the making of wreaths and bouquets. The windows of many florists' shops are often beautifully designed. Cornwall and the Scilly Islands, particularly the latter, are the most important districts of the British Isles for flower growing, although other districts contribute, and Lincolnshire is famous for tulips. Marketing is done mostly through the fruit-markets and merchants, and Covent Garden is the main market for London.

Many people like to give flowers to mark birthdays, anniversaries, and other special occasions.

Constance Spry

PREPARING FLOWER ARRANGEMENTS

After the First World War an organization was set up by which orders for supplies of flowers could be telegraphed from any part of the world to another; it took as a motto 'Say it with flowers'. This organization, which was started in the U.S.A., was called the Florists' Telegraphic Delivery Association. It has been succeeded by Interflora, whose members are the leading florists of every town in the English-speaking world. Its essential feature is a financial clearing system (*see* Clearing Houses) through which money handed in by the sender in one currency may eventually be paid to the actual supplier of the flowers, often in a different currency. There are also several smaller schemes of the same nature, with a more local application.

See also Vol. VI: Market Gardening.

FOREIGN EXCHANGE, *see* Rates of Exchange

FOREIGN INVESTMENT, *see* International Finance.

FREE TRADE, *see* International Trade.

FRETWORK is a form of ornamentation, done by sawing out a number of holes, of more or less intricate shapes, from a thin sheet of rigid material, usually wood. It differs from marquetry (*see* Inlay and Marquetry) in that the holes are not later filled in with contrasting material, though they may on occasion be backed with it. Thomas Chippendale (*see* Cabinet-making) made effective use of fretted brackets and other parts on his furniture. In the Victorian

Crown Copyright

18TH-CENTURY MAHOGANY TABLE WITH FRETWORK DECORATION

Victoria and Albert Museum

age, fretwork, like so many other forms of ornamentation, became over-elaborate, with little regard to general effect. Wood of various kinds, including plywood, is most generally used, and fretworkers can get the wood in ready-planed sheets of different sizes and thicknesses. Fretwork can also be done in the softer metals, such as aluminium, brass, or silver, and in such materials as ebonite, celluloid, ivorine, or perspex.

Patterns are transferred to the work by tracing, pricking through, or by pasting on the wood, the paper on which they have been drawn. The waste part is then sawn away, the blade of the saw being kept at right-angles to the surface of the wood. Interior pieces are started with a drill. A fine saw-blade, no thicker than a piece of wire, is then passed through. When the pattern has been completed, any imperfections are removed with a file, and the work is finished by rubbing with sandpaper. For putting the work together, glue, fine screws, or panel-pins may be used, or close-fitting joints may be cut in the wood. Finally, the work is stained and polished, or painted.

Hand fretwork is still occasionally used by cabinet-makers for certain forms of decoration, although it is mainly popular at the present day as a domestic hobby. Where fretwork has to be used on a commercial scale, it is produced by special machinery.

See also CABINET-MAKING; WOODWORK, HISTORY OF.

FROZEN FOODS, *see* COLD STORAGE.

FRUIT AND VEGETABLE TRADE, *see* GREENGROCERY; CANNING INDUSTRY.

FURNITURE INDUSTRY. 1. WOOD FURNITURE. The furniture industry is one of the smaller of the major industries of Britain. It employs about 100,000 people who produce a volume of furniture worth between £250 and £300 million. But although comparatively small, the industry is very important, for everybody needs furniture in their homes.

The industry grew out of groups of small handcraft workshops, located wherever there were good supplies of suitable timber. These were usually in the vicinity of large towns where the demand for their products was greatest. Furniture has always been bulky to transport, and since its principal raw material, wood, can be found almost everywhere, furniture-making as a local cottage industry established itself in most parts of the country (*see* RURAL CRAFTS, Vol. VI).

Two centres, London and High Wycombe, gradually assumed importance. High Wycombe in Buckinghamshire is largely a furniture town,

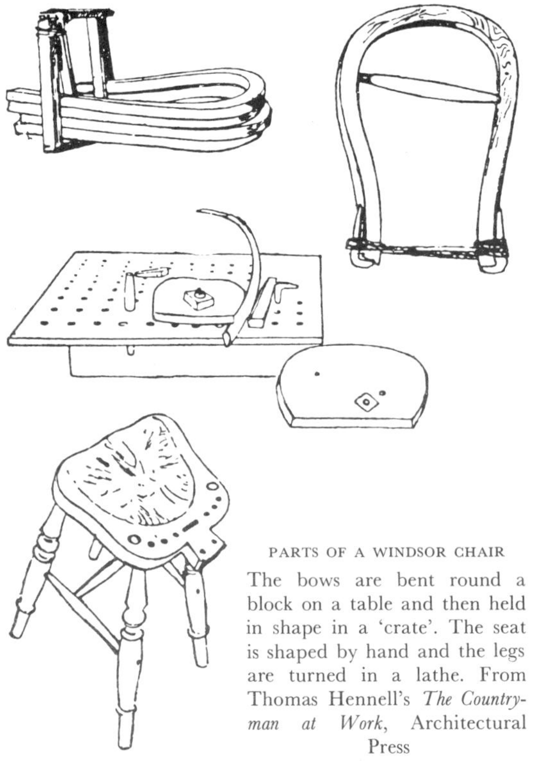

PARTS OF A WINDSOR CHAIR

The bows are bent round a block on a table and then held in shape in a 'crate'. The seat is shaped by hand and the legs are turned in a lathe. From Thomas Hennell's *The Countryman at Work*, Architectural Press

and the growth of the industry there was encouraged by the abundant timber from the local beech forests, and the nearness of the large consumers' market in London. High Wycombe was the birth place of the original 'Windsor' chair, and has always been prominent in chair making. The London industry was first carried on inside the city itself, and when London grew too big for its city walls, the industry moved gradually northwards. Much London furniture-making is now concentrated in the northern suburbs, though in recent years there has been a growing tendency for firms to move outside the London area altogether, in order to escape the high labour charges of the capital.

Today the furniture industry has graduated from hand-craft methods to mass production techniques, and although there are still a great many small workshops specialising in individual items or small batches for a local market, the bulk of production is accounted for by fewer than a hundred large firms, using modern high-speed machinery, with less and less work done by hand. About half of all furniture is still manufactured in London and High Wycombe, and the remainder is distributed throughout the country. Other important centres are the North West, the Midlands, and Yorkshire. The extent of modernisation can be seen from the fact that the number of firms producing furniture has more than halved since 1950, while their turnover has doubled during the same period.

Originally, the commonest furniture timbers were the HARDWOODS (q.v.), such as oak, beech, and mahogany; furniture-making consisted of shaping separate pieces which were subsequently joined, screwed, or glued together and then coated with polish or lacquer. These techniques are still used to some extent, but machines now carry out at great speed almost all the operations previously done by hand. Nowadays, however, very little solid wood is used, except for chair parts. Most cabinet furniture is produced from chipboard, veneered or otherwise surface-coated. Introduced in Britain during the 1950's, chipboard has revolutionized furniture production and largely overcome the problem of maintaining good supplies of timber of a suitable quality. It is made by heating and pressing shavings and wood chips coated with synthetic resin glue; its strength and rigidity makes it perfectly satisfactory for most uses in furniture-making.

Other wood substitute materials such as hardboard (made from wood fibres pressed and heated

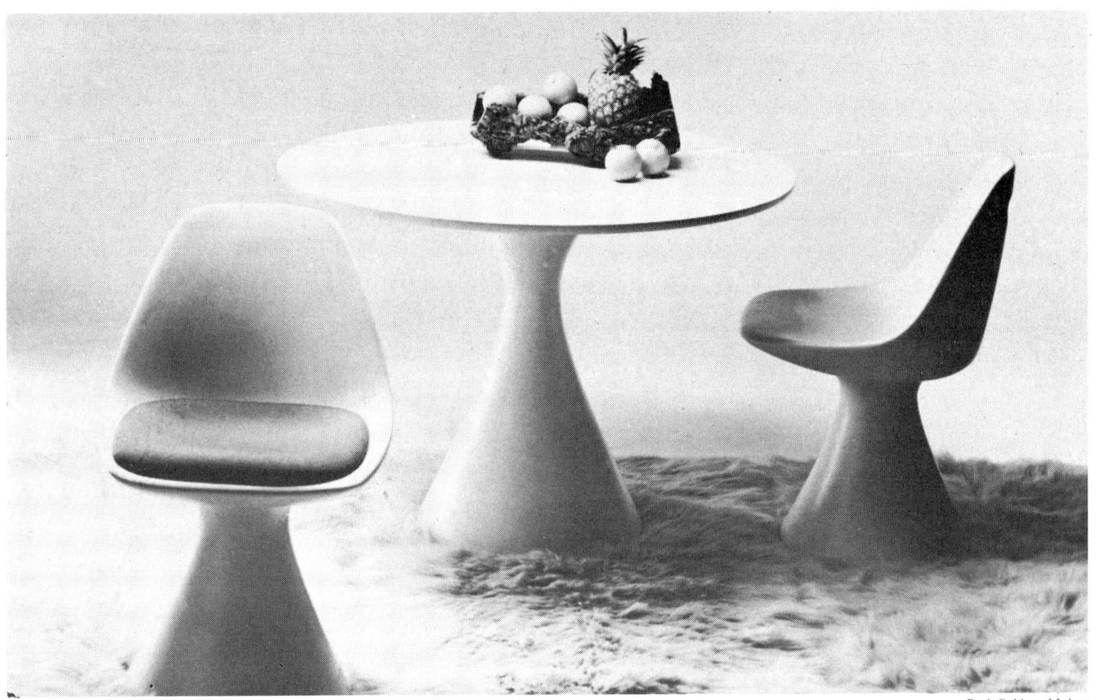

Bath Cabinet Makers

THE 'ARKANA' MUSHROOM COLLECTION, MODERN FURNITURE MADE FROM MOULDED PLASTICS

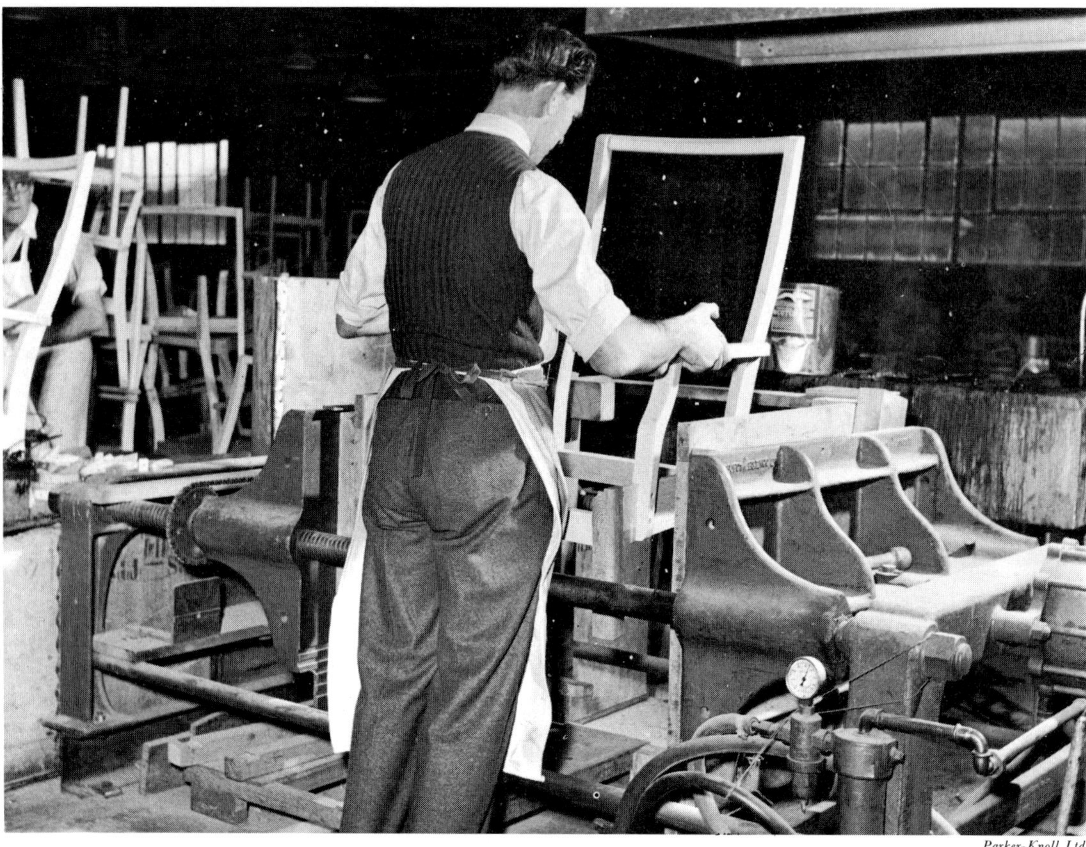

Parker-Knoll Ltd.

A CHAIR FRAME IN A CLAMP WHICH IS WORKED BY COMPRESSED AIR

with resin glue) are now widely used. Similarly plywood (*see* PLYWOODS AND VENEERS) is used for certain curved constructions. It was introduced initially by a Finnish manufacturer who with his designer, the Finnish architect Aalto, was very successful in the late 1930's with furniture made entirely from bent plywood. Laminated plywood shapes can also be made by coating separate sheets of wood with glue, and then pressing them in moulds of the required shape until the glue has set. Moulded plywood is a special variety which is curved both ways.

Since the introduction of plywood, other laminated materials have been successfully developed and used, most notably the hard-surface laminates made from plastics reinforced with paper or fabric; these are widely used in the manufacture of kitchen furniture. Great progress has been made in improving surfacing materials, and modern lacquers are hard wearing and resistant to most forms of domestic chemical attack. They can be applied in a variety of sophisticated spray or coating methods. Synthetic materials, particularly paper and plastic veneer substitutes, are becoming increasingly important, and these and the process of grain-printing have greatly added to the range of effects that can be achieved. In the latter a wood pattern is printed on a base by methods resembling ordinary colour printing, though larger in scale. All these processes produce an acceptable article when finished with a final coating of clear lacquer; in some cases even this can be dispensed with, so hard-wearing is the synthetic material.

These new techniques have been developed in response to the great increase in the demand for furniture, as population and income per head have risen. The range of styles, textures, finishes, and colours is greater than ever before, because not only do people want more furniture, they also want more variety.

2. METAL AND PLASTICS. The use of metal for furniture dates from the early decades of the 19th century. Bedsteads were often made of brass or iron, and steel sheeting was used for park chairs and other outdoor furniture, and later for office, canteen, and factory furniture. The strength and ability of metal to stand hard knocks gradually made it more popular than wood for this kind of furniture.

Metal furniture is built up from a number of flat sheets trimmed to shape, bent in huge presses, and then welded together. Paint is applied to the surface, and it is then dried by heating the furniture in special drying ovens. Chairs made of metal tubes were invented in Germany in 1925. Since then, metal tubes have been used for all kinds of furniture—chairs, tables, couches, stools, and hospital beds. Many such pieces, particularly chairs, are made to 'nest' or fit together, so that they can be stacked compactly when not in use. Metal-tube furniture is made by first bending the tubes in a machine and then welding them together and spray painting or electro-plating them. The materials used to manufacture the metal tubes and sheets are of various kinds. The sheets are sometimes made up of alternate layers of metal, wood veneers, and plastics.

Plastics (q.v.) are also widely used for furniture. Moulded plastics are used for such things as the cases of radio sets, laminated plastics for table tops, and sheet plastics to replace veneers. With the increasing use of synthetic resins, adhesives, and plastic materials, methods have been developed for moulding shapes that would be difficult to obtain by traditional methods. Plastic mouldings can now be produced to replace wooden decorative work in cabinet ware, and wooden frames for upholstered chairs. Flexible plastic foam is also widely used for Upholstery (q.v.). The technology of plastics has developed so fast that today complete chairs, shaped doors, and various components can be moulded from it; structural cabinet panels were first made from plastics in 1969.

See also Cabinet-making; Upholstery; Woodwork, History of.

See also Vol. XI: Furniture, History of; Furniture, Modern.

FUR TRADE. 1. History. The trade in furs is a very ancient one, but throughout the centuries it has changed its character. It began by being a purely local trade in articles of necessity for people living in northern climates: it still is today in such countries. Only where Roman Civilization (q.v. Vol. I) had spread were furs traded outside northern regions with the peoples living in more temperate climates. The trade then ceased to be local and became international, but at the same time it became a trade in luxuries instead of in necessities. As trade in general expanded in Europe during the Middle Ages (*see* Trade, History of), the fur trade expanded also. But it still remained a luxury trade, and this was emphasized by the sumptuary laws allowing only people of high rank to wear furs and rich clothing materials. In the Middle Ages England's sources of supply were north and central Europe, and in the fur trade the Hanseatic League (q.v.) was very prominent: in fact one of its most important depots or 'factories' as they were called, was at Nijni Novgorod (Gor'kiy) in Russia, which has been a big fur market for centuries. Once North America was colonized, the sources of supply of furs became more varied. The early French settlers were very keen fur-trappers. In the 17th century the Hudson's Bay Company (q.v.) was founded to exploit the resources of northern Canada, and it still occupies a leading position in the fur trade of the world.

Since the middle of the 19th century the fur trade, except for the rarest and choicest skins, has ceased to be a luxury trade.

2. Supplies of Furs. The furs most in use today generally come from animals raised on farms or maintained in preserves; some, however, are still trapped in the wild state. The furs are usually consigned to Brokers, and sold by Auction (q.v.) at fixed times every year. These auctions take place in the countries where the furs originate, such as Canada, the United States, Russia, and the Scandinavian countries, as well as in London, which is the chief international market. Public auctions on the London market consist of part of the Hudson's Bay Company's (q.v.) own collection of wild furs and also furs consigned to that company and to other fur brokers by collectors and farmers. Chief among the furs sold at these auctions are Persian lamb from south-west Africa and Afghanistan, farmed or ranch mink from Europe, and part of the Russian fur crop. Furs are sold by catalogue and the actual skins are not displayed in the auction rooms. They are stored in Warehouses (q.v.) where they can be seen by prospective buyers. The same methods are used in the other auction centres.

3. The Furrier. A manufacturer of fur is

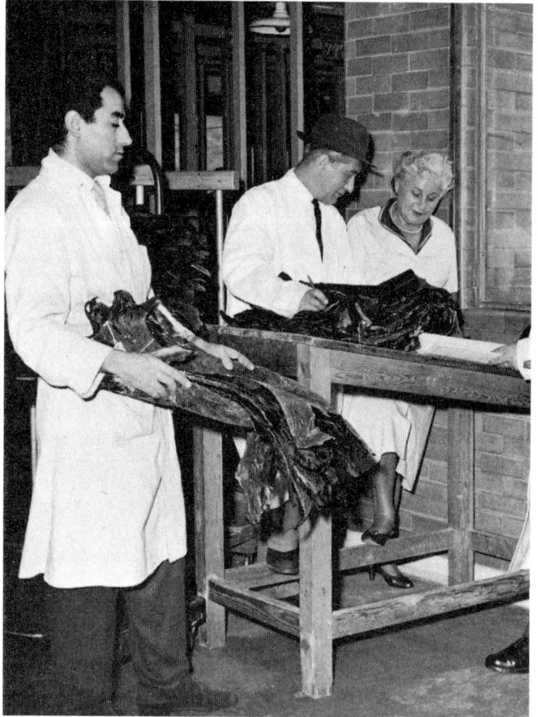

Hudson's Bay Company

BUYERS INSPECTING PERSIAN LAMBSKINS FROM SOUTH-WEST AFRICA

The furs are later sold by auction

called a furrier. Furs are skins with the fur or hair still in place, and before manufacture they need much the same treatment as HIDES AND SKINS (q.v.). The first process is called 'dressing' and is carried out by dressers, not by furriers themselves. It consists of making the skin into soft, pliable leather; thinning down the leathery part of the skin itself, cleaning the whole pelt, removing foreign bodies and dirt; and preserving and increasing the natural shine or lustre of the fur. The processes for furs are like those described under TANNING (q.v.). After dressing, the next process, unless the skin is to be used in its natural colour, is dyeing, also carried out by specialists. In recent years many improvements have been made in the dyes used, and in dyeing methods. Clever dyeing can make many furs look attractive that would otherwise look cheap. The fur going under the trade name of 'coney' is actually dyed rabbit. Dyed marmot and dyed musquash are used to copy the appearance of mink. The final process is the actual manufacture of the garments. Small skins are sewn together by machine to make larger pieces, and the garments are then cut out by hand by highly trained cutters, upon whose skill depends the economical use of the skins.

4. PRINCIPAL FURS. The following are some of the principal furs hunted or farmed.

Beaver. This was the most important fur during the early colonization of North America, when it was used for men's hats. The long guard hair is removed, and the under-wool shorn, and sometimes dyed, after which the skins are used for coats, jackets, or trimmings.

Chinchilla. This is the very soft fur of a small South American rodent, now entirely raised in captivity.

Ermine. Ermine is the white winter coat of the weasel, used for fur garments and sometimes also for ceremonial robes, either in its natural colour or dyed.

Fox. This fur was once enormously popular in its many varieties, and today Arctic white fox and ranched blue fox are still used in considerable quantities. The vogue for 'fun furs' has also revived the demand for red fox.

Lamb. There are two quite different types of lamb used by the fur trade: (i) the small, curly-coated skins, of which the most important are called Persian lamb; these are grown on farms in south-west Africa, Afghanistan, and Russia; they are mostly dyed black or, if grey, left in their natural colour, but a number are bleached and dyed in other colours. The fur is sometimes called astrakhan and, when very young indeed, 'broad-tail'. Indian lambs are similar in type, though not as fine, and are generally white; these can be dyed any colour; (ii) the fur of the merino sheep, which is grown in many parts of the world; this undergoes a variety of processes from which it emerges with various names, of which the best known is beaver lamb. These are used in large quantities for coats, small pieces, and trimmings, and form, with rabbit, the bulk of the raw material of the cheap fur trade.

Mink. This is by far the most important fur of all. More than twenty million mink of various colours are now produced on farms in North America and Europe each year. The price varies from £5 to £50 a pelt, according to size, quality, and degree of rarity of colour. In addition, wild mink is trapped in North America and Russia, but in comparatively small quantities. The finest wild mink is dark in colour, densely furred, and silky in texture. The best small skins, that is, those most suitable for coats, come from

Labrador and other parts of north-east Canada; the larger skins are preferred for stoles and capes, and these come from the northern parts of central Canada, particularly the Mackenzie River district. Good mink are also found in the United States, mostly near the Great Lakes, but they exist as far south as Louisiana where the skins are coarse in texture and poor in colour. These poor-quality skins were formerly used for the lower-priced coats, but their place has now been taken by the farmed, or ranched, mink. Ranched mink were originally bred to produce a very dark brown coloured fur, and skins of this colour are known as 'standard' ranched mink. In the early 1940's, however, certain mutations (changes of type) occurred among a few animals and these were developed into strains of various colours, such as grey, pale brown, gun-metal, and white. Skins from male animals are about twice the size of those from females; up to seventy female skins are needed for a coat. Each skin has to be elongated to form the 'strands' of the garment, and this is achieved by cutting the skin into narrow strips, each of which is resewn slightly lower than its original position. The process is called 'dropping' and involves the use of several miles of cotton for each coat, as well as the highest degree of skill on the part of the cutters and machinists. Cheaper qualities of mink are sometimes dyed, particularly black. Prices for the mutation shades tend to fluctuate from year to year, but the darkest shades of 'standard' mink enjoy a steady popularity.

Musk-rat or Musquash. This is the most important of the moderately priced furs. It comes from North America or, in poorer qualities, from Russia, and is generally dyed to imitate more valuable furs, such as mink.

Nutria. This is the fur of the coypu, found in its wild state in South America but also farmed elsewhere. Nutria looks like beaver, and the method of processing it is the same.

Otter. Many different types exist. The fur of Canadian otter resembles that of beaver. Others, such as those from Brazil, have dense hair, even shorter than a pony's.

Rabbit. Only tame rabbits are used. The skins of those which have been specially bred are used in their natural colour. Most rabbit skins, however, are treated by shearing and dyeing to imitate other furs. In the fur trade rabbit is generally called coney.

Sable. This is a small brown carnivorous animal allied to the marten. The true sable is found only in Russia, but marten from North America is generally called Canadian sable. The finest and darkest are made up in their natural colour and fetch over £100 a skin. The paler sorts are dyed dark brown.

Seal. A number of different kinds of hair seal with attractive markings are used for fur garments of moderate price. Fur seal from the Pribolof islands off the coast of Alaska is known as Alaska fur seal and makes the finer and more expensive coats. It is protected by the United States Government and undergoes a lengthy and complicated process before the skins are offered to the trade by public auction. Fur seals of similar type, but of poorer quality, come from the coasts of South America and South Africa.

Squirrel. Great quantities of skins are used for coats and small pieces, generally dyed brown, although those without any red stripe are sometimes used in their natural colour. The full-furred, soft kinds come from Russia; those from Canada are closer to ermine in appearance.

Most of these animals are described in Vol. II.

See also Vol. VI: FUR FARMING; FUR HUNTING.

G

GAME, *see* Poultry and Game.

GAS INDUSTRY. The Gas Light and Coke Company, formed by Act of Parliament in 1810, was the first concern in Britain to manufacture gas for street and domestic lighting on a commercial scale. When the gas industry was nationalized in 1949, the company owned the largest gasworks in the world, at Beckton on the north bank of the Thames.

In 1659 Thomas Shirley had discovered in Lancashire an escape of inflammable gas from the ground. This came very probably from a seam of 'fiery' coal very close to the surface. His discovery greatly interested an Irish clergyman named Clayton, and led him to experiment with the Distillation of coal (q.v.). He successfully produced an inflammable gas, which he collected in bladders. He would then prick a hole in a bladder and ignite the gas to amuse his guests.

The technical founder of the modern gas industry was William Murdock, a Scotsman, who was in the service of the famous pioneer steam engineering firm of Boulton and Watt, of Birmingham. He was commissioned by his firm to go to Redruth, in Cornwall, to erect some of their pumping-engines for the local mining industry. Here he experimented with the distillation of gas from coal as Clayton had done, and in 1792 he succeeded in lighting his office with the new gas. In 1807 the first street in London was lighted and the Gas Light and Coke Company came into being 3 years later. The plant first used was manufactured for the company by Boulton and Watt. Although the company's early career was difficult and unprofitable, within 10 years from its foundation, many provincial gasworks had been built, and by 1829 there were 200 companies throughout the country.

In these early years there was a good deal of ruinous competition between the different gas companies. Rival companies often ran their mains down the same roads, and sought business from the householders living in them. Shortly after 1850 many rival companies began to amalgamate in self-defence, and to enter into 'zoning' arrangements by which a single company would be alone responsible for supplies in its own allotted district. By the Metropolis Gas Act of 1860 Parliament confirmed these zoning arrangements for London.

To start with, the industry aimed only to supply gas for street lighting and the lighting of factories, warehouses, shops, and public buildings. The early burners were crude, providing a naked jet of flame in the shape of a 'fishtail'. Incandescent lighting, using a 'mantle' of ramie thread, was perfected towards the end of the 19th century. But the companies were greatly interested in other possible uses for gas. James Sharp of Southampton was a pioneer in the use of gas for cookery, and in 1850 he gave a demonstration lecture in Southampton at the Polytechnic Institution. He cooked a meal by gas on the platform, and it was eaten with enjoyment by the audience without any of the ill effects that had been prophesied. The supply of gas for cooking in private houses was soon organized by the companies, and they gradually succeeded in persuading the Catering Industry (q.v.) of the advantages of the new system. Today gas is used for cooking in a very large number of the homes in Britain and equally extensively in catering establishments. Gas fires for the heating of rooms next came into use, but more slowly. They were followed by gas water-heaters of which the first made its appearance in 1863.

Gas is now far more important as a source of heat, both in industrial and domestic contexts; as a source of light, it has been widely replaced by electricity. Both gas itself, and the many valuable coal-tar derivatives which were By-products (q.v.) of the old coal-based gas-making processes played an important part in the development of modern industry.

But today Gas Manufacture and Production (q.v. Vol. VIII) is no longer carried out along traditional lines, using coal as its primary raw material. The industry has undergone a major revolution in the last decade, as a result of two vital developments: first, cheaper production

Gas Council

PONDERS END GASWORKS

On the left are the purifiers and benzole plant, in the centre the boiler house and purifiers, with the water tower and gas holders in the background. On the right are the fitting shop and welfare block

methods based on oil; secondly, the utilization of natural gas deposits under the North Sea. These two factors have caused the industry to expand, so that the wide-spread replacement of existing gas-making plants and methods, and a nation-wide conversion of appliances are now under way. The results have been an average sales increase of about 9% per annum in recent years, and by 1967–8 the industry's total output had reached the record figures of over 4½ million therms. By the mid-1970's, sales are confidently predicted to increase nearly fourfold.

These changes took place because of the growing scarcity of good gas-making coals. Although methods of gasifying low-grade coal at high pressure have been evolved, the only satisfactory long-term solution seemed to be to abandon the old coal-gas plants and adopt the oil-gasification method instead. With this technique gas is obtained more economically and at higher pressure from light petroleum fractions (*see* OIL REFINING). Britain has now overcome the huge industrial problems involved in making the change-over from producing the bulk of town gas from coal, to making it from oil. New gas-making processes, based on oil feedstocks, ensure that gas will continue to be a highly competitive source of energy, and the discovery of large fields of natural gas under the North Sea in 1965 has improved the industry's prospects still further. Natural gas is now expected to meet as much as 15% of the country's total demand for energy by 1975.

Once it was confirmed that there were commercial quantities of natural gas under the North Sea, the industry mounted a massive engineering programme to pipe it ashore, and channel it to the consumer. Research was begun on the conversion of the 40 million existing gas appliances to natural gas; plans were drawn up and people trained to undertake the work.

Full scale marketing and publicity campaigns were launched to ensure that present and potential customers knew of natural gas, and its many advantages. The administration of the Gas Council, and its relationship with its 12 area boards, were revised in order that these operations would be carried out efficiently.

Two big terminals, at Easington and Bacton in

Yorkshire, have been built to receive natural gas pipelined from the North Sea beds. Three feeder mains then carry the gas from the terminals into the Gas Council's national pipe-line network, which by the early 1970's will be 2,500 miles long. The flow of gas will be controlled by a radio microwave system. In addition, the area boards are laying several thousand miles of pipeline to distribute natural gas in their own areas.

The distribution of large quantities of natural gas at high pressure has created new problems in the design, construction, and operation of pipeline transmission systems. These have been studied at a new engineering research station. Special facilities are also required for storing liquefied natural gas to meet extra demand at peak periods; holders are being built both above and below ground for this purpose.

Before natural gas can be supplied direct to consumers, their appliances need to be converted, and while this is taking place, supplies are, of course, maintained by the use of manufactured gas, most of it produced from oil. The conversion programme includes gas appliances in over 12 million homes, and on 500,000 commercial, and 80,000 industrial premises; about 8,500 different models are involved. It is estimated that the whole programme will take about 10 years (*see* GAS, NATURAL, Vol. III).

Although the industry's output has increased, its labour force has remained relatively stable. Productivity per worker has increased at about 7% a year in recent years, and it is expected to increase by about 15% a year over the next five years. While the number of staff employed in gas production has declined, the number employed in consumer services and distribution has increased, as a result of the growth in sales and the natural gas conversion programme.

See also Vol. VIII: GAS MANUFACTURE.
See also Vol. X: STREET SERVICES.

GLASS-MAKING. 1. Glass was long believed to have been the chance discovery of some Phoenician merchants camping on a sandy shore in Syria thousands of years ago. They took some large lumps of carbonate of soda from their cargo and used them to support their cooking-pots over the fire. Next morning in the cold ashes they found lumps of glass, made by the melting of the sand in the presence of the ALKALI (q.v.). This story, related by Pliny the Elder in his *Natural History*, is now discredited, and according to the great archaeologist, Sir Flinders Petrie, glass was being regularly made in ancient Babylonia much earlier than this. Glass is still made today by heating together in a furnace some form of silica (sand, flint, or quartz: *see* MINERALS, Vol. III) with an alkaline 'flux' (usually potash or soda) which helps it to melt. In the great heat obtainable in some modern furnaces no flux is needed, and glass is occasionally made from silica alone.

The earliest glass that has come down to us is in the form of stone beads coated with blue glass, much in the same way as metals are covered with ENAMEL (q.v.). These beads were found in Egypt, and may date from as early as 4000 B.C. For at least 2,000 years after this glass was used only for ornament, in imitation of precious stones. It was coloured, just as it is today, by the addition of various metallic oxides (*see* METAL ORES, Vol. III), such as chromium for green, cobalt for blue, and manganese for pinkish-purple. This very early glass let the light through, but was not transparent; and its natural tint, if not artificially coloured, was greenish. In time it was discovered that greater transparency and crystal whiteness could be given by adding an oxide of manganese, which came to be known as 'glassmakers' soap'.

2. HAND-MADE GLASS. The first glass vessels were made by winding threads of hot molten glass round and round cores of clay, which were then withdrawn. But the great landmark in the history of glass-making was the discovery in Syria, just before the Christian era, that glass could be 'blown'. Hand-blowing, as it is rather wrongly called, is a method still used today. One end of a long iron tube is dipped into a fireclay pot or crucible of red-hot molten glass. When enough of the sticky 'metal' (the word used by glass-blowers) has been gathered on the end of the tube, it is swung clear of the furnace and given a round shape by being rolled on an iron table called a 'marver'. Seated in a 'chair' with long flat parallel arms, the craftsman blows down the other end of the tube, producing a bubble in the glass. With wonderful skill he gives this the final shape he wants, periodically returning it to the mouth of the crucible to keep it soft enough for working. He may make the bubble longer by swinging the rod around him, or shorter by spinning or rolling it along the arms of his chair; he may pinch or shape it with tools or cut it with shears; when he has finished

Crown Copyright

MAKING LEAD CRYSTAL GLASS AT STOURBRIDGE, WORCESTERSHIRE

The man in the centre is 'gathering' molten glass in the furnace; on the right it is placed on the 'marver', and on the left a craftsman is shaping the blown glass in a 'chair'

blowing he may transfer it to an iron rod called a 'punty' (or 'pontil'). All the time he keeps revolving it, so that it retains its round shape and stays in a central position on the tube or rod instead of sagging downwards.

A method of glass-blowing that needs less skill, and so may actually be older than the system just described, is for the bubble to be blown inside a mould of baked clay or stone, whose shape the finished glass vessel then retains. A mechanical form of this process is widely used today for making in metal moulds such articles as bottles and electric bulbs by automatic machinery (*see* Section 3).

Window-glass called for special methods in order to produce flat panes. Although the Romans in their later days had made small panes of window-glass by casting them on a flat bed, window-glass was made by blowing in the Middle Ages and until the invention of glass-making machinery in the 19th century. Very few dwellings had glass in their windows before the end of the Middle Ages; windows were closed with a leather curtain or a wooden shutter (*see* WINDOWS, Vol. XI); glass was, however, used for churches in those days. In making window-glass two methods were used. For 'crown' glass a bubble was blown, transferred to a punty, and then alternately heated and spun until it finally opened out to a flat disk, which might be as much as 4 feet across. It was then cut free from the punty with shears, and into the required size. As glass in those days was very expensive to make, the central piece with the 'bullion' or blob left by the punty was generally used as well as the flat sheets, and this is often seen in ancient windows. By the other method, used for making what was called 'broad' glass, a bubble was blown and then swung round until it lengthened out to a cylinder. The ends of this were cut off, and it was then cut with shears along its length, and flattened. This method is still used to make the old-style glass used for STAINED GLASS windows (q.v. Vol. XII).

In the course of the centuries the peoples of many lands had carried on and improved the craft of glass-making. During the Dark Ages the craft was kept alive by the Franks and the Gauls, to whom it had been introduced by the Romans. Documents of the 7th and 8th centuries tell of requests from Britain for the sending over of continental glass-makers, and in the 13th century the glass industry had become well established in the south-eastern counties of England. The glass-makers had to move about from place to place in search of fresh timber, owing to the great amount of wood burned in melting the glass; and because of this the glass of this time was known as *waldglas*, or 'forest glass'. It had a beautiful greenish tinge.

By the 13th century also the famous glass-makers of the city of Venice had brought to a high state of perfection a glass very different from the *waldglas* of the north. Venetian glass was almost colourless, like ROCK-CRYSTAL (q.v. Vol. III), from which it got its local name of *cristallo*. Venetian glass vessels of this period were very beautiful. The stems of the goblets and glasses were swelled out into 'knops' or bulges, possibly containing an air bubble, or into graceful baluster shapes, and ended in wide firm bases. The glass was often engraved by means of a diamond point. Venetian glass-makers were brought to England, and for over 100 years Venetian glass was made in London.

England contributed the next great advance in glass-making. In 1674 George Ravenscroft invented 'flint glass', sometimes called 'glass of lead' because it used lead oxide as a flux. The new glass was heavier than Venetian and even closer in appearance to natural rock-crystal. Although it melted at a lower temperature than Venetian glass, it never flowed as easily, and so it was not as well suited for blowing thin. By the end of the 17th century nearly 100 glass-makers were making flint glass in Britain, and within the next 50 years English glass reached its highest level of artistic design.

The 18th century saw the introduction into England of an entirely different method of decorating glass, by 'cutting' or grinding it away by pressing it against a revolving copper or iron disk fed with emery and water or else corundum and oil. This method worked particularly well with flint glass, but was checked by a heavy tax levied by the Government between 1745 and 1845, which made it more profitable to make glassware of a lighter design and less suitable for deep cutting. Glass-makers evaded the duty by setting up works in Ireland, and some famous glassware was produced at such places as Waterford, Cork, and Dublin.

3. MACHINE-MADE GLASS. Meanwhile mechanical methods and new processes were being invented. The first large factory for casting plate-glass was opened in England in 1773. In 1810 England was also responsible for the invention of a mechanical method of pressing glass vessels in moulds of the shape of the outside of the vessel. In 1886 the first automatic bottle-making machine was patented.

To-day the highest quality glass vessels are still

1. MOULDED CHAMPAGNE GLASS WITH TWIST STEM, ENGLISH, 1750–80

2. CUT GLASS TUMBLER WITH ENGRAVED DECORATION, ENGLISH, 1791

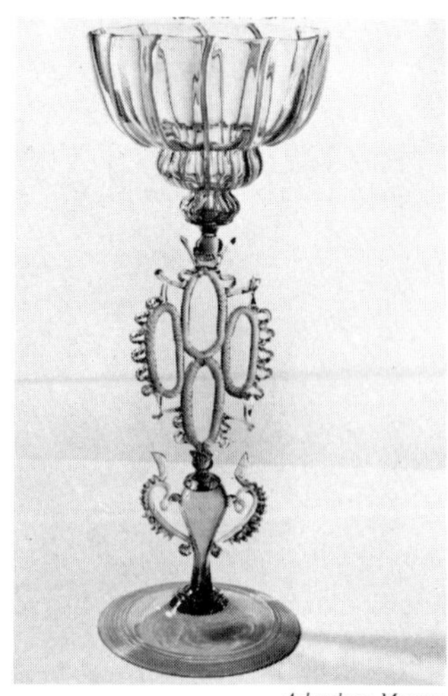

Ashmolean Museum

3. WINE GLASS, VENETIAN, 19TH CENTURY

hand-blown, but most modern glass is produced mechanically. Hollow vessels are made either in pressing or blowing machines, according to their shape. Such articles as dishes, jars, plates, lenses, bowls, and thick tumblers are fashioned by an automatic pressure plunger which descends on to molten glass poured into a mould. Blowing machines are of several types, and are worked by compressed air. What are called 'press and blow' machines make wide-mouthed ware such as jam-jars and milk-bottles. Other blowing-machines, called 'blow and blow' machines, make hollow ware with narrower necks in two stages. The first machine makes what is called a 'parison', which is a glass shape with a neck of the proper size but with the body of the vessel smaller and thicker than is finally desired. The parison is then transferred to a mould, where it is given a second blowing and is finally shaped. Electric bulbs have long been made in Britain on a type of machine which can produce nearly 100,000 bulbs a day, but machinery of American design has now increased output, and one kind of machine has an output of nearly one million bulbs a day.

Sheet glass for windows is drawn out through rollers. Plate glass is poured in a molten state over a casting table of iron. As it pours out it is rolled by a massive iron roller into a sheet, and after being re-heated in an annealing furnace (*see* HEAT TREATMENT, Section 2, Vol. VIII), is cut, ground by water and sand, and polished with rouge by felt rubbers. Thin plate glass is made at less expense by squeezing out a continuous ribbon of glass between two rollers, instead of using a casting table. Pilkingtons' 'float' glass is a high-quality flat glass with many of the qualities of plate glass; it is made by 'floating' a continuous ribbon of glass direct from the furnace on to molten metal. As the surfaces of 'float' glass have not been in contact when soft with anything except a liquid, they have a brilliant finish and are perfectly true. Wired safety glass is made by unrolling wire netting over sheets of glass during manufacture, while a fresh layer of glass is rolled on top so as to 'sandwich' the netting within. Laminated safety glass of patented types is made from sheet or sometimes from well-polished plate glass. A layer of transparent cellulose material (*see* PLASTICS) is sandwiched between two layers of glass and is then subjected to high pressure in a hydraulic press. Such glass is reasonably safe

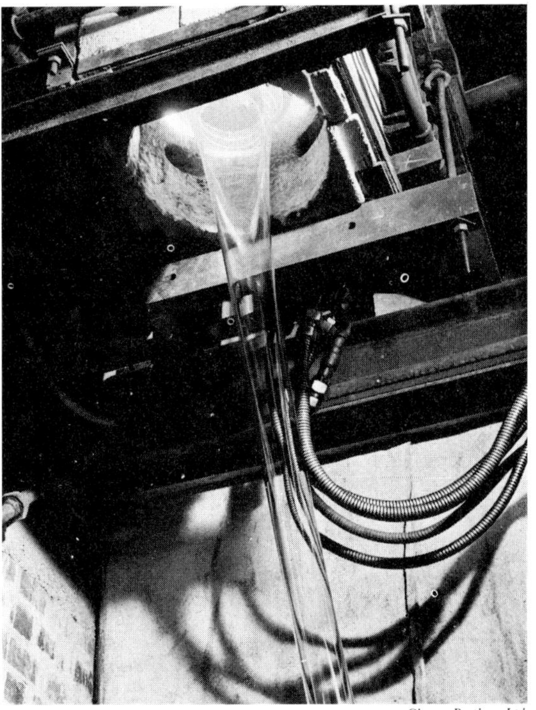

Chance Brothers Ltd.

MOLTEN GLASS FLOWS THROUGH A METAL RING AND IS THEN INFLATED INTO TUBULAR SHAPE BY BLOWN AIR

when fractured, because the splinters stick to the internal layer of cellulose.

Pyrex or fireproof glass is made, by all the methods above described, from a mixture of silica and boric oxide. Optical glass must be of the same consistency and transparency in every part, and it is necessary to stir the mixture constantly during melting and manufacture. The secret of successful stirring was discovered by a Swiss in 1790. Until recently, optical glass could be made only in small clay crucibles, which were broken away when the molten glass inside them had cooled. It can now be made by a continuous process in a furnace, like other forms of machine-made glass.

4. GLASS FIBRE. Thin fibres, a twentieth of the size of a human hair, are made from glass. There are two kinds—wool fibres, which are similar to staple textile fibres, and continuous filament fibres (*see* TEXTILE FIBRES AND FABRICS). To make wool fibre molten glass is poured into a rapidly rotating dish which has many hundreds of small vents round its edge. Glass is thrown out through the holes by centrifugal force to form fibres of random lengths. These are sprayed with a binder, normally resin, to make them stick together, and dried in ovens. Finally the fibrous mass is compressed and cut into the required shape, usually a flexible mat or rigid board. Continuous filament is made by drawing molten glass through very fine nozzles. The filaments which emerge cool quickly as they are so thin, and are drawn down at a speed of several thousand feet per minute to a common collecting point where size is applied to bind them together into a single strand. The yarn is then processed and used either in the manufacture of mats to reinforce plastics, or in textile operations.

Wool fibres are used chiefly for heat, cold, and sound insulation. The insulating material may be in the form of flexible mats, rigid boards, or moulded sections, and all these can be used for insulation, both of heat and sound, in private houses, in factories, and in institutional buildings. Continuous filament products can be woven into tape or cloth for covering electrical flexes, or into non-inflammable furnishing fabrics. They give strength when combined with plastics, and are used to make boat-hulls, car bodies, and chemical vessels.

See also Vol. XI: Table Glass.

GOLD AND SILVER WORK. 1. History. Gold and silver were found and worked almost as soon as man began to use metals at all. Both metals are found in a nearly pure state, often together, and objects were made of the natural alloy as well as of the pure metals.

At first gold and silver were used chiefly for jewellery and small objects (*see* Jewellery, History of, Vol. XI), though the Egyptians covered with gold plate the mummy cases and wooden objects placed in tombs. The Cretans (*see* Minoan Civilization, Vol. I) made gold drinking-cups decorated with scenes in relief. The Greeks made statues with a wooden core covered with gold and set with precious stones. Nearly pure gold was used in early times. This is soft, and was worked principally by beating with a hammer. It was also pulled into wire. Weapons were decorated with gold inlay on bronze, or with gold plates; silver bowls were engraved or embossed.

Few early examples of the goldsmith's work have escaped destruction, but some treasures, buried for safety, have been found. Torques—twisted gold neck-bands—show the characteristic richness of Celtic ornaments. Silver bowls, probably brought from Rome or Byzantium, have been found in Saxon graves.

In the Middle Ages the work of goldsmiths reached a high technical level. Most of the work which survived was made for churches: chalices, crosses, and, richest of all, the Shrines

British Travel and Holidays Assn.

SOLDERING THE SPOUT TO A TEAPOT

The body of the pot, the spout, and the handle are moulded separately

British Travel and Holidays Assn.

'PLANISHING' THE BODY OF A SILVER CUP

The body has been beaten into shape from a flat piece of silver

of saints (q.v. Vol. XII). These were often covered with gold and inlaid with precious stones and decorated with ENAMEL (q.v.).

In the 16th century goldsmiths and silversmiths generally worked for customers who commissioned objects such as salt-cellars and plates to decorate their houses and especially their tables. Hans HOLBEIN and other eminent artists made signs for silverware, and the Italian goldsmith Benvenuto CELLINI (qq.v. Vol. V) made beautiful pieces, including a large golden salt-cellar for the Pope.

The heavy and ornate gold and silver plate of the 17th century gave place to a lighter style in the 18th century. On the Continent objects were decorated in the ROCOCO style of the period (q.v. Vol. XII), but in England a simpler and more classical style was preferred. This was the time when the finest TABLEWARE (q.v. Vol. XI) was produced.

The taste for heavy ornament in the 19th century is seen in the gold and silver work of the period, but in the 20th century there has been a return to simpler designs. The same methods of working the metals have been used continuously since the earliest times, although handwork is now much more assisted by machinery. And the same methods of decoration, chasing, engraving, repoussé, and inlay, are still used.

In the year 1327 the Goldsmiths Company (*see* CITY COMPANIES) was incorporated. It was responsible for the quality of the work of craftsmen, both in material and in design, and for the ASSAYING (q.v.) and hall-marking of gold and silver ware. It still seeks to promote good design and watch the interests of its craftsmen.

2. METHOD. Gold and silver are easily worked; in their pure state they are highly malleable (that is, they can be bent and flattened by hammering), and can be cut with a knife. They may also be cast. The raw material is supplied by the bullion and assaying firms, who smelt the ores (*see* METALLURGY, Section 2, Vol. VIII) and make the gold and silver sheet and wire for the craftsmen. Pure gold and silver are so soft that another metal must be added to make an ALLOY (q.v. Vol. VIII) strong enough for modern manufacture; pure copper is generally used. For instance, 18-carat gold is 18 parts of gold and 6 parts of copper; 24 carat is pure gold. What is called 'sterling' or 'standard' silver is 925 parts silver to 75 parts other metal (usually

Ashmolean Museum

JAMES II GOLD DOUBLE WATCHCASE

Repoussé and pierced work with the bust of the king between the figure of Fame and cherubs; below, a ship and a fortress. (Actual size)

Ashmolean Museum

SILVER EWER, 1727–8

The decoration around the top and foot is chased and engraved, the coat of arms engraved. The applied straps are cast and the handle is cast and chased

copper). Modern silver which bears the 'hall-mark' (*see* ASSAYING) is of this guaranteed quality. Silver is also made in other proportions for other uses.

Silver is generally used for articles for the table and for household use, and for ceremonial occasions. Gold is used for more personal things such as jewellery, or serves to enrich silver objects. The working of the two metals is much alike. Whichever metal is used, it is first cleaned by 'pickling' or 'annealing'. To pickle, the metal is placed in a bath of warm sulphuric acid diluted with water. A few moments of immersion clean and dissolve any dirt which may be on the surface of the metal, which is then ready to be worked upon. ANNEALING (q.v. Vol. VIII) is the process of bringing the metal to a dull red heat (not more than 670–740° C.) on the forge with the aid of a blow-pipe. This burns off any dirt and evens out any stresses and strains in the metal, making it soft enough to work.

To make a beaker or vase, a sheet of metal of the required thickness is marked out, and cut to a circle of the correct size. It is then 'domed' into a cup-like shape by being beaten with a doming-hammer into a hollow block of wood. Before the next process, it must be annealed again. It is next 'raised', by being placed on a steel stake the shape of the finished vase, and beaten with a raising-hammer. In this process the metal is hammered in upon the stake in concentric circles, until the rim is reached. The repeated hammering hardens the metal, and so occasional annealings, to soften it, will be necessary before the shape is perfect. The metal will be covered with the marks from the blows of the raising-hammer, and these have to be removed with the planishing-hammer. This hammer has an almost flat, polished steel face which leaves flat marks on the metal. These are made to overlap each other in concentric rings, so that in time the raising marks are smoothed out.

The foot of the vase is made in a similar way—only, of course, from a smaller piece of metal. A ring of stout wire is generally soldered to it to give it strength and stability, and the foot is soldered to the body (*see* SOLDERING, Vol. VIII). In gold- and silver-work borax is used as a flux to ensure a proper union between the solder and the surfaces to be joined. The borax is ground up and mixed with water to a creamy paste and painted on to the parts where the solder is required to run. The foot is then heated in a forge until the solder melts—which it does at a temperature only just below the melting-point of the metal. When the foot is soldered to the body the work is ready to be decorated. The vase can be chased or repousséd, engraved and carved, inlaid, enamelled, nielloed or colour-treated, gilded or silvered, or embellished by being encrusted with filigree (metallic lacework) and precious stones.

3. CHASING AND REPOUSSE are applied either to beaten objects or to castings. Repoussé work is modelled in relief (from the back) by means of punches and a special hammer. In chasing, which gives a much sharper, clearer effect than repoussé, the design is cut in the face of the metal with chisels or gravers. The term 'chasing' is also used for the 'finishing' of cast surfaces, when blemishes and rough projections are removed, and the surface and ornamentation are cleaned up and sharpened.

4. ENGRAVING is much like chasing. It is usually applied to flat surfaces, the designs being carried out with gravers and scorpers. The designs are first 'pointed' on to the object with a steel point, either freehand or by tracing, and are then followed all over with the graver, which is a very sharp-pointed tool of hardened steel. This removes a thin shaving, or 'sliver' of metal, and leaves in the surface of the metal a thin furrow or trough; this is **V**-shaped, and has a brilliant, glittering look from the sharpness of the cutting tool. The scorper is used rather like a wood chisel, paring away a broad shaving of metal; in this way designs can easily be cut in low relief. For objects afterwards decorated with enamel, particularly rich effects can be got with the graver and scorper, since the flash of the cut metal shows through the transparent enamel.

5. INLAYS are made by piercing and cutting out shapes of different metals, and fitting them into one another to make a design, the whole forming a band or motive which can then be applied to a larger article. 'Damascening' is an inlay of gold and silver wire on iron or steel. The name comes from Damascus, where this art was used at the time of the Crusades for the decoration of weapons.

6. NIELLO is a process of great antiquity, which has for centuries been used in the East. It has even been found on objects taken from very ancient Egyptian tombs (*see* EGYPTIAN CIVILIZATION, Vol. I). Niello is a black alloy of silver, lead, copper, and sulphur, which melts easily.

Ashmolean Museum

SILVER WATCHCASE, EARLY 17TH CENTURY

With design in niello

When melted into the channels left by an engraved design, it shows the decoration as black upon a silver or gold background.

7. Silver Gilt is a way of covering silver with a thin film of gold. The oldest and best method is to apply an amalgam (or mixture) of gold and mercury to the surface. The modern commercial way of gilding is by Electro-plating (q.v. Vol. VIII).

8. Polishing. This process needs great care. After any work in silver has been cleaned in a pickling bath, its surface is 'stoned' carefully all over: that is, it is rubbed with a substance called 'water-of-Ayre stone'. This removes the film of oxide formed on the work during annealing, and all file-marks and scratches. It is then polished with charcoal and oil to which a little crocus powder is added, then with rouge and paraffin. After being washed in hot soapy water and dried, an application of dry rouge on a chamois leather gives it the most brilliant finish. Gold is polished in the same way, except that, after the charcoal and oil process, all plain surfaces are burnished over with steel or agate burnishers and finished with rouge and water. Silver is sometimes oxidised to tone down its glaring whiteness. This can be done by exposing it to the fumes of sulphuretted ammonia or other chemical compounds of sulphur. Ammonium sulphide, the material most generally used, gives a range of colour from purplish-black to a pale golden straw, the depth of colour depending on the strength of the solution and the length of time the article is exposed to it. Gold can be coloured in the same way, if it is first warmed until almost too hot to handle.

See also Gold-mining; Silver-mining; Assaying; Jewellery Trade.

GOLD-MINING. Gold is one of the few metals to be found in the earth's crust in actual metallic form (*see* Metal Ores, Vol. III). Gold neither rusts nor tarnishes, being the most 'noble' of all metals, and it is found in many widely scattered regions throughout the world as 'native gold'.

In ancient times gold possibly first caught the eye of man as bright yellow particles or small nuggets. These would have been found in pockets in the dried-out beds of rivers flowing through regions of gold-bearing rocks. Such rivers, through the centuries, caused the rocks to disintegrate and washed away the resulting sand and mud, leaving the heavy metallic gold concentrated in crevices, particularly in the slower-running reaches of the rivers.

The earliest important sources of gold were probably the river-washed (alluvial) deposits of Abyssinia and various parts of central Africa. Here, and later in India, China, and in many regions of which we have no record, gold was collected through the centuries by simply washing the light sand from the heavy gold. Very infrequently large nuggets of gold occur in river gravels. The Blanche Barkley nugget found in Australia weighed 146 lb. The largest recorded nugget was the Welcome Stranger, found in 1869 in a cartwheel rut in Victoria. This weighed 183 lb.

Most alluvial or 'placer' deposits are soon worked out. In the days when they were the only source of gold, production was scanty and spasmodic. In many countries, therefore, efforts were made to extract the gold from the various hard rocks, in which it existed as 'veins' or 'reefs'. The first operation was to crush the rock. Hollowed-out stones, in which the gold-bearing quartz could be crushed by stone hammers, or by large rocks worked by levers, have been found in Wales, central America, the Pyrenees, and Transylvania in south-east Europe; and the methods used in the mines of Upper Egypt 1,900 years ago have been described by Diodorus Siculus, the Greek historian.

In these early gold-mines the ore was first crushed to a fine powder, and then washed with water. The heavy particles of gold settled to the bottom of the hollow stone-container or mortar, and the worthless lighter material was washed away. It was, however, always difficult to prevent the smaller and finer particles of gold from being carried away with the water and powdered rock and lost. To prevent this, the water and sand were allowed to trickle over raw sheepskins or goatskins, in which the flakes of gold became entangled, and this probably gave rise to the legend of the Golden Fleece.

A big step was taken over 2,000 years ago when mercury was first used as a collector of gold. If a pulp of crushed ore and water is

Canadian National Film Board

PANNING FOR GOLD IN THE YUKON, N.W. CANADA

ground with mercury, the gold forms a stiff amalgam with the mercury. The amalgam is easily collected and washed free from the rocky material, and is then heated in simple retorts. The mercury vaporizes and is removed by DISTILLATION (q.v.), ready to be used again, and the gold is left as a residue, which can later be melted and refined.

Until the middle of the 19th century gold was mined on a small scale by these simple methods. In the Middle Ages Hungary and Transylvania were the most important centres of gold-mining in Europe. Later, from about 1750 to 1850, gold was discovered in the Ural Mountains, Brazil, Mexico, Peru, and Chile. But none of the new deposits was worked energetically, and until about 1830 the world's output of new gold appears to have remained steady at about 12 tons a year, or 400,000 troy ounces by the goldsmiths' measure. From 1830 to 1850 output started to rise slowly, mainly because gold was found in Siberia, where it lay in alluvial deposits of ancient rivers (*see* ROCKS, Section 3, Vol. III).

In 1849 gold was discovered by Colonel Suter in California, and then began the first of a series of 'gold-rushes' which were to recur at intervals for the rest of the century. The inhabitants of San Francisco rushed to the diggings as soon as they heard the news, and were later joined by emigrants from all over the world; ships were diverted from their ordinary routes to bring them from as far away as China or Australia. By the end of 1849 nearly 100,000 emigrants had poured into 'the Golden State', as California was called. People flocked in from the towns in the eastern states, travelling by sea, or overland in trains of covered wagons. The overcrowding caused the most appalling conditions: many, far from making their fortunes, died of starvation or disease before they even reached the diggings. The miners of this period, like the one in the song *Clementine*, were called 'forty-niners'. Two years later, rich deposits of gold were found in Australia by the Californian gold-digger Hargreaves, and in 1884 gold was found in South Africa, in the Transvaal. The Klondike region of the Yukon, in north-west Canada, was first exploited in 1896, and the last of the great gold-rushes took place in 1900, to the Nome area in Alaska, the United States territory beyond north-west Canada.

In all these areas the metal was found in rich but comparatively shallow deposits near the surface, so that gold-mining was an individual operation, and at first a sheet-iron pan was all the equipment needed. This was filled to about one-third of its capacity with 'pay-dirt', and water was added. After the contents had been mixed, the pan was shaken so that the mud slipped over the edges of the pan, leaving the yellow specks of gold at the centre.

Soon after the first gold-rush to California in 1849, a more specialized piece of apparatus, the 'cradle' or 'rocker', was introduced. This was a wooden box, 3 to 6 feet long and about 18 inches wide, fitted in a sloping position on rockers like those then used for children's cradles, and provided with crosswise slats nailed to the bottom. One man shovelled in the sand and gravel through a screen or sieve at one end, and the cradle was rocked by a second man who poured on water from a dipper filled from a nearby water-hole. The sand was thus well mixed with the water, the lighter material was washed away, and the gold particles were trapped in the pockets at the base. Sometimes a little mercury was added to help to catch the gold.

Cradles were soon replaced by 'sluice boxes', wherever water was available in quantities. These often consisted of hundreds of boxes, with slats or 'riffles', nailed in various patterns to the bottom, which trapped the gold from the sand, as this was washed through them by water from a diverted stream. The boxes were 'cleaned-up' at regular intervals, and on these occasions it was often necessary to station a man with a shot-gun to guard against raiders.

As a result of the gold-rushes the world production of gold during the years 1850 to 1890 jumped to an average of 150 tons a year. Nearly all of this was collected by simple means. By 1905, however, the cream of the rich alluvial deposits had been skimmed off, and the Witwatersrand or Rand in South Africa had become the world's chief producer of gold. Here, and in other major gold-producing regions of the world at the present time, it has become necessary to quarry and mine for the gold-bearing rock. Gold-mining is no longer a one-man adventure, but has become a highly organized industry. The first step is, as before, to crush the ore finely and to set free the gold particles; for this purpose heavy mechanically operated stamps were widely used. Although now obsolescent, many thousands of these stamp mills were once in use throughout the world. Each stamp weighed from half to one ton and there were usually several in a line, or 'battery' as this was called. Two stamps were raised to a height of 10 inches by a cam and then dropped on the ore contained in a 'mortar box'. About 60 to 90 strokes a minute was usual. The steady roar of hundreds of stamps in action was heard in gold-mines day and night in South Africa, Australia, and California. Water was fed into the 'box' during stamping and in the early mills mercury was added at the same time to form an amalgam. In later designs the crushed ore and water was led away in channels and the pulp was made to flow over copper plates covered with a film of mercury. The stiff amalgam of gold and mercury which was formed was treated for the recovery of the gold. Even under the best conditions, however, it was not possible to recover all the finer particles of gold by amalgamation; and if the gold in the ore was contaminated with other metals, only a very small proportion of actual gold was recovered.

By far the most important process for treating gold ores is the cyanide process, which was first used in 1890 at a mine in Johannesburg. It rapidly replaced all other methods of treating gold ores, and in a few years cyanide plants were

Transvaal and Orange Free State Chamber of Mines

POURING REFINED MOLTEN GOLD INTO A MOULD

The mould stands on a weighing machine so that the amount of gold can be weighed exactly

to be found in all gold areas of the world. A very weak solution of sodium or potassium cyanide (usually containing only 0·02 to 0·05% of the cyanide) will dissolve gold (and silver). Oxygen must be present, and the solutions must therefore be well aerated. To operate the process, the gold-bearing ore is crushed finely, either by stamps or rollers, or in various kinds of ball or tube mills—rotating horizontal cylinders in which hard steel balls or rods reduce the charge of rock to powder. The method of crushing depends on the nature of the rock. The crushed ore is then transferred to large circular steel vats, where it is treated with the weak cyanide solution.

After all the gold has been dissolved, the cyanide solution is decanted from the ore and powdered zinc is stirred into the liquid. The zinc is attacked and dissolved by the cyanide, and the gold and silver are rejected and thrown out of the solution as a fine mud. The precious metals thus 'precipitated' are recovered by filtering the solutions through cloth, and are cleaned with acids and melted in clay crucibles or open pots.

The gold obtained in this way, as well as the gold obtained by amalgamation or by panning, is never pure, and may contain up to 50% of silver, as well as appreciable quantities of copper, lead, iron, and other base metals. It is usually melted in small clay crucibles placed in a coke fire, and cast into bars of 'crude bullion'. This crude mixture of many metals needs to be refined. The modern method of refining is the chlorine process. The bullion is simply melted again in a clay crucible, and a stream of gaseous chlorine, from a cylinder of the compressed gas, is passed through the melt from a clay pipe which dips below the surface. In these conditions the chlorine combines with the silver and with any of the base metals present, and forms chlorides which collect as a crust on the surface. When all the impurities have been removed, the gold is cast into bars, ready for use.

If platinum metals are present, or if gold of the highest possible purity is needed, the gold may be refined electrolytically by the Wohwill process, a modified electro-plating operation (*see* ELECTRO-PLATING, Vol. VIII).

In 1966, the total world output of gold was approximately 47 million ounces. This represented almost 200 million tons of ore as mined.

See also MINING; ASSAYING.
See also Vol. III: METAL ORES.
See also Vol. XI: JEWELLERY.

GOLDSMITH BANKERS, *see* BANKING.

GOODWILL. In the business world this word means the money value of a firm's reputation and connexion among its customers. This value may have been built up for years by the special qualities of the owners, partners, or directors of a business; or the business may possess secret or patent processes of its own, or have specially valuable connexions, or be situated in some exceptionally favourable place. Notices are often seen to the effect that a firm has acquired the goodwill and assets of another firm: in other words, it has taken over not only its buildings, plant, and other assets, but also this extra earning power built up in the past.

Goodwill may therefore be an extremely valuable asset; but it is seldom entered in the account-books as one, unless new partners are being taken in, or the firm is being taken over by another firm. Partners or directors selling a valuable business can often get the purchaser to pay a large sum for goodwill. This will vary, and will depend on whether the business is steady and solid or merely speculative. Goodwill is usually calculated on the basis of so many years' 'purchase' of average PROFITS (q.v.). Thus, a firm in a steady line of business whose profits have averaged £2,000 a year might reasonably ask £6,000 for goodwill—or '3 years' purchase' of average profits. But no hard and fast rule for calculating the value of goodwill can be laid down: it depends very much on the state of trade, and on business confidence in general, at the particular time when it is being estimated.

See also LIMITED COMPANIES.

GOVERNMENT LOANS, *see* INTERNATIONAL FINANCE.

GRANITE, *see* STONE QUARRYING.

GRAPHITE is of the same chemical composition as DIAMOND (q.v. Vol. III); both are forms of carbon. The great difference between the two is that the diamond is the hardest mineral known and graphite is one of the softest. Graphite occurs in nature in the free state, as veins in igneous or volcanic rocks and limestones (*see* ROCKS, Section 2, Vol. III). 'Plumbago' and 'blacklead', the common names for graphite, are apt to mislead. Plumbago suggests the Latin word for lead, which is *plumbum*, and blacklead

Royal Sovereign Pencil Co.

MAKING PENCILS

The lead slips (made of graphite) have been pressed into shape and are ready for their wooden cases

actually includes the word lead, but graphite has nothing to do with lead.

Graphite is not very widely distributed. The principal deposits are in Ontario in Canada, and in Siberia, Mexico, and Ceylon. There were important English graphite mines at Borrowdale in Cumberland, but they are now almost exhausted. Until recently the world relied on natural sources for its supplies, but graphite can now be made artificially from other forms of carbon. Powdered carbon or powdered anthracite can be hardened into graphite by electrolysis (*see* ELECTRIC CURRENT, Section 6, Vol. VIII). Graphite can also be made artificially from carbon in the high temperature of the electric furnace.

Graphite has long had many uses in industry, but since the 1940's it has become of additional importance as providing essential material in the generation of NUCLEAR POWER (q.v. Vol. VIII). One type of atomic pile consists of radioactive elements surrounded by many tons of pure artificial graphite, which exert a controlling force. In the older industries graphite is used to line crucibles, heat-resisting containers in which molten metals and other substances are handled in furnaces. Lubricants of a semi-solid nature are made from it, particularly those used for the chain-drive of bicycles and motor-cycles. It is one of the principal ingredients of grate-polish and some of the metal-polishes. It is used for electrodes in arc lamps, and in dynamos and magnetos for the carbon brushes which pick up the electric current. The most widely known use of graphite is for making pencils, and for this purpose Cumberland graphite was renowned.

GREENGROCERY. People in Britain buy not only green vegetables, but other vegetables and fruit from greengrocers' shops, so that the greengrocer is more accurately called a fruiterer as well. Today he may also sell some frozen and processed foods, since he has to compete with supermarkets and MULTIPLE SHOPS (q.v.) which have taken away part of his trade.

Before the days of railways the greengrocer had to rely mainly on local growers for his supplies; even markets as famous as Covent Garden only served the people in their own locality. He could not buy fruit and vegetables from other parts of the country where the season was earlier or longer, because they would have

COVENT GARDEN MARKET IN NOVEMBER, 1969

perished on the long journey by cart. This meant that there were times, particularly in winter, when he had little to sell apart from a few vegetables and apples and oranges, which were cheap and popular, and so he was forced to sell other things, such as coal or firewood.

The coming of railways altered this, for it enabled market gardeners to send their produce quickly from one end of the country to another so that a greengrocer in Edinburgh, for example, could sell strawberries grown in Kent. In the 1880's the installation of COLD STORAGE plants (q.v.) in most steamships enabled wholesalers to import perishable fruit such as bananas from distant countries, and in this century the development of motor and air transport has speeded still further the journey between farm and shop.

The result of these advances is that the modern fruiterer and greengrocer can sell at the same time vegetables from a local market garden, potatoes from the eastern counties of England, apples from Australia, pears from Argentina, bananas from the West Indies, oranges from South Africa, lemons from Italy, grapes from Belgium, apricots from Spain, and strawberries flown in from Israel.

No greengrocer could hope to arrange himself for all the varied produce to be delivered to his shop direct from where it is grown. This is done by an intricate distribution system organized by

Meade Collection

COVENT GARDEN MARKET IN THE EARLY 19TH CENTURY

Covent Garden became a fruit and vegetable market in the middle of the 17th century

wholesalers. By this system, farmers and market gardeners in Britain sell their produce to or through wholesalers, who may be established in the big central markets or in the smaller provincial towns. These wholesalers are also supplied by importers of produce grown overseas. The greatest centre for the reception of imported fruit and vegetables is London, where most of it is sold either in Covent Garden Market or by auction in the London Fruit Exchange; a great deal, however, is also received in Southampton, Liverpool, Hull, and Newcastle. At these port markets some of the fruit is bought by local retailers, but the greater part of it by wholesalers in the provinces.

The wholesalers may supply the greengrocer in one of two ways. In London and the larger towns the wholesalers have stands in markets usually owned by the city or borough council, and retailers come there to buy their supplies. In towns where there are not enough wholesalers to make a market possible, wholesalers send out lorries, which call on shopkeepers daily, the drivers acting as salesmen.

This streamlining of distribution means that a greengrocer in Britain to-day can sell you most varieties of fruit and vegetables whenever you want them. You may still be told that celery, for example, is out of season, but with the increased use of cold storage systems in warehouses and shops, Britain is following the example of countries where you can buy any fruit or vegetable you want at any time of year.

See also CANNING INDUSTRY; GROCERY AND PROVISIONS.
See also Vol. VI: GLASSHOUSES; VEGETABLE GARDEN; FRUIT GROWING; CITRUS FRUITS.

GROCERY AND PROVISIONS. The trade of grocer is a very ancient one, although the goods in which the grocer deals have changed much throughout the years. The early grocers in England were called 'pepperers', and the current French word for grocer is *épicier*, which literally means 'spicer'. The early English pepperers dealt mainly in peppers and spices from the East, which were brought over every year by the fleets of Venetian sailing galleys which then did the carrying trade between northern Europe and the East.

Our modern word 'grocer' comes from the French *grossier*, which means 'wholesale dealer'. The first Grocers' Guild or Company was founded in 1345 by a score or more of pepperers of the City of London. Like other guilds it soon developed into a Livery Company of wealthy merchants, who were wholesale and not retail dealers. Later the word 'grocer' was used by retail dealers in what we now call 'groceries', and the older title of pepperer or spicer has been given up.

After the Middle Ages wholesale and retail grocers began to deal in far more goods than before. In the middle of the 17th century tea, coffee, and cocoa were imported from abroad, and became popular new beverages. At that time grocers dealt principally in those three articles; also in spices; in certain cereals, particularly rice; in currants, raisins, prunes, and similar dried fruits, and nuts; and in delicacies such as olives and anchovies, which came from nearby countries and could be sold quickly in the days before it was known how to preserve food. Most grocers were also provision dealers, and dealt in bacon, butter, and cheese.

At the end of the 19th century many more foods were being dealt in by the grocer. Bottling, canning, and other methods of preserving foods had been invented, and certain things that had hitherto been prepared only in the home, such as jam, cakes, biscuits, sauces, chutneys, and pickles, were now made in factories. Improved methods of COLD STORAGE (q.v.) in the warehouse and the shop have in the present century enlarged the range of groceries and provisions still further.

When our grandparents went in search of a grocer's shop they used their noses: the scent of roasting coffee could be smelt far down the street. Inside the shop were more smells: spices and herbs, soaps, polishes, biscuits, tea, cocoa, bacon, cheese, and sometimes paraffin. Teas were stored in large black containers with gold Chinese lettering on them. Sugar, dried fruits, rice, and other cereals came to the shop in sacks or boxes, and the shopkeeper weighed them into stiff paper bags as required. All the world sent its produce to the grocer's shop, and you could see and handle that produce before you bought it. It was fascinating but not very hygienic. The window was shut off from the shop by a partition and in it were piles of merchandise. At Christmas through the steamy window you could see scarlet mounds of glacé cherries, green and gold pyramids of candied peel, boxes of Spanish muscatels, sultanas, crackers, globes of Chinese ginger, Jordan almonds, and a hundred other delights.

Such shops still exist but they are becoming rarer. This is partly because today goods such as flour, lentils, sugar, butter, and margarine, which used to be sold loose, are almost always packed in containers of various sizes before they reach the grocer. Tea was one of the first things to be sold in packets bearing the trade name or 'brand' of the wholesaler or manufacturer. New packing materials, particularly polythene and plastic-coated cardboard, have made it possible to preserve perishable goods for longer periods.

Cadbury Bros.

A MID-VICTORIAN GROCER'S SHOP

At bacon factories, for example, bacon and ham are wrapped in polythene, which is sealed by heating it until the edges fuse together. The factories supply these packs to large shops and in some cases to private traders. CANNING (q.v.) and bottling have also increased the variety of goods a grocer can stock.

Another development in the grocery and provision trade is the increasing amount of refrigeration that is being installed in food shops—not like the refrigerators used in the home, but open-top counters relying on the extra density of cold air (*see* COLD STORAGE). Cooked meats, bacon, fish, and vegetables are sold chilled to temperatures of between 1·6°–4·4° C. The latest introduction to our shops is the frozen food counter, which stores a wide variety of vegetables, fruits, meat, and fish products, even complete cooked meals, at a temperature of minus 1·6° C., so that they keep quite fresh for months at a time.

The biggest revolution in the grocery and provision trade this century, however, have been the growth of firms owning groups of shops and, over the last decade in particular, the growth of self-service stores and supermarkets. Private traders now do less than two-fifths of the country's trade, the greater part of which is shared by the MULTIPLE SHOPS (which often have their own SELF-SERVICE STORES), the CO-OPERATIVE SOCIETIES, and the DEPARTMENT STORES (qq.v.). By placing large orders these trading groups get bigger discounts from the wholesaler and can therefore sell goods more cheaply than the small trader. To overcome this price difference many private grocers are now banding together in 'voluntary groups', working closely with one wholesaler of their own choice and buying almost everything they sell from him in order to get a bigger discount. The wholesaler may help the retailer with window-bills, and 'special offers', and even with modernizing his shop. To be sure of success the private trader now has to offer his customers competitive prices as well as such services as delivering weekly orders and allowing credit.

See also GREENGROCERY.
See also Vol. XI: FOOD, HISTORY OF.

GUILD SYSTEM, *see* CRAFT GUILDS.

GUMS AND RESINS. Gums are organic substances formed in various plants. A gum may trickle through the skin or bark, or it may be reached by making a cut in the bark. Gums are vegetable matter, but resins are either of a vegetable origin or produced artificially. The main difference between gums and resins is that gums will dissolve in water and not in organic liquids (such as alcohol), while resins will dissolve in organic liquids but not in water.

1. GUMS. The best-known gum is gum Arabic, so named because in ancient times it used to be collected at Arabian ports for shipment to Europe, though it has sometimes been called Turkey gum, because in the Middle Ages the trade shifted to Turkey. Today the Sudan supplies most of it. Gum Arabic comes from various species of acacia plant, and is chiefly used as an adhesive, and in the making of cold-water emulsion paints and water-colours.

Gum tragacanth is obtained from wild shrubs which grow in the mountainous districts of Persia and Asia Minor. It is partly gum and partly resin, consisting of a small quantity of gum which will dissolve in water, a little starch and cellulose, and a large proportion of a substance which swells in water. It is chiefly used as a binding material in the manufacture of pastel crayons, and sometimes as a 'medium' for painting on linen.

Dextrin (British gum) is a synthetic product derived from starch, and is largely used as a substitute for gum Arabic. Farina, which is prepared from potato starch, is rather similar.

2. NATURAL RESINS. There are two main types of natural resin. 'Recent resins' have come from living trees, and are obtained by 'tapping' the trees; fossil resins come from trees that have died and decomposed. Fossil resins are usually found buried beneath the ground; they are very hard, and are mainly used in the preparation of oil varnishes (*see* PAINTS AND VARNISHES).

The copal resins are obtained from tropical and sub-tropical regions, and are mostly of the fossil type. Of this type Congo copal is the most important as a constituent of varnish. It is among the hardest of the natural resins. East Indian copals range from varieties as hard as Congo to very soft types. They form a link between the oil varnish resins and the soft resins that will dissolve in spirit. In South America there are varieties of copal whose full uses are not yet known.

New Zealand provides the fossil kauri resin, derived from the large, now rare, tree of the North Island. The bulk comes from the peat swamps, but bush kauri is obtained from the living trees. These kauri gums were at first used in furniture varnishes, particularly for pianos and carriages, for they gave a very high gloss; but they take some time to dry, and Congo copal is now more used.

The hardest resin of all is AMBER (q.v. Vol. III), which is of great antiquity. Most of it comes from the coasts of N. Germany, where it is collected by dredging. Some is also obtained inland by mining.

The most important of the recent resins is dammar, obtained from trees in east Indian forests. This variety is soft, and melts readily at low temperatures; it will dissolve in the cold in turpentine and petroleum spirit, but not in alcohols. It is principally used in spirit varnishes.

A Mediterranean shrub yields the resin known as mastic, which is rather brittle and smells like balsam. It is used in high-class paper varnishes and for varnishing oil paintings. It is put on mixed with a spirit to render it liquid; when the spirit or 'solvent' has evaporated, the film of hard resin which is left behind is waterproof. Its disadvantage is that it darkens in the course of time, but the film can easily be removed by exposing the picture to alcohol vapour. This resin, in the form of alcoholic solutions, can be sprayed as a fixative for pencil and crayon drawings.

Sandarac, known by the other names of pine gum, white pine resin, and gum juniper, comes from North Africa. It is very useful for coating metals, as a thin coat gives a brilliant lustre. Accroides and Dragon's Blood are varieties of the sandarac species, used for colouring spirit varnishes and metal lacquers.

The oleo-resins are soft and easily moulded because, unlike 'recent' resins, they contain a large proportion of what are called 'essential oils' (*see* OILS, VEGETABLE). Typical oleo-resins are elemi, copaiba, and Canada balsam. When the material taken from pine trees is distilled to make turpentine (*see* DISTILLATION) the residue left behind is called rosin or colophony. Because of its method of manufacture, it is a semi-artificial resin. Rosin is a product which finds its way into a wide variety of finishing materials.

Oriental lacquer is a natural resin which, after being applied as a varnish, hardens to a tough dark film, taking a fine polish and being very lasting. It comes from a native Chinese tree, and is the basis of the famous lacquer-ware developed by the Chinese over 3,000 years ago (*see* LACQUER, Vol. XII). Burmese and Indian lacquers are slightly inferior varieties.

British Resin Products Ltd.

RAW MATERIALS BEING PLACED IN A RESIN KETTLE FOR THE MANUFACTURE OF ALKYD RESINS

Shellac, a substance extracted from trees by insects, is described in the article SHELLAC.

3. SYNTHETIC RESINS. Synthetic or artificial resins are products built up by the chemical reaction of comparatively simple compounds. The most commonly used types are alkyds, phenolics, maleics, melamines, and urea-formaldehydes (*see* PLASTICS; PLASTICS IN INDUSTRY).

Alkyds are used in varnishes and enamels for industrial or decorative use where durability is important (*see* PAINTS AND VARNISHES).

Phenolics are used in the preparation of moulding, varnish, casting, laminating, and PLYWOOD (q.v.) resins.

Maleic resins are used for full gloss paints and white stoving finishes. Melamine resins are normally mixed with others for stoving finishes. Urea-formaldehyde resins are used as adhesives, for treating paper and textiles, and in the manufacture of baking-enamels.

See also CHEMISTRY, INDUSTRIAL.

GUNNY, *see* JUTE INDUSTRY.

H

HAIR TRADE. Hair is much used in modern commerce both for spinning into yarn and weaving into fabrics. Human hair has been used for such purposes in the past, but the flourishing trade in it today is entirely due to the demand for wigs. Much of this hair comes from China and Hong Kong. Nowadays the hairs most widely used for weaving are animal hairs, such as mohair, cashmere, horsehair, and camel-hair. There is also a small use for rabbit-hair.

Mohair is the hair of the Angora goat, and is sheared from the coat of the animal once a year, like the fleece of a sheep. As its name suggests, this animal was originally bred in Turkey, one of the most important countries exporting mohair; Angora is another form of the name Ankara, the capital of modern Turkey. The animal has been acclimatized successfully in the Republic of South Africa, and that country now ranks next to Turkey as an exporter of mohair. The U.S.A. is the largest grower in the world, but is also the largest consumer, and has little surplus to export. Turkey still leads other producing countries in quality, but the Republic of South Africa now comes very close. Mohair is chiefly used for making carpets and rugs, and upholstery with a 'pile', or rather thick woolly surface. Fabrics made from it are exceptionally hard-wearing, and are much used for upholstering the seats of railway carriages and motor-cars, which are subject to hard and constant wear. Mohair takes dyes very easily, and makes beautiful rugs and carpets with a very long pile. It is the principal material from which theatrical costumiers make actors' WIGS (q.v. Vol. XI).

Cashmere is the name given to the fine, soft hair of the Kashmir goat. It is not sheared or cut from the body of the animal, but is collected during the moulting season. Some of it is plucked by hand from the animal, and the rest is picked up on their grazing grounds or from the twigs of bushes and shrubs that they have rubbed against. The animal is a native of Kashmir in northern India, and Srinagar, the capital of the country, is an important centre of the spinning, weaving, and embroidery trades. Cashmere shawls are famous, and very attractive bedspreads and other fabrics are produced. Little raw hair is exported from Kashmir. When it can be obtained, the hair is much used by British and American manufacturers for underwear and dress materials of the highest quality. China was formerly the biggest supplier to the world market.

Camel-hair is obtained during the moulting season, in the same way as the hair of the Kashmir goat. Camels must work during the moulting season as well as any other, and hair shed on the march or in camp is carefully collected. China was the biggest exporter of camel-hair before the Second World War, but the trade diminished during the political disturbances that followed it. The principal industrial use of camel-hair is in the weaving of cloth for men's overcoats.

Horsehair, which is coarse and tough, has many uses. The manes and tails were spun into yarn and made into upholstery cloth in Victorian days. Unspun horse-hair is used in Britain for stuffing mattresses and upholstery, and for stuffing and padding garments in the men's tailoring trade.

Rabbit-hair, which is imported mainly from Australia, is sometimes spun into yarn, from which many of the cheaper articles of clothing are made. Sometimes this yarn is mixed with superior yarn to make composite fabrics.

See also CARPET MAKING; FELT; WOOL WEAVING; UPHOLSTERY.

HAIRDRESSING PREPARATIONS, *see* COSMETICS; *see also* Vol. XI: HAIRDRESSING.

HALL-MARK, *see* ASSAYING, Section 2.

HAND-WEAVING, *see* WOOL WEAVING.

HANSEATIC LEAGUE. This was a confederacy of several seaports and trading towns in northern Europe, formed in the 13th century. When the League was founded, trade was exposed to many difficulties and dangers. The sea swarmed with PIRATES (q.v. Vol. IV) and the land with robbers. For some years before the League was formed, princes and other rulers of small states and cities had furnished armed escorts for merchants and their goods. But these armed escorts were so costly to provide that they were eventually withdrawn, and the merchants were left to organize their own protection as best they could. This system of local protection became inefficient and extortionate, and provided no real security. The merchants, therefore, sought a remedy in unity, and the League was formed. The name adopted was *Hansa*, an old Baltic word meaning a league. The title used by Englishmen was either Hanse or Hanseatic League, and its members—all foreigners, of course—were called Hansards.

The League began in rather a small way as a commercial alliance of the two important German seaport and trading towns of Hamburg and Lübeck. This move was so successful that other towns began to join. During the height of its influence it included about ninety towns on the coast and inland, scattered over the length and breadth of Germany, and including towns in what is now Holland. Its area ran roughly from what is now the Russian province of Latvia in the Baltic, southwards to Cracow, westwards to Breslau and Cologne, and then northwards to Amsterdam. Lübeck was its headquarters, and outside its own area it had important trading centres in Novgorod in Russia, in Bergen in Norway, in Bruges in what is now Belgium, and in London. Its London depot was called the 'Steelyard', on the site of what is now Cannon Street Station in the City of London. One of the

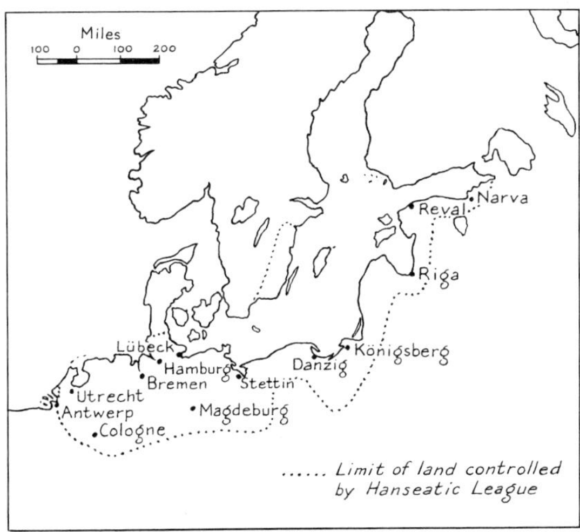

THE HANSE TOWNS

Staatsarchiv, Hamburg

A HANSEATIC PORT

A town crane was provided for loading and unloading ships. 15th-century painting

City Corporation's plaques commemorates this today.

By the 14th century the League had become well established. It had also attained most of its objects, which were to protect its member towns and their merchants from pillage and robbery; to develop overseas trade; to bargain with foreign rulers for trading privileges and concessions; and to organize an administrative machine to control and run its affairs generally.

It opened up in England at a time when the economic development of the country was backward. English merchants then lacked either the organization or the capital for conducting overseas trade on their own. So the League had little difficulty in obtaining privileges from English kings. The trading centres of the League in each country, the London Steelyard for instance, were called 'factories': a name used later by the EAST INDIA COMPANY (q.v.) for its own trading centres in many parts of India.

During the height of their influence in England the Hansards had the same privileged status as the officers of the East India Company later obtained in India, and kept themselves

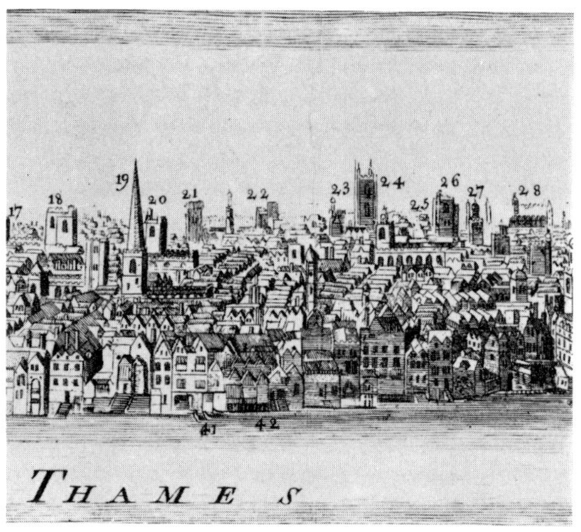

PART OF THE CITY OF LONDON SHOWING THE STEELYARD (NO. 41)

From a 17th-century engraving of London before the Fire

completely aloof from the ordinary life of native Englishmen. They were a kind of alien commercial aristocracy. The League imposed a discipline almost like that of a monastery on the staff of its foreign 'factories', and insisted that certain grades should remain unmarried, like the Roman Catholic clergy.

Such a system was possibly necessary at the time, when English kings were keen to develop overseas trade, and could not turn to any efficient body of English merchants. Yet it was bound to cause much jealousy and friction, and these did not take long to appear. Earlier kings encouraged the League because it represented an easy way of collecting taxes on goods. Later kings encouraged an independent organization of English merchants—the Company of MERCHANT ADVENTURERS (q.v.). The struggle between the Adventurers and the League was long and bitter, and did not end until 1587, when Queen Elizabeth abolished the privileges of the Hansards in London. The League kept the ownership of the Steelyard, but this ceased to be a trading headquarters. On the Continent its organization remained in being, although as the years passed the League gradually lost its commercial privileges in various countries. When the Steelyard in London was finally sold in 1853, the League then existed on the Continent in little more than name, binding together for political and commercial purposes various cities of northern Germany. But before the Franco-Prussian War of 1870 was fought, the German Chancellor, BISMARCK (q.v. Vol. V) formed his North German Confederation, and the League's independent history came to an end.

See also CHARTERED COMPANIES; TRADE, HISTORY OF.

HARD CURRENCY. This term came into use after the Second World War. Any country's money that is scarce abroad is a 'hard currency'. The normal way of obtaining a foreign country's money is by the export of goods; the foreign buyer gets the goods, and the bankers of the exporter's country obtain the price of them in foreign money. A country's imports must be paid for in foreign money, and what a country can import is normally limited by what it can export. But it is not necessary for import and export transactions to be done direct between the two countries concerned; for instance, Britain can obtain dollars not only by selling goods to the U.S.A. direct, but also by selling manufactured goods to, say, Malaysia, using the Malaysian money so obtained to buy Malaysian rubber, and then selling the rubber for dollars to the U.S.A.

Before the First World War, and in a lesser degree between the First and Second, this normal way of obtaining foreign money could be supplemented by borrowing from the bankers and investors, and sometimes from the governments, of the countries whose money was scarce (*see* INTERNATIONAL FINANCE). Some currencies became 'hard' in the period following the Second World War because the volume of international lending and borrowing and the pattern of INTERNATIONAL TRADE (q.v.) had changed. The 'hardest' currency in the immediate post-war period was the United States dollar, mainly because the U.S.A. was very wealthy and needed to import comparatively little. But today, it is no longer hard currency.

During part of this period Britain adopted a policy of strictly limiting imports such as tobacco from areas of hard currency, and of trying to sell increasing quantities of exports to those areas, such as the products of the MOTOR INDUSTRY (q.v.). There are often restrictions on the amount of foreign money holidaymakers may have.

See also CURRENCY; INTERNATIONAL TRADE; RATES OF EXCHANGE.

HARDWOODS. 1. In the timber trade the classification into hardwoods and softwoods is a purely botanical one, and there are timbers in

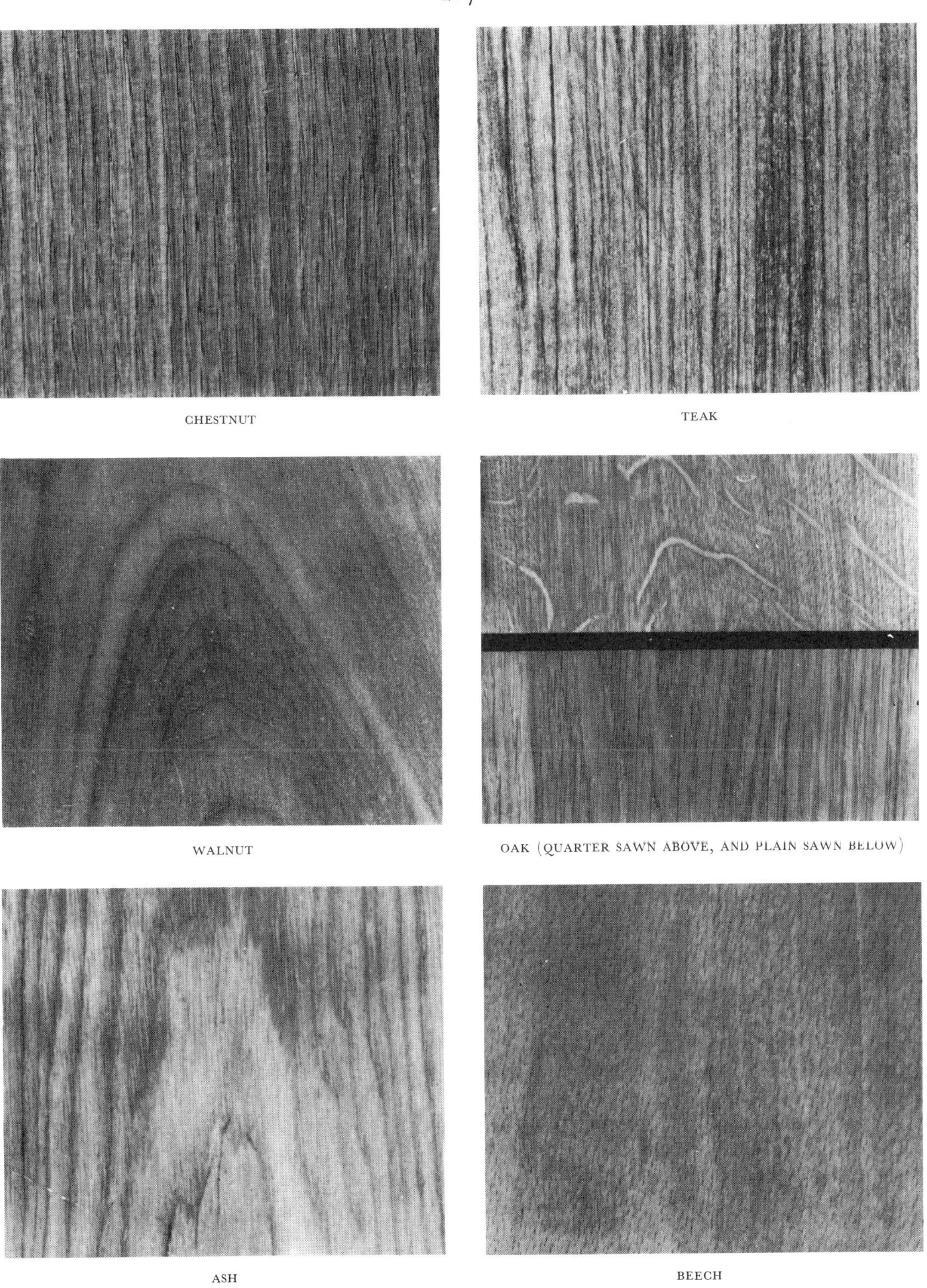

CHESTNUT

TEAK

WALNUT

OAK (QUARTER SAWN ABOVE, AND PLAIN SAWN BELOW)

ASH

BEECH

Timber Development Assn.

HARDWOODS

Quarter sawn means sawn through the centre of the trunk; plain sawn is any other cut

the hardwood class that are really quite soft to work. Hardwoods come from the so-called broadleaf trees such as ash, beech, teak, oak, rosewood, and mahogany (*see* TREES, BROAD-LEAVED, Vol. VI).

Nearly one-quarter of the earth's surface is forest land: 65% of the earth's forests is in hardwoods, and more than half of that is in the tropics. There are many thousands of species of hardwoods, and they are so well distributed that a good variety can be found in most parts of the world.

Timbers produced in a temperate climate are generally of a more even type than tropical woods, and they do not normally show the same extremes of colour, grain, and hardness. Timbers from the tropics are often either very hard and heavy, such as greenheart and lignum vitae, or very light and soft, such as balsa; many are beautifully coloured and figured.

The British Commonwealth has much fine timber. In Africa, for instance, Nigeria, Ghana, Sierra Leone, Uganda, Zambia, and also Tanzania produce a wide range, including mahoganies, beautiful cabinet-woods such as Guarea, Muninga, and African Walnut, and strong constructional woods such as Iroko, Afzelia, and Ekki. British Honduras, in Central America, produces some of the finest mahogany in the world, and Guyana produces the heavy greenheart. About one-fifth of the world's forest resources are in South America, which has the biggest reserve of tropical timber. Burma grows the best teak.

2. PRINCIPAL HARDWOODS. The following are some of the more important hardwoods used in industry:

(*a*) Ash. It is usually considered that the quality of British ash is superior to that of ash grown in other parts of Europe. A closely related timber known as Sen grows in Japan. Ash is very strong and elastic, and is used for many purposes, including tool handles of all kinds and hockey-sticks and other sports goods.

(*b*) Balsa is only half the weight of cork, and is the lightest and softest of commercial woods. Our main supplies come from Ecuador, where the trees grow almost incredibly fast, reaching in 7 years a height of 70 feet and a diameter of 2 feet. Balsa is not strong, but it is an excellent heat insulator, and is used in refrigerators and for making sun-helmets. Its most popular use is for MODEL AIRCRAFT (q.v. Vol. IX), but it has also been used in building real aircraft, including the famous 'Mosquito' aircraft of the Second World War.

(*c*) Beech is a strong hardwood which is easily turned on a lathe and bends well. It is a good all-round timber and much used for domestic articles, such as brush-backs, wooden spoons, and chairs. Supplies come either from British woodlands or from Central Europe.

(*d*) Birch is one of the most important woods in the manufacture of PLYWOOD (q.v.). Finnish birch plywood is made from the silver and common birches, and Canadian yellow birch is also used as a plywood timber. Quantities of birch are used for 'turned' articles, such as bobbins, spools, and domestic woodware.

(*e*) Chestnut. The wood of the sweet chestnut is very like oak in appearance, although it lacks the silver grain so characteristic of oak, and it is not as strong. It is often used as a general substitute for oak, and also for fencing and walking-sticks. The wood of the horse chestnut is white, soft, and woolly, and is little used.

(*f*) Elm. The common elm of the countryside provides a useful, tough timber, but it needs careful seasoning. Its principal use is for coffins, but it deserves a better and wider use. Wych elm is straighter grained and more elastic, and is used, like ash, for tool handles and sports goods. Rock elm from Canada has many uses in the shipbuilding industry.

(*g*) Greenheart is an extremely hard and heavy timber. It is very durable, and is so elastic that it is the best wood for fishing-rods. It is also used for canal lock gates and the timbering of wharves and jetties, as it resists the SHIP-WORM (q.v. Vol. II). Our main supplies come from Guyana.

(*h*) Hickory is a hard, white, very elastic timber from North America. Like ash and wych elm, it is used for the handles of pickaxes, shovels, and other tools, and for sports goods.

(*i*) Jarrah is an Australian hardwood, dark red in colour, strong, hard, and heavy. It strongly resists fire, and is much used for sleepers on the tracks of the London tube railways. It also makes good flooring, and is an excellent wood for heavy structures such as wharves and bridges. The tree is one of the hundreds of Eucalyptus species found in Australia.

(*j*) Lime is a whitish, soft, fine-textured wood that can be worked easily in all directions of the grain. For this reason it is a favourite among wood-carvers. Most of the famous wood carving of Grinling Gibbons, who worked for Sir Christopher Wren, was done in lime. British supplies are either home-grown or come from European countries. A special lime is imported from the U.S.A. under the name of Basswood.

(*k*) Mahogany is of many varieties. The earlier importations were of Spanish mahogany and came from the West Indies, mainly Cuba and San Domingo. Small quantities still come from Cuba and provide the finest quality wood, rich in colour, fine in texture, stable and often richly figured (grained). From Central America comes Honduras mahogany, a close relative of the Spanish but softer and lighter in colour; this also is a fine timber. Most of our mahogany supplies now come from a different (though related) genus in Africa; this wood is coarser textured, and a little less stable than those previously mentioned. It is quite suitable for furniture and interior woodwork and is also used for flooring.

(*l*) Maple. The most important kind is the Rock, Hard, or Sugar Maple of Canada. It provides a white, hard, strong timber. It is very popular for dance-hall and other floors that have to stand hard wear.

(*m*) Oak is probably the most widely used hardwood in Britain, and its uses range from furniture to beer-barrels. For some purposes English oak is the finest in the world. It is strong and well-figured, but needs careful seasoning. Oak from central Europe (Austrian, Volhynian, and Slavonian Oak) is milder, and so is often preferred by joiners and cabinet-makers. Other oaks used are Japanese, which is milder still and not so durable, and the White and Red Oaks from North America.

(*n*) Teak is one of the most useful hardwoods in the world. It is extremely durable, very stable, has little corrosive effect on metals, and resists fire. It is the best timber for ships' decks, and is also excellent for joinery, floors, and constructional work. It is used in the yacht-building and boatbuilding industry. The main supplies come from Burma, but we get teak also from Thailand, Java, and India.

(*o*) Walnut. There are two true walnuts: the European and the American Black walnuts. The first is found in many European countries, mainly in France, Italy, Russia, and Britain. France is the largest present source of supply. Walnut is used mainly for decorative purposes.

A number of unrelated timbers are also called walnut, because of a superficial resemblance: for instance, Australian or Queensland walnut. This is greatly used for veneers in interior decoration (*see* PLYWOOD AND VENEERS); but it lacks the typical grey colour of true walnut and tends to have a rather striped appearance. African walnut is pale brown, with widely spaced, thin, black stripes; it is closely related to the mahoganies, with which it grows in West Africa.

(*p*) Other hardwoods. Some rather interesting hardwoods were once largely used, but have lost their early importance. Rosewood is a dark, richly figured wood which has been used for over 300 years in the FURNITURE and CABINET-MAKING trades (qq.v.), especially as a veneer for pianos. It is still occasionally used for knife-handles and billiard-tables. Satinwood is a beautiful golden-yellow wood, with a high lustre, which was once very popular as a veneer for furniture. It is now little used, except for decorative brush-backs and similar small articles. Sandalwood is now almost unknown in Britain; at one time it was a favourite wood for lining ornamental boxes, because of its fragrant and persistent scent. The sawdust is used for the manufacture of joss-sticks and incense.

See also TIMBER INDUSTRY; SOFTWOODS; CABINET-MAKING; FURNITURE INDUSTRY.

See also Vol. VI: FORESTRY; TREES, BROADLEAVED.

HEMP, *see* ROPE-MAKING.

HESSIAN, *see* JUTE INDUSTRY.

HIDES AND SKINS are the raw material of the leather manufacturer or tanner. When man first used animal skins is not known. Skins, even when preserved by TANNING (q.v.), do not last as long as stone, pottery, metals, and bone, and our knowledge about the early use of skins is vague. The numerous flint scrapers and bone and ivory bodkins in our museums show that tens of thousands of years ago, in the early Stone Age, skins were being prepared and used long before textiles. Today hides and skins are essential raw materials and important articles of commerce.

Any animal skin can be made into leather, but the skins chiefly used come from cattle, sheep, goats, pigs, and horses. To a lesser extent the skins from dogs, deer, kangaroos, reptiles, marine animals, fishes, and birds are also used.

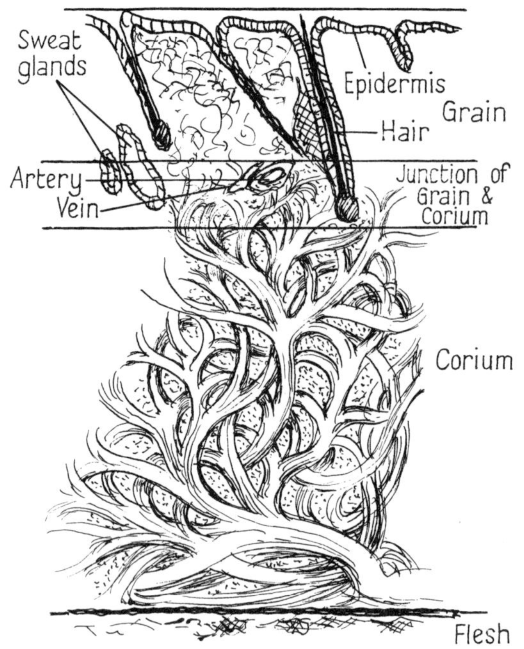

Leather Manufacturers' Research Assn.

SECTION OF HIDE (MUCH ENLARGED)

Snakes, alligators, crocodiles, lizards, seals, whales, walruses, sharks, plaice, dogfish, and ostriches all contribute to leather manufacture. 'Hide' is the trade word for the skins of the larger animals, such as full-grown cattle and horses; and 'skin' for the smaller animals and immature large animals, such as ponies and calves. Some skins are made into leather after the hair or wool has been removed; but the skins of the fur-bearing animals, and sometimes of sheep, lambs, and ponies, are dressed with the hair or wool still in place (*see* FUR TRADE).

Surprisingly large numbers of hides and skins are used in leather manufacture. Each day a fair-sized sole-leather tannery will tan 1,000 hides, and a large 'glazed goat' tannery may deal with 10,000 skins. Britain obtains large supplies from her own cattle, sheep, and horses, but enormous quantities of skins must come from abroad. Most hides and skins are by-products of the well-organized MEAT TRADE (q.v.), but many—especially those from the less common animals—come from remote and primitive parts of the world. Expeditions go to polar waters to hunt seals; and tropical jungles, swamps, and rivers are searched for lizards, snakes, and crocodiles. Cattle hides come mainly from the meat-packing works of the U.S.A., from the *frigorificos* or meat-freezing establishments of South America, and from Australia. Smaller quantities come from East and West Africa, Central America, and the Sudan. Sheepskins are imported from Australia, New Zealand, Argentina, and South Africa. Goatskins come from India, Pakistan, Ethiopia, Arabia, and Nigeria; lizard skins from East and West Africa, India, South America, Indonesia, and Malaysia; crocodile skins from South America, India, Malaysia, and Madagascar; and python skins from India and Malaysia. Veterinary surgeons, flaying instructors, and hide-and-skin inspectors are sent out from Britain to the less advanced countries of the Commonwealth, to supervise the raising, killing, and flaying of animals, and to ensure the production of good-quality hides and skins that will suit the purposes of the leather trades.

There is usually a long interval between flaying the skin off the animal and putting it into work at the tannery. If the flayed skins were left wet they would go bad, like meat; and they must therefore be preserved in some way. The commonest method is salting. This involves sprinkling the skins with salt on their inner side; or immersing the skins in strong salt solution or brine, after which they are drained and sprinkled with solid salt. The salting method leaves the skins slightly moist and heavy, and sometimes the salted skins are dried out. This avoids the transport of useless weight—a consideration in primitive countries, where hundreds of miles of carriage by mule, camel, or even human transport may be involved. A method found convenient in primitive or tropical countries is to stretch the skins out on the ground or on frames, and to dry them in the sun, or preferably in the shade. Sheepskins are often freed from the wool, and then 'pickled' in a solution of salt and sulphuric acid (*see* FELLMONGERING). Beetles and other insects eat skins, and must be kept away by sprinkling the skins with such chemicals as white arsenic, naphthalene, or D.D.T. Large numbers of hides and skins come to England from India and Pakistan in a roughly tanned condition. This 'crust' leather, as it is called, is dressed in England into lining, gloving, shoe-upper, and fancy leathers.

Hides are sold by weight, the trade unit being the pound. Sheepskins are sold by the dozen; python skins are sold by length, and crocodile skins are sold by width.

Not every part of an animal skin is used in leather manufacture. An animal skin is really a structure of three separate layers of tissue. The outermost layer is the 'epidermal' system, consisting of the epidermis proper, the hair or wool, and the sweat or fat glands. The whole of the epidermal system is removed from the skin before tanning, unless it is to be made into a furskin or woolskin for rugs or clothing. The innermost layer is the flesh, which connects the skin loosely to the underlying meat or muscle. This layer is also cut away before tanning. The third, or intermediate, layer is the 'corium' or 'derma' or true skin. It is a fibrous structure, and in its surface layer—just beneath the epidermis—the fibres are very fine, forming the tough grain of the leather which we see. It is this corium layer which the tanner makes into leather. It is to the closely interwoven and interknit fibre structure of the corium that leather owes its virtues: its flexibility, strength, and elasticity; its resistance to abrasion and its non-fraying edges; and its unique power of allowing water vapour and air to pass through it while resisting penetration by liquid water itself.

See also CURRYING; TANNING; LEATHER.

HIRE PURCHASE, *see* CREDIT.

HORSEHAIR, *see* HAIR TRADE.

HOSIERY AND KNITWEAR are both knitted fabrics. They differ from woven fabrics in that they are made from one continuous yarn by the formation of a series of loops, in contrast to the interwoven warp and weft threads of woven fabrics (*see* WOOL WEAVING). The industry began in Britain in the 15th century, when hand-knitting was introduced from the continent of Europe. By the 16th century hand-knitting had spread throughout Britain, and it still survives in parts of Scotland and Ireland as an organized branch of the industry.

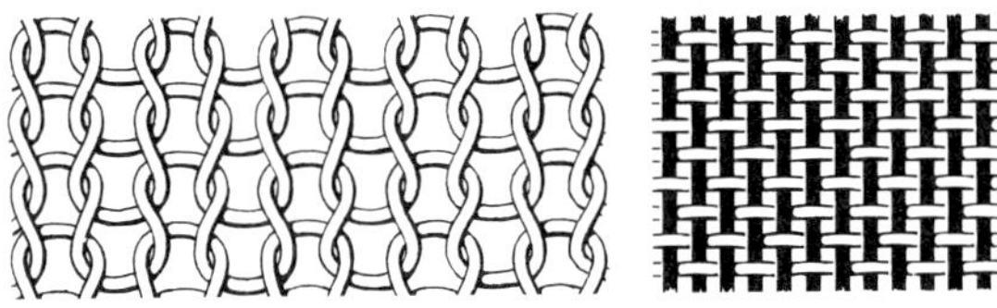

DIAGRAM TO COMPARE KNITTED AND WOVEN FABRICS

Hosiery is the general name for stockings and socks, and was the first textile industry in the country to be mechanized, although at first progress was slow. In 1589 the Rev. William Lee, a country parson who had no mechanical training or experience, invented the stocking-frame. His first invention was fitted with rather coarse needles and could deal only with woollen yarn, but some years later he produced an improved frame with finer needles upon which silk stockings could be made. At this period of British industrial history machinery was very unpopular, and those who invented it met with hostility and often actual violence. Lee and his brother James, together with some workmen, therefore emigrated with their machinery to Rouen, in France. The Lees were no more popular in France than in England, and William died in Paris in 1610. James, however, brought back to England nearly all his brother's stocking-frames, and after setting them up temporarily in London, he transferred them to Nottinghamshire, which

Courtaulds Ltd.

A CIRCULAR TYPE KNITTING MACHINE FOR KNITTING SHAPED UNDERWEAR has since been the great centre of the industry in Britain. The stocking-machine was at first used only for high-quality hosiery, chiefly of silk.

Lee's original machine was improved as years went on, but there was no important improvement until 1869. In that year a patent was granted to William Cotton, a native of Leicestershire, for a machine that has since become known as Cotton's Patent. This machine automatically increased or decreased the number of stitches required to produce a fashioned garment. It is still in regular use in the industry.

It was many years before the industry became fully organized on a factory basis, and even as late as 1870 the bulk of it was organized on the 'outworker' or DOMESTIC SYSTEM (q.v.). From Nottingham, its original home, the industry spread to the surrounding country and to Leicester, and later to Scotland, notably to Hawick, Kilmarnock, Stewarton, Greenock, Glasgow, Lanark, and Airdrie. In recent years other districts have entered the industry, and the greater London area is now important. With the growing demand for silk and rayon goods Leek and Macclesfield—where the yarns are spun—have become prominent towns in the industry. Several seaside towns (particularly Yarmouth, Blackpool, Southport, Bournemouth, and Newquay) have set up knitwear manufacture as a profitable regular alternative to the holiday industry, which is only seasonal.

Fashion changes, and the greater employment and higher earnings of women and teen-age girls have contributed to the industry's rapid expansion in the post-war years. Stocking fabrics are now too fine to be repaired and must be replaced; children's clothes, once home-made, are now more often bought by busy mothers. The increase in stocking sales between 1930 and 1960 reflects these changes clearly. In 1930, for every 100 women in Britain, 150 pairs of fully-fashioned stockings were sold per year. By 1960, the sales of the new seamless stockings had reached 1,100 pairs per 100 women per year.

From 1965, however, stockings' sales began to give way to those of tights and panti-hose, and by 1968 sales of the latter far exceeded 1960 stockings sales. The trend began with young girls in mini-skirts and spread to older women.

The chief natural raw materials of the industry are worsted, wool, cotton, and pure silk yarn, and some Shetland wool, cashmere, angora, and alpaca. Man-made fibres such as rayon, nylon, Terylene, Orlon, Courtelle, and Acrilan (*see* TEXTILE FIBRES, MAN-MADE) are, however, being increasingly used in the manufacture of knitted goods. Many of these modern fibres have the appearance and softness of wool and, since they do not shrink, are most suitable for the manufacture of knitted underwear, jumpers, skirts, and blouses.

Although all branches of the industry make use of the knitting process, different machines are used for different products. Large stocking machines of the modern type are capable of knitting sets of thirty or more pieces of shaped fabric at the same time, each piece being later seamed on other machines to form a fully-fashioned stocking. Small hand-operated 'flat-bar' machines produce single pieces of shaped or unshaped fabric for the making of outer garments. Cotton's Patent knitting-frame, which automatically varies the number of stitches, is used for the making of high-quality fully-fashioned underwear and outer wear. The cheaper type of product is made on circular machines, which knit the stocking or garment in its final circular form. The separate seaming used for fully-fashioned wear is therefore unnecessary, although the various circular sections, such as the arms and body of a man's vest, need to be finally seamed together.

See also WOOL INDUSTRY, MODERN; COTTON INDUSTRY; SILK INDUSTRY.
See also Vol. XI: KNITTING.

HOTEL INDUSTRY. The modern hotel industry is really the product of the transport revolution that began with the railway age (*see* RAILWAYS, HISTORY OF, Vol. IV), and has increased rapidly with the development of the motor-car. Inns and taverns have existed for centuries, and the records of all the ancient civilizations mention them (*see* INNS, Vol. IV). The hotel industry, however, dates from the early 1870's. By that time the habit of railway travel had become general, and for various reasons the railways and their stations had often been built far from the main roads and the old coaching inns. Most of this railway travel was on business, but pleasure travellers began to be attracted by the beautiful inland and coastal scenery through which the railways passed. At the same time many more people from other countries were coming to Britain to buy British manufactures. Social changes also created a

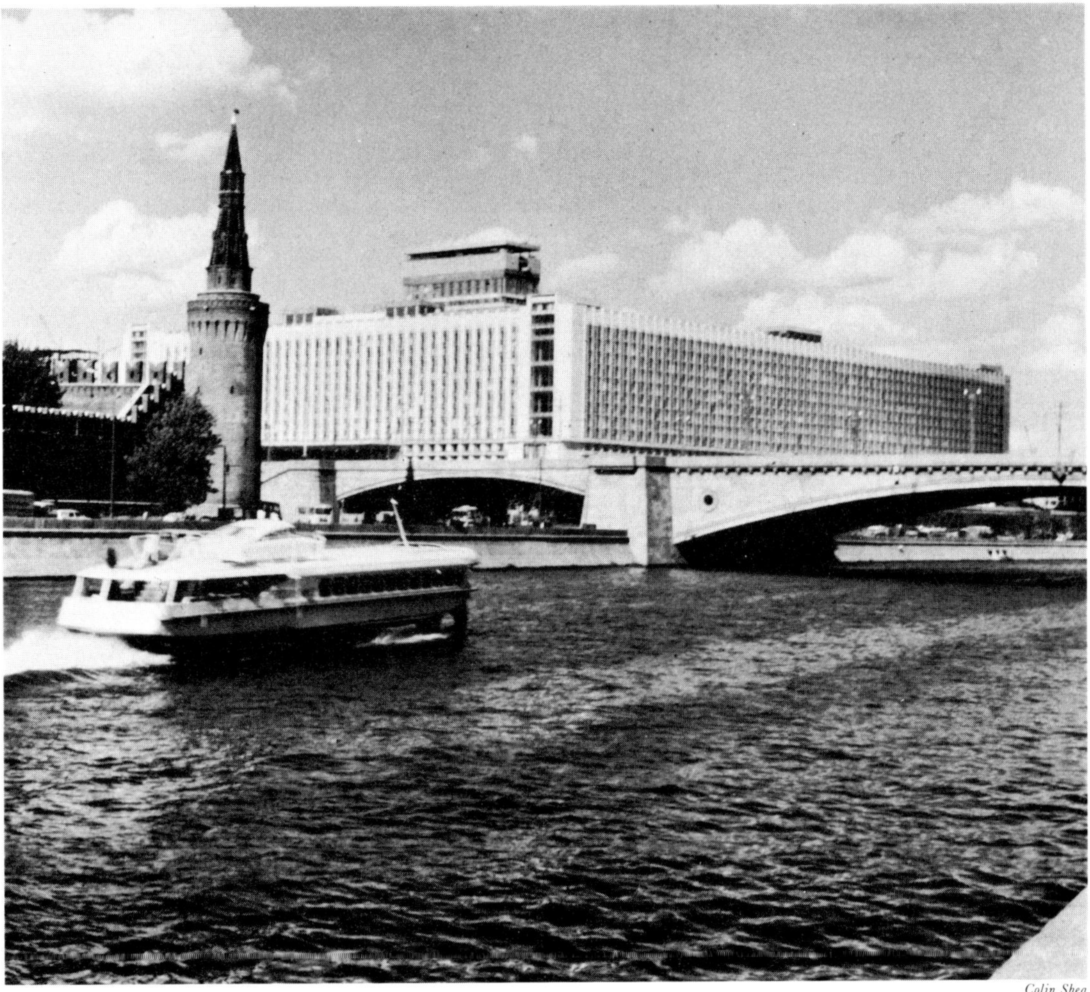

Colin Shea

THE HOTEL ROSSIYA, MOSCOW, WITH 6,000 BEDS, IS THE LARGEST IN THE WORLD

need for hotels. In the early part of the 19th century, as in much earlier times, travellers from abroad were usually put up and entertained in the private houses of their friends and acquaintances. As industry expanded, and wealth became more widely distributed, people who could not previously afford to travel now found themselves able to do so, and not all of them could arrange for private hospitality. All these factors led to the building up of the hotel industry as we know it in Britain to-day.

The railway companies took a leading part in developing hotels in the earlier days; they realized that there would be a direct profit in providing hotels, and they also counted on an increase of passenger traffic when new hotels had made travelling more comfortable.

The earlier railway hotels were planned to be comfortable and convenient for the travelling population, but they did not aim at any very high standard of luxury. Hotels of this sort were the Queen's Hotel, Birmingham, built in 1852, and the North Western Hotel, Liverpool, opened in 1871. It was the Midland Railway (now merged in the London Midland Region of British Railways) which pioneered the 'luxury' railway hotel. The first great hotel of this kind opened in England was the Midland Grand Hotel at St. Pancras Station, London. It was opened in 1873, when the Midland Railway had extended southward and acquired a London terminus. Its architect was Sir Gilbert Scott. He had originally drawn up plans for a new Foreign Office in Whitehall, and when this project was dropped by the Government, the Midland Railway Company bought Sir Gilbert's plans and built their new hotel to his designs. From then on the railways took the leading part in building hotels in the main industrial centres, and their station hotels became the backbone of the industry outside London itself.

The example of the railways was soon copied by private interests. Hotel building on a big scale required a good deal of CAPITAL (q.v.), which was one reason why the railway companies were prominent. The 1880's saw the opening of the Savoy and the Metropole in London, and the Metropole in Brighton. Between the World Wars such hotels as the Mayfair, The Park Lane, Grosvenor House, and the Dorchester were built.

More modest hotels also began to be built. The wealth of the country was becoming more widely distributed among its people. The motor-car and the motor-cycle were becoming cheaper and more numerous. New opportunities, therefore, presented themselves to the hotel trade. In London J. Lyons and Company, who already ran an extensive chain of popular restaurants and cafés (*see* CATERING INDUSTRY), opened the Strand Palace and Regent Palace Hotels shortly before the First World War, and the Cumberland Hotel just before the Second World War. These hotels aimed at comfort and a modest standard of luxury for the traveller of moderate income. The Regent Palace, with eleven hundred bedrooms was then the largest hotel in the world outside America. In the larger provincial towns the railway hotels were already established, but smaller towns sometimes had only the old coaching inns (many of which then required repair and modernizing), the better class of public-house, and the small boarding-house. Two firms, Trust Houses Limited and The People's Refreshment House Association, set about modernizing and improving hotels in the smaller towns and villages. Capital needed for improvements of this kind could not be raised by each hotel singly, and from this time the 'chain' system, or the ownership of branch-hotels by a central body became a feature of the medium-class hotel industry.

During the Second World War hundreds of seaside and country hotels were requisitioned for use by the Government and the Services, and many were damaged by bombing. London alone lost about 10,000 hotel bedrooms. Skilled managers and chefs were recruited for catering in the Services and in factories, while rigorous restrictions and food rationing made it impossible to preserve high standards. These restrictions and shortages continued until 1954.

In the years since, however, the British hotel industry has expanded enormously in response to the massive growth in travel and tourism. Numbers of foreign visitors to Britain have risen from less than a million in 1954, to well over 3 million in 1968, and the total is expected to exceed 5 million by 1970. The tourist industry is Britain's fourth largest source of foreign currency, worth some £350 million per annum; more than a third is spent directly in hotels and restaurants.

London now has many new multi-storey hotels, the outstanding ones being the Royal Garden, the Royal Lancaster, the Europa, the London Hilton, the Carlton Tower, and the Westbury; the last three are operated by American companies. A number of others are under construction or being planned, among them a giant hotel, with 2,000 bedrooms, opposite the Kensington Air Terminal. There are other multi-storey hotels at London Airport (Heathrow), and in Scotland, Manchester, Birmingham, Sheffield, Newcastle, York, Swansea, Coventry, and other provincial cities. The vast majority of these were built by large catering groups, such as Trust Houses, Lyons, Grand Metropolitan, Fortes, the Rank and Oddenino Organizations, and the brewery chains, such as Allied Breweries, Scottish, and Newcastle. Many older hotel companies have been taken over or merged, so that the industry is now dominated by these giant groups. American hotel interests have also invaded Britain, and British companies have, in their turn, extended their operations overseas, to Europe, Africa, Australia, and even America. The major airlines, too, have now entered this field in force, realizing, as the railways did a century ago, that suitable hotel accommodation would be required wherever travellers arrive.

These new hotels are the result of steep rises in the cost of city sites, which force the architect to make the most economic use of what ground he has. A typical hotel of this kind might consist of a multi-storey bedroom tower with restaurants and public rooms on the first and second floors, and an underground garage.

For motorists, motels are being built on main roads, designed on American lines, with groups of rooms or chalets. Many country houses have been converted into hotels and country clubs,

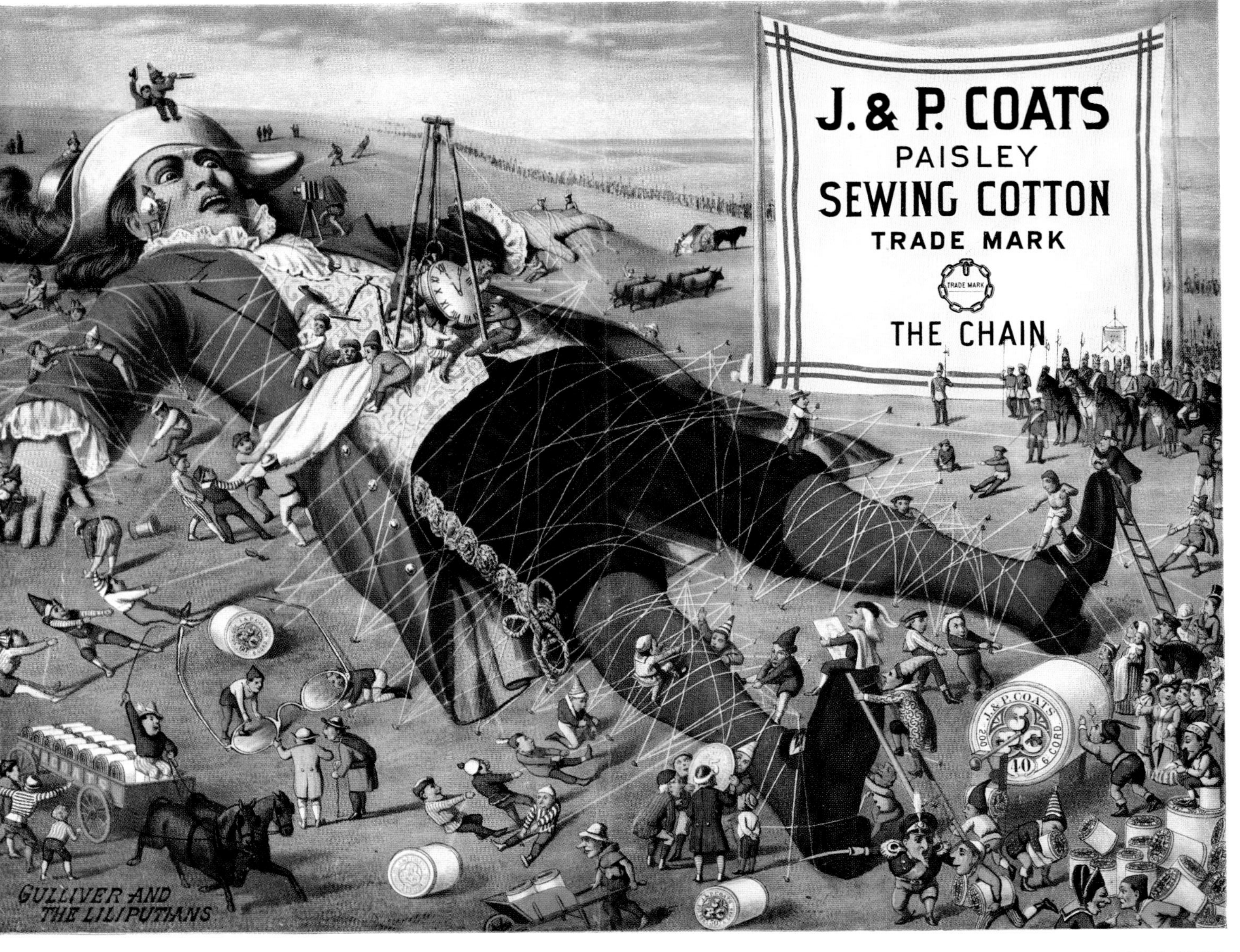

GULLIVER AND THE LILLIPUTIANS. A LATE 19TH-CENTURY POSTER FOR DISPLAY IN SHOP WINDOWS

which cater for permanent guests, as well as those staying a night or two, or having a meal.

Today there are nearly 17,000 licensed residential hotels in Britain, and an unknown number (probably 50,000 or more) of unlicensed hotels, guest houses, and boarding houses. The number of beds available is around 200,000 and it is estimated that about 30,000 more will be needed to accommodate the number of visitors expected in 1970. It seems likely that the hotel industry will continue to expand rapidly.

Whitbread and Co.

THE KITCHEN OF A COUNTRY HOTEL

The tourist business, especially in the country and at the seaside, however, is highly seasonal. Hotels forced to put up 'house full' notices in July and August, may have many empty rooms in January and February. In London the problem is less serious, and has been partially solved by groups of hotels offering special 'package deal' weekends during the winter.

Recently the Government has begun to realise the potential value of the hotel industry to the nation, and in 1968 they announced an incentive scheme which would make grants and loans available for building new hotels, and modernizing and extending existing ones. At present they propose to allocate about £10 million a year to this, but most hoteliers regard this as too little, especially when compared with the financial assistance given to hotels in other tourist countries, such as Spain and Italy. The Government also proposes to make registration of hotels compulsory, so that they may compile an official classified guide to British hotels.

See also CATERING INDUSTRY; TOURIST INDUSTRY.

HOTEL MANAGEMENT. 1. ORGANIZATION. The organization of the smaller hotels is naturally not very elaborate, but that of the leading hotels follows a general pattern. Many of these hotels are grouped into a single large directing company, whose managing director is responsible for policy and for co-ordinating the management of the members of the group. For each separate hotel there is a manager who is its chief executive officer. He often has an assistant manager to act in his absence and assist him generally, but usually without any special functions of his own. Under the manager and reporting direct to him are the accountant and his staff, the engineer and the maintenance staff, and, in larger hotels, the staff manager and the 'house detective', who looks after the property of the hotel and of its guests.

The day-to-day working of the hotel is usually subdivided into three main departments: house, food, and drinks. The house department includes the reception office, the hall-porter and his staff, and the housekeeper and her staff. The reception office is responsible for the booking and letting of rooms, the presentation and payment of accounts, keys, letters, telephone, records, inquiries, and safe-deposit arrangements for guests' valuables. The housekeeper is in charge of the cleaning and maintenance of all the public rooms, including staircases and corridors. She is also responsible for the linen and other furnishings of bedrooms, and for ordering and maintaining stocks of linen, furnishings, and cleaning materials. The housekeeper is also responsible for the service and cleaning of bedrooms, and supervises the staff of chambermaids and valets. The hall-porter is in general charge of all the uniformed staff, including footmen, page-boys, liftmen, luggage porters, and cloakroom attendants.

The food department is usually in two subdivisions, the kitchen and the restaurant. The chef (*chef de cuisine*) is in charge of the kitchen, supervising the ordering, cooking, and dressing of all food and the preparation of the menus. The restaurant manager is in charge of the restaurant and grill-room, and manages the staff of waiters. He is responsible, also, for the stocks of table linen, cutlery, china, and glass.

The drink department is in charge of the cellar manager, who is responsible for ordering and maintaining an adequate and varied stock of wines and spirits, and for controlling their issue to the restaurant, public rooms, and bars.

2. MANAGEMENT. Hotel finance is not at all a simple matter. Most large firms have to borrow money for building and equipping their hotels by mortgaging their property on security (*see* DEBENTURES). High rates have to be paid to local authorities, and the furnishings and equipment have to be kept in good condition and periodically renewed and modernized. A large staff must be engaged and maintained, even if bedrooms remain vacant and the restaurants and other public rooms have few customers. A hotel has therefore to meet very heavy standing or overhead charges (*see* COSTING), and its rate of TURNOVER (q.v.) is low.

The successful financial management of a large hotel depends principally on its having a sufficiently large number of bedrooms for letting. There are hotels in London and the provinces that have never been profitable since they were built, largely because their bedroom accommodation is too small. Even if there are enough bedrooms, a high percentage must be kept constantly occupied, and in this respect Britain is less well situated than other countries, notably the U.S.A. Local conditions have helped the American hotel industry. The United States is a country of long distances, where 'out-and-home' business journeys can rarely be completed in a single day. American business travellers are forced to spend at least one night away from home, and for most of them it is more economical to organize a longer absence and to visit a series of cities in turn. By contrast, the London business man can often do business in a provincial city and return to London the same evening. A British provincial hotel is also under a handicap compared with a London one. London has its attractions, even during the week-end, and the departure of business guests from hotels on Friday afternoons is counterbalanced to a limited extent by an influx of country visitors to London. Provincial hotels, except at holiday resorts, have few week-end visitors.

The 'seasonal' type of hotel, such as the Highland hotels in Scotland, and similar hotels at summer coastal resorts, has its own management problems. These are sometimes solved by the hotel closing down during the 'off' season; sometimes by a scale of different charges at different seasons: the charges are increased during busy times, when the demand for rooms is heavier.

In Britain, a hotel serving alcoholic drinks must be licensed. The licence may be restricted, allowing, for example, service to residents only or to non-residents taking meals. An unrestricted licence, sometimes called a publican's licence, enables non-residents to drink without buying a meal. Residents may drink at any time, but non-residents must observe ordinary licensing hours. The staff in licensed hotels, but not in unlicensed hotels, are protected by statutory wage regulations which prescribe minimum rates of pay, holidays, and so on.

3. TRAINING. Since 1967 the major responsibility for the training of hotel management and staff has been taken over by the Hotel and Catering Industry Training Board, one of a series of such bodies set up by the Government. The Board consists of an equal number of employers and employees, as well as educational representatives, and is responsible for organising the training of all levels of staff in the industry. It is financed by a statutory levy on employers, based on a percentage of their annual wage bill. Those employers who train staff to an acceptable standard receive grants to offset the levy, while employers who do no training pay the levy, but receive no grant. Grants are, however, also made for group-training schemes, enabling small establishments to train staff on a collective basis. The Board has appointed training officers in all areas to give hoteliers and caterers advice and assistance on training.

In addition to this kind of apprenticeship to the trade, there are courses at all levels in hotel schools and technical colleges. These range from 4-year degree courses in management and administration at the University of Surrey (B.A.) and the University of Strathclyde (B.Sc.), through 3-year and 2-year diploma courses, to the City and Guilds' basic cookery course for chefs. Craft certificates are also offered in waiting, housekeeping, nutrition, hygiene, bookkeeping, and reception. Detailed information

Holland & Hannen and Cubitts

THE HILTON HOTEL, TRINIDAD

can be obtained on request from the Hotel and Catering Industry Training Board.

See also HOTEL INDUSTRY; CATERING INDUSTRY.

HUDSON'S BAY COMPANY. After the EAST INDIA COMPANY (q.v.), the Hudson's Bay Company is possibly the most famous of the great CHARTERED COMPANIES (q.v.) founded from the 15th century onwards. It was set up after two Frenchmen had made perilous journeys into the great northern forests of Canada, where the Cree tribe of Red Indians lived, and brought back a valuable collection of furs in 1660. In the French Canadian city of Montreal the Frenchmen could not get the terms they wanted for future trading, so they came to England. Prince Rupert, cousin of Charles II, saw chances of a profitable trade in furs, and in 1668 he organized a voyage from England to test the truth of the Frenchmen's reports. As a result, in 1670 the King granted a charter to Prince Rupert and seventeen others to form the Company of Adventurers of England trading into Hudson Bay. The charter gave the Company exclusive rights of colonization, government, and trade in what are now the northern and western portions of Ontario and Quebec, the whole of Manitoba and Saskatchewan, the southern half of Alberta, and the south-east corner of the North-west Territories. The Company's territory was given the name of Rupert's Land; and the first settlements were made on the shores of James Bay, and on the banks of the Churchill and Hayes rivers on the western shores of Hudson Bay.

As far as trading went, the venture was successful from the beginning. Increasing numbers of Indian traders journeyed to the Company's posts with valuable loads of furs and bartered them for other goods offered by the Company. But it was not found so easy to push into the interior and to carry on with exploration and settlement. There were many difficulties: the severe climate, lack of knowledge of the country, the vast distances to be covered, and, later, the rivalry of French traders from the south. For many years the Company could do little more than hold on to a few isolated posts on the coast; their posts were sometimes attacked and destroyed by French expeditions, for during the Company's early years there was almost continuous war between England and France. The Company was near ruin when England and France signed the Peace of Ryswick.

Later the French adopted a new system of trading which threatened the Company's interests. The Company had hitherto established fortified posts on or near the shores of the Bay, to which the Indian tribes had to bring the furs.

Hudson's Bay Company

TRAPPERS IN NORTHERN MANITOBA, CANADA, ARRIVING AT A HUDSON'S BAY COMPANY STORE WITH THEIR FURS

But in 1731 the French fitted out in Montreal the first of a series of strong expeditions, which penetrated through the prairie provinces to the foothills of the Rocky Mountains and established trading posts in the actual hunting grounds in which the Indians trapped the animals. The Indians often preferred to deal with the French traders, as they were thus saved the long, troublesome, and often dangerous journey to the distant northern posts of the Hudson's Bay Company.

The Company also faced difficulties in England, for in 1749 a hostile group in Parliament tried, but without success, to deprive the Company of its charter. Urgent instructions were sent to the trading posts in Rupert's Land. The Company's men were ordered to push their posts farther inland, to explore the interior with energy, and by living among the Indians to increase the Company's influence over them.

In 1759 General WOLFE (q.v. Vol. V) captured Quebec, and the next year Montreal surrendered. The military power of the French in Canada had been broken. But the Company still had to face the competition of independent traders. As British immigration increased, this competition grew.

The Hudson Bay route was not the only way into the great forests of the north: another route lay by the tributaries of the St. Lawrence river and across the Great Lakes and the prairies. Rival companies were formed which made use of this southern route. In 1784 nine companies, operating from Montreal, amalgamated into a single concern called the North West Company, largely controlled by men of Scots ancestry who had settled permanently in Canada.

The struggle between the two companies became very bitter. At some of the more important centres, trading posts and forts were built by each company side by side; for nearly 40 years there was fierce economic rivalry between them, and often violence and bloodshed. As a result the Indians increased their trapping of animals to a point where normal replacement by breeding could not keep pace with the numbers killed. Competition had become ruinous; and the only remedy was the amalgamation of the two rival companies, which took place in 1821.

The Hudson's Bay Company now entered upon a great period of its history. Exploration, settlement, and administration went ahead peacefully and purposefully. The Company's posts were extended north and west, and as far as the Pacific Ocean.

In 1867 the Canadian Provinces were formed into the Dominion of Canada; so in 1869 Rupert's Land and other settled districts were taken over from the Company. In compensation the Company received £300,000 in cash and the right to one-twentieth of the land in any township settled by the Company, outside the northern forests and within the 'fertile belt' between Lake Winnipeg and the Rocky Mountains. The Company thus acquired 7 million acres of land.

Unlike the East India Company, which had ceased both to trade and govern by 1858, the Hudson's Bay Company still lives on today as a great commercial corporation with a variety of enterprises, which include a number of large department stores situated throughout Canada, a wholesale department, and an oil company. The company's fur trade is now international, raw furs being bought in Europe, Asia, and Africa; and its conservation schemes have replenished large areas with muskrat and beaver. The company also holds mineral rights over several million acres of land in Canada.

See also FUR TRADE; CHARTERED COMPANIES.

I

IMPORTS, *see* International Trade; Overseas Trade.

INDENTURES, *see* Apprenticeship.

INDUSTRIAL ALCOHOL is the liquid known to scientists as 'ethyl alcohol' or 'ethanol'. This chemical is not only the active constituent in alcoholic drinks (wines, beer, cider, whisky, gin, brandy, and rum), but is also very important to industry, which in Britain alone uses over 100,000 tons a year. The pure alcohol has a specific gravity of 0.794 and boils at 78° C.

The substances made from it, or with its aid, include acetic acid (used for Plastics, such as cellulose acetate); polishes, varnishes, lacquers, stains, paints, and enamels; embrocations, tinctures, liniments, and lotions for medical use; soap, perfumes, and Cosmetics (qq.v.); insecticides, plant washes, sheep-dips, and veterinary medicines; the liquid for compasses, spirit-levels, and thermometers; de-icing and anti-freeze solutions; many lubricating and other industrial oils; anaesthetics such as ether and chloroform; drugs such as insulin, and Dyes (q.v.).

The growth of the organic chemical industry during the 19th century created a need for large quantities of alcohol; the need increased after 1929, when Britain began the large-scale making of alcohol-based solvents and of acetic acid for plastics production.

Till recently, most industrial alcohol was made by Fermentation (q.v. Vol. II) of the sugars either in or producible from the starches in cereals (wheat, barley, oats, rye, maize, and rice); in tubers (potatoes, cassava, artichokes, sweet potatoes, and yams); in roots (sugar beet, mangolds, and sugar mangolds); and in molasses. Since cereals, tubers, and roots are needed for food, molasses became the only source of industrial alcohol in Britain. Molasses is the uncrystallizable syrup left after the manufacture and refining of sugar, and contains about 50% of sugars which can be converted into alcohol. Cane molasses comes from the West Indies and Cuba; beet molasses is obtained from the British beet-sugar industry.

The fermentation is caused by the enzyme action of special strains of Yeast (q.v. Vol. II). This is grown in laboratories, in test-tubes and

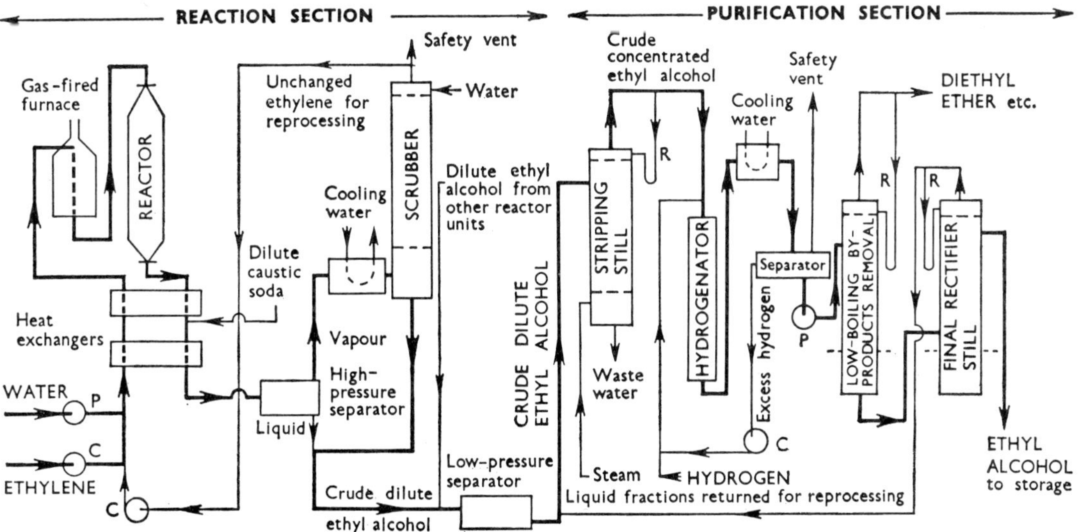

B.P. Chemicals (U.K.) Ltd.

DIAGRAM TO SHOW HOW INDUSTRIAL ALCOHOL IS MADE FROM ETHYLENE, OBTAINED BY A 'CRACKING' PROCESS FROM A LIGHT PETROLEUM DISTILLATE

B.P. Chemicals (U.K.) Ltd.

DISTILLATION (PURIFICATION AND RECTIFICATION) SECTION AT A PETROLEUM CHEMICAL WORKS PRODUCING INDUSTRIAL ALCOHOL

small flasks, and then transferred first to small tanks and then to large fermenting-vessels, each holding up to 100,000 gallons of molasses solution, diluted with water to reduce the sugar concentration to 10–12%, with the correct amounts of acid and nutrients for the yeast. Fermentation takes some 50 hours at 30°–35° C, evolving carbon dioxide gas in the process. The 'wash', as the fermented liquid is called, is then distilled in large copper stills, which may deal with 10,000 gallons per hour. The crude, concentrated alcohol is then purified or 'rectified' by further distillation.

Molasses itself has become valuable for feeding animals, and although fermentation is still used in countries where there is a local surplus of natural materials, scientists have devised other and cheaper ways of making industrial alcohol.

Crude petroleum oil is the basis of the most important modern method, introduced in 1948. In the refining process, the oil is separated into various 'fractions' (*see* DISTILLATION). One of these, mixed with steam, is heated to 730° C in oil-fired furnaces, where it 'cracks' into a mixture of short-chain hydrocarbon gases, particularly ethylene (C_2H_4), propylene (C_3H_6), butylenes (C_4H_8), and butadiene (C_4H_6). To stop these recombining, they are cooled very quickly, and compressed until they liquefy. The liquid is then distilled and separated into its component gases. In contrast to ordinary distillations, the separation plant works at temperatures as low as −100° C and at pressures up to 500 lb. per sq. in.

To make ethyl alcohol (*see* chart) the ethylene (C_2H_4) from the cracking process is mixed with steam (H.OH) and passed through a bank of reactors at a temperature of 190° C and under pressure of 1000 lb. per sq. in. The reactors contain a catalyst of phosphoric acid held in a sponge-like earth, which helps the ethylene and steam to combine, giving ethyl alcohol (C_2H_5OH). After cooling and treatment with dilute caustic soda to remove traces of the catalyst, the vapour is dissolved in water in a 'scrubber', and the dilute ethyl alcohol, containing aldehydes and diethyl ether, is then concentrated in a stripping still. The impure ethyl alcohol is treated with hydrogen in a hydrogenator containing nickel as a catalyst, where the aldehydes are turned into the corresponding higher alcohols. The mixture is then purified by distillation as in the end stages of the fermentation process. Since only about 4% of the ethylene is converted into alcohol each time, the unchanged ethylene is piped back to go through the process again.

Most of the 'Plain British Spirit' thus produced is sold as such for industrial purposes. It is colourless, with a slight, rather pleasant 'spirituous' smell and a sharp taste, but it has little real flavour; the various tastes of alcoholic drinks come from other substances. It is, of course, drinkable, and consequently the excise authorities keep very close watch on its use, to ensure that the tax or 'duty' is paid on any spirit which is not used for an approved purpose. The spirit can be 'denatured' and rendered undrinkable by the addition of wood naphtha (crude methyl alcohol), mineral naphtha, pyridine, diethyl phthalate, and other substances with an unpleasant taste, thus producing the various grades of 'methylated spirits'.

In countries where there is plenty of cheap electricity, calcium carbide can be made from limestone and coke, and on treatment with water this yields acetylene (C_2H_2); if two hydrogen atoms are added to each acetylene molecule, ethylene is again produced, and can be converted to ethyl alcohol as before. Ethyl alcohol has a molecular formula C_2H_5OH.

INDUSTRIAL ART, *see* Vol. XII.

INDUSTRIAL PSYCHOLOGY, part of the general science of PSYCHOLOGY (q.v. Vol. XI), is the scientific study of the behaviour, capacities, and inclinations of people at work, both individually and as members of groups. It is more correctly called occupational psychology. Its practical aim is to improve the contentment, health, and efficiency of people at work, by improving the conditions they work in. It has three main aspects which are closely linked.

1. FITTING PEOPLE TO JOBS. Occupational psychologists give vocational guidance, that is advice to young men and women about the kinds of job most likely to suit them. They also study and give advice on how to select the best applicant for a particular job, and how to allocate an employee to the job most suited to him. They devise methods of training those who have been selected, and methods of assessing and recording a man's performance on the job. With this information, plans can be made for the promotion and further training of individuals to meet an organization's future requirements.

2. ADAPTING JOBS TO PEOPLE. This entails studying the physical environment, and noting the effects that noise, light, heat, colour, music, or vibrations have on work performance. The organization of work is also studied, and this includes the design of machines or tools, the layout of factories or offices, the planning of work periods, hours, and shifts, the DIVISION OF LABOUR (q.v.) or the allocation of tasks, and the effects of automation and computers.

3. RELATIONSHIPS BETWEEN THE INDIVIDUAL AND THE GROUP AT WORK, sometimes called 'organisational psychology'. This includes a great variety of subjects: relations between manager and worker, factory and office, or one department and another; an organisation's policy towards its employees; the 'structure of management', that is, the formal definition of the responsibility attached to a managerial position; the effectiveness of communications, and of different methods used; the attitudes of people at work; the effect of small working groups on output; the morale of different organisations, and its connexion with payment and amenities, the flow of work, the methods of supervision, and the general sense of responsibility, purpose, or involvement.

Occupational psychology became recognised as a science in its own right during the First World War when a Committee on the Health of Munition Workers showed how hours of work can be related to output: if, for instance, workers did too much overtime, their rate of output fell. At this time intelligence tests

Nat. Inst. of Industrial Psychology

A MAN BEING TESTED FOR HAND AND EYE CO-ORDINATION
The man controls the pencil with two handles and has to make it follow a pattern printed on the paper.

began to be widely used in the U.S.A. for selection in the armed forces. In 1921 the National Institute of Industrial Psychology (N.I.I.P.) was formed in Britain to carry out research and advisory work on the topic. It began by studying and practising vocational guidance, and investigating the effects of physical environment and movement on fatigue and productivity.

The importance of the third aspect of occupational psychology, human relations, was brought home by the research of Elton Mayo and his Harvard colleagues at the Hawthorne plant in Chicago, U.S.A., which was first reported in 1933. They examined the possible effects of sympathetic supervision and group loyalties. At the same time the N.I.I.P. was studying workers' attitudes and training methods for semi-skilled jobs. During the Second World War methods of selection and training developed considerably, especially in the armed forces. Since then many organizations have made important contributions to the subject on such topics as the acquisition of skills, aids to learning, joint consultation (between managers and workers' representatives), records of people at work, and the selection and training of computer staff.

Occupational psychologists work in various organizations, for example, in the personnel or training departments of industrial companies, and the armed forces; or in government services, such as the youth employment agencies, the adult occupational guidance or rehabilitation units, and training boards; or they may act as career advisers at universities. Some work for industrial consultants; others undertake field research or advisory work in research associations; others again carry out laboratory research and teach at universities and technical colleges. Occupational psychology is related to many other studies including sociology, medicine, physiology, engineering, and design. The occupational psychologist is concerned with people working, rather than with work methods alone or with habits of spending money, so his interests are wider than those of a specialist in business efficiency or marketing.

He must be able to conduct interviews and construct and interpret aptitude tests; to analyse a job in terms of what is done and the sort of person required to do it; and to design records and questionnaires. He needs to know how to measure and assess performance by the quantity or quality of a man's output, by his absences, his length of service, or his career record, and he must be able to exercise personal judgement. He may have to plan and carry out long or short investigations in order to diagnose problems; in doing so, he must always take into consideration differences between individuals and between their environments, as well as the relationship between the different branches of occupational psychology.

See also FACTORY ORGANIZATION.

INDUSTRIAL REVOLUTION. This is the term used to describe a whole series of changes in the methods of work and in the organizing of industry that have taken place since the 18th century. These changes, which were accompanied by a great increase in the population of England and other European countries, were revolutionary in their effects upon the daily lives of all kinds of people. The steam-engine, which provided a new source of industrial power, has had as striking an influence on human history as any great political upheaval, and inventors such as James WATT and Richard ARKWRIGHT can be compared in historical importance with poets like WORDSWORTH and statesmen like NAPOLEON (qq.v. Vol. V). It was indeed the French Revolution which first suggested another use of the word 'revolution'; a French economist said that while France had had a political revolution, England had had an economic one. But the phrase did not come into general use until it was chosen as the title of some lectures given by the historian Toynbee in 1881.

It is impossible to describe this enormous series of industrial changes as being the result of any single cause. At the beginning of the 18th century, however, two important factors were at work. In the first place, trade at home and abroad increased very rapidly; this increased saving and investment and encouraged business adventure, particularly among British industrialists. In the second place, at the beginning of the 18th century the forests of England were gradually being wiped out, and it became increasingly difficult to find suitable fuel. The shortage of trees, and difficulties in the way of importing foreign timber, led to an increased demand for an alternative fuel. This created a need for technical improvements in the COAL INDUSTRY (q.v.), and for the increased use of coal instead of charcoal for iron smelting.

Coal and iron were the two most important raw materials of the early Industrial Revolution. Without their joint use it would have been impossible to develop either the staionary steam-engine or the locomotive. The result was that the iron and coal areas of the country gained tremendously in importance. Great new industrial regions, such as the Black Country in Staffordshire, developed an entirely new sort of environment for men to live in. The landscape became dominated by industry. A town like Sheffield, which grew up in one of England's beauty spots, became a nest of small workshops and furnaces, which removed the last traces of the earlier natural setting.

Coal and iron took the place of wood, water, and wind, which had provided the industrial power of earlier periods of history. They in turn have been supplanted by electricity, light-alloy metals, and PLASTICS (q.v.), during the course of the so-called Second Industrial Revolution which followed on the invention in 1867 of ELECTRIC MOTORS and GENERATORS (qq.v. Vol. VIII). The widespread use of electric power has affected industry quite as much as steam once did, and we ourselves are living in a period of continued industrial revolution at least as striking as that of the late 18th century. AUTOMATION (q.v.), the electronic control of industrial machines, is our most recent development.

The inventors of this period were backed by the business men who put their inventions to general use. The great technical genius of James Watt was allied with the business initiative of Matthew Boulton, a Birmingham business man, who went into partnership with Watt to make the Soho engine works in Birmingham the most important industrial enterprise of the 18th century.

An inventor was often a very unpopular person. He was frequently accused of taking

Meade Collection

AN EARLY 19TH-CENTURY STEEL WORKS AT SHEFFIELD

bread from out of the mouths of the poor. Hargreaves, for instance, the inventor of the spinning-jenny (see below), had his cottage at Blackburn attacked by an angry mob, intent on destroying his machine. The early manufacturers also had to keep close watch on their factories, to prevent their being attacked. There is a vivid description of such an incident in *Shirley*, by Charlotte Brontë (*see also* LUDDITES).

Changes in the production of coal and iron were followed by others. During the 18th century there was a rapid growth in other industries, such as POTTERY and TEXTILES (qq.v.). The most important maker of pottery was Josiah WEDGWOOD (q.v. Vol. V), who in 1754 invented a 'new green earthenware, having the smoothness and brilliant appearance of glass'. The work of Wedgwood led to a great change in the everyday habits of the people, and began that narrowing of the gap between rich and poor that is still going on. At the beginning of the 18th century ordinary people ate from wooden trenchers or platters, while the well-to-do laid their tables with pewter ware. In this, and in other ways, the Industrial Revolution provided new materials for the consumer, just as it provided new machines and techniques for the industrialist.

The story of textiles is even more spectacular. COTTON (q.v.) was the industry which changed most. There had been big improvements in weaving after the invention of the flying shuttle by Kay in 1733; weavers could now work much more quickly and produce cloth of greater width. But the spinners could now no longer keep pace with the weavers, and the weavers began to complain of being short of material. As early as the 1730's a spinning-machine was invented, and in 1764 Hargreaves patented his new 'spinning-jenny', which he called after his wife. Other inventions followed, one leading to another. The most important were Arkwright's water-frame and Crompton's 'mule'. Inventions for spinning now led to further inventions for weaving. Cartwright invented a loom which was driven by water-power, and eventually steam-power was harnessed first to the cotton and then to the wool industries. There was a widespread demand for cotton cloths, which the new machines helped to meet. There were also opportunities for making good profits; and Richard Arkwright, who had begun as a travelling dealer in hair, realized when wigs went out of fashion that cotton was a far more profitable business. Arkwright was the first big factory organizer, and did much to introduce new machines.

The rise of the factory system produced some of the most important social consequences of the Industrial Revolution. Factories have a relentless discipline of their own; workers must arrive to time, and work side by side for definite hours and for wage-payments. The factories produced a new sort of industrial worker who owned none of his working tools or machines, and was employed for long hours to increase the profits of the factory-owner. There were many good masters, but—as one of the advocates of factory reform stated—'a steam engine in the hands of an interested or avaricious master is a relentless power to which old and young are equally bound to submit'.

The factory system developed most rapidly in the 30 years after the end of the war with Napoleon (1815), and the speed of development and urgency of its expansion led to many abuses, which were only abolished with the making of a national factory code of regulations. This code was extended and improved throughout the 19th and 20th centuries (*see* INDUSTRIAL WELFARE, Vol. X).

But it was a long time before factories were to be found in every part of the country. At first they were mainly situated in the textile districts of the north; by contrast, Birmingham and the midlands were districts of small workshops.

The factory gathered workers together in one place; the new transport system, based first upon roads and canals and then upon railways and steamships, helped first to unify England and then to make the world as a whole a much smaller place. Just as the invention of the steam-engine gave men an increased control over the forces of nature, so the changes in transport enabled them to gain an increased control over the obstacles of distance and time. Long journeys were made easier; oceans and continents were crossed. The world was opened up to industry and trade.

Improvements on the roads were made by such men as John Metcalfe, better known as Blind Jack of Knaresborough, and Telford, and Macadam (*see* ROADS, HISTORY OF, Vol. IV). Some of the improvements can be measured by the shortened times of journeys by stage-coach;

AN EARLY 19TH-CENTURY FACTORY AT TEWKESBURY

The men are making stockings by machine, and children are employed for spinning and unskilled work. The supervisor wears a top hat

even before the beginning of the railway age it had become possible to travel long distances in a single day. Road improvements were preceded by river improvements, and by the building of CANALS (q.v. Vol. IV). Business men played a large part, for the building of canals greatly reduced transport costs. Wedgwood, for example, was largely instrumental in having the Grand Trunk Canal built. Brindley's 7-mile canal from the collieries at Worsley to Manchester halved the price of coal in the city. What had been done by improved road and water transport was magnified many times by the introduction of railways (*see* RAILWAYS, HISTORY OF, Vol. IV). The Stockton and Darlington line was opened in 1825, and the line from Manchester to Liverpool five years later. The great 'railway mania'—the craze for building as many railways as possible—came between 1844 and 1848. By the end of that burst of building there were 5,000 miles of railway in operation in Britain. STEAMSHIPS (q.v. Vol. IV) did for the world what railways had done for England. The first transatlantic steam voyage was made in 1819, and the first steam voyage from London to Calcutta 6 years later. Goods and raw materials could now be transported freely and cheaply to and from all parts of the world, which was fast becoming a single, vast market.

This change-over from a local to a world market has caused some of the most important long-range effects of the Industrial Revolution. Through the extension of markets, countries and peoples have come to know more of each other, and have become more dependent on each other for foodstuffs, raw materials, and manufactures. The building of a world economy has only come about at the price of disputes and anxieties. UNEMPLOYMENT (q.v.) and depression have tended to become international instead of merely national or local, and there is a great deal of quarrelling between governments over such things as trade agreements.

The Industrial Revolution is a challenge as well as an achievement. It provided challenging problems that have appealed to men's hearts and enlisted their energy. It threw a spotlight on many evils and even horrors—smoky, dirty, and overcrowded towns, for instance, and the overworking of women and children. Its abuses were firmly attacked, but not all its problems have been solved, nor all its abuses remedied.

As to its achievement, opinions will always differ, for each generation looks on history with different eyes. If we try to measure the achievement, we must balance the tremendous increase in the goods and services that we can now enjoy—everything from nylons to motor-cars—against a loss of many things that can never be replaced—the green fields of Sheffield, or the pride and skill of the individual hand craftsman.

See also Division of Labour; Exchange and Trade; Domestic System.

See also Vol. X: Industrial Welfare; Poor Law.

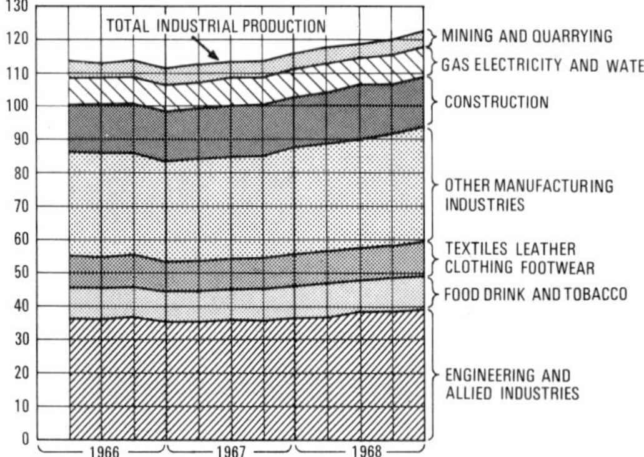

INDUSTRIAL PRODUCTION IN BRITAIN, 1966–68

The width of the bands indicates the contribution of each main industry

INDUSTRY. Most human occupations are either industrial or commercial. Those engaged in industry produce or make things. Those engaged in Commerce buy and sell them, or Transport them from place to place, or provide services such as Banking and Insurance (qq.v.) that assist industry.

Industries can broadly be classified as either extractive or manufacturing. The first, as their name suggests, extract materials from the land or water. Mining (q.v.) is an extractive industry, so also are fishing, whaling, agriculture, horticulture, and forestry, which are dealt with in Vol. VI. Some of these, such as the mining of coal and iron, extract materials whose quantity is limited, and which are not replaced by nature when they are removed. Other extractive industries, such as agriculture or forestry, if they are well managed, do not take more out of the soil than can be restored.

Manufacturing industries are concerned with transforming one type of material into another, or converting a raw material into useful goods. For example, manufacture transforms iron ore, coal, and limestone, which are products of the extractive industries, into iron and steel, which are manufactured products. Similarly, forestry is an extractive industry, but the making of Wood Pulp, and the making of Newsprint (qq.v.) from the pulp, are manufacturing industries.

People often talk of the Hotel Industry, the Catering Industry, and the Tourist Industry (qq.v.). In these, things are not produced or made, but services are rendered; and so they are often classified as the 'services industries'.

INDUSTRY, LOCALIZATION OF, *see* Localization of Industry.

INLAY AND MARQUETRY. Both these crafts are used for the decoration of furniture and wood panels. Inlay consists of gluing in

Crown Copyright

ARMCHAIR INLAID WITH HOLLY, CHERRY, AND BOG OAK, ABOUT 1600

Victoria and Albert Museum

small pieces of different or contrasting material, flush with the surface of the wood. English oak chests or cupboards of the 16th century, for example, often have simple geometrical designs inlaid in holly or poplar (which are much whiter woods than oak) and bog-oak (which, until ebony came to be imported, was about the blackest wood available). Later in the century elaborate patterns and pictures were inlaid in different-coloured woods and other materials, such as mother-of-pearl. In marquetry the whole surface of the wood is covered with a sheet of veneer into which the pattern or ornament, cut from a contrasting veneer, has already been fitted and glued. Veneer, which has been used in British CABINET-MAKING (q.v.) for some 300 years, is a sheet of very thin wood, perhaps no thicker than a postcard, which can be glued over a carcass or panel or less ornamental wood, and then polished. Both inlay and marquetry are flat forms of decoration: they rely for their effect on the colour of the wood, the direction of the grain, and the outline of the inlays. Carving, on the other hand, gets its effect from the shadows thrown by the varying surfaces of the wood (*see* WOODWORK, HISTORY OF).

To inlay a piece of furniture, a piece of paper is first glued to the wood to be inlaid, and each piece is sawn out with a fine saw. Ornamental lines can be made by saw cuts which show up dark when filled with glue. The places in the piece of furniture into which the inlay is to fit are 'chopped down' with gouges and chisels, the recess being made perfectly level with a router (a special kind of plane). The inlay is glued into place; as the glue sets, it shrinks, tending to pull the inlay downwards and to make a perfect join. A final levelling and polishing of the piece of furniture completes the work.

In marquetry the design can be much more elaborate and delicate than in inlay. There are two methods of cutting the veneers for marquetry. In the first the veneer for the background and that for the inlay are fixed together, and the design is sawn through both in one operation. They are then separated, and the pieces of veneer are interchanged; the two make a perfect fit, since a marquetry saw is very fine. A piece of paper is glued over the surface to hold the inlay in place, and the whole is then glued down on to the groundwork. Finally, the surface is cleaned up and polished. In the second method, several different veneers can be used for

Crown Copyright

Above: WALNUT AND MARQUETRY CABINET ON STAND, LATE 17TH CENTURY

Below: WARDROBE MADE BY BOULLE FOR LOUIS XIV, LATE 17TH CENTURY

Made of ebony with marquetry of white metal and brass on tortoise-shell, with ormolu mounts

Victoria and Albert Museum

The Mansell Collection

MARQUETRY PANELLING IN DUKE FEDERICO'S STUDY IN THE PALACE AT URBINO

The illusion of solidity is given by perspective to the marquetry pictures of niche, open door, etc.

the background veneer, and those for the inlay are cut separately. The design is first drawn on paper, and then pricked out with a series of fine holes. By placing this master pattern on a second sheet of paper and dusting a dark powder over it, the design can be transferred, as many duplicates being made as there are to be different kinds of veneer. These are then glued to the veneers, and the design is cut out, assembled, and fixed as in the first method.

In the early days the cutting of the design was done entirely by hand. Later, the marquetry-cutter used a 'donkey', a device by which the veneer could be gripped in upright jaws and turned as the sawing required, the saw being held taut in a frame which was free to move on guides. It was thus always at right angles to the veneer. If the same design is to be used for a number of articles, several thicknesses of veneer can be cut at the same time. For every two veneers two complete designs are produced, both alike in outline but with the veneers reversed.

Marquetry was used in Italy from the 15th century to make elaborate pictures on panels and furniture. In the palace at Urbino the Duke's study has walls veneered to look like open cupboards in which books appear to be standing, and musical instruments lying on shelves seem to stick out from the wall. Marquetry was introduced into England after the Restoration, and by the time of Queen Anne it had developed into a craft of great delicacy and beauty. In France, towards the end of the 17th century, the Italian style of marquetry, with tortoiseshell and metal inlays, had been developed by Boulle, and reached a high standard; it is now known as Buhl-work. French furniture became increasingly elaborate during the 18th century, and was decorated with inlay, marquetry, and gilt bronze carving; but in England the fashion for marquetry did not last long. It was revived in a different form towards the close of the 18th century, and continued until the opening years of the present century, when a tremendous amount of marquetry was used. It then fell into disuse except for reproductions of old furniture.

In recent years there has been a revival in the large landscape panels sometimes used to decorate walls in public buildings.

Many substances other than wood have been used for inlay work. In ancient Egypt and Rome, ivory, mother-of-pearl, and even precious or semi-precious stones were used. Inlay patterns of coloured marbles have been used for all kinds of decoration, and metalwork is often inlaid (*see* Gold and Silver Work).

See also Woodwork, History of.

INNS, *see* Hotel Industry; *see also* Vol. IV: Inns.

INSURANCE. Insurance is the sharing of risks. Nearly everyone is exposed to risk of some sort. The houseowner, for example, knows that his property can be damaged by fire; the shipowner knows that his vessel may be lost at sea; the breadwinner knows that he may die at an early age and leave his family the poorer. On the other hand, not every house is damaged by fire nor every vessel lost at sea. If these persons each put a small sum into a pool, there will be enough to meet the needs of the few who do suffer loss. In other words, the losses of the few are met from the contributions of the many. This is the basis of insurance. Those who pay the contributions are known as 'insured' and those who administer the pool of contributions as 'insurers'.

Not all risks lend themselves to being covered by insurance. Broadly speaking, the ordinary risks of business and speculation cannot be covered. The risk that buyers will not buy goods at the prices offered is not of a kind that can be statistically estimated—and risks can only be insured against if they can be so estimated.

FIRE MARK OF THE ROYAL EXCHANGE ASSURANCE, 1740

Insurance Companies owned their own fire brigades in the 17th, 18th, and 19th centuries and made a charge for attending houses not insured by them. Insured houses had a fire mark nailed to their walls to identify them. (Reproduced by permission)

The legal basis of all insurance is the 'policy'.

AN EARLY 19TH-CENTURY FIREMAN, ROYAL EXCHANGE ASSURANCE

This is a printed form of contract on stout paper of the best quality. It states that in return for the regular payment by the insured of a named sum of money, called the 'premium', which is usually paid every year, the insurer will pay a sum of money or compensation for loss, if the risk or event insured against actually happens. The wording of policies, particularly in marine insurance, often seems very old-fashioned, but there is a sound reason for this. Over a large number of years many law cases have been brought to clear up the meanings of doubtful phrases in policies. The law courts, in their judgements, have given these phrases a definite and indisputable meaning, and to avoid future disputes the phrases have continued to be used in policies even when they have passed out of normal use in speech.

The premium for an insurance naturally depends upon how likely the risk is to happen, as suggested by past experience. If companies fix their premiums too high, there will be more competition in their branch of insurance and

Lloyd's

The bell was salved from H.M.S. *Lutine* which sank in 1799, carrying a valuable cargo insured by Lloyd's. The bell is rung to herald important announcements to Members, one stroke for bad news, two for good

they may lose business. On the other hand, if they make the premiums too low, they will lose money and may even have to drop out of business. So the ordinary forces of supply and demand keep premiums at a level satisfactory to both insurer and insured.

Working out the chances of events happening in the future depends to a great extent on what STATISTICS (q.v.) are available to show how frequently the same events have occurred in the past. Some of the information needed comes from the past experience of the insurers themselves; other information comes from published statistics. The skilled statisticians employed by life assurance companies are called actuaries.

All risks about which there are past statistics lend themselves to insurance. As there are many ways in which these risks can be classified, there are many specialized branches of insurance, the principal ones being: life and pensions assurance, fire, accident, marine, aviation, and engineering.

Fire insurance departments often deal not only with ordinary fire risks, but with damage to property by gales, floods, frost, lightning, and similar natural occurrences. The accident departments insure people against many forms of accident, including personal and motor accidents, burglary, employers' liability, public liability, and fidelity guarantee. Those who run motor vehicles are obliged to protect themselves from claims brought against them by people they may injure in an accident, and this protection is usually provided by insurance. They are not legally obliged to cover themselves against the risk of total or partial loss to the actual vehicle. The law also makes employers, whether in business or at home, liable to pay compensation if, as a result of their negligence, someone who works for them is injured or killed while at work. Employers' liability policies are written to cover such risks. A fidelity guarantee policy compensates business firms for losses through fraud, theft, or embezzlement by dishonest employees.

As its name suggests, marine insurance is concerned with the insurance of ships and cargoes, and in this branch LLOYD'S (q.v. Vol. IV) in London traditionally specializes.

Credit insurance covers merchants and manufacturers against risk of loss through debtors going bankrupt and failing to pay their debts. Credit insurance was once entirely in the hands of private firms, and the companies so engaged covered credit risks in the export as well as the home trade; but in 1962 the British Government, through the Department of Overseas Trade, entered this branch of insurance and set up the Export Credits Guarantee Scheme.

There is one insurance company which also issues an unusual kind of policy—the 'pluvius' policy (from the Latin word meaning 'rainy'), which insures against the risk that an outdoor entertainment or sports event might be spoiled by bad weather. One would think that a risk of this sort could hardly be covered, but the weather statistics of past years allow it to be done.

Life assurance is a very specialized branch of insurance, and while many companies do not touch it, certain others handle nothing else. The earlier policies were written to provide for a man's widow or dependants after his death; but in recent years life insurance has become much wider. Companies now issue endowment policies, by which the insured person is paid a lump sum, or else an income for life, on reaching a specified age. Endowment policies are taken out by many large firms in order to organize pension and superannuation funds for their staffs. Special life policies can now be written to guard against a fall in the value of money between the time when the policy is first taken out and the date on which it becomes payable. The premiums received on such policies are separately invested in a chosen group of ordinary shares (*see* STOCKS AND SHARES) in commercial and industrial companies; such shares normally rise in value as the purchasing power of money decreases.

Of the institutions that carry on insurance, some specialize in only one branch of insurance, while some of them 'write policies' in many branches. In Great Britain there are over 200 insurance companies, some of which have a very large capital, and Lloyd's. Lloyd's is not a company; it is, in fact, a professional association.

Lloyd's at work is an impressive sight. Hundreds of 'underwriters' and their clerks sit in straight-backed and rather uncomfortable-looking pews, while brokers, acting on behalf of would-be insurers, pass from underwriter to underwriter placing their clients' risks. After discussing the risk the underwriter will 'take a line', i.e. he will indicate on the broker's 'slip', which states the risk to be covered, the proportion of the risk he is prepared to underwrite and initial the entry. This proportion could be, say, 5% or 10%. The broker then goes to other underwriters until he has 100% coverage for the whole risk.

The words 'underwriter' and 'underwriting' are particularly associated with Lloyd's, although these terms are also used among the companies and in the capital market (*see* ISSUING HOUSES). The word 'underwriter' came into use because Lloyd's policies were originally initialled at the foot by the various members who joined together to insure the larger risks.

An underwriter may find that on a certain risk he has a greater liability than he is prepared to retain; he may then pass on a portion of it to other underwriters through the medium of a broker. This passing on is called reinsurance, in which some companies specialize. A more specialized form of reinsurance takes place when a vessel has met with an accident. In such a case the underwriters who insured the vessel in the first place will try to reinsure part or all of their original interest with other underwriters who accept this type of business. Sometimes, the chance of successful salvage is so small that rates for reinsurance are extremely high. If one reads that a ship aground off the Cornish coast in February is being reinsured at Lloyd's at a premium of 95 guineas per cent., it is reasonable to assume that her chances of being refloated are negligible.

SOCIAL INSURANCE (q.v. Vol. X) is a national, and not a commercial matter; it covers the death, sickness, disablement, old age, and unemployment of almost all citizens. To a limited extent the national scheme uses the methods of the commercial world; the benefits received bear a reasonable relationship to the contributions paid, but if the contributions fail to meet the cost of the scheme as a whole, the difference is paid for by the general body of taxpayers.

INTEREST. In the business world no person with capital to spare would lend it to anyone else unless he were paid for doing so, because he would naturally consider the money as safe with himself as elsewhere. CAPITAL (q.v.) is, therefore, comparatively scarce. Like everything else that is scarce in economic life, it commands its own price; and this price is known as 'interest'.

The rate of interest which has to be paid will vary with the period for which capital is borrowed and also with the nature of the SECURITY offered (q.v.). To lend money at all involves some risk. The longer the loan, the greater is the risk of its not being repaid, and so rates for short-term loans are generally lower than those for long periods.

Interest is not the same thing as DIVIDENDS (q.v.), which are paid out of the profits made by a business. Interest is arranged in advance, and has to be paid at the rate then fixed. If a business can earn profit at a higher rate than that of the interest at which it can borrow capital, the dividend it can pay to its ordinary shareholders may be higher than it might otherwise be.

Rates of interest seldom remain fixed for long, but vary according to how much capital is being offered for investment and how great the commercial and industrial demand for it is at any particular moment. In times of prosperity or boom, rates of interest may rise; in times of depression they may fall very low. If there is an alteration in the amount of money that is being saved by people generally, interest rates may alter as a result. During and immediately after the Second World War, incomes were high and there was little in the shops to spend money on. Money available was then considerable; and, although the demand for capital was high, the rate of interest stayed low. When money grew scarcer after 1949, interest rates rose. But government control, by limiting the number of industrial and commercial borrowers, can make interest rates lower than they would be in an absolutely free market.

See also DIVIDEND; PROFITS.

INTERNATIONAL FINANCE is the system by which the surplus savings of a more highly developed country are used to assist the economic life of a less advanced country. Within a single country an industry or area short of CAPITAL (q.v.) can borrow from the wealthier parts of the country. For example, in Britain the surplus wealth of London investors and financiers can be placed at the disposal of Birmingham and Glasgow manufacturers. But in the past it often happened that a country's own savings were insufficient to enable it to develop as fast as it wished, and such a country had then either to get the necessary capital from abroad, or remain economically backward. This lending and borrowing between nations is called international finance.

Until 1914, when the First World War broke out, nearly all the lending was done by private investors, and the borrowers were sometimes industries and sometimes governments. International finance first developed on a large scale in the middle of the 19th century, when railways were being built in the U.S.A. In spite of their growing wealth, insufficient capital could be obtained from such cities as New York, and the railways therefore sold their BONDS (q.v.) to private investors in London and other wealthy centres. Later, for the construction of the Canadian Pacific Railway, money was borrowed in New York and many European cities, as the necessary capital could never have been found in Canada itself. The governments of countries where railways were being constructed and operated by the State borrowed in London, Paris, and other wealthy cities, and in this way the money was found to build railways in Russia, India, and Australia. Later in the 19th century London provided an immense amount of capital for the railways of Argentina and Brazil. This assistance helped to develop Argentina, and to make that country wealthy; so that many years later the Argentine Government was able to buy back the railways from the British investors who owned them.

During the First World War governments began to lend direct to each other. The Government of the U.S.A. made loans to Britain so that she could buy American munitions of war for herself and her allies, and Britain made similar loans to her allies. Most of these loans were not repaid, and were eventually 'written off' or cancelled. In 1946, after the Second World War, the U.S.A. made a large loan to Britain for the restarting of British industry after so many years of war. These big loans from one government to another are for sums much larger than could be obtained from private investors, and are now the most prominent form of international finance. All the same, international lending and investment by private individuals still continue.

In the past some of these international transactions have led to friction between governments, usually because interest or capital has not been paid out punctually. But the system of international finance helps the less wealthy or more backward countries to develop their resources and to make them available for the rest of the world, and both the lending and the borrowing countries reap a benefit. For example, by helping to build railways in the Dominions and elsewhere, which opened up new lands for producing wheat and meat and other products, Britain was herself helped to feed her increasing population.

The greatest volume of international financing is now made through two specialized agencies set up by the United Nations: the International Monetary Fund, and the International Bank for Reconstruction and Development, commonly called the World Bank. Although development aid grants are still made to underdeveloped countries by Western nations, these represent only a small fraction of the assistance channelled through such international organizations.

See also FINANCE; RATES OF EXCHANGE.
See also Vol. X: INTERNATIONAL CO-OPERATION, FINANCIAL.

INTERNATIONAL TRADE. 1. Trade between nations is necessary in modern life because most countries are either unable to produce certain things as cheaply or as well as certain other countries, or cannot produce them at all. Climate, raw materials, and the skill and the character of the inhabitants all play their parts in this connexion. For instance, before the invention of the 'humidifier', a machine which provided artificially moistened air, the moist climate of Lancashire was particularly suited to COTTON MANUFACTURE (q.v.), for cotton fibre, which Britain imports in large quantities, is brittle and tends to break if it is spun in a dry atmosphere. Wheat is best grown where a heavy winter snow-fall soaks well into the soil and a short dry summer ripens the plant quickly: so Canada and south-west Russia are specially good for WHEAT growing (q.v. Vol. VI). When different countries specialize in the production of different commodities, so that they have more than enough for their own needs, international trade is the result.

Great Britain is particularly dependent upon overseas trade. Corn crops are grown in Great Britain, but some cereals cannot be grown as well or as cheaply as in other countries. Britain, however, was the first country in the world to develop manufacturing industry on a large scale, and so there are many skilled workers and managers whose knowledge has been passed on from generation to generation. This allowed Britain to increase greatly the output of manufactured goods from the late 18th and early 19th centuries onwards. As the overseas production of food-stuffs increased in about the same proportion, Britain was able to get enough food to provide for a rapidly growing population by selling her manufactured goods to countries overseas and spending the money on buying agricultural products.

2. BALANCE OF TRADE. The difference between a country's 'physical' exports (or exports in actual goods) and its physical imports is called its balance of trade. Physical exports and imports are often called 'visible', because they can be seen and handled, and to distinguish them from the 'invisible' items (*see* Section 3). A country's balance of trade is said to be 'favourable' when the money total of its exports exceeds that of its imports, and 'unfavourable' when the situation is reversed. It is unusual for Britain to have a favourable balance of trade for any calendar year, but of recent years the unfavourable balance has sometimes been reduced. Imports of food, drink, and tobacco account for about 30% of total imports in a normal year, and the raw materials of Britain's manufacturing industries for about 25%. Most British exports are in the form of manufactured goods, the proportion varying between 70% and 85% of total exports in a normal year.

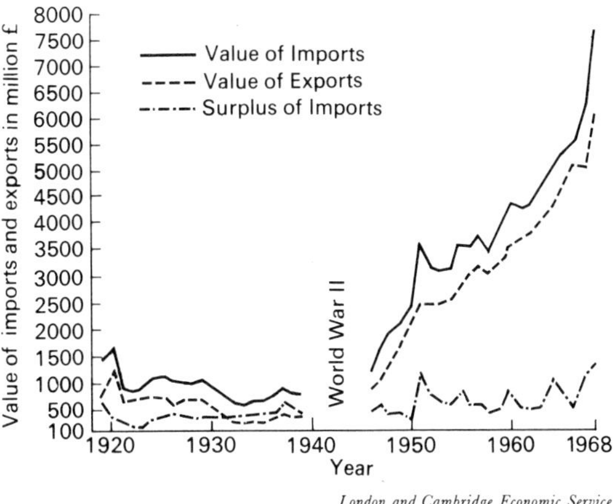

London and Cambridge Economic Service

BRITISH IMPORTS AND EXPORTS, 1920–68

3. INVISIBLE EXPORTS AND IMPORTS. All export transactions are not physical, or visible. For example, if foreigners use British ships to move their goods, her shipping industry earns foreign money just as much as if she exported motor-cars. Or, again, if the underwriters of Lloyd's are asked by foreigners to insure them against fire and marine risks (*see* INSURANCE), they too earn foreign money. All such transactions, which do not involve payments for actual goods, yet which give bankers increased balances in foreign currencies, are called 'invisible' exports; transactions in the opposite direction, giving foreign banks the command of credits in British banks, are called 'invisible' imports. Thus, if people travel abroad, the money they spend in other countries really represents an invisible import. It is for this reason that the amount of money which some governments allow their citizens to spend on foreign travel is strictly limited; for even if invisible exports are added to visible ones, there may still be a gap between a country's total exports and its total imports, and this has to be filled by borrowing foreign money. The American loan granted to Britain in 1946 was arranged to give the British people time to reconstruct their industry after the war and so to bring total exports and total imports more into line with each other (*see* INTERNATIONAL FINANCE).

When all invisible items have been added in, the difference between total exports and total imports, both visible and invisible, is the current account of the Balance of Payments.

4. FREE TRADE. From the 16th to the 18th centuries, most economists and other writers on overseas trade believed that a country should always try to have a favourable balance of trade, which would be paid for by other countries in gold or silver. They argued that those countries with the biggest stocks of precious metals would be the richest and also the best prepared for war (*see* MERCANTILE SYSTEM). But from the end of the 18th century economists began to realize that one could not eat, wear, or live on the precious metals, and that a country's wealth was more likely to be increased, and its STANDARD OF LIVING raised (q.v.), if obstructions to free international trading were removed.

The economists used two main arguments to prove their case. They argued, firstly, that it would pay any country, where a particular commodity cost more to produce than abroad, to give up producing it and to import it instead. From this it followed that all attempts to restrict international trade by import duties (*see* TARIFFS), which made cheap goods from abroad artificially dearer in the home country importing them, were entirely wrong. This took for granted that one country might have an absolute advantage over another in the production of certain goods, and so it was called the doctrine of Absolute Advantage. For instance, in the early 19th century, soon after these ideas had been published, Britain had an absolute advantage over the rest of the world in manufacturing cotton and woollen textiles; whereas Virginia in the growing of tobacco had an absolute advantage over Britain.

The second argument was called the doctrine of Comparative Advantage. This held that it would be beneficial in the long run if a country—even if it possessed an absolute advantage over the other countries in the production of everything—concentrated on the production of those goods in which its comparative advantage over other countries was greatest, so that other countries would be able to concentrate their productive efforts in those directions where their inefficiency was comparatively least.

By the middle of the 19th century these doctrines had led to the political policy of Free Trade. This aimed at removing all taxes and other regulations which restricted both imports and exports. For nearly a hundred years Great Britain practised Free Trade, but very few overseas countries followed her example.

5. PROTECTION. The opposite policy to Free Trade was called Protection. The Protectionist argued that foreign producers, who could undersell home manufacturers, might upset or even ruin whole industries; and so the home manufacturer should be shielded against foreign competition in various ways (*see* QUOTAS; SUBSIDIES; TARIFFS). Early in the present century these arguments became more convincing, because certain foreign industries adopted the habit of 'dumping' or selling their goods abroad more cheaply than at home. In this way they could keep up a high output, which cut down costs and increased profits; and the businesses gained, because what they lost by selling cheaply abroad they made up for by raising their prices at home.

Dumping gradually won more converts to Protection, and so did the growing need to prepare for war. Between the First and Second World Wars Great Britain gradually swung over from Free Trade to a policy of Protection, but not nearly as far as other countries did. Britain still had to import large quantities of food-stuffs and raw materials, and therefore did not tax these; but British industry needed to sell the goods it manufactured, and protective steps were taken therefore against the manufactured goods of other countries.

The industrialization of countries that were previously under-developed, and the general rise in the world's standard of living, have kept Britain's post-war trade at a high level. The tendency in most countries is now towards still freer trade, and an example of this is the reduction of tariffs by members of the European Common Market (*see* INTERNATIONAL CO-OPERATION, SOCIAL AND ECONOMIC, Vol. X).

See also OVERSEAS TRADE; STANDARD OF LIVING; TRADE, HISTORY OF.

INVESTMENTS, *see* STOCKS AND SHARES; DEBENTURES; LOANS; BOND; BANKING.

INVISIBLE IMPORTS AND EXPORTS, *see* INTERNATIONAL TRADE.

INVOICES. Business men use the word invoice for what ordinary people call 'bills'. In modern business invoices are usually forms printed in duplicate or triplicate, with serial numbers. The firm's name and address are printed boldly in the

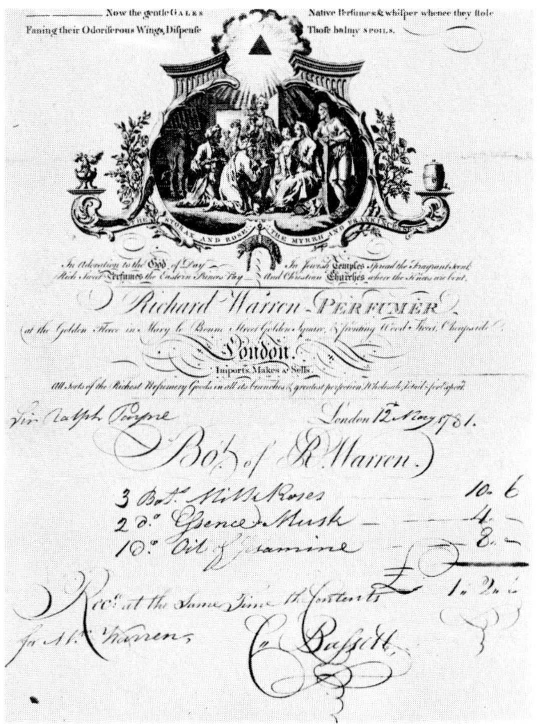

Now the gentle GALES Faning their Odoriferous Wings, Dispense Native Perfumes & whisper whence they stole Those balmy SPOILS.

THE STORAX AND ROSE THE MYRRH AND FRANKINCENSE

Richard Warren PERFUMER

London.

Imports, Makes & Sells

Sir Ralph Payne London 12 May 1781.

Bot. of R. Warren.

3 Botts. Milk Roses	10. 6
2 do. Essence Musk	4. –
1 do. Oil of Jasmine	8. –
£	1. 2. 6

Recd. at the Same Time the Contents for Mr. Warren, C. Bassett.

Meade Collection

AN 18TH-CENTURY RECEIPTED INVOICE

It records the sale in 1781 of Milk of Roses, Essence of Musk, and Oil of Jasmine, by Richard Warren, Perfumer, to Sir Ralph Payne

middle of the form, and above it are lines on which the name and address of the buyer of the goods may be written or typed. The rest of the form is ruled in columns so that the quantities of different goods ordered, their price, the value of each separate purchase, and the total amount, can be clearly seen.

Invoices used in the wholesale trade usually state when payment is expected, and what cash discount will be allowed if payment is made earlier than the stipulated date.

When we buy goods for cash in a shop, the invoice, or bill, is receipted at the time of purchase. If payment is not made at the time of purchase, an account is opened for the buyer, and most of the entries in the seller's account-books are made from the invoices. At the end of the month the purchaser receives what is called a 'statement'. This is a copy of the buyer's account in the firm's books; it includes the total of all invoices issued during the month, together with any balance already owing; from this total payments made during the month and the amounts of any credit notes issued are subtracted.

Credit notes are forms like invoices, generally bound in books with serial numbers and usually printed in red ink, whereas invoices are printed in black. Credit notes are used when a purchaser returns unsatisfactory or damaged articles, or if he complains about the quality of goods and arranges with the seller a reduction in the price. Invoice totals are debited to customers in a firm's books; credit notes and cash payments are credited (*see* BOOK-KEEPING).

Payments of less than the total of a statement are called 'payments on account'. Receipts, stamped with a twopenny stamp, are still necessary when accounts over £2 are settled in cash, but unless insisted on are no longer necessary when such accounts are settled by cheque.

See also PAYMENT; CREDIT.

IRON AND STEEL INDUSTRY, HISTORY OF. Iron is found in the earth's crust in the form of iron ore (*see* METAL ORES, Vol. III), which is a chemical compound of iron, carbon, and oxygen, mixed with impurities such as sand, clay, lime, and compounds of sulphur and phosphorus. Iron ore is of no use to industry until it has been converted into pure iron. Iron is found in an almost pure form in meteorites (*see* METEORS, Vol III), and probably the earliest ironwork was made from hammering meteorite iron. Man did not discover how to release iron effectively from its ore until a long time after he had learnt to use gold and silver, tin, lead, and copper, and to combine tin and copper to make bronze. Perhaps from as early as 2500 B.C. or earlier, men of the Near East experimented with smelting iron ore by heating the ore with charcoal. It is only in this century that we have really understood what was happening when iron was smelted; the men of the Near East experimented on a hit or miss method, and they made a lucky hit when they used charcoal. Charcoal (like coke, used later) is in effect pure carbon, and this, when heated, combines with the oxygen in the air to form carbon monoxide. In smelting, the carbon monoxide combines with the oxygen in the iron ore to form carbon dioxide gas, and iron is left. The early smelters did not know all this—it just happened. But the iron they produced was too soft and brittle to be of much use. It was the HITTITES (q.v. Vol. I) who first discovered, in about 1400 B.C., how to convert this material into a malleable wrought iron hard and tough enough to be useful.

The Hittites found that by vigorously hammering the iron while it was red hot (forging it) they were able not only to bang out almost all the dirt, slag, and ashes but also to weld the particles of metal into lumps which could be forged into useful articles. The process was kept secret for many years, but after the Hittites had been conquered and dispersed, about 1230 B.C., knowledge of iron-making slowly spread into most parts of western Asia and to Egypt, and the true Iron Age can be said to have begun. The technique became known in south-eastern Europe about 900 B.C. and was gradually carried westwards by the Celts; but it was not known in Britain until about 350 B.C. Iron-making was unknown in the Americas until the Spanish conquests, early in the 16th century A.D.

Following the practice in bronze-making, iron was originally smelted in crucibles; then, by about 1000 B.C., more capacious furnaces were made by cutting **L**-shaped tunnels through the brow of a hill and charging a mixture of ore and charcoal into the vertical portion of the **L**. The tunnels caught the prevailing wind which created the strong draughts necessary for raising the charcoal fire to high temperatures. These devices, though effective, depended on natural breezes and were eventually replaced by shaft-furnaces, built of stones and clay, for which the draught was created by hand-worked bellows. Another kind of furnace, the beehive 'bloomery', was common in Europe from 500 B.C. until the Middle Ages and was used in Africa until quite recently. It was made by piling alternate layers of ore and charcoal into a heap and covering the heap with clay, leaving a small opening at the top. Near the base a bellows-draught was forced into the pile and was continued until all the charcoal was consumed, when the 'furnace' collapsed, and the iron—still very impure—lay in the debris.

The actual process of smelting was basically the same in all these furnaces and remained the same for roughly 2,500 years. None of the furnaces melted the iron, and all yielded a soft, malleable, and easily welded material, which, after hammering, was almost indistinguishable from modern wrought iron. But it was not so hard as hammer-hardened bronze and was consequently less useful for weapons and cutting tools.

A technique for hardening this soft metal was discovered about 900 B.C. Blacksmiths found that if they heated wrought iron for a fairly long time in contact with red-hot charcoal to carburize it (that is, charge it with carbon), and then quenched the carburized iron in cold water, they could produce a much stronger and harder metal. They had, in fact, produced 'steel'. Unfortunately, carburizing affects a piece of iron to only a small depth below the surface. So, until the middle of the 18th century, tools and weapons were made by carburizing a number of iron strips and then forge-welding them together into a sword, a dagger, or a knife.

No improvement could be made until higher air-pressures could be obtained to produce greater heat. About A.D. 1350 iron-smelters found they could obtain far higher air-pressures by using bellows driven by water-wheels. This made posible a new type of furnace—the forerunner of the modern BLAST FURNACE (q.v. Vol. VIII)—which is only a heightened version of the older shaft-furnace. The new furnaces produced a different kind of iron—pig iron—which contained much more carbon (about 4%) and consequently became fluid at a lower temperature—at from 1,150° to 1,200° C. instead of at about 1,500° C. This could readily be run into shaped castings. In fact, 'cast iron', so new and exciting to European craftsmen, had been made by the Chinese over 1,000 years earlier (*see* CASTING, Vol. VIII). Few iron castings were, however, made before about 1450, and most of the pig-iron was converted into wrought iron. The increased efficiency of the new furnaces made it possible to burn out the carbon content of the pig-iron in furnaces resembling a smith's hearth and to convert it into wrought-iron bars, which could be quenched in cold water and converted into a kind of steel. By about A.D. 1500 the output of pig-iron in Europe was about 60,000 tons a year.

During antiquity iron from the smelting furnaces was hammered into simple articles with stones held in the palm of the hand, then with bronze hammers, and much later with iron sledges. The Celts, the Romans, and, finally, the British began to make a wider variety of iron goods, including swords, scissors, mirrors, sickles, welded chains, nails, locks and keys, bells, chariot tires, fire-dogs, and currency bars. The old-established tools and weapons were also made, as well as some decorative IRONWORK

Sir Alexander Gibb and Partners

COALBROOKDALE BRIDGE IN 1780, WITH IRON WORKS BEYOND

Painting by W. Williams

(q.v.). In Roman Britain every village had its blacksmith, who forged iron smelted in the forests of Sussex, Kent, Gloucestershire, Shropshire, Lancashire, and Yorkshire. After the fall of Rome, iron production diminished in all parts of Europe and did not revive fully until after A.D. 1000. During this time iron was used to some extent in buildings and in ships, and partially carburized iron, an inferior 'steel', was used to make goods such as scythes, knives, bill-hooks, and sickles.

In medieval times the size of objects made in iron was limited both by the blacksmiths' power to hammer the iron and also by the weight of iron which a smelting furnace could produce at one time, this being usually about 70 lb. After 1250, when water-power was first used for driving forging hammers, craftsmen could produce rather larger works; but even then, when the first iron cannons were created, about 1325, it was still only possible to make them of wrought staves tightly bound with iron hoops like those of a wooden barrel. With the discovery of pig-iron, however, larger weights of iron could be poured directly from a smelting furnace into shaped moulds, and cast-iron guns were being made in Europe by 1400 and in England by 1540. From 1450 onwards more cast iron was used, and for the next 400 years it was considered the most suitable iron for making large objects.

During the 16th and 17th centuries iron production rose, the majority of pig-iron still being converted into wrought iron for blacksmithing. The amount of charcoal used in the industry was enormous, and Britain's timber was being depleted. Indeed, had not Abraham Darby succeeded, about 1710, in smelting iron with coke, supplies of which appeared to be inexhaustible, Britain might have been deforested. As it was, the annual production of British pig-iron rose rapidly during the 18th century. Henry Cort in 1784 invented the dry-puddling process (*see* Iron and Steel, Section 4, Vol. VIII) for turning pig-iron into wrought iron, a method which permitted much larger unit-weights to be produced. Ample supplies of both wrought and cast iron were therefore available to the engineers of the steam age which began in 1770. The Iron Bridge at Coalbrookdale was prefabricated in cast iron at the neighbouring Darby's works and erected within 3 months in 1779. By this time steel tools were being made of 'cast steel', the result of experiments in the 1740's by Benjamin Huntsman in melting mixtures of soft iron and highly carburized iron, casting them into ingots, and then forging these into bars.

For many years, Huntsman's was the only kind of true steel to be made, but since it was produced in crucibles holding only about $\frac{1}{2}$ cwt. of metal it could be used only for tools and hand weapons. All larger engineering structures were still based on wrought iron and cast iron. Then, about 1858, mild-steel, which is steel containing about 0·2% carbon, was produced. Henry Bessemer showed that by blowing a blast of air through the molten pig-iron the temperature could be greatly raised, and the oxygen in the air would combine with the carbon and other impurities in the pig-iron, carrying most of them away as gas. By Bessemer's process, first used commercially in 1859, several hundredweights and, later, up to 20 tons of pig-iron could be converted in a single furnace into mild-steel within half an hour. In 1868, the Siemens brothers invented a different, slower, process of making mild-steel from molten pig-iron, using iron oxide to provide the oxygen. By this process, up to 200 tons were eventually dealt with in a single furnace in 12 to 15 hours. Both Bessemer's and Siemens' methods made steel much more cheaply than Huntsman's method.

For some years these processes could be successfully used only with pig-iron of low sulphur and phosphorus content. Then in 1884 Thomas and Gilchrist showed that the phosphorus and some of the sulphur could be eliminated by using slags containing lime, and by lining the furnaces with basic refractories (*see* Fireclays and Refractories, Vol. VIII). The possibility of producing good mild-steel from phosphoric pig-irons was responsible for the growth of large steel industries in France, Germany, and Luxembourg, and it also greatly widened the scope of British steel-making.

Now that mild-steel could be produced in large quantities, it rapidly replaced wrought iron in engineering work. Demand quickly grew, and the world production of 28 million tons in 1900 rose to nearly 290 million tons in 1957. To provide enough pig-iron, many modern blast furnaces yielded about 1,000 tons a day.

Britain now produces only about 8,800 tons of wrought iron annually; but cast iron is still used widely, and the British output was about $3\frac{1}{2}$ million tons in 1968. Until the end of the 18th century, iron castings were made by running pig-iron directly from a blast-furnace into moulds; but by 1800 it had become the practice to remelt the pig-iron in separate furnaces usually remote from the blast-furnace. To-day most iron castings are made from pig-iron, mixed with scrap, which has been melted in special cupola or reverberatory furnaces.

In the engineering sense, neither mild-steel nor cast iron is a strong enough material for many constructional purposes. Since about 1890 a considerable number of alloy-steels have been evolved which contain various proportions of non-ferrous elements in their composition. These steels are heat-treated, almost always by quenching followed by tempering (*see* Heat Treatment, Vol. VIII). Constructional steels containing nickel and chromium may, after such treatment, have strengths about six times the strength of either wrought iron or mild-steel—as high as 120 or 130 tons per square inch. More important still, these alloy-steels are adequately tough. In the main the Siemens method is used; but, since 1910, electric-furnaces have been increasingly employed for making richly alloyed steels. Depending upon the composition of the steel and the purposes it is intended to serve, either an electric arc or an electric induction furnace is used (*see* Steel-making, Vol. VIII).

See also Vol. VIII: Iron and Steel.

IRONWORK. To-day, this term is generally applied only to wrought iron and cast iron used decoratively and not to their use in engineering. No cast-iron articles were made in Europe before the 14th century (*see* Iron and Steel Industry,

BISRA

CHARGING HOT METAL INTO A 300-TON BASIC OXYGEN STEEL CONVERTER AT PORT TALBOT

National Museum of Wales

CELTIC IRON FIRE-DOG, MADE ABOUT A.D. 25

History of), though the Chinese had produced some large cast-iron statues as early as A.D. 200. Wrought iron was first made about 1400 B.C. but then only for weapons and simple tools. The Celts did the first decorative work in iron (*see* Celtic Civilization, Vol. I), such as the fire-dog produced in Celtic Britain about A.D. 25. The Romans used wrought iron almost entirely for military and utilitarian articles, and after the Romans there was hardly any decorative use of iron until the 9th century. The Anglo-Saxons began to strengthen and embellish church doors with beautifully designed hinges, enriched with scrolls and straps, which covered large parts of the door.

In the Middle Ages the majority of the iron produced in every European country was used for making weapons, tools, and household goods, and then for doors and screens in churches. The Italians led the way in this work, but Germans, French, and Spaniards followed them closely. Iron rods were used to reinforce the outer doors of both churches and fortified places, and grating or trellis made of iron bars replaced wood for interior work. In the 12th and 13th centuries, iron trellis work was widely used for enclosing the choirs and chapels in Gothic cathedrals, and this form of screen was called a 'grille'. Parts of the grilles were hinged to act as gates, the earliest known English examples of this being at Winchester and dating from 1093. These simple structures of rods and rails were lavishly ornamented with more and more complex designs of scrolls, leaves, flowers, and ecclesiastical devices, all made in forged iron. Edward IV's chantry at Windsor has a screen made by an English smith about 1480, but, fine as it is, it is clearly inferior to the remarkable Spanish screen shown in Plate 16 of Vol. XII and dating from 1520.

There is a great deal of beautiful German, Netherlands, and Spanish church ironwork of the 16th and 17th centuries. In England decorative ironwork for the next 150 years consisted mostly of domestic ware, of furniture fittings such as locks, keys, bolts, and handles, of spits, candlesticks, and candelabra, and of inn signs. During this period cast iron was first used in decorative ways, and fire-backs, fire-dogs, and also grave-slabs were cast. Though Sir Christopher Wren had earlier used wrought-iron railings in Oxford, he rather unwillingly surrounded his new cathedral, St. Paul's, with cast-iron railings. About 1725 cast-iron railings were erected outside the Senate House at Cambridge and at St. Martin's-in-the-Fields.

This was the golden age of English decorative ironwork. After about 1750, the quality of the work began to decline, largely because of the

Friends of St. George's Chapel, Windsor

IRON GATES OF EDWARD IV'S CHANTRY CHAPEL IN ST. GEORGE'S CHAPEL, WINDSOR

They were made by John Tresilian, *c.* 1480

Thomas-Photos

WROUGHT-IRON GATE AND RAILINGS IN THE GARDEN OF NEW COLLEGE, OXFORD

Made by Thomas Robinson, 1711

wider use of cast iron instead of wrought iron. Foundries could cast intricate ornaments at far lower prices than blacksmiths could forge them. So practice tended towards making wrought-iron frameworks to which cast-iron decorations could be attached. The Adam brothers and the architects of the Regency period used cast iron extensively in their architectural designs.

By 1850 the quality of decorative ironwork had greatly deteriorated, especially in Great Britain. A host of inartistic monstrosities appeared as grates, for example, and household ornaments. But since 1870 there has been a revival of decorative wrought ironwork, though much modern commercial ironwork lacks the charm of the old because much of it is machine-made instead of hand-made, and consequently looks too uniform and precise.

Before the 19th century, all wrought ironwork was hand-forged from bars of various shapes and sizes and also sheets, which were delivered to blacksmiths in all parts of the country. Wrought iron is a fairly soft and plastic metal, readily shaped and easily welded when hot; so it is an ideal substance for blacksmithing. It contains slag-fibres which run lengthwise in the bars, and consequently it is fairly easily split along the fibres, as wood is; but it is tough and resistant when stressed across the fibres. Blacksmiths take advantage of these properties. They draw out and elongate the whole or part of a bar in a form called a 'swage'. They flatten and point it with hand-hammers; they form a variety of scrolls by hammering bars of various shapes around the horns of their anvils; they split the ends of bars, and bend and hammer the divided ends into floral patterns. They beat out leaves from flat bars or sheets and weld them to rods of suitable shape; they hold bars in clamps and twist them into various patterns, which they then assemble into a decorative design, sometimes by hammer-welding and sometimes by riveting. Today, many of the wrought shapes used in modern, commercial ironwork have been mass-produced in dies and then electrically welded; in such work, mild-steel is sometimes used instead of wrought iron.

ISSUING HOUSES. This is the name given to certain firms in the financial world which make a practice of finding CAPITAL (q.v.) for business firms, public corporations, and governments. No one is obliged by law to make use of the services of issuing houses: any organization is free to decide for itself whether the profits it can earn, or the taxes it can collect (if it is a government), will pay a dividend or rate of interest high enough to attract capital from private investors. It can then put advertisements in the newspapers and invite the public to subscribe the capital needed. But there is always a chance that the investing public may not think the offer tempting enough, in which case those who are seeking capital may find that they have spent a lot of money on publicity and yet have failed to raise the capital they need.

Issuing houses are able to guarantee that the capital wanted will be found. In London such firms are either specialized companies with considerable capital of their own and long experience of this work, or old-established MERCHANT BANKERS (q.v.). An issuing house must know, or be able to get in touch with, a wide circle of firms having plenty of free capital. Its directors or managers must be in close contact with commerce and industry, and be quick to sum up the possibilities of a venture. They must study the financial markets very closely, to know the prices at which shares can be successfully marketed or placed, or the rates of interest at which money can be borrowed successfully.

An issuing house works in this way. Suppose a limited-liability company has already collected subscriptions of £50,000 from its own directors, and now wants to raise an extra £500,000 from the public. It approaches an issuing house, taking with it estimates of the profits it expects to make. These will be studied by the issuing house and, if necessary, corrected. Now the issuing house has to make up its mind whether or not the issue is worth making. If it decides to go on with it, the next step is, with the help of the directors of the company, to draft a 'prospectus'. This is a legal document, giving particulars of the company's directors, the nature of the proposed business, and estimates of profits to be earned. Copies of this will be handed by the issuing house to persons who are asked to 'underwrite', or guarantee, part of the capital required. If they agree, they will sign underwriting agreements.

These underwriting agreements are not definite promises by the underwriters that they will 'subscribe firm', or provide capital up to the number of shares underwritten: if they were, there would be no point in trying to get public subscriptions at all. The underwriting agreements are simply a form of insurance against the risk that the public may not subscribe. What the underwriters actually promise to do is to subscribe for any shares which are not taken up by the public. As compensation for undertaking this risk, each underwriter is paid an agreed commission, usually about $1\frac{1}{2}\%$. Underwriters themselves often 'reinsure' their underwriting risks with sub-underwriters, giving them part of their own commission.

When all the underwriting contracts have been signed, the prospectuses are published in the Press, are put on the counters of all the important branches of the company's bankers, and get more publicity through being recommended by stockbrokers and others. A stated date and time are advertised for the opening of the public subscription list.

If the proposition is a good one the public response is often overwhelming, and more money is subscribed than is asked for; but sometimes this apparent success is deceptive. One kind of City speculator, called a 'stag', makes it his business to fill up applications for newly issued shares that he thinks will go well. As most new shares are paid for by a small initial deposit, and the balance by instalments, a relatively small sum of money can give a 'stag' control of quite a number of shares. These he hopes to sell at a profit, as soon as dealings in the shares commence on the Stock Exchange.

Whether the issue has been 'stagged' or not, everything has gone well for the issuing house and the underwriters so long as public applications have been received for at least as many shares as were offered for subscription. In this event the underwriters would get commission without having to subscribe for any shares at all. But suppose the public did not like the issue, and put up subscriptions for, say, only 50,000 £1 shares instead of the 500,000 offered. In this case each underwriter would have to subscribe for nine-tenths of the shares he had underwritten. If he underwrote 10,000, he would have to subscribe for 9,000; but he would receive commission on the full 10,000 originally underwritten.

Of course, the issuing house must be paid for its trouble and risk. Usually a contract is arranged by which the company gives the issuing house a fixed fee—which might be about £25,000 in the example given. Out of this the issuing house is expected to pay all printing and advertising expenses, the underwriting commission, and all other incidental expenses of the issue.

There are no Government restrictions upon capital issues for British firms and institutions, but issues on behalf of oversea borrowers have to be approved by the Capital Issues Committee, composed of representatives of the Treasury, the Bank of England, and the issuing houses.

See also CAPITAL; FINANCE; BANKING; INSURANCE.

J K

JEWELLERY TRADE. Jewellery has been found in the tombs of ancient civilizations such as that of the Egyptians 4,000 years ago. The principal tool of the ancient jeweller was the hammer. With this he reached a remarkable level of skill in beating out gold and silver into plates and ware of even thicknesses, to be embossed, plated, or twisted later into various objects of beautiful design. By the 14th century B.C. jewellers in Egypt were masters of all the more important processes used today—chasing, engraving, soldering, and enamelling. Some 800 years later Etruscan jewellers in Italy had perfected a technique that no one has since imitated with any success; they were able to produce on the surface of their gold-work a rich grained appearance as though fine gold powder had been evenly sprinkled all over it. There was a decline in jewellery making in the early Middle Ages; but later the art of the jeweller revived, and perhaps reached its peak in the 16th century with the work of Benvenuto CELLINI (q.v. Vol. V).

The jeweller's art has always been closely related to the taste and fashion of the period. In the 19th century, for example, jewellery, like architecture, was often heavy and over-elaborate. Our own times have seen a revival in taste, and the work of the best craftsmen to-day can stand comparison with the past. This work has been helped by the introduction of PLATINUM (q.v.) as a material, in addition to the silver and gold used from time immemorial (*see* METAL ORES, Vol. III). The use of platinum, a more accurate knowledge of the various precious-metal alloys and their strengths, and better standards of design in general, have led to lighter and more graceful work. In modern jewellery-work, particularly when making use of fine stones, the jeweller strives to reveal the beauty of the stones themselves, and to make their setting unobtrusive rather than to smother and dwarf them by elaborate surrounds or settings.

The craft of the jeweller is different from that of the goldsmith and silversmith (*see* GOLD AND SILVER WORK). Broadly speaking, the goldsmith and silversmith make larger articles for household and personal use, while the jeweller confines himself to ornaments that will be worn actually on the person. The jeweller is therefore responsible for such articles as rings, brooches, bracelets, ear-rings, necklaces, lockets, pendants, hair ornaments, buttons, studs, links, badges, medallions, buckles and clasps, charms, tie-pins, hatpins, and similar articles. He also decorates, although less frequently, such articles as watches, clocks, pocket-knives, pens, and pencils. In or on these may be mounted precious or semi-precious stones and other decorative objects in wide variety—plastics, beans and seeds, small shells, birds' feathers, and beetles' and butterflies' wings. Mountings are made from many metals, the precious metals not being the only ones used. Copper, nickel, brass, pewter, and many other alloys, hard enough to be worked upon and suitable for personal wear, are used.

Articles of jewellery are made in many ways. They may be built up into intricate patterns and designs from pieces of plate-metal combined with

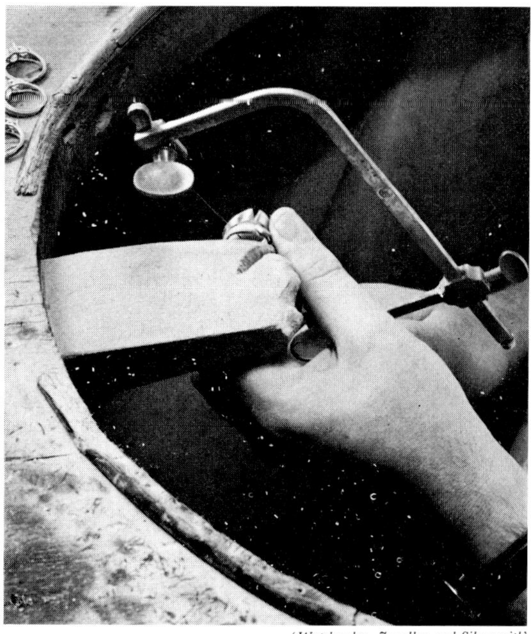

'Watchmaker, Jeweller, and Silversmith'

SETTING STONES IN RINGS

Using a piercing saw to cut a hole for the stone

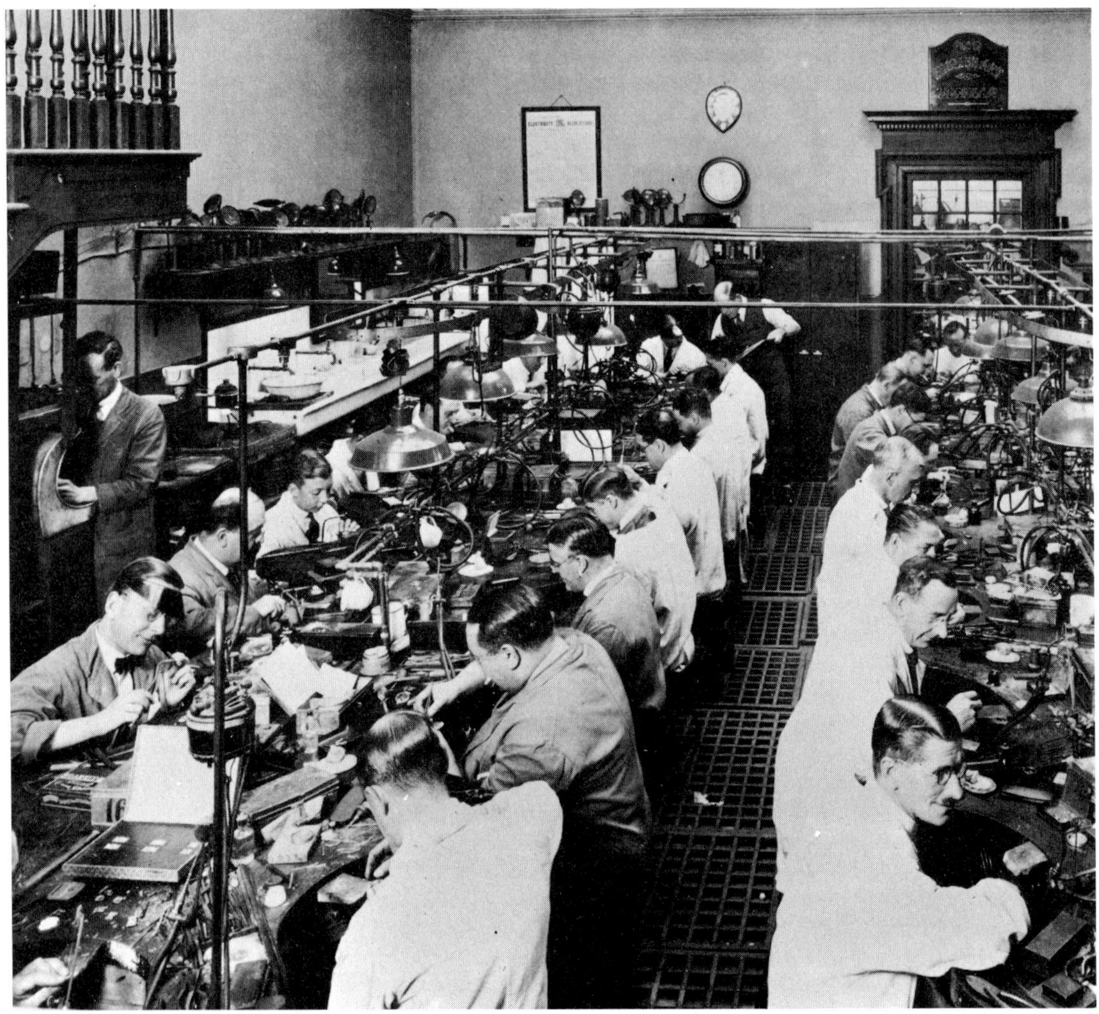

DIAMOND MOUNTERS MAKING PLATINUM MOUNTS FOR JEWELLERY
The worshop is Cartier Ltd.'s subsidiary company, The English Art Works, London

wire. They can be made up in sheet-metal that has already been chased or ornamented with repoussé work (*see* GOLD AND SILVER WORK). They may be cast by various methods which give the effect of carving, chasing, or piercing; and they may be stamped or pressed out of sheet-metal. Any article of jewellery may be further enriched by ENAMEL work (q.v.), or by the addition of the precious stones and other decorative objects just mentioned.

The jeweller's most important tool is the blowpipe, with which he solders the various parts of the finished article together (*see* SOLDERING, Vol. VIII). Soldering is not unlike bricklaying on a miniature scale, solder being the mortar that is used to build up the whole piece of jewellery. The jeweller's other tools are those used by other metal-workers; in some workshops hand-tools are used, and in others power-tools. A piece of equipment used by the jeweller, and not much used by other metal-workers, is the draw-plate—a hardened steel plate containing a series of holes through which wire can be drawn by means of tongs. Wedding-rings, for example, are made by drawing a strip of wire through a draw-plate having a hole of the required section and thickness, cutting the strip into the required lengths, bending each cut piece into a circle, and then soldering the ends together. Casting is the method usually employed when a number of identical articles are required. The master-model is first made in metal, plaster, or wax. From this master-model impressions are made in damp sand, forming a mould. Molten metal is then poured in and allowed to cool and set. The type of metal casting that gives the most faithful copy of the original but involves a good deal of time and expense is what is called the *cire perdu* process (French for 'lost wax'). A wax model is packed round with clay or other moulding material; the wax is then melted out and the hole filled by pouring molten metal into it. A new wax model is of course required for each subsequent casting. Stamping produces objects by pressing the metal between two shaped steel surfaces called 'dies'. As the making of these dies is very expensive, stamping is used only for the large-scale production of jewellery of the same pattern, and not by the jeweller-craftsman. Stamping differs from casting in that it usually produces the object in two halves, which have then to be joined together.

In the high-class trade a piece of jewellery is usually made from start to finish by a single craftsman, who is a master of his art. In that portion of the trade which produces the cheaper and more popular jewellery, repetition work is the rule, and the article being fashioned passes from worker to worker and process to process until it is completed. Jewellery-making is not generally organized on factory lines like other industries, although some firms making costume jewellery are thus organized. This is particularly true of some of the firms in Birmingham, which is the centre of the mass-produced trade in both real and imitation jewellery. The Clerkenwell district of London is the centre of the high-class trade in Britain.

See also Gold and Silver Work; Diamond Industry.
See also Vol. XI: Jewellery, History of.

JOINER, *see* Woodwork, History of.

JOINT STOCK COMPANY, *see* Companies.

JOURNEYMEN, *see* Craft Guilds; Apprenticeship; Trade Union History.

JUTE INDUSTRY. This makes use of the coarse fibres of the jute plant, which is grown almost exclusively in India and Pakistan (*see* Fibre Crops, Section 2, Vol. VI). Cloth from jute has been hand-woven in India for several hundred years, but it is only since the early 19th century that jute fabrics have become commercialized. To those outside the industry jute is usually associated with the material from which sacks and bags are made, but its various uses are more extensive and cover practically every industry. It is used, for instance, in the manufacture of most types of floor-coverings and upholstery, for bags for carrying food-stuffs and grains, and in the steel-components industry for bags for nuts, bolts, and nails; flower-growers use it for shielding plants; and plumbers carry it about for 'lagging' the outside of pipes and water tanks to resist sharp changes of temperature, and for making watertight gaskets at pipe-joints.

British industry first handled jute in the early 19th century, when the East India Company (q.v.) sent samples to Britain to be tested. The coarse fibre had to be softened before it could be spun into a usable yarn. The obvious place to choose for manufacture was Dundee, then the centre of the British flax and whaling industries; for it was found that by soaking or 'batching' jute in an emulsion of whale-oil and water the fibre became soft and could be spun with ease on the existing flax machinery of the Linen Industry (q.v.). By slow steps, and after much trial and error, the jute-weaving industry became firmly established in Dundee by 1838, and for many years that city was the only jute-manufacturing centre in the world. Later, the

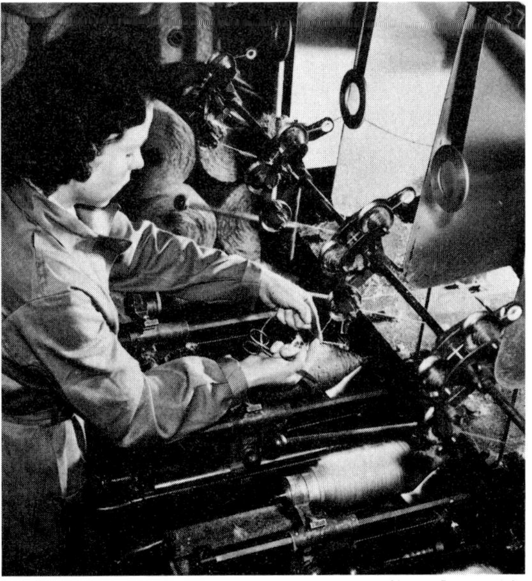

Norman Brown and Co.

WINDING JUTE YARN ON TO 'COPS' BEFORE WEAVING

Norman Brown and Co.

SPINNING HIGH-QUALITY JUTE YARN IN A DUNDEE MILL

industry was opened up in many towns in Europe and America, and many mills were established by British firms in India.

Jute is mainly manufactured into cloth known as 'gunny' or 'hessian'. 'Gunny' is a word of doubtful origin which includes all types of sacking materials woven from jute. 'Hessian' is the word used for the more loosely woven forms of sacking. The term 'hessian' is said to have been first used by the Americans, when during the War of Independence they fought against the Hessians, the mercenary troops brought by George III from the German district of Hesse. These troops followed the old custom of protecting themselves from the rain by placing sacks over their heads. Both kinds of material are now known in India by the name of 'gunny'.

The Crimean War (1854–6) helped the British jute industry. Russia's Baltic provinces were then the main sources of flax. The war stopped these supplies, but increased the demand for sacks and canvas. Dundee stepped in to fill the gap, with jute as a substitute for flax, and from 1854 to 1857 experienced its first boom. Shortly afterwards, during the American Civil War, supplies from the Southern States were cut off by the Northern blockade, and Dundee again did well. As the industry grew, specialization began. The Indian mills made most of the gunny fabrics, while Dundee concentrated on the finer fabrics used for canvas, tailors' interlinings, and the backing of linoleums. Soon the superiority of Dundee jute goods became accepted all over the world, and Dundee prospered reasonably well until the world-wide depression of the 1930's (*see* TRADE CYCLE). Plant had been expanded and methods improved, in both Dundee and India, until more jute goods were being produced than people were prepared to buy. But by 1937–8, when the world production of jute reached its peak, all that was produced could be sold.

Since the Second World War, the demand for jute products has increased, mainly in developing countries which still require packaging materials. But in fully industrialized countries, the use of jute packaging has declined as more modern forms of packaging have developed. Jute manufacturers in countries such as Scotland, therefore, now concentrate chiefly on products required by specialized industries, in particular the yarns and fabrics used as backing material for soft floor-coverings.

In 1947 the separation of British India into two self-governing States raised a serious problem for the jute industry, for four-fifths of the raw jute crop was then grown in Pakistan, while most of the mills were in India. Since then India has started growing more jute and Pakistan has built more mills. Now the two countries compete with one another for world markets.

See also Wool Weaving; Textile Fibres and Fabrics.
See also Vol. VI: Fibre Crops.

KAOLIN, *see* China Clay.

KAPOK. This is a vegetable substance, one of the lightest materials known. It is a kind of floss that can be torn or teasled out from the seeds of a tree that grows in India and farther East. It is used as an upholstery material for stuffing light chairs and cheap mattresses, particularly mattresses used for camp-beds. Kapok is an exceptionally buoyant material in water, and it is much used as a stuffing for ships' life-belts, and as a lining for life-saving waistcoats and similar garments. Seats and cushions for sailing dinghies and small yachts are often stuffed with kapok, and can thus be used as emergency lifebuoys as well as cushions. Cork (q.v.) was formerly used for these purposes, but in certain circumstances kapok has been found more efficient. It is much more buoyant than cork: if tightly compressed, kapok can support more than thirty times its own weight in water. Another advantage that kapok possesses over cork is that after being soaked in water it dries more quickly. For use at sea, where articles may be frequently wetted, Java kapok from Indonesia is generally considered superior to the Indian variety. Kapok is sometimes used for surgical dressings, in place of absorbent cotton-wool and similar materials.

See also Vol. VI: Fibre Crops.

KNITWEAR, *see* Hosiery and Knitwear.

KNIVES, *see* Cutlery Industry.

L

LABOUR. Economists speak of labour as being one of the 'factors' of 'PRODUCTION (q.v.), whose combined effort is needed to make the things on which we live. The other 'factors' are land, CAPITAL (q.v.), and organization or management. Labour includes all people who work for WAGES (q.v.), as distinct from the owners or shareholders of businesses, who receive PROFITS or DIVIDENDS (qq.v.). Labour is sometimes classified as either 'productive' or 'non-productive', the former meaning people who work with their hands in factories or workshops, and the latter those who work in shops or offices. But such a distinction is unfair, for all workers, as well as the other 'factors', share in production. A works cannot run without plans and records, and there must be shops to sell its output.

The size of the labour force depends not only on the size of the total population, but also on the age at which people normally start work, the age at which they usually retire, and the proportion of the population between these ages. It will also depend on the proportion of women in the population, the age at which they normally marry, and the attitudes that exist towards women working.

The STANDARD OF LIVING (q.v.) depends on a large number of factors, including the quality of the labour force and its size in relation to the total population. The flow of labour between jobs also plays an important part here. As new inventions are put on the market, and people alter their spending habits, some industries and occupations develop rapidly, while others decline. Thus people in the labour force have to change their jobs. This flow of labour between different jobs, which often involves moving to different parts of the country, is called the 'mobility of labour'. In Britain the Government does not seek to promote movement merely for its own sake, but it does try to encourage labour to move when such mobility is to the country's advantage. The Employment Exchanges help by informing people of the jobs available in different parts of the country, and industrial training encourages people to move to more skilled and more productive jobs. The creation of new and expanding towns, and the modernization of older areas can also encourage movement between or within regions.

This movement of labour can cause some people to become temporarily unemployed; unemployment may also arise for a number of other reasons, such as a reduced demand for certain commodities. Prolonged unemployment on a large scale has not been common in Britain, except in the less prosperous areas of the North, Scotland, and Wales, since the Second World War. Like most other modern democratic governments, the British Government considers that the achievement of full employment must always be one of the country's most important objectives.

See also UNEMPLOYMENT; WAGES; STANDARD OF LIVING; TRADE UNIONS.

See also Vol. X: EMPLOYMENT AND PRODUCTIVITY, DEPARTMENT OF; EMPLOYMENT EXCHANGE.

LACE-MAKING. 1. HAND-MADE LACE. Lace is a decorative open-work fabric, which in the past was generally made of fine linen thread, although sometimes of gold or silver thread. Since the end of the 18th century, lace has also been made of silk or cotton, and occasionally of wool or mohair (hair from angora goats). There is no sure evidence that any real lace was made before the 16th century, although some net-like fabrics, made by knotting and plaiting threads together, have been found in Egypt, in tombs of about the 4th and 5th centuries A.D. During the early part of the 16th century, lace was used in Europe for the decoration of church vestments and altar-cloths. Later in the century it became fashionable as an enrichment of dress among wealthy men and women (*see* CLOTHES, HISTORY OF, Vol. XI). Less is now made and used than formerly, but it is still an ornament highly prized by those who can afford to buy it.

There are two main classes of hand-made lace. One, made with a needle and thread, like embroidery, is known as 'needle-point' lace; the other, known as 'pillow' lace or 'bobbin-made' lace, is formed by threads twisted and plaited

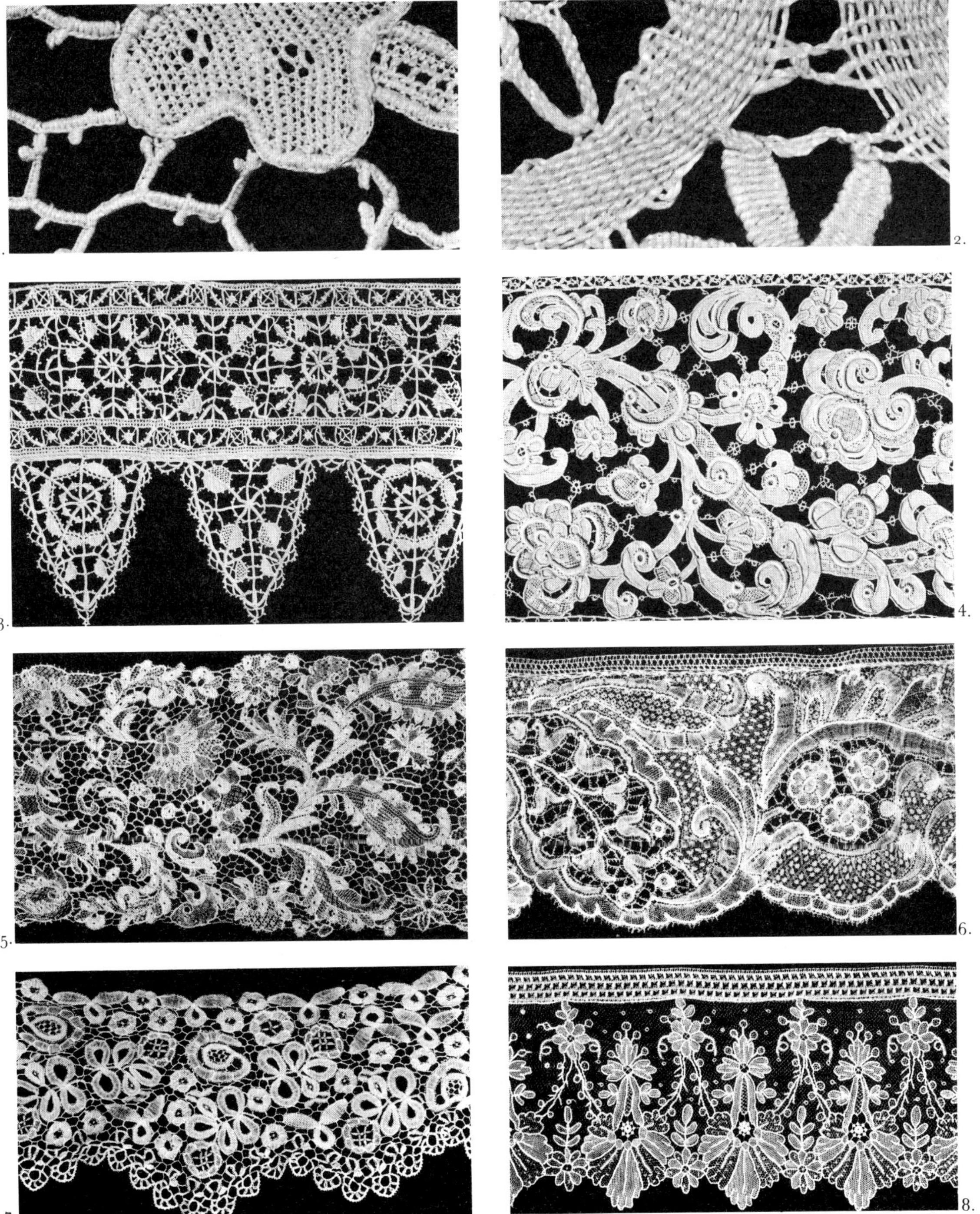

By courtesy of Margaret Simeon

EXAMPLES OF HAND-MADE LACE

1. ENLARGED DETAIL OF NEEDLE-POINT LACE. 2. ENLARGED DETAIL OF PILLOW LACE. 3. RETICELLA WITH PUNTO IN ARIA EDGE, needle-point, late 16th century (7 in.). 4. VENETIAN ROSE-POINT, needle-point, mid 17th century (6 in.). 5. POINT DE FRANCE, needle-point, late 17th century ($3\frac{1}{4}$ in.). 6. POINT D'ANGLETERRE, pillow, early 18th century ($2\frac{1}{2}$ in.). 7. HONITON LACE, pillow, mid 19th century ($3\frac{3}{4}$ in.). 8. BRUSSELS POINT DE GAZE, needle-point, late 19th century ($3\frac{1}{2}$ in.). The measurements are of the actual widths of the specimens

British Travel and Holidays Assn.

MAKING PILLOW LACE AT HONITON

together. The design for bobbin lace is drawn on the form of sheepskin known as PARCHMENT (q.v. Vol. IV), and put over a hard pillow. Pins are stuck into key points in the pattern, and the threads are twisted round the pins, and round each other, weaving the lace as they go. Each thread is held on a long thin bobbin, dozens of which may be used in making one strip of lace.

The *toile* or solid part of the pattern of needle-point lace is made of fine loops or buttonhole stitches, worked row by row into each other; in pillow lace it is made by a regular crossing and weaving of the threads, just like fine darning. The bars or meshes that join the solid patterns also differ in the two types of lace. A close examination will show which town or district the lace was made in, as each had its own traditional way of working.

Needle-point lace developed from drawn-thread and cut-linen embroidery. Rectangular pieces were cut from the linen, and threads were stretched across the open space to form the basis of a geometric pattern, which was worked between them in buttonhole stitches. Sometimes, for a border, practically the whole of the linen was cut away, leaving only a small group of threads at intervals. These were worked over, all the space between being filled with geometric patterns, so that hardly any of the original linen was visible. This is known as *reticella* lace. It is probable that pillow lace was developed from netting. Both Italy and Flanders claim to have been the home of the inventors of this lace.

At the outset the designs were few; they were made rather formal by the rectangular weave of the material on which they were worked; but later lace-makers became more adventurous, and began to construct a needle-point lace without any material as a basis. This is known as *punto in aria*, an Italian phrase which means literally 'stitch in the air'. At first this was made in geometric designs, and was used for the pointed edges that one can see around lace ruffs in Elizabethan portraits. Curved lines could be used in the pattern of *punto in aria* as easily as straight, and during the early 17th century floral and scroll designs began to be worked.

'Venetian rose-point' was the most magnificent and highly developed of the laces. Designs were drawn on parchment, and threads were stitched round the outlines. The pattern was then filled in entirely with buttonhole stitches. 'Rose-point' means 'raised point': the edges of the pattern were decorated by more stitching over bundles of linen thread, which raised them and gave the lace almost the richness of carved ivory. *Point plat* is a similar lace without raised edges. Towards the end of the 17th century design became more delicate: the stems and flowers were farther apart, and the greater numbers of bars or *brides* used to hold them together were more and more enriched with little loops of stitches called *picots*.

North Italy, particularly Venice, was the home of the finest lace-making in the early 16th century, and held this position until near the end of the 17th century. Venetian lace was very fashionable in France, and in 1665 some Venetian lace-workers were persuaded to establish their craft in Alençon and other towns. The early French lace was a copy of Venetian, but soon it became lighter, and more characteristically French. By the end of the 17th century *point de France* was a distinct type. By the 18th century the quality of Italian lace had declined, and French needle-point and French and Flemish pillow lace were supreme.

Pillow lace followed the design of needle-point all through the 17th century. The increasing fashion for lightness and delicacy, and for a mesh ground instead of *brides*, suited pillow lace particularly well. The most beautiful examples of this lace were produced at Valenciennes, Binche, Brussels, and Mechlin (Malines) in the early 18th century.

In England lace was made from the 16th century onwards in styles very like those of Italy, France, and Flanders, but usually less delicate. During the 16th and 17th centuries lace-makers came to England as refugees from religious persecution in France and Flanders. To help the English workers who were taught by these refugees, Charles I and Charles II forbade the import of foreign lace, but there was extensive smuggling. Fine Brussels pillow lace came to be known as *point d'Angleterre* (English stitch)—probably to disguise its foreign origin. Honiton, in Devon, was an important centre, and hand-made lace is still made there. Buckinghamshire and Bedfordshire were also centres of the craft in England.

After the invention of machine lace, the handicraft lost a great deal of its importance. The 19th-century styles were often imitations of old types, such as rose-point. Brussels was the most important centre in Europe, making a fine needle-point lace called *point de gaze* and a pillow lace known as *point duchesse*. A lot of silk lace, both black and white, was made and exported from Malta. In Ireland the craft was established as a relief measure in the famine periods of the early 19th century; Limerick lace is made by embroidering on net. Similarly, in Venice lace-making was re-established to relieve great poverty and unemployment. The fashion for wearing lace died almost completely in the early years of the 20th century, and very little hand-made lace is now produced.

2. MACHINE-MADE LACE. In 1768 net was first made by machinery. It came to be used very frequently by hand-workers, to replace their own hand-made 'ground'. Needle-point and pillow-lace patterns were sewn on to the ground—a much quicker procedure than making the whole piece by hand. The net was also embroidered with 'tambour' stitch, which looks like chain-stitch but is made with a crochet hook.

Between 1770 and 1790 many attempts were made to adapt the stocking frame used in the HOSIERY industry (q.v.) for the production of machine-made lace. It was John Heathcoat's invention of the bobbin-net machine in 1809 that really laid a firm foundation for the machine-made lace industry. Heathcoat set up his first machines at Loughborough in Leicestershire. His original invention was much improved in 1813 by John Leavers (or Levers), and the lace produced was a very good imitation of hand-made Brussels. The first Leavers looms were set up in Tiverton, in Devon, in 1815, and in the following year Heathcoat himself decided to move there when his Loughborough factory, with all its plant, was wrecked by the LUDDITES (q.v.). The Nottingham district, which had been the centre of the hand-made section of the industry since the 16th century, remained the leading locality for machine-made lace. Modified Leavers looms are still used in Nottingham. In 1834 Leavers succeeded in applying the Jacquard machine or harness loom (*see* WOOL WEAVING) to the lace-making loom; it became possible for quite intricate patterns to be produced mechanically. In the early days of these inventions the machine section of the industry was organized on the 'outworker' or DOMESTIC SYSTEM (q.v.); firms owning machines hired them out to workers who made net and lace for their own account. About the middle of the 19th century the industry began to be fully organized on factory lines.

The modern machine-made lace industry of Britain is now organized in six sections, of which the first three are the most important. The Leavers section makes fancy lace, hair-nets, and veilings, and is chiefly located in the Nottingham area. The Leavers loom has been little changed, and only an expert can distinguish between the lace made on it and the hand-made product itself. The section of the industry next in importance makes lace furnishing fabrics and curtain nets; its main centre is now the Irvine Valley in Ayrshire, although Nottingham is still important. The first patent for a machine to make lace curtains was taken out in 1846, and by the middle of the century the Nottingham area alone was operating 100 machines. The machines now used have changed little, although those that use the Jacquard fitment are rather large and complicated. The modern curtain machine can make simultaneously eight curtains up to 5 feet wide, and has been adapted to make cellular or open-texture woollen blankets. A third important section of the industry makes plain net or bobbin net; Tiverton and Barnstaple in Devon, and Chard in Somerset, are the main centres. Bobbin net is a machine-made imitation of plain hand-made pillow lace, and on the

John Jardine Ltd.

THE INSIDE OF A LACE-MAKING MACHINE

The long warp threads come from the bottom of the machine through moving steel bars which determine their position and therefore the pattern of the lace. They are twisted with the threads from the bobbin, the round end of which is seen to their left.

bobbin-net machine is produced *point d'esprit*—a plain net with small decorative spots at regular intervals. The other sections of the industry make warp lace, braid lace, and embroidery. The embroidery section, using a continental process and continental machines, produces machine-made embroidery, either on plain net or on a temporary fabric base of acetate material (*see* TEXTILE FIBRES, MAN-MADE) which can be dissolved away, leaving only the embroidery. Lace trimmings of narrow width are made either by the braid-lace section, or on ordinary Leavers looms. If made on the Leavers loom, the separate narrow widths of lace are connected together during manufacture by draw-threads, which are afterwards withdrawn.

The British machine-made lace industry is much affected by fashion changes. Between 1880 and the outbreak of the First World War, it had to meet very serious competition from French manufacturers, and foreign competition continued after 1918 until foreign imports were taxed in 1925 and the industry was to some extent stabilized. During the Second World War the Government kept certain sections busy with orders for mosquito and sandfly nets for use in tropical and sub-tropical theatres of war.

See also Vol. XI: NEEDLEWORK; EMBROIDERY.

LATEX, *see* RUBBER MANUFACTURE; *see also* Vol. VI: RUBBER.

LEAD occurs as a mineral ore in Derbyshire in England, and throughout Europe, America, Asia, and Australia. The ore most generally found is lead sulphide, known as galena. Lead is one of the few metals in which Britain was once self-supporting, and at the beginning of the 19th century British production was almost two-thirds of the world's output. Spain was then a large producer, and still is. In the late 19th century the famous Broken Hill lead and silver mines of New South Wales were opened up, and in 1888 Australia headed the list of producing countries with an output of 18,000 tons. Today the U.S.A. is the largest producer in the West, but uses nearly all her output herself. The main exporters are Australia, Mexico, and Spain. The Derbyshire mines are still worked.

Lead has many uses in industry. Printing types are made from an alloy of lead and antimony; the stereotype plates used in printing are made from a similar alloy, with the addition of bismuth. Lead, hardened with arsenic, is used to make shot for sporting guns. PEWTER (q.v.) is an alloy of lead and tin. Alloys of lead and other metals—tin, copper, and antimony—are used to line BEARINGS (q.v. Vol. VIII) in engineering work. Lead has been used for many purposes in building, for flat and low-pitched roofs, as piping for plumbing work, and to make vessels which resist corrosion for the chemical industries. The oxides and similar compounds of lead have wide uses as pigments in paint manufacture, and in GLASS-MAKING and the glazing of POTTERY (qq.v.).

Although the softness of lead limits its use, and makes it impossible to decorate it with very fine designs, it has been much used for ornamental work in the past. For this it can be beaten or cast in a mould, casting being the more common method. Lead fonts, with figures and patterns, cast and moulded, were made in the 12th century. From the 13th century onwards lead 'quarries' were often used for ventilation in windows: these were rectangular or diamond-shaped panels, pierced to allow a free passage of air. Decorative tops or 'heads' of rainwater

Ministry of Works
13TH-CENTURY LEAD WINDOW 'QUARRY' FROM RIEVAULX ABBEY

pipes are also quite common. But it was not until the 17th century that lead was used on a large scale for pure decoration. Gardens, then often planned on formal lines, were decorated with lead vases, flower-pots, cisterns, and statues. The well-known statue in Edinburgh of Charles II riding a horse is cast in lead. At the end of the 18th century lead figures and designs were used to decorate wrought-iron gates and balustrades. Today lead is extensively used in nuclear power stations as a shield against radioactive rays.

See also MINING.
See also Vol. III: METAL ORES.

By gracious permission of H.M. the Queen
LEAD CISTERN AT KENSINGTON PALACE, 1746

LEATHER is made from HIDES AND SKINS that have been subjected to various treatments, of which TANNING is the most important (qq.v.). Some materials that are often thought to be leather are not really leather at all. This is true of parchment and vellum, once used for writing, which have not gone through any process of tanning. It is also true of rawhide, a material from which high-class luggage is often made; the hides used for rawhide are not tanned but 'limed', that is, soaked in lime and water.

Leather was one of the first materials used by man for clothes, coverings, and vessels. From the earliest times, until well after the Middle Ages, bottles and drinking-cups were made of leather. 'Black Jacks' were leather drinking-vessels, their insides being covered with pitch to make them watertight. Leather buckets were in regular use until the 19th century; they may still sometimes be seen in churches, where they are kept full of water as a precaution against fire. In early times leather was used for armour. The leather jerkin or loose long waistcoat was the standard outer wear of the English worker and peasant for centuries, and it became a general military garment in the Second World War.

Modern uses of leather still cover a wide range. The footwear industry is perhaps the largest individual consumer (*see* BOOT AND SHOE MAKING). Leather, as well as the untanned rawhide, is used for travelling-luggage, for women's hand-bags, and for document- and note-cases. It is the best material for the permanent binding of books. The most suitable leather for this purpose is Russia leather, which is calf or cowhide tanned by a special process, and with a characteristic grain stamped on the wet leather after tanning. Harness and saddlery, made in England from English leather, have a reputation higher than that of any other country; a modern use of saddle leather is for bicycles and motor-cycles. The glove industry requires soft fancy leathers. Leather has many uses in the CLOTHING INDUSTRY (q.v.). The 'wind-cheater' is a modern variant of the leather jerkin. Coats, jackets, and even skirts and waistcoats are now made in suede or 'nappa' leather. Many belts and dress trimmings are made of leather. It is also much used for upholstering furniture and for decorative wall panelling. It is used to make many kinds of fancy goods, such as cigar- and spectacle-cases and watch-guards. The balls used in cricket, hockey, football, and baseball are made

British Travel and Holidays Assn.

MAKING A LEATHER BAG

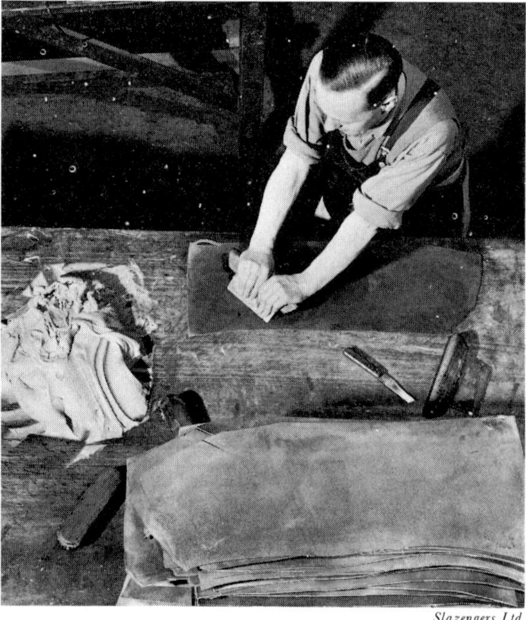

Slazengers Ltd.

HAND SETTING LEATHER FOR FOOTBALLS

The operation removes as much as possible of the stretch from the leather so that the footballs can be as near perfect in shape as possible

of leather, and many sports bags and accessories are either made from it or finished with it. Its purely industrial uses are also very varied. It is much used for pump washers and gaskets, for belting to drive machinery, and for industrial protective gloves. Among its miscellaneous uses are the making of surgical appliances, bellows, and razor strops.

The British leather industry has two sections, heavy and light. As the bulk of their raw materials comes by sea from abroad, the heavy sections are located mainly in seaport towns and cities such as London, Birkenhead, Liverpool, Bristol, Glasgow, and Hull. Some inland Lancashire towns are also important. In the light section the Midland districts are the busiest centres, although London itself is also prominent. Walsall, in Staffordshire, has been for centuries the centre of the saddlery and harness trades, and, with the disappearance of horse transport, successfully switched over to other forms of light leather goods. Northampton, Leicester, Kettering, Nottingham, and Leeds are also important towns in the light section. Glove-making in leather is principally concentrated in the Yeovil district of Somerset, Woodstock, Oxfordshire. and in Worcestershire, although it has of recent years extended into other parts of the country.

Leather can be dyed, moulded, and worked with tools. The *cuir bouilli* process is sometimes used for moulding leather into shape. It is not quite certain how this process was originally worked, but it was probably done, as it is today, by soaking the leather thoroughly in water until it can be hammered or pressed into shape and decorated. It is then heated until it is dry, when it will always retain its shape. Leather bottles, 'Black Jacks', and bags were made in this way, and today the process is used for such things as cigar-cases and the corners of suit-cases.

Leather may be decorated by being modelled, tooled, or incised. For modelling, the leather is damped and the design is pressed into it with a rounded steel tool. To give higher relief portions can be pressed up from beneath. Designs may also be drawn in line or hammered on with a hot tool. The design can also be cut or 'incised'. All these methods can be combined. When the leather is dry, the design can be painted or dyed and then polished. It is then made up by hand, or by machine stitching, or by thonging with thin strips of leather.

See also Hides and Skins; Tanning.

LEATHER-CLOTH. The coating of woven fabric with paint, varnish, oils, and similar substances has been known since the Middle Ages. At first, coating was done for decoration. Later, it was found that fabrics were protected from wear and weather by coating, and materials such as oil-cloth and floor-cloth were introduced. Leather-cloth is one of these materials, coloured and shaped into a grainy surface to look like natural leather.

The making of leather-cloth has enormously increased because there is not enough real leather in the world to meet the demand. There has been a big increase in the demand for leather upholstered furniture, and leather upholstery for cars, aeroplanes, and railway carriages; and as mass-production methods have made it necessary for upholstery to be made in standard widths, in roll form and of known quality, in place of the odd-shaped skins previously used, leather-cloth has proved more practical than real leather for some purposes.

The coating materials are based on drying-oils (*see* OILS, VEGETABLE, Section 4), nitro-cellulose, or PLASTICS (q.v.). If drying-oils such as linseed are used, they are usually thickened by heating, then coloured by the addition of pigments or dye-stuffs, and thinned with spirit to make them spreadable. Lacquer-type coatings are prepared from a mixture of nitrocellulose dissolved in a solvent (*see* PAINTS AND VARNISHES) and mixed with a substance such as castor oil to make it more yielding. Plastic materials consist of rubber-substitutes which are built up from acetylene gas.

The material chosen as the basis of a leather-cloth is usually a woven cotton fabric. Sateen and twill are both popular. There are many ways of applying the coating to the fabric, but usually the material is passed over a long table, and the coating is poured on to its surface, and spread by a metal strip, which extends across the width of the material and nearly down to its surface. The gap between the blade and the material roughly determines the thickness of the film. Then the fabric is passed through a short, heated tunnel for drying. The number of coats varies from three to thirty, and a decorative pattern may then be pressed on to the surface of the coating. A coating of contrasting colour is sometimes put on, to fill the pattern marks.

Materials and fabrics used for leather-cloth are so chosen that the coating lies only on the surface of the fabric: unlike those used for making oil-skin or proofed fabrics, in which the varnish penetrates into the actual fibres of the material. Leather-cloth is a comparatively cheap, hard-wearing, and easily cleaned material. It is free from sweating or tackiness in warmth or heat, and from brittleness under conditions of extreme cold.

See also WATERPROOFING.

LEGAL TENDER, *see* CURRENCY.

LIABILITIES, *see* BOOK-KEEPING.

LIMESTONE, *see* CHALK MINING; STONE QUARRYING; *see also* Vol. III: LIMESTONE.

LIMITED COMPANIES obtain their CAPITAL (q.v.) from many members, or shareholders; if a limited company does not prosper, the loss of each shareholder is limited by law to what he originally invested.

Companies without 'limited liability', as it is called, are rather dangerous concerns for the man of small means to put his money in. A hard-working man who has saved a few thousands of pounds might put only £100 or so into a company with unlimited liability, but if it went wrong and owed more than it possessed, he might be forced to turn the rest of his property into money to help pay the company's debts. He might even have his house seized and sold. The novels of Dickens and other writers about life in England before 1850 mention several hard cases of this kind. There is an example in *David Copperfield*.

Before 1855 limited liability could be granted by the Charter or Act of Parliament which brought a company into being, if the Government thought this right. The liability of the shareholders of the Bank of England, which was founded in 1694 by an Act of Parliament, was limited by a later Act. In the early 19th century the Royal Mail Steam Packet Company and the Peninsular and Oriental Steam Navigation Company were formed by Act of Parliament, and the liability of their shareholders was limited to the amounts they subscribed. This method, however, was expensive, as it meant paying for a Private Act of Parliament, and small concerns could not afford it. The result was that the expansion of commerce and industry, at the end of the 18th century and the beginning of the

19th, was carried out mainly by unlimited liability companies, and many families were ruined when such companies failed.

This situation led to a good deal of political agitation. In 1855, therefore, the first important Companies Act was passed, and this was amended and improved in 1862. These Acts allowed the formation, or 'incorporation', of companies through officials called Registrars of Joint Stock Companies, and liability was limited to the amount of money each person or 'subscriber' invested in shares. These changes greatly helped Britain's industrial development, as capital was less difficult to get when subscribers could judge the limit of their risks. At that time shares of unlimited liability companies were often difficult to buy or sell on the Stock Exchange; this held up enterprise, for people do not like putting up money unless they can get it back in an emergency by selling their shares.

Under the new rules the persons who wished to form themselves into a company first drew up and signed a Memorandum of Association. This stated the company's title and purpose, its 'authorized' capital (or maximum capital considered necessary), and into how many and what classes of SHARES (q.v.) this capital was divided. As well as the memorandum, there was a small booklet, called the company's Articles of Association, giving detailed rules for the management of the company; and also a 'prospectus', stating how the company proposed to carry on its business, and what profits were likely to be. All these documents were then 'filed' or deposited with the Registrar, together with a payment for stamp-duty on the authorized capital, as well as certain registration fees. Most companies incorporated under the Companies Acts had to end up their titles with the word 'Limited', so that traders dealing with them would know that it might be unsafe to give them CREDIT (q.v.) beyond the amount of their capital. The details of registration could be arranged if only a very small amount of capital were subscribed to start with, but it was naturally necessary to obtain larger investments of money (or 'subscriptions') before actual business could be started. This might be arranged privately by the original shareholders, or with the help of one of the ISSUING HOUSES (q.v.). At the end of each trading year the directors and secretary of the company were legally obliged to send a copy of the accounts to the Registrar. The register of shareholders also had to be filed with him, and kept up to date as changes took place.

Early in the present century the business world pressed to be allowed to form companies more easily. So in 1908 a new Act allowed the incorporation of 'private' limited companies, the earlier ones being called 'public' companies. At least seven persons were necessary to form a public company, but private companies could now be formed by a minimum of two persons. Most private companies did not have to file annual reports and accounts with the Registrar, and could thus keep the details of their business private; but the privilege was lost in 1967.

A Board of Directors is responsible for the policy and management of every company formed under the Companies Acts, and the head of the Board is called the Chairman. The necessary decisions are taken at regular Board Meetings, whose proceedings are recorded in a Minute Book. The details of management are usually entrusted to a Managing Director. Every company must have a Secretary, and must register his name, and the address of the company's office, with the Registrar of Joint Stock Companies. The Secretary is the official channel of communication between the company and the Registrar, and he is responsible for seeing that all legal requirements are satisfied. These are now wider than they were, as a new Companies Act passed in 1948 made it necessary for public companies to give much more information than before to their shareholders, or to persons who might become shareholders. Since 1967, further details have been required, such as any gifts made by the company for political purposes.

Britain was the pioneer of the modern limited company, and her example was soon copied by other countries. Although the British pattern is generally followed in the U.S.A., American limited companies are called 'corporations', and the contraction 'Inc.' (meaning 'incorporated') is used at the end of their titles instead of the contraction 'Ltd.' (meaning 'limited') used in Britain. An interesting difference between North American and British limited companies is the 'no-par-value' share. In Britain a share always has a nominal value, which is the figure printed on the share certificate: it may be £1 or 5*s*., or whatever sum was originally paid for the share. This is said to be its value 'at par'. Its real value, or market value, is often quite different. This depends on how much another person is willing to pay a shareholder for his shares. If, for any reason, it is thought that a company is likely to make large profits, then people will pay high prices for its shares, no matter what their nominal or 'par' value. Their market value can change several times in one day (*see* STOCKS AND SHARES). In the U.S.A. and Canada the 'no-par-value' share is really a much more logical idea. The fixed nominal value given to British shares tends to make the original shareholder think that his shares should always be worth at least the money he first paid for them, but he is often disappointed. In Britain, no reduction of the nominal value of a share is allowed without the permission of the High Court.

See also COMPANIES; STOCKS AND SHARES; DEBENTURES; CREDIT; PARTNERSHIP.

LINEN INDUSTRY. 1. Linen is probably the first textile to have been used by man. In ancient civilizations many people were kept busy growing FLAX (q.v. Vol. VI), which is the fibre from which linen is made, and spinning and weaving that fibre into linen yarn and linen cloth. The antiquity of linen can be judged from the many references to it in the early books of the Bible, for example, in Exodus, in Isaiah, and the first Book of the Kings, where it is said 'And Solomon had horses brought out of Egypt, and

Linen Industry Research Assn.

PULLING FLAX BY MACHINE IN NORTHERN IRELAND

Irish Linen Guild

'HACKLING' AND COMBING THE FLAX FIBRES

linen yarn: the king's merchants received the linen yarn at a price.'

It is believed that the original home of linen was ancient Egypt, and that it was distributed throughout the known world by the great trading race of Phoenicians (*see* TRADE, HISTORY OF). As a result, some countries of Europe, including ancient Greece and imperial Rome, gradually took to making linen. The Roman Emperors spread the knowledge of linen manufacture throughout the Roman Empire, and when the barbarians overthrew the western part of the Roman Empire, in the 5th century A.D., this knowledge survived in various parts of the Empire, including Britain.

Records of linen-making in Ireland can be traced back to the 13th century, though linen was made before then; the modern industry was founded in the 17th century by Viscount Wentworth, later to become Earl of Strafford, when he was Lord Deputy of Ireland. The linen industry began to grow when the Irish woollen trade was declining. Although the wool industry was discouraged by taxation, Ireland was given practically a MONOPOLY (q.v.) of the linen trade, which consequently expanded and flourished.

When the French king revoked the Edict of Nantes in 1685, during the French religious strife, tens of thousands of Protestant refugees

Irish Linen Guild

'JACQUARD WEAVING' IRISH LINEN FOR A DAMASK CLOTH

from France, skilled in the making of fine linens and other textiles, fled to England and other countries. Thousands of them settled in Ireland, where their industry and skill greatly helped the linen industry. Today its headquarters are in Northern Ireland (the old province of Ulster), though much of the flax processed there is grown in other European countries, including France, Belgium, and Russia.

2. The flax crop was once sown and pulled entirely by hand. Today the seed is sown mechanically in such a way that the plant grows tall and straight and yields the long fibres essential for smooth linen. The ripe flax stems are pulled from the earth by mechanical harvesters in order that the fibres will not be broken. Before the flax fibres can be spun or woven, they must be separated from their woody stalks by gentle soaking in soft, warm water. This process, known as 'retting', lasts at least 7 days. It used to be carried out in streams and dams, the bundles of flax straw being weighted down with heavy stones, but today it is done in large tanks. After soaking, the woody portions are soft enough to be easily broken and discarded by the 'scutching' rollers at the mill. The bundles of raw fibres are now combed and re-combed, a process known as 'hackling'. At the end of this the silky threads resemble hair.

3. SPINNING. Flax is the only fibre that is spun both wet and dry. For the finest linen fabrics, the yarns must be spun wet, passing through warm water which separates the yarns from their casings of vegetable gum. The quality of the linen depends on preserving its natural characteristics as it is processed. The atmosphere of the spinning and weaving rooms is therefore carefully controlled, and kept warm and moist at all times.

4. WEAVING AND DYEING. The basic principle of weaving, by interlacing two sets of yarns or threads, is described in the article WOOL WEAVING. Elaborate finishing processes follow: first a machine smooths the linen cloth, and removes any loose fibres; then it is ready for bleaching. In the past, this used to be done by boiling the fabric, spreading it out on the grass, and exposing it for weeks or months to the bleaching action of the weather. Then followed steeping in buttermilk, scouring with soap and water, and finally rinsing in pure soft water (see BLEACHING). The 'bleach greens' with acres of grass covered with linen used to be a familiar sight in Ireland. Nowadays this long process is carried out quickly in huge vats, using alkali, acid, and other bleaching agents.

Modern research has discovered techniques for dyeing linens many rich and varied colours, by immersing them in vats or tanks. The DYES (q.v.) used are permanent and colour-fast in water or sunlight. Research has also made possible TEXTILE PRINTING (q.v.) on linen. The silk-screen process is used, the cloth passing over a series of etched rollers.

A further series of finishing machines now smooth, iron, and fix the cloth, whether unbleached, white, dyed, or printed, into its predetermined widths. It is then sent to the warehouses to be made into such household articles as handkerchiefs, table cloths, sheets, and towels; or else it is dispatched on bolts to be made directly into garments.

See also Vol. VI: FIBRE CROPS.

LINOLEUM. This is not the same as floorcloth, a floor covering that was in use for a very long time and only fell into disuse about the beginning of the Second World War. Floorcloth was made by applying many coats of linseed-oil paint to a sheet of hessian or sackcloth—a coarsely woven fabric made from jute. Each coat of paint took several days to dry, and the whole process would, therefore, take many

Linoleum Manufacturers' Assn.

A LINOLEUM CALENDER

The hessian is fed into the machine on the left and the linoleum mix is sprinkled on it before it reaches the rollers on the right

Linoleum Manufacturers' Assn.

LINOLEUM BEING MATURED IN A 120-FT LONG 'STOVE'

weeks to complete. By contrast, linoleum is the result of building up one very thick coat of linseed base. Linoleum has been made since the 19th century and was invented by an Englishman called Frederick Walton. A material based on rubber had been invented earlier as an alternative to floor-cloth; but, as the price of rubber increased, efforts were made to find a cheap substitute. Walton noticed that thick films of linseed-oil paint on the outside of paint cans or on the top of open cans of paint were rubbery in nature; and he conceived the idea of making a rubber substitute by drying large quantities of linseed-oil, which in those days was an exceedingly cheap and abundant raw material. There are now two methods of doing this, each using a treated oil made by dissolving small quantities of lead compounds in hot linseed-oil. The lead makes the oil dry more quickly, so such a treated oil is called a 'driered' oil.

In one of these two processes sheets of thin cotton fabric are hung 6 inches apart in a tall, heated building, and the oil is flooded over the cotton at intervals of 24 hours, which gives sufficient time for each film to dry. In this way, over a period of 6 months, layers of dried oil from 1 to 2 inches thick are built up, and, when a shed is emptied, from 100 to 200 tons of dried oil are taken out to be made into linoleum. The second of the two processes is mechanical. Batches of about 1 ton of oil at a time are heated in vessels fitted with agitators, which whisk the oil into a fine mist through which air is blown. When the oil solidifies, it is quickly emptied out of the vessels. At this stage it is rubbery. To give it a leathery hardness, it is next heated in a pot with about a quarter of its weight of rosin or gum. The product is called 'linoleum cement'.

A composition is made up of about 40 parts of linoleum cement, 40 parts of a mixture of ground cork and woodflour (thin sawdust), and 20 parts of colouring material or 'pigment'. Ochres, siennas, and whiting are typical examples of pigments (*see* PAINTS AND VARNISHES). The mixing of all these materials is done in a series of heavy steam-heated mixers, and the final product is broken down into small particles. At this stage the various coloured materials are called 'linoleum mixes'.

The next process is to sheet the linoleum mix on to a base of hessian. This is carried out on a machine called a 'calender', which is like a gigantic mangle with four rolls, all steam-heated and each about 7 feet long and 2 to 3 feet in diameter. The granulated linoleum mix is sprinkled uniformly on to the hessian, just before it is fed to the first two rolls. In passing through the calender, the heat and pressure make the material plastic, and it fuses together and binds itself to the backing. Different coloured effects can be obtained by mingling the various coloured linoleum mixes before calendering.

The next stage is maturing. As it comes from the calender, the linoleum is soft and crumbly. It is placed in tall, heated buildings called 'stoves' where it hangs in the heat for several days, often as long as a fortnight, until it hardens. It is then taken out, trimmed, rolled, and packed for dispatch. Today linoleum is sold not only in rolls, but also as tiles, as it is easier to lay in this form. Its surface has also been improved by a finish highly resistant to indentation, after the fashion for stiletto heels ruined so many traditional floorings.

Printed linoleum is plain unmatured linoleum, on which a pattern is printed by a rotary printing-press using a particular type of paint called 'print paint'. After being printed, the material is fed to the 'stove', where the linoleum matures and the paint dries.

Linoleum can be made in thicknesses of up to $\frac{1}{4}$ inch and with care it can wear for 20 years. The industry is not a big one. There are four British firms, mainly working in Scotland.

Competition for linoleum comes from the wide variety of vinyl floorcoverings on the market today. These are based on polyvinyl chloride (*see* PLASTICS) which provides a very hard, durable surface, though in some forms its heat resistance is lower than that of linoleum.

LINSEED OIL, *see* Vol. VI: LINSEED.

LITHOGRAPHIC PRINTING, *see* PROCESS REPRODUCTION, Section 5; *see also* Vol. XII: LITHOGRAPHY.

LLOYD'S, *see* INSURANCE; *see also* Vol. IV: LLOYD'S

LOANS. A loan may mean anything lent by a lender to a borrower. In banking and commercial practice 'loan' generally refers to a fixed sum of money, lent to a borrower for a definite period of time; the word distinguishes this kind of lending from a credit or overdraft (*see* BANK ACCOUNTS) which may fluctuate in amount and be repayable at some indefinite date. In Stock Exchange business, however, the word is used for the securities (sometimes called 'obligations') of governments or local authorities. These Government or municipal loans always carry a fixed rate of INTEREST (q.v.).

A register of holders of such loans is kept by the banking firm, which acts as registrar and paying-agent for the borrower. The BANK OF ENGLAND (q.v.) acts for the British Government and for many municipal borrowers. Transfers of ownership are usually arranged by a document called a Transfer Deed, which is signed by buyer and seller. Interest warrants are posted to the registered holders either quarterly or half-yearly.

See also BOND; BANKING; SECURITY; INTERNATIONAL FINANCE.

LOCALIZATION OF INDUSTRY. This term, or the term 'location of industry', describes how certain industries are confined to particular parts of the world, or to particular parts of a country.

Many influences may cause an industry to settle down in a particular place. The presence of raw materials is one of the most important influences. This is especially true of what are called the primary or 'extractive' industries, such as mining, agriculture, forestry, and fishing. For instance, gold-mining must be done where the gold exists; crops must be grown where the climate and soil are best suited to them; fish must be sought in those parts of the sea in which they happen to live. Sometimes Nature herself alters the location of an industry; the departure of herring shoals from the Baltic to the North Sea some centuries ago is an example of this.

The secondary or manufacturing industries are localized for much more complex reasons; there have been several changes in the general pattern over the past few hundred years. At first the tendency was for manufacturing industries, as well as the primary or extractive industries, to settle near the sources of their raw materials. For example, the cloth industry of the late Middle Ages grew up mainly in the towns and villages of the Cotswolds and of East Anglia, where sheep grazed and provided the wool. Location of this kind can continue as long as an industry uses only hand-machinery and local raw materials. But, as soon as power is used, an industry must move towards the sources of power, and as soon as imported raw materials are mainly used, the industry may have to move nearer to a port. For example, as soon as water-power began to be used for the various processes of the wool industry, the worsted industry of East Anglia moved to the West Riding of Yorkshire where there were streams to turn water-mills (*see* WOOL INDUSTRY, MODERN). The cotton industry settled near Liverpool, the port to which the raw material was shipped.

A change in the kind of power used often leads to a change in the location of an industry. It was possible that when steam, raised from coal, replaced water as motive power for heavy machinery, the cotton and wool textile industries might have had to leave Lancashire and Yorkshire, and move towards the coal-fields. Luckily for these industries, seams of excellent coal existed on the spot, and so a change was avoided. For many years the position of the British coal-fields more or less controlled the location not only of the 'heavy' industries (those handling metals and chemicals in great bulk), but of others also (*see* COAL-MINING, HISTORY OF). This is still true of the heavy industries, but new forms of power, such as electricity or oil-fired boilers, have made it possible for the light industries (those which make or assemble most of the ordinary everyday articles) to move elsewhere. This change took place slowly. At first it was cheaper to generate electricity near the coal-fields, where there were already many industries that would want the current. Moreover, until the development of the electricity 'grid' (*see* GRID SYSTEM, Vol. VIII) between the First and the Second World Wars, it was not easy to transmit electricity over long distances, or to transfer the surplus current of one district to one where current was short. But even before the grid was ready, light industries began to move away from the coal-fields and the older industrial districts, and towards London and other southern towns. Here there were two advantages—nearness to a good market and plenty of labour.

These two factors have always influenced location, but their importance has increased. In the 19th century labour was more 'mobile' than today, that is to say, workpeople were more willing to move from district to district in search of work. Also, housing difficulties were much less serious than they are today. Manufacturers have always liked to have a large market 'on their doorstep', for it is easier to distribute and sell goods in a compact and highly populated area like London, with millions of inhabitants, than elsewhere. Between the First and Second World Wars, the attractiveness of London's large market, and its abundant supply of many kinds of labour, caused many industries to migrate towards it. This movement led to some unfortunate results. The building of new factories and housing estates caused much congestion, and slowed down transport. The efficiency of workpeople suffered through long and overcrowded daily journeys. When the Second World War broke out in 1939, many industries had left the older centres, such as South Wales and the Tyne, which had therefore become 'depressed areas', while London had become overcrowded.

Since the war, the congestion in London and some provincial towns has been made worse by the great increase in motor traffic, and natural economic changes have affected the prosperity of other parts of the country. Booming industries, such as motor-car manufacture, have reduced to trifling proportions the amount of unemployment in Birmingham, Coventry, and other Midland towns; while declining industries, such as cotton- and linen-manufacture, have created abnormally large local 'pockets' of unemployment in Lancashire, the Scottish Lowlands, and Northern Ireland.

The Government has therefore stepped in to counteract the tendencies that have created this state of affairs, and deliberately to alter the normal economic pattern of industrial location. In the years immediately following the war the Government relied mainly on the TOWN AND COUNTRY PLANNING Act (q.v. Vol. X), which gave powers to the Central Government and the local authorities to decide where, and to what extent, land might be used for industrial purposes. Under these powers new 'satellite' towns were brought into being between 20 and 50 miles outside London, and also outside some provincial cities, and licences to erect new factories in areas already congested were refused. The earlier powers given to the Government have now been widened through the passing of the Local Employment Act, which came into force in April 1960. The Government can now offer a wide variety of inducements to manufacturers to move to places with 'high persistent unemployment'. Loans may be given, and even actual grants of money that do not necessarily have to be paid back; these grants may now be substantial enough to cover the building and equipment of a whole factory. The Government itself may build factories in selected areas, and let them at subsidized rents (*see* SUBSIDIES) much lower than those which would have to be paid elsewhere. These new powers have influenced some of the large motor-car manufacturers—such as Ford, Standard-Triumph, and Vauxhall—to expand into Merseyside and the Scottish Lowlands; other industries are being similarly influenced.

Natural economic forces and Government intervention are not, however, the only factors affecting industrial location. Tradition is an important influence, for many people are naturally disinclined to change their ways. Apart from the fact that an industry that has always been in a certain place will tend to remain there, the longer it stays the more it will build up around it a supply of labour that thoroughly understands its work and its problems. Birmingham, for instance, has been the centre of the manufacturing JEWELLERY TRADE (q.v.) for over 100 years. Yet there are no particular reasons for this, other than local skill and tradition. This

MAP OF GREAT BRITAIN SHOWING THE POSITION OF THE CHIEF INDUSTRIES, EXCLUDING AGRICULTURE

L

is also true of the clock and watch industry in the Clerkenwell district of London, the TANNING industry of Bermondsey in London, the BOOT AND SHOE industries of Norwich and Northampton, and the CUTLERY trade of Sheffield (qq.v.).

Apart from Government intervention, the strongest influences on industrial location are, (a) natural or geographical advantages, (b) nearness to raw materials, (c) the presence of the right kinds of labour and skill, (d) good facilities for dispatch or for selling, (e) proximity to suitable markets. The SHIPBUILDING INDUSTRY (q.v.) is concentrated on the Clyde, on Belfast Lough, on Tees-side and Tyneside, for natural and geographical reasons. The COTTON INDUSTRY (q.v.) settled in Lancashire originally for other reasons, but has continued there because Lancashire has a damp climate, well suited to the brittle fibres of the cotton-plant. Northampton continues to be a headquarters of boot and shoe making, not because hides are more easily obtained there, or tanning more easily done, but because the local labour has been schooled for many years in the techniques of the industry. Various secondary industries choose ports such as London or Glasgow as their headquarters, some because they are dependent on imported raw materials, others because the large populations of such cities make selling and distribution easier.

No really simple explanation of industrial location is possible. One must consider each industry separately, and weigh up the various influences and counter-influences in its history, before one can work out the precise reasons why it is where it is today.

LOCK-OUT, *see* TRADE UNIONS.

LOOM, *see* WOOL WEAVING.

LUDDITES. In the early 19th century a movement of workers was formed whose object was the wrecking of factory machinery. These men were called Luddites. Little definite is known about this movement. Some historians believe it to have been a widespread national secret society with many branches throughout Britain. Others think that there was no national movement, but only a series of disconnected local movements. There is also no general agreement as to why those in the movement took this particular name. A half-witted worker named Ned Ludd was prosecuted in 1779, more than 30 years before the Luddite riots began, for the wilful destruction of a machine, and the movement may have adopted his name. Although its leader was never identified, he was known as General Ludd or sometimes King Ludd, and he may have taken his name from the earlier Ned.

The first outbreaks occurred in and around Nottingham at the end of 1811. Masked men visited factories in the dead of night, and broke in and smashed up machinery. The members of the movement were all hand-workers, who had either been dismissed because mechanical methods needed fewer men, or were suffering because, on piece-work (*see* WAGES), they could earn very little in competition with factory workers. Their view was that the new machines were taking away their livelihood.

In the Nottingham riots many stocking- and lace-frames were destroyed, and other riots broke out in the spring of 1812 in Yorkshire, Lancashire, Derbyshire, and Leicestershire. The Government put down the movement very severely, and in 1813 many Luddites were brought to trial at York Assizes. In this mass-trial numbers of the accused were sentenced to death, and others were transported to overseas penal settlements for long periods (*see* TRANSPORTATION, Vol. X). After the York trial the movement temporarily collapsed, possibly because General Ludd himself was one of those tried and sentenced. But it was revived in 1816 during the depression that followed the end of the war with France. Nottingham was again the first city to be affected, and, as in 1812, riots broke out elsewhere in the industrial areas of the north. The return of prosperity and rising prices brought the Luddite movement to an end.

See also INDUSTRIAL REVOLUTION; TRADE CYCLE; TRADE UNION HISTORY.

M

MACHINE ACCOUNTING, *see* ACCOUNTING, MACHINE.

MAGNESIUM, EXTRACTION OF. Ores or compounds of the metal magnesium are found in many parts of the earth's crust, magnesium compounds accounting for over 2% of the earth's solid volume (*see* METAL ORES, Vol. III). The commercial ores of magnesium are usually magnesite or dolomite, and the metal is obtained not only by the ordinary smelting and refining processes (*see* METALLURGY, Section 2, Vol. VIII) but also by electrolysis (*see* ELECTRIC CURRENT, Section 6, Vol. VIII). The bulk of the magnesium now used is obtained by electrolysis. In Britain an important method of producing magnesium was formerly the electrolytic treatment of sea-water, which contains 0·125% of the metal. Other methods are now more profitable, though in war-time the electrolysis of sea-water is still important.

In appearance magnesium is a brilliant white metal rather like silver, although if exposed to the air its surface soon becomes dulled by OXIDATION (q.v.), as it forms an oxide with the oxygen of the air. For this reason magnesium for laboratory purposes is usually kept in sealed containers. Magnesium burns with an intense white light, very rich in the violet and ultra-violet end of the spectrum, and the metal wool inside photographers' flash bulbs is an alloy of aluminium and magnesium in an atmosphere of oxygen. It also plays a part in the making of fireworks. Its military uses include the making of incendiary bombs, and of 'tracer' bullets which show the path of their flight.

Light ALLOYS of magnesium play an important part in engineering, particularly AERONAUTICAL ENGINEERING (qq.v. Vol. VIII). Many of the magnesium minerals are of economic importance. Chrysolite ASBESTOS (q.v.) is one; meerschaum is another, this having once been a popular material, particularly in Germany, for the bowls of tobacco pipes.

Some compounds of magnesium are used in medicine. Magnesium oxide, or magnesia, is one of these. Epsom Salts is the common name for magnesium sulphate, whose medicinal value was first discovered nearly 400 years ago in the reign of Queen Elizabeth.

MAIL-ORDER TRADING. This means the sale of goods direct to the customer through the post instead of the more usual system of selling them through shops. Most large city shops, particularly DEPARTMENT STORES (q.v.), have mail-order departments. Goods are advertised in newspapers and periodicals, and catalogues or price-lists are posted to customers asking for them. The customers then post their orders to the store, and the goods are sent off. Payment is made by several methods, varying with the type of store and the customer's standing. If the customer has an account with the store, the goods will be charged against it; if he is not known to them, or cannot be safely given CREDIT (q.v.), he may be asked to send 'cash with order', or the goods may be sent to him by the Post Office C.O.D. (cash on delivery) service. The customer can often safeguard himself against an unsatisfactory purchase by asking for goods to be sent 'on approval'. Mail-order trading of this kind does not differ essentially from ordinary trading. The main difference is that the customer does not inspect and select from a range of goods at the time of purchase.

The vast bulk of mail-order trading is done by specialist firms selling in this way only. A firm of this kind has no shop, and its goods are not open to inspection, but the terms of business are usually 'guaranteed satisfaction or money back'. Such a firm works from a central warehouse or depot in a convenient town or district, and finds its customers by advertising or through representatives. Some specialist mail-order traders deal in one or two limited lines of goods; others deal in a wide range. A feature of specialist mail-order houses dealing in a wide range of goods is their printed catalogues, which are often very elaborate.

Some of the department stores with mail-order departments do not differ greatly from the specialist mail-order traders. Their mail-order departments account for a very large part of their total TURNOVER of sales (q.v.) and, like the specialist houses, they send an elaborate and profusely illustrated catalogue to actual or prospective customers. Gamage's in London have run an important and profitable mail-order department of this kind since the close of the 19th century. Specialist mail-order houses are more prominent in the U.S.A., owing to the vast distances of the country, and the isolation in which most of the farming population live. The largest American firm is Sears-Roebuck, whose catalogue is an enormous volume, covering almost all the American consumer's needs.

Mail-order trading in Britain, especially by specialist firms, is rapidly increasing in importance.

See also RETAIL TRADING; DEPARTMENT STORES; SELF-SERVICE STORES.

MALTING. Barley malt is the basic material in BEER BREWING (q.v.), and the great bulk of the malt is used for that purpose. But malt has other uses: in the production of whisky, malt foods, vinegar, bread, and so on; and the art of the malster is to produce the right kind of malt for each purpose. Distinct types of malt are used for the various kinds of beers; some very light in colour for the pale ales, others so dark that they are called black malt. The colour of the malt affects the colour of the beer.

Malt is barley or other grain which has just begun to sprout. To the eye, a grain of barley and a grain of malt appear to be alike; but, if each is bitten, it will be found that, while the barley is hard, the malt can be crunched easily with the teeth, and tastes rather like a sweet biscuit. This change in texture is brought about by starting the grain of barley into growth, just as it would begin to grow if sown in the earth.

The first step in malting is to steep the barley in water, and then to spread it out evenly, some 6 inches deep, on one of the floors of the maltings or malthouses. Here it germinates, and is allowed to lie for about 5 days. During this time it is frequently turned over, by men using wooden shovels. By this time tiny rootlets have appeared on the grain. The skill of the maltster consists in judging just the right stage to which this growth should be allowed to go, and in deciding when growth should be slowed up by spreading the grain more thinly, or when it should be stopped altogether. The malt is dried and slightly 'cooked' by spreading it on the floor of a kiln, where the heat from the fire beneath can pass up through it; in more modern practice, hot air is passed over the malt. Sieving then removes the tiny rootlets from the grains of

Whitbread and Co.

TURNING THE GRAIN ON A MALTING-FLOOR

The Brewers' Society

BARLEY BEING PUMPED INTO MALTING DRUMS

malt. These rootlets, known as 'malt culms', are a valuable food for poultry and cattle.

There are variations on these methods. In the more modern maltings pneumatic chutes and conveyor-belts are used to lessen human labour. In the 'drum' maltings germination takes place on what is, in effect, a slowly revolving floor, thus eliminating the need for turning the malt over by hand. In the older maltings work had to be shut down entirely from May to September, because the weather is too warm for the process; but modern science has provided suitable means of air-conditioning (*see* VENTILATION, Vol. VIII), which enable the right degree of warmth and humidity to be maintained throughout the year.

See also BEER BREWING.
See also Vol. VI: BARLEY.

MANAGEMENT, *see* BUSINESS ORGANIZATION; SCIENTIFIC MANAGEMENT.

MANILA, *see* ROPE-MAKING.

MAN-MADE FIBRES, *see* TEXTILE FIBRES, MAN-MADE; TEXTILE FIBRES AND FABRICS.

MARBLE AND ALABASTER. The word 'marble' is derived from the Greek *marmaros*, which means sparkling stone. Ever since the times of the Greeks and Romans, it has been recognized as one of the most decorative and beautiful building materials. In a technical sense marble is any kind of limestone which has a crystalline or granular structure and is capable of taking a high polish. It may be snow-white, or it may be brightly coloured. If a piece of white statuary marble is broken, the sparkling facets of the grains that compose it are easily seen. Marble is a form of limestone which is metamorphic, that is, it has changed its original form as a result of pressure and heat within the earth's crust (*see* ROCKS, Section 4, Vol. III). The streaks and veins of colour, which give diversity to all varieties except pure white statuary marble and black marble, come from metallic compounds and impurities in the stone. The colours chiefly found are yellow, orange, red, grey, green, and, more rarely, purple and blue. For building in Britain marble is hardly ever used in the form of large structural blocks, but generally in thin panels or slabs, which are often used as decorative coverings for solid walls of brick. The slabs are usually about ¾ inch thick, and secured to the backing by brass cramps let into the marble and the backing. Damp harms marble, destroying the polish on which the brilliance of its colour depends. Marble is therefore seldom used for the outside of buildings in the comparatively damp atmosphere of England.

Most of the marble used in Britain is imported. It usually arrives by sea in large blocks, which are nowadays sawn and polished by machinery. The machines can saw as many as twenty slabs at the same time (*see* STONE-DRESSING). Grinding and polishing are done by revolving 'rubbers', first with iron and then with felt. Machines have been invented for turning and polishing columns and balusters, and others for making mouldings.

The most famous buildings of Athens, and notably the temples of the 5th century B.C. on the ACROPOLIS (q.v. Vol. XII), were made of solid marble from Mount Pentelicus, cut and polished by hand. The colour was originally white, but in time it weathers to a beautiful golden yellow. Parian marble, which is also white, and was much used by the Athenians, came from the Greek Island of Paros. The Romans used both these varieties chiefly as thin

E.N.A.

A BULLOCK CART TAKING MARBLE FROM THE QUARRIES AT CARRARA, ITALY

wall coverings, but also favoured *verde antica* (old green); its name indicates its colour, and many people consider it to be the most beautiful marble of all. Many famous buildings of the Middle Ages in Italy, such as the Campanile at Florence, and the Cathedral and the Baptistery at Pisa, are entirely faced with marble, as are many of the finest mosques in Cairo and the TAJ MAHAL at Agra (q.v. Vol. XII). The Taj is made of local Indian marble, which in that country is very plentiful; it is often used for flooring offices, public buildings, and private houses. Some of the ancient marble quarries, including Mount Pentelicus in Greece, are still working; but the chief source of white marble today is Carrara, near Pisa, in Italy. Here enormous quarries continue to produce large quantities, for building as well as for statuary.

Black marble, much used for floors, is chiefly obtained from Belgium and Ireland. Fine green marble comes from Sweden, Switzerland, and Connemara in Ireland. Several so-called English marbles are, strictly speaking, merely limestones capable of taking a high polish; examples are Purbeck and Hopton Wood (Derbyshire) marbles, both greyish in colour, and several Devonshire marbles, mainly red.

Alabaster is another form of limestone, pink or red and white, and often beautifully clouded or veined. It is used for decoration in building. The hard Oriental alabaster, used by the ancients, is sometimes incorrectly called onyx marble, but is a stalagmite or stalactite. English alabaster is largely composed of gypsum (a sulphate of lime), obtained especially in Derbyshire and Nottinghamshire. It is very soft when first quarried and can therefore be carved with great detail. It hardens on exposure to the air. In the 14th and 15th centuries it was much used for tombs and statues, which were carved in workshops near the quarries and exported all over England and the Continent. Today English alabaster is used for electric light bowls and other fittings, and also for memorial tablets.

MARGARINE. The modern margarine industry owes a great deal to the enterprise of the Dutch, who were the first to manufacture margarine on a commercial scale. The product was originally invented in 1869 by a French scientist named Mège-Mouriés. This first margarine was a processed mixture of milk, water, and 'oleo', an animal fat produced from suet. Two Dutch families of butter merchants, the Jurgens and the Van den Berghs, took up the new invention, and the first factories of any size were set up in the village of Oss in Holland in 1871. The animal fats used at first came from France and Austria, but later from the meat-packing industry of Chicago, which was rapidly developing 'oleo' as a BY-PRODUCT (q.v.). Rotterdam, a convenient port of entry, has been closely associated with the Dutch margarine industry ever since.

The Dutch had few sources of animal fats and this shortage, coupled with the prevailing economic situation, led to research into the possible use of vegetable oils from GROUNDNUTS and other OIL-BEARING PLANTS (qq.v. Vol. VI) grown in Indonesia. Eventually, ways of using proportions of these vegetable oils in margarine were perfected, and this greatly helped the Dutch industry. Early in the present century it was found possible to convert liquid oils into solid fats by 'catalytic hydrogenation', that is, by treating heated oils with hydrogen gas in the presence of a nickel catalyst (a catalyst helps chemical reaction without being altered chemically itself). This discovery enabled the industry to use the cheaper vegetable oils and whale oil, and freed it from its dependence on animal fats.

In 1927 the Dutch companies, Van den Berghs and Jurgens, who had earlier built factories in the London area, amalgamated with various Continental associates to form the Margarine Union. The same year also saw the first successful production, by a subsidiary of Lever Bros. Ltd. at Bromborough, Cheshire, of margarine containing the fat-soluble vitamins A and D. In 1929 the Margarine Union and Lever Bros. Ltd. amalgamated to form Unilever Limited, the largest margarine-producing organization in the world today.

Following the addition of vitamins, which made possible the production of margarine with a food value in no essential way different from butter, the quality of margarine was greatly improved by changes in production methods.

The oils used in margarine manufacture are principally of vegetable origin—groundnut, coconut, palm and palm kernel, cottonseed and soya bean, as well as whale oil and fish oil. These oils are hardened and are then refined to remove

Unliver

THE 'COMPOUNDING PANEL' IN A MARGARINE FACTORY

The technician measures the exact quantities of the different oils and fats as they go into the pre-mixing tanks

all traces of colour and smell. The refining process is usually carried out in three stages: neutralization with alkali solutions to remove the fatty acidic bodies; bleaching with Fuller's Earth to remove colour, and deodorizing by steam distillation under high vacuum to remove taste and smell. The refined oils thus produced are pure and tasteless.

Specially treated fat-free milk is added to give margarine its flavour. Other ingredients used are water, salt, vitamin concentrates, and vegetable colouring-matters.

In modern factories, a suitable blend of refined oils and other ingredients is emulsified and chilled simultaneously in a machine called a rotator. The chilled mixture is then given a buttery texture and is fed to a packing machine which forms and wraps it into $\frac{1}{2}$-lb. blocks. All these operations are carried out in enclosed machines, so that the highest standards of hygiene are maintained.

See also OILS, VEGETABLE.
See also Vol. VI: OIL-BEARING PLANTS.

MARKET. A market exists whenever there are buyers and sellers of anything for a money price. A market need not be an actual building, although it is often convenient that there should be one. The estate market, for example, in which landed property changes hands, has no single building in Britain set aside for such dealings. The MONEY-MARKET (q.v.) is another market which does not possess a building of its own. All that a market needs is willing buyers and sellers able to get in touch with each other. The foreign exchange market consists simply of the governments and bankers of the world, linked together by a system of cables and telephones.

An exchange is, of course, a market in the general sense of that word; but the term is nearly always used to describe a building in which dealings take place in goods not actually on view there. Buyers and sellers are usually dealing in contracts on paper, entitling them to receive, or binding them to deliver, certain quantities of something at a certain date. On the Liverpool Cotton Exchange, for example, there is no actual cotton displayed for sale; instead dealers contract to buy or sell certain recognized grades for immediate or future delivery (*see* COTTON INDUSTRY).

The word 'exchange' is also used to describe buildings in which purely financial dealings are carried on. Thus the London Stock Exchange deals in documents entitling their possessor to receive a rate of INTEREST, or a rate of DIVIDEND, on an INVESTMENT (qq.v.). The Foreign Exchange Market deals only in bank balances in various countries, but it is called a market rather than an exchange because it has no building of its own.

Exchanges can be further classified into financial exchanges and produce exchanges. The Stock Exchange is a financial exchange. The Baltic Mercantile and Shipping Exchange, in St. Mary Axe, London, is both a financial and produce exchange. On its financial side members are dealing in the 'chartering' or hiring of ships, usually tramp steamers, to carry bulk cargoes. In such transactions no actual goods or contracts concerning any goods are changing hands. But the Baltic also deals in the grain cargoes loaded into those ships, and this side of its business makes it a produce exchange. The Liverpool Cotton Exchange is, of course, a produce exchange pure and simple.

A feature of all exchanges, whether they are financial or produce exchanges, is that business may be done on them in contracts for future as well as for immediate settlement. Such exchanges are generally known as 'terminal markets', because contracts can be arranged either for immediate settlement or for settlement some period or 'term' ahead. On such exchanges contracts to buy or sell are either 'spot' or 'forward'. A spot contract is one which involves buying or selling for immediate delivery and settlement; a forward contract involves buying or selling for delivery and settlement at some named future date. On some markets, the foreign exchange market for example, forward transactions are called by that name; on other markets they are called 'futures'.

As dealings on produce exchanges take place without the buyer ever seeing the goods, business has to be confined to the sort of commodity whose quality can be described beyond all argument—either in words, or by reference to a named grade or quality which all dealers would interpret as meaning the same thing. Obviously, then, it would never do for produce exchanges to deal in such things as meat, vegetables, or fish, which have to be looked at before their quality and value can be known. The places where such commodities are dealt in are therefore generally called 'markets'. Well-known examples in London are the Smithfield Meat Market, the Spitafields and Covent Garden Fruit and Vegetable Markets, and the London Commodity Exchange in Mincing Lane, dealing in tea, coffee, spices, and other Eastern products. But all rules seem to have their exceptions, and one of the most important markets of this kind is called the Wool Exchange; it is near the Guildhall in the City of London.

On some of these markets the dealers do their business after they have already inspected the commodity—either in WAREHOUSES (q.v.) at the docks, or elsewhere—and they fix a price by mutual bargaining. But on most of the commodity markets an AUCTION (q.v.) is the normal way of buying and selling: an auctioneer mounts a raised platform, called a 'rostrum', in the centre of the room, and sells to the highest bidders the various consignments or 'parcels' of commodities offered for sale that day. These are sometimes on show in another part of the market building, or they may be temporarily warehoused elsewhere; sometimes, as at Spitalfields, they are left outside in carts and lorries, and samples are brought into the auction room. As in an ordinary auction of furniture at a sale held in a house, the goods are 'knocked down' by a tap of the auctioneer's hammer on his desk, the last and highest bidder getting the goods.

As well as the permanent markets housed in

Pau Museum

THE NEW ORLEANS COTTON EXCHANGE, 1873
Painting by E. Degas, 1834–1917

buildings, and handling their own limited range of products, there are many auction rooms which are not given the name of market. At the Mart in Queen Victoria Street, London, for instance, there is an auction room for landed property; but naturally only a very small part of the property dealings in the country takes place in it, and it is not called the British Estate Market. Likewise there are the famous auction rooms called Christie's, in London, at which antique furniture, pictures, jewellery, and various other objects of art are auctioned from time to time; but this, too, is by no means the only market of its kind. Throughout the country there are also various fairs and markets, and regular sales of horses and livestock.

This big network of markets is of great service to the commercial world. Business would be far too difficult and expensive if manufacturers, importers, and merchants had to track down individual buyers and get them to buy their goods. The main markets are in the larger ports, such as London and Liverpool, where many of the imported commodities come direct. Purely financial transactions are still centred in London, the principal city for the country's banking, foreign exchange, investment, and shipping dealings. By market organization the seller gets a higher price than otherwise; the consumer benefits because the expense is lessened of transporting goods to the small buyers all over the country; perishable products also reach the customer in better condition. By doing 'forward' business a manufacturer or merchant can cover his future wants for a long time ahead, without having to put down any money until the actual date of his contract. In these big, centralized markets the dealers can detect even small changes in the conditions of SUPPLY AND DEMAND (q.v.); changes in price warn producers of possible over- or under-production, and so they are able to cut down on unprofitable lines, or to open up lines where there is a temporary shortage.

Most market dealings are done through BROKERS (q.v.) who are members of the exchanges or markets in which they specialize. Brokers are told by the manufacturers, merchants, importers, or shippers what goods to buy or sell, and so on; the prices may be either limited or left to their discretion. On the financial and produce exchanges they arrange the necessary contracts with other brokers. If a broker happens to get orders from different customers to buy and sell the same grades and quantities at the same time, he can arrange the whole business inside his own office by drawing up a contract between buyer and seller, and can charge commission to both parties. This practice is called 'marrying' buying and selling orders. Most exchanges, however, have rules limiting the extent to which this may be done.

See also Vol. VI: MARKET TOWNS.

MARKET RESEARCH. This is a scientific way of obtaining information about the taste and preferences of the buying public. The Americans, who have always been more ready than any other nation to use scientific methods as an aid to business, were the first to start market research.

Market research has become almost indispensable for successful business. In the Middle Ages, and until even the early years of the INDUSTRIAL REVOLUTION (q.v.) before the growth of railway communications, most goods were hand-made for a purely local market. The task of finding out what the consumer thought of the goods offered to him was therefore very easy. As the Industrial Revolution went on, factories grew larger and firms made goods for a wider market. By the end of the 19th century a single manufacturer might be selling his goods not only in his own country but over the whole world. It was therefore essential that manufacturers should find out scientifically whether the goods they were turning out were what the consumer really wanted. Research was also necessary to find out many other kinds of information. For example, the consumer might like the article, but not the way it was packed, or the size and design of the package. Moreover, it might be sold on terms which did not suit the shopkeeper, so he might refuse to stock it. A very good instance of what could happen without market research was the experience of the exporter of egg-cups to India, who assumed that hens all over the world laid the same sized eggs. Another manufacturer took care to make inquiries and, finding that Indian eggs were smaller than British, made egg-cups slightly smaller than the standard British size, and thereby captured the Indian market from his competitor.

The marketing problems of all manufacturers are not the same. Some manufacturers are already selling a particular product, and they make use of market research to increase their sales of it. Others are not yet making a particular product, but are thinking of doing so; they wish to learn beforehand what consumers think about existing products, so that if possible they may improve on them. Then there are manufacturers who wish to launch some newly invented product, such as the 'aerosol pack' for packing deodorants, insecticides, and toilet requisites. All these three problems are different, and the methods of market research must vary in each case.

Market research for the first two types of product involves first of all office-work and then 'field' work. The office-work is based on such figures or STATISTICS (q.v.) as happen to be available. A manufacturer of a commodity already on the market will have figures of his total sales in any particular country. These figures must be analysed or 'broken down' in various ways. A useful break-down might be into districts, in some of which the average shopper would be wealthy, in others poor. The trend of these sales figures over several years should then be studied to discover where sales of the product are increasing and where they are falling off. This preliminary office-work will produce ideas to go upon before the 'field' part of the research is started, which involves asking the consumers and shopkeepers to give their opinion. It is impossible to question all customers, even in one district, so the people who carry out the research must rely on a statistical law: if a large enough sample of consumers is chosen at random, the results will differ only slightly from the results obtained if every single consumer had been approached. For field work in market research at least 1,000 persons are often interviewed; if the research is to cover the whole country, 100 persons might perhaps be chosen from each of ten different representative districts. Each person on the list is then asked to give answers to a form or questionnaire containing not more than seven or eight questions, each easily understood and capable of being very simply answered. The questions chosen will naturally depend on the product itself, and on the information the manufacturer wants. A research conducted by one of the big film-producing companies to attempt to gauge the public taste in films would naturally involve totally different questions from those asked in a questionnaire dealing with toothpaste. Answers to the questionnaire can be obtained either by calls on the persons interviewed, or through the post. Interviewers need to be carefully trained and experienced, otherwise they may 'lead' the persons interviewed, that is, they may suggest answers instead of letting the persons speak for themselves. Skill is needed to interpret the replies, as many consumers give different replies to a questionnaire from those they would give in ordinary conversation. So what is called 'interview bias' must be allowed for.

Market research is carried out mainly by highly experienced firms. Some of them may carry out a 'retail audit' every two months in certain kinds of shops, for example, in chemists', grocers', confectioners' and tobacconists'. During the 'retail audit' the stocks of different brands of goods in these shops are counted, and the invoices covering the goods which the retailers have bought since the last 'audit' are carefully studied. From information so gathered the market research companies are able to tell the manufacturers how well their products are selling in relation to their rivals' products. Now, powerful computers can supply regular and rapid reports on the movement of goods at 'the point of sale'. This information can be used to measure the effect of sales promotion and advertising campaigns, often conducted through the medium of television, in selected areas.

New and untried products are sometimes 'test marketed' in a sample of shops in one or two towns. For example, if a manufacturer wants to put a new shampoo on the market, he may ask his market research company to watch the sales of other existing brands and then put his new brand into the town and see how it fares for a month or two. This test helps him to decide whether it is worth his while to manufacture the new shampoo on a national scale.

Some advertising companies who do market research are now employing psychologists to interview customers at some length, not merely asking them which brand of goods they prefer and why, but probing deeply and widely into the underlying reasons for their preference. This is called 'motivation research'.

See also Statistics; Business Organization; Advertising and Publicity.

MARKETS, STREET, *see* Street Markets.

MARQUETRY, *see* Inlay and Marquetry.

MASONRY, *see* Stone Dressing.

MASS PRODUCTION, *see* Production.

MEAT TRADE. Before the days of railways and refrigerated ships, the towns of Britain depended for their meat supplies upon the live cattle, sheep, and pigs that could be driven along the roads to the markets. Butchers who bought animals in the markets took them to their own slaughter-houses for killing and preliminary cutting up. Salting and curing were then the only known ways of preserving meat, and, as far as the poor communications permitted, there was a fairly extensive trade throughout the country in bacon and hams. In many of the large seaport towns the salting of beef and pork, for provisioning merchant ships and the ships of the Royal Navy, was an important activity. The supplies of live animals came only from within the kingdom itself.

By the middle of the 19th century the population had grown so large that Britain was unable any longer to provide all the meat for her people, and live cattle began to be imported from abroad. European countries were the first suppliers, then North America, which sent us over half a million cattle a year at the end of the 19th and the beginning of this century. Smaller numbers also came from South America. Meanwhile the railways had made it possible for British butchers to draw on more distant and isolated parts of the country for their supplies of live cattle, which could now travel in cattle-trucks instead of losing condition on a long walk to market.

During the 19th century public opinion caused many laws to be made in Britain to prevent dirty and unhealthy practices. Local authorities were given power to inspect and license private slaughter-houses, or abattoirs as they were called, and to insist on clean conditions. Towards the end of the century public slaughter-houses began to be set up.

It was not until the invention of COLD STORAGE (q.v.) and the importation of frozen and chilled meat from the U.S.A. that there was any important change in the meat trade, although before this small quantities of salted meat, mostly beef, were imported from that country. The first experimental cargo of beef and mutton from Australia arrived in London in 1879, and two years later New Zealand began to export mutton and lamb. From then onwards the import of frozen or chilled meat began gradually to replace the transport of live animals, but many years passed before the amount of refrigerated cargo-space in ships was sufficient to bring the trade in live cattle to an end, and imports still came in from North America until the outbreak of the First World War. South America, Australia, and New Zealand took up refrigeration on an important scale. Vast abattoirs and freezing-plants—called in South America *frigorificos*—were established at such ports as Buenos Aires in the Argentine, Montevideo in Uruguay, and Christchurch in New Zealand. The famous Canterbury lamb, which has nothing to do with the English city in Kent but comes from the Canterbury plains of the South Island of New Zealand, found a popular and growing market in Britain (*see* NEW ZEALAND, Vol. III).

The average Briton eats about 100 lb. of meat a year compared with over 200 lb. for the average Australian, New Zealander, and Argentinian and 150 lb. for the average American. Home produce accounts for about three-quarters of British meat consumption. Home-bred animals are sold alive at the weekly markets, mostly by auction, but some privately. Others are sold direct to wholesale butchers, who supply retail butchers in the large towns, and to local butchers, who slaughter them and pay for them according to the weight of the carcases (meat) produced. In 1954 farmers formed the Fatstock Marketing Corporation which buys animals from farmers, slaughters them, and sells the meat at wholesale prices to butchers. In addition to the home-bred animals others are imported from Ireland. Some of these are fat and are slaughtered at the ports or in large industrial centres, while others go to

NEWGATE MEAT MARKET, LONDON, IN THE MID-19TH CENTURY
Engraving from the *Illustrated London News*

farms where they are fattened and sold in the same way as home-bred animals. In most of the large inland centres of population, such as London, Birmingham, Manchester, and Leeds, and also in many seaport towns, there are meat markets where the carcases are sold and cold stores where meat, not for immediate sale, may be kept.

In the overseas abattoirs, carcases of the highest-quality cattle are quartered, while those of sheep and lamb are left whole. Mutton and lamb, which can be frozen without losing much of their flavour and tenderness, are shipped in the frozen state. Nearly three-quarters of Britain's imports of mutton and lamb come from New Zealand. Beef can also be shipped frozen, and nearly two-fifths of it is, but it loses quality and flavour much less if it is conveyed as 'chilled' beef at temperatures of about 29°–30° F., which is above the freezing point of meat. Carcases of frozen lamb are loaded into refrigerated ships' holds like any other solid cargo, but each quarter of chilled beef has to hang individually by a separate hook from the deck above. The holds in which chilled beef travels are filled with carbon dioxide gas to kill the tiny organisms of decay, for decomposition cannot be otherwise fully prevented, unless the meat is specially wrapped. The gas needs space to circulate in, and a given weight of chilled beef therefore requires more cargo space than the same weight of frozen lamb and mutton. Some chilled beef, however, is now vacuum packed in plastic film and imported in cartons.

See also Vol. VI: CATTLE, CARE OF, Section 7.

MECHANICAL ACCOUNTING, *see* ACCOUNTING, MACHINE.

MEDIUM OF EXCHANGE, *see* MONEY.

MERCANTILE SYSTEM. This was a name given to a body of economic ideas held by certain British statesmen and economists during the 17th and 18th centuries. These ideas concerned the regulation of trade and industry within Britain itself, and the management and control of overseas trade, to make the nation economically powerful and self-sufficient: that is, only dependent on foreign countries for such goods as Britain was unable to produce herself. The title of 'mercantile system' was given much later, and not by those who conceived the ideas, but

Meade Collection

COVER OF AN 18TH-CENTURY OFFICE FILE

Justice and Britannia are seated one each side of the Custom House. Above is a British merchant ship

by those who thought them wrong. The famous economist Adam SMITH (q.v. Vol. V), although he did not invent the phrase, made great use of it, usually in a hostile and rather reproachful sense. It was Adam Smith's criticisms, in the main, that caused the mercantile system to be replaced by a set of ideas utterly different, namely the Free Trade theories of the 19th century.

The practices were based, to start with, on the idea that it was the business of the Government itself to take control of overseas trade. It was argued that certain kinds of trade, if left uncontrolled and unregulated, allowed imports to come into the country without enough exports going out. This kind of trade meant a drain of money out of the country; the money went out in a very real sense, for in those days money was made of gold and silver, and consequently one country's money could be melted down and recoined by any other nation. The statesmen of the mercantilist period therefore aimed at what we call a favourable balance of trade: a total of exports greater than the total of imports. This would cause precious metals to flow into Britain from the countries that were buying from her more than they sold to her. Everything that would compel the foreigner to pay her in coin, everything that would diminish what she bought abroad, would therefore tend to increase this favourable balance of trade, and would lead to an increasing inflow of the precious metals. So, with this object in view, imports and exports were strictly controlled and regulated. This control did not stop short at goods alone. Any business that meant paying money to foreigners was carefully watched. Payment of this kind, for instance, took place when foreign ships were allowed to carry goods into and out of Britain. Money was not only paid for the goods, but of course, for the use of the ship to carry them in as well. So various NAVIGATION ACTS (q.v.) were passed by Parliament; these forbade the shipment of goods between Britain and certain other countries in any vessels that were not British.

There are other mercantilist practices which go back to earlier periods. As far back as the reign of Henry VII the law compelled French exporters of wine to England to use English ships when they were available. Although England under Edward VI was no longer Catholic, the fishing trade was encouraged by an Act passed in 1548, which enforced fish-eating on the old Catholic days of fasting. The growing of corn in Britain was encouraged by import duties or TARIFFS (q.v.) against foreign corn, so that the country might be independent of foreign supplies and in a position to feed itself from its own production, especially in time of war. Later, to make sure of materials for shipbuilding, Queen Elizabeth ordered the home growing of hemp for rope and cordage, and of flax for sails, and the increased planting of oak trees.

In its later years the mercantile system was seriously criticized, on the ground that it was a policy which made the nation powerful as a whole, instead of making its individual citizens prosperous. Yet serious problems faced British statesmen. Each of the leading nations was struggling to become supreme in the world of that time, and wars were frequent. A Free Trade policy—to which Britain did not become converted until the second half of the 19th century—would have meant that Britain in those earlier days would have depended on foreign nations for food and essential war stores, and this would have been dangerous in war time because of the risks of blockade or attack. The mercantile system was one which kept the nation independent for strategic or military reasons.

The statemen and writers who were keenest to increase the store of gold and silver in Britain were called 'bullionists' by their critics: for these metals, before they are coined into money, are known as 'bullion'. Precious metals had then one great advantage, which they have not fully lost. Men all over the world will accept them, so that in time of war, or of threats of war, a nation that has plenty of these metals can buy from other lands all kinds of necessary and useful stores.

Some of the old ideas of the mercantilists have recently been revived, although in a less extreme form than some centuries ago. British statesmen are still as much concerned with a favourable balance of trade as were their 17th-century predecessors, but their purpose is different: they aim to maintain and protect the value of the country's money, and to have sufficient to lend to Commonwealth countries that are economically underdeveloped. Agriculture, too, is fostered by SUBSIDIES (q.v.) in much the same way as in earlier days, and with the same object: to make the country reasonably independent of overseas supplies in time of war or emergency. But all modern statesmen are agreed that Free Trade, in so far as it may be adopted without grave injury to some of our vital interests, is generally the more advantageous policy, and in this respect their ideas are different from those of their mercantilist predecessors.

See also OVERSEAS TRADE; CURRENCY; RATES OF EXCHANGE; INTERNATIONAL TRADE; SHIPPING; TARIFFS.
See also Vol. X: NATIONAL FINANCE.

MERCHANT ADVENTURERS. This was a powerful organization originally built up in the 13th century round a body of English merchants who traded in the Netherlands, mainly in cloth, at their own risk. To secure greater protection they looked out for special privileges. As early as 1296 they received a charter from the Duke of Brabant, and by 1360 they were an organized company with their own set of rules. They made great strides in the reign of Henry VII, when they were granted a private coat of arms and a new charter, and by that time they had extended the scope of their operations from the Netherlands 'to all the Townes and Portes lying between the river Somme in France and the German Sea'.

The expansion of their trading activities in the 15th and 16th centuries brought them face to face with two serious rivals: the MERCHANTS OF THE STAPLE and the HANSEATIC LEAGUE (qq.v.). They had no difficulty in overcoming the first. The Staplers dealt in wool, the Adventurers mainly in cloth, which was beginning to be far more important than wool in English foreign trade. While the Staplers lost ground, the Adventurers gained it. Furthermore, there was a contrast in the trading methods of the two bodies. The Staplers were content to bring back home the money earned in overseas trade, or to lend it abroad—even to the Adventurers. The Adventurers used their gains to buy foreign goods, such as timber and canvas, pitch and tar, which they then imported into England and resold to increase their profits.

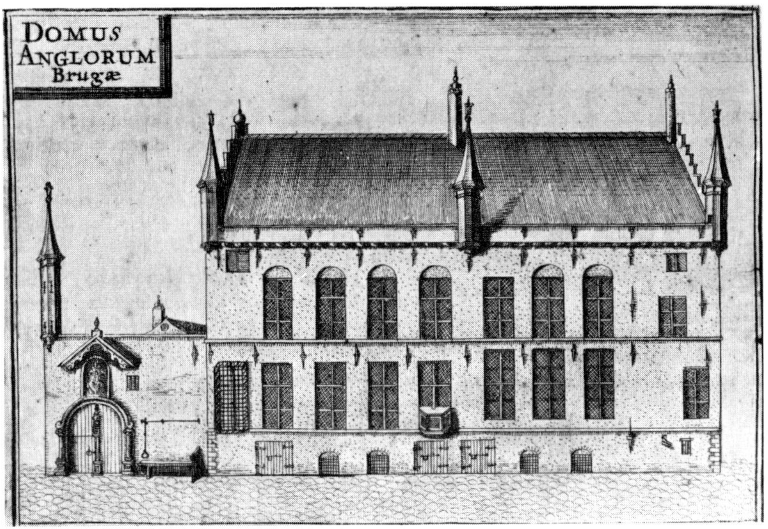

THE HOUSE OF THE ENGLISH MERCHANTS AT BRUGES, BUILT IN 1468
From A. Sanders, *Flandria Illustrata*, 1641–4

The Hanseatic League was a more serious competitor, and rivalry lasted for many years between the two groups. The League had long enjoyed special privileges in London, and owned their own depot, the Steelyard. During the 15th century, in the early stage of the rivalry between the League and the Merchant Adventurers, the League succeeded in securing most of the trade in the Baltic and Scandinavian markets. They even secured from Edward IV a confirmation of their privileges in London. Later, the Merchant Adventurers lost all their trade first in Antwerp, and afterwards in Hamburg. But they never altogether lost their continental foothold. They made vigorous efforts to get trade in German markets, and were finally successful. In 1578 the Germans withdrew all the trading privileges of the Adventurers in Hamburg, but Queen Elizabeth retaliated by revoking the rights of the Hanseatic League in London. The rivalry continued bitterly, and it was not until 1611 that Hamburg finally gave way, and the triumph of the Merchant Adventurers was complete.

Although the Merchant Adventurers were vigorous in their trading activities, much of their energy went into the attempt to secure a complete monopoly in cloth dealing.

Their organization was that of a regulated company, with very strict rules of admittance (*see* CHARTERED COMPANIES). They made a close scrutiny of would-be members, and there were sometimes complaints that their entrance fees were too high. Their restrictions did not end here. Their officers—the Governor and his Court—had great authority over all members, and could levy heavy fines for offences, with no chance of the defendants appealing to civil courts. At times the officers even checked the enterprise of their members by limiting their transactions to a fixed number of cloths. They were allowed to trade in foreign towns only on certain days—Mondays, Wednesdays, and Fridays—and rules were laid down as to the length of time for which they could give CREDIT on their sales (q.v.). They had their eyes wide open for trading opportunities, but their charters were self-protective, providing against too much individual initiative. We find little in their charters about expansion, but a great deal about restrictions and controls.

Because of their wealth and importance the Merchant Adventurers became involved in politics. Kings used the Company to collect export duties and to provide loans. Both Henry VII and Queen Elizabeth were well aware of the uses to which the Company could be put. In the 17th century the Company supported Parliament against the King in the Civil Wars, and contributed heavily towards Puritan expenses. Despite this, in 1661, after considerable financial losses, their rights were restored by Charles II.

With the coming of William and Mary the Company was deprived of its monopoly of the export of woollen manufactures, and its trade was thrown open to all English merchants. This was not, however, the end of the Company. Most of the cloth trade was still in its hands in the 18th century, when its extensive privileges and organization gave it a decided advantage over its rivals. But the continental wars of that period, and the consequent insecurity of trade, drove English merchants to seek new markets in India and America, and allowed much European commerce to fall into other hands.

In the 19th century free competition created a new kind of commercial world. Commerce freed itself of restrictions, and economic expansion was no longer confined within the limits of a single trading organization. There was no place for a body like the Merchant Adventurers.

A 16TH-CENTURY CLOTH MERCHANT'S SHOP

See also CHARTERED COMPANIES.

MERCHANT BANKER is a name used for certain influential banking firms which began as merchants and which do a business different from that of an ordinary banker. They finance international trade by allowing merchants to draw BILLS OF EXCHANGE (q.v.) on them, and they find large sums of money for governments and important industries by acting as ISSUING HOUSES (q.v.).

The merchant bankers of southern and central Europe in the late Middle Ages and Renaissance periods (between A.D. 1100 and 1500) made big profits, and some made vast fortunes. The most successful and well-known firms were the Medici of Florence, and the Fuggers of Augsburg in southern Germany. In those days wealth was mostly in the hands of very few people, so, instead of borrowing the savings of the general public, as modern governments can do, the kings and princes got their money by arranging loans with the big merchant bankers. The bankers naturally insisted upon knowing what the money was for, and it was necessary to let them into many State secrets. They therefore became extremely well-informed on politics and statecraft, and they soon became 'powers behind the throne'. They were shrewd enough not to lend money for war unless they were fairly certain that their borrowers were going to win; and their influence behind the scenes of European politics was sometimes great. *The Fugger News-Letters* is a book that illustrates the knowledge and influence possessed by this Augsburg banking-house in the 14th and 15th centuries. The novel *Romola*, by George Eliot, throws light on the merchant princes of Florence.

From northern Italy and southern Germany merchant banking extended eastwards, westwards, and northwards, particularly during and after the 17th century. In the 18th century the first office of the house of Rothschild was opened in Frankfurt. Branches were opened later in Vienna, Paris, Naples, and London. As trade expanded, London became not only a great international centre but also the headquarters of the merchant banking world. In the 19th century the growing importance of the United States led to the opening of merchant banking houses in New York, some of which were

EMBLEM OF THE AMALGAMATED SOCIETY OF ENGINEERS, 1852

The goddess of Fame stands in the centre on the cornucopia of Plenty. A smith refuses to repair the sword of Mars, the god of War, but an engineer accepts a design from Clio, the Muse of History. The kneeling figures represent Aesop's fable of the bundle of sticks, showing that unity is strength. The busts are Samuel Crompton, James Watt, and Sir Richard Arkwright. The branches of the Iron Trade are depicted below

THE SIGN OF THE MERCHANT BANKING HOUSE OF N. M. ROTHSCHILD AND SONS, ST. SWITHIN'S LANE, LONDON

branches of European houses. Others, like the famous firm of J. P. Morgan and Co., were American firms.

These later merchant bankers continued to keep in close touch with governments, and they were usually as well informed on political matters as statesmen themselves. In fact they often received information long before the statesmen got it: a member of the firm of Rothschild reached London with the first news of the result of the Battle of Waterloo, and his firm greatly profited by it. Each merchant banking house was in close relationship with one or more foreign countries: Hambro's Bank with the Norwegian Government, Baring's with the Argentine Government, Rothschild's with Brazil, Schröder's with Germany, Lazard's with France, and Morgan, Grenfell and Co. (the London house of J. P. Morgan and Co. of New York) with the United States. In fact, before the United States created a State banking system like our own Bank of England, the firm of J. P. Morgan and Co. was the American Government's financial agent. Morgans were also the New York agents of the British Government during and after the First World War.

The profits of merchant bankers from the finance of international trade are possibly less than they used to be, and less government borrowing comes the way of the merchant bankers. They are, however, still extremely wealthy and influential.

See also BANKING.

MERCHANTS OF THE STAPLE. From the 11th to the 13th centuries England's overseas trade was largely in the hands of foreigners. The most important commodity produced—wool—was handled by foreign merchants: Flemings, Italians, and Germans. But gradually there grew up English wool merchants in competition with the foreigners. This group, later called the Merchants of the Staple, were anxious to gain a foothold on the Continent, where they could fight foreign competition and corner the English wool trade.

A 'staple' was a depot, where wool was deposited so that customs duties and tolls on it could be collected. It was obviously useful for the king to have one regular channel through which England's leading exports normally passed, so that he could collect his taxes more easily. It was this royal interest in the staple which turned it from a voluntary body of merchants into an important official organization. Edward I played a leading part in this story. In 1275 Parliament granted him the right to levy a duty on sacks of wool and sheepskins. In order to ensure efficient collection the King encouraged the setting up of staples at fixed points, through which all wool exports were sent.

There were two big problems, however. Where should the staples be, in England or abroad? And how many staples should there be, one or several? The English wool-growers, and many of the small merchants who dealt in wool as a sideline, would have preferred to have had no staple at all. This opinion was shared by many of the foreign merchants, who did not want to see Englishmen gain a privileged control of the trade. On the other hand, the wealthy English merchants wanted one single staple, preferably abroad, where they had powerful connexions. The English country wool-dealers and clothiers would have preferred an English staple, where they could gain complete control of the market.

Different groups used their influence to suit themselves, and so, from the end of the 13th century down to 1363, the staple town was frequently changed from one place to another.

In particular Edward III, who fought complicated continental wars, switched it about to suit his political programme. At one time it was in St. Omer, at another in Bruges, then in Antwerp, and then in Middelburg. Between 1326 and 1327, and between 1332 and 1334, it was in England, in a set of different scattered staple towns. In 1363 it was moved to Calais—a French port which then belonged to England—and, with a few intervals, it remained there until Calais ceased to be English in 1558. By that time cloth and not wool had become England's most important export, and the Merchants of the Staple had given way in importance and influence to the Company of MERCHANT ADVENTURERS (q.v.).

The Staplers were organized from the start as a company of merchants with their own Mayor and Council. Originally they comprised the whole body of English merchants engaged in foreign trade. The wool merchants who made up the organization were the wealthiest merchants in England, drawn from all over the country. In 1313 they were officially recognized as the central wool-trading body. Fifty years later, when the staple was set up in Calais, it secured a virtual monopoly of the export of wool and leather, and as time went by the Staplers in Calais became not only traders but also effective rulers. Although they did not live in Calais, they paid the Calais garrison and controlled the government of the town, and remained a body of great importance until they were challenged by the new cloth-manufacturers. The change from wool to cloth as England's chief export was the most important factor that destroyed their position. There is a pathetic note in their records 7 years before the fall of Calais. 'At thys day the hoole fellowshippe be so discomforted that they are mynded to forsake the staple for to seke theire poore livynge some other way.' They could only comfort themselves with the thought that, in face of such trials, 'there is no fellowship of merchants under any Christian

British Museum

CALAIS, THE STAPLE TOWN FROM 1363 TO 1558
Drawing, about 1525 (*Cotton MS. Aug. I, ii,* 70)

prince that could have so sustained like burden and damage'.

The Merchants of the Staple, before their importance dwindled, competed strongly with the Merchant Adventurers, and contended that the latter should pay admission fees for the right to trade in cloth. The Merchant Adventurers were too successful for the Staplers, however, and in the end got complete control of the cloth trade.

See also CHARTERED COMPANIES.

MERCURY, or quicksilver, is one of the most interesting metals, as it remains liquid at any temperature likely to be met with in most parts of the world except the very coldest. It only becomes a solid when it has been cooled down to below the temperature of 38° below zero Fahrenheit, that is, 70 degrees of frost. It was first mentioned about 300 B.C. in Greek literature, and was then prepared from the ore called cinnabar, or the red sulphide of mercury (*see* METAL ORES, Vol. III). Later it was much used by the alchemists in their experiments with metals (*see* CHEMISTRY, HISTORY OF). Most of our modern mercury still comes from the red sulphide, which is found principally in Spain, Italy, and Yugoslavia in Europe, and in California, Oregon, Nevada, and Arkansas in the U.S.A. Very often small quantities of metallic mercury are found in these deposits in a free state (that is, not chemically combined with other substances). There is the famous Almaden mine in Spain, 140 miles south west of Madrid, which has been producing mercury for 2,000 years and is still the biggest individual mercury mine in the world (the name Almaden comes from Arabic words meaning 'the mine'). Until 1938, when the Pinchi Lake mine in British Columbia was first worked, no mercury was mined in Canada at all. Mercury fumes are dangerous to health, and the air in mines, and also in refining and manufacturing plants, is constantly sprayed with a chemical which corrects the poisonous effect of mercury, and makes it possible for men to work there.

Bodleian Library

AN INDIAN LEGEND OF QUICKSILVER

The metal was supposed to spring up from wells when a virgin passed. Early 18th-century painting of the Rajput School

Mercury is transported and sold in iron flasks containing 76 lb. of the metal. Since it expands or contracts a good deal on being heated or cooled, it is a useful liquid to use in THERMOMETERS (q.v. Vol. VIII), although alcohol thermometers must be used for POLAR REGIONS (q.v. Vol. III) or wherever very low temperatures are met with; even where mercury freezes, alcohol will remain fluid. Mercury is much used in metal refining, particularly in the refining of the precious metals, because it is able to absorb many of them and to form with them what are called 'amalgams'; for this reason it is also used in ASSAYING (q.v.). Until the cyanide process replaced it, mercury was used to separate the gold from the dross in GOLD-MINING (q.v.). A compound of mercury known as fulminate is much used in making detonators for setting off explosives. The metal itself is also used for THERMOSTATS (q.v. Vol. VIII) or automatic heat controllers, and for many forms of electrical contacts and switches (*see* SWITCHGEAR, ELECTRICAL, Vol. VIII): in fact, these uses account for just under one-fifth of the total world output of mercury. Mercury compounds, such as calomel, are much used in medicine, both for internal use and in preparing ointments.

See also Vol. III: METAL ORES.

METAL ORES, *see* Copper Mining; Mercury; Tin Mining; Lead Mining; Platinum; Nickel; *see also* Vol. III: Metal Ores.

See also Vol. VIII: Iron and Steel.

METHYLATED SPIRITS, *see* Industrial Alcohol.

MICA is a mineral which is easily split into flakes or leaves, sometimes as thin as a very thin sheet of paper. These can be bent without breaking. There are several varieties of mica, and these are called by different geological names. Most kinds are transparent, and some are of a whitish or neutral tint while others are coloured. The mineral is found principally in India, but also in the U.S.A., Brazil, Canada, and Ceylon. India is the main producer and exporter, the most important mines being at Hazaribagh and Nellore. Hazaribagh produces a reddish mica, and Nellore a mica of a greenish tint. Mica is very little affected by heat, and for this reason, and also because of its transparency, it is much used for the windows of stoves, lanterns, and industrial furnaces, for the chimneys of lamps and gas burners, and for the eyepieces of gasmasks and goggles. The ordinary kitchen hot-water boiler, or anthracite sitting-room stove, often has mica windows. In the past mica has been much used for window-panes in remote regions, as in parts of Russia, which were then far from industrial centres and where glass could not be bought.

The mining of mica is done in India by rather primitive methods, which often result in damage to the large sheets found underground. For many years these damaged portions were looked upon as useless and wasted, but in recent years uses have been found for ground and powdered mica. Ground mica is used in the manufacture of wallpaper and is used for giving the frosted effect to Christmas decorations and stage scenery. Powdered mica is used in paint manufacture.

One important property of mica is that it is a very good electrical insulator. This is true even when it is split into extremely thin sheets; it is therefore of use in Electrical Engineering (q.v. Vol. VIII), in the construction of electric motors and dynamos, in some types of condensers, in radio and television receivers, and electronic equipment.

An artificial mica has been produced in German and British research laboratories, but not cheaply enough for general use. The Americans have also undertaken research on artificial mica, for the U.S.A. is the biggest importer of natural mica from India, her own mines producing only a tiny fraction of her requirements.

See also Mining.

MICROFILM PHOTOGRAPHY, *see* Photography, History of.

MILK PASTEURIZATION, *see* Pasteurization of Milk.

MILLING, FLOUR, *see* Flour Milling.

MINING. As long ago as the Stone Age, men extracted minerals from the earth by mining. In Britain at that time the southern and eastern parts were regularly mined for flints (*see* Chalk). But no detail of how mining was done in those days has been handed down to us. The Greeks in the 4th and 5th centuries B.C. mined extensively in the silver-mines at Laurium, inventing mining tools and methods of smelting heavy ores (*see* Metallurgy, Section 2, Vol. VIII). They used the silver to make the coins which were known all over the then known world (*see* Coins). The Romans developed mining wherever they could in those parts of the world which they conquered, for example in Italy itself, in Britain, and especially in Spain which at that time was rich in gold, silver, and lead.

Minerals in the earth occur either as seams or as lodes. A seam is a horizontal layer of mineral or mineral ore, usually at a good depth below the surface. Coal is practically the only mineral that occurs in seams; most others occur in the form of lodes. A lode is a streak or vein which may be found in the earth at all sorts of angles, varying from the horizontal to the vertical, according to the way in which the movements of the earth's crust have twisted it. Lodes are often called 'reefs', notably in South Africa. The angle of a lode is important: if it is vertical its presence may be missed, unless a borehole happens to be sunk right on top of it or unless it is found quite by chance.

In fact, throughout the history of mining, chance has played a very large part. The famous Bolivian silver-mines of Potosi were discovered because an Indian stumbled and held on to a bush, which came away in his hand and disclosed

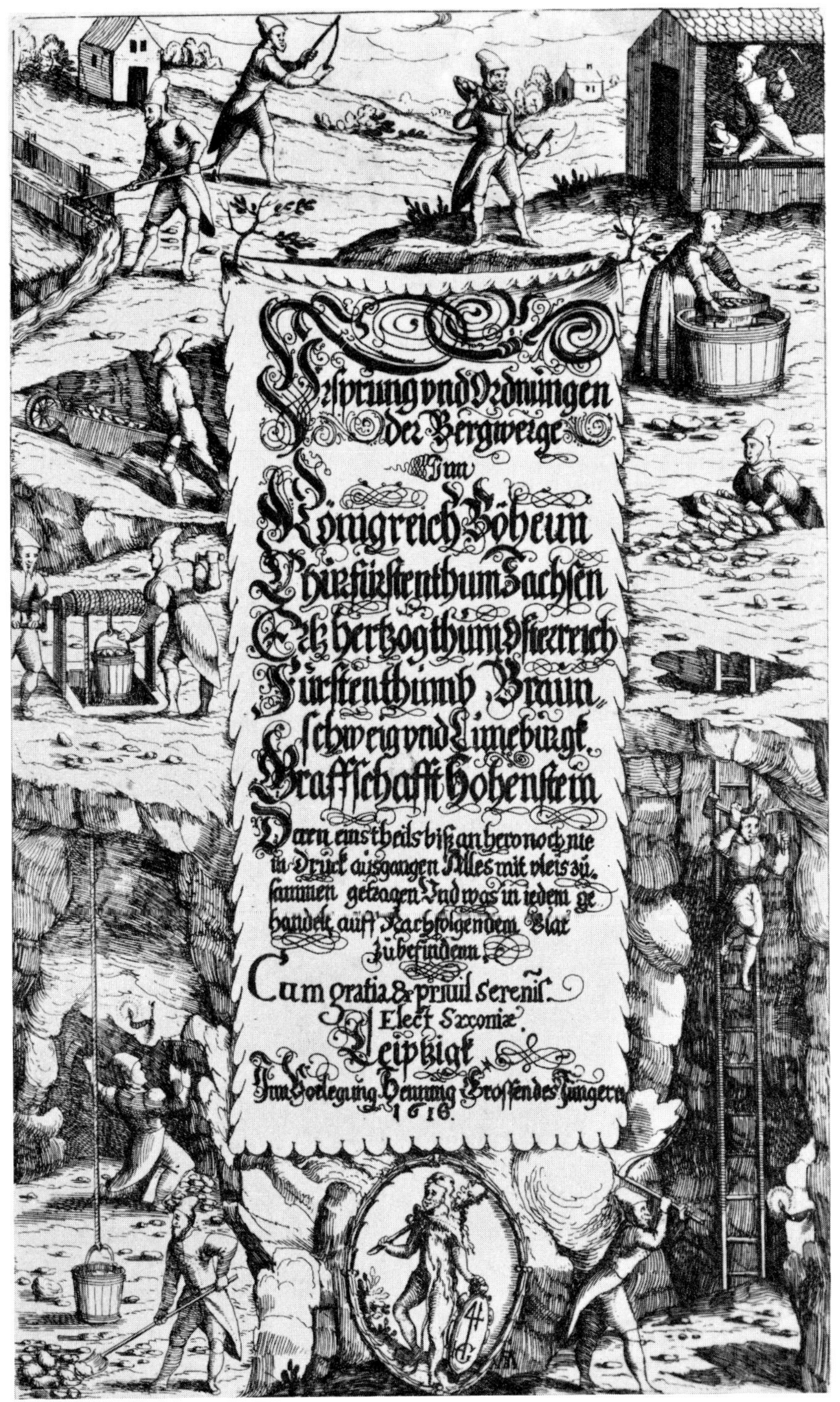
Vrsprung vnd Ordnungen der Bergwerge
Im Königreich Böheim
Churfürstenthum Sachsen
Ertzhertzogthum Osterreich
Fürstenthumb Braunschweig vnd Lünebürgk
Graffschafft Hohenstein
Daran eins theils biß an hero noch nie in Druck ausgangen Alles mit vleis zu sammen getragen Vnd was in iedem gehandelt auff Nachfolgendem Blat zu befinden.
Cum gratia & priuil. serenis. Elect. Saxoniæ.
Leipzigk
In Vorlegung Henning Grossen des Jüngern
1616.

ALLUVIAL, DRIFT, AND UNDERGROUND MINING

Title-page of a German book on mining, 1616

a deposit of metallic silver. It is only in the present century that chance has given place to science in the search for useful minerals. Searching for mineral deposits which are 'payable', that is, which will pay to work, is called 'prospecting'. The old-time prospector of the 19th-century adventure stories was a figure more romantic than scientific, although he had a good practical grasp of his trade. He had a working knowledge of geology, knew the appearance and properties of the different minerals, and was able to apply simple chemical tests to find out their precise nature. Nowadays he has been replaced by mining geologists trained in the sciences of geophysics and geochemistry, with modern methods and highly complicated instruments. But even today it is sometimes difficult to detect mineral lodes unless they are exposed on the surface as an 'outcrop', and chance still plays some part in mineral PROSPECTING (q.v. Vol. VIII).

When prospectors think there is a mineral deposit in a piece of ground, they try to find it by drilling narrow boreholes deep into the ground. From different levels samples are brought up to the surface and tested or assayed (*see* ASSAYING). Often many years pass before a series of boreholes, 'sunk' at various points, proves the existence of an underground lode. If the samples disclose the existence of payable ore, mining is begun.

Mining can take four main forms. The first and simplest is open pit mining; the lode is exposed on the surface or lies just beneath it, and can be worked after the top soil or 'overburden' has been removed. Some methods of open mining are not essentially different from those used in STONE QUARRYING (q.v.).

The second form is alluvial mining (or 'placer mining' as it is called in America). Alluvial soil is formed by mud washed down the course of a river or stream (*see* ROCKS, Section 3, Vol. III). Alluvial mineral deposits are found in pockets or pools in existing or ancient river-beds or watercourses. 'Diggings' of this kind still account for a small proportion of the gold and diamond production of the world.

Drift mining is the next form of mining. It involves driving towards the lode a slightly sloping tunnel or gallery. In the early days of the British COAL-MINING industry (q.v.) many of the mines in Northumberland were drift mines. With the advent of very powerful conveyor belts, large new drift mines have recently been sunk in many parts of the world.

The fourth form of mining takes place in underground workings, and accounts for about half the world's metal mining: this consists of underground mines at great distances below the surface, opened up by shafts.

Once the existence of payable ores has been proved, the first three methods of mining are not difficult. The ways in which alluvial deposits of ore are dealt with are described in the article on GOLD-MINING (q.v.). Drift mining also is comparatively simple. Along the drift, or inclined plane driven below the surface, conveyor-belts or self-discharging trucks travelling on an endless cable keep up a continuous delivery of ore from the working 'face'. Underground mining, however, involves sinking main shafts before the lode can be reached and worked. Main shafts are usually big enough to provide sufficient room for skips or cages, used both for lowering men and materials to the working face and for hoisting ore to the surface. A section of the shaft is generally set aside for compressed-air mains, electric cables, and an upward discharge pipe by which underground water can be pumped away from the workings. To sink shafts and drive tunnels underground is very expensive. From the main shaft horizontal galleries or passages called 'levels' are driven towards the lode, usually about 60 feet apart. Unless the lode is absolutely vertical, these levels are seldom directly above each other, and each level is connected with the next by small shafts called 'winzes'. Very often, if the lode is irregular, 'raises' are driven upwards from one of the levels towards it. When the lode is reached, a 'stope' or big working-place is dug out, and this is often timbered (supported by wooden props) to hold up the roof and protect the workers at the face. From these stopes the ore is taken away, and this process is called 'stoping'. Holes are drilled in the rock, and filled with explosive and fired to bring down the ore. Drilling is usually done by rapidly moving compressed-air drills called 'jackhammers'. The ore is sent along the nearest convenient level to the shaft, in modern mines usually by continuous conveyors. At the surface the ore is crushed mechanically until it reaches its final size, which varies according to subsequent treatment; for example, gold ore is reduced to tiny particles. The crushed ore, often in powder form, passes through chemical, mechanical, or heat processes; these either 'concentrate' it so that much metal is contained in small bulk for overseas shipment, or they smelt the metal out from the ore (*see* METALLURGY, Section 2, Vol. VIII). If there is enough fuel and labour on the spot, it is cheaper to smelt near the mine; otherwise the mineral is shipped as a 'concentrate' to the country where the smelting process will be carried out.

See also COAL-MINING; COPPER-MINING; GOLD-MINING; SILVER-MINING; ASSAYING; MINING IN BRITAIN.

See also Vol. III: METAL ORES; COAL.

See also Vol. VIII: MINING ENGINEERING; MINING MACHINERY; PROSPECTING.

MINING IN BRITAIN. Although COAL-MINING (q.v.) is still the biggest such operation in Britain, substantial amounts of iron ore, china clay, tin anhydrite, gypsum, etc., are excavated as well. Sand and gravel mining has also increased significantly since the war, and the total tonnage of these other minerals now exceeds that of coal. Our mining records go back to the days of the Roman occupation, when the Romans did much to develop British tin and lead mining. A writer in the 1st century A.D. describes how smelted tin was exported from the island of Ictis—probably St. Michael's Mount in Cornwall—to Marseilles, then called Massilia. Lead was mined in considerable quantities, probably in the Mendip Hills and in Derbyshire, Flint, and West Shropshire. Pliny, the Roman writer, mentions the large supplies of lead pipes and sheeting from Britain that were imported into Rome for building. The Romans also mined copper in Anglesey—probably at Amlwch, where a little mining is still done—and in Shropshire.

Long after the Romans left, lead and tin mining continued on a large scale. In the 12th and 13th centuries lead was in great demand, particularly for the roofs and guttering of churches and monasteries. Some centuries later, mining was encouraged by Queen Elizabeth, who was anxious to make her country as self-supporting as possible. She brought many continental mining engineers to England. Two CHARTERED COMPANIES (q.v.) were formed to foster mining, the Mines Royal Society being the larger. CORNISH MINING (q.v.) much expanded after 1730, when the invention of a method of

Scunthorpe Division, British Steel Corporation

OPENCAST MINING OF IRON ORE ON THE LINCOLNSHIRE ORE FIELDS AT SCUNTHORPE

South Crofty Mine

CORNISH TIN MIN, HEADGEAR AND ORE CONVEYORS

tinning steel plate was the beginning of the South Wales TINPLATE industry (q.v. Vol. VIII). About the same time an improved method of extracting zinc from its ores led to the opening in Bristol of the first British smelting-works. The ores came mainly from the Mendip Hills, and by the end of the 18th century nearly 100 zinc-mines were being worked.

Throughout this period the old Roman mines in Anglesey and Shropshire continued to produce copper, and newer mines in Devon and Cornwall were opened up. In the early 19th century Cornwall and Devon together produced about half of the world's copper. When immense supplies of rich copper ores were discovered in Chile and the U.S.A., the English mines ceased to pay. Mining for other non-ferrous metals (metals other than iron) has also declined. The peak period of British lead-mining was between 1850 and 1870, principally in Derbyshire, Durham, Cumberland, and Dumfries. There is no mining now in the last two districts, although there is a little in Flint, Durham, and Derbyshire, and also in the Isle of Man, where the ores are rich in silver. Zinc production reached its peak in 1881, but has since greatly declined; and tin-mining is no longer an important Cornish industry, though new mines are being opened.

Small quantities of other minerals are still mined in Britain. In some of the limestone areas, particularly in Derbyshire, the heavy minerals barytes and stroniamite are mined or quarried. These are used as filling material in high-class PAPER-MAKING (q.v.). Derbyshire also has deposits of fluorspar, which is used in some metal processes and is the base for producing hydrofluoric acid. This acid has the property of eating away glass, and it is therefore used for etching designs on glass. Nottinghamshire and South Durham have deposits of gypsum, a soft, chalky mineral which, when ground up and evaporated, becomes plaster-of-paris. To the west of Edinburgh there are deposits of SHALE OIL (q.v.), but they are now no longer worked.

Gravel and sand are quarried on a large scale for use in building and in METALLURGY (q.v. Vol. VIII). A special metallurgical sand, used for CASTING molten metal in metal-works (q.v. Vol. VIII), comes from Mansfield in Nottinghamshire. In some parts of the country there are sands, consisting mainly of quartz, that are very useful in GLASS-MAKING (q.v.). Though many such deposits have failed, mining

South Crofty Mine

CORNISH TIN MINE, UNDERGROUND WATER PUMP STATION

National Coal Board

THE ENTRANCE TO TILLICOULTRY DRIFTMINE, CLACKMANNAN

for sand and gravel is flourishing, and many millions of tons are now extracted from the sea-bed.

See also Mining; Coal-mining, History of.

MINTING COINS, *see* Coins; *see also* Vol. X: Mint.

MOHAIR, *see* Hair Trade.

MOLASSES, *see* Industrial Alcohol.

MONEY. 1. Money came into existence to answer a need of mankind, but this need did not arise until civilization had grown beyond its earliest stages. Primitive man lived by hunting, each hunting only for himself and his family or tribe. At such a stage, when strangers were avoided or driven away, money and even trade were unnecessary. Later, when he had learned to domesticate wild animals, man lived a nomadic and pastoral life, constantly wandering as he drove his flocks and herds to new pastures. As the road to wealth was then the possession of beasts, money in its modern form was still not necessary, although the beasts themselves were really a form of money. It would suit what few craftsmen there were to be paid for their wares in cattle, and farmers and herdsmen to pay in that way. To this day some of the people in parts of Africa still regard their cattle as their money, and every bridegroom has to pay the bride's family a price in cattle for his wife.

When human communities began to settle down and cultivate the land, instead of wandering over it with their flocks and herds, the Division of Labour (q.v.) increased, and people specialized in crafts and trades. Most men specialized in growing or producing something, of which only a very small portion was necessary for their own wants. So they had to get rid of their surplus. In exchange for it they wanted something which would give them the power to choose what they wanted from the surpluses of other people. A few transactions might take place by straightforward exchange, or barter, but only certain things could be treated in this way. It is unlikely, for instance, that a cobbler needing supplies of corn for his family from time to time would always find that the farmer would take shoes in payment. It would be more convenient if there were some other object that would always be useful to both the shoe-maker and the farmer.

Once people have agreed what this other object is to be, and once they are prepared always to accept it or to offer it in payment, then we have money in its primitive form. It is the go-between in all business transactions or, as the economists say, a 'medium of exchange'. We have seen that in the pastoral stage of human history cattle themselves were this generally acceptable commodity; it is therefore not strange that the Latin word for money, *pecunia*, comes from a similar Latin word, *pecus*, meaning cattle. In modern English we still use the adjectives 'pecuniary', meaning concerned with money, and 'impecunious', meaning having no money.

The trouble about cattle is that they are subject to disease, are easily driven away while their owners are asleep, require a lot of land on which to graze, and cannot easily be concealed. Worst of all, they cannot be subdivided without being killed and so losing their value. The precious metals, such as gold and silver, do not suffer from any of these disadvantages. A small weight of gold has cost a good deal of labour and effort to produce, and so it is equal in value to other things that have taken about the same amount of labour and effort to produce. It can be buried and hidden away easily; it does not rust or lose weight through storage; it can be weighed out into quite small quantities without loss of value. Even some modern communities have used the precious metals by weight as their standard money, although they have used coins for pocket-money and for small change. For many years the standard money of China was the tael, which was not a coin, but a weight of silver; the dollar and the 'cash' were used for small change and minor transactions.

There are, however, disadvantages in using weighed quantities of these metals. Dishonest persons may mix them with less valuable metals of the same appearance and weight. In time, so many mixtures might then be passing from hand to hand that every business man would need to be accompanied by an assayer to test and weigh every piece presented to him. The obvious way out of this difficulty is for the State to make coins of a standard shape, weight, and fineness which are then called CURRENCY (q.v.).

Anything which passes from hand to hand as money, and which is thus 'current', is called currency, although in modern countries the word is usually reserved for money issued by the State. BANKING (q.v.) creates another kind of money, in the form of bank accounts withdrawable by cheque. It is comparatively easy for a powerful government to make certain of the purity of its coinage, although, when governments were not powerful, the coinage often got into very bad condition. This was so when William III came to the throne in 1689, and re-coinage was needed to put things right. A strong government can also control the quality and quantity of the bank-note currency; in modern days the right to issue notes is usually given only to a Single State bank, called a Central Bank. If the Central Bank is also given power to control the extent to which the banks can create bank money, withdrawable by cheque, then some control over the value of money can still be maintained. For if the quantity of money in a country, particularly bank-notes and bank money, is allowed to increase without check, money will follow the economic rule that the more common a thing is, the less valuable it will become.

Ashmolean Museum

MIDDLESEX TOKENS, HALFPENNIES 1795–6, THE UPPER ONE SHOWING A LACE MAKER, AND THE LOWER ONE ANTISLAVERY PROPAGANDA

In the 17th and 18th centuries there was such a shortage of coins issued by the Royal Mint that token coins were made for tradesmen and local authorities. These were used for small payments in the district in which they were issued. They were engraved with illustrations of subjects of topical interest

2. CHANGES IN VALUE. Very serious social results follow changes in the value of money. A fall in its value is the same thing as a general rise in prices; a rise in its value means a general fall in prices. On the whole, rising prices are good for trade. Manufacturers and merchants can make or buy almost anything, in the certainty that its price will rise, and go on rising, and that profits will be almost automatic. In times of falling prices the possibility of loss discourages enterprise, and leads to general trade depression. But apart from these short-period changes in the value of money, there are the long-period changes. Wars cause prices to rise and to stay high, and this has serious consequences. People with fixed incomes and pensioners are particularly badly hit. It is therefore the duty of a government to keep the value of money as steady as possible.

There is a way of measuring changes in the value of money. It is not absolutely perfect, and must be used carefully. It is called a Price Index Number. By means of an Index Number we can compare prices now with what they were in some earlier year of steady prices (known as a 'base year'), and we can measure from this the percentage of change in the value of money between one year and another, or even between one month and another (*see* COST OF LIVING).

If a country's money is made out of some

THE MONEY CHANGER

German woodcut, 1539

precious metal, it will always be worth (by weight) an equal amount of the money of another country made from the same metal. But the value of paper money depends upon what one can buy with it if it is spent in the country that issues it. The value may vary from time to time within the issuing country; it is also possible that when the value of one country's paper money goes up, that of another country's may go down. There is no certainty that the values of different nations' moneys will always keep level. The reasons for such variations are discussed in the article on Rates of Exchange.

See also Primitive Money; Exchange and Trade; Currency; Banking; Coins.

MONEY MARKET. This is the name given to the activities of a number of banking firms dealing in money. In London, it has no special building of its own. 'Money' is not a very good name for what is dealt with in the Money Market, because its members are not buying and selling actual bank-notes: they are borrowing or lending money for various periods—generally for short periods.

In the London Money Market the principal lenders of money are the ordinary commercial banks. They lend money, usually from day to day, but sometimes on weekly agreements, to firms called Bill Brokers or Discount Houses. These firms earn their profits by investing the borrowed money for a short time in Bills of Exchange (q.v.) and short-dated Government securities. Before the First World War, most of the bills arose from ordinary trading business, either within Britain or in connexion with international trade. Since 1914 many of the bills have been British Government Treasury Bills.

Rates of interest on loans to the Money Market, and rates of discount on bills of exchange, naturally depend on the amount of free money that the banks feel able to lend, and on the quantity of bills coming into the market for discount. Generally, money is lent at about $1\frac{1}{2}\%$ per annum below Bank Rate (q.v.), and bills are discounted at 1 to $2\frac{1}{2}\%$ per annum above the borrowing rate, according to their quality and period. Discount rates on bank bills are always lower than on bills payable by ordinary merchant firms.

The Bank of England is the leader of the London Money Market. It is able, fairly

The Times

MEMBERS OF THE LONDON DISCOUNT MARKET MAKING THEIR DAILY CALL AT A LONDON CLEARING BANK

effectively, to control the rates at which business is done, and also its extent.

MONOPOLY. The word 'monopoly' comes from two Greek words meaning 'a single shop' or 'a single seller'. A firm or group of firms or a State organization is said to have a monopoly when it is the sole producer or seller of some article or service. Few firms possess a perfect monopoly, extending over the whole world. But there are many firms that have a monopoly within their own country. The National Coal Board, which is the only producer and seller of coal in the United Kingdom, is an organization of this kind. So is the Post Office, which has the sole right to carry letters and to provide other services. There are today many public monopolies of this kind.

In the middle of the 19th century competition in Britain was practically unrestricted; firms were small and numerous, and were keen rivals of each other. Competition kept prices down, which was, of course, often to the benefit of the consuming public. It was not long, however, before these numerous small firms began to form themselves into Trade Associations, bodies which laid down standard prices throughout the whole country and forbade price-cutting. This move had much the same effect on prices as if a single firm had possessed a monopoly to produce and distribute the article.

A firm possessing a monopoly is called a 'monopolist'. The object of a monopolist is to make his total profits as large as possible, and he can do this in one of two ways. If there is no real substitute for his product, he can probably raise its price, without suffering any falling-off in sales (*see* SUPPLY AND DEMAND), to that figure which will make the highest profits. He has another choice: he can decide to restrict output, and to sell only to his better-off customers who will pay a higher price. Usually a monopolist will make higher profits if he restricts output below what it might be if there were free competition.

A monopoly in the hands of private firms may,

therefore, greatly injure a country's consumers, who are the ordinary members of the public; they may pay a higher price than they would pay if competition were free, and they may also find fewer goods to buy. In Britain, as industry has tended more and more towards large COMBINES (q.v.), consumers have agitated for some form of Government control of monopoly. There is now a Monopolies Commission which investigates and reports on alleged monopolies and a special new court of the High Court of Justice in London—the Restrictive Trade Practices Court—before which complaints may be brought.

MORTAR, *see* CEMENT.

MOTOR INDUSTRY. Until 1914, the production of motor vehicles in Europe remained a small and modest industry, carried on in moderate-sized factories whose layout and methods differed little from those of the earlier coach-building works. Many British firms made chassis only, and left bodywork to firms that still called themselves coach-builders. In Britain, the leading makers were Lanchester, Rolls-Royce, Napier, and Thornycroft; in France, Citroën and Renault; and in Italy, the Fiat works in Turin. Even in the U.S.A. the annual production of passenger cars did not exceed 4,000 until 1900. Many of the present American makes were then being produced, but on a small scale and by the same general methods of production as in Britain and other European countries.

Just before the First World War Henry Ford began at Detroit (U.S.A.) the manufacture of mass-produced cheap cars. His first model became famous, and his example was soon followed by other makers in the U.S.A. After the war there was a large demand for cars and lorries; new firms joined the industry, each producing a few hundred vehicles a year. The American motor industry had gone ahead rapidly during the first 3 years of the First World War when America was still neutral; and so the U.S.A. was practically the only country represented in the growing world export trade in motor vehicles. General Motors Corporation, a big COMBINE (q.v.) embracing several producing plants whose scale was constantly increasing, was formed to organize the production of the medium-priced car, in much the same way as Ford had popularized the production of the cheaper model.

One reason for the success of the Americans was the way in which production was organized. Most of the big producers merely assembled cars from a number of component parts, including even engines, turned out by specialist firms on mass-production lines. In Britain an enterprising car-maker named W. R. Morris (who later became Lord Nuffield) was the first man to adopt this system, and the early Morris-Cowleys were similarly assembled from components, the original engine being a Hotchkiss. Between the two World Wars the Ford Motor Company, which at that time merely assembled American components at Trafford Park, Manchester, and Cork, Ireland, built a large works on the American model on the north bank of the Thames at Dagenham, near London. In spite of its American ownership and control, there were distinctive British features in the models turned out, and Dagenham produced not only passenger and goods vehicles but also agricultural tractors (*see* TRACTORS, Vol. VI).

Since the Second World War, the British motor industry has become much more like its American counterpart, for with the general rise in the standard of living there has come a huge demand for cheap and medium-priced cars—a demand which the manufacturers could only satisfy by adopting mass-production methods and standardization. Smaller firms have merged to form big units, and models that were quite different have now become minor variations on a single basic car. One very typical example of this trend was the merging of Morris and Austin to form the British Motor Corporation, with the result that four basic engines now power the entire Morris and Austin ranges, and, for instance, the Austin Mini and the Morris Mini are virtually the same car. Though today the major firms make their own engines, the tendency to buy the components from specialist firms is a logical consequence of concentration and mass-production. Thus pressed steel bodies (which have almost entirely replaced the old coach-built bodies), doorhandles, propellor shafts, shock absorbers, radiators, and electrical equipment are all examples of components made by specialists such as Lucas and the Pressed Steel Company. The latter firm, like other component manufacturers, was itself absorbed into a larger group, that of British Motor Holdings, which also included B.M.C. and Jaguar. In 1968 an even larger merger joined this group to British

B.M.C.

AN ASSEMBLY LINE IN A MOTOR FACTORY

The car body is being lowered on to the chassis and engine

Leyland to form the British Leyland Motor Corporation, the fifth largest motor manufacturers in the world. Co-ordination such as this has enabled the British motor industry to compete successfully in foreign markets, and provide one of our most valuable exports.

The manufacture of cars for a mass market has brought other changes, too. In the old days, cars were bought to be kept until they were worn out. But to sustain today's vast industry and to keep hundreds of thousands of workers fully employed, once the original demand for cars has been satisfied, it is necessary that users shall buy a new car as often as possible—certainly long before the old one is worn out. For this reason British manufacturers are beginning to adopt the American practice known as 'styling for obsolescence'—the deliberate design policy that makes cars look out of date in a couple of years. In America the point has been reached that old cars handed-in in part exchange for new ones are broken up rather than re-sold, in order to keep up the demand for new models.

See also TRANSPORT.
See also Vol. IV: MOTOR-CAR, HISTORY OF.

MULTIPLE SHOPS are chains of more than ten shops owned by companies whose names are often nationally known. With the exception of the CO-OPERATIVE SOCIETIES (q.v.), most of the multiples started as one-man businesses, for example, Lipton's, which made its name by the low prices and high quality of its provisions, such as bacon, cheese, butter, and cooked meats. Multiple shops or 'chain stores' were opened in growing numbers in the U.S.A. and Britain towards the end of the 19th century, at a time when the population of big towns was growing fast. These new firms were large concerns, and most of them were LIMITED COMPANIES with large CAPITAL behind them (qq.v.). Their usual policy was to expand by buying up other shops, and today some own hundreds of shops, many of which are now being converted into SELF-SERVICE STORES (q.v.).

One of the earliest chains in Britain was the grocery and provision firm of Sainsbury, formed in 1869. Freeman, Hardy, and Willis, the boot and shoe distributors, were formed in 1876, and the 1880's and 1890's saw the opening of many grocery chains, such as the United Kingdom Tea Company, the International Stores, and Lipton's. By the beginning of the present century the whole country was covered with a network of multiple shops, in the grocery and provisions, tobacco, sewing machine, cheap tailoring, drug, bookselling, boot and shoe, china and glass, and meat trades.

Before and after the First World War the multiple shops of Britain increased in number and variety. The American firm, Woolworth, opened many branches, later forming a British company. Its shops sold a wide variety of goods with a price limit of 3*d.* and 6*d.* Marks and Spencer started a growing chain of popular multiple department stores, but without the low Woolworth price limit. The war had increased the number of women at work earning independent incomes, and multiple firms selling women's shoes, hosiery and underwear, and millinery opened up in growing numbers. Since the war, this trend has increased, aided by the mass production of standardized goods, and today many of the chains have passed into common ownership. Firms of football-pool promoters have found a use for their growing profits by opening their own chains of multiple shops.

Big concerns of this kind can buy in very large quantities, and thus obtain from the manufacturer or wholesale merchant a lower price or a larger discount. The extension of multiple shops has lowered prices. The multiple department store of the Woolworth type can sell cheaply not only because it buys in immense quantities, but also because its operating costs are low (*see* COSTING). It comes very close to being a SELF-SERVICE STORE, with a big TURNOVER (qq.v.) and a relatively small staff.

The head offices of the multiple shops exercise very close control over their branches. In many trades the branches are allowed to sell only for cash; and in those firms where credit is allowed, the branches must make to head office regular returns of unpaid bills. Usually the accounts of the branches are kept at head office, and it then becomes easy to control each branch, whose cash remittances to head office and unsold stock on hand must always equal the selling value of the stock received from head office. Branch accounts and results are closely analysed and compared at head office, and are used to estimate the efficiency of the various branch managers.

See also GROCERY AND PROVISIONS; RETAIL TRADING.

N

NAVIGATION ACTS were laws passed in Britain and some other countries, from the 14th century onwards, to develop native shipping by allowing goods to be carried to and from that country in that country's own ships only.

In earler years any increase in a nation's merchant shipping was linked with its strength in naval vessels; changing a merchant vessel into a naval one was a comparatively simple matter in those days of light weapons and absence of armour. The first English Act was passed in 1381, in the reign of Richard II, 'to increase the navy of England which is now greatly diminished'. The Act provided that 'none of the King's liege people do from henceforth ship any merchandise in going out or coming within the realm of England in any port but only in ships of the King's ligeance'. Anxiety about the decay of the navy was continually being stressed. The first Navigation Act of Henry VII's reign in 1485 laments 'the great diminishing and decay that hath been now of late time of the navy'. This Act ordered that the wines of Guienne and Gascony in France, which were then coming to England in big quantities, should be imported only in English, Irish, or Welsh ships. Later, these ships were obliged to have English masters and mariners.

Henry VIII strengthened his father's laws, and this led to retaliation by other countries. Elizabeth, who wished to reduce her enemies to a minimum, tactfully repealed the Navigation Acts, adopting instead the principle that goods imported in foreign ships should pay higher customs duties than those carried in English ships.

Then came the famous Navigation Act of 1660, which remained in force for the best part of 200 years. It sought 'the encouraging and increasing of shipping and navigation', and ordered that 'no goods or commodities whatsoever shall be imported into or exported out of any lands . . . to his Majesty belonging or in his possession . . . in Asia, Africa or America . . . but in such ships or vessels as do truly and without fraud belong only to the people of England or Ireland, Dominion of Wales or town of Berwick-upon-Tweed . . . and whereof the master and three-fourths of the mariners at least are English'. This Act was aimed chiefly at the Dutch, with whom England was then beginning to dispute the mastery of the world's carrying trade.

There has been much argument as to whether the great increase of British shipping during the following 100 years was due to the 1660 Act, or would have taken place anyway. The figures are impressive. Between 1663 and 1774 the tonnage of British ships leaving Britain increased eight times, whereas the tonnage of foreign ships increased by only a half. Modern historians think this advance was due to other causes. During a long struggle between the Dutch and the French, British shipping took the lead. It is now believed that it was not the Navigation Acts that established Britain's lead, but her enterprising and aggressive policy of developing colonies.

It was a long time, however, before the Navigation Acts were finally repealed. The deep-sea traffic to and from British ports was thrown open to the ships of all nations in 1849, although the coastal trade around the British Isles remained reserved to British ships and British owners. In 1853 the British coastal trade was opened to the ships of any nation, largely in the hope (which was not fulfilled) that the United States would copy the British example and allow coastal competition in their own home waters. The growth of British shipping since then does not suggest that the repeal of the Navigation Acts was a mistake.

See also Shipping; Trade, History of.
See also Vol. X: Royal Navy.

NEWSPAPER INDUSTRY. During the course of the 20th century, the principal British daily and Sunday newspapers (with their magazine and television interests) have reached a leading position in British industry. For example, the giant International Publishing Corporation owns three morning, four Sunday, and half a dozen weekly newspapers, and over 200 periodicals, and its sales exceed £131 million a year. It has interests in every aspect of publishing, from the trees from which the paper is made, to the retailers who sell the newspapers.

A newspaper is an unusual industrial product in that its income comes from two very different sources. It costs more than the reader pays to produce a single paper, and unless the paper sells some of its space to advertisers it cannot pay its way. Of the price paid by the reader—whatever that price may be—more than a third goes to the retail and wholesale newsagents. The most expensive item in the production of a newspaper is NEWSPRINT (q.v.), of which a national newspaper with a large sale may use over 300 tons (at £66 10*s.* a ton) every night. In one way and another it may cost £450,000 or more a week to produce an important daily paper.

The total money paid by readers and by advertisers is closely related, for advertisers find that it pays them to advertise in the papers with the largest numbers of readers. The cost of the advertisement, averaged over the number of readers who will see it, tends to be cheaper when the circulation is larger. For instance, an advertiser of bicycles might wish to hire an entire column of a newspaper for one day. A paper with a million readers might charge him £220, but a paper with two million readers would only charge him, say, £400. So his advertisement would be seen by twice as many people for less than twice the cost.

The development of newspapers to the status of a leading industry is fairly recent. Although newspapers have a long history—some news-sheets or news-books began to appear regularly in 1622—for a long time they were merely one of the by-products of printers' shops. During the Napoleonic wars *The Times* consisted of a small sheet of paper, folded in two; fewer than 250 copies an hour could be printed on hand-presses. In 1814 a steam-driven machine made it possible to print 1,000 copies an hour. Newspapers were then heavily taxed, and few people could afford to buy them. Taxes were paid on all paper supplies and on advertisements, while each copy of a newspaper had to bear a stamp as well. In the 1830's a single copy of a newspaper might cost as much as sevenpence—a sum then worth several times its present value—and $5\frac{1}{2}$*d.* of this would represent taxes. By degrees Parliament reduced these taxes, and in 1861 the last of them was abolished. Until then, few daily

London Express

FLEET STREET, THE CENTRE OF LONDON'S NEWSPAPER PRODUCTION

papers had a circulation of 5,000 copies, and few dailies were published outside London. *The Times* was unique in selling 50,000 copies of each issue. With the removal of taxes the circulation of newspapers began to increase, and many new papers were established. In 1855 *The Daily Telegraph* was reduced to a penny, and it thus became the cheapest daily paper in London. Soon it was competing successfully in circulation with *The Times.*

From the middle of the century, when it became worth while to print large numbers of papers, many technical improvements made fast printing possible. The rotary press, first devised by *The Times*, enabled both sides of an endless band of paper to be printed (*see* PRINTING, HISTORY OF, Vol. IV). A newspaper firm that could afford to install rotary presses could print many hundreds of thousands of copies of a paper in a single night. Although this new machinery lowered the cost of each paper and made cheap newspapers possible, it was itself very expensive, and caused the total costs of production to rise very considerably. It cost as much to equip a newspaper office as to equip a large factory.

It was Alfred Harmsworth—later Lord Northcliffe—who first regarded newspaper production as a branch of manufacturing industry. At the age of 23, with hardly any money, he started a weekly magazine called *Answers*. It was first published in 1888, when many more people had been taught to read as a result of the recent compulsory Education Acts. *Answers* was very popular, and was soon selling a million copies a week. With his profits Harmsworth bought cheaply the goodwill and plant of an unsuccessful London paper, the *Evening News*, and caused it to be so brightly edited that it became profitable too. Then, in 1896, he launched the *Daily Mail*. Within 4 years the halfpenny *Daily Mail*, which made a novel popular appeal, was selling nearly a million copies a day, which was more than any newspaper had ever sold before.

The cheap Press which quickly grew up in imitation of the *Daily Mail* was made possible by advertising. Most of the earlier newspapers had carried advertisements (*see* ADVERTISING AND PUBLICITY), but they had been rather restricted in quantity and appeal. As the nation prospered during the late 19th century, and the number of people with middle-class incomes increased, there were many more customers ready to spend their money in the shops, and shopkeepers became anxious to advertise their goods to them. The removal of the various newspaper taxes made it possible for more papers to be sold, and advertisers benefited by the greater number of customers who read their advertisements. In the course of time advertising by shopkeepers was partly replaced by advertising by manufacturers. A bicycle shop could spend a pound or two on advertising in a local paper, but a bicycle manufacturer supplying hundreds of bicycle shops could spend hundreds of pounds on a single advertisement in a national paper read all over Britain.

When the cheap Press began to grow early in the present century, the national newspapers set out to compete for advertisement fees. A paper selling 600,000 copies every day could charge larger fees than a paper which might have been much better edited, but only sold 300,000. In the 30 years that followed the first success of the cheap Press, it became the business policy of most newspapers to achieve the largest possible circulation, so as to possess an advantage over rival newspapers in obtaining advertising contracts. Circulation was important for another reason. Papers that received larger advertisement fees could spend much more money on development. They could install faster and better printing machines. They could set up branch works in big cities, and save the time of sending papers from London by train. They could pay famous authors large sums for writing articles, and they could send their staffs of journalists all over the world in search of exciting news. They could also print more copies than they would sell, so that there were always copies on view in every bookstall in the land, while hundreds of paid canvassers went round to people's doors, persuading them to take these papers regularly. Newspapers with a smaller circulation can, however, succeed commercially if they are of sufficiently high quality. The growing strength in recent years of *The Times*, *The Guardian*, *Daily Telegraph*, the *Observer*, and the *Sunday Times* has proved this.

The papers which secured the lion's share of the many millions of pounds spent on newspaper advertising made large profits for their owners. In the past, most newspapers had been owned personally by one individual; now most were formed into limited companies. As in other industries, the companies began to be associated in big groups and combines, which tended to become bigger still by absorbing other companies. In the 1920's various London groups began to buy up provincial newspapers, and many were closed. Since the end of the First World War Britain has lost about 60 daily papers, but more recently, several provincial evening newspapers have been launched. The view that television is a serious threat to the survival of the Press is now widely challenged, and many newspaper proprietors have some financial interests in commercial television.

See also Vol. IV: NEWSPAPERS, HISTORY OF.

NEWSPAPER PRODUCTION. The making of an issue of a newspaper is an act of team work strictly limited by space and time, and by the capacities of printing-machines. Tens of thousands of copies of each edition of a national morning paper must be loaded on to trains which leave their railway stations at precise times. In the printing-works each page of metal type, completely ready for printing, must be passed to the machines at a given minute. In each column of every page, a precise number of inches is available for the journalists' work.

Evening Standard

ROTARY PRESSES PRINTING 40,000 COPIES OF A NEWSPAPER PER HOUR

The paper is printed in one continuous strip and then cut into sheets which are assembled and folded

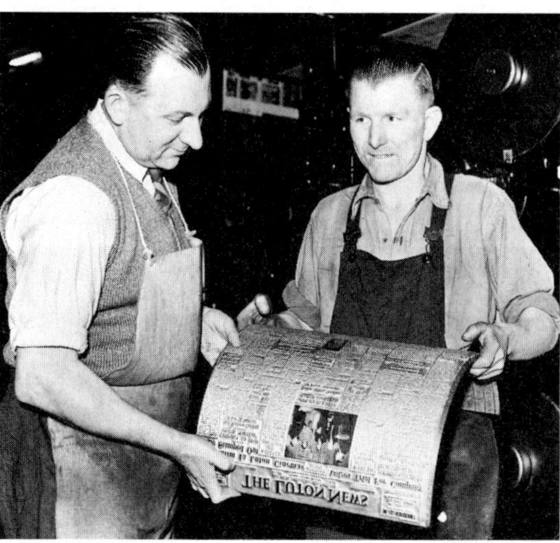

The Luton News

THE CURVED PLATE OF A PAGE OF A NEWSPAPER

Therefore the rigid industrial process involved in manufacturing a million or more copies of a morning newspaper in a printing-works every night governs the whole business of editing.

A London printing plant, which may produce a morning and evening and a Sunday paper, requires a vast organization. Printing plant must be maintained in central London (within easy reach of all the terminal railway stations) and in Manchester and sometimes also in Scotland. As many as 3,000 men and women may be employed by one newspaper firm. The editorial office may need to be equipped with 40 or more telephone lines to the exchange and perhaps 200 extensions within the office. Private telegraphic and picture transmission apparatus links the London office with its Manchester branch and with the Post Office telegraph system in London. A fleet of perhaps 150 vans carries the firm's evening papers through London at any one time, requiring a permanent garage organization like that of a bus maintenance depot. Foreign correspondents may be costing the firm £2,000 a week, and bank credits have to be arranged in all the capitals of the world for the use of these correspondents and of cable companies serving the paper. Only when all these arrangements are in working order can the editor and his staff set about their daily work.

When the news has been prepared by reporters, sub-editors, and editors (*see* NEWSPAPER, Vol. IV), it is sent to the printing department in written or typewritten sheets, and there composed in metal type. No matter how important the news or how incomplete the information, an even flow of reports from the sub-editors must reach the printing operators throughout the evening, otherwise steady production would break down. After the type has been corrected for printers' mistakes, various senior journalists read the proofs to detect journalists' mistakes, and the proofs are often read by a lawyer also, to ensure that there are no LIBELS (q.v. Vol. X) or other wrongful statements about people, which might involve the paper in the payment of legal damages. Throughout the evening all items of news are sent by wire on private TELEPRINTER machines (q.v. Vol. IV), by means of trunk lines rented from the Post Office, to the newspaper's chief offices in the provinces. Carbon copies of all reporters' work are available for this service, as well as all messages telephoned from correspondents. Proofs of every few inches of type are supplied by the printer as they emerge from every composing-machine. Local editors of the various regional editions of newspapers controlled from London have a good deal of freedom to print local news in place of news supplied from London. These provincial offices, however, have to achieve as strict a schedule in both the editorial and printing departments as the London headquarters.

Finally in London (as in provincial centres) the metal type is assembled into the shape of pages, the news and pictures are fitted together according to a plan provided by the chief sub-editor, and the advertisements are placed as directed by the advertisement manager. If news items are too long to fit the space allotted after being composed in type, sub-editors indicate to the printing staff where the text may be cut. The responsibility for the composition, correction, and accurate assembly of each page at the right time belongs to the manager of the composing department, who is always known as 'the printer'. When the pages are ready, moulds are taken, in which molten metal is cast to make the curved plates actually used for printing the newspaper (*see* PRINTING, Section 5, Vol. IV).

The rotary printing presses that carry the four-mile-long reels of NEWSPRINT (q.v.), produce eight pages at a time, and print 40,000 to 50,000 copies of the newspaper an hour, folding them and counting them in batches. A big newspaper has several such printing units. As the batches of newspapers emerge, they are tied into bundles, labelled, and distributed by conveyor belts to the vans, which take them to the railway stations.

Technical developments in the collection of news and the production of newspapers occur constantly, but inventions sometimes take several years to come into general use as the larger newspapers have such exacting requirements, due to their big circulations and high speed of production. In recent years, there have been two outstanding developments in colour printing for newspapers: colour printing by rotary presses, and web-offset lithography, that includes colour. Web-offset is widely used among local newspapers which do not print so many copies. It offers special advantages, both in black and white reproduction and in colour. The system is basically photographic, it dispenses with metal type, and requires new designing techniques.

See also NEWSPAPER INDUSTRY.
See also Vol. IV: JOURNALIST; NEWSPAPER; NEWSPAPER, HISTORY OF; REPORTER.

Evening Standard

REELS OF NEWSPRINT

Four papers can be printed side by side on each reel, which is approximately four miles long

NEWSPRINT. This is the name given to the paper on which most newspapers are printed. This kind of paper—a paper of cheap quality—is made in larger quantities than any other kind, to provide for the enormous number of NEWSPAPERS (q.v. Vol. IV) printed every day. Wood pulp is the basic raw material used. Newsprint is generally made from about 85% of ground wood pulp, made by a mechanical process, and about 15% of sulphite pulp, made from spruce wood by a chemical process (*see* WOOD PULP). CHINA CLAY (q.v.) is also added to make the paper more opaque and give it a smooth surface for taking print. Britain imports half of the 800,000 tons of newsprint it uses annually, and possesses the largest newsprint machine in the world.

If the newsprint mill is near the pulp mill, both kinds of wood pulp are kept in a slush form in separate tanks, and are then drawn off by pumps to the refining engines, as needed. But if the pulp has to be taken some distance, the chemical sulphite pulp is transported almost dry, and the mechanical ground wood pulp with about 50% moisture in it; and, on reaching the paper mill, the bales go into breaking engines to convert them again into slush form.

The paper-machine for newsprint is a very large Fourdrinier machine (*see* PAPER-MAKING, Section 1), of a width up to 26 feet. The pulp, or 'stuff', goes into the machine chest from which the paper-machine is served. It is then strained to remove coarse lumps, and passed on to the paper-machine, which spreads it evenly over a fast-moving wire cloth so that the water can drain away. To draw out yet more water the pulp then passes over suction boxes and a suction roller, by which time the pulp is in a thin sheet, which, though still wet, can hold together. It is then carried on woollen felts to presses which compress it into a fairly smooth, even sheet of paper. To remove the rest of the moisture, it is passed over drying cylinders heated by steam, the wet web of paper being held against them by cotton felts. The paper is then rolled up, 'calendered' (that is, given a smooth shiny surface) if many illustrations have to be printed on it (*see* PAPER-MAKING, Section 2 *b*), and cut up into rolls of the required width. It is then ready to be sent to the printer.

See also PAPER-MAKING; WOOD PULP.
See also Vol. IV: NEWSPAPER.

NICKEL was recognized as an individual metal in about 1694 but was not produced pure until 1775, though it had been isolated in an impure form in 1751, by the Swedish metallurgist Cronstedt. Although traces of nickel are found in many rocks throughout the world, the relatively few deposits that are commercially worthwhile

International Nickel Ltd.

DRILLING HOLES TO TAKE EXPLOSIVE CHARGES

The roof of this Canadian nickel mine has been made safe with wire netting, and long bolts fastened into the rock

were all originally formed by processes of natural concentration. There are two main types of ore: sulphide ores, which were probably concentrated when molten rocks cooled, are found in one-time volcanic areas such as Canada, Northern Russia, Scandinavia, and Australasia; lateritic ores, however, were concentrated by weathering and are mainly found in tropical rainbelts such as Australasia, the Caribbean, and South America. With both types of ore, elaborate processes are necessary to extract and refine the nickel. More than half the world's supply comes from Canadian mines. Russia is the second principal producer, followed by New Caledonia.

Nickel is a strong, tough metal, resistant to corrosion, heat, and wear. Its principal use, unalloyed, is in ELECTROPLATING, (q.v. Vol. VIII) where it is deposited by itself or under a thin top layer of chromium. Nickel is also used in the chemical industry for equipment for handling caustic ALKALIS (q.v.), and also as a catalyst for speeding up chemical reactions. Many countries make COINS (q.v.) from it, either as a pure metal or as cupro-nickel.

About 75% of all nickel produced is used in ALLOYS (q.v. Vol. VIII) with other metals because of the valuable properties it imparts. The largest consumption is for nickel stainless steels, used throughout industry because of their corrosion resistance; for the handling, storage, and transport of food and pharmaceutical products, and also as an architectural material. Nickel is also added to heat-resisting steels and to many tough engineering steels. Many corrosion-resistant or high-strength cast irons also contain nickel. Nickel-chromium-based alloys are highly resistant to the effects of very high temperatures and are used in all GAS TURBINE (q.v. Vol. VIII) engines, as well as most electric heaters and furnaces.

Nickel forms several useful alloys with copper. Alloys containing about 70% nickel are strong and highly resistant to corrosion and are used in chemical plants where sulphuric and hydrofluoric acids are handled. Copper, alloyed with 10–30% nickel, is much used for steam condensers and piping to carry polluted seawater. Other copper-based alloys containing nickel include nickel-aluminium-bronzes for making ships' propellers, and nickel-silvers, containing copper, nickel, and zinc, and mainly used as the underlying metal in silver-plated cutlery, or for decorative architectural metalwork.

Controlled-expansion nickel-iron alloys are used in making thermostats, and the glass-to-metal seals of radio transmitting valves.

NUCLEAR POWER, *see* Vol. VIII: NUCLEAR POWER.

NYLON, *see* TEXTILE FIBRES, MAN-MADE.

O

OFFICE EQUIPMENT. Nearly all modern business is done in offices, and the bulk of office work consists of some form of communication. Reading, writing, talking, telephoning, and typewriting are essential forms of business communication. It is important to save time and labour over all this, as office expenses are not what is called 'productive' expenditure: that is, they do not lead directly to the production of goods. Office communications may be classified into two groups: first, the linking of people and things so that they can make contact easily, and the standardizing of written communications for the sake of speed and clarity; secondly, the compiling of information, and its rapid and ready presentation so that nothing is overlooked or lost.

1. COMMUNICATIONS. The TELEPHONE (q.v. Vol. IV) is a vital link because it provides quick and simple communication. Telephones within an office may be part either of the General Post Office system or of a private intercommunication system, which can be bought or hired. Small firms may have only one outside G.P.O. line with one or two external extensions; larger organizations have many outside lines and hundreds of internal extensions as well as a private telephone system. In a large modern business many full-time operators and engineers may be needed to maintain a telephone service of this kind. Most of the private intercommunication telephone systems are of the automatic type, requiring no operator. By using a special amplifier, several members of an organization can be signalled, and short conferences can be held between them without their having to leave their own offices.

Loudspeaker systems are used to call people who may be away from their offices, or the staff may carry small radios on which they can receive messages.

The TELEPRINTER (q.v. Vol. IV) is also much used by large business firms with a central head office and many provincial branches, and teleprinter messages have the advantage that they provide a definite record of what has been said. In large offices rows of coloured lights on the walls or ceilings of corridors and other places are used to catch the attention of important officials and to warn them that they are urgently needed at some point in the building; different officials are identified by different combinations of lights.

Large shops, particularly DEPARTMENT STORES (q.v.), often have special means of communication to enable their sales staff to send customers' money to a central cash desk, from which change and receipts are sent back to the counters. Earlier in the century this was often done by placing the money in a hollow wooden ball which ran 'downhill', moved by its own weight, on gently sloping rails. Later, a small container, hanging from a wire, was 'shot' across the shop by a spring. Pneumatic tubes, in which containers are propelled by compressed air, are the more modern system. They are much used in newspaper offices to send 'copy' from the editorial to the printing departments, and to send other communications about the office. In Paris the principal post offices are linked by pneumatic tubes, through which express letters—called locally *bleus* or *pneumatiques*—can be sent for a special fee.

Much time and labour is saved in modern business by standardizing written communications, generally through the use of forms. All printed forms such as invoices and receipts are standard ways of communicating information in a quick, easy, and accurate way. Departments and branches of banks, shops, factories, and other large concerns keep their records by standardized means, often on standard printed forms or by punched cards.

2. INFORMATION. In modern business the compiling or recording of information has now become very systematized and is often mechanized. Many documents that would be bulky to handle are now filed in a compact and orderly way by being photographed microscopically. A roll of film 1½ inches wide can carry a record of hundreds of documents. When a document has to be consulted, it can either be viewed through an enlarger or be projected on a screen in the same way as a cinema film.

Conversations can be recorded and stored on

tapes or disks. A good filing system is important to keep records in good condition and to make them easily and instantly accessible when required. Systems may be arranged alphabetically or, like library catalogues, on a system of decimal figures (*see* CATALOGUING AND INDEXING, Vol. IV). Files are kept in cabinets, drawers, cupboards, trays, boxes, shelves, or folders as may best suit their use; lateral filing is often preferred as it has the advantage of saving space in crowded offices. Folders, papers, and cards can be indexed so that all information on a given subject can be found at once. Centralized filing departments are used in large firms. Out-of-date files which need to be kept can be safely held in collapsible or rigid storage cases suitably indexed. Private or secret documents can be completely destroyed by electric shredders which cut the paper into very fine, completely unreadable strips. The presentation of STATISTICS (q.v.) is made easier with a 'punched card' system described under ACCOUNTING, MACHINE (q.v.); sorting machines group the information contained on the cards in any way required and deliver it automatically. Adding and listing machines and calculators are a great help in compiling statistics, and the analysis of statistics can also be done on book-keeping machines.

It is important to know exactly what stage a firm's production has reached at any given time. Production charts have movable indicators which can be adjusted daily to show progress.

3. EQUIPMENT FOR LETTERS. Typewriters are used in all modern offices. Both electric typewriters and standard typewriters fitted with electric carriage-returns save typists much unnecessary fatigue. Most business letters, except those that are purely formal, need to be dictated

Spirella Co.

LATERAL FILING IN A SALES OFFICE

A large number of files can be reached by the correspondent without moving from her chair, and they can be filed from the back of the cabinet by a responsible member of the firm's staff, and a dictaphone or similar machine—which is really a recording gramophone—makes it possible for letters to be dictated at any time and typed when a typist is ready. Another machine that saves much time in a busy office, and retains the goodwill of the customers of a business, is the automatic typewriter. One of the problems that many businesses have to solve is how to send out a letter that is really a 'form' or circular letter, but which must appear to the recipient as if it has been dictated and written especially for him. It is impossible to convey this impression if this kind of letter is prepared in quantities in advance, the name and address and the opening greeting being typed on to it afterwards. Even if the same typewriter which typed the original is used, the alignment and adjustment of the address and greeting can never be perfect. The automatic typewriter solves the problem. It works on much the same principle as the PLAYER-PIANO or pianola (q.v. Vol. IX), typing automatically from a perforated paper record of the original that has been made beforehand. The typist loads the machine with a record of the appropriate form letter, types in the name and address and the opening greeting, and then switches on the machine, which completes the letter automatically.

For the preparation of ordinary circular letters which do not need such careful attention as this there are many efficient types of duplicator. The most common is the stencil duplicator. The stencil is a wax-coated sheet of tissue which is cut by the sharp impact of the typewriter keys (with the ribbon not engaged). The stencil is put on to the drum of the duplicator, and ink on the drum is forced through the typed portions of the stencil on to the copy paper.

A duplication process in which a master copy is made by using a special carbon is becoming increasingly popular. Sheets of paper are dampened by a roller moistened with colourless spirit and are then passed through the duplicator into which the master copy has been clipped. Carbon impressions from the master copy are made on the damp sheets, and thus copies are produced.

Facsimile copies of documents, letters, plans, and deeds, are very quickly and easily made by photocopying processes. Other forms of duplication used for very long runs work on the same principle as ordinary printing machines. A problem that arises in connexion with the dispatch of circulars is the addressing of large numbers of envelopes. If the same people are written to frequently, addressing by machine is much quicker and more accurate than individual typing. An automatic machine works from small metal plates or silk stencils large enough for several lines of type. Plates can be inserted into the machine either individually or in batches, according to the machine, and the envelopes inserted in the same way. The 'window' type of envelope, with the opening covered with transparent paper, solves the problem in another way, provided that the address is already on the enclosure. Automatic folding machines can be used to fold letters and invoices quickly.

Opening incoming letters and sticking the stamps on outgoing letters are tasks which can take up much time. There are now efficient machines that will open letters automatically at a high speed, and other machines that will automatically stamp envelopes passed through them.

See also Vol. IV: COUNTING INSTRUMENTS.

OIL-CLOTH, *see* LINOLEUM.

OIL, MINERAL. The technical name for the mineral oil that comes from the depths of the earth is petroleum. Petroleum is a mixture of chemical compounds consisting almost entirely of hydrogen and carbon, and is therefore a 'hydrocarbon' oil. Mineral oil as it comes from the well is called 'crude oil', and contains many different substances, which boil at varying temperatures. It is therefore possible by DISTILLATION (q.v.) to separate the crude oil into many different 'fractions', such as petrol (called 'gasoline' in the U.S.A.), lubricating oil, and asphaltic bitumen. The products of distillation can also be treated by further refining processes which alter their arrangement of molecules or 'molecular structure', and thus change them into entirely different substances (*see* OIL REFINING).

Bitumen was the earliest mineral oil product used by man. Seepages of crude oil escaping to the earth's surface had become weathered by sunlight and exposure, and had left deposits of bitumen—as in the famous Trinidad lake in the West Indies, which still produces important quantities of bitumen. Where the seepage oil remained in liquid form, other uses were found

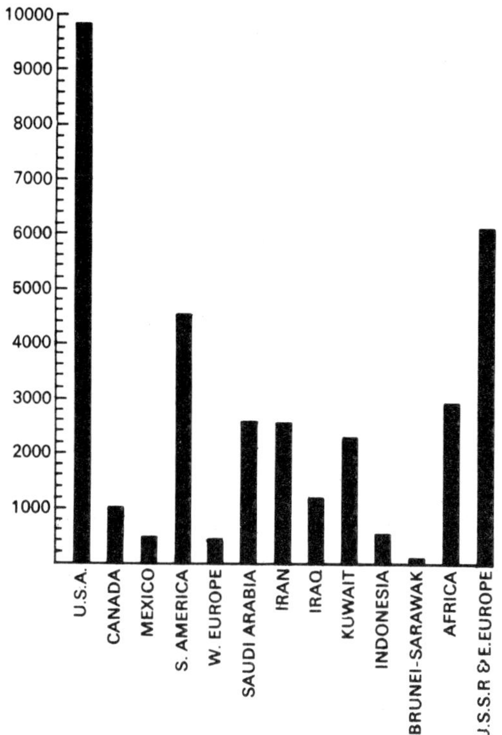

WORLD PRODUCTION OF CRUDE OIL AND NATURAL GASOLINE IN 1967

Daily average in thousands of barrels

for it: the Red Indians of North America, for instance, used it as a medicine. In fact, almost all the early users of mineral oil made use of it in the form in which it was found naturally at the surface.

The modern mineral oil industry dates from 1859, when a well was bored at Titusville in Pennsylvania, U.S.A (*see* OIL WELLS). The first efforts to convert this crude oil into other products were made by borrowing methods of distillation and refining from the SHALE OIL industry (q.v.), which had flourished (particularly in Scotland) since the middle of the 19th century.

In the year following the boring of the first well, the total production of crude oil in the world was under 80,000 tons, or about 18 million gallons, and most of this was produced in the U.S.A. By the outbreak of the First World War the world's annual production of crude oil had risen to 58 million tons; United States production accounted for almost two-thirds of this, and the rest came from many other countries, of which Russia, Mexico, Roumania, and Indonesia (then the Dutch East Indies) were the most important. By the end of the Second World War, world production of crude oil and natural gasoline had increased to more than 375 million tons.

Although crude oil today is produced in some sixty different countries, the great bulk of this output comes from five main areas—North America, North Africa, the Middle East, the U.S.S.R., and Latin America. Of these, the largest single producer is still the U.S.A. Her output in 1967 approximated to 491½ million tons. Second came the U.S.S.R., with almost 290 million tons, Venezuela being third with some 185 million tons. In the Middle East the two leading producers were Saudi Arabia and Iran, virtually equalling each other with outputs of around 129½ million tons. Kuwait, tiny in area, but enormously rich in oil, followed with 115¼ million tons. Africa was chiefly represented by Libya (83¾ million tons) and Algeria (39 million tons).

For about the first 50 years of the industry, lamp oil (paraffin or kerosine) was the most important product distilled from crude oil, though some lubricating oil was also produced. The remaining products of distillation, especially petrol, were regarded as a nuisance, and were burned or thrown away. About 1900 the early motor-cars were being made, for the INTERNAL COMBUSTION ENGINE had taken a practical form (q.v. Vol. VIII). Petrol ceased to be a waste product, and the oil industry began to find uses for many new substances refined from crude oil. The First World War increased the demand for petrol and lubricating oil, and for fuel oil to replace coal-firing afloat and ashore.

Until after the First World War the industry remained dependent on the range of products that could be obtained by simple distillation and refining. The thermal 'cracking' process (*see* OIL REFINING), to increase the yield of petrol, was first used on a commercial scale about 1912. From about 1920 the cracking process became more efficient, and products in great demand (such as petrol) could be made by 'breaking down' other products (such as gas oil and fuel oil) in less demand.

By 1930 the high-speed Diesel engine (*see* INTERNAL COMBUSTION ENGINE, Vol. VIII) was becoming more used for buses and heavy lorries, and the demand for diesel oil rose rapidly. Developments of the aero-engine also called for improved lubricating oils and aviation spirits. Scientific discoveries responded very well to all these changes in the types of oil needed, and also satisfied the increasing demand of the chemical industry for special products and solvents.

See also OIL WELLS; OIL REFINING; OILS, VEGETABLE.
See also Vol. VIII: FUELS.

OIL REFINING. Crude oil, obtained from the earth by drilling OIL WELLS (q.v.), contains many separate substances. Most of these are liquids which boil and turn into vapour, but they do not all boil at the same temperature. Some will turn to vapour at almost normal air temperature; others may have to be heated to more than 315° C. These various substances can be separated by gradually heating up the crude oil and condensing in different stages the various vapours that come from it. In the early days of the oil industry this DISTILLATION (q.v.) was done by heating the crude oil in a still and then passing the vapour from it through a water-cooled condenser. The liquid coming from the condenser changed from one product to another as the temperature in the still was raised. Nowadays a more efficient and economical method of distillation is used: a continuous flow of crude oil enters the plant at one end and the separated 'fractions' (*see* DISTILLATION) are drawn off at different levels. The crude oil is heated to a high temperature by passing it through tubes in a furnace. The hot oil then goes to the lower section of a large cylindrical steel vessel, called a 'fractionating tower', which may be as much as 120 feet high. This contains large metal plates or baffles (called 'bubble-trays') at intervals between 1 and 2 feet all the way up. The temperature in the tower is high at the bottom and becomes lower towards the top. The mixture of different vapours rises up the tower; as the temperature gets lower, more and more vapour condenses into liquid and is collected on the bubble-trays, from which it drains away through pipes to storage tanks. Each bubble-tray delivers a liquid with a different boiling-point: thus the liquids from the lower trays may be gas oil or lubricating oil, while that draining from the upper trays will be paraffin. Petrol will generally be condensed with the vapours leaving the top of the tower. In practice, it is usual to

British Petroleum

NIGHT VIEW OF B.P.'S REFINERY AT LLANDARCY, SOUTH WALES

The process plant contains fractionating towers, storage tanks, etc. The large towers (centre) are for cooling water

employ two fractionating towers, so as to recover the full range of products by distillation and redistillation.

The raw products from this first distillation need further treatment, each being treated in a different way. Some processes involve 'cracking': this means creating new products by regrouping the atoms of a product into different molecular arrangements. Some forms of cracking require high temperatures and pressures of 1,000 lb. per sq. in. or more. There are also other special processes, many of great complexity.

A wide range of products is obtained from the raw materials of the oilfields and used in modern industry. The list includes synthetic rubber, plastics, detergents, textile fibres, explosives, anaesthetics, spirits and solvents, insecticides, carbon black (used as a dye in the manufacture of printing inks, and also in RUBBER MANUFACTURE (q.v.)), asphaltic bitumen or asphalt, lubricating oils (including medicinal paraffin) and greases, paraffin or kerosine, highly refined colourless and tasteless oils (for lubricating machinery used in the manufacture and packing of foodstuffs), paraffin wax, petroleum jelly, petroleum coke (much used for making carbon blocks and rods for electrical uses, such as electrodes in arc-lamps), and various forms of light and heavy fuel oils.

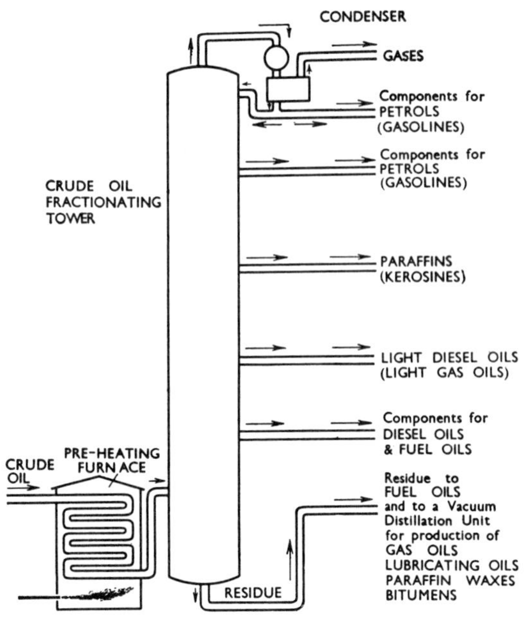

DIAGRAM TO SHOW SYSTEM OF REFINING OIL

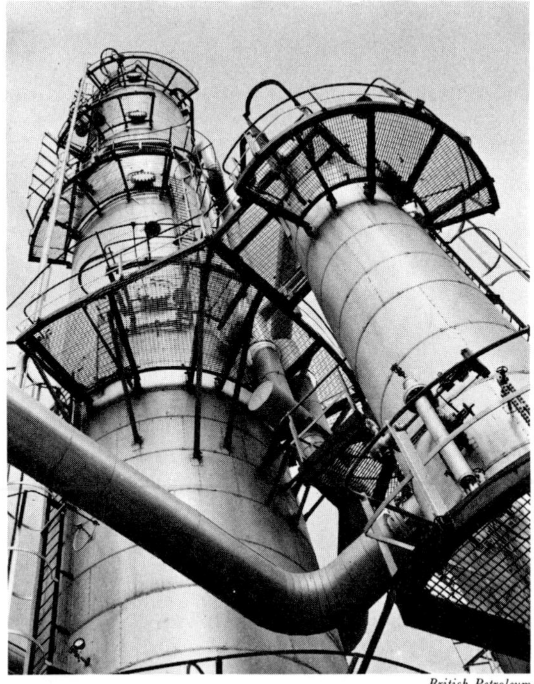

British Petroleum

THE DISTILLATION COLUMNS, ALSO CALLED FRACTIONATING TOWERS (SEE DIAGRAM), AT EUROPOORT REFINERY, ROTTERDAM

See also OIL WELLS; OILS, VEGETABLE.
See also Vol. VIII: FUELS.

OIL, SHALE, *see* SHALE OIL.

OIL WELLS. Nowadays immense quantities of oil are needed for making various FUELS (q.v. Vol. VIII) to drive ships, aircraft, and all forms of land transport, as well as for industry, agriculture, and domestic heating. Those countries which have their own oilfields have an advantage over those which have not, although the world-wide operations of the international oil industry have made petroleum products available to all countries which can pay for them.

One of the most important post-war developments has been the introduction of offshore production, perhaps a hundred or more miles from land, and in hundreds of feet of water. These wells are drilled from huge mobile barges. There has been much recent drilling off Britain's North Sea coast.

Oil usually lies thousands of feet below the earth's surface, and is contained in the pores of rock strata (*see* OIL, NATURAL, Vol. III).

The earliest method of discovering this underground oil was simply to sink a well at a point where oil had seeped out on the surface, and to bore downwards until oil was found. Later on, this rather 'hit and miss' method was replaced by more scientific methods, based on a careful study of the geology of the region where oil was being sought. In particular, it was necessary to study what lay below the earth's surface, because oil occurs only in certain types of underground rocks and sands. The nature of the rock formation below the earth's surface could often be judged from 'outcrops' (where a ridge of rock broke through the surface) or from what could be seen on hill-sides or in river valleys or gorges. The invention of aerial photography helped these surveys a great deal. What are called 'geophysical' methods are now also being used, and most of them involve the use of delicate scientific instruments. Different rocks have different 'gravitational pulls': that is, the earth's force of gravity is not the same everywhere. By using very delicate instruments experts can measure these differences in gravitational pull, and estimate whether the rock-structure below the surface is of the type in which oil will probably be found. Another property of rocks is also made use of. Some types of rock reflect sound-waves differently from others; and by producing a minute artificial earthquake (through the explosion underground of a small charge of dynamite), and measuring how quickly the sound-waves are reflected from the different layers of rock below the surface, the rock most likely to yield oil may be discovered.

But the actual existence of oil in any area can be proved only by drilling boreholes or wells. While a well is being drilled, samples of the rock or sand below the surface at different levels can be obtained by using a 'drilling bit', which is rather like the sharp end of a carpenter's drill but on a smuch larger scale. It has a hollow centre, and the material from the earth which collects in this centre is called a 'core sample'. After the well is drilled, an instrument that measures the electrical resistance of the rock-layer may be lowered down it: different rocks and sands have differing electrical resistance, and those that contain oil have a particularly high resistance. This process is called 'electric logging'. As more and more wells are drilled, it becomes possible to compare an increasing number of core samples and electric logs, and eventually a good plan can be drawn of the layer below the surface. By studying such a plan, geologists can often decide on the most likely direction in which to extend drilling, and on the depth to which wells should be sunk. The big steel framework structure over an oil well is called a 'derrick', and serves to raise and lower the drilling machinery and other instruments.

The diameter of an oil well varies. Very deep wells may have a diameter of 24 inches at the top, tapering to as little as 3 or 4 inches at the bottom. Many oil wells are very deep: oil has even been produced from a well nearly 4 miles deep. The world's deepest borehole, which was drilled in an unsuccessful attempt to find oil, went to a depth of almost 5 miles. At such depths the temperature of the oil is sometimes over 200° C., and the pressure may be as high as 3,500 lb. per square inch.

There are three stages in getting oil from a well. First, the oil flow must be started or 'brought in'. Then the flow must be controlled throughout the months or years during which oil continues to come from the well. This period is known as the 'life of the well'. Individual wells must not be allowed to flow too freely, or the output of other wells in the oilfield will decline very seriously; and care must be taken not to drill wells too close together, or one may 'steal' another's oil. Even when the natural flow of a well declines, and the oil has to be brought to the surface by pumping, only a portion of the oil will be recovered, the greater part remaining in the oil-bearing layer underground. The third and final stage is to bring some of this to the surface by what are called secondary recovery methods, i.e. by injecting water or gas.

The force that pushes the oil up the well to the surface is called the 'drive'. This may arise from the pressure of natural gas dissolved in the oil, or from the pressure of the 'gas-cap' above the oil (*see* Gas, Natural, Vol. III); it may also arise from the pressure of a layer of water below the oil; or it may arise from all these influences working together. Before it is decided to bring an oil well into production, the oil at the bottom of the well is kept under control by filling the well with a heavy mud. When it is decided to start production, this mud is thinned out or removed, so that the oil, forced by the 'drive', is free to rush up the well in a bubbling mass to the surface. When, as in some formations, the oil does not flow freely through the pores of the

British Petroleum

CONTROL VALVES, CALLED A 'CHRISTMAS TREE', FITTED AT AN ALASKAN WELLHEAD TO REGULATE OIL FLOW

rock, production may be improved by various methods. For example, hydrochloric acid is often pumped down wells to dissolve limestone; and explosives are sometimes used to break up the rock formation at the bottom of the well, and so help the oil to flow more easily.

During the life of an oilfield the 'drive' loses its initial vigour, and the natural flow arising from the 'drive' gradually ceases. When this happens, the oil must be pumped to the surface. This is usually done by a pumping engine on the surface, which operates a plunger at the bottom of the well. Most wells today produce 'on the pump', because the natural flow generally ceases long before the life of an oilfield ends; but in some oilfields it is necessary to pump from the beginning. This applies to England's oilfields in Lincoln and Nottinghamshire, which produce about 80,000 tons of oil annually.

See also Oil Refining; Oil, Mineral; Oils, Vegetable.

See also Vol. III: Oil, Natural.

OILS, VEGETABLE. 1. Oils are derived from practically every part of a plant, although not all plants yield oil. Most vegetable oils come either from the sap of trees or from seeds. They are widely used for making soap, perfumes, paints, and flavourings.

All vegetable oils consist of compounds of carbon and hydrogen. They fall into two main classes: the 'essential' or volatile oils, which give a distinct odour to the plants in which they are found, and evaporate easily; and the 'fixed' oils, which are greasy and do not easily evaporate. These include the oils which can be used in food ('edible' oils) and those used in paint manufacture, known as 'drying oils'. Some edible oils can also be used as drying oils.

2. Volatile Oils. The most important are the turpentines, which are made by distilling the resin of pine trees. In the paint industry the turpentines are used as thinners and solvents (*see* Paints and Varnishes) and the essential oils are used in waxes and polishes (*see* Cleaning Materials, Vol. XI). A volatile oil which is popular in the U.S.A. is wintergreen, which is used in medicine, in cosmetics, and for flavouring. A kindred oil is sweet birch, from the tree which grows in Canada and the northern United States. It is a rather heavy oil. From the mountains of India comes sandalwood, which is cultivated in dry open spaces. It is a parasite on the roots of trees, and, before it can be obtained, a tree has to be felled and the roots dug up (*see* Parasitic Plants, Vol. II). The best grades of sandalwood are used in India for carvings and in making incense, but most of the wood is used for the distillation of sandalwood oil. The 'soft drinks' industry uses sassafras oil in their manufacture, and it is also used in medicine. Volatile oils used as flavouring include peppermint and anise. Other volatile vegetable oils are lavender, eucalyptus, and nutmeg (*see* Oil-bearing Plants, Vol. VI, Section 2).

The modern methods of isolating an essential oil from an aromatic plant are by distillation and by solvent extraction (*see* Perfumery).

3. Edible Oils. These have always served mankind as important items of diet. They are basically compounds of organic acids and glycerine; they may also contain small amounts of other substances, including pigments and vitamins. Many vegetable oils are used for cooking. Several oils are used in the making of margarine, including cottonseed, coconut, soya bean, palm, and peanut (or groundnut) oils, together with flavouring materials. Corn oil is used as a salad and cooking oil, and in lard-like cooking-fats; it comes from maize. In the U.S.A. Cotton is a large crop, and refined cottonseed oil is used to make lard compounds, margarine, and cooking and salad oils. The kernels of the Coconut palm yield coconut-oil, again used for margarine. The Soya Bean (qq.v. Vol. VI) yields an oil which has been used for many years in the East for cooking. It is now used all over the world in the making of margarine and mayonnaise.

Groundnut oil can be used for margarine and salad and cooking oils, and for cooking sardines when they are tinned. Schemes for growing Groundnuts (q.v. Vol. VI) on a large scale have been tried, especially in Tanzania, for there is a demand for them in many countries.

The fruit of wild African palms and cultivated Sumatra palms yields two kinds of oil. From the fleshy part of the fruit palm oil is obtained, and it is the nut which provides palm kernel oil. Both these can be used in margarine. The seeds of Muscat grapes give us another edible oil called raisin oil. This is mainly used for coating raisins, to prevent their sticking together when they are packed. An important oil comes from the Olive (q.v. Vol. VI). Other edible oils are poppy seed oil, sunflower oil, and rapeseed oil.

4. Drying Oils. The standard by which all drying oils are judged is linseed oil, which has been the mainstay of the paint industry and has great importance in the manufacture of soap and linoleum. The oils known as 'semi-drying' absorb sufficient oxygen from the air to dry to a tough, elastic substance, and are much used to add bulk to the more expensive linseed oil. Examples are sunflower seed, soya bean, cotton-seed, kapok, and hempseed oils and—rather less well-known—tomato-seed and pumpkin-seed oil.

Linseed (q.v. Vol. VI) is the oily seed of the plant whose fibres, known as flax, are woven to make linen cloth. Before 1939 the main producers of linseed were Argentina, the U.S.S.R., India, and the U.S.A., but the Second World War disorganized its production and distribution. The post-war shortage was overcome by extensive production in the U.S.A., Canada, and Argentina, but the dollar shortage limited exports from these countries to the sterling area. In Britain linseed has been grown sporadically for many years, and the Ministry of Agriculture has attempted to stimulate production by guaranteed prices to farmers. The pre-war

United Africa Co.

PALM OIL STORAGE INSTALLATION AT PORT HARCOURT, NIGERIA

The oil is shipped in barrels or pumped straight from the storage tanks into tanker ships

cheapness of the imported product discouraged its growth in the United Kingdom.

After the First World War tung oil was developed as a substitute for linseed oil. It had long been used in China for painting and weather-proofing boats.

Although castor oil is a non-drying oil, it can be made by chemical processing to resemble tung oil in its drying properties. It is much used in making leathercloth.

The soya-bean is mainly grown for food, but its oil is used for lamp oil and soap making. In America it is used in paint. Candlenut, sunflower, safflower, and chia oils are other drying oils, less known and less important. Walnut, poppy, and hempseed oils have been used for artists' colours from very early times (*see* Oil Bearing Plants, Vol. VI, Section 1).

5. Extraction. After the oil-seeds have been cleaned, they are prepared for extraction of the edible or drying oils by being crushed, to break down the walls of the oil-containing cells. A typical crushing-plant consists of iron rollers ranged one above the other in an iron frame. The seeds are passed in turn between the first and second rollers, the second and third rollers, and so on, the pressure increasing each time. The seeds are then cooked, so that a clean separation will take place in the actual process of extraction.

There are three different methods. One is to 'express' the oil by subjecting the 'meal', which is obtained by cooking, to heavy pressure in a hydraulic press. Another is to expel the oil by subjecting the meal to increasing pressure in a screw-press working in a perforated cylinder. The most modern process is solvent extraction, by which a petroleum spirit, acting as a solvent, is brought into contact with the meal. The solution of oil in the solvent is run off, and the operation is repeated several times. The solvent is then removed by distillation. This method produces about one and a quarter tons of oil for every ton produced by pressing.

After the oil has been extracted by any of these methods it is refined, bleached, and deodorized by a series of heat treatments that remove impurities.

See also Oil, Mineral; Oil Refining; Margarine; Soap; Paints and Varnishes.

OPENCAST MINING, *see* Mining.

ORGANIZATION, *see* Business Organization; Factory Organization.

OVERDRAFT, *see* Bank Accounts.

OVERHEAD CHARGES, *see* Costing, Section 2.

OVERSEAS TRADE. Britain's overseas trade has now returned to its pre-war pattern, after a period in which the import side was almost entirely controlled by the Government (*see* Bulk Purchase). Most of the goods dealt in are imported and exported in large quantities on a wholesale basis (*see* Wholesale Trade). As well as the goods exported from Britain and imported for manufacture or consumption within Britain there is also a large 'entrepôt' trade: that is, trade in imported goods which are later re-exported to other countries. Such commodities as wool, tea, coffee, hides and skins, rubber, many metals and metal ores, and various spices and essences figure in this 'entrepôt' trade, and London is still the biggest centre of this trade in the world.

The largest firms engaged in overseas trade conduct export, import, and re-export business. Typical firms of this kind are the big Eastern merchant houses, with London offices and branches in India, Burma, Malaysia, and Hong Kong. There are similar firms in the Australasian and West African trade. The overseas branches of these firms act as managers and Agents (q.v.) for many local enterprises. The Indian merchant firms, for example, control and manage coal-mines, jute mills, cotton mills, tea and coffee plantations, light railways, and river steamers. They export produce to their British houses and in return import through them machinery and stores for their mines, mills, and plantations, as well as any other goods for which they can find a market. They are not now as active or influential as they were before India and Pakistan became independent in 1947.

The small firms of merchants or manufacturers usually handle exports or imports only. Export firms are organized in many different ways. Some firms open overseas branches for the sale of their goods. Some of these branches are wholesale branches, dealing in large quantities of goods in bulk; others are retail branches selling through shops to the public. But many manufacturers and merchants do not sell enough in any single 'territory'—as any particular district or province of a country is called in business language—to justify opening a branch in it. Such firms therefore often send out members of their staffs as local Representatives (q.v.) in each important territory. A representative has to get as many orders as possible for his firm's goods, and to post or cable the orders to his head office in Britain, which then dispatches the goods direct to the actual buyer. In some ways, and for some lines of goods, the resident representative system works well; but it is often found better to appoint for each territory a well-established local firm as sole agent. Usually an agreement between the home exporter and the overseas sole agent contains a condition that the agent shall not sell the products of any firm whose goods compete with those of the exporter; the agreement also states the amount of Commission (q.v.) that the agent will receive on the orders he obtains. Many firms working through sole agents appoint

EUROPEAN 'FACTORIES' (TRADING HOUSES) AT CANTON, CHINA, ABOUT 1815

The trading houses of the various foreign companies flew their national flags. The goods were brought to the warehouses in Chinese native boats

resident representatives as well: for example, a British firm exporting to Australia might have its own resident representative for the whole of Australia, and might also appoint sole agents in each of the separate States of the Australian Commonwealth. It would then be the representative's duty to travel round the country at regular intervals, and to visit the sole agents so as to satisfy himself that they are doing their best for his firm.

Sometimes a firm does so little business in any single territory that it is not worth while appointing a resident representative or a sole agent. Such a firm then usually works through a manufacturer's agent or an export agent in London or one of the big British provincial cities. These agents are in touch with overseas firms which send orders to them, and they pass on the orders to the merchants or manufacturers they think most suitable. The firm actually executing the order then dispatches the goods direct to the overseas buyer, and pays the export agent a commission on the value of the goods ordered and sent.

Many firms make a business of rendering special services to exporters. The larger exporting firms run special departments of their own for all these services, but smaller firms often find that it does not pay them to do this. One such service is the special packing of goods for export, to satisfy the strict requirements of the shipping lines and marine insurance underwriters, and to resist heat and insect pests. There are several specialist firms of export packers. The trade of shipping and forwarding agent is another speciality: these firms collect goods from exporting manufacturers or merchants, have them specially packed for export, and attend to all the details of shipment, including loading the goods into the ships and obtaining signed BILLS OF LADING (q.v.) from the ships' officers.

The organization of the British import trade is on much the same lines, although for many goods the organization at the non-British or export end is controlled by foreign firms. But Britain is so outstandingly the largest importer in the world, particularly of foodstuffs and raw materials, that the import trade often copies the export trade's system of resident representatives abroad. Resident 'buying agents' are appointed for certain countries, and sometimes such agencies are turned into local branches of the British importing firm, particularly when the goods have to be processed in some way before they are shipped.

Overseas trade has always been complicated by official regulations made by the various governments of the world. Many countries, including Britain, levy import duties or taxes on goods coming in from abroad (*see* TARIFFS), and if these duties are calculated on the cost of the goods they can often be partly evaded if INVOICES (q.v.) are made out for less than the true cost. Certificates of value, called Consular Invoices, have therefore to be signed at the port of shipment by the importing country's consul. Some countries make their import duties lower for particular countries than for others, for example, members of the Common Market (*see* INTERNATIONAL CO-OPERATION, SOCIAL AND ECONOMIC, Vol. X), and the favoured countries are then said to enjoy a 'preferential tariff'. The true origin, or place of manufacture, of such goods has therefore to be vouched for in a document called a Certificate of Origin, signed by a responsible government official in the exporting country.

During the Second World War all overseas trade came under strict Government supervision by means of Board of Trade import and export licences. This system is still in existence, although in many cases a licence is very easily obtained and its grant is largely a formality. But should a war or other emergency recur the licence system would enable the Government rapidly to control overseas trade very strictly once again.

See also INTERNATIONAL FINANCE; TRADE, HISTORY OF; SHIPPING.

OXIDATION. This is the name given to chemical reactions on which many important industrial processes are based. The simplest form of oxidation occurs when an element (*see* MATTER, Vol. III) absorbs oxygen from the air and thus forms what is called an 'oxide'. This may take place at ordinary temperatures, as with phosphorus, or at higher temperatures, for example, when coal is burned and the carbon of the coal goes up the chimney as carbon dioxide; or when metallic mercury is heated, and forms red oxide of mercury. Another form of oxidation takes place when a substance absorbs oxygen from another substance, and not from the oxygen of the air. In the BLAST FURNACE (q.v. Vol. VIII) oxide of iron, containing oxygen, gives up its oxygen to the coke with which it is mixed, and the carbon in the coke passes off as carbon monoxide or 'blast furnace gas'.

P

PAINTS AND VARNISHES. Paint consists essentially of three parts—pigment, binding medium, and thinners. The pigment gives it colour and the binding medium forms a protective, glossy film. The thinners make the paint easier to put on and they evaporate completely as the paint dries.

1. Pigments. The first pigments used were made of natural earths, which were easy to find. In the Stone Age, 20,000 years ago, pictures were painted with earth pigments on walls of caves in southern France and northern Spain (*see* Prehistoric Art, Vol. XII). Among the earths are yellow ochre, siennas (yellow and brick red), and umbers (brown), all of which are iron oxides.

Other pigments made from pulverized minerals, such as malachite (green) and cinnabar (red), were used by the Eypgtians. In the Middle Ages ultramarine was made from lapis lazuli, and the pigments called lakes were made by dyeing powdered chalk and other substances with dyes obtained chiefly from plants and insects. In the 19th century many brilliant pigments were made from Dyes (q.v.) extracted from coal tar. In addition, gold has been used, especially for medieval manuscript illumination and altarpieces.

Pigments are either transparent, that is, the background on which they are painted shows through the colour, or opaque, when they completely obscure the background. In water-colour painting the brightness of the paper shines through the transparent colours; if white is added they become opaque.

For house-painting, pigments are of two kinds: 'prime' pigments, which must be completely opaque, and have colour and brightness, and 'extenders' which give bulk to the paint and strengthen the film. They must cover the surface completely and protect it, and so must be stable, that is, resist chemical action and not dissolve in the medium.

The following are examples of prime white pigments. White Lead (basic carbonate of lead) has been widely used since Roman times and, while it has excellent colour and protective properties, it has now been superseded because it is poisonous and tends to blacken in industrial atmospheres. Lithopone (zinc sulphide and barium sulphate) was in great demand from the end of the 19th century until recent times, but other colours tend to show through it. Zinc Oxide, sometimes called Chinese White, gives a hard film. Zinc Sulphide is very opaque. Titanium Dioxide, used for finishes of high quality, is bright, very opaque, and keeps its colour well. It is used in all paint nowadays, extended with cheaper pigments of little or no opacity which help to strengthen the paint film.

Natural pigment materials are mined or quarried, then ground up. Other pigments are prepared chemically.

2. Medium. The binding medium may be glue, egg white, or natural or synthetic resins. The Egyptians used glue, and gums are still used in water-colours. In the Middle Ages egg was the medium used for tempera (*see* Painting Methods, Vol. XII). In the 15th century oil began to be used as a medium and oil painting gradually replaced tempera.

Nowadays the binding media in oil paints are drying-oils and resin mixtures, or synthetic resins dissolved in solvents. A drying-oil absorbs oxygen from the air when applied as a thin film, and then dries into a tough and elastic substance. The oils come from oil-bearing seeds and nuts, and from plants, fish, and animals (*see* Oils, Vegetable). The seed of the flax crop yields linseed oil, which is widely used for house paints and for varnishes. In varnishes it has the disadvantages of turning yellow and of drying slowly, but it is the only oil that meets all needs in oil paints. Tung oil, the best varnish oil for all purposes, comes from the Chinese tung nut, which is now also grown in the U.S.A.

The addition of natural resins (*see* Gums and Resins) to an oil-based paint improves the gloss, increases the hardness, and shortens the drying time.

Synthetic resins (*see* Plastics) have largely superseded natural gums, and are often used as media with drying oils. Alkyd resin, made by the reaction of an alcohol with phthalic acid

Imperial Chemical Industries Ltd.

BALL MILLS BEHIND SLIDING GATES TO ENSURE SAFETY

The mills contain steel balls which grind the pigments and varnishes when the cylinders rotate. Safety precautions protect workers from contact with the revolving drum

and acids derived from drying oils, is a synthetic resin, used extensively for many kinds of paint; others are epoxide and polyurethane.

Nitrocellulose is used as the basic raw material of quick-drying lacquers. It is prepared from cellulose derived from wood pulp or cotton linters. It is highly explosive and great care is taken to keep it moist during manufacture.

3. Thinners. These are used to make paint less 'gluey', more even, and easier to put on: they are solvents which evaporate quickly, and include naphthas, turpentine, kerosine, pine oil, and various coal tar hydrocarbons.

A 'drier' is a chemical which makes the paint dry quickly. Until modern times, litharge (monoxide of lead) was almost always used, but today compounds of lead, manganese, cobalt, and zinc are often used.

4. Varnishes. These liquids are transparent or translucent (letting light pass through), and protect a surface and improve its looks. Varnish is, traditionally, a mixture of oil and resin. A high proportion of oil gives an elastic varnish, while a high resin content produces a hard, brilliant, but brittle varnish. Nowadays, the resin constituent of a varnish can be natural or synthetic, or the whole varnish may consist of a synthetic 'syrup' that contains no oil at all.

5. Paint Manufacture. Until the 19th century artists and housepainters alike made their own paints, grinding the pigments in a mortar with the media. Nowadays paints are made in factories.

In large-scale paint manufacture, the pigments are first thoroughly ground with part of the binder and solvent in a ball mill. This is a large revolving cylinder, lined with steel or porcelain and half filled with steel balls or pebbles, which grind the ingredients as the mill rotates. The well-ground mixture, known as a mill-base, is then mixed with the remainder of the binder and solvent in a rotary mixer and adjusted to the exact colour before filling into tins.

6. Types of Paint. Of the many types of paint used for decorating and preservation, the following are the most important:

(*a*) Priming paints are used for the first coating on unpainted surfaces. They usually consist of white-lead pigments in linseed oil vehicles. For painting on metal, red lead is used, because it prevents corrosion. For paints on cement or plaster surfaces, a tung-oil resin is usually favoured.

(*b*) Undercoats or flat paints are put on to hide the original surface; they have a large proportion of white pigments. They may be put on after the priming coat, or, alternatively, two coats of undercoating may be painted on.

(*c*) Gloss paints are finishing paints, with a smooth surface. They contain heat-treated oils, which make the paint flow better, and resins to give brilliance and hardness to the surface. There are many kinds of gloss paints. 'Enamel' is a trade term for the more brilliant types of hard-gloss paint, though it must not be confused with the art of Enamel work (q.v.).

(*d*) Emulsion paints give a matt surface; they can be used on plaster and woodwork. They contain particles of solid binding medium and pigment held in suspension in water. As the water evaporates the particles coalesce to form the solid paint film.

(*e*) Stoving finishes are used for metal articles such as motor-car bodies. They are made with alkyd or other synthetic resin media, with pigment added for colouring. They are dried in heat which brings about chemical changes which do not occur in air-dried varnishes, and this makes them more permanent.

(*f*) Stone paints are used extensively for outside work, and dry with a surface like stone. They are mostly made with tung oil, and have sand or finely ground rock in place of a pigment.

(*g*) Anti-fouling paints contain materials poisonous to marine growths and need renewing regularly. They are painted on ships' hulls and the underwater parts of bridges and similar structures on which organisms are likely to develop.

(*h*) Fungicidal paints, containing special chemicals, are used in such places as greenhouses and dairies, to prevent the growth of fungi in damp atmospheres.

Other special paints in common use are heat-resisting paints, fire-retarding paints, and aluminium or bronze paints, which contain metallic powder as a pigment. Luminous paints are of great importance in the instrument industry. They are usually composed of a special type of zinc oxide and barytes powder.

PAPER-MAKING. Modern paper is composed of the fibres of wood, esparto grass, flax, cotton, straw, repulped waste paper, and rags, felted together into a pulp which is pressed and dried into a sheet. All these raw materials, or a mixture of them in varying proportions, produce different kinds of paper; the actual constituent of any particular kind of paper may also vary slightly according to the individual custom of the particular paper-maker.

1. History. The art of making paper was discovered by the Chinese 2,000 years ago. For raw materials they used such things as old rags and worn-out fishing-nets, which they made into a pulp by soaking them in water and then stamping them with a pestle in a stone mortar When the soaking and stamping had reduced the rags to individual fibres, the fibrous pulp was spread thinly on to pieces of cloth and dried in the sun. These first sheets of paper were very rough; but soon the Chinese invented a better method. They used a bamboo mould, rather like a sieve, which they dipped into a tank or vat containing the fibrous pulp. When the mould was lifted out, it was covered with the wet pulp, and, as the water drained through it, a thin sheet of pulp was left on top. This sheet, after being dried in the sun and polished with a smooth stone, made a much finer paper. The Chinese made very beautiful paper in this way, pieces of which survive today in perfect condition. They also made coloured papers which were 'sized' with a gummy substance to give them a surface on which it was possible to write with ink or paint.

It was not until the 8th century that the art of paper-making spread from China. Some Chinese paper-makers were captured by the Arab army at Samarkand, and, during their captivity, they taught the Arabs how to make paper. The art spread westwards through Baghdad, where there was a street of paper-makers in the 8th century in the time of Haroun al-Raschid of *Arabian Nights* fame. Thence it came to Egypt, where many paper mills were set up in Cairo; and from Cairo the art spread along the shores of the Mediterranean to Fez in Morocco. The Moors brought it to Toledo in Spain in the 13th century; from there it spread northwards into Italy, France, Germany, and Holland, and finally it came to England in the 15th century. Water power began to be used for driving the stampers, or pestles, about the 12th century. Paper-making did not become established in Britain for a long time, and it was not until 1588, when John Spielman started his mill at Dartford, that the industry began to spread: although John Tate had actually made paper at Stevenage in 1490.

At that time paper was made entirely by hand, by methods very little different in principle from those used by the ancient Chinese. Indeed, some papers are still made by hand today in Britain and other countries: for example, the most beautiful papers for water-colour painting and drawing, and for banknotes. For making paper by hand a sheet of wire cloth is used as the mould, and this is dipped into the vat of pulp. If a watermark is to be put in the paper, a piece of wire or wire cloth bearing the device is stitched or soldered on the wire mould before dipping. When the mould is lifted out covered with pulp, the vatmen shake it from side to side and backwards and forwards to make the fibres mat evenly together and allow the water to drain through, until a wet sheet of paper has formed on the mould. The mould is then lifted, and the wet paper deposited on a sheet of woollen felt. When a pile of alternate sheets of wet paper and felt has been assembled, the whole is squeezed in strong presses to remove the water. The paper sheets are then dried, sized with gelatine 'size' to prevent their being too absorbent (like blotting-paper), and calendered (that is, a form of ironing rather like being put through a mangle) to make them smooth.

At the beginning of the 19th century a paper-making machine was invented by a Frenchman, Nicolas Louis Robert, who brought it to

England, where it was taken up the Fourdrinier brothers. The modern paper-making machine is called the Fourdrinier machine after them, and the large modern machine, making perhaps 200 tons of paper a day, is simply a development of this original machine.

2. Modern Paper-making. (*a*) *Raw Materials.* Until the middle of the 19th century the only raw materials used for paper-making were linen, hemp, and cotton. Paper was very scarce, as there was not enough of these materials to meet the demand. But in the middle of the 19th century esparto grass (*see* Fibre Crops, Section 8, Vol. VI) began to be brought from Spain and North Africa and used, as it is today, for very fine paper. There followed an even more important discovery—it was found that wood could be made into a pulp which could be used for paper (*see* Wood-pulp). The wood-pulp used in British paper-mills is almost entirely imported from abroad, and in a condition ready to go into the beating engines. But the linen, cotton, esparto grass, or straw is made into pulp at the paper-mill. To pulp them, they are boiled in water and chemicals to remove any colour, and impurities such as grease, from the rags; then they are washed in clean water, and put into a machine called a breaking-engine, which breaks up the bundles of fibres or rags into a pulpy mass.

As well as wood-pulp and the pulp made from the other fibrous materials, a certain proportion of waste paper is repulped, purified, and used to make new paper. It is possible to make paper entirely from repulped waste paper, and most papers contain a good proportion of repulped waste paper, especially when wood-pulp and other modern materials are scarce; so it is important to salvage waste paper.

Thomas-Photos

PULP BEING MIXED WITH WATER IN A HYDRAPULPER

(*b*) *Manufacture.* The mixture of pulp and waste paper goes first into a hydrapulper, where water breaks it down into a fibrous mass. It then passes to beaters and refiners where the fibres are cut and bruised by revolving knives according to the kind of paper required. The majority of papers are 'loaded' with some mineral matter, usually China Clay (q.v.), to make the paper opaque and its surface smooth; various chemicals are also added, for example, dye to make the paper the right colour, starch to give it strength, resin 'size' to make it take ink without absorbing the ink like blotting paper.

The fibrous mixture is next put into a storage chest, from which it is fed on to the paper-machine. The modern paper-machine consists of three main parts: the wire part, where the wet sheet of paper is formed; the press part, where the wet sheet is made firm by pressure and suction; and the dry part, where any remaining water is taken away by heat. Paper-making is a continuous process from one part to the next, the machines running for many hours without stopping.

When the pulp from the storage chest, diluted with water, is fed on to the machine, it looks rather like milk. It is carried along a moving belt of woven wire cloth through which the water drains, leaving the fibres on top. The wire belt is shaken mechanically from side to side to make the fibres in the pulp lie evenly in all directions and so 'felt' together. At the end of the wire cloth the pulp is firm enough to hold together in a sheet and to be lifted off and placed on a woollen felt, on which it is carried into the presses. There the fibres are squeezed together under high pressure, making a smooth, but still wet, sheet of paper. The sheet is then carried alternately between felt and hot cylinders until it is quite dry and can be wound upon a wooden or metal cylinder at the end of the paper-machine.

The paper is then treated in various ways according to the type of paper needed. If a highly polished surface is needed for printing or reproducing pictures, it is usually 'calendered': that is, it is damped and passed through a machine consisting of a stack of polished steel

Thomas-Photos

THE WET END OF A PAPER MACHINE

rolls, pressing against each other. If the paper is needed in rolls (which are usually narrower than the machine roll) for a printing press, the roll from the machine is cut up and rewound into smaller ones. If the paper is required in sheets, several machine rolls are put into a cutting-machine, and the paper is unwound into the cutter and chopped off to the right size. The number of sheets cut is usually counted on the cutter, and reams of the required number of sheets are kept separate by marking-tabs.

Watermarking, when required, is done at the stage when the wet pulp is passing along the wire cloth. The name or device is sewn or soldered on to a revolving 'dandy roll', which compresses the fibres in the pulp when they reach it. This makes the paper thinner and leaves a clear impression when the paper is held to the light.

A kind of thick paper known as cardboard or folding boxboard is made on a different machine. This machine has a series of vats or tanks in which metal cylinders, covered with wire-cloth, revolve, picking up a layer of fibre and transferring it to the underside of a felt which is travelling along the top. Layers of fibres are pressed on to the felt until a thick paper is formed. The sheets of paper then go through presses and over drying-cylinders in much the same way as in the ordinary process. These boards are used for cartons and folding boxes for packing fruit, and so on.

Papers which are to be used for reproducing half-tone illustrations (*see* PROCESS REPRODUCTION) need to have a highly finished smooth surface. Art paper is a high-quality paper usually made from wood-pulp and esparto grass which is then coated with a film of white mineral matter such as china clay or calcium sulphate held together with an adhesive, usually casein, and heavily calendered to give it a smooth, highly polished surface. The colour plates in this

Thomas-Photos

THE DRY END OF A PAPER MACHINE

Encyclopaedia are printed on art paper. The rest of the book is printed on process-coated paper. This is similar to art paper except that the coating is applied to the paper during its passage through the paper machine instead of on a separate coating machine. There are many other varieties of paper, with different types of finish for different purposes.

See also Wood-pulp; Newsprint; Printing.
See also Vol. IV: Paper.

PARTNERSHIP. Firms jointly owned by two or more persons, unless they are private Limited Companies (q.v.), are called Partnerships. They have the advantage over one-man businesses of being able to draw on, not only the capital, but also the brains and experience of more than one person.

Partnerships may be formed without the signing of any special agreement, and are then bound by the Partnership Act of 1890, which lays down that all partners shall contribute and share equally and that the partnership shall be automatically ended by the death, bankruptcy, or retirement of any one of the partners. Partnerships formed by the drawing up of a partnership deed, however, are not bound by the provisions of the Act: capital can be provided, and profits or losses shared, in different proportions; interest on a partner's capital, and salaries for one or more of the partners, can also be paid.

But partnerships, being unlimited liability associations (*see* Limited Companies), suffer from the disadvantages of this form of enterprise. For instance, if such a firm gets into difficulties and owes more than it possesses, a partner with spare money will have to pay up for those who have none. Early in the present century, therefore, Britain adopted the continental device of the 'limited partnership', by which partners may be classified as either general or limited partners. Limited partners contribute capital to the firm, and get a share of the profits or bear a share of the losses; but they may not take any part in the management of the business or withdraw any part of their capital without the consent of the other partners. Limited partnerships must be registered with the Registrar of Joint-Stock Companies. They are not at all common.

The great disadvantage of a partnership is that it becomes dissolved on the death of any partner, and a promising business may then have to be 'wound up' simply for lack of the capital lost in this way. So it is usual for partnerships whose business would be seriously affected by such an event to insure the lives of the partners for a sufficient sum of money to replace a deceased partner's capital (*see* Insurance). This allows the surviving partners to re-form the partnership with the same amount of capital as before.

See also Co-partnership; Limited Companies.

PASTEURIZATION OF MILK. 1. Nature of Process. The value of heat for the preservation of foods has been known for thousands of years, but it was not realized until the 19th century that a very mild heat treatment, far below the boiling-point, made liquid foods such as milk keep much longer. The discovery followed the work of the French scientist Pasteur (q.v. Vol. V) on wine and beer. The process, called after him 'pasteurization', is a carefully controlled mild-heat treatment. It was found that the process served two purposes: it prevented the souring of milk, and it destroyed the dangerous disease germs which occur in some samples of milk. These germs include the bacteria causing tuberculosis, undulant fever, typhoid and paratyphoid fevers, dysentery, diphtheria, scarlet fever, and septic sore-throat (*see* Epidemic Diseases; Infectious Diseases, Vol. XI). It was known to bacteriologists that the tubercle bacillus was the germ which most strongly resisted heat treatment. To destroy this organism it is necessary to heat milk to about 60° C. for 15 minutes, and its destruction has always been taken as a way of testing the efficiency of pasteurization. A heat treatment of this kind destroys also about 99% of the common bacteria in milk, including nearly all those which cause milk to get sour—the lactic streptococci and the coli-aerogenes bacteria.

2. Technique. To ensure the certain destruction of tubercular and other disease germs in milk, it must be held at a fixed temperature for a fixed time, and in 1923 these conditions were officially defined in Britain as 63° to 66° C. for 30 minutes. This became known as the 'holder' process. Properly carried out, it was a thoroughly reliable method, but for the dairyman it had certain disadvantages. The raw milk had to be heated to just over 63° C., pumped into a tank, held there for half an hour, and then pumped out and cooled. This was a slow process and required a very bulky plant. For many years scientists and engineers experimented to try to devise a continuous-flow method by which the milk would only need to be held for a much shorter time; by 1949 a method known as 'high-temperature short-time', or H.T. S.T., was officially recognized. Most of the milk now pasteurized is treated by this process, which involves the following stages:

(*a*) The heating of the cold incoming milk by the returning hot pasteurized milk in a 'heat-exchanger', in which the liquids are separated by a thin sheet of metal.
(*b*) Filtration or clarification.
(*c*) Heating by hot-water pipes to just over 72° C.
(*d*) The holding of the milk at this temperature for at least 15 seconds.
(*e*) The cooling of the hot milk by the cold incoming milk in the heat-exchanger.
(*f*) Further cooling by brine or chilled water outside the compartments which contain the milk.

A flow-control valve maintains a constant rate of flow of milk through the plant to keep the temperature precise. An ingenious device,

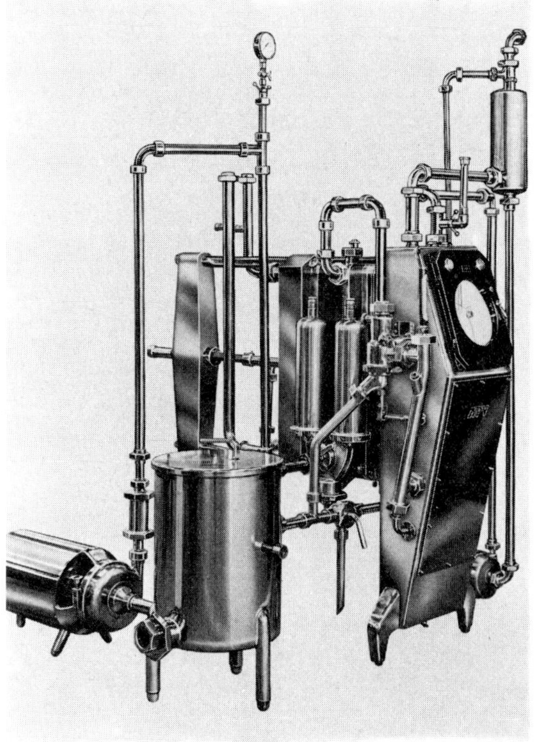

The A.P.V. Co. Ltd.

A PLATE HEAT-EXCHANGER TYPE H.T. S.T. PASTEURIZING PLANT

The instrument panel is mounted on the head of the machine

known as the flow-diversion valve, makes it impossible for milk to pass through the plant unless it has been properly pasteurized. The bulb of a very sensitive thermometer is held in the milk at the end of the 15-seconds holding-pipe, and if the temperature of the milk at this point falls below 72° C., the flow-diversion valve is brought into operation by pneumatic or electrical control, and the under-pasteurized milk is diverted back into a raw-milk tank, ready to pass through the plant again.

In one type of heat-exchanger in use in Britain, the liquid to be heated flows in a thin film between two stainless steel plates, the heating liquid being on the other sides of the plates. Thus there are thin films of cold and hot liquids arranged alternately. In another type the pasteurized milk is finally chilled by an ammonia Refrigeration unit (q.v. Vol. VIII).

Efficient pasteurization may reduce the bacteria in raw milk from, say, one million to only a few thousand per cubic centimetre. The remaining bacteria are biochemically mostly of the inert type: that is, they either do not sour milk at all, or sour it only slowly. In certain cases, however, pasteurized milk in a commercial plant may become contaminated by souring-bacteria in the tanks, pipe-lines, and bottle-filling machines; and unless these are most efficiently cleaned and sterilized the advantages of pasteurization may be wasted. If milk is pasteurized in the bottle, with a securely fitted cap, contamination after pasteurization is impossible. Milk treated by this so-called 'in-bottle' method has an extremely good keeping quality, although the process involves serious practical difficulties.

See also Dairy Industry; Cold Storage.
See also Vol. XI: Tuberculosis.

PATENTS. The word 'patent' is a contraction of Letters Patent, a document, signed by the King or someone acting on his behalf, conferring some right or privilege. Letters patent are still issued when commoners are raised to the Peerage or Governors are appointed to overseas Colonies (qq.v. Vol. X). From the reign of Queen Elizabeth onwards, letters patent were granted by the Crown to many persons or companies, giving them a Monopoly (q.v.) to produce some kind of goods, or exclusive rights to trade and explore in overseas territories. By the time of James I the number had grown so big that laws were passed to abolish them, on the ground that they were 'grievous and inconvenient to the subjects of this Realm'. An exception, however, was made in favour of letters patent granted for the 'sole working or making of any manner of new manufactures'.

This exception is the origin of our modern patents, which are rights of monopoly granted to any person who invents a new machine or a new process, or the apparatus for carrying out the process. A patent cannot be granted for an idea, but only for putting an idea into practice.

Patents are granted by the British Patent Office, which is a government department, for a first term of 16 years. The person to whom a patent is granted is called a patentee. At the end of 16 years patentees may apply to the law courts for an extension, usually an additional 5 years, but sometimes an additional 10. Patenting an invention or process is a highly technical matter. To be worthy of a patent, an article or process must be something entirely new, which has never been the subject of a previous patent. For this reason there are firms called Chartered Patent Agents, who specialize in the law concerning patents and in the details of applications to the Patent Office; these firms are usually consulted by would-be patentees. British patents cover Britain only, and patentees who wish to prevent foreigners from copying their inventions abroad should take out patents in all other important countries, according to the laws prevailing there. A patent is a form of Property (q.v. Vol. X), and can therefore be bought or sold, or assigned or leased to other persons. Inventors of articles or processes, who do not wish to take the personal risk of developing them commercially or industrially, may allow other firms to use their patents under licence. The licensees may pay for this privilege in various ways: a lump sum, an annual rent, or a Royalty (q.v.).

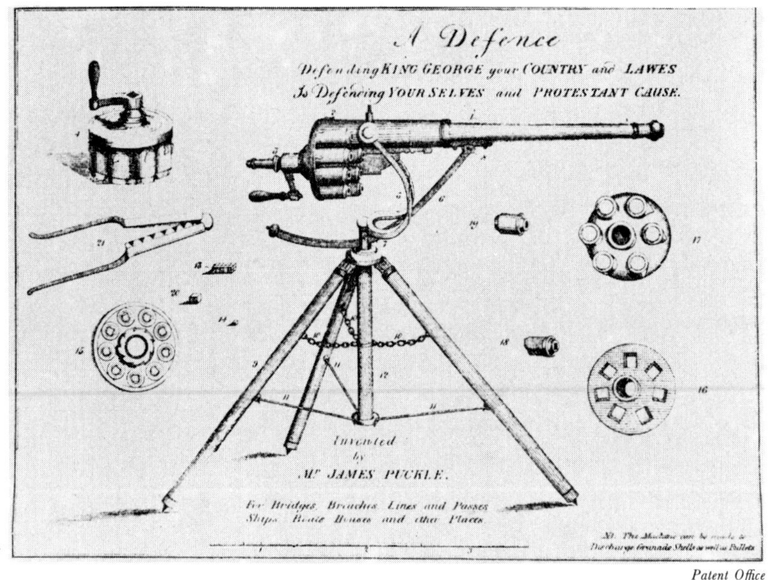

Patent Office

ILLUSTRATION FROM THE SPECIFICATION FOR PUCKLE'S MACHINE-GUN, PATENTED 1718

The gun was designed to shoot square bullets against Turks and round bullets against Christians

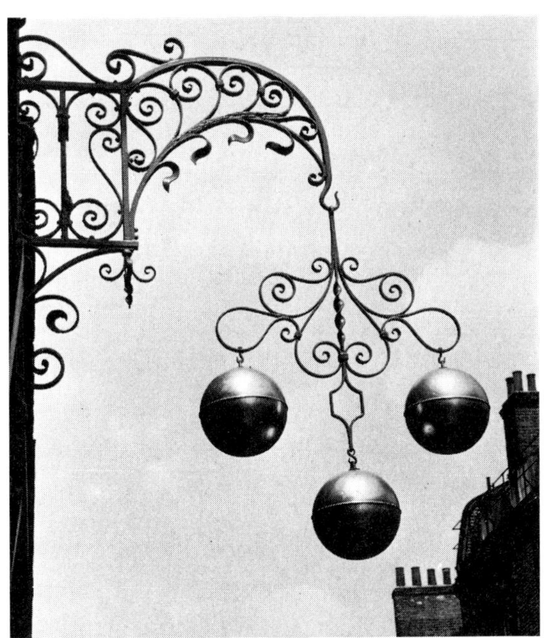
Fox Photos

THE THREE GOLDEN BALLS OUTSIDE A PAWNBROKER'S SHOP

PAWNBROKERS are persons or firms who are permitted to lend money against the security of goods deposited with them. Their methods of business are extremely ancient, and are rigidly controlled by law. The pawnbroker's sign is three golden balls: these have sometimes been held to be the arms of the Medici family of Florence, but this is denied by many historians, who consider the device to be the general sign of the bankers of Lombardy who came to England in the late Middle Ages (*see* BANKING).

Goods left as security with pawnbrokers are called 'pledges'. The interest that may be charged on loans is limited by law. On top of this, a halfpenny (or, on loans of over 10*s*., a penny halfpenny) is usually charged for the pawnticket, which states the terms of the contract between pawnbroker and pawner. If the pawner has failed, by a certain date, to 'redeem' his pledge, that is to say, to repay his loan with the interest due, the pawnbroker can sell the goods left with him. For loans over £2 pawnbrokers may issue special tickets which usually give the pawner the right, if the goods have been sold, of searching the pawnbroker's books and claiming the difference between the amount due and the sum received from the sale.

In the 19th and early 20th centuries the pawnbroker's sign was frequently seen in Britain. People who suddenly needed money would take personal jewellery or household valuables to a pawnbroker in the hope that he would lend them the sum they wanted. Many poor people were regular customers of pawnbrokers, and would even pawn their clothes.

Today, owing to the great improvement in the STANDARD OF LIVING (q.v.), pawnbroking is a declining trade.

PAYMENT. In Great Britain, by far the largest value of payments is made by transferring money from one bank account to another. Coins and bank notes are still used when making ordinary purchases, but cheques, especially when accompanied by a bank's cheque-guarantee card, are increasingly replacing cash payments in shops.

A cheque may be unacceptable if the person offering it is not known to the person receiving it, as the cheque's value depends on whether the drawer has enough money in his bank account to meet its value. If the drawer is carrying a bank's cheque-guarantee card, however, any cheque he writes up to the value of £30 is absolutely guaranteed by that Bank. In the next few years cheques will probably tend to displace notes and coins for making large purchases; though cash will still be necessary for small buys, the need to carry pockets full of notes will be outdated.

Even cheques themselves may one day fall into disuse and be replaced, through computer techniques, by 'electronic money'. In future, it may be possible to pay for a new suit by presenting a card and dialling a number on a telephone. This procedure may well be sufficient to transfer £25 from one person's account to another's.

Until recently, a person drawing a cheque could have it certified by the bank from which it was drawn, but this practice has now fallen into disuse. It is still possible, however, to obtain a bank draft, that is, a cheque drawn by a bank upon itself. Such an arrangement naturally offers greater security than a privately-issued cheque. Bank drafts are still occasionally used when buying real estate, but are no longer common for internal trade. They are also sometimes used overseas, but the majority of international payments are now made within the banking system by direct mail transfer, or telegraphic transfer. By these methods, the payer's bank (which has its own bank account in an overseas bank in every financial centre throughout the world) instructs

5D R.12.67.
30th June 1969
Date

CODE NO.
98-76-54

LLOYDS BANK LIMITED
BANK GIRO CREDIT

TO: BANK EVERYBANK LTD.,
BRANCH NORTHTOWN

ACCOUNT HIRERIGHT LTD.

PAYEE'S ACCOUNT NUMBER
54-76-98

CASHIER'S STAMP AND INITIALS

Paid in by John Brown. HTA 4032

	£	s.	d.
£10 NOTES			
£5 NOTES			
£1 NOTES	8		
10/- NOTES			
SILVER		3	6
BRONZE			2
COPPER			
TOTAL OF CASH	8	3	8
CHEQUES, P.O.'S ETC.			
£	8	3	8

Lloyds Bank

A BANK GIRO CREDIT TRANSFER FORM

John Brown has paid in £8.3.8. in cash at a branch of Lloyds Bank, which will be transferred through the Giro to the account of the payee, Hireright Ltd. The name and branch of the payee's bank must be included on the form

its overseas correspondent to pay the person named. This system is cheaper, faster, and safer than using bank drafts.

When paying a number of bills at the same time, one can use the Banks' Giro Transfer Services. Instead of making out individual cheques for each payment, a giro transfer form is completed, giving particulars of the bank account of each person to receive payment, and the amount to be received. The transfer form is handed to one's bank with a cheque for the total sum. The bank deals with everything else.

The Post Office has recently introduced a Giro service, but to use this one must open a giro account at a Post Office. Other methods of payment are also available through the Post Office. For small sums, 'postal orders' are suitable. The name of the person to whom the money is being sent, and the name of his nearest Post Office, may be filled in before posting an order: there is thus some protection against theft if the letter should get into the wrong hands. For larger sums 'money orders' may be used. These are only paid across the Post Office counter if the receiver of the money can say who the sender is, and this is a great protection against fraud. If payment is urgent, money orders may be telegraphed. People with a Post Office Savings Bank account can ask for a draft to be made out in favour of someone to whom they wish to send money.

As an extra safeguard, postal orders, money orders, cheques, and bank drafts may be 'crossed'. A 'crossing' consists of two parallel lines drawn across the face of the document. Sometimes the words '& Co.' (a relic of the days when all banks were private partnerships) are added at the right-hand end of the crossing; but a crossing consisting of two parallel lines is legally sufficient. No crossed cheque will be paid in cash across the counter: its value will only be paid to a banker, usually the banker of the person to whom it is made payable.

Greater protection can be given if the crossing is a 'special' instead of a 'general' crossing. Thus, if a cheque is crossed 'Account Payee only', the money may only be placed to the credit of the actual bank account of the person to whom it is made payable. Another form of special crossing is to write the name of the payee's bank between the lines of the crossing: the money then becomes payable only to the bank named. Another special crossing is the inclusion of the words 'Not Negotiable' between the lines; a person cashing such a cheque for someone who has stolen it cannot legally recover the money if he passes the cheque on to someone else.

The technical term for sending money by post, by the methods described, is 'remitting'; the sums sent are called 'remittances'.

See also BANKING; CURRENCY.

PEDLARS AND HAWKERS. The street salesman has existed since very early times. Though he no longer fulfils the important function he once did, he still survives; and in some countries, particularly in the East, a great deal of the normal day to day trading takes place in the street and at house doors. In Europe, from the Middle Ages until well into the 18th century, the streets of towns were full of street hawkers, sellers of flowers, fruit, fish, and various kinds of cooked food, besides menders of chairs, knife-grinders, and so on, many of them with a traditional cry or song to advertise their wares. Some of these, such as the muffin man with his bell, were to be seen in some parts in the 19th and even the 20th centuries, and the wandering rag-and-bone man is still a common sight in most towns. Mainly, however, street selling, apart from that of the regular STREET MARKETS (q.v.), is confined to flowers and fruit, though, in the streets of big towns, there are still to be seen not only girls with baskets of flowers and the 'barrow boys', but also sellers of matches, bootlaces, and other small goods, and men who demonstrate clockwork toys on the pavement.

The pedlar, the wandering salesman of mixed wares, is a character rather distinct from these street vendors of the towns, though his ancestry goes back quite as far. Early names for him were 'huckster' (related to 'hawker', and still sometimes used of a 'huckster's store' where miscellaneous goods are sold) and 'chapman'. The word 'pedlar' is probably derived from the old Scottish word 'ped', meaning the basket he carried. The verb 'to peddle' came later, and was derived from 'pedlar'. Pedlars were common in the Middle Ages, and valuable, since there were no shops where people could buy the household and other wares in which they dealt. Often, like Autolycus in Shakespeare's play *The Winter's Tale*, they sold BALLADS (q.v. Vol. XII), as well as trinkets of every kind. As with the street traders, there seems to have been no special legislation to govern pedlars, though they were no doubt included in the laws against vagrants. The earliest special reference to them in English law comes in a statute of Edward VI's reign, which insists that every 'pedlar, tynker, or petty chapman', selling such articles as 'pins, points (suspenders), laces, gloves, knives, glasses, tapes', should hold a licence issued by a J.P. In Queen Elizabeth's reign, when special laws were passed to clear the streets of vagrants, unlicensed

Bodleian Library

AN EARLY 19TH-CENTURY PEDLAR

pedlars were included in the list of vagabonds upon whom strict penalties were imposed (*see* STREET ENTERTAINERS, Vol. IX).

Apart from GYPSIES (q.v. Vol. I), who generally sell goods they have made themselves, pedlars are rarely seen in the 20th century. They were common, however, until the end of the 19th century, and in 1871 a special Act, known as the

Fine Oat Cakes fine
The Water Bearer
White Yeoung parsnips
Old Shoos bye any Broomes

Bodleian Library

EARLY 18TH-CENTURY LONDON STREET CRIERS

R. Gorbold

A WATER-SELLER IN BAGHDAD

Pedlars Act, was passed to govern their position. This Act, which is still in force, defines a pedlar as 'any hawker, pedlar, petty chapman, tinker, caster of metals, mender of chairs, etc.' who 'without any horse or other beast bearing or drawing burden, travels and trades on foot and goes from town to town or to other men's houses carrying to sell or exposing for sale any goods, wares, or merchandise—or selling or offering for sale his skill in handicraft'. A tax of 5*s*. a year is imposed on him, entitling him to a certificate. He must be over 17 years of age, and able to produce references as to his character. His pack is subject to inspection by the police.

In 1888 a further act, the Hawkers Act, was passed, which makes a legal distinction between a pedlar, who travels on foot, and a hawker, who is defined in this Act as anyone who 'travels with a horse or other beast of burden, selling goods, etc.'. The hawker, like the pedlar, must produce a certificate of good character signed by a responsible person, and must pay a tax of £2 before he is granted a licence. He must have the words 'licensed hawker' legibly written, painted, or printed on every box, package, and vehicle.

These two Acts, however, apply only to travelling salesmen dealing in their own wares. They do not cover the REPRESENTATIVES of firms, nor people who sell goods at STREET MARKETS (qq.v.); nor do they apply to vendors of food, or traders such as rag-and-bone men, who buy to sell again. Also exempt are all street traders who do not travel from place to place. Legally a trader who remains at a certain pitch is neither a pedlar nor a hawker, and does not need a licence unless this is required by a local bye-law in the place where he is working. There is, in fact, no special legislation to govern him, and such regulations as there are are purely local, being usually framed to limit the number of traders, and to prevent obstruction. In some towns, for instance, the bye-laws may prohibit trading in the busiest parts of the town, or after certain hours at night. In London, where the numerous street traders have made tighter regulations necessary, trading is only allowed by those holding special street traders' permits.

See also STREET MARKETS.
See also Vol. VI: MARKETS.

PERFUMERY. This was originally the art of extracting the scented essences of plants and other fragrant substances and of combining them with other materials, such as grease, spirits, starch, and soaps, that had no odour or only an unattractive one. The art of the perfumer is very ancient. The Assyrians, ancient Egyptians, Phoenicians, and Persians made much use of perfumes. Tyre, on the shores of the eastern Mediterranean, was a famous export market for perfumes to be sent away by sea, and Babylon was an equally important inland market for supplying the country around. Perfumes were much used by the Greeks and Romans, and they used them in ways in which we do not use them today: for example, they perfumed their wines with roses, violets, and hyacinths, in much the same way as rosewater is now used in making Turkish coffee. Pliny, the Roman writer, gives many details of the trade in perfumes in ancient Rome. Like many other arts, that of the perfumer had come to Rome from Greece, and most perfumers in the time of the Roman Empire were Greeks. Their shops occupied a special quarter of the city, and were a fashionable resort; they were supplied with perfumes from all parts of the then known world.

In the Middle Ages the use of perfumes spread

from the southern and eastern Mediterranean towards the west. The Arabs introduced them into Spain, and France and Italy became the most important countries that made them. Many modern perfumes are mixed with alcohol, and perfumes of this kind are believed to have been first made in the 14th century. Hungary Water, the earliest of which we have any record, was distilled from rosemary in 1370 by Queen Elizabeth of Hungary. Italy, the centre of culture and luxury of those days, was a leader in this new trade, but when Catherine of Medici left Florence for France in 1533 she took with her a famous perfumer, and ever since then the French have been the real leaders of the industry, in quality if not in quantity.

Fragrances can be extracted from flowers and plants by four methods: distillation, solvent extraction, enfleurage, and maceration. In distillation, the petals, leaves, and stalks of the plant are packed in a still, and water added. Steam is then injected, and the influence of the hot water and steam frees the oil from the glands in the plant tissue. Sometimes mixed oils have to be separated by a process known as 'fractionation' (*see* DISTILLATION). Modern stills can often take up to a ton of leaves or flowers, and may hold 1,000 gallons or more of liquid perfume.

Solvent extraction is a newer industrial technique, increasingly used in larger factories. The leaves or flowers are put into sealed containers with a solvent that will evaporate at a fairly mild temperature; petroleum ether is normally used. The solvent penetrates the plant cells and dissolves the natural perfume, together with some natural waxes and colouring matter. Then the solvent is allowed to evaporate, leaving in the still the mixed flower essence and waxes. The waxes are removed by filtering, and what is left is, after a little further refining, the true essential oil or absolute essence of the flower. The solvent process is expensive and requires elaborate plant; distillation is simpler and cheaper and can be carried on in remote parts of the world with portable stills.

Goya Ltd.

FILLING PERFUME BOTTLES

In earlier times flower scents were extracted by means of fats. Some flowers continue to give out perfume after having been picked, and if their petals are placed against cold meat-fat the aromatic oil is absorbed by the fat: this is the enfleurage process. Other flowers die on being picked, yielding no more oil than is in the flower at the time; such flowers are immersed in hot fat, which dissolves out their oil; this is the maceration process. In each case the scent is recovered from the fat by washing in alcohol. But these old hand processes are now little used, except in parts of India and southern France.

Whatever the process, the absolute essence of a plant is the most expensive raw material of the perfumery trade, and the highest classes cost many pounds per ounce. Over 1,000 tons of essence of jasmine alone are used in the world's perfume industry every year.

As well as flower extracts, certain animal extracts are used. The three most important are musk, which comes from the glands of the musk deer, a native of China; ambergris, from the sperm whale (*see* WHALING INDUSTRY, Vol. VI); and civet, which is a glandular secretion from the civet cat.

Natural flower extracts are no longer used by themselves, and synthetic or artificial perfumes are the basis of the modern industry. Most natural flower fragrances have been imitated synthetically, particularly violet, lily, lilac, hyacinth, narcissus, clover, may blossom, orange blossom, carnation, heliotrope, peach, and gardenia. The cheaper perfumes are entirely synthetic. Better-class perfumes are a blend of synthetic essences, animal extracts, and certain gums and balsams. In all good perfumes a small quantity of natural flower essence is always used. In the making of perfumes, the synthetic essence or essences (for many perfumes are a blend of two or more fragrances) are first dissolved in alcohol. They are then 'toned' or blended with gums and balsams, which prevents too much evaporation and thus makes the finished perfume last longer. For the better-class perfumes natural extracts are added. The liquid is then allowed to mature in glass-lined tanks, often for many months.

The main world centres of modern perfume manufacture are Paris, London, New York, and the Mediterranean towns around Grasse in the south of France. Some of the most expensive perfumes are marketed by famous fashion houses in Paris.

See also OILS, VEGETABLE.
See also Vol. VI: OIL-BEARING PLANTS.

PEWTER. This is a silvery-grey alloy, once much used for TABLE WARE (q.v. Vol. XI) and other domestic articles. It is composed principally of tin and lead, although lead is sometimes replaced by COPPER (q.v.) or antimony. The antiquity of pewter is shown by the reference made to it by the Hebrew prophet, Ezekiel, when the city of Tyre is said to have laid up riches of silver, iron, tin, lead, and copper, which were made into pewter vessels.

In England, pewter gradually superseded wooden platters and porringers during the Middle Ages. It supplied articles for the table for people who could not afford real silver. It went out of general use in the early 19th century when cheap china and EARTHENWARE (q.v.) became common, but it is still used today for such vessels as beer tankards.

Tin Research Institute

SOLDERING A HANDLE ON TO A PEWTER TANKARD

The pewter-making industry was recognized by royal charters as early as the 13th century. Its chief centre was London, although the craft also flourished in York and Newcastle, and extended later to other towns. The reputation of English pewter on the Continent was second to none, although there were important centres of manufacture in France and Germany. The first written records of the Pewterers' Company date from 1348.

In those days pewter consisted of tin with the addition of as much brass or copper as it would take up in the melting process—the proportion being about 4 parts tin to 1 part copper. This was called 'Fyne Peauter, No. 1', and from it were made such things as salt-cellars, platters, chargers, and ribbed or 'fluted' vessels. 'Fyne Peauter, No. 2', consisting of about 112 parts tin to 26 parts lead, was used for commoner household articles such as pots, pans, bowls, cruets, and candlesticks. This alloy is very similar to that used by the Japanese in the 17th and 18th centuries, and also to that prescribed by law for the manufacture of spoons and candlesticks in France today. The metal was worked either by hammering or casting. Craftsmen using the first method were called 'sadware' men ('sad' being used in the sense of 'heavy'—like 'sad cake'); those using the second were called 'hollow-ware' men. The two classes belonged to quite distinct crafts. It was the custom of those days for travelling pewterers to recast all worn-out and damaged pieces, and this accounts for the disappearance of much medieval pewterware.

Today, pewter is still manufactured by casting and hammering. The pewter is melted in iron pots, and before it is ready to pour into the moulds it is stirred with a 'green' stick. This can be any piece of living shrub or tree, the theory being that the sap in the green stick generates steam when plunged into the melting pot and distributes oxygen throughout the molten metal, thereby purifying it. The green stick is also used to clear the dross from the top surface of the molten metal. The casting is generally done in gunmetal moulds. When the cast is removed from the moulds, the pewter has a white, frosted appearance. This is removed in the finishing processes, which are generally done on a lathe. Tankards and mugs are cast in two or three pieces; large dishes are made entirely by hand from rolled sheet metal which is hammered and fashioned on an anvil and on a metal pattern (a 'swage') covered with soft leathers. Some pewter vessels with roughened surfaces, particularly beer tankards, are first cast, and then finished by hand-hammering.

The old regulations of the Company laid down that pewter vessels should always be stamped, like silver, with the maker's mark (*see* ASSAYING, Section 2), but the regulations seem to have been very often ignored. At one time the Pewterers' Company used to lend out moulds to its members, and this accounts for articles of the same shape being found with different makers' marks on them. The Company still have some of these moulds, and moulds 300 years old are still in use.

PHARMACY. This means the preparation and dispensing of DRUGS (q.v. Vol. XI), and the knowledge of their properties and action.

1. HISTORY. In Saxon and early Norman England there was no differentiation between an apothecary (a man who prepared and sold drugs), a physician, and a surgeon, the practitioners known as leeches performing the functions of all three. During Norman times drugs, one of a group of commodities known as 'spicery', were sold by a 'mercer', a term originally meaning a dealer in small wares. In the 12th century the trade in drugs passed to the pepperers and spicers who later united and eventually became the Grocers' Company. The apothecaries evolved as a specialized group of this guild until they were granted full independence as the Worshipful Society of Apothecaries of London by a charter from James I in 1617.

From about the time of Henry VIII the apothecaries gave medical advice as well as dispensing, and this led to bitter disputes with the physicians. The apothecaries strengthened their position as medical practitioners during the plague of 1665 when they remained in London to treat the sick. In 1703 the physicians brought a case against an apothecary for practising medicine, but they lost their case, and apothecaries continued to practise both pharmacy and medicine. In 1815 the Apothecaries Act gave them complete control of medical education throughout England and Wales, a power which they held until the General Medical Council was set up in 1859.

As the apothecaries devoted more of their

Boots Pure Drug Co.

A LABORATORY WHERE DRUGS ARE ANALYSED AND TESTED

time to medicine, chemists, who prepared chemical remedies, and druggists, who were mainly wholesalers of crude drugs, gradually took over the practice of pharmacy, and in 1841 they and some apothecaries founded the Pharmaceutical Society of Great Britain, which became the examining and registering body of pharmacists. Today only those on the Pharmaceutical Society's Register of Pharmacists may run a pharmacy or chemist's shop. The Society of Apothecaries became a professional medical society, and still offers medical diplomas and the certificate for pharmacy technicians. It is one of the 84 City Guilds still in existence.

2. LEGAL CONTROL OF DRUGS. In medieval times the guilds appointed searchers and tasters to control the purity of drugs. In 1540 the power to visit apothecaries' shops to inspect the quality of drugs was given to the College of Physicians, and they exercised this right for more than 300 years. Similar power was given to the Society of Apothecaries by the Charter of 1617. In 1530, the first law on poisons was passed; it decreed boiling in oil for the crime of poisoning. In Scotland a law of James VI restricted the sale of poisons to apothecaries.

Standards for drugs and medicines are specified in books known as pharmacopoeias, the first in Great Britain being the London Pharmacopoeia of 1618. This was superseded in 1864 by the first edition of the British Pharmacopoeia, a work which is revised every 5 years and is supplemented by the British Pharmaceutical Codex and the British National Formulary. The purity of drugs is now controlled by the Medicines Act of 1968. From 1969, all medicines are being dispensed in milligrams; the five-milligram spoon has replaced the teaspoon.

Before 1923 it was possible to buy opium and other habit-forming drugs quite freely: the poet De Quincey (q.v. Vol. V), for example, easily obtained opium to relieve the pain of neuralgia and so became an addict. Today dangerous or habit-forming drugs may only be supplied on a doctor's prescription. Both the Home Office and the Pharmaceutical Society have teams of inspectors to enforce the laws, the former being responsible for the control of dangerous drugs, and the latter for medicines and poisons.

3. Pharmacy as a Career. To qualify as a pharmacist, a candidate must obtain a degree in Pharmacy or Science (specializing in Pharmacy) at a university, or from the Council for National Academic Awards (*see* Examinations, Vol. X). To study for these examinations, the student must have passed advanced level chemistry, physics, biology, and botany or zoology, and must then take a 3-year course at the school of pharmacy of a university or at a technical college. Pharmacy is related to many branches of science, and the course includes not only a study of bacteriology, physiology, and chemistry, but also pharmaceutics—the study of the preparation of medicines; pharmacognosy—the study of natural sources of drugs; pharmacology—the effect of drugs on living tissues; and forensic pharmacy—the laws governing the purchase, storage, and sale of drugs. After completing the course, the candidate must serve a year of practical training under a registered pharmacist in general practice, in a hospital, in industry, or in a research laboratory. Pharmacy graduates may then study for a Master's degree or for a doctorate in their subject if they wish.

Most pharmacists are engaged in the general practice of pharmacy, which consists of dispensing National Health Service and private prescriptions and selling drugs, medicines, dressings, medical and surgical appliances, and sundries. Many pharmacies (or chemists' shops) also sell toilet requisites, cosmetics, photographic equipment, and sometimes agricultural and horticultural requirements such as fertilizers or insecticides.

Those who prefer a more academic career may choose hospital pharmacy where they will be responsible for dispensing medicines for in-patients and out-patients, for supplying the hospital with drugs, dressings, medical gases, etc., and, in larger hospitals, for a considerable amount of manufacturing, especially of fluids for injections and of tablets. Hospital pharmacists act as advisers to the medical staff on the properties of drugs. In teaching hospitals experienced pharmacists lecture on pharmacology to nurses and students, and may also carry out pharmaceutical research.

Today most of the advances in pharmacology come from the laboratories of industrial pharmaceutical firms, though pharmacists lecturing in universities and schools of technology usually carry out research as well. Pharmacists, because of their training in chemical and biological sciences, are now being employed in the foodstuffs industry, forensic science, and clinical biochemistry. In all branches of pharmacy there are equal opportunities for men and women.

PHOTOGRAPHY, HISTORY OF. Photography consists of the action of light-rays focused through the Lens of a Camera (qq.v. Vol. VIII) on to a plate or film coated with light-sensitive chemicals, and chemically 'fixed'.

Since the middle of the 16th century, artists had used an instrument called the *camera obscura* as an aid in sketching. This is a small box with a lens which focused an image on to a sheet of ground glass on the top of the box. In principle it was like a camera, but the image, seen through the ground glass, had to be traced by hand instead of being recorded on a negative. In 1727 a German professor discovered that light caused chemical changes in a mixture of silver nitrate and chalk, but he did not know how to make use of this knowledge. About 1800 Thomas Wedgwood attempted to make photographs by coating paper or white leather with a solution of silver nitrate, but failed to produce pictures in the *camera obscura* in a short enough time to be practical, and he also could find no way of 'fixing' the images, which darkened all over when further exposed to light.

The world's first photograph (Fig. 1) was taken in 1826 by a Frenchman, Joseph Nicéphore Niépce, on a pewter plate coated with bitumen of Judea, which hardens—not darkens—under the influence of light. After exposure in the camera, the parts of the bitumen which had not been hardened by light were dissolved away with a mixture of oil of lavender and white petroleum, leaving a permanent positive picture, even though a very indistinct one by modern standards. But the exposure time was 8 hours, too long to be practicable. In 1829 Niépce formed a partnership with L. J. M. Daguerre who had also been experimenting, with the object of speeding up the process, and some 7–8 years later Daguerre succeeded in making clear and permanent photographs on silvered copper plates sensitized with iodine vapour. After an exposure of 20–30 minutes, mercury vapour was applied to the plate to bring out the latent image.

Gernsheim Collection

FIG 1. THE FIRST PHOTOGRAPH EVER TAKEN

View from his window at Gras taken by Nicéphore Niépce, 1826

This process, called 'daguerreotype' after its inventor, was first demonstrated in detail in 1839 before a joint session of the Academies of Science and Art in Paris. In this year the word 'photography' was first used for this new art. The process was applicable only for pictures of still objects such as buildings or sculpture, for the exposure was still too long for portraits; but by using improved lenses and more sensitive chemicals the exposure time was soon reduced, and in March 1840 the first photographic portrait studio was opened in New York. A year later a second was started at the Royal Polytechnic Institution in London by Richard Beard, who could take portrait photographs up to 2½ in. by 3 in. in 10–20 seconds according to lighting conditions.

In the meantime an English amateur scientist,

Crown Copyright

FIG. 2. AN EARLY CALOTYPE BY FOX TALBOT

From the Fox Talbot Collection, Science Museum, London

W. H. Fox Talbot, had been working on his own invention. He made his first pictures on ordinary letter paper sensitized with silver chloride, and then improved his 'calotype' process by using paper prepared with silver iodide and developed with gallic acid—an idea he learned from another independent inventor of photography, the Rev. J. B. Reade.

Talbot's paper was about as sensitive as the daguerreotype and, although it did not give as fine detail, it had one great advantage. Whereas each daguerreotype was a unique positive picture from which no copies could be made, Talbot's were paper negatives from which a large number of contact copies could be printed. This is the principle on which modern photography is based. The terms 'negative' and 'positive' were introduced by Sir John Herschel in 1840. The history of photography from this point consisted mainly of improvements of Talbot's work.

Paper as a negative had the disadvantage that it was always to some extent opaque and so light could not easily pass through it. Several experimenters tried using glass, but at first they could find no coating which would adhere firmly to the glass. In 1847, however, it was discovered that if white of egg (albumen) was mixed with silver salts, glass made a very satisfactory 'plate' for photographs of still objects—landscapes, for example, or buildings—where a long exposure of 5–15 minutes could be given.

In 1851 F. Scott Archer discovered that if another chemical mixture called 'wet collodion' was used with the silver salts, the result combined the advantages of the negative/positive principle with short exposure and fine detail. The 'wet-plate' process was universally used for nearly 30 years; but it had the disadvantage that the photograph had to be taken while the collodion was still moist, otherwise it lost its sensitivity. The plate had also to be developed immediately. For studio portraits this did not matter, but the landscape photographer had to take with him, in addition to a big camera, a tripod, and a stock of glass plates, a complete darkroom outfit, a total weight of equipment which amounted to 100 to 120 lb. Some photographers had a carriage fitted up as a travelling darkroom: in fact, this was the way that Roger Fenton photographed the Crimean War in 1855.

It was a long time before any alternative to the wet-plate process could be found, for any alternatives always had the disadvantage of being less sensitive. In 1871, however, R. L. Maddox showed that by using a gelatine silver-salt emulsion a satisfactory dry plate could be made. By 1880 gelatine dry plates twenty times more sensitive than wet collodion were being mass-produced and used all over the world. The greatly simplified photography encouraged enormous numbers of amateurs to take it up, particularly after the introduction of the roll-film camera.

As early as 1856 the first flexible film was made and used instead of a glass plate, and films were manufactured commercially in the U.S.A. In 1888 the Eastman Co. of Rochester, U.S.A., produced a small, cheap, and simple roll-film camera known as the Kodak; the next year they introduced nitro-cellulose roll-film; and in 1891 a light-proof paper backing to the film which made it possible to load the camera by daylight. Developing and printing firms came into existence to process the amateur's photographs.

Before 1880, enlarging of photographs was little practised, though small cameras were used for taking double pictures to view in the STEREOSCOPE (q.v. Vol. VIII) which, since the Great Exhibition of 1851, had become a craze. From 1880 onward, however, enlarging of small negatives by artificial light was possible on fast gelatine/bromide paper, and consequently the sizes of both negatives and cameras were gradually reduced from hand to pocket size, and eventually to miniature models. The modern miniature camera as a scientific precision instrument came into widespread use in the late 1920's with the introduction of the Leica and Rolleiflex.

In 1873 a German chemist, H. W. Vogel, found that by adding certain dyes to the photographic emulsion, a truer translation of natural colours into the photographic grey tone could be obtained; this led to the development of orthochromatic and panchromatic PHOTOGRAPHIC EMULSION (q.v. Vol. VIII), and made the development of colour photography possible.

The development of colour photography was based on the experiments in 1861 of Clerk MAXWELL (q.v. Vol. V), who found that every COLOUR in nature (q.v. Vol. III) could be matched by mixing varying proportions of the three primary colours of light—orange-red, yellow-green, and blue-violet. He noted that different colours had different effects on a photographic negative. If an object containing blues, greens, and reds was photographed, the greens and reds came out darker and the blues lighter than they would appear to the human eye. This led experimenters to use different-coloured light filters to record the amounts of the three primary colours reflected by each part of the object being photographed. At first the object was photographed through the three different colour filters, making three separate negatives. A positive transparency was prepared from each negative, each with its appropriate colour, and the three images were projected simultaneously on to a white screen. The overlapping colours produced an effect of natural colour. Now, these three processes are combined by using one film which is coated with three layers of specially prepared photographic emulsion, each layer being sensitive to a different primary colour. The negative is then developed by a very complicated process of exposures through different light filters.

PHOTOGRAPHY (q.v. Vol. IX) is not only a hobby but of great importance in science and industry. In medicine it is the basis of cardiography, recording movements of the heart, and of radiographs (*see* X-RAYS, Vol. VIII). Aerial photography is of military value and is also used in ARCHAEOLOGY (q.v. Vol. I) and in SURVEYING (q.v. Vol. VIII). Most astronomical observations are recorded photographically. The taking of photographs on tiny negatives, microphotography, is invaluable for storing a vast quantity of information in a very small space. Its first practical use was in Paris during the German siege of 1870, when microphotographs of important documents were attached to the legs of carrier pigeons and flown out of the city. The opposite procedure, photomicrography, is the photographing of minute objects through a microscope so as very greatly to enlarge them. This is used, for example, for photographing bacteria and for studying the quality and structure of metals and alloys.

The technique of reproducing photographs as illustrations in books and magazines is discussed in the article PROCESS REPRODUCTION.

See also Vol. VIII: CAMERA; LENS; PHOTOGRAPHIC EMULSION.
See also Vol. IX: PHOTOGRAPHY.

PHOTOGRAVURE, *see* PROCESS REPRODUCTION.

PIECE-WORK, *see* WAGES.

PLASTICS. Since the 1920's the term 'plastics' has been used in industry to denote synthetic substances (that is, artificially made from chemicals as distinct from natural substances) which can be moulded or extruded by pressure and heat. 'Plastics' is a confusing term, which is used in at least three different ways by technologists. First, it can mean the complete moulded article. Secondly, it can mean the moulding compound from which the article is made; this consists of the basic synthetic material (often called a synthetic resin), colours, and fillers, such as powdered wood. Thirdly, it can mean the basic synthetic material alone. Many plastics are called synthetic resins because they resemble natural GUMS AND RESINS and replace the latter in such products as PAINTS (qq.v.) and glues.

Most plastics are either 'thermosetting' or 'thermoplastic'. A thermosetting plastic is one in which the process of shaping and moulding under heat creates a permanent change in the material; that is, it cannot be dissolved, melted, or moulded again. By contrast, a thermoplastic resin is one which can be shaped under heat, but which does not undergo an irreversible change; the article can be again rendered plastic by heat and re-shaped. There are also some synthetic plastics that do not fall within either of these two groups.

(*a*) Thermosetting materials. The firm establishment of the plastics industry is probably due to phenolic resins, which were developed rapidly between the First and Second World Wars, after many years of preliminary research. Phenolic resins are produced by combining phenol with formaldehyde. Phenol, a BY-PRODUCT (q.v.) of coal tar, is now mainly derived from petroleum; formaldehyde comes from methyl alcohol. In 1872 a hard resinous substance was first made by combining these two materials. Early in this century Dr. Leo Baekeland showed that this chemical process could be controlled to make useful commercial products. As a tribute to his work the word 'bakelite' is still used for this type of resin, for which 'phenolic resins' is the more correct technical name.

The phenolic resins are dark in colour. The demand for articles in pale and pastel shades led to the setting up of another group of thermosetting materials, known as the amino, urea, or 'beetle' plastics. Commercial production began

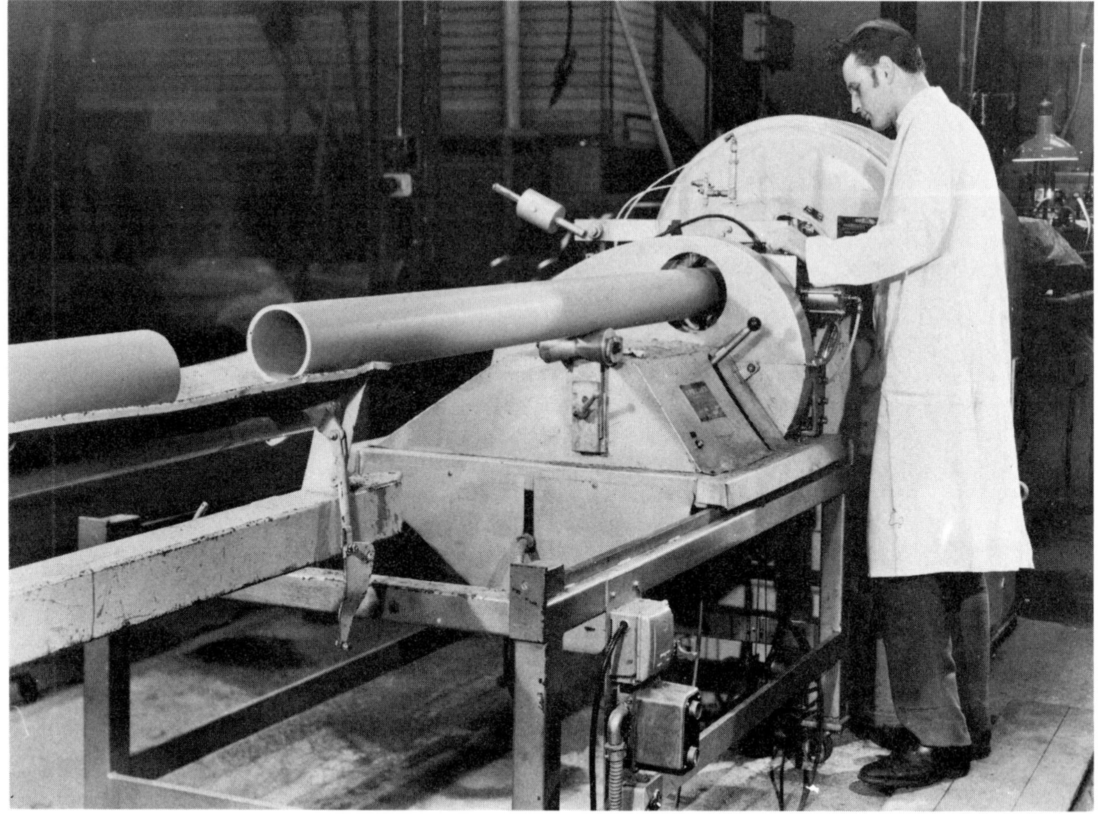

Imperial Chemical Industries Plastics Division

EXTRUSION OF A PIPE MADE OF THERMOPLASTIC

in the early 1930's, and later a similar resin called melamine was made.

(*b*) Thermoplastic materials. The first important synthetic material of the thermoplastic group was based on nitrocellulose. Nitrocellulose was known in Switzerland in 1846, but the first cellulose plastic was not produced until an English scientist, Alexander Parkes, discovered in 1864 that a horn-like solid could be produced by combining nitrocellulose, camphor, and alcohol. Americans had similar success in searching for a suitable material for billiard balls. In this way the highly inflammable 'celluloid' came into use.

Research for a non-inflammable celluloid led to cellulose acetate in 1865; this was produced commercially by the end of the century. Acetate film was used in 1912 for photographic purposes; sheet, rod, and tube were available in 1927 for bending into certain shapes; powders were made by 1934 for moulding into more complicated shapes. It was, however, bulk production for spinning into 'acetate' rayon that made this plastic so important (*see* TEXTILE FIBRES, MAN-MADE). In more recent years two others, cellulose butyrate and cellulose propionate, have been produced; for some purposes they are superior to the acetate, as when an article has to resist damp. Ethyl cellulose is another thermoplastic material of this type.

Other important thermoplastic resins produced commercially include the acrylic, polystyrene, and vinyl resins, the nylons, and the polyethylenes. The best-known example of an acrylic resin is 'Perspex'. Polystyrene is similar in appearance to the acrylics, but is less expensive and more brittle: it rings rather like glass when dropped or struck, and is much used for inexpensive combs, beakers, toys, etc. Of the vinyl resins, polyvinyl chloride or P.V.C. is the best known. Flexible P.V.C. is made into such products as hosepipes, rainwear, and imitation leather; rigid P.V.C. is used for rainwater gutters and non-corrodible piping.

Nylon, developed just before the Second World

War, and now available in many varieties, first reached the general public in the form of extruded fibre in nylon stockings. It is very strong and resists wear, so is now increasingly used for engineering components: gear wheels, lock-nut inserts, sheathing for wire ropes, and driving belts. Two types of nylon are Type 66, made from hexamethylene diamine and adipic acid, and Type 610, made from hexamethylene diamine and sebacic acid (derived from castor oil). Polyethylene is made from ethylene gas and is a very tough, wax-like plastic with superb electrical properties—and also very familiar around the house in the form of buckets and washing-up bowls.

Plastics are what chemists call polymers. These are chemical substances in which individual molecules, or monomers, are joined together—often by means of heat and pressure—to form much larger molecules. Polyethylene, sometimes called polythene, is the simplest example of a polymer; it is made from ethylene gas by forming larger molecules from the smaller individual molecules of ethylene. Similarly, polystyrene is a polymer of styrene, polyvinyl chloride a polymer of vinyl chloride, polypropylene a polymer of propylene, and so on. Nearly all monomers nowadays are made by chemical reactions from oil.

The thermoplastics all soften when heated, and at a temperature greater than 80–90°C. many of them risk being distorted. However, many thermoplastics have now been developed which withstand much higher temperatures, examples being polytetrafluoroethylene, polyformaldehyde and polycarbonates.

Plastics of a different class are the 'regenerated' celluloses. Purified wood cellulose is dissolved in one of several chemical solutions, and squirted through a small opening into another solution, where the cellulose takes form again as a thin strand which can be spun into viscose rayon yarn. Film of the 'cellophane' variety can be made in this way. Paper and pulp can be partially treated to produce 'hydrated paper', 'parchmentized paper' and 'leatheroid'; treated papers can be built up to yield 'vulcanized' or hard fibre, which is tough and leathery, and is used for making suitcases.

See also Plastics in Industry; Chemistry, Industrial.

PLASTICS IN INDUSTRY. 1. Manufacture. Most Plastics (q.v.) are combined with other substances in the manufacture of plastic articles. To give it bulk, a plastic is often combined with a 'filler' or filling material, such as glass fibre, wood flour (sawdust), chopped cotton or fabric, inorganic powders such as China Clay, Mica dust (qq.v.), slate dust, or mixtures of these, and also with colouring matter. Plastic moulding powders (thermosetting powders) are pressed in hot moulds and thus become rigid articles. Thermoplastic powders coalesce and soften when heated, and are injected into cool moulds, to set to the desired shapes. Plastic solutions can soak into paper or textile sheeting, and a number of layers can be built up and pressed hot, to make sheets or boards. Used in this way, the thermosetting resins produce hard, rigid boards which do not soften with heat and which are known as laminated from their layer-like formation. The phenolic resins can be cast into rods, sheets, and other shapes.

Thermoplastics can be 'extruded', that is to say, squeezed out through a narrow opening on the same principle as toothpaste leaving a tube. The hot material can be forced under pressure through a die of the required shape. It can also be extruded and hot-rolled into film or sheet. Film can be made in another way by continuous evaporation from solution fed on to rollers. Threads and fibres can be made by extrusion and spun into yarn or woven into fabric sheets. Many thermoplastics can be filled with air bubbles and expanded into light-weight sponge-like products, such as expanded polystyrene.

2. Electrical Articles. The electrical industry has greatly encouraged plastics because their electrical properties are so good. Mouldings are used for insulators, boxes, and cabinets. Telephone hand-sets and cabinets for radio receivers are moulded from bakelite or melamine resins, or a range of other new materials, such as polymethyl methacrylate, or acrylonitrile-butadiene-styrene polymers. Polythene, which helped to make Radar practicable (q.v. Vol. VIII), is used for insulating cabling. The fluorinated polythenes (PTFE) were essential to the development of Nuclear Energy (q.v. Vol. VIII). Silicones enabled smaller transformers to be built for war-time aircraft. P.V.C. was substituted when rubber was short during the Second World War, and later came into use for cable insulation. Cellulose acetate film is an improvement on paper and fabric for coil insulation. Laminated phenolic resin paper or fabric is the main insulation in board form. Moulded

British Industrial Plastics Ltd.

MAKING PARTS OF A PORTABLE RADIO

Lumps of a dough-like material are placed in the moulds. When the ram of the press, which can be seen above the man's head, is lowered, the plastic is forced into the shape of the moulds

bitumen compounds are used for battery cases. Grey vulcanized fibre is used in railway track insulation, and red fibre provides the fronts of switch-boards.

3. Building Industry. Bakelite and urea-laminated sheets are used for panellings. The coloured and patterned walls of many milk bars are made from this material: their surface can imitate polished woodwork. It is used for counter-tops and table-tops, and also for furniture. Its qualities are permanence, freedom from damage by moisture and fungi, and great strength. Mouldings in bakelite or urea are used for knobs, handles, light-switches, and clock-cases. Coloured forms of P.V.C., cellulose acetate, or polythene, some of them patterned, embossed, or crinkled, make lamp shades, and the methacrylates are used instead of glass for transparent shades.

4. Chemical Industry. Metal tanks are lined with polythene, P.V.C., or hard rubber to resist corrosion by chemicals. Tanks are also made entirely of hard rubber or mineral-loaded bakelite. The vinyls and polythene are used for containers, for pipe-lines and ducts, and for cocks and valves; and they can be fitted together by welding in much the same way as metals are welded. PTFE has become important in making gaskets, to prevent leakage of gases or liquids at joints; it plays a part in making fluorine compounds, such as uranium hexafluoride for atomic energy. Polythene bottles, beakers, flasks, and buckets are used in laboratories.

5. Wrapping. Plastic films of regenerated cellulose (cellophane), cellulose acetate and butyrate, rubber hydrochloride (pliofilm), P.V.C., and polythene are used for wrapping and packaging. Polythene is particularly important for 'cold pack' foods, such as refrigerated fruits and vegetables. Various forms of closure for bottles, tubes, pots, and jars are moulded in bakelite or cellulose acetate, while beer-bottle stoppers are moulded in bitumen compound. Containers or boxes are moulded or shaped in transparent plastic. Firms packing goods for the tropics use polythene, heat-sealed, to give an airtight closure. Vinyl solutions can be sprayed to give a complete envelope around an article and enable it to resist the weather. War stores were protected in this way when shipped during

the Second World War from America to the Far East; aircraft were carried as deck cargo, and, when the plastic films were peeled off on arrival, the aircraft were ready to take the air.

6. Constructional. Wood joined together or 'bonded' with phenolic resin is a light but strong constructional material. It made the design of the Mosquito R.A.F. aircraft possible, and has been used for air gliders and small boats, such as canoes and motor launches, and even for aeroplane propellers. Synthetic resin adhesives enable waterproof plywood to be made, and are also used in aircraft construction for cementing light alloys together. This improves flying, for the joints are as strong as those made by riveting, and have less wind-resistance.

7. Liquid Uses. Solvent solutions form the basis of adhesives, cements, paints, varnishes, enamels, and coating materials. Practically all modern lacquers, varnishes, and enamels used in industrial finishing have a synthetic plastic base. Nitrocellulose yields lacquers and enamels, including the finishing materials for furniture and other woodwork, and for metal surfaces such as motor-car bodies. Melamine resin enamels are used in making refrigerators. Cellulose acetate is used for the lacquers which protect the cores of Cables (q.v. Vol. IV). The phenolics, ureas, and melamines form the basis of air-drying and stoving enamels and varnishes.

8. Miscellaneous. Plastics are widely used in cars for dash-boards, head-trim, and steering joints, as well as increasingly for upholstery; in future, plastic car-bodies, also, could come into more general use. Both polystyrene and polymethylmethacrylate are used for lenses, on account of their admirable optical properties. (See also colour plate opposite p. 96.)

PLATINUM is almost invariably found in nature in metallic form, and not as a compound or ore (*see* Metal Ores, Vol. III). It is, however, never found in absolutely pure form, but generally in company with one or more of five other metals, which together with platinum are called the 'platinum metals'. These others are iridium, osmium, palladium, rhodium, and ruthenium. The platinum metals are found principally in Brazil, Central America, Russia, Australia, Borneo, California, and the Union of South Africa. Tasmania is now the chief source of osmiridium, a mixture of iridium and osmium.

The platinum metals are important in industry, mainly for two reasons: they are very little affected by heat, and do not melt until heated to very high temperatures; they also possess excellent powers of catalytic action: that is, they can speed up chemical processes without themselves being affected by them. Owing to their high melting-point, which enables them to glow brightly without melting, they were originally much used for electric bulbs, and the trade name 'Osram' was adopted because osmium was the principal constituent of the filaments used in these lamps. Platinum itself, usually reinforced with one or other of the platinum metals to give it added toughness, is much used for laboratory work in chemistry, because it resists Acids (q.v.). One of the main modern uses of platinum is in the Jewellery Trade (q.v.). It is used either by itself, or in the form of an alloy called 'white gold', which is a mixture of gold with a small quantity of platinum or palladium. Platinum salts are also the basis of the platinotype process of photographic printing, which gives pleasing results in portraiture.

PLUMBAGO, *see* Graphite.

PLYWOOD AND VENEERS. Before plywood was thought of, thin sheets or veneers of expensive and rare woods had been used as facings on less costly wood, particularly for furniture. This use of veneers is very old—archaeologists have found evidence of it in Egyptian sculptures dating from about 1500 B.C. How the original veneers were cut has not been discovered, but they were fixed with some kind of animal glue and weighted down with sandbags until the glue had set. After these earlier uses there was a long interval during which only solid wood was in general use; but veneering was revived in the late 17th century in France and Holland, whence the practice of the craft spread to England (*see* Cabinet-making). The exact date when ornamental veneering suggested the idea of using plywood for more general purposes is uncertain; but in the second half of the 19th century plywood was used for tea-chests in the China tea trade, and for curved perforated seats for railway stations and tramcars.

Plywood in its simplest form consists of three or more thin layers of wood glued together, so that the grain of one veneer runs at right angles to that of the next. This arrangement gives the piece of plywood equal strength in both directions. There are other advantages. Shrinkage is reduced to a minimum; there is little or no tendency to split; and as the layers can be cut from big logs at their greatest width, plywood can be made in large sizes. It can be moulded to various shapes and will keep them indefinitely. The so-called 'water-proof plywood' made with special glues will not come to pieces even when alternately boiled and baked for 28 hours.

Three-ply is the simplest type of plywood. Multi-ply may have any odd number of veneers. Blockboard has blocks of solid timber with thick veneers glued to each side. Diagonal plywood has the grain of each layer running at an angle of 45° to the grain of the next. Laminated board has a core of strips of wood glued together with the grain running at right angles to the veneers. Plywood may itself be faced on one or both sides with a decorative veneer, or even with thin sheets of metal such as steel, copper, or zinc.

Birch from Finland, pine from Sweden and Douglas fir from Canada are used for the manufacture of plywood. Other woods used are alder, beech, and poplar from European countries. Gaboon, Limba, African mahogany, Makore, Obeche, Sapele, and Utile from West Africa and quantities of Japanese Lauan plywood are also imported.

Most wood for plywood is cut from a log on a rotary cutting machine. This is a kind of giant lathe, in which a round log is revolved against a stationary knife, and the layer comes off in a thin continuous sheet. This process is called 'peeling', and logs suitable for it are often called 'peelers'. Peeling is a highly skilled operation, for much good wood may be wasted if the knife angle is incorrect or the speed of rotation is wrong. After the wood has been peeled off it is trimmed to size, and then dried in a drying-kiln, into which the damp wood is fed at one end and from which it emerges dry at the other. Then any defects are cut out and solid patches glued into their place.

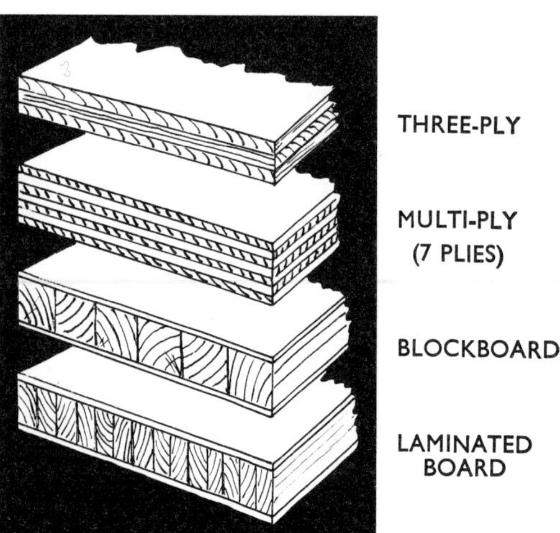

TYPES OF PLYWOOD

There are two main ways of sticking the layers together. An automatic glue-spreader may be used, looking like a clothes mangle with a trough of glue at the bottom. The rollers pick up glue from the trough and the wood becomes covered with glue as it passes through the rollers. The other method requires 'glue film', which is thin paper impregnated with glue. This is put between the layers and becomes liquid under heat in the presses. When glued and arranged in the necessary number of layers, the panels of plywood are carried to the press. This is usually a hydraulic press (*see* Vol. VIII, p. 208), and can press several panels at once; steel sheets or 'plattens' keep each panel separate from the next. Some glues require the pressing process to be cold; others require heat treatment, and the plattens are then heated by steam. Heat treatment reduces the setting time of certain synthetic resin glues from hours to a mere matter of minutes. On coming from the press the plywood boards have their edges trimmed and their faces surfaced by scraping or sandpapering; they are then inspected for defects, and graded. Large-sized boards are made by glueing several smaller boards together by long taper joints. This process is known as 'scarfing'.

Much of the success of modern plywood construction arises from improved glues. The early vegetable glues made from starch, and animal glues made from bones or skin, were apt to be spoilt by Bacteria and Mould (qq.v. Vol. II), and they failed to hold if the plywood got wet. Casein, made from milk, is still widely used; it resists water, but it can be affected by mould. Since 1930, synthetic resin adhesives have been used (*see* Gums and Resins). There are two main types: the urea formaldehyde (or U.F.) resins, which are moderately, but not entirely, resistant to moisture; and the phenol formaldehyde (or P.F.) resins, which can be exposed to the weather, or even submerged in water for long periods, without being affected at all. The choice of glue naturally depends on the use to which the plywood is to be put. The P.F. resins are principally used in the manufacture of plywoods for exterior use in boat-building and aircraft construction and in all cases where the plywood is to be exposed to the weather.

John Wright and Sons

A PEELING-MACHINE FOR CUTTING SHEETS OF VENEER FROM A LOG

Plywood lends itself well to being moulded into various shapes. The simplest way to bend it is to press it while the glue is still wet against a solid block shaped to the desired curve, and to keep it there until the glue has set. This was the earliest method used, and it is still used for simple bends; but it will not work when bends in more than one direction are required in the same sheet of plywood. For this kind of bending or moulding a new technique has been evolved. A mould in the desired shape is made from wood or other materials, and the freshly glued plywood is placed upon it. The whole is then covered with a sheet of rubber or plastic, and put in a pressure chamber called an 'autoclave'. Here it is subjected to heat and air-pressure, by which the rubber sheet is forced against the plywood and the plywood against the mould. The heat hastens the setting of the glue. This process, which is often called the 'rubber bag' method, can be used for boat hulls, which can thus be made in one pressing.

Plywood is still used for tea-chests, and for boxes and packing-cases of all kinds. It is used in boat-building and ship-building for many purposes, from the hull of small boats to the bulkheads of ships. In the building trade it is used for interior walls and partitions in shops, offices, and factories, and sometimes even for exterior walls, for floors, doors, kitchen cabinets and fitments, and as shuttering for the construction of concrete walls. It is used in the FURNITURE INDUSTRY (q.v.), and for making cheap buildings and sheds on farms. It is much used for the construction of railway carriages and wagons, and in the construction of certain aircraft. It is widely used for sports goods—table-tennis bats and laminated skis are examples—and also for making trunks and other baggage. Manufacturers of wireless and television sets make much use of it.

See also TIMBER INDUSTRY; FURNITURE INDUSTRY; CABINET-MAKING.
See also Vol. VI: TIMBER.

PORCELAIN. This term includes all POTTERY (q.v.) which is translucent, that is, through which light may be seen. Porcelain can be classified into three main types: the hard or 'true' porcelain of China and Europe; the soft porcelain of the 18th century, now no longer made; and 'bone china', the distinctive product of Staffordshire, which comes between the two. The term 'china' was first used for all kinds of pottery imported from the Far East, and for pottery made in Europe in imitation of it; properly the term refers only to porcelain.

The porcelain of the Far East was a development of STONEWARE (q.v.), from which it differed mainly in being whiter and more translucent. It was made from kaolin or CHINA CLAY (q.v.) and petuntse or china stone, and was glazed with the same materials. At first it was made in strong sculptural shapes; but gradually these became more graceful and were painted with colours. A beautiful blue-and-white painted porcelain, which had great influence on delftware (*see* EARTHENWARE), and early European porcelain, was made during the Ming dynasty of Chinese emperors (A.D. 1368–1644), and was at its best during the reign of K'ang Hsi (1662–1722). At the same time, delicate monochrome (one-colour) glazes were used in greens, blues, yellows, and the red glaze known by the French name *sang-de-bœuf* (ox-blood). Later we find decoration in bright coloured 'enamels' painted over the glaze, and known by the respective ground colours as *famille verte* (green), *famille noire* (black), *famille jaune* (yellow), and *famille rose* (pink). In the 18th century, Chinese porcelain reached that final stage of refinement and fragility which was to impress itself on European wares for a long time.

The first successful attempts to produce hard porcelain in Europe were made near the German town of Dresden about 1709, and soon after porcelain was made at Vienna, St. Petersburg (Leningrad), and elsewhere. Experiments in Florence in 1575, and much later in Venice and in France, resulted in the production of soft-paste porcelain (*pâte tendre*) which was quite different in composition, being really an opaque glassy material. Beautiful table and ornamental

Leonard Gow Collection

PORCELAIN JAR WITH 'FAMILLE VERTE' DECORATION

Chinese, K'ang Hsi period

Wallace Collection

ROSE POMPADOUR SÈVRES PORCELAIN

Flower Bowl dated 1757

wares were made in soft porcelain at the French factory at Sèvres under the patronage of the Marquise de Pompadour. After the discovery of china clay at Alençon (France), about 1758, French potters experimented with making hard porcelain, and after 1771 *pâte tendre* was gradually replaced at Sèvres by *pâte dure* (hard-paste).

In Britain, soft porcelain was made from about 1745 at Chelsea and Bow, and, soon after, Lowestoft, Derby, Longton in North Staffordshire, and Worcester were making it. In 1755 china clay and china stone (which gives porcelain its translucency) were discovered in Cornwall. Experiments were made at Plymouth by William Cookworthy, and, later, some hard porcelain was made at Bristol and Shelton (North Staffordshire). 'Bone china' takes its name from the large proportion of ground burnt animal bone that is added to the china clay and china stone mixture. It requires a lower heat to fire it than is needed for hard porcelain, and a soft glaze is applied to it. Josiah Spode the younger perfected the recipe for this about 1795 and, until 1959, it was the only kind of porcelain made in Britain. When porcelain was first made in London, Chinese and German influences were strong. Decorations were painted with great freedom and refinement. In the 19th century, when the porcelain of Sèvres was fashionable, pictorial painting and the use of coloured grounds and gilding became over-elaborate and ornate. The best-known Staffordshire producers of 'bone china' to-day are Mintons, Copelands (formerly Spode), and Doultons. In 1959

Doultons announced the introduction of an entirely new porcelain called 'English translucent china'; this differs in composition from bone china and hard porcelain, and is almost as cheap as the best earthenware.

Although the making of porcelain has been much less mechanized than earthenware, large quantities are made in Stoke-on-Trent for home markets and for export.

See also Vol. XI: TABLE DISHES.

POTTERY is the general name given to all kinds of ware made from clay and other minerals when they have been 'fired', that is, hardened by heat in the potter's kiln. Articles made of pottery include tableware, fireproof ovenware, wall and floor tiles, chemical storage jars, bathroom fittings, filters, water closets, drain pipes, electrical insulators, and ornaments.

Pottery is one of the oldest crafts, practised as soon as man learned to control fire, and long before the smelting of metals. It enabled him from prehistoric times to make vessels for storing and cooking food, for carrying water, and for ritual and burial purposes. Such vessels were shaped by hand and probably 'fired' in a big bonfire by covering them over with dried grass and brushwood, which were then set alight.

A great advance in pottery-making followed the invention of the potter's wheel and the kiln. It is not certainly known where the potter's wheel was first used, but it is thought that about 3500 B.C. potters in Central Asia were using some kind of wheel, from whence its use spread west and east, to Egypt, Crete, China, and the Far East, and to Greece and Rome. At first it was nothing more than a small circular disk turned on a pivot by hand, something like a big top, but later it was improved by raising it and providing it with a larger circular platform near the ground which could be rotated by the feet of the potter as he sat at his work. Such a wheel was in use in Egypt from about 150 B.C. and was still in use in Europe at the beginning of the 19th century. In the 18th century, however, the potter's wheel was improved so that it could be worked by a treadle or turned by an assistant. Modern pottery wheels are power-driven.

Although the Egyptians are known to have constructed ovens for firing pottery, little is known about firing techniques until the time of the Greeks and Romans, who used a small bee-hive-shaped construction. It consisted of two chambers separated by a perforated platform resting on a centre post and ledges at the sides. The pots were placed on this platform, and the fuel for firing the oven was fed through a short passage into the space below. When the oven was ready for firing, the upper chamber was covered over with a dome of clay and straw, care being taken to leave an opening at the top to serve as a chimney and to create the draught to draw up the hot air among the pots. This simple up-draught kiln was made larger in medieval times and provided with four or more fire-mouths instead of one. These were the fore-runners of the giant bottle ovens, sometimes as high as 30 feet, which until recently formed such a feature of the North Staffordshire land-scape.

Josiah Wedgwood and Sons

'THROWING' A VASE ON A POTTER'S WHEEL

There are three principal ways in which articles may be made of pottery: shaping by hand, 'throwing' on a potter's wheel, and moulding. Shaping by hand is the earliest method and is still used by native peoples in Central America, parts of Africa, and the South

Crown copyright

EARTHENWARE LOVING-CUP DECORATED WITH COLOURED 'SLIP'

English, late 17th century. Victoria and Albert Museum

Sea Islands. Pots are made by coiling ropes of clay, and pinching and pressing it to the desired shape. Sometimes a primitive form of moulding is used, as when the potter shaped his ware with the help of a big smooth stone, a stout bamboo pole, or by lining a hollow in the ground or the inside of a basket. Such handmade pots are often well made, 'true' in shape, and thin, smooth, and light in weight. Little figures of men and animals were also made by 'pinching out' the shapes with soft clay.

Throwing on the wheel is the most interesting and characteristic of pottery processes. It makes the fullest use of the clay's peculiar quality of being both plastic and tensile (able to be pulled out or stretched). A ball of soft clay is deftly thrown on to the centre of the wheel, which is set in motion. The potter works the clay with his hands into a wet mound, hollows it out with his fingers into a cup shape, draws the side of the cup upwards until it forms a straight-sided cylinder, and finally shapes this into the springing curves typical of the process. All this is done within a few minutes. The term 'throwing' refers to the potter's control of the spinning clay against its 'throw' or centrifugal tendency to fly off the wheel.

The moulding of pottery involves the preliminary modelling of a shape or statuette, the preparation from it of master moulds, and from them a series of working moulds in which the article or object can be made. This is done by pressing into the mould a lump of clay, or by pouring into the mould slip (clay made into a liquid batter), from which the moisture is gradually absorbed, leaving a thin shell having the shape of the required article. The process of moulding is an ancient one. Moulds were used by the Greeks for coarse pottery as early as the 7th century B.C., and the Romans used moulds extensively for their red-gloss pottery. The process seems to have been forgotten in the Middle Ages but was revived in the Renaissance. In Staffordshire, pitcher moulds made from fired clay or moulds cut in alabaster by the 'block-cutter' were originally used, but after about 1740 absorbent plaster-of-Paris moulds became general.

After the pots have been made they are thoroughly dried and are then ready to be fired. Firing means the gradual heating of the ware to the temperature necessary to effect certain chemical changes in the clay, and an equally gradual cooling down. 800° C., a bright red heat, is enough for common pottery; but harder kinds may need up to 1400°, a bright yellow heat. The time taken for firing pottery varies with the size of the kiln and the temperature needed, from about 24 hours to 2 weeks. In Staffordshire for generations potters have fired their ware in bottle-shaped kilns. For this kind of firing the ware is placed in oval or circular fireclay boxes (*see* FIRECLAYS AND REFRACTORIES, Vol. VIII), called 'saggars'. The even firing of these large kilns required great skill and judgement. The bottle-shaped kiln is called an 'intermittent' kiln because the ware has to be packed

Brighton Museum

MODELLED POTTERY GROUP, STAFFORDSHIRE, 18TH CENTURY

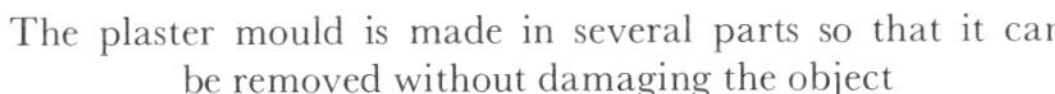

Josiah Wedgwood and Sons

REMOVING A TEAPOT FROM A MOULD

The plaster mould is made in several parts so that it can be removed without damaging the object

Josiah Wedgwood and Sons

TAKING A PAPER PRINT FROM AN ENGRAVED PLATE

The pattern is then transferred from the paper on to the pottery

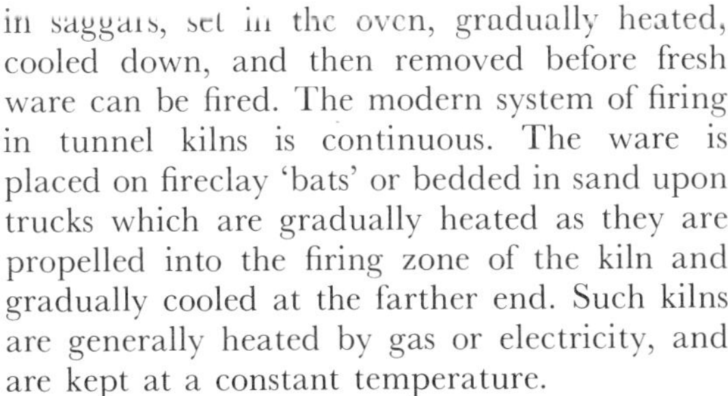

in saggars, set in the oven, gradually heated, cooled down, and then removed before fresh ware can be fired. The modern system of firing in tunnel kilns is continuous. The ware is placed on fireclay 'bats' or bedded in sand upon trucks which are gradually heated as they are propelled into the firing zone of the kiln and gradually cooled at the farther end. Such kilns are generally heated by gas or electricity, and are kept at a constant temperature.

Ware is often fired more than once. The first firing is called the biscuit firing, and the unglazed ware is called biscuit. It is now ready to be glazed. Glaze is really a glass which makes the surface of pottery smooth and non-porous. The art of glazing pottery was discovered by the Egyptians, who produced a beautiful turquoise blue glaze. The Greeks did not use a glaze for their painted pottery, nor the Romans for the glossy Samian ware, but in the Near East and China, and in Europe from medieval times, glazes of various kinds, translucent, opaque, or coloured, have been widely used. Peasant potters frequently glazed their pots by sprinkling powdered lead ore upon it, but from about 1730 a glaze solution has been used. This liquid glaze consists of the raw materials of glass ground together and mixed with water to a creamy consistency, or of materials which have first been melted together to form a kind of glass called 'frit', which is then ground up and mixed with water. The glaze is applied by dipping ware into it, or by spraying glaze upon the ware.

Some pottery is decorated while it is in the soft clay state, either by incising it with a pointed tool, by coating it with slip, that is, clay reduced to a liquid batter, usually of contrasting colour, and scratching through to show the colour of the clay underneath (this is called *sgraffiato* or *sgraffito*), or by trailing slip upon the ware like icing a cake. Most decorations, however, are applied after the biscuit firing. Painting which is

Josiah Wedgwood and Sons

LOADING TRUCKS FOR FIRING IN AN ELECTRIC TUNNEL OVEN

done on biscuit pottery is called underglaze painting. This is more permanent and generally more attractive than painting over glaze, which requires a further firing at a comparatively low temperature. The pigments used for pottery painting are all derived from the oxides or salts of metals. Iron gives red; copper, green; cobalt, blue; manganese, purple-brown; antimony, yellow; chrome (not used before the 19th century), green; and gold, crimson or pink. These same metallic oxides used as stains for glazes produce a variety of other colours according to the nature of the glaze and the conditions of firing. For example, copper in a glaze fired in an atmosphere from which oxygen is excluded (a smoky or 'reducing' atmosphere) yields a splendid crimson called *sang-de-bœuf* (ox-blood). The painting on tin-glazed pottery was done on the 'raw', that is unfired glaze, and required great skill and certainty of touch. This technique is not in general use to-day. Metals have also been applied to pottery either in the form of iridescent lustres (ruby from gold, yellow from silver) or thin films of gold and platinum. These, too, require a further firing at a lower temperature.

Pottery is no longer entirely made by hand. Many processes have been partly, and some entirely, mechanized. The clay itself is prepared by scientific means. Fine sieves and electric magnets extract particles of iron and other impurities. Air is extracted in a mixing machine with converging blades (called a de-airing pug mill) which churns up and kneads the clay into a homogeneous mass entirely free from pockets of air and in good condition for use. At many factories round articles are no longer made by hand on the potter's wheel and smoothed on the lathe. In the 19th century a mechanical wheel called a 'jolley' was invented, which has been greatly improved and made automatic in the post-war years. It consists of a revolving metal head shaped like a flower-pot into which a mould for a hollow vessel is placed. A ball of clay, weighed out to the right size, is placed inside the mould, and the shape of the vessel is formed by a metal profile attached to a lever arm which is brought down upon the clay, forcing it against the sides of the mould. The inside of the vessel is formed by the profile tool, the outside by the mould. Cups, bowls, and teapots are made with a 'jolley'. Plates and dishes are formed in a similar manner, although in this case the back of the article is formed by the profile tool and the front by the mould. At one or two factories plates are mass-produced by an elaborate machine operated on continuous automatic principles. Slices of clay are fed into it from the pug mill and emerge at the other end as finished articles ready for drying and firing. Some decorating processes have also been partly mechanized, particularly the rubbing down of engraved and lithographic transfers, and the application of coloured bands and edges to tablewares.

See also PORCELAIN; STONEWARE; EARTHENWARE.
See also Vol. XI: TABLE DISHES.

Meade Collection

AN EARLY 19TH-CENTURY POULTERERS' SHOP

POULTRY AND GAME. 1. POULTRY. Even before the Second World War the rearing and marketing of turkeys, geese, ducks, and chickens was a popular and paying occupation for farmers. Turkeys from Norfolk, chickens from the Lancashire districts round Preston, and ducklings from Yorkshire were sent in large numbers, especially at Christmas time, to Smithfield Market, in London, the main centre of the poultry trade. Today, however, far-reaching developments, largely introduced from America, have entirely changed this agricultural occupation into a highly mechanized and competitive industry, in which intensive methods of rearing birds, improved plucking equipment, deep freeze, pre-packaging, and barbecues for roasting birds set up in poulterers' shops are all playing their part.

Though turkeys are still reared in Norfolk, they are also being produced in many other parts of the United Kingdom. Broad-breasted strains of both bronze and white turkeys are the most popular, and it is now possible to rear these intensively and to market them at about 16 weeks old, thus satisfying the family demand for birds of small and medium weight. The British Turkey Federation exists to foster better breeding and to encourage the public to eat turkeys all the year round.

Although large chickens and capons are still produced for the table, new strains of table poultry and highly intensive methods of rearing have led to the development of a British broiler industry on American lines. These birds are marketed for roasting, frying, and grilling at around 10 to 11 weeks of age, and they often weigh up to 5 lb. and over. In 1960, 100 million broiler chickens were bought by the British public. To-day, the annual total comes close to 250 million—and the broiler industry is still expanding.

Geese have declined in popularity since the Second World War, and the demand for ducks has increased very little.

Poulterers used to be the only type of retail shop to sell poultry, but now fishmongers, butchers, provision merchants, supermarkets, and SELF-SERVICE STORES (q.v.) all sell poultry.

2. GAME. This is the word generally used to define pheasant, partridge, grouse, black cock, and hares, but various Acts of Parliament include woodcock, snipe, quail, and deer among English game, and ptarmigan among Scottish. (All these game animals are described separately in Vol. II.) The Game Laws control the trade in game, and make a licence necessary to kill or deal in it. These laws differ slightly in their application to the four countries of the United Kingdom.

Game and wild birds may not be taken during the breeding season, and there are statutory 'close' seasons when they may not be killed or sold. The grouse season opens on 12 August, and is followed by partridge on 1 September and pheasant on 1 October. The close season for other birds is governed by the Wild Birds Protection Act, and varies from country to country. Details can always be seen at the local police station (*see* GAME SHOOTING, Vol. IX).

As in the poultry trade, London is also the centre of the game trade. Buying and selling on Smithfield and Leadenhall markets fixes the day-to-day prices of game for the whole country. Prices sometimes change rapidly, as good or bad weather for shooting affects the ebb and flow of supplies.

There is not enough game in Britain to supply all her wants. Icelandic and Norwegian ptarmigan, Dutch wild duck, and Danish pheasants add to the supplies from abroad. All these importations play a part in the negotiation of trade agreements between Britain and other countries. Although rabbits are not strictly game, they form a sizeable British import from Australia; strains of domestic rabbits have also been developed there for the table.

Grouse are Britain's only export of game birds, since the British red grouse is not to be found anywhere else. The United States are willing buyers at all times. Britain once exported a large number of hares to France, but the trade declined with the advent of better prices for hare in this country.

See also Vol. VI: DUCKS; GEESE; POULTRY; TURKEY.
See also Vol. IX: GAME SHOOTING; DUCK SHOOTING.

PREFABRICATION, *see* Vol. VIII: PREFABRICATION.

PRESERVATION, FOOD, *see* Vol. XI: FOOD PRESERVATION.

PRICE, *see* VALUE AND PRICE; SUPPLY AND DEMAND.

PRIME COST, *see* COSTING, Section 2.

PRIMITIVE MONEY. 1. Aristotle, the Greek philosopher, summed up the four chief qualities of money some 2,000 years ago. It must be lasting, and easy to recognize, to divide, and to carry about. In other words, it must be 'durable, distinct, divisible, and portable'. When we think of money we picture it either as round, flat pieces of metal which we call coins, or as printed paper notes. But there are still parts of the world to-day where coins and notes are of no use: they will buy nothing, and a traveller might starve if he had no native 'money' to exchange for food.

A collection of primitive money from all parts of the world will show hundreds of different objects of differing materials, shapes, and sizes. There are the feather coils of the Santa Cruz Islands, the 'millstones' (some of them 10 to 12 feet high) from the Caroline Islands; the copper plates of British Columbia, the 'drums' of Indonesia, the 'tin hats' of Malaya, the brick tea and squirrel skins of Siberia, the boars' tusks of New Guinea, the dog, porpoise, or fish teeth of the Solomons, the silver 'fishhooks' of the Persian Gulf, or the 'mat-money' of West Africa, the New Hebrides, and Polynesia.

Among backward peoples, who are not reached by traders from outside, commerce usually means barter (*see* EXCHANGE AND TRADE). There is a direct exchange of fish for vegetables, meat for grain, or various kinds of food for pots, baskets, or other manufactured goods, and money is not needed. But there is often something that everybody wants and everyone can use, such as salt to flavour food, shells for ornaments, or iron and copper to make into tools and vessels. These things—salt, shells, or metals—are still used as money in out-of-the-way parts of the world to-day.

2. SALT. Salt seems a rather uninteresting thing to us. But it is rare in the inland parts of Africa, and wherever the food of the people is mainly vegetable there is a desperate craving for it. African carriers and road-makers are often paid in salt, which they can exchange for food in the markets, although some of the lump may be licked away before it gets there! Until recently salt bars were the ordinary money of Abyssinia, and bars of exact weights had definite values. Cakes of salt, stamped to show their value, were money in Tibet; and cakes of different sizes, worth from a penny to a shilling, still buy goods in Borneo.

3. SHELLS. Cowrie sea-shells have been used as money over the greater part of the Old World. They were collected mainly from the beaches of the Maldive Islands in the Indian Ocean, and were traded to India and China. Here they were used either singly as coins or, for larger sums, were weighed up into bags. In India, in the 19th century, they were accepted by traders in payment for goods, and by Government in payment of taxes. Four or five thousand went to the rupee (about 1*s.* 6*d.*) yet revenue

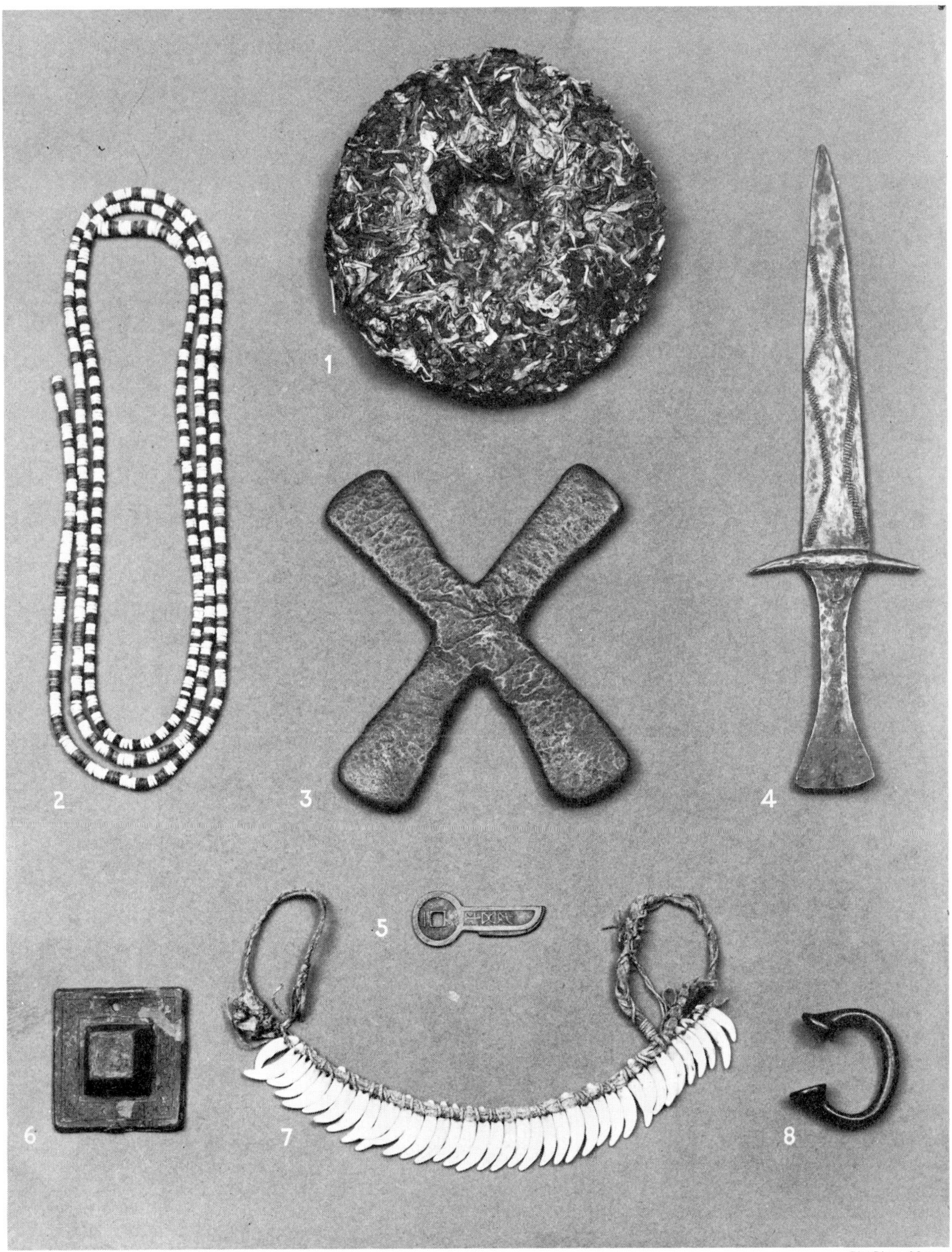

Pitt Rivers Museum

PRIMITIVE MONEY

1. Brick of tea made in Yunnan, China. 2. String of shell and coconut discs, New Guinea. 3. Copper ingot, Congo Free State. 4. Copper dagger, Congo Free State. 5. Knife, China. 6. Tin hat, Siam. 7. Dog's teeth necklace. 8. 'Manilla', West Africa (about $\frac{1}{3}$ size)

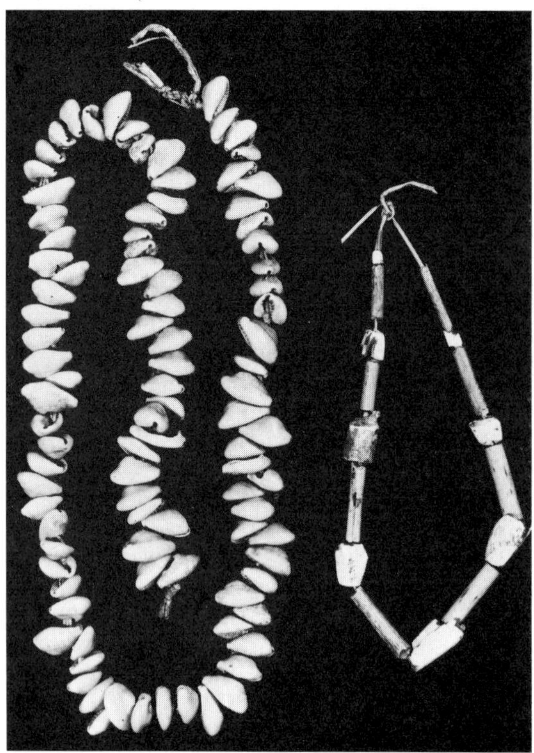

Pitt Rivers Museum

COWRIE SHELL MONEY FROM UGANDA (LEFT), AND A STRING OF BEADS, SHELLS, AND BAMBOO USED AS CURRENCY IN THE NAGA HILLS, ASSAM, INDIA

was still collected in cowries. Huge buildings were needed to store them, and fleets of boats to float them down river to Government headquarters, then at Calcutta.

In Africa cowries were traded right across the continent from east to west. The 'cowrie counter' was a necessary official in the Sudanese markets, where he had to count many thousands daily in fives, with fingers and thumbs. Four or five thousand went to the Maria Theresa dollar, an Austrian silver coin which had become accepted as currency in many parts of Africa. Cowries were used for large payments as well as small. When the Arabs brought the first cowries to Uganda they were so highly prized that two cowries were worth a woman, or four to five cows. But cowries very like the Indian ones could be picked up on the East African shores, and millions more were brought in by merchant ships. They soon became too common to be worth much in the market, and when small coins were introduced cowries were no longer used as money.

They lasted longer as money in West Africa. In Nigeria during the present century cowries could still be seen in the markets, although a thousand were worth only about sixpence; and a woman on her way to market, seeing a cowrie in the sand, would pick it up with her toes and add it to her store. In up-country districts, off the trade routes, cowries are still in use and the people often prefer them to coins.

In the islands of the Pacific Ocean, from New Guinea to New Caledonia, cowries are used here and there in place of money. In some inland parts they are very valuable, ten cowries being the price of a capable young woman or a full-grown pig in Dutch New Guinea, while many useful objects can be bought with a single shell of the right size and shape. Travellers tell of inland natives coming down as carriers to the coast and hunting for shells in the sand as eagerly as gold-miners hunt for lumps of gold.

But the native money of the Pacific islands is usually made of different shells which are broken up, ground down into disks, and threaded on strings like beads. The strings are sometimes short, in bunches; more often they are long, and measured by the fathom (6 ft.). They are usually made in the outlying islands where food is scarce, and used for trading with the mainland. They may be coarse or fine, and are of many colours. The red are usually more valued than the white (perhaps because the red shells are less common), and each island has its own preferences.

The best known shell money, the *diwarra* of New Britain in the Bismarck group of islands, is not strung. The little cowrie-like shells are pierced, and forced on to a stiff piece of cane. They are evenly spaced and do not touch each other; any desired number of shells can thus be counted and the cane broken off. *Diwarra* is used widely. A hundred to two hundred fathoms buy an expensive object such as a wife or a canoe, half a fathom buys a fowl, and only two or three shells have to be paid for a purchase of vegetables.

Wampum is an example of shell money from America, and it was used by the colonists as well as by the native Indians. Long cylindrical beads were cut out of white and purple clam shells (like oyster shells) and strung together; these strings were 'legal tender' (*see* MONEY). But when wampum began to be manufactured by the white man, who could make fifteen to twenty strings a day on a lathe, its value as money came to an end.

4. Metal. Metal, valued by weight, preceded coins in many parts of the world. Iron in lumps, bars, or rings is still used instead of money over parts of Africa. It can be exchanged for goods, or made into tools, weapons, or ornaments by the smith. West coast 'manillas', 'Kissie pennies', Congo spears, and Fan 'axes' are examples in collections of primitive money, and may still be seen sometimes in local markets. Copper crosses are used in place of, or together with, coins in the Congo and Zambia.

The early money of China, apart from shells, was of bronze, in the shape of spades, knives, hoes, and other familiar objects, and also in flat round disks with a hole in the middle, which we know as 'cash'. The date of the earliest of these is uncertain, but some are believed to be between 3,000 and 4,000 years old—older than the earliest coins of the eastern Mediterranean.

Metal lumps and bars formed the primitive money of prehistoric Europe before the coming of coins, although wealth was commonly counted in cattle or slaves, as in Greece in Homeric times. 'Currency bars' were of iron, copper, or bronze, and gold wings—sometimes in a series of definite weights—were used in trade as well as for gifts.

Greece in early times had its 'talents' of copper and bronze as well as of gold, and also rough lumps and bars, which could be broken in pieces. In the course of time these rough bits became more shapely, and when stamped may properly be called coins. These early examples, whether from the Greek island of Aegina or (as Herodotus reports) from the Lydian coasts of Asia Minor, are held to be the models from which European coinage is derived (*see* Coins).

In the civilized world coins and notes have taken the place of all the picturesque forms of primitive money. In the less civilized parts the beads, cloth, and tobacco of the trader are often preferred to the native money, and drive it out of use. Although it is still often hoarded for ceremonial occasions such as weddings and funerals, examples of primitive money will soon be found only in museums.

PRINTING. 1. This is a method of making many copies of a design which may consist of letters, words, and sentences, or of a picture or some sort of decoration. Whether the printing is used to produce books, newspapers, showcards, wallpaper, fabrics, wrappings for chocolates and tins of food, or any other use, the principle is the same—all printing is done from an inked pattern pressed on a prepared surface.

There are three main methods of printing—relief, intaglio, and planographic—each being distinguished by the different kind of surface used.

2. Relief Printing. This is the oldest and still the commonest way of printing books and newspapers (*see* Printing, History of, Vol. IV). A good example of a printing-surface in relief is a woodcut. In this the background has been hollowed out, leaving the lines of the design on a higher level, so that they are the only part of the wooden block capable of receiving ink and leaving their image (turned left to right) on paper pressed against it. Type for printing words is a number of metal castings reproducing letters cut in relief (*see* Printing-type).

The lines of type are generally set by composing-machines which cast type for the letters and arrange it in lines of the right length. Until 100 years ago all type-setting was done by hand; and it is best to understand hand type-setting before trying to grasp how composing-machines work.

A compositor working by hand sits in front of a pair of cases in which the type is laid, each letter and kind of space (thin, middle, thick, etc.) in a separate compartment, the capitals, small capitals, and accented letters in the upper case, and the small letters, figures, and spaces in the lower. He holds in his left hand a tool called a composing-stick adjusted to the length of his line. With his right hand he picks up letter after letter and fits it in his stick, following each word with a middle-sized space. When his line of letters and spaces has almost filled the stick, he has to consider whether to squeeze in one more word by changing the spaces for thinner ones, or to bulk out his line by using thicker spaces, or to divide the next word with a hyphen. Making the type exactly fill the line is called 'justifying'. When the compositor has set and justified as many lines as his stick will hold—about eight lines of type of medium size—he lifts them out of the stick and stands them in a 'galley', which is a small metal tray with sides rather lower than the type. He goes on composing until his galley is full; and then he secures the type against falling by putting strips of metal along the exposed sides, and inks the face of the type in order to print a galley-proof.

All the type needed for a book is generally set and kept standing in galleys until it has been proof-read and corrected by the printer's proof-reader and by the author. When the compositor is given corrected proofs he makes the necessary alterations to his type and proofs it again. When correcting is finished, the type is made up into pages with the addition of blocks for illustrations and type-set page headings and page-numbers; then it is proof-read again. When the pages are passed as correct, they are assembled and made into 'formes'.

A 'forme' is a unit of type and blocks to be printed on one side of a sheet. One forme may hold as many as 64 or even 128 pages at a time, though 16 or 32 are more usual. The pair of formes for the two sides of a sheet have to be planned and arranged so that the sheet, when it has been folded and cut, will give the pages in the right order. The type and blocks for each page make a rectangle surrounded by strips of wood or metal not high enough to print, and the whole forme is securely wedged in a steel frame so that it becomes rigid enough to be lifted up and carried about (*see* BOOK, Vol. IV).

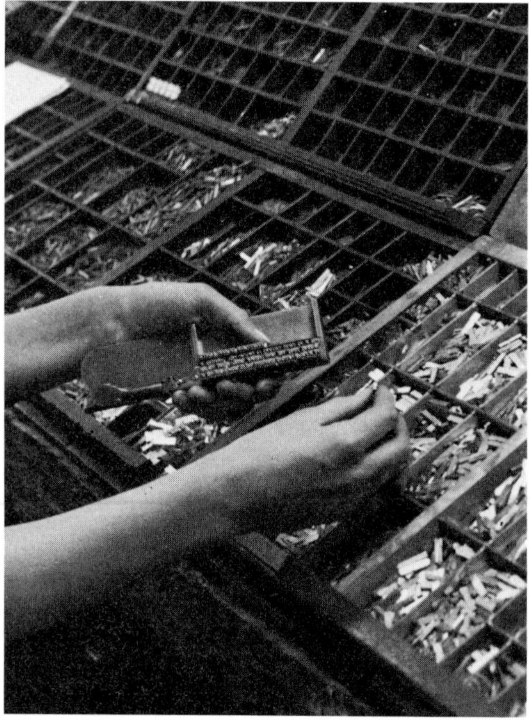

HAND COMPOSING

The compositor arranges the letters in the 'stick'

Oxford Jun. Ency. VII—17281J 169–12

THOUGH a veriety of opinions exist as to the individual by wrom the art of printing was first discovered; yet all authorities concur in admitting Peter Schoeffer to be the person who invented *cast metal types*, having learned the art of of *cutting* the letters from the Gut-tenbergs, he is also supposed to have been the first whoengraved on copper plates. The following testimony is preseved in the family, by Jo. Fred. Faustus of Ascheffenburg. Peter Schoeffer of Gernsheim, perceiving his master Fausts design, and being himself desirous ardently to improve the art, found out (by the good providence of God) the method of cutting (*incidendi*) the characters in a *matrix*, that the letters might easily be singly *cast* instead of bieng *cut*.'

THOUGH a variety of opinions exist as to the individual by whom the art of printing was first discovered; yet all authorities concur in admitting PETER SCHOEFFER to be the person who invented *cast metal types*, having learned the art of *cutting* the letters from the Gutenbergs: he is also supposed to have been the first who engraved on copper-plates. The following testimony is preserved in the family, by Jo. Fred. Faustus of Ascheffenburg.

'PETER SCHOEFFER of Gernsheim, perceiving his master Faust's design, and being himself ardently desirous to improve the art, found out (by the good providence of God) the method of cutting (*incidendi*) the characters in a *matrix*, that the letters might easily be singly *cast*, instead of being *cut*.'

THE CORRECTION OF PROOFS

Above, proof with corrections, and, below, corrected proof

In order that the forme may be rigid, all the lines of a page must be exactly equal in length, and any blanks, such as short lines at the ends of paragraphs, must be packed tightly with spacing material too low to show in the printing.

Mechanical typesetting replaces hand-work as far as the galley stage. In this country the Monotype machine is generally used for books. It has two parts: a keyboard instrument and a casting-machine. The keyboard instrument is worked like a typewriter and produces a reel of paper punched with holes; these control the operation of the casting-machine so that it not only casts type and spaces arranged in words but justifies the lines. The holes controlling the thickness of spaces are made after those for the letters; so the casting-machine begins at the end of the line and works backwards, learning first how thick to make the spaces.

Linotype and Intertype machines are used for newspapers and in some countries for most books. In these, keyboard and casting-apparatus are one machine. Tapping the keys releases 'matrices' (small pieces of metal containing a hollow mould of the letters required), and these fall into line. Words are separated by wedges, and justification is done by pushing in the wedges to make the line tight. The line of matrices is then cast as a single unit. This is much quicker than casting each letter separately, but correcting one letter in the line means re-making the whole line.

For centuries relief-printing was done on hand-operated presses with which two skilled men could print 250 sheets on one side every hour. Early in the 19th century, power-driven presses were introduced for printing small sheets, and machines were invented to print large sheets by rolling over the forme a cylinder to which the paper is gripped during printing. These machines carry the forme on a moving bed which takes it first to the inking-rollers and then under the cylinder. Books are generally printed on machines of this kind, which can make up to 3,000 impressions in an hour. A machine which keeps the cylinder continually printing works much faster; but it must have the forme curved to fit round a second cylinder. This so-called 'rotary printing' only became fully practicable when stereotyping was perfected. By this process a thin plate is cast reproducing the surface of the forme, and the plate is curved to fit the cylinder. Rotary machines printing reels of paper on both sides at once are used for newspapers and cheap books and magazines. These can produce as many as 70,000 copies an hour printed in two colours, folded, and made into batches of a given number.

A MONOTYPE KEYBOARD

The copy to be printed is on the left, and the paper punched by the striking of the keys is at the top

A MONOTYPE CASTER

The punched tape is at the back of the machine: the operator is examining the cast type

3. INTAGLIO PRINTING is a method of printing from images recessed instead of raised in the printing-surface. The simplest example is copperplate printing from an engraved or etched metal plate in which the lines have been cut out with a pointed tool or eaten out by acid. Engravers and etchers heat the plate and dab stiff ink into the lines. They have to wipe surplus ink off the surface; and they print by squeezing the plate with paper on it between the cylinders of a press made like a mangle (*see* ETCHING AND ENGRAVING, Vol. XII).

Photography and mechanical etching (*see* PROCESS REPRODUCTION, Section 4) made it possible to develop copperplate printing into 'photogravure', a quick way of multiplying photographed images, including those of such diverse things as paintings and pages printed from type. They are etched in cylinders made to fit in rotary machines. The process is used for large editions of illustrated booklets and leaflets: it is excellent for fine work in colours and for postage-stamps.

4. PLANOGRAPHIC PRINTING. Early lithographic prints were made on hand-worked presses from stones on which artists or copyists had drawn in greasy crayon or ink (*see* LITHOGRAPHY, Vol. XII). The use of lithography for commercial printing was enormously increased when it could be made to reproduce photographed images and adapted to fast rotary machines. It was found that metal sheets could be treated so that they repel water and take greasy ink in the same way as stone. The metal plates are easily bent to fit round cylinders.

Nearly all lithographic printing is done in two stages: first on india-rubber, and then from the rubber on paper. This is called 'offset' printing. The machines for it have a rubber-covered cylinder which, as it revolves, is continually taking inked impressions from the lithographic plates and depositing them on paper. This saves wear on the plates, and it is not necessary to use the very smooth paper needed for printing direct.

This kind of printing has great advantages. It produces clear impressions at high speeds; the plates cost less than cylinders for gravure and very much less than the type and blocks for relief printing, and are easy to store. A great deal of text set in type is now photographed and printed by lithography.

5. PHOTO-COMPOSITION. The use of type to make an impression on sheets of paper which are then photographed for lithographic, gravure, or relief printing is expensive. Type is heavy, bulky to store, made of expensive metals by highly skilled labour using expensive machines. So the tendency now is to dispense with it by developing photo-setting. Photo-composing machines build up words by photographing a letter at a time, space the words apart, and justify the lines. Prints of pages so assembled are used to make lithographic or gravure plates, or very finely etched blocks for printing in relief. Correction, which has proved to be the chief difficulty, is done by cutting a line out of the PHOTOGRAPHIC EMULSION (q.v. Vol. VIII) and putting in its place a strip of emulsion bearing the corrected line.

See also BOOKBINDING.
See also Vol. IV: PRINTING, HISTORY OF; BOOK; NEWSPAPER.

PRINTING-TYPE is a collection of small metal castings on each of which is formed in relief one of the letters, figures, and signs used in PRINTING (q.v.). Ornaments called 'printers' flowers' (Fig. 2), designed to be often repeated, are also cast as type. Type is cast in a mould fitted with a copper matrix in which the shape of a letter or other character has been struck with a punch or hollowed out with fine drills. As many castings as the printer may need are cast from each matrix. The type is made of a soft metal alloy, a compound of lead strengthened with antimony and tin. All type must be the same height so that it forms a level surface for printing; in England it is made almost one inch high (0·917 in.).

A complete set, or 'fount', of type contains all the letters and signs needed in one size and design: CAPITALS and SMALL CAPITALS, small letters, figures, punctuation marks, and signs:

ABCDEFGHIJKLMNOPQRSTUVWXYZ
ABCDEFGHIJKLMNOPQRSTUVWXYZ
abcdefghijklmnopqrstuvwxyz
æ œ & ff fi fl ffi ffl
1234567890.,;:(-)"!?[–]/+@&

FIG. 1

Some letters are used more than others; and a fount of 10,000 pieces of type for setting English, for example, has about 783 of e, 167 of m, 16 of z, and 36 of M. To adapt his fount for another language, say French or Spanish, the printer would have to get more of certain letters and add type for letters with accents.

The alphabets in Fig. 1 are called Roman. In addition founts of *Italic* and **Bold** alphabets are used, matching the Roman in size and to some extent in design. Italic type is so called because it imitates an Italian style of handwriting.

So that the Roman, Italic, and Bold letters may be set side by side and make perfectly even lines, the 'body' (Fig. 3) of each piece of type must be uniform. It is usually made just big enough to contain the heads and tails of the longest letters, such as *f* or Q, but sometimes type is cast on a body bigger than it need be in order to produce a space between the lines of a page. Printers measure the bodies of types in 'typographical points'; there are 72 points to an inch. The alphabets in Fig. 1 are cast with a body of 12 points; the letters used for this book are called '10- on 11-point', because they would fit on a 10-point body, but they have been cast on an 11-point body in order to leave a space of one point between the lines, which makes them easier to read.

TYPES OF VARIOUS BODIES

hj hj hj hj hj hj hj hj hj hj hj hj hj

72 pt 60 pt 48 pt 36 pt 24 pt 18 pt 14 pt 12 pt 10 pt 8 pt 6 pt 5 pt 4½ pt

SIX ROMAN TYPES OF DIFFERENT DESIGN

10 point CENTAUR

In a strict sence, a good Compositer need be no more than an English Scholler, or indeed scarce so much; for if he knows but his Letters and

10 point BEMBO

Characters he shall meet with in his Printed or Written Copy, and have otherwise a good natural capacity, he may be a better Compositer than

10 point PLANTIN

another Man whose Education has adorn'd him with Latin, Greek, Hebrew, and other Languages, and shall want a good natural Genius:

10 point PERPETUA

For by the laws of Printing, a Compositer is strictly to follow his Copy. *From* MOXON, 1683. In a strict sence, a good Compositer need be no more

10 point CALEDONIA

than an English Scholler, or indeed scarce so much; for if he knows but his Letters and Characters he shall meet with in

10 point GILL SANS

his Printed or Written Copy, and have otherwise a good natural capacity, he may be a better Compositer than another man whose

DECORATED

Bold sanserif *Brush Script*

RUSSIAN

АБГДЕФЖИIКЛМНОПЧР

HEBREW

אבגדהוזחטיכלמנסעפצקרתש

GREEK CAPITALS

Α Β Γ Δ Ε Ζ Η Θ Ι Κ Λ Μ Ν Ξ Ο Π

Ρ Σ Τ Υ Φ Χ Ψ Ω

FIG. 2. EXAMPLES OF TYPE FACES AND 'FLOWERS' (DESIGNS IN THE BORDER)

Types of many different sized bodies are used in printing. Twelve bodies are most commonly used, ranging from

type as small as this, which is 6 point

up to 72 point;

this is 24 point

Type larger than 72 point, used, for example, for posters, is carved out of wood. Italic founts are usually on bodies from 6 to 18 points.

There are many different designs of type, each with letters of characteristic shapes. The earliest founts, designed in the 15th century (*see* PRINTING, HISTORY OF, Vol. IV), copied the manuscripts of the period. In northern Europe most of them imitated late medieval handwriting and were what printers call **black-letter,** but some Italian printers preferred what we call Roman, based on an earlier form of the Latin written alphabet (*see* HANDWRITING, Vol. IV). Germans and Scandinavians continued to print mostly in Black Letter until recent times, but the other peoples of western Europe changed over to Roman between 1525 and 1600. Types for Roman and Italic vary in design. Some are copied from types used long ago by famous printers: examples are Centaur, based on a type made in 1468 by Nicolas Jenson, a French printer who worked in Venice; and Bembo, based on one used by the Venetian, Aldus Manutius, in 1495. Baskerville, the type used for this book, derives from one designed by an Englishman, John Baskerville, about 1750. Examples of modern designs are Perpetua and Gill Sanserif, designed by Eric Gill (1882–1940). Most types are designed to imitate penwork in having thick and thin strokes, and the tops and bottoms of the letters are finished with serifs. Gill Sanserif, and a few other modern designs, have all the strokes of the same thickness and no serifs (Fig. 3).

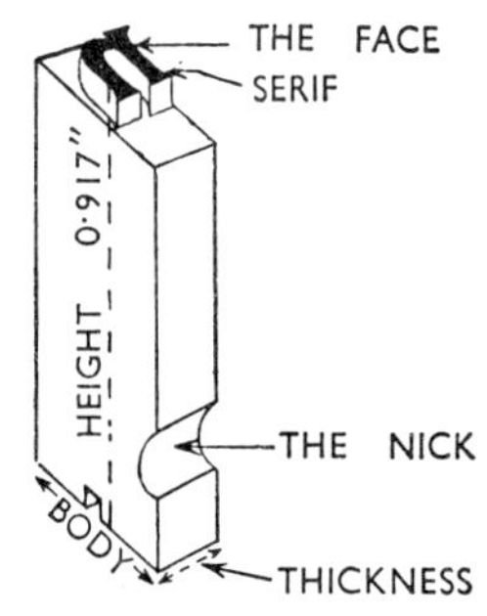

FIG. 3. A PIECE OF TYPE

The nick enables the compositor to feel which way up to set the letter

Printers generally have other styles of type besides Roman, Italic, and Bold, such as Black Letter, script, decorated—even typewriter. They may also need type for foreign alphabets, Hebrew, Greek, Russian, and hundreds more. The number of alphabets and designs for which type can be had is believed to be over 2,000.

See also PRINTING.

See also Vol. IV: PRINTING, HISTORY OF.

PROCESS REPRODUCTION. 1. This is the reproduction for printing purposes of various kinds of illustrations for newspapers, books, and posters. The term 'process engraving' is often applied to this, although other methods than engraving can be used. Designs or pictures are reproduced by three different basic methods, as described in PRINTING. They are: relief printing, in which the design stands up in relief; engraving or intaglio printing (after an Italian word first applied by jewellers to engraved gems), in which the design consists of grooves filled with ink; and lithographic or planographic printing, in which the printing is done from a smooth or plane surface, the design or picture being defined by chemical rather than mechanical means.

2. AUTOGRAPHIC PROCESSES. Apart from mechanical and photographic methods, printing surfaces for designs or pictures may be prepared autographically, that is, by the hand of the artist who composes the picture or design. Designs are engraved or cut in wood or metal or 'bitten' by acid into metal, or drawn on stone (*see* WOOD-ENGRAVING AND WOODCUTS, ETCHING AND ENGRAVING, LITHOGRAPHY, Vol. XII), and prints are taken from them in a printing-press. But work of this kind, done by hand, takes time and much skill; it is costly and otherwise unsuitable for commercial production in large quantities.

Although most modern methods of reproduction are based on photography, some autographic methods can be adapted for mass production. Wood engravings, for example, can be reproduced in large quantities if 'electrotypes' of the original are made of copper. A mould is made from the wood block in plaster softened by heat. After it has been cooled the block is withdrawn, and the mould sprayed with a solution of silver nitrate. It is then hung in a liquid solution through which an electric current is passed. In the same solution there is a piece of copper, and the current causes a layer of tiny particles of copper to be deposited on the surface of the silvered mould (*see* ELECTROLYSIS, Vol. VIII). Then the mould is taken out, and the thin copper layer or shell peeled from it. The

1.

2.

3.

1. HALF-TONE REPRODUCTION OF A LINE BLOCK. 2. PRINT FROM THE LINE BLOCK IN (1). 3. ENLARGEMENT OF THE HALF-TONE BLOCK FROM WHICH (1) IS PRINTED

copper shell is next backed by a softer metal and planed to produce a 'plate' of even thickness. It is then strong enough to be used for making many prints, and even larger numbers may be taken if a coating of nickel is deposited upon the copper face. In the same way, original engravings made by an artist on copper plates can be given a steel or nickel face.

3. Relief Processes. For most modern purposes, process engraving has taken the place of the older autographic methods. All designs to be reproduced fall into two broad classes: (*a*) those made up solely of lines and other solid areas of ink, such as pen-and-ink sketches, engineering drawings, and statistical diagrams; (*b*) those made up of tones, such as photographs and oil paintings, water-colour drawings, pastel sketches, and any other pictures or patterns which are mainly without sharp lines and which convey their effect by gradual changes of tone—some parts being white, some light grey, some darker grey, and some black. The first kind of design is printed from a line block, and the second kind from a half-tone block. Printers use the term 'block' for any surface of wood or metal from which an illustration is printed by the relief process.

(*a*) Line Blocks. To make a line block, the original black-and-white drawing is photographed, and a clear negative obtained (*see* Photography, Vol. IX). The negative is then photographically printed by strong artificial light on to a plate of polished zinc coated with a layer of emulsion sensitive to light. The light passes easily through the transparent parts of the negative (the dark lines of the original drawing), and, where it reaches the zinc plate, hardens the emulsion on it. The thick black parts of the negative (the white or blank parts of the original drawing) allow no light through, and so the emulsion underneath them on the zinc plate remains comparatively soft. The plate is then covered with ink and soaked in water, when the softer emulsion, which has not been affected by the light, dissolves. The plate, after being dried, is dusted with finely powdered resin, which sticks to the inked parts where the emulsion has not been dissolved. The plate is then put into a tank or bath of acid, and the parts unprotected by resin (representing the blank white parts of the original drawing) are etched or eaten away by the acid. Etching goes on until the etched parts of the plate have become fairly deep hollows. Thus, when printing takes place later, those parts will not be touched by the inked rollers, nor will they touch the paper that is being printed on (*see* Fig. 1).

(*b*) Half-tone Blocks. The method used for line blocks is not suitable for pictures with grey tones because it can print only black. For a half-tone block the original picture must be photographed through a 'screen'. A screen is prepared from two sheets of plate glass, each marked with extremely close parallel lines. There may be 100 lines or more to every inch in the glass. The two sheets are fixed at right angles to each other with transparent cement, forming a screen like trellis-work with tiny square 'windows' of glass. Each window may be only $\frac{1}{200}$th of an inch across. In that case there would be 40,000 dot-like windows to every square inch of the screen. Half-tone blocks in a newspaper will have a screen of 60 or 80 lines to the inch, that is to say, 3,600 to 6,400 windows to a square inch, while those in a book or art magazine will have 133 or more lines to the inch, making more than 17,000 windows to a square inch. This half-tone screen is placed in the camera in front of the photographic plate; the original picture is then illuminated and photographed through the screen. From those parts of the original which are dark in tone, very little light will pass through the square windows of the screen, and the photographic plate will be hardly affected. But where the original is pale in tone, the light will pass through the square windows. When the light passes through a window, it tends to fan out to form a cone; thus it reaches the photographic plate in the form of a round dot: the stronger the light, the bigger the dot. The sensitive, photographic emulsion on the plate will register these dots of varying sizes which will even run into each other where the light is strongest; in this way the plate or negative will show masses of nearly solid black where the original picture is lightest. The half-tones of the original will become smaller dots, varying from black to grey, and becoming smaller where the original is lighter. When the negative is developed, all these varying sizes of dots will be clearly seen: as, in fact, they can be seen if a magnifying glass is held over a newspaper photograph. From this negative a block or zinc plate is then prepared in the same way as for line blocks. That is to say, from the negative a 'positive' is photographically made in zinc, and this is etched in a bath of acid. Photographs make very good originals for half-tone blocks, particularly those on glossy paper.

4. Intaglio Processes. Photogravure is the only kind of printing from recessed surfaces that is done on a large scale. Rotary machines are used, and the image to be printed is etched on the surface of a copper cylinder. The first step in the process is to make two photographic prints, one of a very fine screen and one of the picture to be reproduced. The print of the screen is made in close contact, so that the light passing through forms squares, not circles as it does on half-tone blocks for relief printing. A combined print of the screen and the picture is made on a tissue coated with emulsion, which is stuck on the cylinder. The cylinder is then put into an etching bath so that the tissue is destroyed and the less resistant parts of the two prints are bitten into the copper. The effect of this process is to make the surface of the cylinder a network of crossing lines enclosing square cells of various depths.

Odhams Press

DRAWING ON A LITHOGRAPHIC STONE

On the right is a print taken from the stone

Three operations are essential in gravure printing: to ink the plate or cylinder, to wipe off ink, and to press the plate or cylinder against paper. The network of lines on a photogravure cylinder prevents the mechanical wiper from taking off too much ink. Printing transfers ink held in the cells to the paper; and the print is a close likeness of the original picture because the deeper cells produce darker tones and the shallower cells lighter ones. To some extent the process depends for success on the use of ink made of dyes in spirit which evaporates quickly, and an absorbent paper.

5. Planographic Processes. These are worked on the chemical principle that grease and water will not mix. The earlier lithographs were done on limestone, a porous stone which absorbs grease. The design was drawn direct on the stone by the artist, with a greasy black 'chalk' or with a pen and greasy lithographic ink. The stone was then moistened with water, and a roller of greasy printing-ink passed over it. This ink was absorbed by the greasy portions of the stone but it left no mark on the wet portion on which there was no design. From this stone numbers of sheets of paper could be printed. For modern lithographic work stones have now been replaced by thin pliable metal plates; these can be used in rotary presses, and are therefore suitable for rapid reproduction in large quantities. The image to be printed is put on to it photographically, as in the line and half-tone processes, and the process is called photo-lithography. Nearly all lithographic printing is done on 'offset' machines (*see* PRINTING, Section 4), the impression in the ink from the plate being made on rubber and transferred from the rubber to paper. This means that the print is not a reverse of the design on the plate as it is in the other processes.

Collotype is a process which has been developed from the water-and-grease principle of lithography. The image to be printed is photographically transferred to a film of hardened gelatine on a sheet of plate-glass. When water is applied, the 'light' parts of the image absorb more moisture than the dark parts. Then, when ink is applied, the driest parts take most ink and therefore print heaviest. Only about 1,500 copies can be taken from a collotype plate, but as no screen has to be used there is no dotted 'screen grain' on the prints, which come out as very faithful reproductions of the original. It is an ideal process for reproducing works of art. Collotypes can make very good colour copies.

6. COLOUR PRINTING. When a printer wants to print some lines on a page in red and others in black, he makes up a forme of type for black and another for red and prints one after the other on the same sheet. The same principle may be employed in reproducing illustrations using only a few colours. A block or plate is made from a drawing for each of the colours used, and the blocks are then printed one over another in inks matching the colours of the original. By making many drawings and blocks it is possible to print a fair reproduction of a painting in mixed colours or even of a colour-photograph, so long as the successive impressions are made to fit accurately.

It is cheaper, however, to reproduce such things by a 'panchromatic' (all-colour) process using photography to separate the colours. The original illustration is photographed in turn through three different colour 'filters', one for each of the primary colours of light—green, red, and violet (*see* colour plate, Vol. III facing p. 96). Each filter cuts out its complementary colour; a positive print is made which shows only those places where the complementary colour was in the original. Three half-tone blocks are made to be printed in the primary colours of pigment—magenta-red, blue-green (called 'cyan'), and yellow—one over another to build up a single print which gives approximately the 'all-colour' effect. The print in three colours is often overprinted with another block for black ink to make the shadows darker (*see* colour plate, opposite p. 368).

See also PRINTING; ENGRAVING.
See also Vol. IV: ILLUSTRATION.
See also Vol. IX: PHOTOGRAPHY.

PRODUCTION. 1. THEORETICAL. The economic life of mankind depends upon the production of goods and services. To produce either of these things, use must be made of land and human labour, and also of at least a modest amount of CAPITAL (q.v.) with which to buy tools and raw materials. Moreover, as all except very primitive production depends on teamwork by several people, there must be someone to manage or co-ordinate production. Land, labour, capital, and management are therefore the four things concerned in practically all production, and economists call them 'the factors of production'. To the manager or co-ordinator of any act of production, economists have given the technical name 'entrepreneur', which is a French word from which comes the English word 'enterprise'.

Just as so many processes in industry depend on the correct mixture of ingredients, so efficiency of production depends very much upon

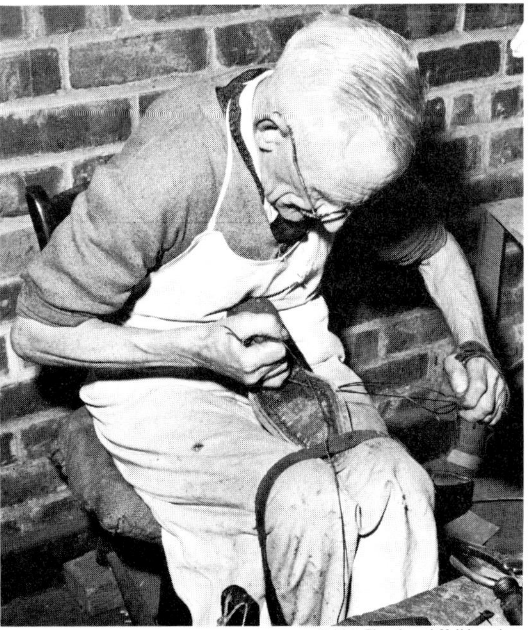

British Travels and Holidays Assn.

JOB PRODUCTION: THE HAND CRAFTSMAN

A shoemaker sewing on the welt of a shoe

Ekco Radio and Television Ltd.

RADIOS BEING ASSEMBLED ON CONTINUOUSLY MOVING ASSEMBLY LINES

the way in which the quantities of land, labour, and capital are combined or mixed together. The most efficient mixture or combination—called by economists the optimum (or best) combination of the factors of production—is that which reduces the cost of production to the lowest possible figure. At any given moment the best combination depends on the price of each 'factor'. At certain times, land may be relatively more expensive than capital or labour. For example, in some countries land and labour are plentiful and cheap, but capital is scarce and can be borrowed only at a very high rate of INTEREST (q.v.). Such countries use much land and labour, and very little machinery. Other countries may find it more profitable to make great use of capital and to reduce the amount of labour to a minimum. One such country is the U.S.A., where the WAGES (q.v.) of labour are extremely high, and capital reasonably cheap because the people are well off and much money is saved. In the amount of machinery used Britain does not approach the U.S.A., but she is far ahead of many other countries of the world.

2. PRACTICAL. In a practical sense production takes three forms: job production, batch production, and continuous or mass production. 'Job production' means producing a single article, usually specially ordered: for example, a suit from a West End tailor, or an architect-designed house from a builder. SHIP-BUILDING (q.v.) is mainly job production. 'Batch production' is, as the name suggests, the production of a batch of articles, all of the same type, size, and design. Production in the textile industries, for example, is often batch production, certain weaves or patterns of cloth being run through the loom for days on end. Batch production is naturally cheaper than job production. 'Continuous production' may take two forms. Production of pig-iron in a steel-works, or of glass in a glass factory, is truly continuous, because work goes on during the whole 24 hours and only ceases for a time when furnaces have to be relined or repaired. The term is often applied, however, to continuous production of the same pattern—for instance, in the MOTOR INDUSTRY (q.v.)—although work is interrupted at the end of the usual 8-hour day. There is continuous production of models of the same type, and the work moves from worker to worker and process to process, often along a conveyor (*see* FACTORY ORGANIZATION). 'Flow production' is another and perhaps better term for this kind of production. 'Mass production' is a term in common use for what is very often merely line or continuous production. Strictly, the term should be used only for such production at a rapid rate and on an immense scale.

See also LABOUR; FACTORY ORGANIZATION.

PRODUCTION COSTS, *see* COSTING, Section 1.

PROFIT SHARING, *see* CO-PARTNERSHIP; PROFITS; WAGES.

PROFITS. Profits are normally taken to be the difference between cost and selling price, and they may be stated 'gross' or 'net'. Cost includes not only the actual purchase price of the goods, but the expense of their being taken to the WAREHOUSE (q.v.), any customs duties or taxes, and the wages bill and expenses for unloading and arranging the goods in the warehouse. Gross profit is the difference between what the goods have cost and what is received from their sale. Net profit is gross profit less all the 'overhead' expenses (*see* COSTING) such as ADVERTISING, travellers' COMMISSION, and office salaries (qq.v.). A manufacturer usually makes a distinction between his profit on manufacture and his profit on trading.

To the economist, profit is what is left to the owners of any business after they have paid for land and labour (rent and wages), and INTEREST on borrowed CAPITAL (qq.v.). Profit to the economist is, therefore, much the same thing as the merchant's or manufacturer's net profit. If profits are made, they are the reward to the owners for successfully taking on the risks of production. In modern business, which is conducted mainly by LIMITED COMPANIES (q.v.), the owner who assumes the risks of trading or manufacturing is really the body of persons holding ordinary shares, whose DIVIDEND (q.v.) fluctuates with the profits earned.

See also ECONOMICS; BOOK-KEEPING; COSTING.

PROMISSORY NOTE, *see* BILLS OF EXCHANGE.

PROSPECTUS, *see* ISSUING HOUSES.

PROTECTION OF CONSUMER. When a customer buys goods in a shop he is protected by the law against certain frauds. It is illegal, for example, for shopkeepers and manufacturers to sell unhygienic food, or to give short measure, or to make false statements on labels. In all other matters, *caveat emptor*—the customer must look after himself, and see for himself that he gets what he pays for.

Until recently, this was fairly easy to do. Goods were made from only a few materials, all well-known and easy to judge. When a housewife bought a sheet, she could tell by feeling it whether it was made of linen or cotton and whether the quality was good or bad. But now in nearly every range of commodity there are many materials to choose from. In household equipment, for example, the development in such things as SOAPS AND DETERGENTS, PLASTICS, and synthetic TEXTILE FIBRES (qq.v.) has been so vast that it is not easy even for shopkeepers themselves to know the quality of the goods they sell.

Customers throughout the world felt that they needed more protection than the law afforded them. In 1928 a number of shop-goers in the U.S.A. formed an association which used the subscriptions from its members to buy goods and to examine, test, and report on them. If they bought an electric iron, for instance, and found it unsafe, they said so, giving the name of the iron. If they bought six kinds of soap and found that, though all of the same quality, two were cheaper than the others, they said so. In this way customers had the opportunity of learning in advance the real value of the goods offered them in shops.

In Sweden, Norway, and Denmark, the Government took on this job of protecting the consumer by financing institutes to advise shoppers. These institutes not only do a certain amount of testing and reporting on goods, but also deal with complaints and help manufacturers to improve their goods.

There are now organizations of consumers, independent or supported by the Government, in many other countries including Holland, Belgium, Israel, New Zealand, Jamaica, and Japan. In Britain, shoppers can obtain information from the independent Consumers' Association, the government-financed Consumer Council, and, in some places, local consumer groups and local authority-sponsored information centres. Citizens'

Advice Bureaux help with complaints, while the British Standards Institution sets certain, mostly voluntary, standards for consumer goods.

The privately organized Consumers' Association, founded in 1957, has over half a million subscribers to its monthly magazine *Which?* Financed entirely by the sales of its publications, it carries out comparative tests on goods and services, distinguishing between what is good value for money, what is satisfactory, and what is not. It also presses for improvements in consumer protection at every level.

In 1959, the British Government set up the Molony Committee to consider changes in the law for the protection of the consumer. Parliament, at their instigation, established the Consumer Council to investigate the consumer's further protection, and extra money was given to the Citizens' Advice Bureaux to deal with complaints. The Trade Descriptions' Act of 1968 prohibited false or misleading descriptions of goods for sale, of facilities available, and of their prices; it is now illegal to claim that goods are reduced in price, if they are not.

PROVISION TRADE, *see* GROCERY AND PROVISIONS.

PUBLIC UTILITY COMPANIES. These provide services such as gas and electricity, necessary to all the inhabitants of a city or area. To carry out their business they have to have powers to interfere with the private rights and property of ordinary citizens; and so most public utilities are not ordinary LIMITED COMPANIES (q.v.) but are incorporated by special Acts of Parliament. Before NATIONALIZATION (q.v. Vol. X) the railways were a good example of public utility companies, for in order to lay their tracks they had to be given compulsory powers to acquire land. Similarly gas, electricity, and water undertakings have to break up public and private roads to lay their mains; when the 'grid' electricity system was organized (*see* POWER STATIONS, Vol. VIII), the Central Electricity Board had to be given permission to carry overhead cables across the countryside. Most public utilities possess a MONOPOLY (q.v.), having been given exclusive rights in their areas by Acts of Parliament. It would be an impossible situation, for instance, if roads were constantly being broken up by a succession of competing gas companies.

Some public utilities are national: the British BROADCASTING CORPORATION (q.v. Vol. IV) is an example. Others are local: of these the best examples are the dock authorities, such as the Port of London Authority and the Mersey Docks and Harbour Board. Another local public utility is the Thames Conservancy, which is responsible for the Thames from Teddington Lock upwards. The majority of local public utilities (which are not usually referred to as 'companies') obtain their capital by successive issues of BONDS or DEBENTURES bearing fixed rates of INTEREST, or of STOCK entitling the holders to DIVIDENDS payable out of earned profits (qq.v.). But there are some utilities which adopt the ordinary limited-company method of finance: that is, they have a fixed authorized capital.

When consumers have to buy their services from a monopoly, they are largely at its mercy, because it has no competitors to whom they might go if dissatisfied. So the parliamentary charters of public utilities usually contain restrictions which enable the State to look after the interests of the public. Sometimes maximum charges or rates are laid down, and these must not be exceeded without reference to a Minister, or to some neutral body such as (in the days before nationalization) the Railway Rates Tribunal. A maximum rate of dividend is often fixed, and this can only be exceeded if the price of the service concerned is lowered at the same time.

A nationalized or State-owned industry is simply a public utility on a grand scale. The National Coal Board, formed in January 1947, is the largest public utility in Great Britain at the present time. The greatest in the U.S.A. is the T.V.A., or TENNESSEE VALLEY AUTHORITY (q.v. Vol. VIII), which was organized by President Franklin Roosevelt's administration as part of the unemployment relief programme in the great period of depression which preceded the Second World War. This was an immensely ambitious scheme of development for a vast tract of land in the Southern States of the U.S.A., including among much else the buildings of great dams and electric power-stations, and the reclamation of hundreds of thousands of acres for agriculture and forestry. (*See* SOIL EROSION, Vol. III.)

See also COMPANIES.
See also Vol. X: NATIONALIZATION.
See also Vol. VIII: POWER STATION.

COLOUR PRINTING: FLOWER PIECE BY PAUL GAUGUIN

The four-colour print in the centre is made from the four surrounding blocks. The yellow is printed first, then red over it (bottom left), then blue (bottom right). Finally, the black gives the finished print

THE AUTHOR AND HIS PUBLISHER

By gracious permission of H.M. the Queen

A satirical drawing by Thomas Rowlandson (1756–1827)

PUBLISHING. It is only recently that publishing became a separate trade. Early publishers (for example, the existing firms of Longmans and John Murray, both founded in the 18th century) opened up as booksellers, but later found it profitable to arrange for the publication of works of their own choice. The trade in books is now shared by the publisher, the printer and binder (who are often firms distinct from one another), and the bookseller; each of these is an independent branch of the trade. The publisher takes the commercial risk on the production of the book; the printer prints the book to the publisher's order; and the bookseller distributes it to the buying public. There are both wholesale and retail booksellers. The wholesale booksellers receive a larger discount than the retailers, because they buy in big quantities and supply the smaller booksellers and newsagents with whatever books they may require, from their own stores.

Some books are written by their authors in the hope that a publisher may be found for them; many are 'commissioned', or ordered by publishers themselves. The creation of a book is described in detail in the article Book in Vol. IV. In the early days of publishing, publishers usually bought authors' works outright for a lump sum, which very often was extremely small. It has been said that Milton received only £5 for *Paradise Lost.* The usual arrangement nowadays is for the publisher to finance the production of the book and to pay the author a percentage Royalty (q.v.) on the sales. But sometimes authors, or in these days more often institutions, merely use publishers as Agents (q.v.) for the production and distribution of their works, the publisher merely receiving a Commission (q.v.) on the sales. For many years George Bernard Shaw arranged for the publication of his own works in this way.

When a publisher has decided to publish a

work, he signs the contract with the author, and usually instructs a firm of printers to produce the actual book. Some publishers print their own works, but these are few. After batches of the book have been bound in quantities decided by the publisher (*see* BOOK-BINDING), they are distributed to firms of booksellers. Until 1900, when a Net Price Agreement was signed, there was much under-selling and price-cutting among retail booksellers. This agreement laid down that every book should be sold at the exact price which had been decided by its publisher and advertised by him, and not at any lower price, and that publishers would not supply books to retailers who refused to sign the agreement. The Net Price Agreement was largely due to the persuasion of two large firms in the trade, Dent and Macmillan. Dent's brought out the 'Everyman's Library' series, originally sold at a shilling a copy, and were the pioneers of the modern cheap book. Within a few years the principle of the net price became generally accepted, and is still upheld. Although Resale Price Maintenance has recently been abolished in most trades, the Restrictive Practices Court judged it in the public interest that the book trade should retain it.

Announcements of books which are due to be published are made in *The Bookseller*, which is the trade journal of the publishing world. These announcements contain what is known as the 'blurb', or the publisher's own opinion of the merits and attractions of his books. These announcements are usually made before the books are printed, and publishers are prepared to take orders from booksellers immediately. Such orders are called 'subscription orders', and booksellers who give the orders receive a larger share of the selling-price, as they are then to some extent sharing the risk of production with the publisher. The average share or 'discount' allowed to the bookseller ranges between 17½% to 35% according to the type of book and circumstances.

Publishing is a highly speculative business. First novels, by unknown authors, are the most speculative books of all, and one in nine is unprofitable. No one has yet discovered what it is that makes a 'best-seller', and those publishers who bring out best-sellers are fortunate. Most publishers bring out a mixture of profitable and unprofitable books. Some books, such as expensive and scholarly works with a limited appeal, are almost certain to be unprofitable, but as their publication adds to a publisher's reputation, he is often prepared to bring them out, and to cover his loss by his profit on more popular works. Unsuccessful books are often 'remaindered' when sales have dropped to a low figure: that is, the unsold copies are sold in bulk, usually at a very low price; they are then often 're-pulped' to make new clean paper from them (*see* PAPER-MAKING).

Book publishing is not only a speculative trade, but is also one of the first to suffer when bad times come, for books seem to be one of the first things on which people economize.

Publishers' costs are almost impossible to set out in a hard-and-fast way, as they vary so much with types of books and even individual books, and with different editions of one book. Broadly speaking, it may be said of a new book with a moderate sale that about a third of the price paid by the public is kept by booksellers, about a quarter is paid by the publisher for printing, binding, and warehousing, and the remainder is left for advertising, for the general working expenses of the publisher's office, for his own profit, and for the author's royalty.

There are other methods of distributing books than through booksellers. Very expensive books, such as some encyclopaedias, may be sold directly to the public, either by newspaper- or direct-mail advertising, or by a salesman going from door to door. Another method is the Book Club, which distributes to its members through the post books that are likely to have general popularity.

See also PRINTING; BOOK-BINDING.
See also Vol. IV: BOOK.

PUNCHED CARD SYSTEM, *see* ACCOUNTING, MACHINE.

Q R

QUICKSILVER, *see* MERCURY.

QUOTAS. A quota (which is a Latin word meaning proportion) is a means used by governments to protect home producers of goods against foreign competition. For example, British flour mills may be ordered by the government to mill a quota of 40% of English wheat in every 100 tons of wheat they mill. Or the importation of foreign steel may only be allowed up to 80% of the total imported in some previous year. Quotas have the effect of giving the home producer an assured sale for his goods, or of so limiting the quantity of imports from abroad that his interests cannot be damaged.

During and after the Second World War, quotas were used as a means of rationing certain things that were very scarce. For example, public-houses, wine merchants, and hotels were restricted to a quota of the whisky supplies that they had been receiving in 1939.

RADIO-CHEMICAL INDUSTRIES, *see* Vol. VIII: RADIO-ACTIVE ISOTOPES.

RAILWAYS, *see* INDUSTRIAL REVOLUTION; TRANSPORT; CLEARING HOUSES; *see also* Vol. IV: RAILWAY SYSTEMS; RAILWAYS, HISTORY OF.

RATES OF EXCHANGE. In the days before bank-notes and banking accounts became general, money used to be made of gold or silver; and, although coins of one country would not usually circulate in another country, they could always be melted down and recoined. So the 'rate of exchange' between one country's money and another's would be roughly the ratio of the weights of gold or silver in their coins; and the rate of exchange between any two moneys made from the same metal would only alter whenever one of the countries altered the weight of metal in its standard coin.

Nowadays there are few countries with their standard money in the form of coins made of the precious metals; most money today is made of paper. The rate of exchange between the paper moneys of two countries depends mainly upon the purchasing power of the money within its own country. Trade is, of course, the main reason why paper money is exchanged between citizens of different nations. Obviously the value put upon the money will vary according to what it will buy in the way of goods and services. If, for instance, owing to the raising of all wages and costs, the prices of all goods in a certain country became double what they were before, then the value of that country's money would be halved in the eyes of another country whose prices had remained steady. If wages and costs remain steady in two countries, the rate of exchange between the two paper moneys will settle down at a figure at which one country's money will buy in the other country roughly the same as it will buy at home. The reason statesmen so dislike rising wages and costs is that these always make their own country's money worth less in other countries.

Rates of exchange are arranged between dealers in the foreign-exchange market, and are simply the prices at which the brokers acting for the banks find themselves able to buy and sell. Rates of exchange are quoted each day in certain newspapers—but not always in a very clear manner. If the rate for American dollars is quoted as being $2{\cdot}39\frac{7}{8}$–$40\frac{1}{8}$, it means that a person having pounds and wanting to buy dollars would receive $2{\cdot}39\frac{7}{8}$ for each £, and a person with dollars wanting to buy pounds would pay $2{\cdot}40\frac{1}{8}$ for each £. But the rate of exchange between London and Ceylon might be quoted the opposite way round—as 1*s.* $4\frac{15}{16}$*d.* —1*s.* $5\frac{1}{16}$*d.* per rupee. This means that a person with sterling who is a buyer of rupees would have to pay 1*s.* $5\frac{1}{16}$*d.* for each rupee, while a buyer of sterling with rupees would only get 1*s.* $4\frac{15}{16}$*d.* for every rupee.

The two prices quoted are the market's buying and selling prices, and the difference between them is the market dealer's profit.

Sometimes the governments of States take action to 'peg' or fix a rate of exchange at some desired level. This is described in the article on CURRENCY CONTROL in Vol. X.

See also INDEX, p. 98.

RAYON, *see* TEXTILE FIBRES, MAN-MADE.

RECEIPT, *see* INVOICE.

REFINING is a word used to describe many different industrial processes. In metallurgy it means purifying or separating metals from dross or dirt or other unwanted matter; converting impure metals, such as pig-iron or unrefined copper, into a purer form; and separating a metal from an alloy or mixture of two or more metals, as for example the separation of silver from lead. The term is also used for any process of purifying or clarifying a substance: for example sugar (*see* SUGAR REFINING), or fats for MARGARINE (q.v.). It is also applied to the series of processes by which crude mineral oil is converted into petrol, paraffin, and other products (*see* OIL REFINING).

See also ASSAYING.

REFRIGERATION, *see* COLD STORAGE; *see also* Vol. VIII: REFRIGERATOR.

REPRESENTATIVES. This is the modern term for 'commercial travellers'. The word is also used for any person acting on behalf of his own employer, even if he is selling nothing; thus, an insurance company may send round its 'representative' to inspect the wreckage of the sitting-room carpet after an accidental fire. This article deals with representatives concerned with the sale of goods.

The sales representative is the spear-head of the manufacturer's marketing organization. Although his efforts are supported by advertising, packaging, brochures, and other selling aids, it is usually he who must finally persuade the customer to buy.

Today greater efforts are made to train the sales representative and to plan his task more scientifically. Market research can help a firm to assess which calls will be worthwhile for their representatives. In this way greater efficiency and economy are achieved, because unprepared calls are eliminated, and all the efforts of representatives are guided towards those outlets which offer the best prospects. Such planning is all the more necessary since consumers tend to buy more and more from supermarkets and chain-stores and other large organizations (*see* RETAIL TRADING). The smaller retail outlets are therefore increasingly served by wholesalers and other intermediaries.

Each sales representatives has his own defined territory to cover. He must be carefully briefed by the regional or head-quarters manager on the product and its performance, and on the advertising and promotion plans. Moreover, in marketing products such as computers and machine-tools, the representative needs enough technical knowledge to allow him to negotiate with specialist clients at managerial or even Government level. Similarly, a sales representative working in the expanding export market needs a knowledge of the appropriate foreign language.

Sales representatives who are directly employed by a manufacturer will normally be paid a basic salary with an important additional COMMISSION (q.v.) or bonus, which is based on the sales achieved. Representatives are also paid expenses, or a fixed monthly travelling allowance. Free-lance representatives, whose earnings consist entirely of commissions earned on sales made for one or more suppliers, are declining in numbers. Such a free-lance representative is really a travelling AGENT (q.v.).

See also AGENT; BROKER; BUSINESS ORGANIZATION; MARKET RESEARCH.

RESINS, *see* GUMS AND RESINS.

RESTAURANTS, *see* CATERING INDUSTRY.

RETAIL TRADING. This is the branch of commerce which distributes goods into the hands of the people who finally buy them. Retail trade is not restricted to actual shops. Everybody who sells goods to the final customer is a retail trader. Kerbstone men, hawkers, and barrowmen (*see* PEDLARS AND HAWKERS) also are retail traders just as much as the shopkeeper himself.

Modern retail trade includes those firms—prominent in the U.S.A.—that specialize in selling by post direct from their warehouses to the public (*see* MAIL-ORDER TRADING). One branch of retail trade includes canvassers who pay personal visits with their firms' wares to the homes of people to whom they hope to sell. Another branch includes automatic delivery-machines, better known as 'slot machines';

15TH-CENTURY SHOPS

Painting from the manuscript *Les Chroniques de Jérusalem*

when a coin is inserted, a tray is released, and a small packet of some foodstuff or other commodity can be drawn out.

All the same, shopkeeping is the branch that distributes most goods. Shopkeeping has always been necessary since man gave up a wandering life, settled down to agriculture, and began to live in villages and towns. As the population has increased, the number of shops has too. It is probable that in the United Kingdom there is now one shop for every eighty people, or putting the average family at four people, there is one shop for every twenty families. There might seem to be too many, but this figure covers all kinds of shops, including the very small ones.

Shops may be classified as specialist shops, selling a single line of goods, and compound shops, selling a variety of different goods. On the whole, the tendency today is for specialist shops to decrease and compound shops to increase. Even butchers' shops now mostly also sell poultry, tinned soups and vegetables, sauces, stuffings, and other sundries which formerly had to be bought elsewhere. But certain trades still keep to the specialist shop, in particular the boot and shoe, jewellery, and furniture trades. Craftsmen's shops, run by electricians, plumbers, and painters and decorators, sell materials for anybody to buy and use, but they also offer the trained services of the craftsman proprietor or manager, or of his assistants.

Shops may also be classified, not by the goods they sell, but by the type of shop that sells them: the small personal or family business, the chain store or MULTIPLE SHOP, and the DEPARTMENT STORE or co-operative store (qq.v.). In Britain the most numerous type of shop is the small personal business, staffed by the proprietor and his wife and family, with perhaps one or two paid outside assistants if the business grows. Between the small family business and the multiple shop comes the small local chain of shops; this may have grown up because a single parent shop has done so well where it was first opened that its owner has opened other branches nearby on which he can keep a personal eye. There are many more of these small local chains than is generally realized. The pattern of retail trade is changing fast. Multiple shops, often of the self-service type, are increasing both in numbers and in their share of the trade, particularly in foodstuffs, footwear, and medicines. Private shops are declining in number somewhat faster than the multiples increase, because the latter are larger. In some trades, particularly grocery, private shopkeepers have formed co-operative buying groups in order to compete with the multiples.

It is fairly easy to set up a shop; less easy to succeed. Moreover, the qualities which ensure success in a small shop may be unsuitable

AN EARLY 19TH-CENTURY DRAPER'S SHOP

Meade Collection

for managing a big one. Statistics show that in no branch of British commerce is the percentage of business failures or bankruptcies so great as in retail trading. There are many risks involved in opening a new shop. There are often right and wrong streets, and even a right and a wrong side of the same street. Wrongly sited shops may do a reasonable business, but may not handle a sufficiently large TURNOVER (q.v.) of goods to enable them to buy goods cheaply from manufacturers and WHOLESALERS (q.v.), who will only cut prices for those who can place big orders. Retailers compete in price, in the services they provide, and in the range of stocks they carry. Price competition is now rather more important than in the past, because it is now illegal, in most trades, for manufacturers to fix retail prices. For many classes of goods, therefore, retailers now try to increase their turnover by charging attractive prices.

See also SELF-SERVICE STORES; DEPARTMENT STORES; MULTIPLE SHOPS; WHOLESALE TRADING.

ROPE-MAKING. 1. HISTORICAL. No one knows who first twisted strips of hide, hair, or other materials to make rope. References occur in the Bible and in classical histories. Crude ropes were used in China about 2700 B.C., and early followers of BUDDHISM (q.v. Vol. I) used ropes made of women's hair while building temples. In the tombs of ancient Egyptian kings ropes have been found made of flax, date-palm fibre, halfa grass, bulrushes, and camel-hair. The most ancient rope yet discovered was found in an Egyptian tomb, and is now in the Cairo Museum in an almost perfect state of preservation. It is made of flax, and is about 5,200 years old.

The ropes made in ancient times, though crude, were constructed on the same principles of twist balance that operate today. The balance is obtained by reversing the direction of twist of each component of the rope: for example, rope yarn twisted right hand, strand twisted left hand, and rope twisted right hand.

Ropes were being made commercially in Britain 500 years ago, and until the second half of the 19th century they were still being made by hand, in long narrow outdoor alleys called 'rope-walks'. One man, with the raw fibre wound round his waist would walk backward down the rope-walk, often a third of a mile long, paying out and twisting together small quantities of fibre, which he gauged for grist by the touch of his fingers. The rope yarns so formed were attached to hooks on a wheel at one end of the rope-walk and this wheel, turned by a man or a boy, formed the rope yarn into strands and ultimately into rope. Rope-walks are still in use, but are now indoors, and the process is a mechanical one.

2. Raw Materials. The basic material for rope-making is fibre; before the introduction of man-made fibres in the 1940s, only vegetable fibres were available. There are two main types, known as soft and hard, and almost all are long fibres. Soft fibres are hemp, cotton, flax, and jute (*see* Fibre Crops, Vol. VI), the principal one being hemp (*Cannabis sativa*), a bast or stalk fibre, grown in many parts of the world. The highest quality is cultivated in Italy; crops are also grown in Southern and Eastern Europe, India, and the U.S.A.

Hard fibres are manila, sisal, henequen, New Zealand hemp, and coir; with the exception of coir, all are leaf fibres. Manila (*Abaca* or *Musa textilis*) is obtained from a plant of the banana type, which is a native of the Philippine Islands, although plantations have been developed in Central America, Borneo, and some other tropical locations. Sisal (*Agave sisalana*) is obtained from a spiny, prickly plant, that comes mainly from East Africa and Brazil. Henequen (*Agave fourcroydes*) comes from a plant resembling sisal, grown mainly in Mexico, and mainly used there and in the U.S.A. New Zealand hemp (*Phormium tenax*), obtained from a plant native to New Zealand, is also grown in St. Helena; it resembles sisal, but is rather whiter, for sisal has a brownish tinge. Coir (*see* Coconuts, Vol. VI) is made up of very short fibres spun into yarns. The fibres are obtained from coconut husks, in India, Ceylon, and the Philippines.

Today man-made fibres are the commonest rope-making materials because of their high strength, low weight, and their resistance to rot and mildew and to certain chemicals. The principal fibres are nylon (polyamide), terylene (polyester), polypropylene, and polyethylene (polythene). Nylon and terylene yarns for rope-making are usually spun as continuous filament, with many fibres twisted together to make multi-filament (*see* Textile Fibres, Man-made). Polypropylene may take the form of single-thread continuous yarn (monofilament), or staple fibre, or plastic film, broken up (or fibrillated) into many small fibres. Polyethylene is normally used in monofilaments.

The comparative properties of the main rope-making materials are given below. Taking manila, grade 1, as equivalent to 100%, the relationship of weight and strength is shown:

Materials	*Weight Comparison*	*Breaking Load Comparison*	*Melting points*
Manila (grade 1)	100	100	Do not melt, but
Sisal; manila (grade 2)	100	88	char at 150° C.
Nylon	93·5	250	250° C.
Terylene	115	200	260° C.
Polypropylene	65	167	165° C.
Polyethylene	71	133	135° C.

3. Manufacture. For vegetable fibres, the initial stages of ropemaking are preparing, followed by spinning or twisting operations. Soft fibres (hemp) are fed through rollers, a process known as softening, and then through rotary carding machines. The resultant sliver passes through drawing frames until the desired evenness and grist is obtained. Carding and drawing are essentially combing operations, the combing pins becoming finer and closer together as the preparing proceeds.

About 100 years ago, soft fibre (hemp) ropes were superseded by ropes of manila fibre which are better for marine use, needing no tarring to protect them against rotting. Today, soft fibres are used only for special-purpose ropes where soft texture and flexibility are required.

Manila and sisal fibres are received in bales consisting of bundles (sometimes termed 'heads' or 'sticks'). These are manually separated and fed through machines with sets of chain- or screw-operated fuller bars, fitted with steel spikes called hackle pins. Each machine has a set of slow and fast pins, and the fibre is held in the slow-moving pins and combed by the fast. It then passes through further machinery of progressively finer pinning, until the desired sliver fineness is reached. The final sliver is spun right-hand into rope yarns on multi-spindle machines, known as gill-spinners, to the desired number of turns per foot, usually 12. When making ordinary helical structure ropes, the rope yarns are collected through a tube or

Meade Collection

A MID-19TH-CENTURY ROPE-WALK

die, and twisted left-hand. The left-hand strands are then twisted into 'right-hand' ropes. If 'left-hand laid' rope is required for a specialised application, the direction of twist is reversed at each stage.

Nylon and terylene polyester are made from continuous multifilament yarns; a collection of threads are first twisted into the primary material, and then into rope yarns. After that, rope-making methods are similar to those of manila and sisal, except that after rope-laying, the ropes are heat-set to stabilize them (as nylon yarn is, see p. 431).

Polypropylene rope is made from mono- or multi-filament, or from staple fibre, or fibrillated film. The two continuous filament yarns are processed much as nylon and terylene polyester, or polyethylene monofilament, are, but there is normally no heat-setting. Staple fibre is prepared in the same way as manila and sisal fibres. Polypropylene film is melt-extruded (*see* PLASTICS IN INDUSTRY, Section 1), and fibrillated at the rope-yarn twisting stage.

4. DEFINITIONS. 'Cordage' is the word used to describe all ropes and twines, irrespective of size. Rope is cordage over 1 inch in circumference (the common method of measuring rope is by circumference).

'Hawser-laid rope' is three strands twisted together, and is the general construction.

Hawser lay, 3 strand

Shroud lay, 4 strand

Cable lay, 9 strand

Plaited, 8 strand (4LH, 4RH)

Braid-on-braid, (braided sheath over braided core)

TWISTS OF ROPE

'Shroud-laid rope' is four strands twisted together over a central 'heart rope'. It is more resistant to surface wear than the three-strand hawser, but is somewhat weaker than a three-strand rope of equivalent size.

'Cable-laid rope' is normally made of three

British Ropes Ltd.

SLIVERS OF FIBRE BEING FED INTO DRAWING-MACHINES TO BE COMBED TO PRODUCE FINER SLIVERS

British Ropes Ltd.

ROPE YARN BEING THREADED THROUGH METAL PLATES TO BE FORMED INTO STRANDS

hawser-laid ropes twisted together, although other combinations can be used. Cable-laid rope is weaker than three- or four-strand rope, but more elastic.

'Eight-strand plaited rope' is made up of four left- and four right-hand strands, plaited in pairs in opposite directions. This type of rope is non-kinkable and is almost as strong as three-strand rope of equal weight. For marine application, it has many advantages over helical construction ropes.

'Braid-on-braid ropes' consist of a braided sheath over a braided core, and are of man-made fibres only. They combine great strength with flexibility, and resistance to abrasion.

Rope is dealt in commercially by weight, and not by length.

See also Vol. IV: KNOTS.

ROYALTIES. These are a form of payment-by-results; royalties are paid for the use of land for mining, or for the use of some special process or machine (*see* PATENTS). The word is also used for payments made by publishers to their authors, and by play promoters to playwrights.

In many countries, particularly the U.S.A., the owner of land owns the mining or mineral rights below the surface as well, and mining companies pay a royalty to the ground landlord (*see* PROPERTY LAW, Vol. X) for the privilege of mining beneath his land. British mineral rights were owned by private landlords until the passing of the Coal Mines Act of 1938. The State then arranged to buy out the royalty-owners for a cash compensation of £66,450,000; it also became the owner of all future mineral rights: not only for coal, but also for other metallic ores, china and other clays, and slate and building stone. The most general arrangement for mining royalties is a payment either on the tonnage mined or, if the mineral is coal, on the acreage and thickness of the coal seam being worked (*see* COAL-MINING). The average royalty paid to landlords for coal-mining in Britain before the 1938 Act was just under 6*d.* a ton. This payment included what are called 'way-leaves', or the right of access to the mine across the owner's land.

Royalties are still frequently paid for the use of secret or patented processes, or for the use of special machines with which to carry out the processes. In the history of British industry one of the earliest arrangements of this kind was made in the early 19th century by Boulton and Watt, of Birmingham, for James Watt's steam-engines. Boulton and Watt could not make in their own works all the engines the world needed; they therefore allowed other engineering firms to make them, under licence, provided that they paid a royalty on each engine turned out. Similar licences are often granted by owners of patent processes to other firms that make use of them. Sometimes a fixed annual payment is made for the use of the process; sometimes a percentage royalty is paid on the goods manufactured and sold. Royalties are also often paid to inventors. The firms that take up the inventions often have to spend much money on making them profitable, and the usual arrangement is that the inventor is paid a royalty on every machine produced and sold. As actual sales are the only proof of the commercial success of an invention, such an arrangement is fair to both parties. For much the same sort of reason, royalty arrangements are the customary way in which publishers pay their authors (*see* PUBLISHING), and theatrical promoters those who write their plays. Neither in the publishing nor in the theatrical world is it possible to estimate accurately in advance what the revenue from a book or a play will be.

RUBBER MANUFACTURE. In modern industry, 'rubber' goods are manufactured either from natural rubber or from various synthetic alternatives made, very commonly, out of crude oil.

Most natural RUBBER (q.v. Vol. VI) is obtained from a tropical tree called *Hevea brasiliensis* which is grown in large plantations in Indonesia, Malaya, Burma, Ceylon, and Nigeria. The tree is 'tapped', and a milky liquid called 'latex' oozes out and is collected in a bucket. Acetic or formic acid is added to the latex to make it coagulate, and the white 'curd' which is formed is washed and dried. Sometimes latex is shipped in the liquid state direct to the manufacturing factories.

During the First World War, when natural latex was difficult to obtain, the Germans invented a substitute for rubber which they used for making tires. Since then, the quality of synthetic rubbers has been so greatly improved that for some purposes they are better than the natural product. Styrene butadiene rubber, made from crude oil, is used extensively in the tire industry.

There are three main processes in the manufacture of rubber goods: the preparation of a suitable rubber compound; shaping or forming the article; and vulcanizing it.

The Dunlop Co. Ltd.

MIXING RUBBER WITH SULPHUR IN AN INTERNAL MIXER

1. COMPOUNDING. Raw rubber must first be worked into a soft, warm, pliable condition in a large mixing machine; and other ingredients, depending on the use to which the rubber is to be put, are added. The most important of these is sulphur—more or less being used according to whether a 'hard' or a 'soft' rubber is to be made. Softening agents such as pine tar, soft asphalts, or petroleum jelly are used to make the rubber more plastic; and reinforcing agents such as carbon black are used where a very tough rubber is wanted.

2. SHAPING. The rubber is shaped in four ways.

a. Extrusion. Tubing, hose pipes, tire treads, beading, and various kinds of rubber strips are produced by forcing the rubber compound under pressure through a specially shaped nozzle or 'die', like squeezing toothpaste out of a tube, so that it emerges in a continuous strip the same shape as the die.

b. Rubberizing. Some rubber goods, including tires, waterproof clothing, and footwear, are made of proofed or rubberized fabric. These may be prepared by 'spreading' or 'calendering' the rubber on the fabric. For light-weight fabrics a soft rubber 'dough' is spread evenly over the dried fabric, which is then passed between consolidation rollers. The dry fabric absorbs almost entirely the first application of the rubber, and the process is repeated several times until the desired weight is reached. Calendering is used for heavier materials such as tire fabrics. A much stiffer compound is forced between the cords in the fabric by making one consolidation roller turn faster than the other. Quite heavy films of rubber may be applied at a time.

c. Dipping. For making articles of fairly simple shape and light weight, such as rubber gloves or Wellington boots, the latex dipping process is used. To make Wellington boots, for example, a fabric base is made up on a wooden or metal frame, and the whole is dipped several times into a bath of liquid latex until the correct thickness is attained. After each immersion the latex coating is dried or coagulated in an acid solution.

d. Moulding. This is the simplest way of shaping rubber. A suitable weight of rubber compound is placed in a steel or aluminium mould, the surface of the mould having been lubricated. The whole is then put in a steam-heated press so that the rubber softens and flows evenly over the mould. The mould is then closed by hydraulic pressure until the rubber has become set in the required shape.

The Dunlop Co. Ltd.

VULCANIZED TIRES BEING REMOVED FROM THE MOULD

3. VULCANIZATION. After being shaped, rubber articles must be vulcanized to give them durability and resilience. Vulcanization consists essentially in mixing sulphur into the rubber under heat so that a chemical change takes place in the material and its properties are altered. It was an invention made by an American, Charles Goodyear, in 1838, and it solved the problem that rubber goods previously tended to become soft in heat and to absorb oil and grease and become almost jellified. Vulcanization is done in different ways according to the article being vulcanized. Very thin rubber articles such as gloves or toy balloons are dipped in a solution of sulphur chloride which penetrates the rubber in a few seconds. Vulcanizing thick rubber is a much slower process.

4. USES OF RUBBER. Over half the rubber used by British industries in 1968 was used in the manufacture of tires. In making a tire, layers of rubber and rubberized rayon or nylon fabric are built into a casing. Different rubber compounds are used for the various tire components—one type for the tread which has to stand hard wear, and another for the sidewalls, which must be able to bend under the weight of a motor-car or lorry without cracking. 'Beads' or rings of steel wire which hold the tire on to its rim are fitted at the edges. The tire is then shaped and vulcanized in a mould. With modern methods a motor tire which one took several hours to vulcanize is now done in about 20 minutes.

Modern motor-car tires are now 'tubeless', that is, do not have inner tubes as they used to. The air used to inflate them is kept in the tire by a thick layer of rubber, which makes an airtight seal with the wheel rim. Bicycles or motorcycles cannot have tubeless tires because the rims, drilled with spoke-holes, are not airtight.

Foam rubber, now used a good deal in upholstery, was first made by beating natural rubber latex into a froth, pouring it into a mould, and vulcanizing it. Many foam-rubber articles are now made by causing a certain kind of synthetic rubber to froth while it is being made.

S

SALES, *see* AUCTIONS; COMMISSION; RETAIL TRADING.

SALT MANUFACTURE. The world has almost inexhaustible supplies of SALT (q.v. Vol. III), which has always been one of man's chief necessities for himself and his animals as well as for his industries. Supplies exist in two main forms—rock-salt and sea-water. Sea-water contains a large percentage of soluble salts, but the proportion of sodium chloride or 'common salt' (the kind used for food) is only 3%. In earlier days most salt was usually obtained by allowing sun and wind to evaporate sea-water in shallow pans or 'salterns' constructed by the side of the sea or estuaries. This system is still followed in warm countries, particularly in India and China, and on the shores of the Mediterranean and the Red Sea. Evaporation of the water leaves the salts concentrated as a solid, and this is collected usually once a year. A drawback to the evaporation of sea-water is that pure 'common salt' is not left behind; it is mixed with other salts. The bulk of the present world production of salt is therefore rock-salt.

This is either dug out by mining, or pumped as brine from underground workings. There are large deposits of rock-salt in Europe, North America, Russia, and India; Polish mines near Cracow have been worked since the 13th century. Stassfurt in Germany, where much natural potash is produced (*see* ALKALIS), has deposits of rock-salt also. The largest British deposits are in Cheshire, around Middlewich, Northwich, Nantwich, and Winsford; this area contains reserves sufficient for several centuries. At Winsford the salt is only about 200 feet below the surface and is mined. In other parts of Cheshire, and also

Imperial Chemical Industries Ltd.

TWO EVAPORATORS IN A VACUUM EVAPORATION PLANT AT A SALT-WORKS in Droitwich and elsewhere, the salt is produced by pumping brine.

Where rock-salt is mined, ordinary mining methods are followed, as in COAL-MINING (q.v.). Pillars of rock-salt are left unhewn, to support the roof. There are no poisonous or explosive gases; the mines are electrically powered and lighted, and working conditions are safe, cool, and comfortable. If mining is impossible, there are two ways of pumping brine. Sometimes natural water has trickled down from the surface of the land towards the salt deposits, and natural or 'local' brine is already present below. This merely has to be pumped to the surface. If there is no natural water below, some must be led down through shafts or boreholes. This water dissolves the salt, and is left for some time to settle before it is pumped to the surface again as brine. The brine must then be evaporated.

Some 2,000 years ago the Romans mined the Cheshire salt deposits, and mining has been continuous ever since. They got solid salt by evaporating the brine in open pans over furnaces. Nowadays the vacuum process is generally used: that is, the evaporation takes place at less than normal atmospheric pressure and therefore at a lower boiling-point (*see* DISTILLATION). Whichever method is used, as the water boils the salt crystallizes, falls to the bottom of the evaporator, and is removed.

Cheshire rock-salt is about 95% pure and, like most rock-salt, is a light reddish-brown, owing to the presence of iron. Most rock-salt, whether mined or evaporated, is disposed of in unrefined form as a solid, but liquid brine is also sent in tanks from Cheshire salt-works to the chemical works of Cheshire and Lancashire. Purity is increased by REFINING (q.v.). Salt, particularly in refined or powdered form, is very liable to get damp in an ordinary atmosphere; table-salt is therefore usually mixed with about 1% of magnesium carbonate, which prevents it from caking. Apart from the large quantities consumed by the chemical industry (*see* ACIDS, ALKALIS), salt is also used for many industrial purposes, including the preserving of hides and skins and of foodstuffs.

SAVINGS. The money that people save is the most important source of CAPITAL (q.v.) for governments, local authorities, and industries. People used to save their money by hiding gold and silver coins, but such hoarding earned no interest and by withdrawing money from circulation it diminished trade and employment.

Even in these days of paper money some people hoard their savings, but most people place them with the many institutions which handle savings. The commercial banks allow interest on savings and deposit accounts. The Post Office Savings Bank is one of the most important national collectors of savings (*see* BANK ACCOUNTS). The Trustee Savings Banks, like the Post Office Savings Bank, accept deposits which bear interest; their normal limit is £5,000. Amounts up to £100 may be withdrawn in cash on demand, and larger sums after giving notice. The way in which they employ their depositors' money is rigidly controlled, and nearly all of it is lent to the Government or to local authorities. The BUILDING SOCIETIES (q.v.) offer a higher rate of interest, but the security is not quite so good. Life insurance is a sound form of saving, and insurance policies can be arranged so as to compensate for future falls in the value of money (*see* INSURANCE).

Government loans offer higher rates of interest than are obtainable on bank deposits. The risk of loss of capital through inflation can be largely guarded against by buying loans repayable on a fixed future date at a higher price than the original purchase price. For the small investor there are the various issues of savings certificates and the premium bonds (*see* NATIONAL SAVINGS, Vol. X).

Savings can also be invested in STOCKS AND SHARES (q.v.), but these are not so secure because the value of shares varies according to economic conditions and the prosperity of the enterprise. However, some shares are sounder than others, and the investor can make his choice according to the amount of risk he is prepared to take. Unit investment trusts spread their capital over a range of selected securities, and each 'unit' sold to investors represents a share in the whole range. Investment Trusts may aim at achieving capital growth on the one hand, or high income on the other.

SCIENTIFIC MANAGEMENT. 1. This means using scientific methods in the management of business firms. The need for scientific management only became clear when the old DOMESTIC SYSTEM (q.v.) of industrial organization had developed into our modern factory system.

Management was a comparatively simple

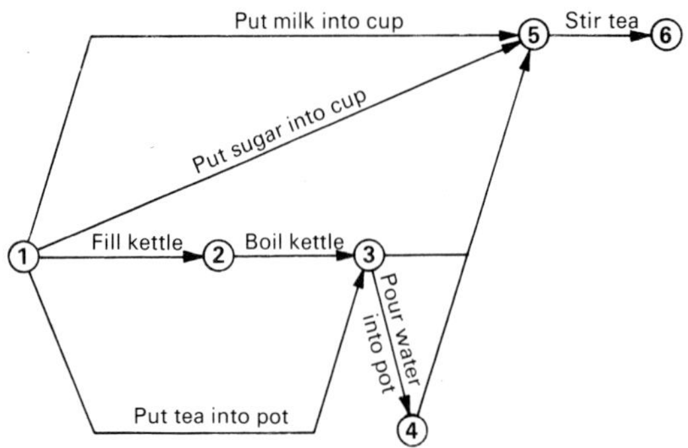

A SIMPLE EXAMPLE OF A 'NETWORK' DIAGRAM, ANALYSING THE MAKING OF A CUP OF TEA

matter when industry was in the domestic stage. Workers were then their own managers, and worked in their own homes; although an employer controlled the pattern and design of the goods turned out, and provided the materials for making them, he did not in our modern sense 'manage' those who worked for him. Management remained fairly simple in the early days of the INDUSTRIAL REVOLUTION (q.v.), when the factory system was just beginning. Most of the employers of the period were practical working-men who had risen in life; and, as they often worked side by side with their workers and were in close daily contact with them, the problems of management solved themselves by 'give and take' as they arose. Now that factories are much larger, with an orderly array of managers and foremen controlling large bodies of workers, the problems of management are much less simple, and the need has arisen for a scientific approach. The branch of scientific management which deals with human beings at work is called 'personnel management'. It makes much use of the modern science of INDUSTRIAL PSYCHOLOGY (q.v.).

There are other aspects of scientific management. No business can go on providing work, even for the most contented workers, unless it is fully efficient in other ways. Even if it happens to have a MONOPOLY (q.v.), every business has to meet competition and must constantly be trying to improve output and reduce its cost of production. Management, therefore, is concerned with costs of production, output, and sales, and makes use of such techniques as BOOK-KEEPING, COSTING, STATISTICS, and MARKET RESEARCH (qq.v.). Historically, an important part of scientific management is what is now generally called 'work study'. This includes measuring and assessing the job to be done, and fixing rates of payment for them (*see* WAGES); the simplifying of goods and processes, so that the cost of production can be reduced to a minimum; time and motion study, that is, observing the motions which workers go through in doing a job, planning the least fatiguing and most efficient motions, and calculating the 'standard' or ideal times that various tasks should take; and the organization of a factory so that those employed there may work as efficiently and contentedly as possible (*see* PRODUCTION ENGINEERING, Section 4, Vol. VIII).

With the advent of computers, which can deal with large quantities of information, more sophisticated techniques are coming into use, for example, network analysis, an approach which is of great value when planning construction jobs. A network diagram can show the sequence, timing, and relationship of a series of jobs that have to be done. A simplified example of such a diagram is illustrated on this page.

2. HISTORY. Modern scientific management owes more to an American engineer, Frederick Winslow Taylor, than to anyone else, but there were pioneers of modern management in Britain long before Taylor's ideas were published. Boulton and Watt, the famous Birmingham engineering firm of the early 19th century, was one of the first to work out a scientific costing system. Personnel management goes back as far as ROBERT OWEN (q.v. Vol. V), the father of the co-operative movement, who discovered over 100 years ago that if workers were treated well their work improved. Richard ARKWRIGHT (q.v. Vol. V), who invented the water-frame for textile spinning, was also a clever manager and organizer. Even time and motion study is not an entirely modern idea, for Charles Babbage, a Cambridge mathematician and the inventor of the Babbage calculating machine, wrote about it over 100 years ago, and also made some important suggestions about costing.

Taylor, however, was the first to see clearly that the principles of management could be worked out by studying industry in general, and that such principles could be applied to all industries and not merely to one. On the whole, his observations were restricted to firms in the engineering and allied trades, but his principles were worked out so soundly that later on they were found to apply equally well to other industries, and even to firms that merely traded in goods and did not manufacture them. Taylor emphasized that there must be good relations between management and employees, and he suggested that there would have to be in the future a scientific study of the causes that led human beings at work to think and act in the ways they did. He stressed the importance of selecting workers for particular jobs, and of transferring 'misfit' workers from jobs that did not suit them to others which they might perform brilliantly. Years before such a science came into existence, Taylor clearly foresaw the necessity of what is now called industrial psychology. He was also the first to emphasize the importance of what we now call 'work measurement', that is, the careful definition of what each individual in a factory has to do, and the calculation of the rate that will be paid for doing it. Taylor improved upon Babbage's ideas about time and motion study, and was the first to work out 'standards' of work and performance which all workers in a factory should attain. He also made important suggestions for drawing up what are now called 'organization charts' (*see* BUSINESS ORGANIZATION), giving the detailed chain of responsibility from the top of a business downwards, and defining the duties of each person or group of persons in the chain. Finally, the very term 'scientific management' was invented by Taylor and his assistants. They did not claim too much for it. They believed that management was not a science but an art: an art, however, that could be more effectively acquired if various scientific techniques—such as organization, accounting, costing, statistics, time and motion study, and industrial psychology—were used also.

3. MANAGEMENT TODAY. Great advances have been made in this field since the Second World War. Not only have new techniques been devised, but the whole approach to business problems has been the subject of a great deal of research. Specialized firms of consultants now advise business managements on the improvements they might make in the interests of greater efficiency. Graduate business schools teaching management studies have now been established in this country, as they have been in the United States for over 50 years. Both these types of organization are evidence of a more widespread scientific approach to business problems. Courses and conferences for business men also help to disseminate new ideas more widely.

See also BUSINESS ORGANIZATION; FACTORY ORGANIZATION.

SECURITY. This word is often used in the world of finance, and has two meanings. Its more important meaning is some kind of document, stating that the person named in it is the owner of stock or shares in a limited company (*see* STOCKS AND SHARES), or is entitled to receive interest on a LOAN (q.v.) made to an industrial concern, to a government, or to a local authority. Such 'securities' can be bought and sold on the stock exchanges, and are called 'negotiable' securities.

The other meaning of the word is some form of guarantee given to a lender of money that the promise to repay it will be carried out. This may take the form of negotiable securities deposited with the banker or lender, so that if the loan is not repaid he may sell the securities and repay himself the amount due. But sometimes bankers are quite satisfied if they receive written guarantees, signed by responsible persons, that they will themselves repay the loan if the original borrower fails to do so. Title-deeds of houses and of PROPERTY (q.v. Vol. X), life-insurance policies, and other documents are often put up as security to bankers and other lenders. Such security is called 'collateral'.

See also BANKING; DEBENTURES.

SELF-SERVICE STORES. The idea of self-service is to cut costs by letting the customers search for their own goods. It was also found that, if all goods were displayed either on shelves round the walls or on gondolas (island counters on the shop floors), people bought more than they did when only some of the goods were on show, the rest being out of sight in the warehouse. So far, in most countries this system has been adopted principally in the grocery trade.

In a self-service store the customer takes a basket and fills it with goods from the stands. When she has completed her shopping she passes through what are called 'check-out lanes', where she pays a cashier-assistant for her purchases.

Goods sold in self-service shops have to be pre-packed and price-marked, and indeed such shops would not be possible were it not for canning, and the almost universal pre-packing of food at the factory. Cheese and bacon, for example,

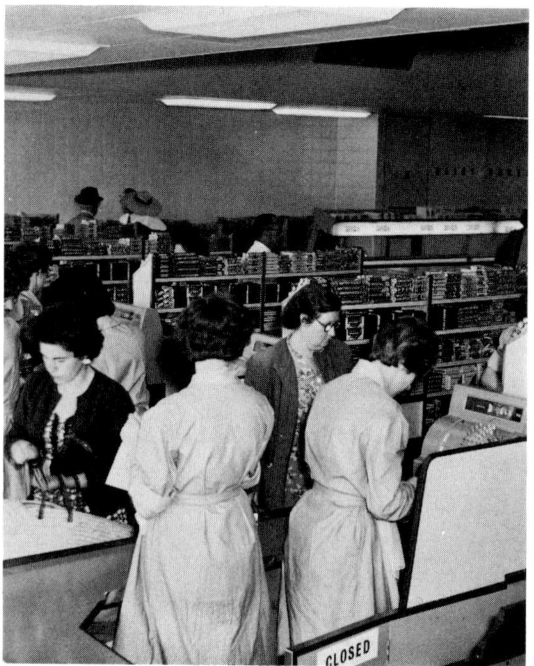

L.N.A.

CUSTOMERS PAYING FOR THEIR PURCHASES AS THEY LEAVE A SELF-SERVICE STORE

are weighed into pounds and half-pounds, and their weight and price marked on the wrapping.

The cost of running this type of store is low because only a small staff is needed to keep the stands filled with stock and to work the cash registers. The supermarket, or self-service store of 5,000 square feet or more, caters particularly for the shopper by car, who can buy in bulk, storing the food in a refrigerator or deep freeze. In addition to groceries, provisions, and frozen foods, it sells fresh fruit and vegetables, meat and fish, hardware, clothing, books, and even furniture and garden equipment. This is the most rapidly growing section of the food trade, and it is estimated that by 1970, 70% of the grocery trade will be self-service.

See also MULTIPLE SHOPS; DEPARTMENT STORES.

SHALE OIL comes from oil shale, a type of rock (*see* CLAYS AND SHALES, Vol. III). The United States has the largest reserves of shale oil, followed by Brazil, the U.S.S.R. (Estonia), Canada, China, the Congo, and Sweden. There are Scottish deposits, principally in West Lothian, Midlothian, and Fife, but work ceased on these sites in 1962 since the cost of processing makes it uneconomic to produce (*see* OIL, MINERAL). One of the earliest shale-oil industries is that of France, which was started in 1830, but the first large-scale works was opened in Scotland in 1862.

Oil shale is mined in much the same way as coal, either in open-cast workings or by underground mining (*see* COAL-MINING). Chemically, oil shale contains both organic and inorganic compounds (*see* CHEMISTRY, Vol. III); the inorganic portions turn to ash when heated, and the organic portion (known as the 'kerogen') decomposes into crude oil. The mined shale is crushed into small pieces, put into large cast-iron retorts similar in principle to those used in GAS MANUFACTURE (q.v. Vol. VIII), and heated to a high temperature. The 'kerogen' decomposes into crude oil and what is called 'retort gas'; from this gas some crude petrol can be obtained. The process produces a large quantity of AMMONIA (q.v.), which is treated with sulphuric acid to form sulphate of ammonia, a valuable soil fertilizer. The crude oil is then distilled and refined into various products, including solvent spirits, petrol, paraffin or kerosine, and paraffin wax (*see* OIL REFINING).

SHARES, *see* STOCKS AND SHARES.

SHEFFIELD PLATE. This silver-plated ware, which included mainly articles for domestic use, such as dishes, tea-caddies, biscuit-boxes and snuff-boxes, decanter-stands, and candlesticks, was made by a special process that was practised for about a century, and then died out. The general level of taste and design in England stood very high during that particular period—from the middle of the 18th century onwards. Sheffield plate possesses a beautiful quality of its own, which is absent in articles silvered all over by the process of ELECTRO-PLATING (q.v. Vol. VIII) which took its place.

Silversmiths had long looked for a way in which wares made of cheap metal or alloy could be 'plated', or given a coating of silver, so that they would appear to be made of the solid metal. Two methods were widely practised: 'amalgamation', a chemical process, and 'French plating', in which thin silver-leaf was made to adhere to the copper or brass underneath it by means of heat and friction. The first of these methods gave rather a poor effect, and the second required immense labour if a thick enough layer were to be built up by repeated heating and burnishing. In 1752 Thomas Bolsover, a Sheffield workman, while mending a knife handle made of copper and silver, discovered that by accidentally overheating it he had fused the two metals so closely together that no later working could part them. He began the manufacture of what came to be called Sheffield plate, though he confined himself to small articles, which he first made in base metal and then plated. The method finally adopted was to produce first of all a strip or small ingot of copper and brass alloy, about 12 inches by 3, and about an inch thick. It was carefully filed and scraped dead flat and clean on its upper face, great care being taken to prevent any dirt—even a fingermark—from reaching it. On this was placed a slightly smaller piece of silver, the under surface of which had been similarly cleaned and flattened. The thickness of the silver was between about $\frac{1}{16}$ and $\frac{3}{16}$ of an inch, according to the thickness of plating finally required. A sheet of iron, washed with whiting to prevent its sticking during heating, was then placed over them, and the three pieces of metal were bound tightly together with iron wire. Finally, the edges of the silver were painted round with borax ground to a paste, and the whole was put into a small furnace and brought to a red heat. As this temperature was approached, the edges of the silver (helped by the borax) began to show signs of melting; and just at that moment the metals were taken from the furnace and laid aside to cool. It was on the great precision of this that the chief success of the process depended; for, if correctly done, it

Meade Collection

18TH-CENTURY LABEL OF A SHEFFIELD PLATE MANUFACTURER

Crown Copyright

ONE OF A PAIR OF LATE 18TH-CENTURY SHEFFIELD PLATE CANDELABRA
Victoria and Albert Museum

made so perfect a join between the silver and the base metal that no subsequent operation, however violent, could separate them. To reduce the twin ingot to sheet-metal of the required thickness, it was passed repeatedly through iron rollers (not unlike a mangle in operation), being 'annealed' (or softened by being reheated) as necessary (*see* HEAT TREATMENT, Vol. VIII).

In early Sheffield plate only one side of the alloy was silvered, the other being usually tinned; later on, both sides were plated. In each case there remained the raw copper edge, which had to be concealed. This was done by soldering silver wire over it or along it. Various ornamental sections of wire were used, and at times they were further treated by being hammered so as to overlap above or below. Articles were further decorated by having mounted on them ornaments either of solid silver or of silver filled with pewter. These, too, were soldered into place. The presence of these joints, beautifully concealed as they are, is one of the features distinguishing Sheffield plate from electro-plate, in which the covering of silver is deposited uniformly everywhere; another is the pleasant characteristic texture and colour of the metal itself, the result of the process of manufacture.

For some years the makers of early Sheffield

plate were forbidden to stamp their 'mark' on it, as was done with solid silver, but in 1784 the right to mark plate was granted by law. Marking is by no means a sure guide to the genuineness or quality of Sheffield plate, because many of the finest speciments carry no mark at all.

Sheffield plate was made not only in Sheffield, but to a very large extent in London and Birmingham also. Birmingham used a copper base, which was not only softer, but shows as a much redder metal where the silver has been worn or polished away. From 1850 onwards the commercial manufacture of Sheffield plate ceased, but the method is occasionally revived for special orders.

See also GOLD AND SILVER WORK.

SHELLAC is one of the natural resins (*see* GUMS AND RESINS). The natural resins are divided into two classes: those of woody origin, obtained as a rule from tree-tapping, and those of insect origin. The insect group includes the lac resins, of which shellac is the best known.

There are about sixty varieties of trees which act as hosts to the grubs or larvae of the lac insects, a variety of the SCALE INSECT (q.v. Vol. II). These larvae feed on the sap of the trees, and produce a kind of resin which they then exude to protect themselves from weather and enemies. The larvae encase themselves in resinous shells, allowing only a narrow tube to protrude for breathing. The trees become covered with the lac, which, at the proper season, is collected by rolling and sifting. It is called 'sticklac' in the crude form and is purified by being kneaded in warm water and 'fused' over a fire.

Resins of insect origin occur chiefly in India, where shellac is first recorded as being used. In the 16th century shellac lacquer work and shellac varnishes were widely known in India. Since then the uses of shellac varnish and sealing-wax have increased throughout the world. About 95% of shellac still comes from India, the remainder coming from Burma, Thailand, and Indo-China.

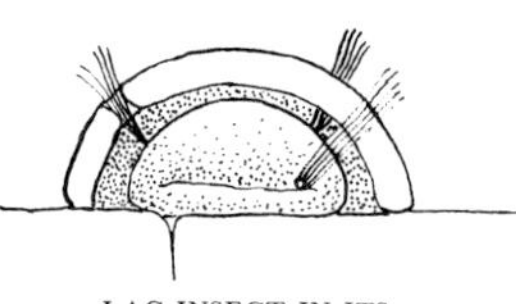

LAC INSECT IN ITS RESINOUS COVERING

The mouth parts point downwards into the plant. Three sets of breathing tubes pass through gaps in the resin

Besides yielding resin, shellac also contains some dyestuffs and waxes. There are two types of colouring matter in shellac, of which only one is a true dye.

Shellac is chiefly needed for making varnishes, lacquers, inks, wax emulsions, sealing-wax, and 'fillers' or filling-material for certain woodwork. In the United States alone some 14 million lb. of shellac varnish is used on wood floors every year. Varnishes account for 60% of the known uses of shellac; shellac mouldings, mostly in the form of gramophone records, account for 30%; shellac cements and adhesives use 2% of the world's output; the remaining 8% is useful for many purposes, ranging from fireworks to the chocolate industries. Although synthetic materials, such as cellulose acetate and vinyl chloride, have been used increasingly in recent years for gramophone records, shellac is still the most important material for this industry.

See also GUMS AND RESINS; PAINTS AND VARNISHES.

SHIPBUILDING INDUSTRY. From very early times men have been building ships (*see* CLASSICAL SHIPS, Vol. IV). Wood was the chief material used, and there is plenty of evidence that these early shipbuilders—Egyptians, Phoenicians, Cretans, Greeks—had a good deal of practical skill.

At the close of the Middle Ages, when there are more plentiful records, ships, still of wood and propelled by sails, were usually built at ports which were near large forests. Some of these early shipyards were on such narrow waters that launching had to be done sideways. By Elizabeth I's time London was a great shipbuilding centre, depending on the oak forests of Kent and southern England, which were carefully preserved. The shipyards were at Deptford; there were anchorages at Greenwich, and a naval arsenal at Woolwich. In those days masts and spars were imported from Scandinavia, and also such things as resin and tar. As well as the big centres, there were small building yards at almost every busy port around the coast, and each district produced its own local designs. The woodworker who specialized in shipbuilding, called a shipwright, was a person of importance, and in 1612 this was recognized by James I when he granted a charter to the Worshipful Company of Shipwrights, a body which still exists to-day.

By the 18th century world trade had increased so much that there was competition between

National Maritime Museum

A SHIP ON THE STOCKS AT DEPTFORD, POSSIBLY THE *Buckingham*, A 70-GUN SHIP LAUNCHED IN 1751

Painting by J. Cleveley in the Greenwich Hospital Collection

nations for better and faster ships. Shipbuilders had to keep up with the increasing demand. The sturdy traders of north-eastern America and Canada began to build fast ships as good as or better than those built elsewhere. The ships were still wooden sailing ships, though often with bottoms sheathed with copper, but with continually improving designs. The design of the wooden ship reached its height about the middle of the 19th century, the period of the great CLIPPER SHIPS (q.v. Vol. IV), which were able to hold their own even against the early steam-driven ships.

During the first half of the 19th century a great change came over the shipbuilding industry, and this was the increasing use of iron for building ships' hulls. By 1855 iron shipbuilding had so far developed that Lloyd's Register of Shipping (the body which lays down standards for shipbuilding) first published rules for iron construction. The use of iron, and later steel, instead of wood meant that shipyards no longer needed to be within reach of forests: instead, they had to be near coalfields and iron foundries. So during the 19th century the industry steadily drifted away from southern England. There was still a good deal of shipbuilding on the Thames; the GREAT EASTERN, for example (q.v. Vol. IV) was built there in 1856. But new centres opened up on the Clyde at Glasgow, the Tyne at Newcastle, the Wear at Sunderland, and the Mersey at Birkenhead, as well as at Belfast.

The change from wood to iron and then steel altered the industry in other ways besides locality. The shipwright no longer reigned supreme; many other skilled craftsmen—platers, riveters, drillers, and caulkers—became essential to the industry. It also became usual for each yard to specialize in one kind of ship, and only the very large yards built their own marine engines (*see* MARINE ENGINEERING, Vol. VIII).

At first most of the iron-built ships were still driven by sail, and so their design was not greatly changed; but as STEAMSHIPS (q.v. Vol. IV) developed, designs also changed. Britain was well placed to become the world's leader in shipbuilding. She had the knowledge and the raw materials (coal and iron), and her enormous overseas trade meant that she needed ships more

Vickers Ltd.

THE BUILDING BERTHS IN A SHIPYARD

In the foreground are the bottom plates of an *Empress* liner and next to that a 37,000-ton tanker

than any other nation. Again, after 1856, when Bessemer had shown how to make steel cheaply and in large quantities (*see* IRON AND STEEL INDUSTRY), Britain took the lead in the construction of steel ships. By 1867, when Lloyd's Register of Shipping accepted steel as a standard material for shipbuilding, companies such as the Cunard already had steel vessels. British shipbuilders were among the founders of famous shipyards abroad—at Gothenburg in Sweden and Copenhagen in Denmark, for example. By 1890 Britain was building about four-fifths of the world's shipping and owned about three-fifths of it.

By the end of the 19th century Britain's lead in the shipbuilding industry was being seriously challenged by Germany, and later by Japan. The Thames yards were no longer able to compete, and the last big ship to be built by the Thames Iron Works, the battleship *Thunderer*, was launched in 1911. After the First World War, when the demand for shipping was enormous, Britain could not spare time or materials to build for foreign buyers and consequently foreign shipyards were opened or enlarged. Then, when the demand began to fall off, Britain had lost her foreign markets, and the 1930's were years of great depression and unemployment in the industry. The Second World War produced a boom again in shipbuilding with much development in modern methods. The use of welded construction was extended, particularly in the United States, where a manufacturer named Henry Kaiser developed a process which almost amounted to the mass production of ships (*see* SHIPBUILDING, Vol. VIII). These modern methods made it necessary to reorganize the lay-out of the yards and to install much new equipment. For a period British shipyards were handicapped in this development by a serious steel shortage and also by a lack of skilled craftsmen; and by the time the yards were fully modernized, orders for new shipping were beginning to fall off again.

Today the leading shipbuilding countries are Japan, Britain, Germany, and Sweden. Britain builds every type of ship afloat—from tugs to tankers, and from fast container ships to nuclear submarines. In 1967, five giant tankers, $\frac{1}{4}$ million tons each, were ordered, and a new Belfast dock is designed to build tankers of up to a million tons. In 1968, British yards completed 152 merchant ships (about £120 million worth), in addition to warships. Over 70,000 workers are employed in shipbuilding and another 40,000 in repairs, apart from those working in Royal Dockyards, or related supply industries.

Today, almost without exception, everyone in the shipbuilding industry completes either an apprenticeship or a training course of one sort or another. The skilled workers—shipwrights, platers, sheet-metal workers, welders, riveters, caulkers, joiners, plumbers, painters, and electricians—all serve 5-year craft apprenticeships, which they begin between the ages of 16 and 17. Those on the technical and management side also usually begin with an apprenticeship. Drawing office or technical apprenticeships, for example, start when a boy is between 16 and 18, and the apprentice must hold a General Certificate of Education, with passes in mathematics and at least one physical science subject. Student apprenticeships are available for those with advanced-level G.C.E., and are usually started between the ages of $17\frac{1}{2}$ and $18\frac{1}{2}$. This type of course provides practical training, combined with full-time study courses at university or technical college, with a view to obtaining a degree in Naval Architecture or Engineering (q.v. Vol. VIII). Finally, there are 2- or 3-year courses provided for graduates who have no previous practical experience.

See also Vol. IV: Ship; Primitive Ships; Classical Ships; Sailing Ships; Steamships, History of.
See also Vol. VIII: Marine Engineering; Shipbuilding.

SHIPPING. The history of Ships (q.v. Vol. IV) is very closely bound up with the history of trade, for it is cheaper to carry goods by sea than by land. Britain's greatness as a mercantile power has depended very largely upon the efficiency and size of her merchant navy. By the end of the 17th century the English had succeeded the Dutch as leaders of the world's carrying trade by sea. They improved upon this lead in the 18th and 19th centuries; and, although in the 20th century competition from other countries has become very keen, the British merchant fleet remains the largest single fleet that is still truly national.

The position has varied over the centuries. In the Middle Ages the seaborne trade of the western world was chiefly restricted to the Mediterranean, the Channel, and the North Sea, and was largely in the hands of the Venetians and the Hanseatic League (q.v.), the ships of the League being based on north German ports such as Lübeck and Hamburg. In the north the Viking pirates had ceased to exist, and it was reasonably safe to cross the seas. But in the Mediterranean the famous Barbary pirates, from what are now the Algerian and Moroccan coasts, were still a menace to shipping, and compelled the Venetian galleys to travel in convoy (*see* Pirates, Vol. IV). The arrival of these galleys in Spithead and the Solent was a great spectacle every year.

It took a long time for England to get a start as a merchant-shipping nation, and longer still to achieve a leading position. The start was made during the later Middle Ages, when the ships of the Merchant Adventurers (q.v.) began to challenge the supremacy held by the Hanseatic League. By the 15th century the Venetians were being so much occupied by troubles at home—by wars with other Italian republics such as the Genoese, and by the attacks of the Turks—that they were no longer serious rivals. At the end of the 15th century English shipping was firmly established in north European waters; but by that time the Portuguese and the Spaniards had begun to voyage into the remoter and unknown waters of the world.

England's Tudor rulers had foreseen the coming struggle with Spain and they encouraged seafaring, not only in home waters but also abroad; even before the defeat of the Spanish Armada in 1588, the number of English ships on the more distant seas was considerable. After this defeat Spain was so crippled that the seafaring people of the Netherlands, who had struggled under Spanish domination, succeeded in their fight for independence. For a time the Dutch fleets were occupied with overcoming the Spanish and Portuguese fleets, and this gave England an opportunity to build and man more ships and to send them all over the world. But as soon as the Dutch had settled with their other enemies, they turned their attention to England; and there began a long period of Dutch–English

SHIPS LOADING TIMBER IN A NORTHERN EUROPEAN PORT *National Maritime Museum*

Painting by H. C. Vroom, 1566–1640

rivalry at sea, which occasionally resulted in open war, and which never really came to an end until a Dutch prince, William III, became King of England in 1689. But Britain even then could not fully consider herself 'mistress of the seas' until TRAFALGAR (q.v. Vol. X) had been fought in 1805.

After the Battle of Waterloo Britain enjoyed nearly 100 years of freedom from wars in western Europe, when she could develop her industry at home and her shipping abroad. The owners of her diverse fleet of sailing-ships found themselves in a favourable position to run their ships cheaply in competition with the rest of the world, and so to make a good profit. In a country where few towns were more than 40 or 50 miles from the sea, the sea was in the people's blood. The fishing industry and a series of naval wars had bred a magnificent force of trained seamen, whose skill and knowledge were handed down from generation to generation.

By the beginning of the 19th century, the pattern of British shipping organization had become established, and it did not in fact alter greatly when steamships began to replace sailing-ships. There were famous lines of fast and well-found ships trading regularly between British and overseas ports, and there were also the sailing 'tramps' which picked up cargoes when and where they offered themselves, and which ran on no regular schedules. There was also a large fleet of coasting vessels, using the smaller ports.

Towards the end of the sailing-ship period competition began to be serious, particularly from the U.S.A., whose total tonnage in 1861 was almost equal to that of Britain, and from Finland, Sweden, Norway, Denmark, and Holland. The crews of these foreign ships were prepared to work for lower wages and under less attractive conditions than British crews. To counter this, many British shipowners put British officers, boatswains, and quartermasters in charge of foreign crews from these northern countries. But this undercutting of freight and passenger rates by foreign competitors might have seriously injured Britain's supremacy in the world's seaborne carrying trade, had not the coming of the steamship saved the situation. For Britain was at this time so much in the lead in the production of iron, steel, and machinery that she had an overwhelming advantage in the building of STEAMSHIPS (q.v. Vol. IV).

There were, however, many British and American shipowners who did not believe in steam for long deep-sea voyages. They argued that steamships would have to carry so much coal that there would be little space for a paying load of cargo; also that, if sailing-ships could be redesigned for speed and given the fine lines of yachts, they might hold their own against steam. Although in the end these arguments proved unsound, especially as steam technique improved, for a while they were believed in, and in consequence there followed the magnificent period of the CLIPPER SHIPS (q.v. Vol. IV). But clippers were superseded by steamships.

Britain became the largest producer of the new stronger and lighter steel ships, because she had iron and coal and skill in smelting. When the screw propellor replaced the paddle wheel, and the compound steam engine, invented in Britain, was introduced, these ships became immeasurably better than sailing ships both in cargo capacity and speed. Since Britain was the principal source and market for many of the goods which made up their cargoes, she also maintained her lead in running them. The old distinction between the 'line' of ships plying regularly between port and port, and the tramp ship, picking up cargoes wherever they offered, became more marked in the age of steam. LINERS (q.v. Vol. IV) may carry passengers only, cargo only, or mixed cargo and passengers; their voyages are planned and advertised beforehand, and they run, as trains do, to a time-table regularly and punctually. The tramp ship, on the other hand leaves port with a cargo for a particular destination; on reaching it, it picks up another cargo. Tramp ships are 'chartered' either to undertake a particular voyage, or for a period of time during which the charterer can, subject to agreed conditions, use the ship in any trade that suits his requirements. They usually carry a single bulk cargo, but they may be chartered on a liner service by a shipowner, in which case they may carry a variety of smaller consignments, as liners do.

The liner proprietors soon found that the tramp ships were taking over their traffic by undercutting freight rates when trade was good. They therefore organized themselves into associations or conferences, sometimes consisting of shipowners of more than one nationality, to provide regular services at fixed rates, and to establish permanent contracts with cargo shippers, who in return agreed to use their services at all times.

At the beginning of the 20th century Britain's leading position in world shipping was again challenged by the merchant fleets of other nations, including Germany, Norway, and France. But the most immediate threat came from an

Cunard Steam-ship Co. Ltd.

CUNARD'S NEW CONTAINER SHIPS. THE CONTAINERS ARE QUICKLY LOADED ON BY CRANE

American combine, the International Mercantile Marine, which planned to control all the North Atlantic liner traffic. After it had taken over a number of British companies, the Government intervened for the first time since the repeal of the NAVIGATION ACTS (q.v.) by supporting the building of two huge transatlantic liners, the Mauretania and the Lusitania.

Between the wars the practice of registering ships under 'flags of convenience', such as those of Liberia or Panama, which had little or no sea-borne trade themselves, grew up. In this way the ship owner could avoid taxes and the various conditions imposed by his native country, thus reducing his costs. But the governments of traditional maritime countries felt anxious to maintain their merchant fleets since they are an important source of foreign currency. Many have therefore attempted to encourage shipping by granting tax allowances, directing cargo, building liners, or lending money for such building at special rates of interest.

Two recent technical developments have made a major impact on the organization of the shipping industry. The first is the increase in size of the average cargo ship, particularly those carrying bulk cargoes. Specially designed bulk carriers can now take up to 150,000 tons of dry cargo, such as ores, coal, or grain, and oil tankers carry 200–300,000 tons of crude oil (*see* NAVAL ARCHITECTURE, Vol. VIII). These ships are so large, and consequently so expensive, and pose so many management problems that the shipowners have formed pools or consortia with the aim of making huge contracts with producers and shippers. The owners then charter their own ships (and others, if necessary) to the pool on a long-term basis, and the pool uses them to fulfil its contracts. Tankers, however, are mainly owned or chartered by the international oil companies.

The second development has taken place in the handling of all cargoes other than bulk commodities and oil. These general cargoes are increasingly being conveyed by the unit-load system, described in TRANSPORT (q.v.). Special container ships carry the goods, pre-packed in standardized cases; but they form only a part of a wider operation which takes the goods in their containers from the factory or depot, right through to their final destination. Loading or unloading the container ship can be done at high speed, though special dock facilities are needed to cope with the rapid turnover. But the system requires far greater investment and a more elaborate organization than the old liner service did. Companies which once ran separate transport services are now forming national or international consortia to organize a single-route unit-load service.

In spite of the losses of two wars, and great economic changes in the world as a whole, British shipping has managed to maintain its prestige, even though its proportion of the world merchant fleet has gradually declined. Today British shipowners are showing enterprise by investing in unit-load services and special bulk carriers on a large scale.

See also SHIPBUILDING INDUSTRY.

See also Vol. IV: SHIP; MERCHANT SHIPPING; PORTS AND HARBOURS.

SHOP, *see* RETAIL TRADING; MULTIPLE SHOP; DEPARTMENT STORES; SELF-SERVICE STORES.

SILICONES is the name given to a particular group of synthetic compounds of silicon having properties which are valuable in industry. Silicon is a non-metallic element (*see* MATTER, Vol. III) which occurs abundantly in the earth's crust combined with other elements. Sand is a compound of silicon and oxygen, and many rocks consist of various silicon compounds. Bricks, pottery, and glass are among the things made from natural silicon compounds. But silicones do not occur in nature; they are made by combining silicon with other elements (especially hydrogen and oxygen) in a large number of very complicated ways to give whole families of different products—just as whole families of organic chemicals (*see* CHEMISTRY, INDUSTRIAL) can be built with carbon, hydrogen, and oxygen.

Many of the silicon compounds formed in this way are similar to carbon compounds—oils, waxes, varnishes, and insulating materials, for example—but they have two useful properties of their own: they are exceptionally stable at temperatures that would destroy the carbon-based materials, and they are extremely water-repellent. So silicones are increasingly used for greases and insulating materials that have to withstand high temperatures, for treating anything from brickwork to clothing to make it water-repellent, and as furniture and car polishes which last longer than ordinary polishes and do not show finger-marks so easily.

SILK INDUSTRY. 1. According to Chinese legend, the breeding of SILKWORMS (q.v. Vol. VI) for their silk thread goes back more than 4,000 years. For centuries the Chinese kept their knowledge of this craft to themselves. A silk industry existed in India by 1000 B.C. or even earlier, but it is very likely that 'wild' silk was used, produced by the tussah-moth and not by the cultivated silkworm. This tussore silk, as it is now called, is still made in India. Silk goods do not appear to have been brought to Europe until about 325 B.C. after Alexander the Great's campaign against the Persians; whether the goods were of Chinese or Indian origin is not certain. Nearly 300 years later silk was being imported into Rome, and silk garments were worn by the wealthy. They probably came overland by camel caravan from China. In the third century silkworms and the art of weaving silk were introduced into Japan. During all this time European merchants bought silk goods but knew nothing of how they were made. The Roman Emperor Justinian (A.D. 483–565) is believed to have introduced the silkworm to Europe. It is said that two Russian monks who had travelled in China told Justinian about the silk industry, and that he sent them back to China with instructions to bring out its secrets. They are reported to have returned about A.D. 550 with a collection of silkworms' eggs hidden in a hollow bamboo staff. In any event, in the later years of Justinian's reign silk manufacture became a MONOPOLY (q.v.) of the Emperor, and weaving looms were set up in part of his palace. By the 8th century A.D. the knowledge of silkworm breeding (or sericulture, as it is sometimes called) had spread to countries which were then under the influence of the MOORS (q.v. Vol. I), including Sicily and Spain. By the 12th century silkworms were being bred in Italy, and by the end of the 13th century in France also. The climate and vegetation of many countries were not suitable for silkworms. In the 16th century the Spanish conqueror Cortés took silkworms to Mexico, as well as the mulberry trees which are their natural food. But nothing came of this. Later attempts elsewhere in North and South America had no greater success, and the chief modern producers of silk on a commercial scale are still the countries that were producing in the Middle Ages—China, Japan, Italy, and France. By far the largest producer is Japan.

Silk Centre

SILKWORMS ON THEIR FEEDING TRAYS

They are ravenous feeders and must be given fresh, dry mulberry leaves at frequent intervals

The threads spun by silkworms and by spiders are very much alike; in fact, spider-silk is used where silkworm-silk would not be fine enough, as for marking the centre line of lenses in optical instruments, such as those used for surveying or for directing gunfire in war. Attempts have been made, notably in the U.S.A., to 'farm' spiders on a commercial scale.

2. MANUFACTURE. The silkworm spins the silk round itself in the form of a cocoon, and the manufacturing processes begin with the reeling of the silk from the cocoons; this takes place in a silk-reeling establishment, or *filature*. (The words

Silk Centre

SILK REELING MACHINE

The cocoons are in troughs of hot water

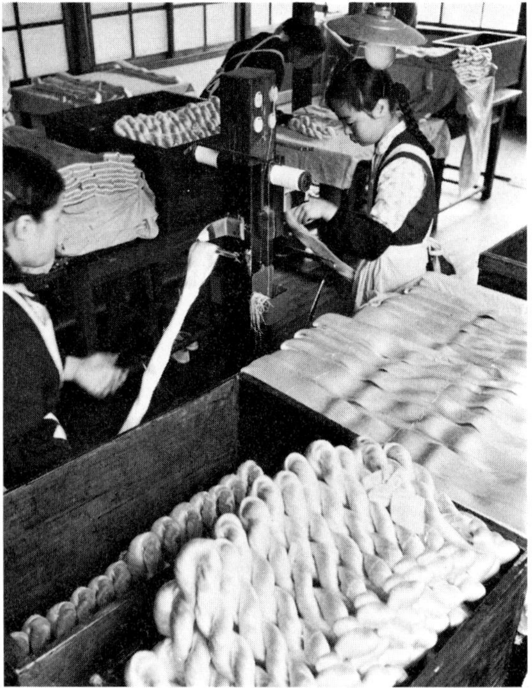

Silk Centre

TWISTING SKEINS OF RAW SILK

They are packed in bundles for export

used in the industry are largely French, as for centuries the city of Lyons has been the centre of the European industry.) The cocoons are placed in a basin of nearly boiling water to soften the silk gum which coats the silk filament. They are brushed, and the brush fibres catch up the end of the thin thread of the cocoon. This end is then picked up by hand. Series of threads, sometimes six or more, are reeled into a single stronger thread; this is known as the 'raw silk', the form in which the material is usually exported. If a thread breaks, the natural gumminess of the silk makes it possible to press the broken ends together. During the brushing a good deal of fluff or floss is caught up from the cocoons by the brushes. This is silk waste, and is later made into what is called 'spun silk'.

Before manufacture the reeled silk is soaked in oil or in an emulsion of soap. This softens the thread and reduces, but does not entirely remove, the natural gumminess which is a feature of the silk. The reeled silk is then wound on to bobbins and is ready for the process called 'throwing'. Reeled silk does not have to be spun. Spinning, in which short slender fibres have to be drawn out straight and twisted together to form a continuous yarn or thread, is peculiar to cotton and wool and similar fibres (*see* Wool Spinning). Reeled silk is already a continuous thread, although a very thin one, and 'throwing' either gives a twist to the single thread or twists several threads together. The word 'throw' is probably derived from the Anglo-Saxon *thrawan*, meaning to turn or twist. A silk-thrower is called a 'throwster'. Not all silk is thrown; some fabrics are made from unthrown silk.

After throwing, there follow the various weaving or knitting processes by which fabrics are made from the yarns. The fabrics then go through the usual textile finishing processes, such as bleaching, dyeing, and printing, although sometimes the yarns are bleached and dyed before being worked up into fabrics (*see* Bleaching, Dyes, Textile Printing). The finishing processes sometimes include the 'weighting' of silk. This consists of dipping yarns or cloths in a solution of tin or another of the metallic salts to give the silk fabric an added stiffness.

A silk thread is found to be very strong if pulled or stretched (tensile strength); it is also very elastic. Silk is used for knitted garments, which are comfortable to wear because they 'give' to the wearer and yet return to their own shape when taken off. Silk has excellent insulating properties and is therefore cool in summer and warm in winter. It has many industrial and military uses. Cloths and tapes for electrical insulation and filter cloths in the flour industry are made of silk, and some medical supplies such as dressings and sutures. Its great strength makes it a suitable material for parachutes and cartridge bags for naval guns, and also for fishing lines and the strings of tennis racquets and musical instruments.

3. Silk Weaving in Britain. Since synthetic fibres (*see* Textile Fibres, Man-made) have been produced, the British silk industry has become less important. Its most prosperous days were the 18th and 19th centuries, when there were no artificial substitutes, and when men as well as women sometimes wore silk outer garments (*see* Clothes, History of, Vol. XI). As with other British industries, silk owes much to foreign immigrants, and particularly to those from France and Flanders. In the 16th century Flemish weavers made bombazines, of mixed silk and cotton, in Norwich and Colchester. They settled also in Sandwich and Macclesfield, and made silk ribbons in Coventry. The knitting-frame was invented in the 17th century (*see* Hosiery and Knitwear) and Nottingham and Derby began to make quantities of silk stockings for wear by men and women. Many French Protestants or Huguenots (q.v. Vol. I) were driven from France by the loss of their religious rights in 1685, and those who were skilled in silk weaving settled in Spitalfields, which was then a suburb just outside the City of London, and already an important centre for woollen fabrics.

By 1700 silk weaving was one of England's most flourishing industries, and Spitalfields had become its principal centre. From 1713 onwards, the industry was encouraged by protective Tariffs (q.v.) imposed by the Government to keep out silk fabrics woven abroad. The reeled or thrown silk used in England was imported, principally from the eastern Mediterranean, India, and Italy. The technique of silk throwing was not known to British manufacturers until John Lombe, of Derby, brought the knowledge of it from Italy in 1717. He is believed to have disguised himself as a workman and to have worked in an Italian throwing-mill, where he could make drawings of the machinery. Soon after his return the Huguenot family of Courtauld, now famous in the textile industry, began silk-throwing at Braintree in Essex; throwing-mills were opened later in Malmesbury, Sherborne, and Taunton, in the west of England.

The industry reached its highest prosperity in the first half of the 19th century. In Spitalfields weaving was organized largely on the Domestic System (q.v.), and hand-work was the rule. As machinery was invented and applied to the many processes, there was less work for Spitalfields and neighbouring parts of London, but in Macclesfield and other towns of northern England mechanical weaving increased. In 1857, Lister of Bradford rendered the industry a great service by discovering a method of spinning silk waste. During most of the processes, from reeling onwards, much fluff or waste was brushed or rubbed off, and there had hitherto been little or no use for it. The West Riding of Yorkshire became the centre of waste-silk spinning, and for weaving plain and mixed 'spun silk' fabrics. In 1860 the Government tariffs were removed. British makers could no longer compete with imports from France, and the industry gradually declined.

In 1887 the Silk Association of Great Britain and Ireland was formed; today its work of uniting and representing all branches of the industry is carried on by the Silk and Man-Made Fibre Users' Association. The main centres of manufacture are Macclesfield in Cheshire, Sudbury in Suffolk, and Dunfermline in Scotland.

See also Vol. VI: Silkworm.

SILVER-MINING. Silver is the whitest of all metals and, like gold, does not oxidize or scale when heated. Unlike gold, however, it combines with Sulphur (q.v.) and therefore rapidly tarnishes in industrial atmospheres, in the fumes from gas or coal fires, and when kept near vulcanized rubber.

Native silver is not nearly as common in the earth's crust as gold (*see* Metal Ores, Vol. III), but scattered deposits have been found in central Africa, Spain, Armenia, Norway, and North and South America. The palace decorations of the ancient cities of Tyre, Nineveh, and Babylon, and the silver used for coinage in countries between the Indus and the Nile many centuries B.C., were possibly made from silver collected from such sources. The Athenians obtained silver from silver-mines at Laurium, from which they made silver coins used all over the known world (*see* Coins).

Silver also occurs in many parts of the world in the form of a black, soft ore called Argentite (silver sulphide), and the wax-like Kerargyrite or Horn Silver (silver chloride), as well as other more complex minerals. As long ago as 1500

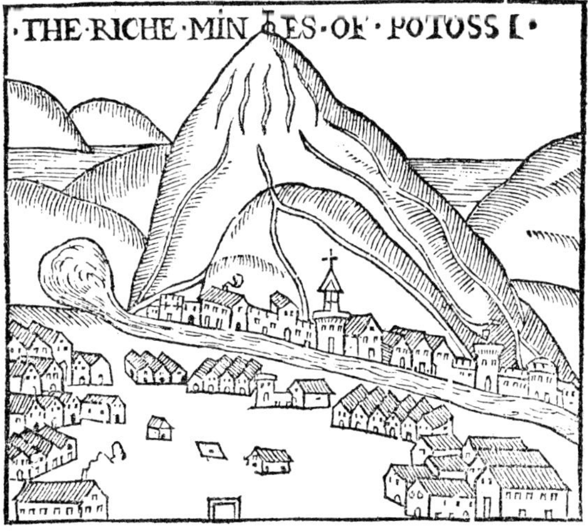

POTOSI, BOLIVIA, WHERE THERE WERE SILVER MINES IN THE 16TH CENTURY

Woodcut from the title-page of Augustin de Zarate's *History of Peru*, 1581

Compania Fresnillos, S.A.

A MINE IN MEXICO PRODUCING SILVER, GOLD, LEAD, ZINC, COPPER, AND IRON

Most of the silver is extracted from the lead ore. The copper and iron ore also contain silver

B.C. the Babylonians and Myceneans found that it was possible to obtain metallic silver from these ores. They used the process known to-day as 'cupellation', which is still practised for refining some types of impure bullion. In this process the ores were heated with lead on a shallow hearth, where they formed a lead-silver ALLOY (q.v. Vol. VIII). Heating was then continued with free access of air. In these circumstances the lead oxidized to form molten lead oxide (litharge), which was run off from the top of the bath (*see* OXIDATION). After some hours all the lead oxidized (as well as any copper, iron, and other base metal impurities, whose oxides dissolve in the litharge); and, on raising the temperature, a pool of molten silver, which might be as much as 99·8% pure, was left on the hearth or 'cupel'. The silver was ladled out, and poured into moulds.

This simple method was practised universally until early in the 16th century, when Mexico became the foremost source of silver. In many Mexican districts fuel and water are scarce, and in 1557 an 'amalgamation' method—a modification of the process used for recovering gold from ores (*see* GOLD-MINING)—was devised, using mercury, common salt, and 'magistral'—an impure form of copper sulphate.

Early in the 20th century the cyanide process (*see* GOLD-MINING) was introduced in South Africa for recovering gold from its ores. It soon became apparent that, with few modifications, the process would prove just as economical for treating silver ores. Before many years, all the principal Mexican mines, which then produced more than half the world's output, were using weak solutions of sodium cyanide to dissolve the silver from the crushed ores, the pulp being agitated with the cyanide solution for about 3 days. The silver was subsequently removed from the solution by adding powdered zinc, and was then collected for melting and refining.

Mexico has remained the chief source of straight silver ores, but by the middle of the 20th century about three-quarters of the world production of silver was obtained, not from silver-miles, but as a BY-PRODUCT of the extraction of LEAD and COPPER (qq.v.). It has been estimated that of the world's production of silver only 20% is derived from straight silver ores;

45% is recovered from lead-zinc ores, 18% from copper and copper-nickel ores, 15% from gold-silver ores, and 2% from tin ores. The important producers of silver are still in the New World: Mexico, the 'Silver' States of America—Montana, Idaho, Colorado, Utah, Nevada, California, Arizona, and New Mexico—and South and Central America. But these producers are now essentially large base-metal refiners, each of which has perfected special methods for recovering the traces of silver present in the products dealt with.

Pure silver is the best known conductor of electricity, and in industry very large quantities are used for electrical contacts. As silver resists corrosion by food acids and many chemicals, it is used to line machines used in food-processing and in the manufacture of such chemicals as acetic acid (*see* ACIDS). Its best-known alloy is standard or sterling silver, containing $7\frac{1}{2}\%$ of copper. This was used for the British silver coinage from the reign of Henry II until 1920, as well as for silverware of all kinds, for hundreds of years. The total world output of silver is about 250 million ounces per year.

See also ASSAYING; MINING.
See also Vol. III: METAL ORES.

SILVER WORK, *see* GOLD AND SILVER WORK.

SLATE INDUSTRY. Slate was formerly much used for the roofs of houses and factories. But during the present century coloured tiles, made of clay or concrete (*see* BRICKS AND TILES), have proved cheaper and more popular, and the output of slate has fallen.

1. DEPOSITS. Slate began as a muddy sediment deposited on the bottom of the sea (*see* ROCKS, Section 4, Vol. III). During later geological ages these beds became deeply buried under other layers. The resultant pressure and heat forced the particles in the sediment into parallel positions (*see* MINERALS, Vol. III), with their broader sides lying all in the same direction, and altered them into hard slate rock which could be easily split.

The presence of slate in certain areas is the joint result of movements in the earth's crust—when the slate beds were crumpled into alternating arch-like and trough-like folds—and the natural process of DENUDATION (q.v. Vol. III). Slate beds that were once horizontal, and buried thousands of feet down, are now often steeply inclined or even vertical, and are exposed on the earth's surface. Where the beds are fairly vertical, and 'outcrop' on level ground or at the bottom of a valley, they are worked in deep open quarries. If they outcrop on a steep mountain-side, quarrying is done in a series of terraces or galleries, and there may sometimes be as many as twenty of these, each providing a working face about 20 yards high. Where the slate beds are not so vertical, open quarrying soon becomes unprofitable because of the cost of removing the increasingly thick layer of useless rock on top of the slate, and it is found cheaper to work it in underground mines. A slate-mine consists of a series of long parallel chambers—which are in effect underground quarries—divided by pillars of slate rock, left in place to support the roof of hard rock covering the slate bed. Most of the slate in Britain is produced in open quarries.

Slate is mainly quarried in Britain in North Wales. The two largest quarries, the Dinorwic Quarry, Llanberis, and the Penrhyn Quarry, Bethesda, are linked by private railways with their own miniature ports in the Menai Strait; together they produce more than half the total British output. Practically all slate is sent to market by rail, but before 1850 all Welsh slate was shipped coastwise, and even in 1900 half of it was still being sent by sea. The other main centres of production in Wales are the Nantlle district of Caernarvonshire, and the slate-mining area of Festiniog, in Merioneth. In England production is concentrated in the Lake District and the Cornwall-Devon-Somerset area. In Scotland the only commercially important slate region is Argyllshire.

2. TECHNIQUE. The first step in the production of slate is to get the blocks out of the rock face and cut them to a size convenient for transport. 'Rockmen', using pneumatic drills, make holes for blasting. The blasting dislodges large blocks, and these are further split and 'pillared' into smaller ones. (Slate rock will fracture at right angles to the line of cleavage.) The small blocks of slate are transported along inclined planes or aerial cableways to 'sheds'. Here they are split into slabs, and then sawn by circular saws into blocks of a convenient size for making into roofing slates by the 'splitters' and the 'dressers'. Splitting is invariably done by hand, and is a difficult task that calls for great skill and long experience. Using steel chisels and wooden mallets, the splitters divide each block into sheets of the required thickness, which are then trimmed to rectangular shapes. There are three methods of trimming: by hand, by a foot-operated machine acting on the principle of a printer's guillotine, or by mechanically driven rotating blades. There are some thirty standard sizes of trimmed slates, and there are other colours than the dull blackish grey so well known in England. The Dinorwic quarry, in particular, produces a variety of colours, including attractive greens.

3. Uses. About 97% of the total output of the industry is roofing slates. The remainder of the output consists of slabs and By-products (q.v.). Slate slabs are used for monumental work, such as gravestones or memorial panels, billiard-tables, brewery and chemical vats, laboratory benches, and blackboards. The Penrhyn quarry produces slate granules and 'flour' out of crushed slate waste. This may be used as a filler or filling material to give bulk to gramophone records, and to such products as plastics, rubber, linoleum, paints, and insecticides. Its main use is as a filling material for the tarry coating given to prefabricated road surfacings. The Dinorwic quarry has produced a kind of mineral wool out of waste rock.

The peak of British slate production was reached in 1898, when 634,000 tons were produced and 19,600 people were employed. In the next 50 years production dropped to a quarter of this amount, for lighter and more colourful roofing materials, far cheaper to produce, had come into use in place of the universal slates which had given a grey look to so many towns in the 19th century.

See also Bricks and Tiles; Stone Dressing; Building Industry.

SLAVE TRADE. A slave is someone who is not free, who is deprived of rights enjoyed by others, and who is compelled to obey a particular master under fear of punishment (*see* Slavery, Vol. X). An extensive trade in human slaves went on from the earliest times until the 19th century. Even in 1935 there was evidence that the trade was still going on in some of the more distant parts of Africa, and in the remotest parts it may still survive even to this day. The earliest slave-markets mentioned in historical records

Topix

SPLITTING SLATE IN A CORNISH QUARRY

Parker Gallery

H.M. BRIG 'BLACK JOKE' ENGAGING A SPANISH SLAVE SHIP OFF THE WEST AFRICAN COAST

Coloured engraving, 1829

were those in the cities of Greece and Asia Minor, around the Aegean Sea. Most of the slaves sent to these markets were people conquered in war: 150,000 slaves are said to have been sold in 168 B.C. after the defeat of Perseus of Macedon. Dealings in slaves regularly took place in the days of ancient Rome. Later, during the DARK AGES (q.v. Vol. I), many slaves were sold in the markets of Spain, and most of these were of Slav race, from beyond the eastern frontiers of Germany. A big trade in these Slavonic captives (from whose name comes the word 'slave') flourished in continental Europe during the Middle Ages, mostly under the control of Jewish dealers. Lyons and Verdun in France, Civita Vecchia and other towns in Italy, Kiev in Russia, and Constantinople (Istanbul) were the main European markets; there were also many markets in Africa, where slavery, which had existed from time immemorial, was widespread.

Slavery as an institution died out in western Europe with the passing away of the FEUDAL SYSTEM (q.v. Vol X) at the close of the Middle Ages, but the trade in African Negro slaves continued. At first it was merely an internal trade, supplying Africa itself and adjoining Moslem countries. But after the period of the 'Discoveries', when Portuguese and Spanish navigators explored Africa and other new lands (*see* EXPLORATION, Vol. IV), European dealers entered the African trade. The Portuguese were the first, and they drew their supplies of slaves from the west coast of Africa. There were big slave-markets in Benguela and Loanda, from which Negro slaves were shipped to Brazil and to the Spanish possessions in the West Indies and South and Central America. By agreement with the local African chieftains the Portuguese at first had a MONOPOLY (q.v.) of this trade. This was disputed by other nations, and in 1563 the English navigator, Sir John Hawkins, carried out a successful raid, and made a profitable shipment of slaves to the West Indies. Later, Dutch and English dealers entered the trade in large numbers, and in the 18th century it reached its peak. These were the days of the famous 'triangular trade' out of the ports of Bristol and Liverpool. Ships went out with gin and cheap finery to the West Coast of Africa, voyaged with cargoes of slaves from Africa to the West Indies and the British colonies in North America, and did the homeward voyage to Bristol with sugar and tobacco. In those days the prosperity of Bristol and the growth of Liverpool were largely founded on this triangular trade, for it was very profitable. The price of the slaves was trifling, and they were sold in the West Indies and on the American mainland at an average price of about £25 per head. During the 18th century nearly 2 million were imported into the British colonies in America. Towards the end of the 18th century a great agitation against the cruelties of the slave trade grew up in Britain, and in 1807 an Act of Parliament introduced by William WILBERFORCE (1759–1833) (q.v. Vol. V) made it unlawful to deal in slaves. Other European nations, and also the northern States of the American Union, soon copied the example of Britain. Until the close of the American CIVIL WAR (q.v. Vol. X) slavery continued in the Southern or Confederate States; in 1832 the price of a young Negro fit for active work on a Southern plantation was well over £100. This rise in prices was largely the result of reduced supplies, for by an American federal law of 1809 no new slave was allowed to be imported into the country. But Arab dealers still continued to deal in African slaves. Zanzibar, off the coast of East Africa, was the big central market; thousands of slaves were sold there every year, and distributed through various other markets all over the Moslem world. At last an agreement was made with the Sultan of Zanzibar, by which his territory ceased to be the centre of the African slave trade; but it still persisted on the mainland of Africa, and was only gradually abolished as the various European nations occupied more territory.

See also Vol. I: AMERICAN NEGROES.
See also Vol. X: SLAVERY; PRISONERS OF WAR.
See also Vol. XI: DOMESTIC SERVICE.

SOAP AND DETERGENT MANUFACTURE. A detergent is a cleansing agent (*see* CLEANING MATERIALS, Vol. XI). There are soapy and soapless detergents, though the word is usually applied to the soapless products. Though the manufacture of the two involves quite different processes, they are usually both made by the same firm; in fact, the old-established soap works first made soapless detergents as a side-line, and later built full-scale plant as the demand for these new products increased.

The demand for soap and detergents in industry is great. All textile trades use soap and other cleansers at almost every stage, and strong detergents are frequently used in engineering and metallurgical industries. Special detergents are made for laundries, for dish-washing machines in canteens and restaurants, for scouring milk, beer, and medicine bottles, for the cleaning of plant in factories, and for cleaning trains, buses, and such things.

1. SOAP. This is made from fats or oils combined chemically with the ALKALIS caustic soda or potash (q.v.). The making of soap is an old industry. It was important in Italy and Spain in the 8th century, and in the 13th century Marseilles in France was a soap-making centre, using olive-oil as the main raw material. Soap works in England appear to have existed by the 14th century. The methods of manufacture were rather haphazard until the 19th century, when a greater understanding of the chemistry of oils and fats led to a more scientific approach. The raw materials are tallow and grease from animal fat and vegetable oils from coconut, cotton-seed, soya bean, palm kernel, and groundnut. At

SAPONIFICATION

A jet of mixed oil and alkali enters the soap for heating

first vegetable oils were considered too soft for use, but a method of hardening oils (hydrogenation) was discovered early in this century.

'Saponification' is the technical name for soap-making. Soft soap, the simplest soap to make, is produced by boiling the oil with water and caustic potash or with a mixture of potash and caustic soda. Hard soaps are made either by the boiling or by the cold process. The latter, which is far the cheapest, can be done only with coconut or palm kernel oil; its chief disadvantage is that glycerine, a valuable substance in fats and oils, remains in the soap instead of being separated and sold as a by-product.

For the cold process the materials are well mixed and slightly warmed. As the soap begins to form it affects the rest of the mixture chemically, speeding up the saponification and causing a further rise in heat. For the boiling process, the boiling of the fats or oil with a quantity of alkali (usually caustic soda) brings about saponification; the impurities can be skimmed off, and a repeated boiling in brine separates the glycerine, which is used, for example, in making drugs and explosives.

For household soap the boiled soap is cooled by evaporation, and refined twice. Toilet soap is refined four times, perfumed, and then cut. For soap flakes a thin film of soap is run on to a cold steel drum where it cools into a sheet which is slit into ribbons and dried. The ribbons are then passed over rotating steel rolls placed one on top of another, on which they form a very fine skin. This skin, marked out as diamond-shaped flakes by sharp rotating knives, is skimmed from the top roll.

2. Soapless Detergents. Most synthetic detergent powders are formed by the chemical interaction of certain mineral oils and oleum, a form of sulphuric acid—a process called 'sulphonation'. The resulting sulphonic acid is neutralized with caustic soda. The molecules of a detergent consist of two parts, one attracted by water and repelled by oil, and the other part attracted by oil and repelled by water. This allows a solution of the detergent in water to get past any grease barrier and wash away dirt.

The sulphonated and neutralized liquid is made into a powder by spraying the liquid, mixed with detergent aids such as phosphates, through a rising current of hot air. This solidifies the drops.

See also Vol. XI: Fats and Oils; Cleaning Materials.

SOFTWOODS. The word 'softwoods' is used by the timber trade to mean wood coming from conifers, such as pine, fir, and spruce (*see* Trees, Coniferous, Vol. VI).

The softwoods of the world are distributed in a fairly well-defined belt running from the northern part of the British Isles and the Baltic countries to the northern half of Russia and Siberia, and continuing across the Bering Strait to the northern half of North America. Although softwood trees are not common in tropical countries they are often found there at a high elevation in the mountain ranges, where the climate is permanently colder. The world's two great reserves of softwoods are in Canada and other parts of North America, and in Russia and Siberia; in each of these localities there are coniferous forests so vast that great areas of them are still untouched.

Only two of our principal softwoods come from European countries. The first of these is the European Redwood, also called Red Deal, Yellow Deal, and other names depending upon the exact source of origin. Trees producing this timber grow in Britain, where they are known as Scots Pine. The second is the European Whitewood, also called White Deal; it is the product of a spruce-tree which in this country is known either as Common or Norway Spruce. Most of the timber from Europe comes already sawn into boards and planks; but there is a considerable proportion of pitprops and round poles, most of these being telegraph poles.

Softwoods are bought and sold commercially by the 'standard'; a standard is 165 cubic feet of timber, and the term is used for softwoods only. About a quarter of the British imports of softwoods go to the Building Industry (q.v.), and a similar amount is used in the manufacture of boxes and packing cases, largely for the export trade. The coal-mines also use quantities of softwood pitprops, which are treated by a preservative process to protect them from attack by wood-rotting fungi. British Railways use a great deal of softwood and hardwood, principally for sleepers. Sleepers are treated with creosote before being laid on the track and for that reason have quite a long life. Softwood poles are used for overhead electric transmission, by the Post Office for telegraph and telephone services, for the cargo derricks of ships, and for the masts and spars of yachts; and softwood planks and baulks are used as shuttering for concrete construction,

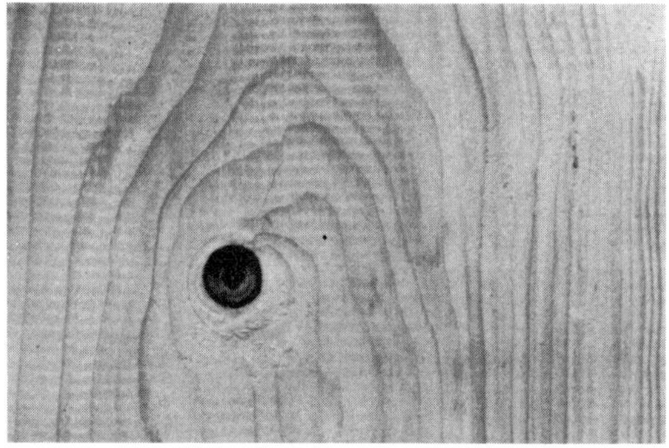

COMMON SPRUCE

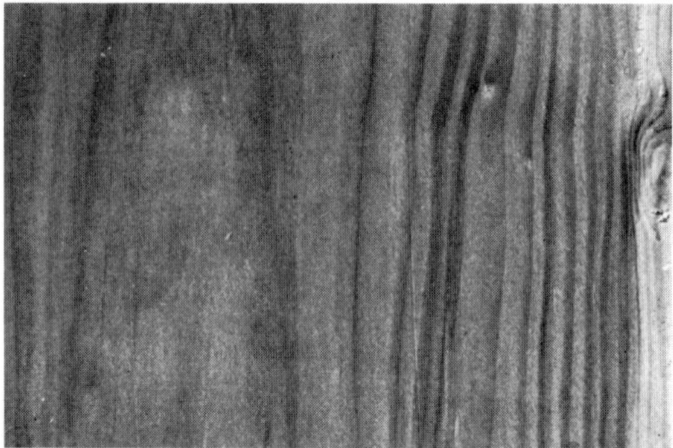

EUROPEAN LARCH

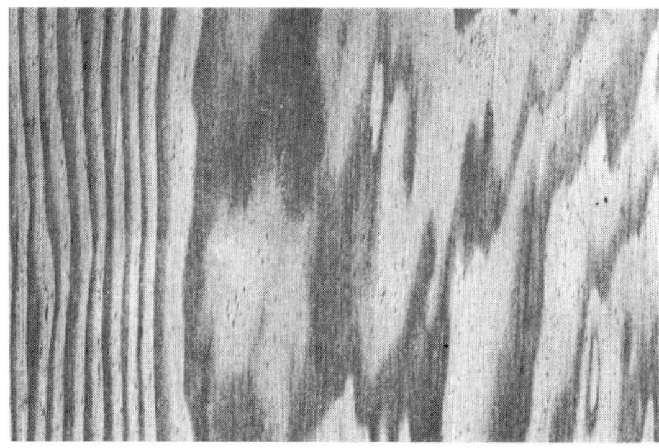

Timber Development Assn.

DOUGLAS FIR

in dock and harbour work, and for sea defence works.

See also TIMBER; HARDWOODS.
See also Vol. VI: FORESTRY; TREES, CONIFEROUS.

SOUTH SEA BUBBLE. 'Bubble' is a word that used to be applied to SHARES OF COMPANIES (qq.v.) when they were pushed up to unjustified prices by wild promises and speculative rumours —'blown up by the air of great words' (*see* SPECULATION). The name was first used in 1636, when there was a big boom in Dutch tulips. Tulips were bought and sold in Amsterdam like mining shares, and rose rapidly in price, only to collapse equally rapidly later on.

'South Sea Bubble' is the name given to the speculation in the shares of the South Sea Company and other concerns in the early 18th century. The Company was formed in 1711 as a CHARTERED COMPANY (q.v.), its objects being (according to its charter) 'trading to the South Seas and other parts of America and encouraging the Fishery'. The South Seas meant Central and South America, and 'fishery' referred to whaling. The original stock or CAPITAL (q.v.) issued was increased in 1714 and 1717, and speculative dealings in the Company's shares began in earnest in 1719, when the directors of the Company suggested that they might take over the responsibility of gradually paying off Britain's NATIONAL DEBT (q.v. Vol. X). They offered the Government £7 millions in cash (to be subscribed by the Company's stockholders) for this privilege, and, as the Government had greatly increased the National Debt by the cost of the War of the Spanish Succession, they accepted the proposal eagerly. A Bill was passed through Parliament in 1720, with Government support, and before it reached the House of Lords each £100 of the Company's stock was being dealt in at a price of £400—four times its nominal value. The support given to the project by the Government, over-optimistic calculations of profits, and wild rumours led to still further speculation, and the stock rose in the end to ten times its nominal value. At the height of the boom Change Alley and Cornhill in the City of London were almost impassable. The directors of the Company, taking advantage of this boom, issued a further £1 million of stock at three times its nominal value, and another £1 million worth at four times its nominal value, the second offer being all bought up in a few hours. The speculative fever that attacked the investing public, and the general feeling of optimism that came from the rapid rise in the Company's stock, led to the starting-up of other concerns. Some only lasted for a few days; one promoter advertised in a newspaper for subscriptions 'to a certain promising or profitable design, which will hereafter be promulgated'. On this extremely vague prospectus, the promoter of the enterprise sold in a few hours 1,000 £1 shares for £2 each, and then disappeared and was never heard of again.

When such a feverish stage is reached booms of this kind usually collapse. The South Sea Bubble soon 'burst', and the prices of the Company's stock and of the shares of other companies collapsed. Thousands of speculators were ruined, and the directors of the Company had to meet big claims out of their own private estates. The South Sea trade gave few opportunities of profit, and the Company turned its attention to the whaling fishery. But after eight successive annual voyages the Company had made no money out of whaling, and in 1750 an arrangement with Spain deprived the Company of any advantage in the South American trade. In 1807 the Company's exclusive trading rights were formally taken from it by Parliament, and after some years it was finally wound up.

See also Speculation; Stocks and Shares.

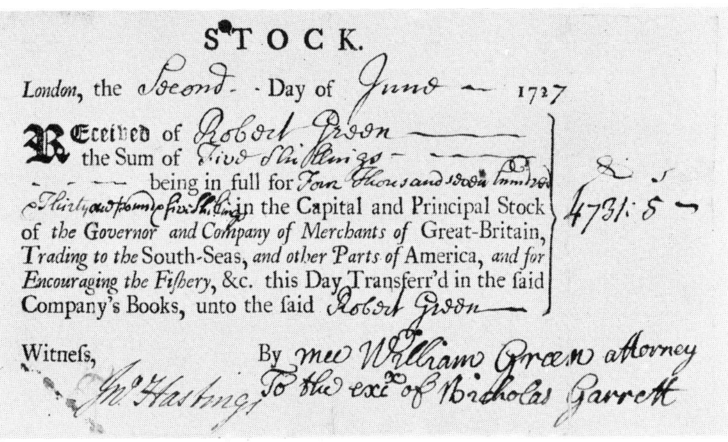

STOCK.

London, the Second Day of June 1727

Received of Robert Green
the Sum of Five Shillings
being in full for Four Thousand Seven hundred Thirty one pounds five Shillings in the Capital and Principal Stock of the Governor and Company of Merchants of Great-Britain, Trading to the South-Seas, and other Parts of America, and for Encouraging the Fishery, &c. this Day Transferr'd in the said Company's Books, unto the said Robert Green

£ s
4731: 5

Witness, By mee William Green attorney
Jn. Hastings To the exr of Nicholas Garrett

RECEIPT FOR AN INVESTMENT IN SOUTH SEA STOCK, DATED 1727

SOYA BEAN, *see* Oils, Vegetable.

See also Vol. VI: Soya Bean.

SPECIALIZATION, *see* Division of Labour.

SPECULATION. By speculation we usually mean market dealings (buying or selling) by persons who are neither manufacturers nor merchants, and who are out to make profits for themselves. There is obviously nothing to be said for the unintelligent gambler; but the intelligent speculator has had his place and his use in the world of business.

An example may make this clear. Let us suppose that a speculator has made a careful study of the production and consumption of plantation rubber all over the world, and that he forms the opinion that there is likely to be serious over-production. He sells fairly large quantities of rubber (which he does not yet possess) by promising to deliver it on the London market a year ahead (*see* Market). His action in selling such large quantities causes the price to fall. Other people join in the selling movement, and lower the price still further. A year later, when the speculator has to buy rubber to fulfil his earlier contract to deliver, he can therefore buy it more cheaply than he sold it—and so he makes a good deal of money.

During the year, as the result of his action and that of other people, the price of rubber has been steadily dropping; and this may have had two effects. It may have stopped someone planting still more rubber-trees; and it may have led business men to buy rubber for some useful purpose which could not have been afforded at the earlier high price. It is true that the over-production of rubber would have produced these results in time, without the action of the speculator, but he has helped to hasten the changes.

The markets in 'futures', in which goods can be bought or sold for delivery many months ahead, can be useful to merchants and manufacturers, and could not be so easily or freely organized if there were no speculators. For example, a miller can buy wheat on 1 January in order to mill it into flour during the next 3 months. But during that time the price of flour may fall. So the miller, on 1 January, promises to sell a quantity of wheat for delivery on 1 April. If by 1 April wheat has fallen in price, the price of flour will also have fallen in sympathy; so the miller must sell his flour more cheaply, and make a loss on his milling. But what he has lost on milling will be made up by what he gains when, on 1 April, he buys cheap wheat to fulfil his earlier contract to deliver. Dealings of this kind are called 'hedging' contracts.

A dangerous form of speculation is that in 'foreign exchange' or Currency (q.v.). Speculation in commodities or in Stocks and Shares

Neck or Nothing, or the downfall of ye Missippi Company.
IAT JUSTITIA,
UERUNT REGNA
Should Law be just to unjust Laws,
And all his proud Directors,
The Law must hang up Laws, because
The vilest of Projectors,
Let this invite you to behold
Their decent Execution,
Who basely, for the Sake of Gold,
Have brought us to confusion.
A Sermon, you shall allso hear,
From Jerry's Lamentation,
To comfort suff'rers that appear
Upon this Sad Occasion
The words appointed for the Text are
Lamentations Chap. iv. verses the 5. & 18.
They that did feed delicately, are become desolate in the Streets They that were brought up in scarlet, embrace dunghills. They hunt our Steps that we cannot go in our Streets: our end is near; our days are fulfilled, for our end is come.
Engrav'd by Mons.r Duchange Engraver to the Missippi Company in France.
Sold by ye Printsellers of London & Westminster Price 6

AN 18TH-CENTURY PRINT SHOWING THE FATE DESERVED BY THE PROMOTERS OF SPECULATIVE COMPANIES

The figure of Justice presides over the execution of the promoters

(q.v.) is subject to certain natural economic checks: in the long run prices are bound to come back to what the goods or the shares are really worth. But speculation in foreign money is quite different. If an international ring of speculators were to put down the value of British money (the pound sterling) from 2 dollars 40 cents to only 2 dollars, by selling large quantities of pounds, the results would be that all imports to Britain from the United States, and from countries financially connected with the United States, would cost about one-sixth more in British money. Wages paid in Great Britain would then buy less, and there would be trade union pressure to have them raised; this would cause an increase in the prices of our exported goods, and so the new and lower value of the pound in foreign countries, being now economically justified, would be maintained (*see* RATES OF EXCHANGE). This kind of speculation must be prevented, and the method adopted in Britain since 1932 has been to provide the Bank of England with a fund of gold, dollars, and other foreign currencies sufficiently large to counter the activities of the speculators. The total gold and dollar reserves are published soon after the end of every month, and the variations in the monthly figures are closely watched by statesmen and others responsible for the stability of the pound sterling.

See also INTERNATIONAL FINANCE.

SPINNING, *see* WOOL SPINNING; COTTON MANUFACTURE; LINEN INDUSTRY.

STANDARD OF LIVING. The 'standard of living' of any country means the average person's share of the goods and services which the country produces. A country's standard of living, therefore, depends first and foremost on its capacity to produce wealth. 'Wealth' in this sense is not money, for we do not live on money but on the things that money can buy: 'goods' such as food and clothing, and 'services' such as transport and entertainment.

A country's capacity to produce wealth depends upon many factors, most of which have an effect on one another. Wealth depends to a great extent upon a country's natural resources, such as coal, gold, and other minerals, water-supply, and so on. Some regions of the world are well supplied with coal and minerals, and have a fertile soil and a favourable climate; other regions possess perhaps only one of these things, and some regions possess none of them. The U.S.A. is one of the wealthiest regions of the world because she has vast natural resources within her borders, her soil is fertile, and her climate is varied. India, on the other hand, has fewer such advantages.

Next to natural resources comes the ability to turn them to use. China is perhaps as well off as the U.S.A. in natural resources, but has suffered for many years from civil and external wars, and for this and other reasons has been unable to develop her resources. Sound and stable political conditions, and freedom from foreign invasion, enable a country to develop its natural resources peacefully and steadily, and to produce more wealth than another country equally well served by nature but less well ordered. Another important factor is the technical efficiency of a country's people. Old countries that have, through many centuries, trained up numerous skilled craftsmen and technicians are better placed to produce wealth than countries whose workers are largely unskilled. Wealth also begets wealth. As a country becomes wealthier, its people have a larger margin for saving, and can put their savings into factories and machines which will help workers to turn out more goods in their working day.

A country's standard of living does not only depend upon the wealth that is produced and consumed within its own borders, but also upon what is indirectly produced through INTERNATIONAL TRADE (q.v.). For example, Britain's wealth in foodstuffs and other agricultural products would be much less if she had to depend only on those grown at home. Trade makes it possible for our surplus manufactured goods to be traded abroad for the agricultural products that would otherwise be lacking. A country's wealth is, therefore, much influenced by its manufacturing capacity, provided that other countries can be found ready to accept its manufactures.

Population is also an important influence. A country's population may be, to start with, too big or too small for the best use of its resources. Countries such as India and China are generally thought to be overpopulated. Their immense populations put a great strain upon the available natural resources, particularly agricultural land. There are so many people growing foodstuffs on a limited quantity of land, and foreign trade and manufacturing are so underdeveloped, that the standard of living of the masses of the population is extremely low. A smaller population would make it necessary to farm only the more fertile land, and there would consequently be a larger average share of food for each person. But a country may even have too small a population for the full development of its natural resources. If, for example, the population of North America were only one-tenth of what it is today, the much smaller market for goods would make it more difficult to manufacture them cheaply on mass-production lines, and the standard of living of the average American—particularly in such things as motor-cars and labour-saving household goods—would be lower than it is today.

But it is not only the quantity of a country's population that influences its wealth. The quality of the population needs also to be taken into account. Skill and craftsmanship have been already mentioned as important, but a great deal depends upon what proportion of the population is engaged in useful work. Other things being equal, less wealth will be produced in a country with a large non-working class than in another where most people work. For example, the average standard of living in 18th-century France was far lower than it might have been; and the high standard of living of the U.S.A. owes much to the long-standing tradition that even the sons and daughters of the rich should work. The proportion of young people to old people affects considerably the number of a country's workers. If the population of any country is gradually getting larger, it will have a smaller proportion of old people than one whose population is falling; and old people who are no longer fit to work must be supported by the work of those who are younger.

To calculate the average standard of living of any country, one divides its 'national income' by the number of people in it. Strictly, the term 'national income' means the total of goods and services produced for consumption in that country in a year; but such a total cannot be divided unless it is expressed in money. There are in the United Kingdom over 50 million people to share the national income; if its money value is divided between them, the average share of each person in 1967 was approximately £550, increasing yearly by about $2\frac{1}{2}\%$ in real terms. Averages, though convenient to use, do not always show clearly the true facts (*see* STATISTICS), and some groups of our population receive more than the equivalent of £550 a year, and other groups less. Tradition and habit influence the standard of living of different kinds of people, and once a group has got used to a certain standard of living, it does not like to give it up. Just as there are varying standards of living for different groups within a country, so also there are varying standards between different countries. Britain's standard of living, for example, is below that of the U.S.A., but it is higher than that of south-eastern Europe, the U.S.S.R., and the countries of the East.

See also COST OF LIVING.

STATEMENT, *see* INVOICES.

STATISTICS. 1. The object of statistics is to find out information about groups of people or things by collecting facts about them, and arranging these in an orderly way. Those who compile the figures, and make a scientific study of them, are called statisticians.

Statistics are very important to business men, as well as to statesmen and government officials. A merchant who buys and sells goods is interested particularly in comparing past and present trading results, and often in trying to forecast future trends (*see* MARKET RESEARCH). He may also want to compare the result of one branch with those of another, or of one department with another's. Manufacturers are also interested in knowing how the sales of some products are progressing as compared with the sales of others, and also in checking the quality and standard of the goods turned out.

Some businesses use statistics for more definite purposes. INSURANCE (q.v.), for instance, is really based upon the belief that the future will follow fairly closely the pattern of the past. For example, a life insurance company must know the number of people who die in any given year compared with the total number of the population, and also the average ages at which death has taken place. From statistics of past experience they can make fairly accurate estimates of the future, and can construct what are called 'mortality tables'. Similarly, companies insuring against accidents at sea or on land, or against other events (such as rain on a Bank Holiday), must know what lessons the past has to teach before they can work out how much they must charge for insuring against such risks in the future.

2. METHODS OF PRESENTATION. Statistics can be set out in a number of different ways. One method is to tabulate the figures in several sets of columns. Figures presented in this way, however, do not very easily draw attention to the really important points; the eye and the other senses do not quickly take in their meaning. Figures are therefore often more effective if they are expressed in the form of diagrams. The 'bar' diagram is one of the most useful. Thus we could represent a firm's sales on a bar diagram (*see* Fig. 1).

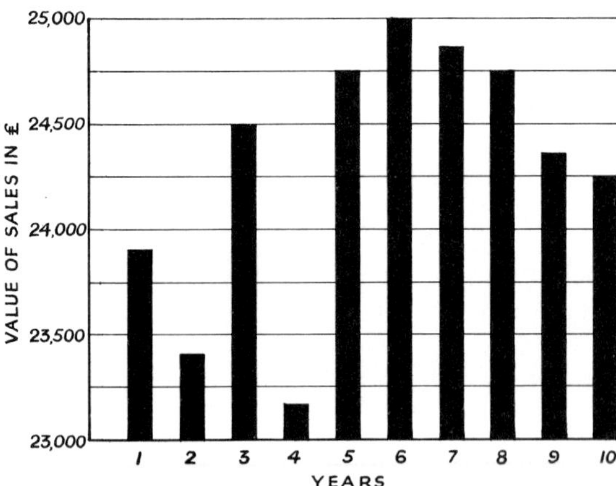

FIG. 1. A FIRM'S YEARLY SALES SHOWN IN A BAR DIAGRAM

This diagram arranges the history of the firm's sales over the past 10 years in a way that hits the eye, and enables anyone studying the diagram to take in at a glance the years that have been most or least successful. The diagram could also be used to build up a curve showing the up-and-down movements of sales over the 10-year period.

If we join the tops of each of the bars by a connected series of lines, we get an up-and-down curve, rather like a hospital patient's temperature chart (*see* Fig. 2). We can then, if we wish,

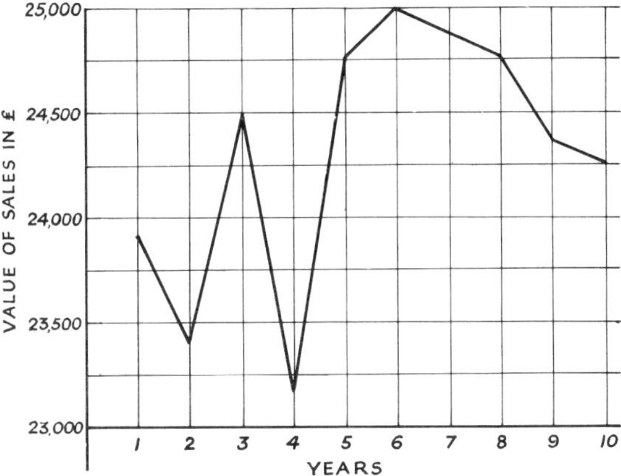

FIG. 2. THE SAME YEARLY SALES SHOWN IN A GRAPH

plot on the same graph any other figures which may help to explain the changes in sales. The percentage of insured workers employed in any year would be a useful figure, as sales in general would be very likely to vary with the total of workers' money incomes (*see* Fig. 3).

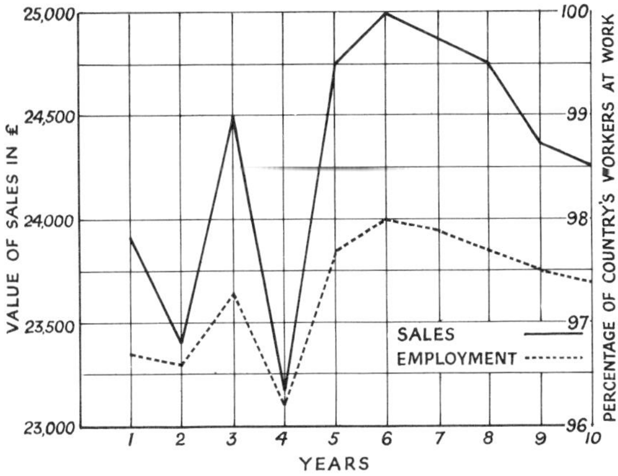

FIG. 3. THE YEARLY SALES (AS IN FIG. 2) COMPARED WITH EMPLOYMENT

The employment curve in this diagram follows the sales curve very closely: as indeed it should. If there are big differences between the sales curve and the employment curve in particular years, this indicates that sales per worker are fluctuating. When two or more sets of figures are compared in this way, their relationship to each other is called a 'correlation'. The closeness of this relationship is called the 'coefficient of correlation'. Fig. 3 shows a very close correlation between the two sets of figures.

Statistics can also be presented in the form of pictures. We could thus compare, say, the average output per man in one country with that in another, or the average output per man of one factory in a big business with that of another. Diagrams to show these might take the form of a black-shaded or coloured picture of a worker, drawn to scale in such a way that the taller the man the greater is the output represented. This method is much used in government posters and publications, particularly those connected with matters of production and output, and designed to appeal to the ordinary man or woman. Care must be taken in the preparation of such diagrams, and in the scales used. For example, if comparative figures are represented by circles or squares, it must be remembered that a circle and a square of the same width will have different areas.

Only limited information can be given in simple statistics of this sort. For example, a curve, showing the movement in yearly sales over a series of years, does not take account of changes in circumstances which may have affected sales in certain years. The CAPITAL (q.v.) of the firm, for instance, may have increased, the number of factories at work may be larger, or the total number of workers may have grown; for such reasons the yearly sales are likely to go up in any case. What is really wanted is a diagram which will show, not the yearly sales, but the way in which the average sales for a period of years are moving. If we worked out for each year the average sales for, say, the past 5 years, each time dropping the first year and substituting the last, we should obtain what is called a 'moving average'. Using the figures of Fig. 2, and plotting a curve from them, we should obtain the diagram shown in Fig. 4, which gives more complete information.

3. THE MODE. There are other business problems which statistics may help to solve. To take an example, a boot and shoe manufacturer is interested in knowing how many pairs there ought to be of each different size out of, say, every hundred. It is not possible for him to send REPRESENTATIVES (q.v.) into every household in the country, and to take a sort of census of sizes and fittings. Statistics can help here, by using what is called 'the law of statistical regularity'. If a reasonably large number of items is

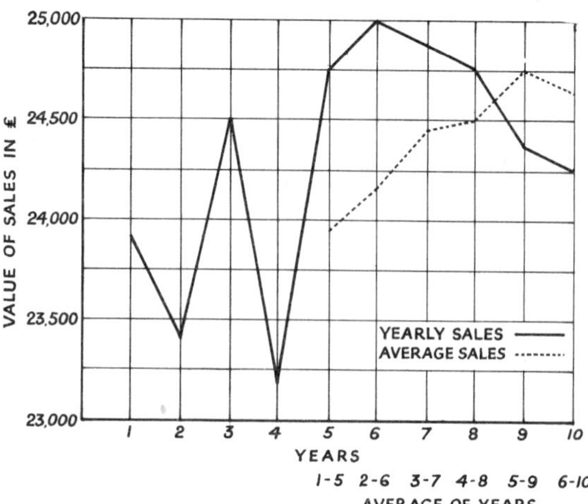

FIG. 4. THE YEARLY SALES (AS IN FIG. 2) AND THE AVERAGES OF SALES OVER PERIODS OF 5 YEARS

chosen at random from a very much larger number of items, the difference between what an analysis of the smaller number can tell us, and what we should learn if we examined the whole, is likely to be extremely small. Our boot-manufacturer could therefore solve his problem by taking several 'random samples' of the population (say, 100 families in each of ten different districts of the country), and then assembling and arranging the result. Naturally, success would largely depend on the random way in which the instances had been chosen. All kinds of social groups and classes must be more or less equally mixed together in each sample. The results of such an investigation might be: size 6, 109 pairs; size 7, 141 pairs; size 8, 343 pairs; size 9, 232 pairs; size 10, 134 pairs; size 11, 41 pairs.

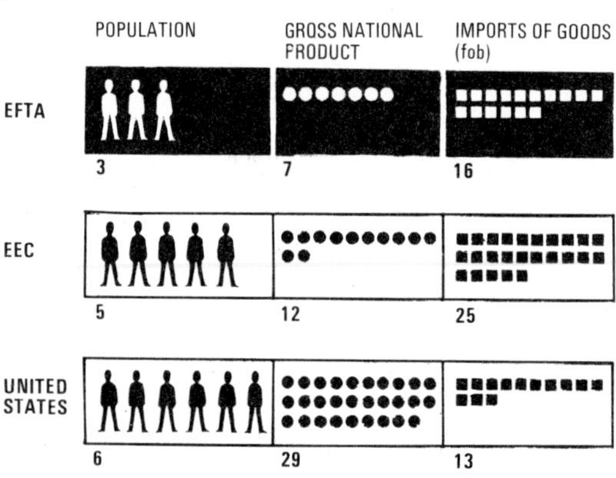

FIG. 5. PICTORIAL DIAGRAM SHOWING COMPARISON BETWEEN EUROPEAN FREE TRADE ASSOCIATION, EUROPEAN ECONOMIC COMMUNITY, AND UNITED STATES, IN THREE RESPECTS—POPULATION, GROSS NATIONAL PRODUCT, AND IMPORTS

Our manufacturer would be interested in working out the average size of shoe worn. A layman might say that the average size of shoe, calculated from the above figures, would be $8\frac{1}{2}$: that is, the various sizes added up, and divided by 6, which is the number of different sizes. This is called the 'arithmetic average', and is useless for our purposes, if there is no such actual size as $8\frac{1}{2}$. It is more important for our manufacturer to know which is the size that most frequently occurs out of the whole thousand samples taken. This is obviously size 8, and statisticians would call size 8 the 'mode', or 'modal' size: namely, that size likely to be most frequently met with in actual practice. The 'mode' is, therefore, of more use to the manufacturer than any average, because he could arrange to manufacture more pairs of the modal size than of other sizes, and by applying mass-production methods to their manufacture to reduce their cost, and thus to reduce the average selling price of shoes in general.

The 'mode' is being found of increasing use in business statistics. For instance, in comparing the trading results of a MULTIPLE SHOP organization, it might be found useful to find out the 'modal' profit expressed as a percentage of TURNOVER (qq.v.): that is, the figure which is attained by the largest number of branches. It would then be possible to investigate 'sub-modal' branches, so as to find out why they did not do so well; and the 'super-modal' branches might also be studied, so as to find out what made them more efficient than the others. In a manufacturing industry, using large numbers of similar machines, a modal output for a machine could be established; this could be used to detect and check inefficiency, and to increase efficiency by discovering what features there were about the super-modal machines that made their performance so outstanding.

Modern statistical technique also assists manufacturers in another way. Most factories have an inspection department, which examines the products to see that they are of a standard quality and finish. This department cannot, of course, examine every single article produced; it must work by the 'random sampling' method, described above. An analysis of such results will establish the modal size and finish. It may then be necessary to work out to what extent goods can be allowed to be inferior to the mode.

4. THE INDEX NUMBER. This is another

statistical device used in the modern world. It is much used in government and other economic statistics, particularly those which show changes in wholesale and retail prices and in the Cost of Living (q.v.). A mass of figures for different articles would convey little information; and, for any cost-of-living graph, the number of items appearing in an average person's normal weekly list of purchases would be so immense that the number of lines and curves would merely create confusion. But if a representative collection of items were priced in any year, and the result called 100 (which would be the index for that year), the same collection of goods could be priced at later periods and the cost expressed as a percentage of the cost in the standard year. For instance, if goods became slightly cheaper in one year, the index number might fall from 100 to 94; if, in a later year, prices rose a good deal, the index number might become 110 or more. The index number has been found so useful in practice that, in certain industries, wages are regulated upwards or downwards according to the movement of the cost-of-living index.

See also Scientific Management.
See also Vol. X: Vital Statistics.

STEEL INDUSTRY, *see* Vol. VIII: Iron and Steel.

STOCK EXCHANGES are regular associations of dealers in Stocks and Shares (q.v.). An association was not formed in London until late in the 18th century, although dealings had previously taken place among bankers, brokers, and financial houses. The members of the new association met regularly at a coffee-house in Change Lane, known as 'Jonathan's', and early in the 19th century they acquired a building of their own. The New York Stock Exchange had even humbler beginnings, for at the end of the 18th century it started as a street market under a spreading tree in Lower Wall Street.

Early dealings were limited mainly to Government loans or gilt-edged securities (so called because of the gold-bordered paper on which they were printed) and the stocks of the larger Chartered Companies (q.v.). As the Industrial Revolution (q.v.) went on, dealings began to take place in the shares of the unlimited liability companies (*see* Limited Companies) which came on to the market in growing numbers. The limited liability companies which followed the Companies Acts of 1855 and 1862 greatly helped the development of the London Stock Exchange, and in America Wall Street began to develop at the same time.

The organization of the London Stock Exchange is different from that of other stock exchanges and of the continental exchanges or 'bourses'. In London there is a rigid division of membership into those who act as jobbers or dealers and those who act as Brokers (q.v.); in most other stock-markets all members carry on both functions. In London the jobber or dealer is really a kind of shopkeeper in securities. Just as there are different shops for different commodities, so there are different firms of jobbers in different markets. Usually a firm of jobbers specializes in one market, such as the gilt-edged market, the miscellaneous industrial market, or the 'Kaffir' market (which is the market in South African mining shares). The broker is just an intermediary between the jobbers and the outside public, since non-members are not admitted to the 'House', as the Stock Exchange is called.

A broker, wishing to deal for a client, goes down to the House and asks perhaps several jobbers what prices they are 'making' in the shares concerned. The price quoted by any jobber will actually be a pair of prices, such as $5–5\frac{1}{16}$. This means that if the broker's client wants to sell the shares named, the jobber will buy them at £5 each; but if the client wants to buy them, the jobber will arrange to sell them at £5 1*s.* 3*d.*. The difference between the two prices is the jobber's 'turn', or profit. A broker may approach several jobbers before deciding where he can get the best terms for his client. The 'bargain', as it is called, is entered in the jobber's book, and the broker posts off that evening to his client a Contract Note, which gives details of the transaction at the price arranged and also includes the broker's commission or brokerage. If the client is a buyer, he has to pay Government transfer stamp duty, and also a small transfer fee to the company (if he is buying other than Government securities) for a new share certificate. All the routine details of settlement are arranged through the Stock Exchange Clearing Department.

On the London Stock Exchange dealings in gilt-edged securities take place 'for cash': that is, the buyer must settle for his purchase as soon as his broker delivers his stock. Dealings in other securities take place 'for the Account'.

Fox Photos

THE LONDON STOCK EXCHANGE
Members are seen dealing in gilt-edged securities

Each 'Account' is a trading period of 14 days; when a bank holiday comes within the period of an Account the period is usually extended to 21 days. The ordinary investor buying securities dealt in for the Account is expected to settle for them on or before the Account Day or settling day, but much more latitude is given to speculators. Speculators are either 'bulls' or 'bears'. A bull is a person who buys shares—often beyond his capacity to pay—hoping that they will go up in price and that he will be able to sell them at a profit. A bear is a person who sells shares which very often he does not possess, hoping that by the time settlement has to be made he will be able to buy them in at a lower price than the figure at which he originally sold them. It is very unusual for bulls or bears to be able to achieve these ambitions within a single Account, and they usually wish to 'continue' their transactions over several Accounts. It is generally possible for their brokers to arrange this. Towards the end of each Account a 'making-up' price is fixed for each security. The speculator pays or receives the difference between his original price and the making-up price, and the transaction is 'continued' or 'carried over' until the Account Day next following. For this privilege bulls have to pay a rate of interest, called 'contango', while bears normally receive a smaller contango. Contango rates are generally much above the rates at which loans or overdrafts are granted by the banks, and many speculators pay for their shares on Account Day in the ordinary way and get their banks to finance their dealings.

Stock exchanges are useful to business in that they provide a free market in stocks and shares, and offer a means by which the worth of investments can be valued. Capital for industry would not be found so easily if investors did not feel that they could sell their shares when they wished. In recent years the Government and the Stock Exchange Committee have done much to prevent reckless SPECULATION (q.v.).

See also FINANCE; STOCKS AND SHARES.

STOCKING MANUFACTURE, *see* HOSIERY AND KNITWEAR.

STOCKS AND SHARES. These are investments that can be bought and sold on stock exchanges. Formerly the word 'stock' nearly always meant an investment on which a fixed rate of interest was paid, and 'share' meant an investment receiving a dividend paid out of profits which varied from time to time. But this distinction no longer holds good. Whether a company calls its capital 'stock' or 'shares' is of no real importance. A share is a fractional part of the capital of a company; stock is so many £s worth of the capital. Thus a company with a capital of £100,000 might arrange for its capital to be in 100,000 shares of £1 each, or it might arrange for it to be in 20,000 shares of £5. On the other hand, it might decide that its capital should be in stock. A person with 1,000 £1 shares in a company with a capital of £100,000 in £1 shares owns a one-hundredth share in the prosperity or misfortune of the company; a person owning £1,000 worth of stock is in exactly the same position.

Government LOANS (q.v.) are usually stocks which are transferable from one investor to another in multiples of £1. The older Government stocks, such as 2½% Consols, can be transferred in multiples of a penny. The loans of foreign governments and the capital of overseas railways are mostly stocks, and nearly all DEBENTURES (q.v.) are stocks. The bulk of the capital of other concerns dealt in on the Stock Exchange is in shares.

Stocks and shares may be of different classes: that is, the legal and voting rights and the interest or dividend rights of the various stockholders and shareholders may vary. Debentures, and the priority rights of their holders, are explained in the article DEBENTURES. (In any case, debentures are not shares in the fortune of a business, but loans made to it against the security of its assets.) Apart from debentures, stocks and shares can be divided into two main classes, 'preference' and 'ordinary', although there is a variety of names for each class. A preference share gives the holder the right to be paid a dividend out of the earned profits of a company before any dividend is paid to a non-preference shareholder, that is, an owner of ordinary shares. The limit of a preference dividend is stated in the title of the share. This might be, say, a 6% or 7% preference share, which means that earned profits will first be used for paying the preference shareholders their 6% or 7%, as the case may be, and that any profits then left over will be divided among the ordinary shareholders, as the directors decide.

Naturally, preference shares are a steadier kind of investment than ordinary shares, and are not so liable to changes of price on the Stock Exchange. There are various types of preference share. The most solid is the 'cumulative preference' share: if the fixed dividend due to the holders of these shares cannot be paid in any one year because there are not enough profits, the amount which is left unpaid becomes 'cumulative', that is to say, it accumulates as a debt and has to be paid out of the profits of later years. After a long trade depression, one sometimes reads that certain cumulative preference dividends are 3 or 4 years in arrear, but they may one day be paid, whereas a 'passed' ordinary dividend is not paid later. Another type is the 'participating preference' share, which entitles the shareholder to a fixed preference dividend and also to a 'participation' or share-out with the ordinary shareholders in what is left over, according to the terms on which the shares are issued.

Ordinary shareholders are entitled to dividends paid out of earned profits after the dividends due to the preference shareholders have been paid. Ordinary shareholders are said to own the 'equity' of a company: that is, the whole of its earning power after all fixed obligations have been met. Usually the rates of interest on debentures, and the fixed rates of dividend on preference shares, are lower than the percentage a good company can earn on its ordinary shares. If this is so, the equity owned by the ordinary shareholders becomes very valuable, and they may receive high dividends. Companies with a large amount of debentures or preference shares in proportion to ordinary share capital are said to have their capital structure 'highly geared'. Just as there are many types of preference share, so there are different types of ordinary share. 'Preferred ordinary' shares are really another name for preference shares. In some companies there are 'deferred' shares, which do not receive a dividend until the ordinary shares have received a fixed maximum. This device really turns the ordinary shares into preference shares, and the deferred shares become the real equity shares of the concern. Today, however, it is very rare.

The market-prices of stocks on the STOCK EXCHANGES (q.v.) are quoted on a percentage basis. Two prices are given, the lower being that at which jobbers (or dealers) are prepared to buy stock from brokers who wish to sell, the higher being the price at which brokers can buy from the jobbers. Thus, $2\frac{1}{2}\%$ Consols might be quoted in the Stock Exchange Official List at $49\frac{1}{2}$–50, and $3\frac{1}{2}\%$ War Loan at $62\frac{1}{2}$–63. These prices mean that a buyer of Consols would pay £50 for £100 nominal value of that stock on the Register at the Bank of England, and a buyer of War Loan would pay £63 for £100 of War Loan stock on the Register. Sellers, however, would receive the lower of the figures quoted, the difference between them being the jobber's profit. For each £50 paid, the buyer of Consols is really buying the right to an annual income of £2 10*s*., and the buyer of War Loan the right to an annual income of £3 10*s*.

The market-price of a stock depends on the rate of interest on money invested which will satisfy the investing public. If people thought that just over £2. 10*s*. on every £100 actually invested was a reasonable rate of interest, they might be prepared to pay nearly £100, say £96, for £100 of $2\frac{1}{2}\%$ stock; but they would pay only £48 for a $1\frac{1}{4}\%$ stock, which at the price they paid would give them the same income as that obtainable on a $2\frac{1}{2}\%$ stock bought at £96. But if the investing public change their ideas about what they consider to be a reasonable rate of interest, and require at least £5 on every £100 invested, they would be prepared to pay only £50 for £100 of $2\frac{1}{2}\%$ stock. If this were so, we should find the $2\frac{1}{2}\%$ stock changing hands at a price around £50.

The market-prices of preference shares vary in much the same way as the prices of Government stocks. Such shares receive a fixed rate of dividend, just as gilt-edged stocks receive a fixed rate of interest, and their market-prices depend on what the investing public consider, at the time, to be a satisfactory yield on money invested in them. In times of 'dear' money, when Government stocks are selling at prices which yield, say, $5\frac{1}{2}\%$ on money invested in them, a £1 preference share receiving a fixed dividend of 6% might sell for less than £1, and in times of 'cheap' money the market-price might be well over £1.

The method of quotation of market-prices of shares differs sometimes from that of stocks, and much depends on what the actual market-price is. As a general rule, shares with prices below 100*s*. or £5 a share are quoted in shillings and pence: for example 74/3–74/9, or 8/6–9/–. Those shares with prices exceeding £5 are usually quoted in much the same way as stocks: that is, in £s and fractions of £1. The reason is the awkwardness of such quotations as 222/6

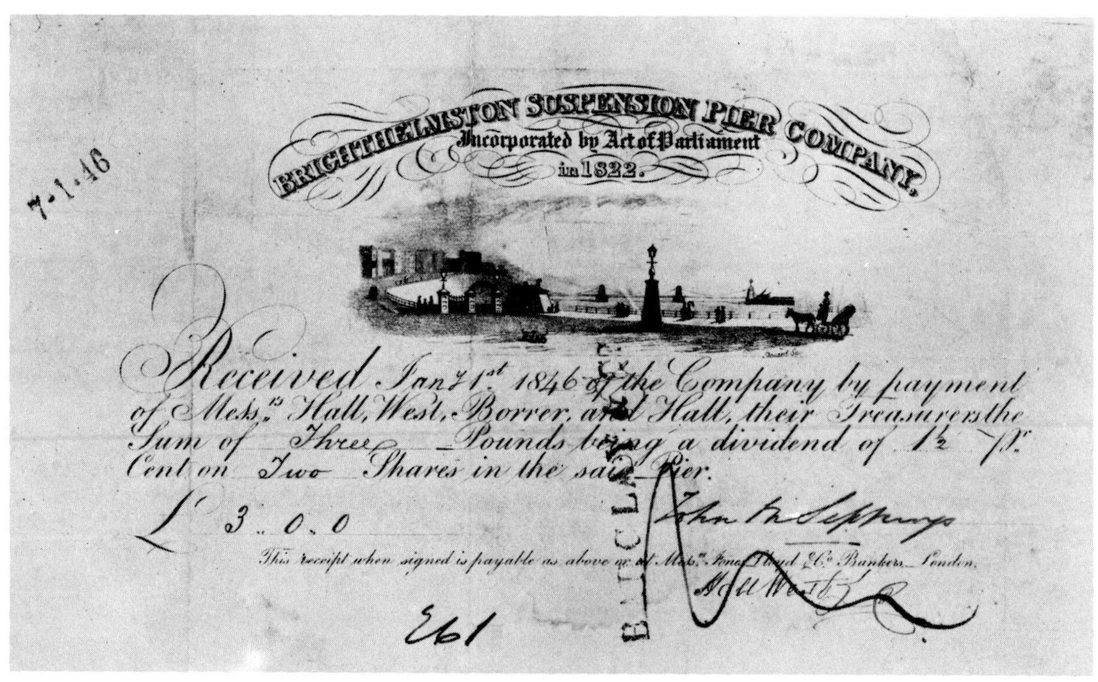
Brighthelmston Suspension Pier Company
Incorporated by Act of Parliament in 1822.
7·1·46
Received Jany 1st 1846 of the Company by payment of Messrs. Hall, West, Borrer, and Hall, their Treasurers the Sum of Three Pounds being a dividend of 1½ per Cent on Two Shares in the said Pier.
£3. 0. 0
This receipt when signed is payable as above or at Messrs. Jones Lloyd & Co. Bankers London.
E61

RECEIPT FOR A DIVIDEND ON SHARES IN THE BRIGHTON PIER COMPANY, 1846

or 380/–. Such shares would be quoted in the Official List, which gives the jobbers' buying and selling prices, as $11\frac{1}{8}$–$11\frac{1}{4}$, or 19–$19\frac{1}{8}$.

If no profits are earned by an industrial firm, its ordinary shares, whatever might be their nominal value, may become worthless and almost unsaleable. Let us take an opposite case—one of high profits. If a company is able to pay the high dividend of 24% on its £1 ordinary shares, it is quite possible that these £1 shares might be quoted in the market at £6 each, for even at that price the yield on money invested would still be 4% per annum. It is, therefore, impossible to obtain any idea of what the market-price of an ordinary share ought to be unless one knows what rate of dividend the company is paying, and what rates it is likely to pay in the future.

Another factor which affects the value of a share is what is called the 'break-up' value of the company, or what would be left in cash if the company's assets were disposed of, and all liabilities settled. The shares of companies which cannot pay dividends are often valued in the market simply on their break-up value; but the shares of dividend-paying companies are more often valued solely on the basis of their yield, as explained above.

Certain technical terms may be explained here. The word 'par' means the nominal value of a share of stock. Thus a 3% stock standing in the market at £100 would be said to be quoted at par. If the price is below £100, say £95, then the stock is said to be standing 'at a discount'. If a stock is standing at over £100, it is said to be 'at a premium'. The same terms are applied to shares.

See also Stock Exchanges; Debentures; Dividend; Speculation.

STONE DRESSING. The ancient industry of stone cutting forms a branch of Masonry (q.v. Vol. VIII) and is one of the building 'trades'. Nowadays the hand dressing of stone on a bench or 'banker' has been largely superseded by machinery. The machines are so large and costly that they either adjoin the quarries or are found only in workshops belonging to building contractors.

Building in stone is one of the most cherished traditional crafts in Britain, creating her greatest monuments of architecture—cathedrals, abbeys, parish churches, colleges, and mansions, as well

SAWING AND PLANING STONE

Drawing by W. H. Pyne, 1802

as some of her most beautiful old cottages. One finds these especially along the belt of fine limestone that runs from Dorset to Lincolnshire, including the Cotswold country that has given this distinctive style of rural building its name. But the mason's craft is dying. Even in the Cotswolds it is cheaper to build cottages of imported brick or of concrete than to use the cream-coloured stone that lies beneath the soil. In 1949 Italian workmen had to be brought to Britain to carry out the masonry work of a new dam in South Wales, for the number of skilled British masons was then only half of what it had been in 1938. The greatly increased use of machinery for stone dressing has led to a saving in skilled manual labour, and so has the use of 'reconstructed stone' in place of natural stone. Reconstructed stone is really concrete, usually mixed in the proportion of 4 parts gravel to 1 part of Portland cement (*see* Cement) and then faced with chips of stone or stone dust from the works at the quarry. Reconstructed stone, therefore, looks very much like the natural stone with which it is faced, and there is no need for dressing, either by machinery or by hand.

Natural stone is quarried in large blocks. Bath stone blocks average 4 to 6 feet long, and weigh from 2 to 3 tons. The blocks are first cut into parallel slabs of convenient thickness by a horizontal frame-saw. This has a swinging frame, into which are wedged a series of large steel blades, continuously fed with sharp grit, steel shot, and water. The next process is sawing the slabs into blocks of the required size by a vertically fixed circular saw, fitted either with diamonds set into dovetailed sockets or with a carborundum rim (this is an abrasive mineral with a cutting edge which is hard enough to go through stone). This gives the block its final finish, assuming that a plain 'ashlar' finish is desired. Water is used to keep the stone and saw wet. Other machines, very elaborate in design, are capable of planing the blocks when a very smooth finish is needed, or of producing stone mouldings. Large masonry workshops, whether at the quarry or at the contractor's own premises, have a battery of these great machines, arranged in an orderly sequence. Machinery seems to have been first used for working stone as long ago as 1730, at the Aberdeen granite works, but the dressing of hard granite differs considerably from that of the relatively soft limestones, such as Bath and Portland stone. Granite, like MARBLE (q.v.), is often polished. This is done by machinery. Shot, sand, and water are first used to produce a smooth surface; a felt disk then does the polishing, or 'glassing' as it is called.

All ornamental work—including carving and curved mouldings—must be done by hand, even when machinery is used for shaping the plain blocks; and, if a special finish is desired for the blocks, hand work is also needed. Apart from dressing, the processes of cutting which involve precise geometrical accuracy, such as the stones of a Gothic traceried window, are known as 'stereotomy', a word of Greek derivation meaning 'solid cutting'. The masons who actually fix the stones in position on a building are called 'setters' or 'wallers'.

See also STONE QUARRYING; BRICKS AND TILES; SLATE INDUSTRY.

STONE QUARRYING. 1. BUILDING STONE. Stone for building is generally one of five kinds —granites, sandstones, limestones, slates, and marbles (*see* SANDS AND SANDSTONE; LIMESTONE; ROCKS, Sections 2 (*b*) and 4, Vol. III). Many building stones are also used to make rollers for paper-making machines and for grinding-mills. Building stones are usually identified by the names of their type, sometimes varying from one locality to another; and knowledge of where they come from is very useful to the builder or architect, in judging the purposes for which they can best be used. The chief British building granites come from Cornwall, North Wales, and Scotland, and limestones from Bath and Portland. Sandstones are found in Devon and Herefordshire.

Large regular lumps of stone are required for building, preferably with parallel faces. ROCKS, in their natural form (q.v. Vol. III), are divided by cracks or fissures, which are known in the trade as 'joints'. These joints often enable quarrymen to separate masses of stone with their faces roughly parallel to each other. Some types of stone, known as 'freestones', can be cut easily in any direction. Bath and Portland stones are of this type.

If the stone which is to be quarried shows above the surface of the ground, as an 'outcrop', or exposed at the edge of a cliff or the side of a valley, direct quarrying work can be begun. But more often the useful stone is covered by debris or by inferior stone, called the 'overburden', which must be removed before the good stone is reached. The best stone is often found at lower depths, and quarries are therefore often deep. To get down far enough, MINING (q.v.) is sometimes necessary, but the methods of working underground are very like those used in surface quarries. Some of the softer stones can be removed, in the required sizes and shapes, by the use of wedges and crowbars; but the normal method of releasing blocks of stone from the face of the quarry is more complicated. A row of holes is made with a pneumatic drill, and two steel plugs, each of a semi-circular section, are inserted in each hole. A long thin steel wedge, known as a 'feather', is driven between the flat surfaces of the two plugs (*see* picture). The feathers are gradually driven farther in, until the pressure breaks away the stone. Sometimes the pressure is applied by water-power (*see* HYDRAULIC POWER TRANSMISSION, Vol. VIII). In some quarries each individual bed of stone may be cut through with a wire-saw, which is really an endless thin wire rope passing over pulleys. The rope is driven by steam or electric power, and is forced against the stone to be cut. Where the constantly moving rope touches the stone, a mixture of abrasive sand and water is fed on to the rope, and this enables the rope to eat its way

U.S. Information Service

QUARRYING GRANITE IN VERMONT, U.S.A.

Wedges or 'feathers' being driven into the drill holes to split the stone

gradually into the stone. The lumps of stone, when broken away from the face to about the right size, are lifted by cranes and sent to the dressing-sheds, where they are shaped more exactly (*see* STONE DRESSING). Lumps of building stone may weigh several tons, and if the dressing-sheds are far away the stone is often taken to them by aerial cableway, in skips or containers running on a rope.

There is still a demand for the best quality stone for use in building work. Clipsham stone from Rutland was used for the new House of Commons after it was bombed in the Second World War. Granite is in demand for harbour walls, and was used for the new London embankment on the south bank of the Thames. So far, no manufactured substitute has been found for granites or marbles. A very fair substitute for Bath, Portland, and similar stones is now produced by mixing chips or dust of these stones with concrete. This 'reconstructed' or cast stone can be worked in the same way as natural stone and at much lower cost.

2. BROKEN STONE. In Britain this is mostly either granite or limestone, but it seldom comes from the same localities as building stone. There is very little stone to be found east of a line drawn from Lyme Regis in Dorset to Flamborough Head in Yorkshire. Good deposits of granite are found in Devon and Cornwall, and in the Midlands and many parts of the North. There are scattered deposits of granite in South Wales, and some large granite quarries in North Wales. In the north of Scotland some of the finest granite in the country is found, particularly in Aberdeenshire. Limestone is more widely distributed. There are small deposits in Devonshire, and a good deposit of carboniferous limestone in the Peak District of Deryshire. As this is near the centre of the chemical industries, the limestone is mainly used in the chemical and steel trades. There are large deposits of limestone from Yorkshire northwards, up to the Scottish Border, and there are scattered deposits of limestone in Wales. There is also a fair amount in the lowlands of Scotland.

Broken stone ranges in size from 12-inch lumps to dust. Dust has many uses in modern industry. Granite and the harder stones are used almost exclusively as road metal or railway ballast. Limestone is used to some extent for the same purposes, but in much greater quantities in

OLD LIMESTONE QUARRY ON THE DORSET CLIFFS

The stone was let down the cliff face into boats

chemical manufacture, as a flux for smelting iron-ore (*see* BLAST FURNACE, Vol. VIII), and for certain processes of STEEL MAKING (q.v. Vol. VIII). A good deal of limestone is also converted into lime by being burned in kilns.

The methods of quarrying broken stone are different from those used in quarrying building stone. After any overlying soil has been removed by scrapers, excavators, bulldozers, and similar equipment, the stone itself is blasted with explosives to loosen it. There are three main methods of blasting, and the nature of the quarry decides which shall be used. By the first method a compressed-air drill is used to drill holes in the rock, from $1\frac{1}{2}$ to $2\frac{1}{2}$ inches in diameter and up to 20 feet deep. These holes are filled with explosive to within about 2 feet of the face. This space of 2 feet is then filled with 'stemming', consisting of dust or clay. The explosive is fired from some distance away by means of an electric wire, and the stone is blasted away from the face of the quarry. A second method, which is finding favour in large quarries, uses the 'churn' drill. This drill makes a vertical hole, from 5 to 9 inches in diameter, to any depth up to about 250 feet. A series of holes is drilled some feet back from the existing face, and parallel to it. These holes are then filled, to about 10 feet from the top, with a quantity of explosive, and the 10-foot space is filled with 'stemming'. The explosive is then fired. The advantages of this method are that the explosive is well distributed in the rock, and a large quantity of well-fragmented stone is brought down at a time. A third method, which also produces larger quantities, is the system of tunnel-blasting. This can be used if the stone is fairly well broken up beforehand into thin layers. A small tunnel, about 3 feet by 2, is driven in at right angles to the face of the quarry. When some way in, the tunnel is turned again at right angles, and continued parallel to the face. The tunnel is driven as far as required, and a series of sinks or cavities are made in it for the explosive. When this is in position, the tunnel is filled with loose stone as 'stemming' before the charge is fired.

Usually the blasting produces large pieces of stone, which have to be again drilled and blasted before they are small enough to be taken to the breaking-plant. It is only comparatively recently that the old system of breaking down stone on the quarry floor with a sledge-hammer has ceased. The big lumps were thus broken down to the size a man could handle—about a hundredweight. The stone was then loaded by hand into 'trams', or small trucks. But in a modern quarry the stone is loaded by mechanical 'navvies' into railway wagons, lorries, or dump wagons, and taken to the breaking-plant to be broken up by machines known as primary crushers. Mechanical handling enables much larger lumps to be dealt with. Lumps of stone weighing from 3 to 5 tons can now be handled by the primary crusher, whereas before the use of handling-machines the size of a lump was limited to what a man could lift. If the stone is required for chemical-works or steel-works, it is broken by the crusher into lumps about the size of a 4-inch cube. For railway ballast or road metal, it is broken down to about $2\frac{1}{2}$ inches. The stone is sorted into various sizes by screening, and each size is stored in a separate bin.

See also STONE DRESSING; MINING; SLATE INDUSTRY; MARBLE AND ALABASTER.

See also Vol. III: LIMESTONE; SANDS AND SANDSTONE; ROCKS, Sections 2 (*b*) and 4.

See also Vol. VIII: QUARRYING MACHINERY.

STONEWARE is POTTERY (q.v.) which is so hard that it cannot be scratched with a knife. It has been fired to a temperature sufficient to 'vitrify' the clay; its texture is therefore no longer earthy, but vitreous, that is, of the nature of glass, and consequently non-porous, as distinct from EARTHENWARE (q.v.). It is also opaque. There are two main types: the salt-glazed stoneware of Europe, and that of the Far East, which in some respects resembles PORCELAIN (q.v.).

Salt-glaze stoneware originated in the Rhine-

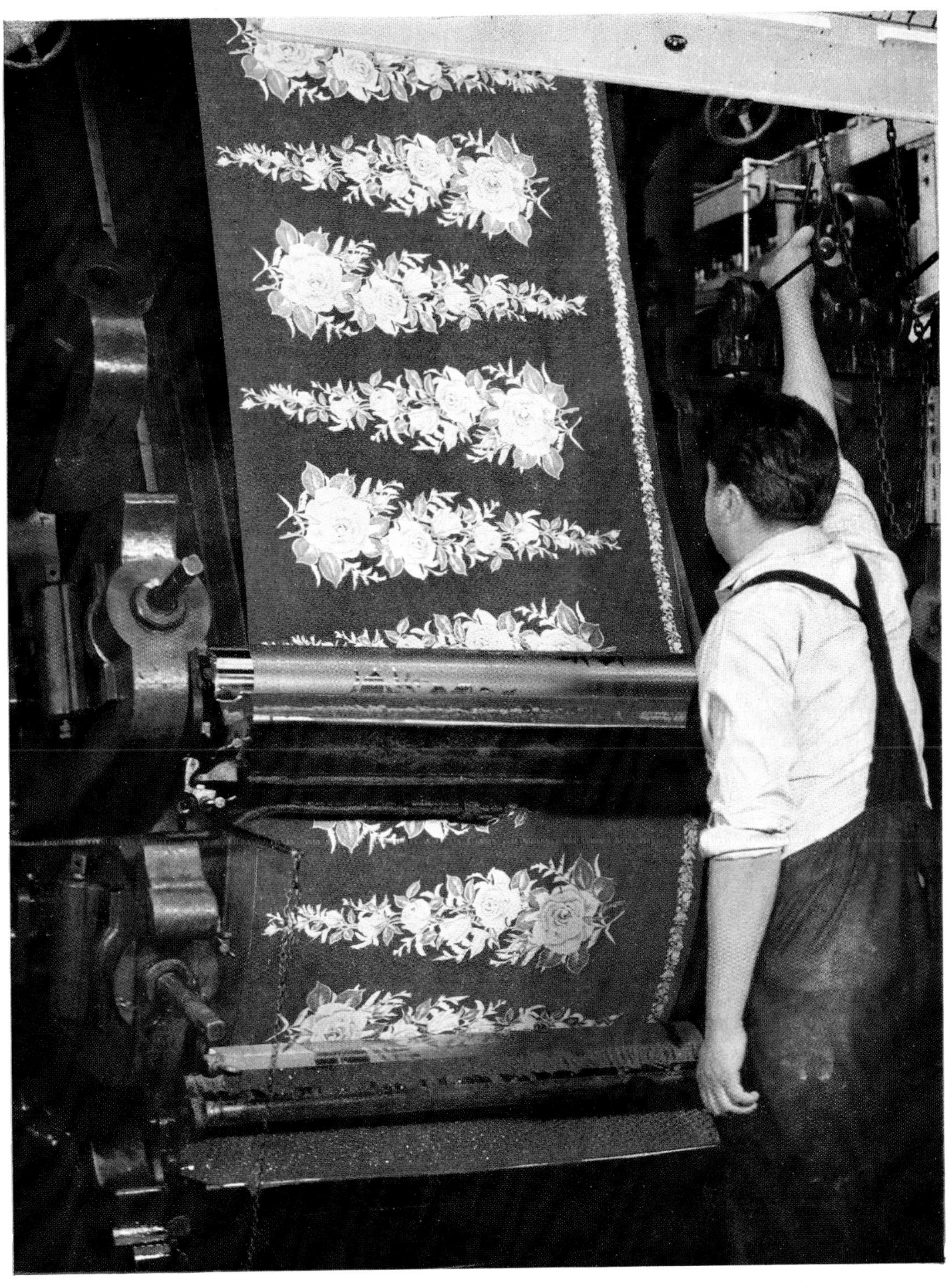

PRINTING COTTON IN THREE COLOURS AT THE SAME TIME

The operator is adjusting the registration by means of a lever above his head which controls the engraved rollers at the bottom. Each roller prints a different colour

land in the Middle Ages, and has been made there ever since. The glaze was produced by throwing common salt into the kiln when it reached its greatest heat (about 1,200° C. or over). The salt volatilized, or turned into gas, decomposed, and attacked the clay of the pots, forming on their surface a thin skin of very hard glaze, with an 'orange-peel' texture. These wares, blue-grey, buff, or dark brown, were often decorated before firing with incised patterns or with applied 'low reliefs', that is, ornaments modelled in clay and stuck on to the pot. The only colouring pigments used were cobalt blue, managanese purple, and iron brown.

Dr. Dwight of Fulham, about 1670, was one of the first to make stoneware in England; it was made later at Nottingham, in Derbyshire, and also in North Stafford, where from about 1700 it became a flourishing industry. Astbury, Whieldon, and others, using Dorset clay and flint, produced English grey or white salt-glazed ware in the first half of the 18th century. But the smooth cream earthenware perfected about 1760 by Josiah WEDGWOOD (q.v. Vol. V) had many advantages over white salt-glaze, and

Brighton Museum

SALT GLAZED STONEWARE JUG MADE AT FULHAM ABOUT 1720

eventually drove it out of production. The coarser kinds of salt-glazed stoneware continued to be made for certain purposes, such as sewer pipes, chemical containers, and sanitary and bathroom fittings. In the 19th century, stoneware was given a new importance by the firm of Doulton of Lambeth, who made a wide range of stoneware, from drain-pipes to heat-proof dishes. Large articles, such as drain-pipes, are made by squeezing a continuous length of plastic clay through a wide nozzle. In the centre of the nozzle is a steel disc, whose diameter is the same as the interior diameter of the pipe.

See also POTTERY; EARTHENWARE; PORCELAIN.

STREET MARKETS. A street market is usually held once a week, although some street markets are open daily. 'Street market' is the term generally used for a market in groceries and provisions, fish, fruit and vegetables, clothing, and household necessities; weekly markets for the sale of livestock are now usually held on properly regulated market grounds, and are called 'fairs' or 'marts' (*see* MARKETS, Vol. VI). The large-scale market held once, or at most two or three times, in the year is also called a 'fair' (*see* TRADE FAIRS).

Some markets held in streets and squares of towns are centuries old (*see* colour plate opp. p. 176), survivals from an age when agriculture and stock-raising were the main industries of the country (*see* AGRICULTURE, HISTORY OF, Vol. VI), and when country folk visited their nearest town once a week for shopping, as they still do in many parts of Britain today. Some of our British street markets are so old that the original rights or charters under which they are held cannot be traced. Others are more recent, and their rights are based on a Royal Charter or special Act of Parliament. Since 1847 the authority of Parliament has been necessary to start any new market. Some street markets in Britain are not properly constituted markets of this kind, but are merely selected 'pitches' where numbers of hawkers or barrowmen stand their barrows and trade with the passers-by. Lewisham High Street in south-east London is a hawkers' market of this kind. Hawkers have to take out a licence as such, whether they trade singly or in groups, whereas traders in a regularly organized market, held in a street or any similar public place, need no licence. They may, however, have to pay a

The Times

BERWICK MARKET, LONDON, AT NIGHT

'stallage' or rent to the owner of the land, or to the local authority, for the privilege of running a market stall, which is usually a horse-drawn or motor van that can be opened out into a booth where goods may be displayed and sold.

'Petticoat Lane' (Middlesex Street) in East London is one of the most famous London street markets, and another important though less well-known market is that in Berwick Street, Soho, not far from Oxford Street. Street markets are not as numerous as they were even 50 years ago. Owing to the growth of motor traffic and the congestion of town streets, many of them have been shifted to enclosed sites, either in the open or under cover. Most of these sites have been provided by the local authorities, and the markets have thus become ordinary municipal markets.

See also PEDLARS AND HAWKERS.

STRIKE, *see* TRADE UNIONS.

SUBSIDIES are payments made by the government of a country in order to lower the cost or selling-price of some particular goods or services in the national interest. Their purpose is generally to protect an industry against foreign competition; but subsidies are also given to support some nationally essential industry, such as railway or air transport, which cannot make both ends meet. There are other kinds of subsidies, mostly in connexion with social welfare: for example, school meals, schoolchildren's fares, and rents of council houses. Subsidies are occasionally paid for reasons of prestige or in connexion with national defence: for example, the subsidy paid to the Cunard Steamship Company for building the huge and fast passenger liners, the *Queen Mary* and the *Queen Elizabeth*, which were invaluable as troop transports during the Second World War.

During this war, and for some years after it ended, the British Government adopted the policy of subsidizing the market-prices of certain essential foodstuffs to keep down the cost of living. This meant that people could buy food such as bacon and butter in the shops for less than it had cost the importers or producers, the loss on such trading being made up by the amount of the subsidy. These subsidies have now been discontinued, except for such items as orange-juice for infants; but much the same result has been achieved by the large subsidies to farmers and fishermen, which enable their produce to be sold in the shops for far less than it would otherwise cost.

See also QUOTA; TARIFFS.

SUGAR CONFECTIONERY. This is the trade name for sweet-making in which sugar forms the main part. We know that the Egyptians as early as 2000 B.C. made sweets, using honey as their chief sweetening ingredient. They mixed the honey with flours, spices, crude starch, sweet herbs, and fruit, making a sweetmeat not unlike nougat. At much the same time the Chinese also made sweets which they spun into sticks and rolled in toasted sesame seeds. Ancient references have been found to a marzipan sweetmeat made from almonds, and also to a confection, similar to Turkish Delight, and made from grape juice and starch cut into squares and strips. All these were made before the use of SUGAR-CANE (q.v. Vol. VI) became widely known.

Although sugar-cane had been grown in the East for centuries and had been introduced into Europe during the Crusades, it was still an expensive luxury in Europe in the Middle Ages, and honey was the main sweetener. In the 17th and 18th centuries, as sugar became more generally available and, therefore, cheaper, small manufacturing confectioners set up their businesses, using hand methods of production.

The development of the SUGAR-BEET industry (q.v. Vol. VI) and the expansion of sugar-cane plantations in nearly every tropical country of the world have led to an enormous increase in the making and eating of sweets in the 20th century. Today, the average consumption of sweets each week in Britain is $7\frac{1}{2}$ oz. per head, purchases being divided about equally between chocolate and sugar confectionery. Nearly every other shop in Britain sells sweets, and their sale, together with that of ICES (q.v. Vol. XI), in cinemas and theatres has become one of the principal sources of profit to the entertainment industry. Wrapped in aluminium foil or plastics, sweets can now be kept fresh for a considerable period of time; so they can be sold in large quantities from automatic machines.

The confectionery manufacturer uses many different kinds of sweeteners besides cane and beet sugar. Maize starch, known as 'confectioner's glucose' or sometimes as 'corn syrup', is used a great deal, and also sweeteners possessing a characteristic flavour, such as treacle, maple syrup, molasses, and honey. To these basic sweeteners are added such ingredients as nuts, starches, milk products, and butter or hardened vegetable oils, which all help to give the confectionery texture and flavour. Natural gums, pectin, gelatine, or isinglass (a substance obtained from a type of seaweed) are used to make gums and jellies set. Fruit pulps and essential oils, such as lemon, lime, orange, and peppermint, are used for flavouring.

From such ingredients many different kinds of sweets are manufactured. Boiled sweets, of which acid drops are examples, are ordinarily made from a solution of sugar and confectioner's glucose. This is boiled until most of the water has evaporated, leaving a thick syrupy liquid. This when cooled becomes plastic, and colours and flavours are worked into the mass. It is then cut up into sweets of the required shape, allowed to harden, and wrapped ready for dispatch.

In a modern factory these processes are for the most part carried out by machines, but certain products still need the individual attention of the craftsman. Lettered rock, for example, is still made partly by hand. Letters made from coloured sugar are assembled in long strips around a core of sugar about 8 inches in diameter. More sugar is overlaid, and the rock is finally rolled and cut into its familiar shape. Similarly, stripes are put into humbugs by combining white and coloured sugars.

Toffees and caramels are closely related sweets, which depend for their flavour on the sugar, which is cooked until it begins to turn brown and 'burn'. Confectioner's glucose, butter, and condensed milk are commonly added to enrich the final product. Toffees are much harder than caramels because the toffee mixture is boiled at a higher temperature and therefore, owing to evaporation, has a lower water content.

Fondants are confections made from a combination of sugars formed into a syrup which is then beaten into a creamy paste and poured into starch moulds. Sugar-coated sweets, such as aniseed balls, hundreds-and-thousands, and sugared almonds, are manufactured by a process called 'panning'; the sugar syrup is poured into heated revolving pans containing the centres, which become sugar-coated and are then dried. If a thicker coating or successive coatings of different coloured sugars are wanted, the process is repeated. Much the same process is used for sugar-coating pills.

James Pascall Ltd.

MAKING FONDANT

James Pascall Ltd.

MAKING MINT LUMPS

A long twist of candy is fed into a machine which cuts it up and wraps the pieces

Marshmallows are a blend of sugar, glucose, gelatine, and white of egg. Peppermints are made by compressing flavoured sugar granules in a steel die. Liquorice allsorts consist of alternate layers of cream paste and liquorice made up in large sheets, sandwiched together, and then cut into small pieces. The cream paste in them is similar to the 'dough' used in lozenges, and the usual recipe includes icing sugar with gum or gelatine as a binding agent.

Varieties of gums and pastilles containing fruit were first manufactured in Britain by Rowntree & Co. Ltd. They are made from a syrup consisting of sugar, flavoured and boiled up with gum arabic, gelatine, or pectin to make the sweets set. The syrup is poured into starch moulds to set.

See also Cocoa and Chocolate.
See also Vol. XI: Sweet-making.

SUGAR REFINING. In earlier days few who used sugar bothered about its natural colour being brown, but during the Italian Renaissance (q.v. Vol. I) in the 14th and 15th centuries people became more particular and the idea of white or 'refined' sugar became attrac-

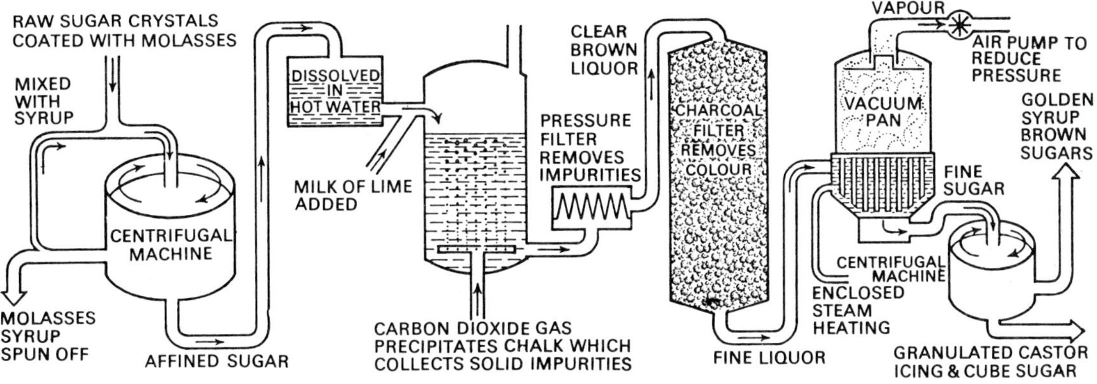

STAGES IN THE REFINING OF SUGAR

The process starts on the left

tive. The practice of importing raw sugar (*see* SUGAR-CANE, Vol. VI) and refining it started in Venice about 1400. In England the first refinery opened in the 16th century. Major changes have taken place since then.

In a modern refinery the brown raw sugar is first mixed with a warm syrup and then spun and water-washed in a centrifugal machine. This produces a light-coloured sugar, known as 'affined', and a dark syrup. The affined sugar is next dissolved in hot water. Next, milk of lime is added and carbon dioxide gas is bubbled through the liquid. The chalk produced by the reaction collects the minute impurities present in the sugar. The solution is then forced through pressure filters, which remove both chalk and impurities. Sugar is also recovered from the dark syrup and later refined in the same way. After being filtered, the liquid, now brown and clear, trickles downwards through large beds of bone charcoal, which removes the brown colour by adsorption. Today either activated carbon or ion-exchange resins are used with the bone charcoal. When their decolourizing power fails, it is restored by treatment: for example, the bone charcoal is heated to 600° C. in a kiln without air.

The sugar then passes on to the evaporation stage. The 'fine liquor' produced after the colour has been removed is evaporated in steam-heated vacuum pans, from which some air has been withdrawn and so the boiling temperature lowered, until the white sugar crystallizes out. The crystals and syrup are separated in a centrifugal machine, and then the sugar is dried and cooled in rotating drums or 'granulators', and finally stored and packed as required. Cube sugar is formed by pressing together a mass of small crystals while still moist and then drying in hot air.

See also SUGAR CONFECTIONERY.
See also Vol. VI: SUGAR-CANE.

SULPHUR or brimstone (from Anglo-Saxon words meaning 'fiery stone') is a MINERAL (q.v. Vol. III) which burns easily. It is yellow and brittle, and is found in a more or less pure state in regions near both active and extinct VOLCANOES (q.v. Vol. III). There are deposits in Italy, Iceland, Mexico, the U.S.A., New Zealand, and Japan. On the Pacific island of Vanus Lava in the New Hebrides there is a mountain of almost pure sulphur, nearly 2,000 feet high. For many years Italy produced most of the sulphur used in the world's industries, but in the late 19th century supplies began to come from big underground deposits in Louisiana and adjacent American States, which now supply nine-tenths of the world's needs. Sulphur is mainly used in the manufacture of the important industrial chemical, sulphuric acid (*see* CHEMISTRY, INDUSTRIAL), and of sulphite WOOD PULP (q.v.). It is also used in medicine, and as 'flowers of sulphur' in substances used for killing insects, moulds, and other fungi and parasites. Sulphur plays a big part in the vulcanizing processes of RUBBER MANUFACTURE, and a gas made from sulphur is used for BLEACHING (qq.v.).

The choking fumes and unpleasant smell given off by sulphur when burnt have impressed man's imagination for centuries. Some of the ancient philosophers believed that it was one of

THE CRATER OF SOLFATARA, ITALY, WHERE SULPHUR WAS FOUND IN THE 17TH CENTURY

The sulphur was prepared in the huts. Sick people came to be cured by the sulphur fumes

the prime elements out of which all things were made (*see* CHEMISTRY, HISTORY OF).

SULPHURIC ACID, *see* ACIDS.

SUPPLY AND DEMAND. The expression 'demand', expressed in terms of money, means the wish of a number of people to buy certain articles. 'Supply' is the quantity of articles put on sale to satisfy these wants.

The prices of goods in the market move upwards and downwards in accordance with changes in supply and demand (*see* VALUE AND PRICE). The supply of any commodity is not always constant, and changes in supply come often from causes outside human control. Climatic and seasonal influences, for example, may affect the supply of foodstuffs and other agricultural products. The world price of wheat alters greatly from one year to another, falling when harvests are good and rising when they are poor. Fish is another commodity whose supply changes considerably because of changes in the weather. The supply of manufactured goods is more constant than that of natural products such as wheat and fish, and tends to rise or fall as people want more or less of them. If supply and demand are sensitive to alterations in prices, they are said to be 'elastic'; if not, they are called 'inelastic'. As a general rule, the supply of manufactured goods is elastic, and of natural products inelastic. If the price of some manufactured articles goes up, and its manufacture therefore becomes more profitable than it was, it is usually fairly easy for its manufacturers to turn out more of it, and thus to increase the supply coming on to the market. But, in the short run at any rate, it is not easy to increase the supply of, say, wheat or meat. More wheat will be forthcoming only if more is sown, and even if more is sown there is an interval of months before it can be harvested, always provided that the weather is favourable to the crop; and an increased supply of meat may only be possible after many years.

In normal times, demand does not alter as much as supply. People's tastes and preferences remain very much the same, and do not greatly depend on changes of climate and seasons, although of course there are many things whose demand depends on the weather. Changes in demand arise mainly from changes in people's incomes, and we must not forget that changes in supply may alter these incomes. North American business men, for example, are well aware that the demand for many of the things they sell depends on the incomes of the farmers of the Prairie provinces and the Middle West; and these incomes depend in their turn on the supply of the crops they have grown and livestock they have bred and sold. UNEMPLOYMENT (q.v.) is another great influence on demand, for the demand for all kinds of goods decreases very much when millions of people, perhaps, are out of work.

The demand for most necessities is so urgent that upward or downward changes in price (coming, perhaps, from changes in supply conditions) are likely to have little influence on the quantity demanded or bought. Bread is an example. If its price were doubled, there would be greater economy in its use, and demand might decrease slightly; but it is almost certain that demand would not be halved or anything like it. Similarly, if its price were halved, it is very unlikely that people would want twice the quantity of bread; demand might increase by a fraction, but little more. The demand for necessities is, therefore, generally inelastic. On the other hand, the demand for luxuries, and for other things that most of us can do without if forced to, is elastic. This is particularly true of such things as books and theatre and cinema seats, and very true of things like fruits and flowers out of season and similar purely luxury goods. Whether a rise or fall in the price of any article will cause demand to alter very much depends, therefore, on the elasticity or inelasticity of the demand for that particular thing.

See also COMMERCE; EXCHANGE AND TRADE; VALUE AND PRICE.

SWEET MANUFACTURE, *see* SUGAR CONFECTIONERY.

SYNTHETIC PRODUCTS, *see* PLASTICS; CHEMISTRY, INDUSTRIAL; DYES; RUBBER MANUFACTURE; OIL, MINERAL; TEXTILE FIBRES.

T

TANNING. 1. This is, strictly speaking, only one of the processes of leather manufacture, but the term as used in the trade means the art of converting animal skin into leather. Tanning makes skins and hides supple and elastic, and protects them from damp and decay. In a rather primitive form, the art of tanning goes back more than 15,000 years in the history of mankind.

Leather manufacture has three distinct stages. There are, first of all, the 'wet-work' processes. In these, the corium or true skin is separated from the hairy outside layer (the epidermis) and the fleshy inside layer (*see* HIDES AND SKINS). Next come the tanning processes proper, in which chemical treatment makes the corium proof against damp and against the growth of BACTERIA and MOULDS (qq.v. Vol. II). Finally there are the finishing processes, which improve the appearance of the leather and make its outer surface more fully waterproof.

Barrow, Hepburn, and Gale Ltd.

HAIR BEING REMOVED FROM THE HIDE BY MACHINE

2. WET-WORK. These processes vary with the type of skin or hide, but the treatment of ox-hides for shoe soles provides a good example. They are first soaked in water to remove dirt and blood and any salt that may have been used in 'curing' the hides for preservation, and also to restore any moisture in the hide which has been lost in curing. To loosen the hair and epidermis, the hides are then steeped in a chemical solution chiefly composed of lime. This treatment takes place in rectangular pits of wood, brickwork, or concrete, sunk into the ground. After a few days in this liquid, the hides are taken out and the loosened hair is scraped off by machine. Next comes 'fleshing', or cutting away the loose underlayer of the hide, also by machine. 'Scudding', or working over the grain of the hide with a blunt tool to force out dirt, is then done by hand or machine. The corium or central layer of the hide has now been separated, as a flat white sheet. The shoulder or foremost portion and the two bellies or side portions are cut off to be tanned separately for such uses as straps and cycle-saddles. This is called 'rounding'. The central portions, or 'butts', are treated with a little weak boric or lactic acid to kill any lime left in the surface, and are then ready for tanning.

After the wet-work processes, it may be necessary to divide the skins or hides horizontally into two or more layers. This is done in a splitting machine in which the skin is pressed, edge on, against the sharp edge of a travelling band-knife, a thin, ribbon-shaped blade that goes round and round like a bicycle chain. Sheepskins are often split; the uppermost layer, or grain, is vegetable-tanned for fancy leathers known as 'skivers'; the lower layer, or flesh, is oil-tanned for chamois leather. Cattle hides are also often split, when the whole thickness of the hide would be too great for such uses as upholstery leather or shoe uppers.

3. TANNING CHEMICALS. These fall into five main classes. (*a*) Vegetable tannins are extracted by water from the bark, leaves, roots, and other parts of certain plants. Oak-bark is the traditional English material, but is now very scarce and little used. Important modern materials are chestnut wood from France and Italy, oak wood from Yugoslavia, quebracho wood from Argentina and Uruguay, mimosa or wattle bark from Natal, myrobalan nuts from India, valonia acorn-crops from Turkey and Greece,

Barrow, Hepburn, and Gale Ltd.

SOLE LEATHER IN COURSE OF TANNING

and sumac leaves from Sicily. Vegetable tannins produce leathers varying in colour from pale cream to reddish-brown. (*b*) MINERALS (q.v. Vol. III) provide such tannins as salts of aluminium, chromium, and zirconium. ALUM (q.v.) is one of the oldest tannins, and produces a white leather which is not very waterproof. Chrome tanning was introduced in 1884, and produces a greenish-blue leather, extremely waterproof. The use of zirconium is recent; it produces a white leather suitable for gloves, handbags, and sports shoes. (*c*) Fish oils, of which the most used is crude cod-liver oil, produce the well-known wash-leather or chamois. (*d*) Formaldehyde, made from wood alcohol, produces a white washable leather, much used for gloves. (*e*) The modern synthetic tannins made from coal-tar products (*see* CHEMISTRY, INDUSTRIAL) produce leathers resembling in many ways those made with vegetable tannins. Sometimes more than one tannin is used—chrome after vegetable, for example, giving semi-chrome leather.

The details of the tanning process, the time taken over it, and the chemicals used vary with the class of leather being prepared. A typical process is the treatment of ox-hide butts for vegetable-tanned sole leather. The butts are hung in a tanning pit to soak in the 'liquor', and are moved every day to a pit containing a slightly stronger liquor. Later soakings last one week and two weeks. In the end, a pit of strong liquor is filled with alternate layers of butts and tanning material. This stage of the process takes a month. Tanning is completed by 'hot pitting' the hides for a week in a warm strong liquor. Contrasted with this lengthy process is chrome tanning, used for the two chief types of shoe upper leather: box calf, and glazed goat or kid. The unhaired limed skins are first washed and the lime removed with a weak acid, such as boric. Then comes a cleansing process called 'bating', or steeping in a mixture of ammonium chloride and digestive juices from animal pancreatic glands. The bated pelt is then 'pickled' in a solution of salt and sulphuric acid. The pickled skins are placed in a revolving drum with salt and water, and green chrome liquor (basic chromium sulphite) is fed through the hollow axle of the drum. Tanning is complete in about six hours.

4. FINISHING PROCESSES. These are varied,

and include washing, the introduction of lubricating oil, dyeing, drying, and glazing or giving a high gloss. Some leathers, for special uses, have to go through a process of CURRYING (q.v.).

Much sheep leather is embossed or stamped with the grain patterns of rare and expensive skins, such as lizard, crocodile, and python, and is dyed to the right colours. Parchment and vellum are made respectively from sheep or calf skins, without tanning (*see* PAPER, Section 3, Vol. IV). Morocco leather is goat skin, sumac-tanned by a special method, with a pattern produced by graining in several directions. Glacé kid for women's gloves is made by treating prepared kid skins with a mixture of alum salt, flour, and egg yolk. The leather is not proof against water, and this process is called 'tawing' rather than tanning. Suède and velvet leathers are made by holding the leather against a rapidly revolving wheel covered with carborundum, a gritty substance which teases up the fibres of the leather. Upholstery leathers are mostly made from cattle hides split into two or more layers. The top layer is vegetable-tanned. It may be merely stained and given a plain finish; or it may be stained, embossed, and otherwise worked up to give antique and other effects. Patent leather is now usually made by varnishing leather with polyurethane lacquers.

See also HIDES AND SKINS; BOOT AND SHOE MAKING; UPHOLSTERY; LEATHER.

TAPESTRY. This is a textile with a woven pattern, and it is generally used for wall hangings and some kinds of carpets (*see* CARPET-MAKING). The pattern is not applied after the cloth has been woven, as in EMBROIDERY (q.v. Vol. XI); it is made by the weft threads themselves (*see* WOOL WEAVING). Sometimes the two crafts are confused; the famous BAYEUX TAPESTRY, for instance (q.v. Vol. XII), which was made soon after the Norman Conquest, is actually an embroidery of wool on a linen foundation. The tapestry method of weaving is very early in origin, and small pieces of tapestry used for garments and wrappings have been found in ancient Egyptian tombs (*see* EGYPTIAN CIVILIZATION, Vol. I). But we know little about the craft until the Middle Ages. Tapestry hangings then began to be made chiefly for rich people and for churches, for they have always been very expensive to produce. They were often kept for special occasions, such as state ceremonies, pageants, and festivals, when they were used to enliven the buildings and the streets.

Tapestry, like other weaving, is done on a frame or 'loom'. The warp is either upright or horizontal, and the warp threads, usually of a dull neutral colour, are completely covered by the weft threads which form the pattern. These, which are in various colours, are not thrown completely across the warp, but are woven backwards and forwards, each colour across the appropriate part of the warp (*see* p. 78, Fig. 1). In this way is built up a pattern that may be of a simple geometrical kind, or a complicated picture with figures. The original design (called a 'cartoon') is worked out in detail on paper, and the weaver follows it closely. This design is seldom the work of the weaver, being usually commissioned from an artist. Famous artists, including RAPHAEL and GOYA (qq.v. Vol. V),

Ashmolean Museum

DETAIL OF TAPESTRY CUSHION COVER MADE BY WILLIAM SHELDON IN THE 16TH CENTURY

The warp runs horizontally and is covered by the weft threads whose different colours form the design

designed tapestries. Raphael's cartoons for a set woven in the Netherlands belong to H.M. the Queen and are on loan to the Victoria and Albert Museum. In the early work the range of colours is small, little more than a dozen shades being used; but by the 18th century several hundred might be used in a panel.

The Edinburgh Tapestry Co.

WEAVING THE COAT OF ARMS OF H.M. THE QUEEN (NOW H.M. QUEEN ELIZABETH THE QUEEN MOTHER)

The weavers work from the back of the warp. The original design for the tapestry is at their left

The finest medieval tapestries were made in France and Flanders. Arras was so famous a centre in the 14th and 15th centuries that in England and Italy all tapestries came to be called 'arras'. The subjects were generally biblical or scenes from romances. Later all kinds of subjects became popular —mythology, history, hunting, sport, landscape, heraldry, and decorative panels of all kinds.

In the 16th century Brussels became the centre of importance, and for two centuries dominated the whole field of tapestry production, after which it declined. William Sheldon established a small English factory in Warwickshire in the 16th century which lasted for 100 years and produced some fine maps and heraldic tapestries among other subjects. About 1600, a factory was founded at Mortlake (now part of south-west London), and weavers were brought over from the Netherlands. During the 19th century William MORRIS (q.v. Vol. V) started a small factory at Merton, south of London, and this is still in existence.

In 1662 the Gobelins factory was inaugurated in Paris under royal patronage. It was here that most of the finest French tapestries were made. Famous artists directed the factory and designed tapestries, which were used for upholstering chairs as well as for hangings. Beauvais, in the north, and Aubusson and Felletin, in central France, have also been important centres for hundreds of years and are still flourishing, now producing tapestries designed by modern artists.

See also CARPET MAKING; WOOL WEAVING.
See also Vol. XI: FURNISHING MATERIALS.

TARIFFS. A tariff is a list of duties or taxes on goods imported, and is published by the government of a country for the information of international traders. The word 'tariff' is also commonly used to mean an individual tax in this list.

Some governments impose a tariff purely for revenue purposes—that is, to collect money to meet their normal costs. If this is the purpose of the tariff, duty will be charged on goods in the list even if they are produced inside the country itself. Duties imposed on such home-produced goods are called Excise Duties.

Some countries may impose a tariff in order to protect home industries against foreign competition (*see* INTERNATIONAL TRADE). The tariff of Britain is arranged both for revenue and for protective purposes. The tariff on imported tobacco is for revenue only, because there is no tobacco-growing industry in Britain. But the British import duties on clothing manufactured abroad are mainly protective, although they are also useful in providing some revenue.

Import duties may be either 'specific' or *ad valorem*. A specific duty is a duty of so much per ton, gallon, bushel, or whatever the measure of weight or size may be. An *ad valorem* duty is one of so much per cent on the money value of the goods imported. If the money values of imported goods subject to *ad valorem* duties were declared at a false figure, the country's revenue would suffer; and so invoices for such goods must be certified by a British Consul abroad as representing fair and reasonable market values in the country from which they come. Such invoices are called Consular Invoices, and must be shown before the goods can be cleared through the Customs.

Import and excise duties are collected by the Board of CUSTOMS AND EXCISE (q.v. Vol. X).

See also QUOTA; SUBISIDES.

TEA TRADE. Chinese legend suggests that tea was first grown and drunk in that country about 3,000 years before our first written record, which belongs to the 9th century. It was grown in Japan from the 9th century A.D. onwards. Centuries passed before it was known and appreciated in Europe. In the early 17th century some officers in the distant stations of the EAST INDIA COMPANY (q.v.) in Japan and the Philippines in the Pacific introduced tea to the Indian stations of the Company. At the end of the 17th century the Company made a trial shipment of a small quantity to England. This was green China tea, of the type generally drunk in China and Japan today. This first consignment was sold in London at about £8 a pound. Even at this immense price many liked the new beverage, and other small shipments followed. The tea was brought direct in Chinese junks to the Company's trading stations, or 'factories', in India, and was then re-exported. As the taste for tea increased, the Company decided that the tea trade had a promising future, and set up in Amoy, in China, a buying depot for direct purchases of tea from that country. As the trade developed, the demand for tea in London grew with it, and towards the end of the 18th century the average price had fallen below 20*s*. This was still high, but the Company had a monopoly of the new trade, and at that time there was no known source of supply outside China itself. By the beginning of the 19th century the annual consumption of tea in Britain had risen to over 2 lb. per head of the population.

Ceylon Tea Centre, London

TEA COMING OFF THE ROLLING MACHINE IN WHICH THE LEAVES ARE CRUSHED

It was obvious to London merchants that sales of tea could be considerably increased if supplies came forward in greater quantities at a reduced price. The Company agreed to look into the possibility of growing tea locally in India itself. In 1813, the Company was forced by Parliament to give up its MONOPOLY (q.v.) of Indian trade and commerce, but it still retained its monopoly of the China trade. Its officers believed that by selling a comparatively small quantity of China tea at a high price more profit could be made than by encouraging the growth of the plant in India and selling larger quantities at a more popular price. The experiments in transplanting Chinese tea-bushes in India were therefore rather half-hearted. But between 1823 and 1834 the tea plant was discovered growing wild in the Assam province of north-east India (*see* TEA, Vol. VI). In 1833 the Company lost its Chinese monopoly, and Calcutta business men were anxious to develop Indian tea-gardens; so in 1834 the Governor-General set up a committee to arrange for the cultivation of tea in India on a commercial scale. In May 1838, the first consignment of tea from India was shipped to London and auctioned there on 10 January 1839, prices ranging from 16*s*. to 34*s*. a pound. Indian tea-gardens were established not only in Assam, and the Sylhet and Darjeeling districts adjoining, but also in Travancore and the Nilgiri Hills. The finest teas came from the Darjeeling district. India became the most important producer of tea for the British market, and for 30 years shared with China the export tea trade of the world. Other countries then turned their attention to tea-growing, but the world market was steadily expanding and the prosperity of the Indian tea industry was not affected.

With the partition of India in 1947, the tea-growing areas in Sylhet and in the Chittagong area became part of Pakistan.

In 1869 the coffee plantations of the island of Ceylon were largely ruined by blight. Through the combined energies of the Government, which helped financially, and the planters themselves, the ruined coffee estates were replanted with tea. By the end of the 19th century there were over 300,000 acres of tea-gardens in Ceylon. Tea seed from Assam had also been planted in the Dutch East Indies, now Indonesia, and a big local industry was established.

A more recent development has been in Africa where the growing of tea has expanded rapidly during this century in Kenya, Uganda, Tanzania, Malawi, and Mozambique, is making headway in the Congo and Rhodesia, and has been planted experimentally in Rwanda. There are extensive tea areas in the U.S.S.R. and also in the Asian countries of Malaysia, Burma, Vietnam, Iran, and Turkey, in the island of Mauritius, in the Azores, and in several countries of South America.

Two main varieties of tea have a world-wide popularity—black tea and green tea. Black tea is the most commonly known and is in general use in Britain and the U.S.A. It forms the main output from India, Pakistan, Ceylon, Indonesia, Africa, and other less important producing countries, and part of the output from China, Japan, and Formosa. One of the principal characteristics of black tea is that the leaves are fully fermented (subjected to oxidation) in the process of manufacture. The principal characteristic of green tea is that the leaves do not undergo any oxidation during manufacture. It is now mainly produced in China and Japan, and, apart from home consumption, is principally used in the Levant, North Africa, U.S.S.R., and Afghanistan. There are other specialized types of tea for particular markets not in general commercial use. Oolong tea, a semi-fermented type standing halfway between

Ceylon Tea Centre, London

A TEA-TASTER

black tea and green tea, is produced in China and Taiwan but is not now much drunk elsewhere, although at one time it was popular in the U.S.A. 'Brick' tea in tablet form used to be exported in large quantities from China to the U.S.S.R. by camel caravan. This rather curious form of tea was widely drunk throughout the whole of Central Asia and Tibet and was even used as a form of currency there.

Black tea supplies the bulk of the world's requirements, practically all of which is sold at public auction. The oldest and still the most important market is London where auction sales are held weekly in Plantation House. Regular auctions are also held in Calcutta and Cochin in India, in Chittagong in Pakistan, in Colombo in Ceylon, and in Nairobi in Kenya.

Although tea as a commodity changes little, it is now sold in teabags, and in 'instant' (powdered) form, as well as in the normal way.

See also Grocery and Provisions.
See also Vol. VI: Tea.

TERYLENE, *see* Textile Fibres, Man-made.

TEXTILE FIBRES, MAN-MADE. As long ago as 1663 Dr. Robert Hooke, then Curator of the Royal Society, observed that raw silk in the cocoon (*see* Silkworms, Vol. VI) has a gummy nature. He thought that it might be possible to make a gummy substance artificially, and then to spin it into an imitation silk filament. But it was not till late in the 19th century, when the demand for textiles increased tremendously, that scientists tried to make artificial fibre, mainly from cellulose. By imitating in machinery the action of the silkworm's spinneret in forcing a viscous or syrupy liquid through minute holes (a process known as extrusion), they produced the cellulose fibre which used to be called artificial silk and is now known as rayon. The most successful method for producing rayon was developed in 1892 as a result of the discovery of viscose (cellulose dissolved into a viscous liquid) by three British chemists, Cross, Bevan, and Beadle. Courtaulds, then a prominent silk-weaving concern, took over the world rights of the viscose process. They started their first factory at Coventry in 1905 and also established the industry in America some 4 years later. In 1932 American scientists invented nylon which is made from chemicals derived from coal and oil. There are now many different fibres and they fall into two groups: regenerated fibres made from carbohydrates and proteins which are found in nature, and truly synthetic fibres which are made from simple chemicals built up into a complex substance.

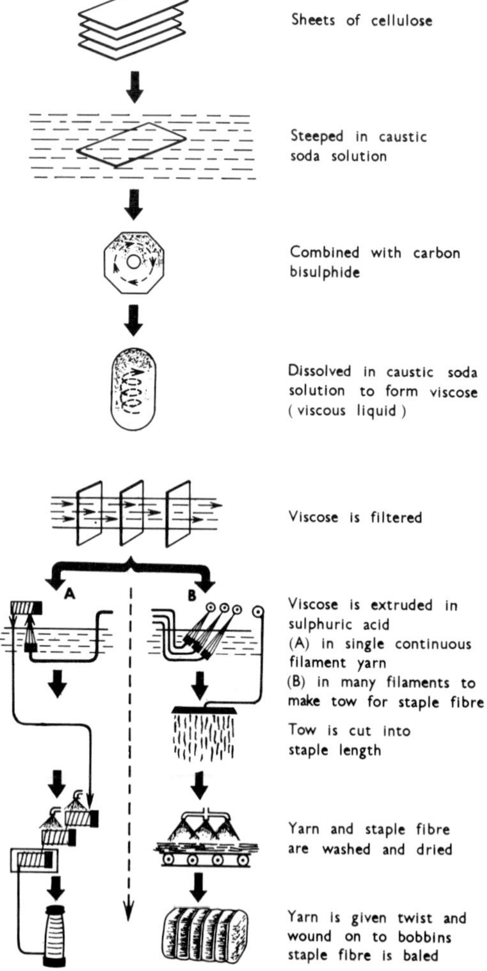
Sheets of cellulose
Steeped in caustic soda solution
Combined with carbon bisulphide
Dissolved in caustic soda solution to form viscose (viscous liquid)
Viscose is filtered
A
B
Viscose is extruded in sulphuric acid
(A) in single continuous filament yarn
(B) in many filaments to make tow for staple fibre
Tow is cut into staple length
Yarn and staple fibre are washed and dried
Yarn is given twist and wound on to bobbins staple fibre is baled

THE PRODUCTION OF VISCOSE RAYON YARN AND STAPLE
The yarn is ready to use but the staple must be combed, drawn, and spun

The most important raw material for making regenerated fibres is the carbohydrate cellulose. Viscose rayon is made from the cellulose extracted from WOOD-PULP (q.v.), acetate and triacetate (Tricel) from cotton linters (the short, unspinnable hairs of the cotton boll). Another carbohydrate fibre is made from alginate, which is extracted from certain kinds of seaweed. It is used for surgical purposes and in some weaving and dyeing processes. Fibres are also made from proteins which are extracted from natural substances such as egg albumen and soya beans. The first protein fibre was Lanital, produced in Italy in 1937; it was made from casein, a protein which comes from milk. Fibrolane, another protein fibre from casein, was much used once.

The synthetic fibres are derived from coal and oil. Nylon is made by combining benzene (a product of oil or coal-tar), oxygen, nitrogen, and hydrogen; Terylene, a British invention, is made from ethylene glycol (known to motorists as anti-freeze) and terephthalic acid, which are compounds of chemicals obtained from petroleum. Fibres made in this way are classified according to their chemical composition; the main groups are polyamides (nylon), polyesters (Terylene), acrylic fibres (Acrilan, Courtelle, and the American fibre Orlon), polyethylene fibres (Courlene), and polypropylene (Ulstron and Cournova).

The processes for making man-made fibres are all basically the same. First the raw material is made into a viscous liquid either by treatment with chemicals or by heating it. The raw materials for regenerated fibres are usually treated chemically; for example, the cellulose for viscose rayon is soaked in caustic soda, and for acetate it is treated with acetic acid, acetic anhydride, and sulphuric acid. Most synthetic fibres are made first in the form of solid PLASTICS (q.v.) which are melted by heating. The second stage is to extrude the liquid through a spinneret and then solidify the fine threads: viscose rayon and protein fibres by chemical treatment, acetate by drying, and synthetic fibres by cooling.

The fibres can be used in two ways, as continuous filament yarn or as staple fibre. Con-

I.C.I. Fibres Ltd.

WHEELING A BATCH OF NYLON YARN INTO THE SETTING CABINET TO STABILIZE IT BY HEAT

tinuous filament yarn consists of a few fibres from the spinneret which are twisted together slightly and wound straight on to a bobbin ready for weaving or knitting into fabrics such as taffeta or fine jersey for lingerie. The filament can be fluffed to give it extra warmth and absorbency: this is called 'texturing' or 'bulking'; it is then used for fabrics which are light and soft, yet thick and warm, suitable for jerseys, dresses, curtains, and carpets. Stretchy, elastic yarn, used for stretch stockings, tights, and swimsuits, for example, is made by stretching and twisting or crimping the filament.

Staple fibre is more important than filament yarn, for it can be made into a wider variety of fabrics. Thousands of filaments from a number of spinnerets are drawn together to make a continuous thick rope called a 'tow', which is cut into short lengths. This forms a mass of 'staple fibre' which is combed, drawn, and spun into yarn, in much the same way as yarn is made from natural fibres (*see* TEXTILE FIBRES AND FABRICS). Spun or staple yarns are used for fabrics which are thick and warm to the touch, for example, suitings and blankets. Different staple yarns may be blended with each other or with natural fibres before they are spun to produce fabrics in a very wide range of textures and weights.

Continuous filament and staple yarns are frequently dyed during the chemical process by injecting particles of dyestuff into the spinning solution just before it passes through the spinneret. This gives the fastest possible colours. But large quantities of yarn are made in the natural white state and dyed or printed at a later stage, for greater variety of colour and pattern can be obtained in this way.

Man-made fibres are used for many kinds of fabric, though they all have characteristic qualities which make them especially valuable for certain purposes. At the present time, about one half of the world's production of man-made fibres is viscose rayon. It is used for clothes, furnishing, and in industry for such things as tire cord (*see* RUBBER MANUFACTURE) and conveyor belts. Acetate is used chiefly for clothes and furnishings, for it has a rich appearance and drapes well; Tricel is similar but stronger.

Nylon is very strong and naturally elastic, which makes it suitable for stockings and for the strings of musical instruments and racquets. Terylene is also very strong and, like nylon, keeps its shape. It does not rot in strong sunlight so is good for curtains, and in its spun form is warm to the touch. Both nylon and Terylene are also used for ropes, crash nets on aircraft carriers, and fishing nets, among other things. Acrylic fabrics such as Acrilan and Courtelle are soft and warm and also very light, so are made into jerseys and blankets; they are also blended with wool or cotton to make suit and dress fabrics. Polyethylene fibres such as Courlene are non-absorbent and resistant to chemicals, and are used for stiffening collars and cuffs, for bathroom curtains, and for deck chairs.

Most man-made fibres wash easily and dry quickly, and, being crease-resistant, need little ironing; a hot iron, in fact, will melt them. Many can be permanently pleated and they keep their shape. They are moth-proof, and as they absorb little water they will not rot; they therefore wear well. The latest man-made fibre, polypropylene, derived from petroleum products, is very light and strong, but, owing to dyeing problems, the filament is used mainly for ROPE-MAKING (q.v.). Polypropylene film, however, is fibrillated, or slit. The resulting strips are twisted into yarns and twines used for tying parcels, etc., or woven into fabrics for backing tufted carpets. Glass fibre is an entirely different kind of synthetic fibre, used for making some furnishing materials and for insulation (*see* GLASS-MAKING, Section 4).

TEXTILE FIBRES AND FABRICS. The word 'textile' comes from the Latin *texere* 'to weave', but it is applied today to knitted fabrics as well as to woven ones, and to all fibres from which such fabrics are made. These textile fibres may be natural, such as the animal fibres of silk and wool and the vegetable fibres of flax, cotton, and hemp; or they may be man-made (*see* TEXTILE FIBRES, MAN-MADE). Man-made fibres are made from chemical compounds called polymers which are capable of being changed physically—that is to say they can be made solid or liquid, hard or soft—without altering their chemical structure. Regenerated man-made fibres are made from polymers which occur in nature, such as cellulose and casein; while synthetic fibres are made from polymers which do not occur in nature but are built up from other chemicals.

1. NATURAL FIBRES. Natural fibres were the first to be used by man, and they are still the most important. Fibres from flax stems, from the cotton plant, and from sheep come in short lengths called 'staples', and the first problem that faced our early ancestors was to discover how to turn these staples into a continuous yarn capable of being woven. This process is called spinning. The findings of archaeologists suggest that man first learnt to spin during the New Stone Age, perhaps about 5000 B.C. Flax was probably the first slender textile fibre that he used, and from this he spun linen thread and wove linen cloth.

The next natural fibre to be used was probably wool. There are records of the existence of a wool-weaving industry in Mesopotamia about 4000 B.C. Cotton has a long history in India, although it was some time before it was introduced into Europe; and silk is perhaps almost as ancient. Legend suggests that its use in China dates from about 2700 B.C.

Many other natural fibres have been used for textiles. The Scythians are believed to have made ropes and nets from hemp as early as 500 B.C., and today jute as well as hemp is used for coarse fabrics, sacking, and some furnishing materials. The early Swedes used the fibre of the stinging nettle plant for ropes and sailcloth, and in South America and the Philippine Islands fibre from the leaves of the pineapple plant has been much used. Some textile yarns are spun from the hair of various animals (*see* HAIR TRADE), and even the downy feathers of birds can be used in this way.

Silk is the only natural fibre that does not come in short lengths, or staples, but in one long continuous filament. To prepare silk for weaving all that has to be done is to twist the single strand from the silkworm into a thicker thread of sufficient strength to be usable. This process is called 'throwing' and is described in the article SILK INDUSTRY (q.v.).

2. MAN-MADE FIBRES. Late in the 19th century the shortage of certain natural textile raw materials and the desire for something new made chemists try to produce fibres synthetically. The first and most important of these fibres, rayon, has been followed by many since, based on various synthetic polymers, such as nylons on polyamides;

polyesters, such as Terylene; and acrylics, such as Orlon, Courtelle, and Acrilan. All of these fibres are produced by forcing a more or less liquid substance through small holes. Thus man-made fibres are all produced initially as continuous filament; as such they can be treated either by processes similar to those traditionally used in the silk industry, to give silk-like yarn which can be woven or knitted into silk-like fabrics, or, by cutting the filaments into staples, they can be spun on machinery used for other textiles. Short staples of man-made fibres are now more important than filament yarn, for they give a greater variety of fabrics and can be used alone or blended with natural fibres. Rayon staple, first developed for cotton spinning, can now be spun on most other spinning systems, as can many synthetic fibre staples.

3. Textile Processes. The names given to the basic textile processes date from the times when only natural raw materials were available, but today they apply equally to fabrics made with synthetics. We start either with staple or continuous filament, and the first step is to produce yarn. With continuous filament materials this simply consists of 'throwing'.

With staple material the first step is to prepare the staple by carding and combing. The prepared staple must then be spun into yarn, and the three main methods of doing this are the cotton process (*see* Cotton Manufacture) and the woollen and worsted processes (*see* Wool Spinning). Nearly all the man-made fibres can be subjected to all these processes; it is a matter of cutting up vast masses of continuous filaments specially prepared for the purpose into staple of the right lengths, thicknesses, and characteristics. It is thus possible to produce woollen-spun nylon or worsted-spun nylon, while cotton-spun rayon is familiar to everyone. In some cases two or more yarns (they may be of different materials) are twisted together; this process is known as doubling.

The final stage is the conversion of yarn into fabric by weaving (*see* Wool Weaving), knitting (*see* Hosiery and Knitwear), or Lace-making (q.v.). The fabric will derive its nature from the yarn or yarns used on the loom, in the shuttle, or in the knitting machine, and from the method of weaving or knitting employed. The finished fabric is then usually dyed or printed (*see* Dyes and Textile Printing). In many fabrics the yarns are dyed before they are woven; indeed man-made fibres may derive their colour from dye injected into the polymer used to prepare the continuous filament. Patterns such as checks are made by weaving yarns of different colours.

See also Vol. XI: Costume, History of.

TEXTILE PRINTING is the quickest and cheapest way of decorating fabric. It is not

Council of Industrial Design

HAND-BLOCK PRINTING

Photowork Ltd.

SILK-SCREEN PRINTING

Men are pressing the colour through the screens

Miller and Harris

A ROTARY SCREEN PRINTING MACHINE

The amount of colour pumped into each screen is controlled automatically

known who invented the process, nor when it was first used.

Until the 18th century hand-block printing was the only method known, and it is still used for certain kinds of work. For this the design is drawn or traced on a block of wood (generally sycamore, plane, or pear wood), and the parts not to be coloured are cut away to a depth of about a quarter of an inch, leaving the rest of the design standing up in relief. Details too fine for woodwork may be built up by brass or copper strips driven edgeways into the wood. The block is then pressed on a pad covered with pigment or dye; next, it is placed on the cloth, and given a blow with a heavy mallet to make sure that the design is pressed hard against the cloth. A separate block has to be cut and used for each colour in the design. The pattern cut on the block is called a 'repeat', and the whole design on the cloth is made by printing the 'repeat', over and over again. Pins, set at each corner of the blocks, are used to ensure that designs and colours produce a pattern without gaps or overlaps.

In the 18th century textile printers began to use engraved copper plates instead of wooden blocks; in this way they did much finer and more delicate work. Before long, however, the textile trades became mechanized. Machines for printing from engraved copper rollers instead of flat plates were invented in 1783 and 1784. This process greatly speeded production, and made it much cheaper; it is still the basis of modern textile printing (*see* plate opp. p. 416). Yet the old hand craft is still practised, not only in the studios of craftsmen-designers, but also within the industry itself. The cost of engraving rollers is very great, and it is more economical to produce by hand small quantities of the more experimental designs. In this way good artistic standards are maintained. One form of printing which is more akin to dyeing is 'batik' (*see* Dyes).

Textiles are also decorated by the silk-screen process which is a form of stencilling rather than true printing. Colour is pressed on to the cloth through a screen made of fine silk gauze stretched on a framework. The pattern is made by covering parts of the screen with a substance through which the colour will not pass. Different screens are used for each colour. Screen printing is not only used for textiles but also for wallpapers, posters, and coloured labels.

The fastest method of screen printing in use today is by the rotary machine. Here the continuously-turning cylindrical screens revolve in contact with an endless belt. The belt carries the cloth through the machine, and on into the drying chamber. Such machines can print 2,400 yards of material per hour, as compared with the 350 yards of the traditional flat screen process.

See also Cotton Industry; Linen Industry; Wool Industry, Modern.

See also Vol. XII: Design.

TILES, *see* Bricks and Tiles.

TILES, ORNAMENTAL. These are thin sections of baked clay, generally glazed, which are principally set into floors, walls, and fireplaces. They are usually 5 or 6 inches square, and $\frac{1}{4}$ to $\frac{1}{2}$ inch thick. Larger sizes than these are difficult to keep flat during the drying and baking or 'firing' processes.

Ornamental tiles are very ancient. Wall tiles with coloured glazes and relief ornament have been found in the ruins of ancient Egypt, Assyria, and Babylon. The Louvre Museum in Paris contains parts of two magnificent friezes of tiles from the palace of Darius, the great Persian king, at Susa (*c.* 500 B.C.). They are glazed in several colours, and decorated with life-size figures of men and animals in relief.

The Near East seems to have been a centre for glazed and painted tiles, and Persia in the 13th century produced some of the finest. These were usually not squares, but were hexagons, stars, and crosses: in fact, almost any shapes that would fit together into a repeating pattern. They were enriched with painting in various colours. China was another country which made great use of glazed and ornamental tiles, not only for walls and floors but also for the roofs of important buildings. By placing at gable ends or elsewhere matching figures (such as dragons) in glazed earthenware, their artistic effect was enhanced.

The art of making ornamental tiles travelled to Europe. The MOORS (q.v. Vol. I) introduced it when they conquered and occupied Spain, and it spread from there to Italy and northward. Some of the finest English tiles of the Middle Ages were made in a monastery at Chertsey, on the Thames. Both in England and in France the floors of many churches in the Middle Ages were paved with glazed tiles of elaborate design, inlaid, embossed, or incised. Fragments of these lovely old tiled floors can still be seen in old churches. The tiles varied in colour from golden brown to dark chestnut, through the use of different local clays.

In the 17th century the potters of Delft and other places in the Netherlands produced a large range of ornamental tiles, which found their way into every house of importance in the country. The paintings of Dutch artists, particularly VERMEER (q.v. Vol. V), show that they were used on the skirtings of walls as well as in fireplaces and elsewhere. These Delft tiles were imported in vast quantities into England, and were soon being made in this country at Lambeth (London), Bristol, and other places. They were usually about 5 inches square, and were made by pressing clay into wooden moulds. They were then dried, fired, coated with glaze, and painted over the unfired glaze. Sometimes a little transparent glaze was spread over the painting, and the tiles were then fired again. The earlier Delft tiles were patterned all over in lines and curves in several colours. The later tiles were pictorial, and were painted usually in blue or purple.

Ashmolean Museum

13TH-CENTURY PERSIAN TILES

Crown Copyright

FOUR 17TH-CENTURY DUTCH TILES

Victoria and Albert Museum

Modern ornamental tiles are mostly machine-pressed from almost dry materials. The machine-pressing process was invented in the 19th century. They look harder and more mechanical than hand-made tiles. A certain number of artist-potters still produce tiles decorated with hand-painted designs.

See also POTTERY; BRICKS AND TILES.

TIMBER INDUSTRY. 1. Before the Romans came to Britain the country was thickly forested, and there was more than enough timber

Wm. Mallinson and Sons

YUGOSLAVIAN BEECH-WOOD SEASONING

for the needs of the people. As the population grew, many of the woodlands had to be cleared to make room for arable and pasture land (*see* AGRICULTURE, HISTORY OF, Vol. VI). Then, as industry developed, it began to use a tremendous amount of timber; in fact, the Sussex iron industry, which smelted its ores with CHARCOAL (q.v.), cleared large forests, completely changing the original face of Sussex. Soon, timber ran short, and by the 17th century it was being imported, mainly from Scandinavia. Since then Britain has imported increasing quantities of timber from overseas.

During and immediately after the two world wars it was difficult to import timber, and home woodlands had to be felled; but today Britain is again buying large quantities of wood from abroad. In 1955 she was the largest importer of timber in the world, buying 309 million cubic feet, valued at over £190 million—almost one-tenth of the cost of British imports of all raw materials. At the same time Britain's own woods are being replanted and cared for under the general supervision of the FORESTRY COMMISSION (q.v. Vol. VI).

'Timber' has two distinct industrial meanings, one indicating the world's wood usable by man in any way (*see* TIMBER, Vol. VI), and the other, the trade in sawn boards, logs, and poles—the subject of this article. The North American expression 'lumber' is often used to describe timber sawn from the log. Timber operations include the felling of trees, the extraction of logs from the forest, the sawing of logs into sawn timber, the conversion of logs into veneers and plywood, and the sale and export of logs, sawn timber, and processed timber.

Of the world's production of timber (trees cut down each year) two-fifths are used as fuel. The remainder is classified as industrial wood, of which approximately one-fifth is used in WOOD-PULP (q.v.) for making paper, plastics, and other substances. The rest is cut for veneers, for plywood manufacture, or sawn into boards. Commercial timber is divided into two main groups—SOFTWOODS and HARDWOODS (qq.v.). Softwoods are those derived from coniferous trees, such as pine and fir; hardwoods are those derived from non-coniferous trees, in the main broad-leaved, such as oak and mahogany. Britain imports about five times as much softwood as hardwood, buying about half her requirements from Sweden and Finland and the rest mainly from the Soviet Union and Canada. Hardwoods come from North and Central America, the Far East, central Europe, Africa, and a number of Commonwealth countries.

2. SEASONING. New-cut timber contains a great deal of moisture, and if used in this state will shrink unduly and may split or warp. Seasoning is a carefully controlled process of drying out this surplus moisture. The traditional method is that of air-seasoning, in which the boards coming from the sawmill are stacked in a manner which allows a good flow of air underneath and between them; then they are left to dry slowly for a long period. Hardwoods take longer to season than softwoods which, if stacked in the spring, will be seasoned in about 3 months. A quicker and more easily controlled method is kiln-drying. The boards are stacked on a trolley in the same way as for air seasoning, and the trolley is run into a kiln. A kiln is a brick-built room with heating pipes, fans, and steam jets, and with an air-tight door, so that the temperature and humidity can be regulated precisely and the wood dried to the exact condition required. During the drying, samples of wood are removed from time to time to test the moisture content.

Timber seasoned in the open has from 18% to 23% of moisture in it, according to the humidity of the atmosphere; the moisture content of furniture in a warm, dry house may be as low as 10%. Since air-seasoning will never reduce the moisture in wood much below 20%, timber to be used in centrally heated buildings should always be kiln-seasoned to ensure against shrinking or warping. Well-seasoned wood is stronger than natural wood and, provided it does not subsequently become damp, will not decay. It is easier to work and finish with polish or paint and can more easily absorb preservatives.

3. PRESERVING. Even the most careful seasoning will not prevent wood from deteriorating if it is allowed to get damp. This deterioration is principally caused by the attacks of wood-destroying insects or fungi. Several preservatives are used to prevent the attacks of these pests. They are classed according to the liquid the chemicals are dissolved in; the liquid may be water, tar oil, or a mineral oil. Creosote is used to treat external timbers such as railway sleepers, telegraph poles, and fences. The other types of preservative are used to treat wood indoors, as they have less smell (*see* FURNITURE, CARE OF, Vol. XI).

4. TIMBER ENGINEERING. In recent years, research into the basic properties of timber and advances in the science of adhesion, mechanical connexions, and timber technology have led to the development of new forms of construction in which timber is used as an engineering material for structures of all kinds.

Timber is important today not only for its use as timber but also for the many commercial products which are made or extracted from it. Among these are wood INDUSTRIAL ALCOHOL, GUMS AND RESINS, turpentine, chemicals used for TANNING, and cellulose (*see* WOOD-PULP) for synthetic textiles.

See also HARDWOODS; SOFTWOODS; PLYWOODS AND VENEERS; WOODWORK, HISTORY OF.

See also Vol. VI: FORESTRY; TIMBER; TIMBER MEASUREMENTS.

TIME AND MOTION STUDY, *see* Vol. VIII: PRODUCTION ENGINEERING, Section 4.

Seaboard Lumber Sales, Canada

CUTTING TIMBER INTO BOARDS IN ONE OPERATION WITH A POWER-DRIVEN SAW

TIN, one of the metals in bronze, was much used in prehistoric times during the Bronze Age. Tin is not found in nature as a free metal, but only as an ore (*see* METAL ORES, Vol. III). The most important ore is tinstone or cassiterite, which is dioxide of tin. Five-sixths of the world's tin now comes from alluvial or river-bed workings, but underground mines are still worked in Cornwall and Bolivia, and in the Waterberg district of the Transvaal, in South Africa. Until about 1870 Cornwall was the world's leading producer of tin (*see* CORNISH MINING), but tin was then discovered in Malaya, and the production from that region has since increased steadily. Malaysia produces about one-third of the world's tin (200,000 long tons a year), Bolivia an eighth, the U.S.S.R. a tenth, and Indonesia one-sixteenth.

Tin has many industrial uses. It is used for lining iron cooking-pots, stills for DISTILLATION (q.v.) and other such devices, particularly those that have to deal with foods. Tinfoil is much used for wrapping chocolates, confectionery, and some forms of cheese.

Tin plays a part in several important ALLOYS (q.v. Vol. VIII). Solder consists of equal parts

W. J. Bennetts and Sons

19TH-CENTURY TIN DRESSERS AT A CORNISH MINE

The tin ore, mixed with water, flowed along the central troughs, where the men are standing, and down the sloping 'decks'. The heavy ore stuck to the decks and was swept up

of tin and lead. Tin and copper in varied proportions make different types of bronze, such as gunmetal and the bronze used for coinage (*see* COINING). Tin alloys are much used in engineering for making bearing metals (*see* BEARINGS, Vol. VIII). Various types of bell metal, out of which church bells and other big bells are cast, contain 16 to 20% of tin. A large quantity of tin is used to coat the steel sheet in TINPLATE (q.v. Vol. VIII), whose main use is the packing of preserved foods and other perishable goods.

TINNED FOODS, *see* CANNING.

TOBACCO INDUSTRY. 1. Tobacco is made from the leaves of the plant *Nicotiana* (*see* TOBACCO, Vol. VI). Only two of the sixty or more species are grown for smoking purposes—*N. tabacum*, the main tobacco of commerce, and *N. rustica*, which is grown in Russia for smoking under the name Makhorka and is also smoked locally in some other parts of the world. Britain's main sources of supply of leaf tobacco are the U.S.A., Canada, and India; Turkish or Oriental tobaccos come mainly from Turkey and Greece; while cigar tobaccos come chiefly from the West Indies, Indonesia, Brazil, and the U.S.A.

When harvested, the leaves must be 'cured'—the process by which the green leaf is dried—on the plantation, before being sent for sale. A great deal of tobacco, especially for cigars, is air- or sun-cured by being hung in sheds with the ventilation carefully controlled. But most tobacco is cured by artificial heat, usually by flue-curing; a certain amount of it is fire-cured. By the fire method an open fire is used, and the smoke gives a distinctive flavour to the leaf. Most tobacco coming to England is flue-cured in drying houses, where the heat is distributed by pipes and no smoke reaches the leaf. It takes about 4 days and turns the leaf yellow or even orange. After curing, the leaf is put into heaps, which are known as 'bulks', to mature for about a month, during which time the heaps are turned several times, and the leaves soften. The tobacco is then graded according to quality and often the mid-rib of the leaf removed (though this may be done at a later stage). It then goes to the sales warehouse, and from there to the packing factory, where it is redried and packed firmly into casks (hogsheads), cases, or bales, ready for shipping.

On arrival in Britain the casks are stored in bonded WAREHOUSES (q.v.), where the leaf continues to mature until the manufacturer, having paid the heavy duty, transfers the

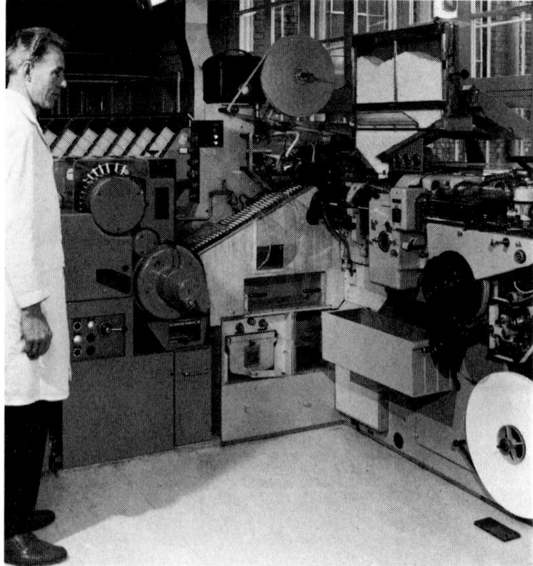

W.D. and H.O. Wills

A MACHINE MAKING FILTER-TIP CIGARETTES

It produces 2,000 cigarettes per minute, and joins together 4 miles of cigarette paper and tobacco per hour

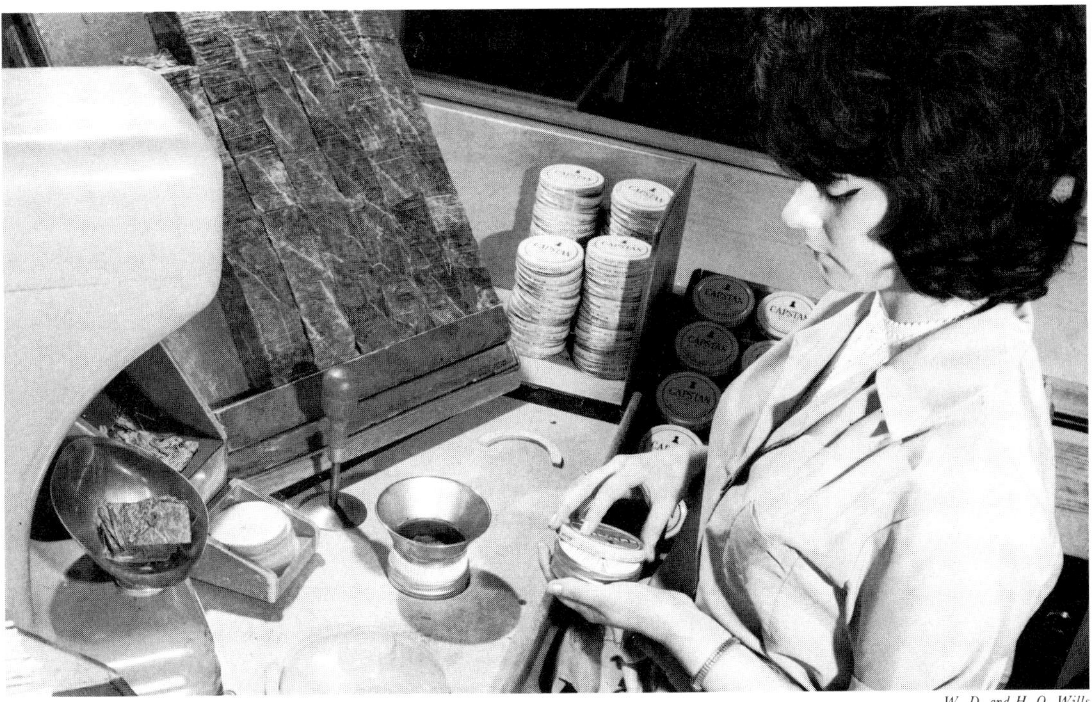

W. D. and H. O. Wills

WEIGHING AND PACKING TOBACCO BY HAND

Here flakes of Navy Cut, a medium tobacco, are being weighed out individually. They are then packed into 2-ounce vacuum tins, ready for despatch to the shops

tobacco to his factory. There he has to moisten the leaf in a steam-heated chamber to make it soft and pliable enough for manufacture.

2. MANUFACTURE. An important part of the manufacturing process is the blending of leaves of different types to give a brand its special characteristics, and this requires skill and experience. For cigarettes, the prepared blended leaf is first finely cut by high-speed cutting machines. The cut tobacco, known as the 'rag', is then passed through a heated rotary cylinder, which reduces the moisture and brings out the flavour and aroma. It is then cooled and stored for about 24 hours, after which it is fed into the cigarette-making machines. The tobacco is drawn on to an endless ribbon of cigarette paper, which is automatically printed with the name of the brand. The tobacco and paper are shaped into a cylinder and sealed to form one endless cigarette; this is then cut by a fast revolving knife into individual cigarettes. Modern cigarette-making machines produce perfectly made cigarettes at speeds of up to 2,500 a minute. The finished cigarettes pass to the packing room where a packing machine packs them into cartons, boxes, or tins, at a rate of over a million cigarettes a day.

For Shags and Fine Cut pipe tobaccos the prepared leaf is finely cut on machines and, after being stoved and cooled, is ready for packing. Flakes, Navy Cuts, and Cut Plugs are compressed into cakes, bars, or plugs, which are then placed in retaining presses, sometimes under heat. Afterwards they are cut into thin slices or flakes. Mixtures are blended from various types of tobacco, types with a strong and distinctive flavour such as Latakia from Syria and Perique from Louisiana being used to give piquancy.

Roll, Twist, and Pigtail are made by spinning the leaves by machinery into 'ropes' varying in diameter from about $\frac{1}{8}$ in. to $1\frac{3}{4}$ in. The 'ropes' are wound into coils, which are wrapped and corded and sometimes pressed and stoved.

A cigar consists of a 'filler', which is the inner core and forms the body and shape of the cigar; a 'binder', which is the leaf wrapped round the filler to form what is known as the 'cigar bunch'; and a 'wrapper', which is the leaf rolled spirally round the bunch to complete the cigar.

Nearly 99% of the cigars smoked in Britain are made in Britain, and the best British brands compare well with the famous Havana cigars imported from Cuba.

Snuff is a powder made from tobacco leaves and 'stem' (the mid-rib of the leaf). These are fermented in bins and ground in snuff mills. Snuff recipes are jealously guarded trade secrets. Snuffs are often scented by using essential oils such as those used in PERFUMERY (q.v.). There are also menthol-flavoured snuffs which clear the head in somewhat the same way as eucalyptus does.

3. DEVELOPMENT OF THE INDUSTRY. At the beginning of the 19th century most of the tobacco consumed in Britain consisted of shag and roll tobaccos and snuff. Early in the 19th century British officers returning from the Peninsular War in Spain brought the cigar to England, and gradually cigar-smoking superseded snuffing in fashionable society.

Cigarettes came to Britain from the Continent, and troops returning from the Crimea brought with them the habit of cigarette-smoking which they had learnt from their French and Turkish allies. Robert Gloag started the first cigarette factory in England at Walworth, London, 1856; the cigarettes were made by hand and were extremely crude, with cane mouthpieces, and the tobacco used was Latakia dust. Around 1870 Virginian cigarettes began to come on the market, and in 1883 Messrs. Wills of Bristol installed the first really efficient cigarette-making machine. This was the beginning of the popularity of cigarettes. By 1900 cigarettes were accounting for one-eighth of the total tobacco sales in Britain and pipe tobaccos for over four-fifths; by 1961 more than nine-tenths of the tobacco smoked was in the form of cigarettes.

In 1901 some leading British tobacco firms formed The Imperial Tobacco Company (of Great Britain and Ireland) Limited, in order to resist powerful American competition. Today the Imperial Tobacco Company supplies over two-thirds of the total quantity of tobacco products consumed in Great Britain and Ireland. Because of the very high import duty on tobacco and the undoubtedly bad effects on health of very heavy smoking, tobacco consumption is no longer maintaining its former rate of increase.

See also Vol. VI: TOBACCO.
See also Vol. XI: SMOKING, HISTORY OF.

TOKEN CURRENCY, *see* CURRENCY.

TOURIST INDUSTRY. The religious PILGRIMAGES of ancient and medieval times (q.v. Vol. I) were often organized by agents, but no details are known of how they ran their businesses. In those days, and indeed down to the coaching days of the 18th and early 19th centuries, travel was looked upon generally as an unavoidable necessity and not as a recreation, although a few pleasure trips were organized, such as the 'grand tour' of the cities of Europe and excursions to such beauty spots as the English Lake District. But until the time of the railway and the steamship, the organization of travelling cannot be said to have become a proper industry.

At first the beginnings of this new industry were slow. Its pioneer was Thomas Cook, a young man who organized the first railway excursion in 1841, and who later founded the firm of Thomas Cook and Son (*see* TRAVEL AGENCIES, Vol. IV). The railway companies paid Cook a share of the fares actually charged to the passengers. No other arrangement would have been legally possible, as the railway tickets, being legal contracts between company and passenger, could not have been issued by Cook himself at his own price. A share of the passenger fare, or a COMMISSION on it (q.v.), is still the way in which Cook's and other travel agencies are paid for their services. Originally the parties of passengers who took part in 'Cook's Tours' were in charge of leaders or 'couriers', who could usually speak several languages. The charge to the traveller for the whole tour was fixed and paid in advance, previous arrangements having been made with innkeepers on the route for food and accommodation at fixed prices. From the innkeepers and restaurant proprietors, as well as from the railway and steamship companies, Cook received a commission or discount on the actual charge to the traveller. Later, Cook established 'inclusive independent travel'. His agency quoted an inclusive charge for travel, food, and accommodation for a fixed period over any chosen route; and the traveller, having paid his money, made his own way independently. At first independent tourists were restricted in each town to a single hotel or restaurant with which arrangements had been made in advance; but in 1866 'inclusive independent travel' was made easier by Cook's invention of the 'hotel coupon'. A traveller, when he booked his tour, received detachable coupons in a counterfoil book, each coupon being valid for a meal or a night's lodging at any one of a large number of hotels and restaurants on Cook's list.

Cook had many imitators, at home and abroad, and the firm he founded is now only one of a large number. Since the later years of the 19th century, the only important development in the travel industry has been the increase in its size. Nowadays there is more time and money for pleasure travel. New means of travel have also become available—air travel, PLEASURE CRUISES (q.v. Vol. IX), and inland and continental motor-coach tours. Cultural societies and organizations now promote tours of their own, particularly to such countries as Italy and Greece; some of these promoters make their own arrangements, while others rely on the ordinary travel agencies. Some begin as cultural societies and end by becoming travel agencies themselves.

For many years economists have known the tourist industry to be an important factor in a country's balance of payments (*see* INTERNATIONAL TRADE). A country such as Spain now depends largely on foreign tourists, for almost as much of her foreign currency is earned that way as by the export of actual goods. Until recent years British Government policy was not greatly concerned with the tourist industry. It is now realized that the encouragement of tourists from abroad is a most useful way of increasing the country's earnings of foreign currency, and an organization sponsored by the Government, the British Travel Association, is now helping the British tourist industry by advertising Britain's attractions in other countries. The tourist trade has in recent years become one of the biggest earners of foreign and overseas currencies; in 1967, for example, 3¼ million overseas visitors came to Britain, and foreign currency earnings amounted to about £351 millions.

See also Vol. IV: TRAVEL AGENCIES.

TRADE, *see* EXCHANGE AND TRADE: INTERNATIONAL TRADE; OVERSEAS TRADE; TRADE, HISTORY OF.

TRADE CYCLE. This is the name given to the up-and-down movements of business activity, from good times to bad times, that have been a feature of economic life since the early 19th century. The typical cycle begins with a general collapse of business activity, followed by depression and UNEMPLOYMENT (q.v.). There follows a gradual recovery from depression, beginning at first very slowly and acquiring momentum as the years go on. At the end of the recovery phase, business activity increases more swiftly, and there is a good deal of speculation in goods and raw materials on the commodity markets, and in STOCKS AND SHARES on the world STOCK EXCHANGES (qq.v.). Later still, speculation and business activity increase to a feverish height, which another general collapse brings to a sudden end. This series or cycle of events then repeats itself.

The average period of the cycle has been about 10 years. For example, 1825, 1837, 1847, 1857, and 1866 were years in which active, or 'booming', business conditions suddenly came to an end. The passing of over a hundred years seems to have made little difference to this average 10-year period, and nearer our own times 1920 and 1929 were both years in which boom conditions suddenly collapsed. Before the outbreak of war in 1939 there were signs that the normal pattern of the cycle would be repeated, but the money spent on rearmament and war preparations succeeded in checking the tendency towards depression.

Serious unemployment is a feature of the trade cycle, which is thus intimately linked with the welfare of those who earn their living in industry and commerce. Professional economists have studied the cycle very carefully, in order to find out its causes and possible cure. Its regular rhythm, and its recurrence about every 10 years, are the strangest things about it, and these are just the features that many of the theories fail to explain. All schools of thought, however, are in general agreement that during the 'boom' phase of the cycle people are spending too much and saving too little, and that during the 'depression' phase they are spending too little and saving too much. The real differences between economists lie in their explanations of the remoter causes of this alternation of overspending and underspending.

Most modern economists now agree that a possible cure for the trade cycle may be found in government intervention. It is suggested that at the beginning of any depression the business 'pump' should be 'primed' by government expenditure on public works, house building

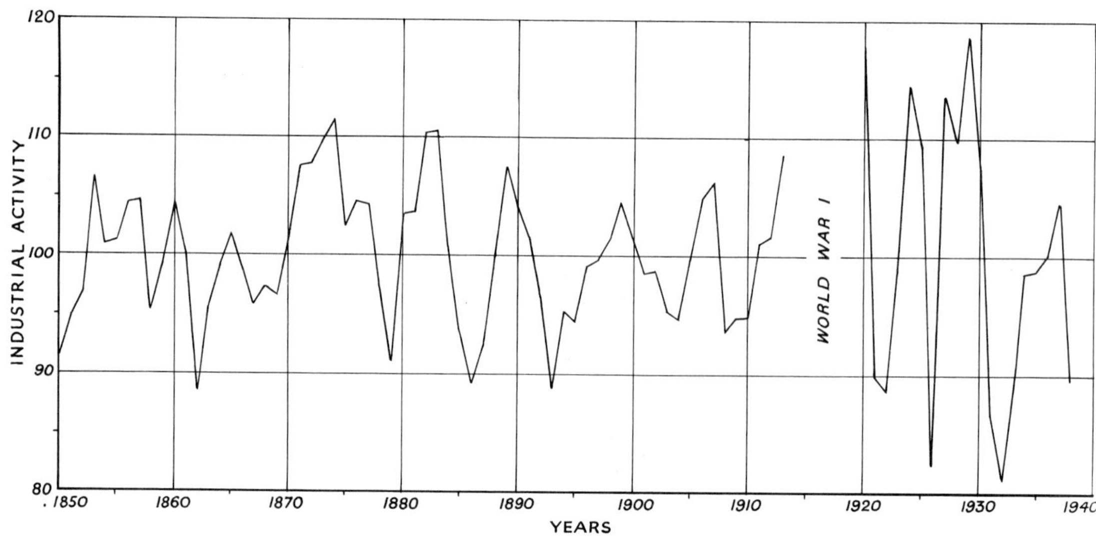

CHART OF INDUSTRIAL ACTIVITY IN BRITAIN, 1850–1938

100 is taken as the average activity. Boom years are indicated by the crests and depressions by the troughs. From Beveridge's *Full Employment in a Free Society*

programmes, and modernization and renewal of the plant and machinery of nationalized enterprises; also, that at the same time governments should assist private enterprise by making loans and capital freely available, if necessary by government guarantee. Further, taxation should be increased, and a budget surplus built up, in years of active business; and taxation decreased, and the budget surplus allowed to run off, in years of depression. Government intervention would thus work in a direction exactly opposite to that of the cycle itself.

Whether such measures can be effective still remains to be proved. Depressions on the pre-war scale have not affected Britain since the war ended, but there have been minor recessions (periods of lessened business activity) in the U.S.A. in 1949 and 1954, and early in 1958 unemployment in that country exceeded 5 millions, and there were many signs of a real depression. It is probable that the trade cycle has not been fully conquered, but that its worst effects can now be much reduced.

See also UNEMPLOYMENT; ECONOMICS.

TRADE DISCOUNTS, *see* WHOLESALE TRADING.

TRADE FAIRS arose in past centuries just as much for religious as for commercial reasons, and in the German language the word *Messe* is used for both a religious SACRAMENT (q.v. Vol. I) and for 'fair'. In Europe, fairs were at first held on days that were important festivals of the Christian Church, when many people gathered together in some cathedral city or other shrine of the faith. Merchants and traders saw in such gatherings good opportunities of doing business, and either petitioned local Church dignitaries for permission to set up stalls in the cathedral square or on Church lands, or obtained a municipal or Royal charter granting a similar privilege. Gradually these fairs came to be associated not only with religion and business, but also with entertainment and amusement (*see* FAIRS, Vol. IX). Fair days began with religious services, continued with business, and often ended at night-time in riotous gaiety. Many fairs of this kind now survive only for purposes of amusement. The annual 'Mop Fair' at Stratford-on-Avon is one of these. Its name shows that farm labourers and domestic servants (with their mops) went to the fair to find employment for the following year.

Fairs of the mixed religious and commercial kind go back a long way in the history of most countries. Sidonius Apollinaris, who wrote in the 5th century, mentions fairs then being held in the Roman province of Gaul. The big Mohammedan fair at Mecca dates from the early days of ISLAM (q.v. Vol. I), and the Hindu fair at Hardwar, in India, is of very long standing.

By the time of CHARLEMAGNE (q.v. Vol. V) English merchants visited fairs at St. Denis, near Paris, and Rouen. In England the number of fairs increased after the Norman invasion in the 11th century: one of the most famous was Stourbridge Fair, which was first held in 1211. Most important of all were the fairs of Champagne, the main meeting-place between the merchants of northern and southern Europe. Such fairs continued to flourish for many centuries, but gradually changed their character. Some, which were held at first only on Church feast-days, became street or municipal markets, held weekly, as the population and trade of their district expanded (*see* STREET MARKETS). Others, held in large towns or cities, became in time international trade fairs. Leipzig, for instance, began as a local fair at the end of the 12th century, but soon became a large annual market in furs, hides and leather, glassware, and linens and woollens. At the end of the 17th century the *Ostermesse*, or Easter Fair, at Leipzig became the annual gathering of the merchants and agents interested in the German book trade, and later this fair became the main European centre for dealings in Russian and East European furs (*see* FUR TRADE). The big Russian fair at Nijni-Novgorod (Gor'Kiy) was at its height in the late 19th century, and was revived under Communist rule in 1923. Other important European trade fairs are those of Lyons and Prague.

These large international trade fairs are still held, although improvements in communications and in trade organization have greatly changed their character. In trades that are seasonal, such as books and furs, a fair such as Leipzig is still largely what it once was: a centre for the actual sale and purchase of goods. But, in general, trade fairs are nowadays organized advertising displays on a large scale, where manufacturers and merchants may see the latest designs in goods, and in machines with which to manufacture them. As at the earlier fairs, however, large orders are often booked and much actual business done. The British Industries Fair (B.I.F.), organized by the British Government until 1954, continued until 1956–7 when

LEIPZIG FAIR IN THE 18TH CENTURY

Merchants discuss business while pedlars sell their wares to the women

L.N.A.

BUSINESS EFFICIENCY EXHIBITION AT OLYMPIA, LONDON

Office furniture, electric typewriters, adding machines, and filing systems are displayed

it was discontinued mainly because of the growing emphasis on the importance of international trade fairs.

See also EXHIBITIONS.

TRADE, HISTORY OF. 1. The beginnings of trade in the primitive days of mankind are difficult to trace, for the only evidence we have is from digging by archaeologists. For example, excavations in the early CHALK workings (q.v.) in south-eastern England and discoveries elsewhere have shown that, even in the New Stone Age (about 2500–2000 B.C.), there was a widespread trade in flints and stone axes, and an axe workshop in Cumberland supplied axes as far away as the Oxford region. This period was the beginning of agriculture and close settlement, which favoured the growth of trade. But it was a long time before trade became organized along regular routes, and developed by systems of MONEY, BANKING, and CREDIT (qq.v.). These things belong to a later period, when man began to live in towns and cities.

2. THE ANCIENT WORLD. The trade about which we first know something definite is the caravan trade across the Asiatic deserts, to and from the cities of Mesopotamia, Egypt, and Arabia (*see* TRADE ROUTES, Vol. IV). In those days traders could rely on protection from robbery or murder only when near the cities, as is the case in parts of Asia today. Caravans had to carry not only their cargoes, but also fodder for the animals and food for the drivers, merchants, and guards, for foodstuffs were not easy to find or buy in the lands they travelled through. As the space left for merchandise was not large, the goods carried by the merchants tended to be light and yet valuable: that is, luxuries and not necessities. The oases along these routes became first of all trading depots, and later big commercial centres. Mesopotamia, particularly the valleys of the Tigris and Euphrates rivers, and north-east Africa, particularly Egypt, became in those days the main trading regions of the known world.

A big advance was made when, in some parts of the world, sea-borne trade became usual. The Phoenicians of the coast of Syria are usually thought to have been the first to have developed sea-borne commerce, but this is not certain. It is quite possible that about 3,000 years ago the coastal trade of China was equally important, but we have no records that can prove this. The Phoenicians traded from ports in Syria to Crete, Cyprus, Rhodes, and other Greek islands, to North Africa and later to the western Mediterranean and beyond. Tyre and Sidon were important bases for their activities, but greatest of all was their colony of Carthage. The Phoenicians were manufacturers. The outward or export trade was mainly in manufactured goods, notably metal ware, glassware, and textiles. These were traded for raw materials, principally metals, and especially tin, copper, and silver (*see* PHOENICIAN CIVILIZATION, Vol. I). This trade was mainly in luxuries, for the sea was no safer from marauders than the land, and ships were small. The western peoples with whom the Phoenicians traded were primitive and uncivilized, and had not adopted the regular use of money. The basis of these Phoenician dealings was the direct exchange of goods for goods, or barter (*see* EXCHANGE AND TRADE).

The Phoenicians were contemporary with the Greeks and the Romans. The Athenians were the most advanced of the Greeks in the matter of trade. In their trading relations the Athenians looked east and the Phoenicians west, and there was no real conflict of interest between them. Athens was the first big commercial city of the European mainland, and its importance was assisted by sound money and an efficient banking system. Athens itself was not a seaport, but not very far away was the port of Piraeus. Athens was the first community to import necessities in any quantity. Grain came in for her increasing population from the shores of the Black Sea, then called the Euxine, and her exports included figs, olive oil, wine, honey, pottery, metal ware, and textiles. Athens lost the political leadership of the Greek world after the Peloponnesian War (about 400 B.C.), but her trade was not greatly affected. When ALEXANDER THE GREAT (q.v. Vol. V) gained the leadership of the Greek peoples and fought his way into Asia, the trade of Athens and Piraeus increased, and they are still commercially important cities. Alexander's marches into Persia, Mesopotamia, Central Asia, and India opened up more of the caravan trade, and Antioch and Alexandria became big commercial cities. Many inland caravan routes converged on Antioch, which had a port, Seleucia, not far off. Alexandria was a base for sea-borne trade. The trade of both cities was mainly in luxuries, principally in spices, drugs, and silks.

British Museum

ROMAN POTTERY, CALLED 'SAMIAN WARE', MADE IN GAUL AND EXPORTED TO BRITAIN IN THE 1ST CENTURY A.D.

The Roman Empire was the next big trading community. The city of Rome produced little; it was a political capital and the financial centre of the Empire. Before Rome could expand, Carthage had to be reckoned with; for Carthage controlled the cornlands of North Africa, which were vital to the growing population of the city of Rome, and was an influential sea-power which could endanger Rome's communications. So, before the Empire was founded, the two Punic Wars were fought, which ended in the destruction of Carthage in 146 B.C. Rome's rise to the rank of the world's leading power did not much affect the nature of trade or the main centres where it was carried on. Increasing quantities of luxuries were imported from the East and from North Africa. These imports were what we should nowadays call 'unrequited imports': they did not have to be paid for by exports, but were the tribute paid to Rome by the various peoples she conquered. Most of the trade tended to come from the Eastern Mediterranean, as can be seen from the number of Jews and Greeks in the business life of the Roman Empire. These races are still the merchants of the eastern Mediterranean today.

In the 5th century A.D. Byzantium, rebuilt and renamed Constantinople (and today called Istanbul), became the political capital of the Roman Empire, and remained the world's

Bodleian Library

EUROPEAN MERCHANTS AT AN INDIAN COURT

Members of Sir Thomas Roe's embassy to the Emperor Jehangir, 1616–17. Detail from a Mogul painting (MS. Douce Or. D. 3. f. 21)

commercial capital from the beginning of the Dark Ages until the time of the Crusades (*see* BYZANTINE EMPIRE, Vol. I). The commercial importance of Constantinople was founded on solid hard work, and the surrounding district was a busy manufacturing centre. Textiles, leatherwork, armour, pottery, and artistic metal work were manufactured and exported. Imports included not only the raw materials of these trades, such as wool, metals, wax, furs, and amber, but also a considerable amount of grain. Big TRADE FAIRS (q.v.) were held annually at Constantinople and Thessalonica. The leadership of Constantinople in world trade rested largely, like that of Athens many centuries earlier, on a sound system of currency and banking. The standard Byzantine coin, the 'bezant' (*see* COINS), kept up its international value, and it became the currency of European business. The use of BILLS OF EXCHANGE (q.v.) for making payments in distant countries (without the risk of carrying coin over routes infested with bandits and pirates) was developed to a high degree. The Emperor Justinian made the SILK INDUSTRY a State MONOPOLY, and joint-stock COMPANIES (qq.v.) were formed by groups of private traders and manufacturers. A good deal of the commerce of Constantinople was done by sea, and risks were greater than they are today. So the Byzantine merchants invented a very efficient system of marine INSURANCE (q.v.).

3. THE MIDDLE AGES. Many foreign merchants, principally those of Venice and Genoa, took part in Byzantine trade and in the 12th century the Venetians and Genoese succeeded the Byzantines as the world's leading traders. Venice was well placed to be the main European commercial centre. There were overland routes to southern Germany, the Rhineland, and the Netherlands, and there was, of course, the sea. It was by sea that imports arrived from the East, and from the early 14th century onwards a fleet of galleys (*see* SHIPPING) took exports once a year to north-west Europe. Bruges, in Flanders, was then a port capable of berthing the largest ships, and was the main objective of these annual voyages; Southampton, Sandwich, and London were also visited. The exports were mainly luxuries, principally spices and silks. Raw materials, particularly wool, hides, and metals, were imported from the West, worked up in Venice and the interior of Italy, and re-exported to the East as manufactured goods: particularly Florentine cloths and silk fabrics from Lucca. The Venetians improved on the Byzantine banking system, and developed the science of double-entry BOOK-KEEPING (q.v.). In northern Europe in the Middle Ages the HANSEATIC LEAGUE (q.v.), which had a large trade in grain and salt fish, occupied much the same position as Venice in the south, the depots or 'factories' of the League extending as far east as Nijni-Novgorod in Russia and as far west as London.

4. THE MODERN WORLD. In 1453 the Turks conquered Constantinople, and the interruption to trade with the East encouraged the search for alternative trade routes. World trade could not grow into its modern pattern until people had more knowledge of the world itself; the period when this knowledge was acquired is known as the 'Age of Discoveries' or 'Navigations' (*see* EXPLORATION, Vol. IV). Spaniards and Portuguese made voyages more or less as State projects: in fact, one of the kings of Portugal at this time acquired the name of HENRY THE

Navigator (q.v. Vol. V). Britain and other countries of northern Europe countered by forming big Chartered Companies (q.v.), each being given a certain part of the world as its exclusive domain. The new companies penetrated into distant lands and brought back their products, many of which were new and unknown. The Russia Company, for instance, opened up a route into the very south of Russia, from Archangel in the north and thence southward by land and river. The Levant Company, operating in the eastern Mediterranean, was the first to introduce the currant into Britain. But Spain and Portugal, particularly Spain, rather scorned trade. They merely imported silver and gold from Mexico and Peru, and bought the goods they wanted from the trading nations; and so they helped to make their enemies more wealthy and powerful. By the 17th century the Dutch dominated the world's trade, with the French and the English as their closest rivals. All three nations opened up the tropical and sub-tropical lands of the East and West Indies, and imported into Europe sugar and tobacco, and tea and coffee, which gradually ceased to be luxuries and became the necessities of the masses of the people. In the course of the 18th century the Dutch fell behind, and the commercial and naval rivalry between the French and the British was settled in Britain's favour by the Napoleonic Wars (q.v. Vol. X).

Manchester Art Gallery

PUNCH BOWL MADE IN BRISTOL TO COMMEMORATE THE ARRIVAL THERE OF THE SWEDISH MERCHANT SHIP *Vigilantia* IN 1765

Ashmolean Museum

PLATE MADE IN CHINA FOR THE DUTCH MARKET

It illustrates the destruction of Rotterdam in 1693 during the French wars. In the 17th and 18th centuries large quantities of blue and white porcelain were exported from China to Europe

During the following century, the 19th, the Industrial Revolution (q.v.) led to greater production, and the pattern of world trade started to become what it is today. Luxuries still entered into world trade, but formed a smaller and smaller part of it. North-west Europe—Britain, Belgium, France, Germany, Sweden, and Switzerland—became a concentrated manufacturing region, to which raw materials came from all parts of the world, and whose growing populations came to rely more and more on imported foodstuffs. In the present century the U.S.A. has also become an important trading nation, but her trade within her own borders is vastly greater and more important than her external trade. Most of the world's trade is now in articles of common use rather than luxuries for the few, although what would now be considered necessities would have been the undreamed-of luxuries of even a few centuries ago.

See also International Trade.

TRADE MARKS are distinctive names or designs applied to goods manufactured or sold by the owners of the trade mark. A trade mark is carefully protected by law; the right to it is obtained through the Government Patent Office in London, where it must be registered, in much

Meade Collection

THE WRAPPER OF AN EARLY SALMON TIN

The illustration is the trade mark of the manufacturer

the same way as a PATENT (q.v.). Under the rules a trade mark will be granted for a representation of the name of the individual or company in some 'special or particular manner': for example, in Gothic lettering, or in some symmetrical pattern of differently-sized letters. A signature can also be used, such as, for example, the signature 'King C. Gillette' on a packet of Gillette razor-blades. The most successful and well-known trade marks rely on an invented word or words, for example 'Bovril', 'Kolynos', or 'Glaxo'. But any ordinary word in general use will satisfy the regulations, provided that it does not refer to the character or quality of the goods, and is not a geographical name; for instance the word 'skipper' is lawfully applied to 'Skipper' sardines. A trade mark will also be granted for the use of a 'distinctive mark', such as the drawing of a swan on a 'Swan' fountain-pen. In this case the trade mark contains not only an ordinary word ('swan') but also a distinctive mark.

Many trade marks, when granted, become valuable pieces of property. If a trade mark is an invented word (such as 'Bovril') or a clever design (such as 'Mr. Peek and Mr. Frean'), it may lend itself to very successful ADVERTISING (q.v.) and lead to big sales of the product. It is for that reason that owners of trade marks are protected by law against any infringement of their rights by other firms. The owner of a trade mark may sell it to someone else, but the new owner cannot use it for any other article than that for which it was first granted. The trade mark 'Bovril', for example, could not be sold for use with a toothpaste.

Goods sold under a trade mark are called 'branded goods', or 'brands'. It is fairly easy to advertise a brand successfully, if it has a short and 'catchy' name or a clever design. Since trade became highly competitive in the second half of the 19th century, more and more of the goods sold in British and American shops have been branded goods bearing registered trade marks.

See also PATENTS.

TRADE SIGNS. In the days before most people could read, shop fronts did not display the names and trades of the shopkeepers, and it was their custom to indicate their business by some sort of emblem. This practice certainly goes back to the days of ancient Rome, for many of these old signs have been dug up by archaeologists. The signs were sometimes painted, but more commonly were made of stone, or stamped on *terra cotta* or baked clay, and embedded in the walls, usually above the entrances. In the days when the goat, and not the cow, was the more usual source of the household milk (as it still is in many Mediterranean countries) the dairyman's sign was a goat; the baker showed a mule driving a flour mill, the surveyor a measuring rule, the tavern-keeper a bunch of grapes.

In the same way medieval shops proclaimed their business by models of what they sold, or by tools and utensils, or by signboards painted to represent such objects. As long as trade was limited, a simple device was enough for each tradesman. The cutler displayed a knife, the tailor a pair of scissors, and the hosier usually a carved wooden shape painted to look like a stocking. Later, when there were several people of the same trade doing business together in the same part of a town, they might find it necessary to adopt some sign to distinguish, say, Brown the Tailor from Green the Tailor. Brown might, therefore, exhibit a signboard showing a brown bear, and Green a signboard with a green dragon. Brown's address would come to be known generally as 'at the sign of the Brown Bear'; Green's address, similarly, would be 'at the sign of the Green Dragon'. A tradesman could choose any sign he liked: animal, vegetable, or mineral; but often he would advertise his name by a pun or 'rebus' (*see* PUZZLES, Vol. IX), Mr. Haywood's sign being a haystack and a bundle of sticks, and Mr. Hancock's a hand and a cock.

As trade rivalry increased and town life developed, painted signs became more elaborate and beautiful. Not only were the designs themselves artistic, but the ornamental ironwork on which they hung reached a high level of craftsmanship.

As more people learnt to read, signboards became fewer, and the practice of numbering houses and shops in streets increased. A few tradesmen's symbols still survive. The best known are the barber's pole and the three brass balls of the PAWNBROKER (q.v.). The merchants from Lombardy, in northern Italy, who settled in England in the 15th and 16th centuries as pawnbrokers and money-lenders, brought this symbol with them as the sign of their trade. It may have represented three gold coins, although the real origin of the sign is obscure. The barber's pole was once commonly seen, striped in red and white, and sometimes in blue as well. Before 1745 barbers were members of the Barbers' and Chirurgeons' (Surgeons) Company, and also practised blood-letting, tooth-pulling, and rather rough surgery; the stripes round the pole indicated the material used for bandaging.

Some of the private bankers of the City of London, whose businesses were founded in the 17th or 18th centuries when trade signs were more usual than numbers, remained true to the old tradition, and in Lombard Street the golden

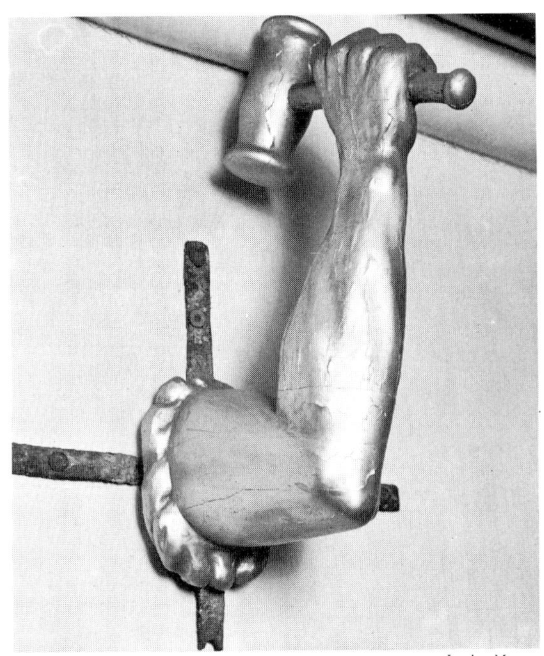

London Museum

18TH-CENTURY GOLD-BEATER'S SIGN

London Museum

18TH-CENTURY SIGN FROM A TOBACCONIST'S SHOP

A FRENCH GLASS-BLOWER'S SIGN *Musée Carnavalet, Paris*

grasshopper of Martins Bank and the anchor of Glyns, the Admiralty agents and bankers, still hang today. The newer bankers have followed this old custom, and Lombard Street is full of

TRADE MARK OF THE BOWATER PAPER CORPORATION

symbols or heraldic signs such as the prancing horse of Lloyds Bank, or the full coats-of-arms of other houses (*see* picture, p. 31).

See also Vol. IV: INN SIGNS; SYMBOLS.

TRADE UNION HISTORY, BRITISH. Trade unions are essentially associations of wage-earners, unlike the CRAFT GUILDS (q.v.) of the late Middle Ages, which included all persons engaged in a trade, and not wage-earners alone. The guilds were joint associations of masters, workers (then called 'journeymen' because they were paid by the *journée* or day), and apprentices in any particular trade. When industry began to form itself into larger units, most of the craft guilds split up into two separate bodies: companies of masters, and associations of workers or journeymen. There is no real historical continuity between these early workers' guilds and modern trade unions.

In the reign of Elizabeth the Government took over the functions of both the masters' and the workers' guilds. The workers' guilds largely disappeared. The masters' guilds gradually transformed themselves into livery companies (*see* CITY COMPANIES). The Government took over the duty, hitherto performed by the craft guilds, of regulating wages and conditions of work and apprenticeship. The Statute of Artificers (or the Statute of Apprentices—both words appear in the title) laid down conditions in 1563 in regard to working hours, standards of work, and the period of apprenticeship, and also made the local JUSTICES OF THE PEACE (q.v. Vol. X) responsible for fixing the wage-rates of the various trades in their districts.

Such of the journeymen's or workers' guilds as survived became mere benefit or FRIENDLY SOCIETIES (q.v. Vol. X). They did not exist to bring pressure against employers to grant concessions in regard to hours and wages, and they thus had little in common with modern TRADE UNIONS (q.v.). It was not until the local justices began to disregard the duties laid upon them by the Act of 1563 that any movement towards the modern trade union began. During the 18th century fewer and fewer people accepted the old view that the regulation of working conditions and wages was rightly a matter for the King's Government or the local justices. By the end of the century the Justices of the Peace were still carrying out their bare duty of fixing wages, but all that they attempted to fix was the maximum wage which might not be exceeded. No attempt was made to fix minimum wage-rates, below which no worker could legally be engaged. This favoured the employer and not the worker.

By the 19th century the general view was that wages and hours should work themselves out by what ADAM SMITH (q.v. Vol. V) had called 'the higgling and bargaining of the market'. The 18th century had been, on the whole, a time of expanding trade and increasing prosperity, but there were periods of bad trade, and many unions of workers were formed. Strikes were not unknown. All these new unions had no real legal status, and as early as 1721 a Combination Act was passed which made associations of workers illegal. Similar Acts were passed in 1726 and 1749. The effect of these Acts was to drive the budding trade union movement underground.

In 1793 war broke out with France. The British Government became frightened of secret societies, which might possibly be working against the safety of the State. An Act was therefore passed in 1797 which prohibited seditious or subversive societies, and forbade any society whatever to administer oaths to its members which would bind them not to inform or give evidence against fellow members. This Act was followed by the Combination Acts of 1799 and 1800, which made associations of workmen generally illegal, whether seditious or not.

War against Napoleon made labour scarce and wages high. It was not until after Waterloo that times began to get bad and the movement towards trade unionism began to grow again.

In 1824 and 1825 the Combination laws were repealed. This was largely due to the influence of Francis Place, himself a journeyman tailor of London and a pioneer leader of the movement to organize working people. The Act of 1797, forbidding criminal societies and oaths of secrecy, was left on the Statute Book. Between 1825 and 1834 many more small unions were formed. On the whole, these were years of business activity and general prosperity, and the new movement made quiet headway without worrying either employers or government. In 1834, however, one incident touched the conscience of the nation. Some workers at Tolpuddle in Dorset had formed a 'Friendly Society of Agricultural Labourers', and although the ban on such societies had been removed, it was found possible to prosecute under the Act of 1797 for 'administering an illegal oath'. Six of its members were tried at Dorchester, found guilty, and sentenced to TRANSPORTATION (q.v. Vol. X) to an overseas penal settlement for 7 years.

There was general sympathy throughout the country with the victims of this prosecution, which took place during the rise of another workers' movement—Chartism. Although the repeal of the Combination Acts in 1824 and 1825 meant that trade unions were no longer 'criminal associations', no precise legal status had been conferred on them, and the law gave them no rights, even against their own officials if they happened to be dishonest.

The harsh treatment of the six Dorset labourers (who became known as 'the Tolpuddle Martyrs', although they had been reprieved in 1836) virtually put an end to union organization among agricultural workers until the 1870s, and some of the other unions had difficulty in surviving a long depression in trade.

An important forward move happened in 1852 (*see* colour plate opp. p. 288) with the formation of the most famous of the large trade unions—the Amalgamated Society of Engineers, embracing the unions of fitters, millwrights and machinists, and others. From the first it was strong and influential and provided a 'new model' for organization, in that it covered the whole country and amalgamated into one society separate crafts, each sharing in the same general activity. Another large union was formed in

Protection

FOR THE

INDUSTRIOUS

Weavers.

INFORMATION having been received that a great number of industrious Weavers have been deterred by threats and acts of violence from the pursuit of their lawful occupations, and that in many instances their Shuttles have been taken, and their Materials damaged by persons acting under the existing Combinations:

Notice is hereby Given,

That every Protection will be afforded to persons so injured, upon giving Information to the Constables of Stockport: And a Reward of

FIFTY GUINEAS

Will be paid, on conviction, to the person who will come forward with such evidence as may be the means of convicting any one or more of the offences mentioned in the Act of Parliament, of which an Extract is subjoined: And a Reward of

TWENTY GUINEAS

Will be paid, on conviction, to the person who will come forward and inform of any person being guilty of assaulting or molesting industrious and honest Weavers, so as to prevent them from taking out or bringing in their Work peaceably.

Stockport, June 17th, 1808.

PETER BROWN, T. CARTWRIGHT, CONSTABLES.

By the 22nd, Geo. 3, C. 40, S. 3.

It is enacted, "That if any person enter, by force, into any House or Shop, with intent to Cut and Destroy any Linen or Cotton, or Linen and Cotton mixed with any other Materials, in the Loom, or any Warp or Shute, Tools, Tackle, and Utensils, or shall Cut or Destroy the same, or shall Break and Destroy any Tools, Tackle, or Utensils, for Weaving, Preparing, or Making any such Manufactures, every such Offender shall be guilty of FELONY, without Benefit of Clergy".

J. CLARKE, PRINTER.

Meade Collection

ANTI-COMBINATION NOTICE, 1808

A local order under an anti-combination law

N.U. of General and Municipal Workers

CELEBRATING THE REDUCTION OF THE WORKING DAY TO 8 HOURS IN 1889

Invitation to a breakfast given by the Amalgamated Society of Gas Workers and General Labourers at Birmingham

1861—the Amalgamated Society of Carpenters and Joiners. At the same time the unions in the bigger industrial towns were beginning to work together in permanent associations (Trades Councils) for mutual support, and their determination to secure the full legal recognition of trade unionism led to various groupings of unions for common activity on a national scale.

None of these national groups were thoroughly representative of trade unionism; indeed, at times they competed with each other. Few of the important unions sent delegates to the first Trades Union Congress, convened by the Manchester and Salford Trades Council in 1868 to meet the attacks then being made upon them, and to campaign for reforms in the laws affecting trade unions. In spite of this poor support, the second Congress (in 1869) decided to elect a permanent Parliamentary Committee to act between the annual assemblies.

Steadily, over the next few years the Congress attracted increasing support; and between 1871 and 1876 it won legal protection for the funds and property of unions and generally strengthened their legal position.

'Picketing' of works where a strike was in progress became lawful (*see* TRADE UNIONS, MODERN), provided that there was no intimidation or violence. The law also made clear that a strike, or any similar combined action, would no longer be regarded as a conspiracy against the security of the State.

Up to this time the main strength of trade unionism, except in mining, textiles, and a few other industries, was to be found among apprentice-trained craftsmen and other skilled workers. During the last quarter of the century there was a rapid growth of unions for labourers (notably in the docks and gas works), railway workers began to organize themselves, clerks and other non-manual workers, teachers and other public servants formed unions, and the Women's Trade Union League was founded.

In 1906 an Act was passed protecting union funds against legal actions brought by employers for compensation for losses caused by strikes. In the same year the Labour Party was founded (*see* POLITICAL PARTIES, Vol. X). In those days Members of Parliament received no salary, and many of the larger unions supported financially those of their members who gained seats in Parliament, and also the Labour Party itself. The right of the unions to do this was challenged in the law courts by W. V. Osborne, a member of the Amalgamated Society of Railway Servants, who was not a member of the Labour Party, and in 1909 the judges of the House of Lords decided in his favour. The 'Osborne Judgement' threw a doubt upon the lawfulness of trade union activity in politics, but in 1913 an Act was passed allowing the unions to spend money for political purposes, provided that unsympathetic members not wishing to pay the 'political levy' would be entitled to 'contract out' without prejudice to their general membership of the union.

In 1926 a general strike took place in Britain, an attempt by all the great unions in industry to help the miners to resist the reduction of wages and increase of the working day with which they were threatened. A large part of British industry, including transport, was brought to a standstill, but the Government received so much help from volunteers, many of whom regarded the strike as a challenge to the authority of Parliament, that after 9 days the General Council of the T.U.C. called off the strike. Financial support from other trade unionists helped the miners to continue their own strike for about 6 months before they admitted their defeat. A consequence of the general strike was an Act of Parliament the following year which imposed new restrictions on strikes and picketing, forbade the unions of civil servants to remain in the T.U.C., and made it necessary for members who wished to pay the 'political levy' to 'contract in' by an agreement in writing. The Act of 1927 was repeated in 1946, and since then trade unions have been free to engage in politics.

See also TRADE UNIONS, WORLD; WAGES.
See also Vol. X: INDUSTRIAL WELFARE; ARBITRATION.

TRADE UNIONS, MODERN. Members of a trade union generally form branches in various towns or districts, and elect certain members as officials (such as branch secretary). Delegates are also elected to national conferences and committees of the union to decide its rules and policy. Every member of a union pays regular subscriptions to meet the cost of running his union and to provide a fund to help members whose wages cease if they 'strike' against the employers or are 'locked out' by them.

Trade unions can be classified as craft, industrial, and general labour unions. The members of a craft union, such as the Pattern-makers, practise a single skilled craft or trade. An industrial union includes different types of craftsmen and other grades of workers, all employed within the same industry: the National Union of Railwaymen is a typical union in this class. A general labour union includes workers, many of whom may be unskilled or semi-skilled, from several industries: for example the General and Municipal Workers' Union. In 1968 the total membership of the unions affiliated to the T.U.C. (Trades Union Congress) was more than 8 millions, and there was only one large union that was not affiliated. Trade union membership in Britain is, therefore, not far short of 10 millions. The largest individual union is the Transport and General Workers, with a membership of over 1,450,000.

British trade unions began to assume their present form as national organizations in the middle of the 19th century, and have been generally successful in attaining their main object, which was to raise the STANDARD OF LIVING (q.v.) of their members. This success is largely due to their having replaced 'individual bargaining' by 'collective bargaining'. Before trade unions became lawful in the 19th century, age-rates and working conditions were decided by bargaining between each employer and each workman. If a workman thought the wages offered were too low, he had two choices: to continue to work discontentedly at that wage; or to leave his work, which usually meant leaving his home and district and taking his chance elsewhere. He could not apply much pressure on his employer, especially in times of serious UNEMPLOYMENT (q.v.); he could only hope to persuade his employer that he was a valued and almost indispensable employee, as he usually had no money to fall back on if he decided to stop working. Moreover, it would be too big a risk for all the workers of an employer to agree to stand together, without the backing of a trade union and of the money it could pay the members as 'strike pay'.

This situation was completely changed when wages and other conditions (such as hours of work) came to be negotiated between employers and unions. Employers were then faced with the chance that all the workers in a trade or industry might stop working, or 'strike', if they were not satisfied with the wages and conditions offered.

N.U. of General and Municipal Workers

BANNER OF NORWICH BRANCH OF THE NATIONAL UNION OF GENERAL AND MUNICIPAL WORKERS

Sometimes the threat of a strike was sufficient to force employers to raise wages, but often it was not; and, if the union felt itself strong enough, an actual strike might take place. A strike would not achieve its aim unless all the members of the union (or of the branch concerned) joined in it, and unless the majority of workers in the industry belonged to the union. Therefore, when a strike took place at a factory, the strikers appointed some of the members as 'pickets'; their task was to stand near the factory gate and to persuade members of the union who wanted to work, and often non-union men also, to change their minds and join the ranks of the strikers.

What is called a 'General Strike' is rare in Britain. This is a stoppage of all work in all or many industries throughout a country. It is generally more political than industrial in nature. A general strike occurred in Britain in 1926 (*see* TRADE UNION HISTORY).

Collective bargaining led to a slow yet steady improvement in the welfare of the worker, which individual bargaining would not have achieved. Once a higher wage-rate had been agreed upon, in a district or in a whole industry, it became very difficult for employers to reduce it. If the union members would not agree to lower wages, employers sometimes decided on a 'lock-out', a weapon which they used in the same way as their workers used a strike. A lock-out meant that an employer or group of employers shut down the works, and lost money for the time being, so that the workers would earn no wages and would be forced in the end to accept the conditions offered by the employers. Usually a lock-out was only declared when general trade depression or foreign competition made the prevailing wage-rate in an industry too much for the majority of employers to pay.

Wages have never been the only concern of the trade unions. Hours of work and general working conditions have long been matters of negotiation between unions and employers, and in recent years holidays with pay have been added to these. The unions are also vitally interested in the technical efficiency of their members, and the rules for APPRENTICESHIP (q.v.) and training in the skilled trades are drawn up with the help of the unions. These rules may be relaxed when new entrants to the trade are falling off, or when the trade itself is expanding. At other times the rules for the admission of learners are tightened up, the unions being anxious to protect their members against the risk of future unemployment. To deal with disputes promptly, in the actual workshops where they arise, union members in most works elect a 'shop steward' as their spokesman to negotiate with the management, and as one of the links between themselves and the executive committee of the union.

British trade unions may register under the FRIENDLY SOCIETIES Acts (q.v. Vol. X), for they are in a true sense friendly or 'mutual benefit' societies for their members. During a strike that is officially ordered by the union committee, the union pays out 'dispute benefit' or strike pay. If a member is unemployed, his union usually pays him money, which is additional to the unemployment benefit paid by the State (*see* UNEMPLOYMENT INSURANCE, Vol. X). Unemployment benefit is not paid by the State during a strike. Many unions also pay sickness and disability benefit, in addition to the payments now made by the State. Most unions also pay out a lump sum for the funeral expenses of members who die, and some have pension schemes to supplement the pensions paid by the State. Another important function of British unions is the giving of free legal advice to their members, and the payment of solicitors or counsel if a case has to go to court. A union is generally prepared to fight a member's case as far as the House of Lords, the highest Law Court in the land, whenever it involves a point of law vital to the interests of the union (*see* APPEAL COURTS, Vol. X).

During the Second World War British trade unions were consulted by the Government on all matters likely to affect workpeople, and their advice did much to lessen the hardships and frictions of a large number of people working very long hours and under difficult conditions in munition factories, mines, and other essential industries. To save any damage to the country's war effort, an Act of Parliament was passed in 1939 (and agreed to by the Trades Union Congress) laying down that any dispute on wages or conditions should go before an Arbitration Tribunal composed of a trade unionist and an employer and independent members, one of whom was the chairman (*see* ARBITRATION, Vol. X). This agreement not to use the strike weapon nor the equivalent employers' weapon of the lock-out continued in force for some years after the war.

Although, in wartime, the unions were moderate in their claims for higher wages they did not fail to secure advances which could be won without hindrance to the war effort. Agreements, for instance, were signed to guarantee a week's pay to men taken on for work which might be brought to an end (by bad weather, for example) before the week ended. The unions decided that directly the war was over and they were free once more to demand improvements for their members, their chief aims would be to press for a shorter working week and longer holidays; to improve the national insurance and health schemes and the educational services; to expand their own educational and other services to members; to secure an extension of public ownership or control of industries; and to maintain full employment.

The Government has continued to consult the T.U.C. and the employers' organizations on problems of manpower and production, and the unions have shown great interest in efforts to make industry more efficient. In the past, workers have feared that greater mechanization

Blackpool Gazette & Herald Ltd.

THE 100TH ANNIVERSARY OF THE T.U.C. CONFERENCE, OCTOBER 1968

in factories would lead inevitably to the dismissing of large numbers of men and consequent unemployment. In the early 19th century, it was the dismissal of hand-workers that led the LUDDITES (q.v.) to wreck stocking- and lace-frames in Nottingham. Today, however, a period of full employment over most of Britain has helped workers to overcome this fear, and it is now widely believed that higher productivity (output per worker), achieved by more efficient methods and introduced after full consultation with workers' representatives, can lead to higher standards of living. The T.U.C., the employers' organizations, and the nationalized industries formed the British Productivity Council to stimulate a wider understanding of modern industrial techniques. Many teams of trade union leaders, often in company with industrial managers and technicians, have visited the United States of America and various European countries in search of new ways of increasing productive efficiency; and return visits have been made from America and Europe to study British methods and, in particular, to gain first-hand knowledge of the British pattern of relations between unions and management.

The machinery of negotation which settles problems of wages, hours of work, holidays, apprenticeship, dismissals, and leave for illness, varies from industry to industry. It does not always work perfectly, and union members do not always follow the advice of their leaders; but in general Britain suffers less dislocation from strikes and lock-outs than most of the other industrialized countries of the world.

See also TRADE UNION HISTORY; TRADE UNIONS, WORLD; WAGES.

See also Vol. X: INDUSTRIAL WELFARE; SOCIAL INSURANCE.

TRADE UNIONS, WORLD. Trade unions have a long history in many other countries besides Britain, and in most cases have had similar struggles to become recognized by law. In most countries it was skilled craftsmen who formed the earliest unions, which functioned generally as benefit societies, uniting occasionally into larger groups for campaigns in defence of wages and conditions of work. In both France and Germany their history goes back to the 18th century, but they had little influence until the second half of the 19th century. In France they were suppressed by law after the Revolution of 1789, and, though they revived, were given no legal recognition until 1884. In Germany they were active in the mid-19th century, chiefly among skilled craftsmen, but became highly organized only towards the end of the century. The Roman Catholics of Germany organized a rival Christian Trade Union movement, open to both Catholics and Protestants, especially in the Rhineland and Ruhr, and this remained separate until 1933, when Hitler's Nazi Government suppressed both movements. Separate Christian trade union movements exist today, for instance, in Belgium, France, Holland, Germany, and Switzerland, sometimes working with the larger non-religous movements. In France and Italy sections of the movement are under Communist control.

The organization of trade unions varies from country to country. In Britain, for example, the movement is less centralized than in Germany, Sweden, or Austria. The Scandinavian countries have strong trade union movements, fairly closely associated with Social Democratic political parties. Democratic trade unionism in Spain was suppressed when General Franco came to power after the Spanish Civil War of 1936–39.

In Russia, trade unions started at the beginning of this century, but, between 1908–12, the majority of them were suppressed by the Tsar. Some continued to exist secretly, and others carried on under a different guise. The Revolution of February 1917, followed by the abdication of the Tsar, gave back to workers their liberty to combine. Very soon there were $1\frac{1}{4}$ million trade union members, and by the time of the October Revolution of 1917, membership had increased to over two millions (*see* Russian Revolution, Vol. X).

In the U.S.S.R. today trade unions have a very large membership, though they are in effect part of the State machinery without rights of independent action, and so not trade unions in our sense of the term. The Government allows them to take part in the social administration and inspection of factories, and they run extensive social services for their members. All over Eastern Europe trade unions, except on a very small scale, are of recent growth; only Czechoslovakia and the former German part of Poland have trade union movements of long standing. Trade unions in the communist-controlled countries of eastern Europe are now under Government control and are, therefore, not independent trade unions at all.

In the United States, trade unions have made rapid progress in recent years. They were largely set up by emigrants from Europe in the early 19th century. For a time there existed two main trade union groups in the country: the American Federation of Labor, founded in 1886, had its main strength among skilled workers and in the older industries; the newer Congress of Industrial Organizations, founded in 1935, enrolled mainly workers in the growing mass-production industries (such as steel, oil, motor-cars, and rubber). The two groups merged in December 1955. The three largest unions outside the AFL-CIO are those of the mineworkers, the teamsters, and the auto-workers. The Canadian Labour Congress includes unions which are entirely Canadian and others which are sections of United States unions. Latin America has its own movements, fairly strong in certain countries, but highly unstable. Australia and New Zealand have well-organized movements; that of South Africa is weaker because of the division between white and African workers. India's movement is developing, and in recent years there has been a rapid growth of trade unions in other Commonwealth countries, for example, the West Indian countries, Malaysia, and East and West Africa.

There are three main international organizations to which, according to their outlook, trade union groups of different countries belong. The International Confederation of Free Trade Unions (I.C.F.T.U.) was founded in London in 1949. The large majority of unions in western Europe and North America, as well as movements from Asia, Africa, Latin America, the West Indies, and Australia are affiliated to it. The communist-dominated World Federation of Trade Unions (W.F.T.U.) was founded in 1945, the bulk of its membership being derived from the U.S.S.R., China, and the communist-controlled countries of eastern Europe, but with some members in other parts of the world. The International Federation of Christian Trade Unions (I.F.C.T.U.) is the body to which are affiliated the Christian trade union movements in various countries.

Individual unions may also belong to international federations of workers in a particular trade or industry, such as miners or transport workers. Each of the three above-mentioned international organizations, I. C. F. T. U., W.F.T.U., and I.F.C.T.U., is associated in one way or another with a group of specialized industrial federations. The W.F.T.U. has always called these specialized bodies Trade Union Internationals, the first being founded in 1901. Those associated with the I.C.F.T.U. and I.F.C.T.U. are known as International Trade Secretariats and International Federations respectively.

TRAINING, *see* APPRENTICESHIP; FACTORY ORGANIZATION, Section 4.

TRANSPORT is often a costly item of expense to a manufacturer or merchant, and he tries to reduce it as much as possible. To some manufacturers using large quantities of bulky raw materials the cost of their transport would otherwise be so great that the factory is located near the source of the principal raw material. This is particularly true of iron and steel works, which are usually built near ironstone mines or deposits, or on a coalfield (*see* LOCALIZATION OF INDUSTRY). If a firm's raw materials come in by sea, transport charges can be reduced if the factory stands at the waterside, with wharves or jetties for unloading sea-going ships of deep draught. A site of this kind is still more economical when the goods manufactured are for export and can be sent away from the factory by sea. The Ford Works at Dagenham, on a deepwater reach of the Thames, is ideally sited for these purposes. Freight charges by sea, particularly for cargoes in bulk, are so much cheaper than railway charges that a distant waterside site involving long journeys often proves cheaper than a much nearer inland site. Canal sites have the same general advantages as sea or river sites. Canal communications are slow but, unlike railway goods services, they provide a form of transport that is free from shocks and vibration. The heavy and bulky raw materials used in the Staffordshire pottery industry, and the brittle nature of the finished articles, had much to do with the decision to build a canal to serve this area (*see* CANALS, BRITISH, Vol. IV). If, however, a firm decides to rely on railways, it may be cheaper to place the works in open country, and to build private sidings connecting it with the main line, than to pay the cost of road transport to and from a railway station.

Most light industries, and nearly all trading businesses, need not consider transport charges quite so seriously. But to handle their goods they must choose one of three methods of transport: (*a*) public-service transport (railway or publicly run road services); (*b*) their own road vehicles; (*c*) hired road vehicles. The decision can only be made when the comparative costs have been carefully worked out for that particular business, for a method that would suit one business would not necessarily suit another, even in the same trade or industry. A firm deciding to run its own vehicles must then decide which type of vehicle suits its requirements best.

Today, scientific research into new sealing and insulating materials has solved some major transport problems. The use of non-porous polythene sheets, or of light but rigid expanded polystyrene (*see* PLASTICS) has simplified the packaging of many perishable or delicate articles. But the most dramatic development has taken place in the handling of cargo, with the concept of 'through-transport'. Any goods except oil and bulk commodities such as ore, coal, and grain, may be transported by this method.

The goods are packed into road trailers or large boxes called 'containers' at the factory, or at inland depots, or they may be secured to moveable platforms or pallets. These are taken to the port and are driven or loaded directly on to a specially-designed container ship (*see* SHIPPING). At the other end of the voyage the process is reversed, the 'unit loads', as they are called, being taken straight through to their destination. Cars and machinery for export can be transported in this way, and most of the general cargo travelling by sea between Britain and Europe is now handled thus.

While the system saves much time—and consequently money—previously spent in loading and unloading a variety of individual packages and consignments, such a big operation requires greater outlay, a larger organization capable of providing transport facilities by land and sea, and new docks to cope with faster loading techniques. Unit-load transport is now widely replacing more traditional methods.

See also Vol. IV: MOTOR TRANSPORT; GOODS TRAIN; SHIP; CANALS; AIRCRAFT, SPECIAL USES; HORSE TRANSPORT.

TRAVEL AGENCIES, *see* TOURIST INDUSTRY.

TRUST, *see* COMBINES.

TURNOVER. 1. The 'turnover' of a business is the value of its 'net' sales during any chosen period, say a month or a year: that is, its 'gross' or total sales, less the selling price of any goods returned by the customers as unsatisfactory. One way in which a business can increase its net profit is by increasing its turnover. In most businesses the gross profit margin, or difference between the selling price and the cost price of each article sold, remains fairly constant. Many overhead charges (*see* COSTING) seldom change: for example, rent, lighting and heating, and office salaries. The advantage of a high turnover can be seen from a comparison of the trading results of a business in two distinct periods, one showing a low turnover and the other a high turnover. In the following example the proportion of gross profit remains the same; half the overhead charges remain the same, or are 'fixed'; the other half (for instance, delivery charges and stationery and printing) rise as turnover increases, and form the variable overheads. The advantage of a higher turnover can be seen from these figures. Not only has the net profit risen from £5,000 to £13,000, but it has risen from being 10% of turnover to 13%.

PERIOD I—TURNOVER £50,000

	£		£
Cost of goods sold	40,000	Net Sales	50,000
Gross profit	10,000		
	£50,000		£50,000

Constant overheads	3,000	Gross profit	10,000
Variable overheads	2,000		
Net profit	5,000		
	£10,000		£10,000

PERIOD II—TURNOVER £100,000

	£		£
Cost of goods sold	80,000	Net sales	100,000
Gross profit	20,000		
	£100,000		£100,000

Constant overheads	3,000	Gross profit	20,000
Variable overheads	4,000		
Net profit	13,000		
	£20,000		£20,000

2. STOCK TURNOVER. The word 'turnover' is also used in business for the number of times a year the average stock of goods on hand is sold or 'turned over'; this is called the 'stock turnover'. Different trades vary greatly in this respect. If a jeweller's or furniture dealer's stock turnover were 1, that is, if he just managed to sell within the year the stock with which he started, he would consider himself reasonably fortunate, for in these trades the sales are slow. But a fishmonger or butcher might worry seriously if his stock turnover fell much below 50, or a complete turnover of stock about once a week; and a milk retailer would naturally expect a stock turnover of 365. Other things being equal, a high stock turnover will enable a trader to cut his 'profit margin': that is, his gross profit, or difference between cost price and selling price; it is, of course, equally possible that cutting the profit margin, and thus lowering the selling price, may lead to a higher rate of stock turnover than before. Stock turnover and sales turnover are usually closely connected with each other, and move together; sales turnover is very often increased when the prices to the customer are lowered.

TYPE, *see* PRINTING-TYPE.

U

UNDERWRITER, *see* INSURANCE; ISSUING HOUSES.

UNEMPLOYMENT. In more primitive days, before industry had become highly organized, unemployment was much less serious. Workers then mostly worked at home (*see* DOMESTIC SYSTEM). Some grew or made things for their own families, and would naturally never throw themselves out of work. Others, who made goods to sell, could always cut their prices and be content with a smaller 'wage', rather than become unemployed. In those days there was also less DIVISION OF LABOUR (q.v.) or specialization in one type of job; all except highly skilled craftsmen could easily adapt themselves to other jobs, moving from one to another as the demand for goods changed.

In modern industrial countries there are four main types of unemployment: seasonal, technological, transitional, and cyclical. Much unemployment is due to two or more of these causes acting together.

1. SEASONAL UNEMPLOYMENT. This may be of two kinds. The first arises from the fact that some occupations can be carried on only at certain seasons of the year. Boatmen, yacht hands, and others engaged in the seaside holiday industry are examples of people following seasonal occupations. The only way in which they may avoid prolonged unemployment is to combine a summer with a winter occupation. Many persons following seasonal occupations do so merely to supplement retired pay or pension or earnings from running a business. The Scots girls engaged ashore during the British herring fishing season regard this employment as a part-time activity only. The second type of seasonal unemployment arises from weather conditions, and particularly affects those engaged in the building trades; wet weather, or hard and prolonged frost, make some kinds of work temporarily impossible.

2. TECHNOLOGICAL UNEMPLOYMENT may be caused in many different ways. One cause is the occasional necessity to re-equip a factory throughout with new or improved machinery, as happened before the war when Henry Ford of Detroit went over to the production of a new-model car. Technological unemployment also occurs when the demand for some particular article falls off permanently, or ceases entirely; when the Government, as a matter of policy, closes down dockyards or substitutes atomic weapons for aircraft; or when machines replace men in some industry which cannot hope to enlarge its output by thus cheapening the cost of production. These last types of technological unemployment are nowadays called 'redundancy', but unless the country is in the grip of a cyclical depression (*see* Section 4 below)

ALL

UNEMPLOYED

SHOULD ROLL UP

ON

WEDNESDAY NEXT, the 13th,

FOR THE

THIRD GREAT MARCH

We are going to see the Chairman of the L.C.C. to inquire why they do not push on with their works faster. Rates are being saved while men are starving for want of work, which could and should be done.

Don't forget that JACK WILLIAMS is at home to the Unemployed on TOWER HILL every Monday, Wednesday, and Friday (bar the 13th, of course) at 12.30.

Contingents should assemble from all parts every Friday.

We are going to St. Paul's, Sunday, 17th.

COMING?

MEET AT TRAFALGAR SQUARE AT 2, AND MARCH TO THE CATHEDRAL.

Twentieth Century Press, Ltd. (T.U. and 48 Hours), 37a, Clerkenwell Green, E.C.

UNEMPLOYED MARCH NOTICE, 1905

Daily Herald

UNEMPLOYED MEN MARCHING FROM JARROW TO LONDON IN 1936

Jarrow, County Durham, was one of the 'depressed' areas badly hit by the slump of the 1930's

redundancy is likely to be only a rather long-lasting type of transitional unemployment.

3. TRANSITIONAL UNEMPLOYMENT. A worker is transitionaly unemployed when, owing to some personal circumstance, he has left one job and has not yet started on a new one. This kind of unemployment, which is less serious than other kinds, forms the largest category of the persons registered as unemployed in Britain. The average period of transitional unemployment is not more than a few weeks.

4. CYCLICAL UNEMPLOYMENT. The most serious kind of unemployment is cyclical: so called, from the Greek word for 'circle', because it tends to come round again every time business becomes slack in what is known as the TRADE CYCLE (q.v.). Unemployment of this kind tends to last a long time; it usually begins with the 'heavy' industries (such as iron and steel, and shipbuilding) and spreads to others. The men dismissed have less to spend; this creates further unemployment in the industries turning out goods for which the demand has thus decreased. Cyclical unemployment is therefore cumulative; during the worst year of the depression of the 1930's it rose in Britain to over 2,600,000, in Germany to nearly 7,000,000, and in the U.S.A. to 10,000,000. Preventing unemployment on this tragic scale involves preventing the trade cycle from recurring as it did before the Second World War.

See also TRADE CYCLE.
See also Vol. X: SOCIAL INSURANCE.

UPHOLSTERY is the production of furniture such as chairs, settees, and beds by covering a framework with springs, padding, and fabric so that they are comfortable to sit or lie on.

The earliest British form of upholstery, known at least as far back as the 14th century, consisted simply of strips of leather stretched across the top of a kind of X-shaped camp stool, with strips of the same kind across the back. For 3 centuries this was the only kind of upholstered chair used until about the middle of the 17th century, when padded upholstery of the modern type gradually came into use. Steel springs were used later to give added resilience.

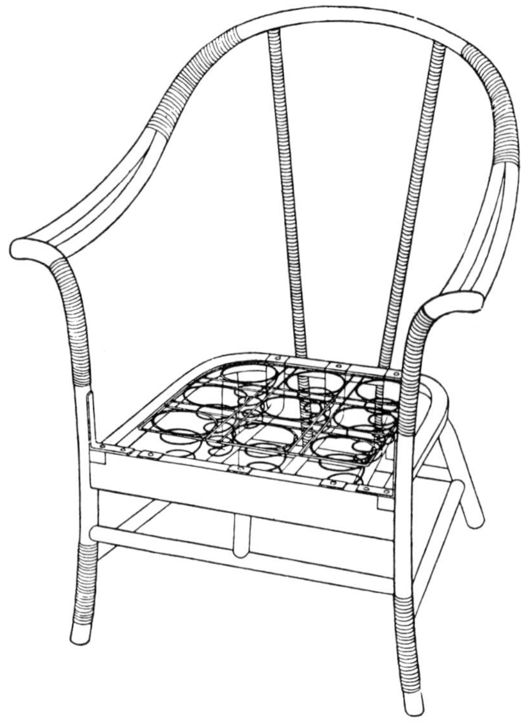

Gordon Logie

FIG. 1. THE SPRINGS OF AN UPHOLSTERED CHAIR SEAT

The traditional upholstering method was a combination of steel springs and padding, and this method is still used for renovation. The steel springs, usually in the shape of a cone, or a double cone, are joined to each other by wire clips or fabric, and rest on a network of canvas tapes fixed to the bottom of the chair. Similar tapes hold the springs in position at the top. The tapes form a basis on which padding is sewn (Fig. 1).

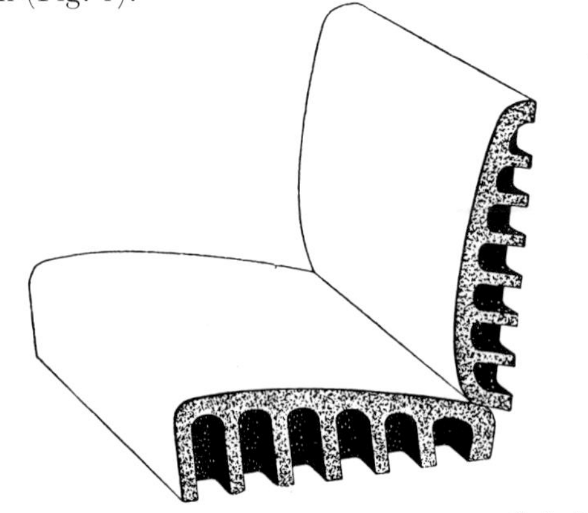

Gordon Logie

FIG 2. THE CONSTRUCTION OF FOAMED LATEX UPHOLSTERY

This method is now rarely used. Vertical springs have been replaced by horizontal springs made from rods of metal shaped in continuous wave-like curves, or by rubber webbing, or flexible rubber platforms. These support the cushioning which is usually made from foam, or occasionally rubberized hair. The principal cushioning materials are latex or polyester foam, the former produced from natural or synthetic rubber (*see* RUBBER MANUFACTURE), the latter by purely chemical methods. They can be readily cut to the shape required and can be manufactured in a variety of structures such as honey-comb (Fig. 2), or pin core.

The final upholstery process is covering the springs and cushioning with fabric. For many years upholstery fabrics were made exclusively from wool and cotton, but the development of man-made fibres has greatly extended the range of materials available to the upholsterer. A wider variety of colours and patterns is now possible, and fabrics with a high degree of elasticity have been developed which can be stretched tightly over frames difficult to upholster by traditional methods.

At the same time there have been considerable developments in frame design; traditional beech-wood frames are in some instances being replaced by plastic frames, particularly for highly-curved shapes. Plastic frames are produced by chemical reactions in closed moulds, the end product being a 'rigid foam' which assumes exactly the shape of the mould. Today it is possible to produce both the flexible foam cushioning and the rigid foam frame within the same mould; with such rapid, labour-saving methods the mass production of upholstered chairs is becoming increasingly common.

See also FURNITURE INDUSTRY.

See also Vol. XI: CHAIRS; FURNITURE, HISTORY OF.

USURY. Nowadays this means lending money at an excessive rate of INTEREST (q.v.), but in medieval times it meant not only moneylending of any kind, even at very low rates of interest, but also a good many commercial transactions that are regarded today as normal and reasonable. Aristotle, one of the famous philosophers of ancient Greece, considered money itself, as distinct from goods, to be 'unproductive', and he condemned as immoral not only money loans but also the earning of interest on them. Many of Aristotle's ideas were later adopted by the

National Gallery

TWO BANKERS OR USURERS

Painting by Marinus van Reymerswael, 1497–1567

Schoolmen, or medieval philosophers of the Catholic Church, who at first condemned the lending of money at interest as usury, just as Aristotle had. But they were living in a period of rapidly expanding business and enterprise, and gradually their earlier ideas became changed. At first they condemned not only moneylending but also certain forms of trading; it was lawful, they argued, to buy goods in order to manufacture or fashion them into something else, or to keep a shop, but unlawful to buy goods speculatively in order to re-sell them at a profit —this was looked upon as only one degree better than usury. As trade enlarged and specialization developed, the Schoolmen adapted their views to the changing times, and St. Thomas AQUINAS (q.v. Vol. V), the greatest of the Schoolmen, admitted that there was such a thing as 'trading for the public good'. Gradually, in place of the complete condemnation of trading and moneylending, there grew up the theory of the 'Just Price', under which trading became lawful provided that the trader made no more profit, and charged no higher selling price, than would enable him to maintain himself in his own station in life. Later, some new ideas were put forward on the vexed question of moneylending. The Church, which in those days had immense influence, began by removing its previous objection to the earning of profits by persons who put up CAPITAL (q.v.) for a trading or manufacturing venture; it was now accepted that these people were merely partners with the trader or manufacturer himself, and shared his risks; but it was still held to be wrong to charge a fixed interest on money loans which involved no trading or manufacturing risk. Business, however, was advancing still more rapidly, and at last the Church agreed that interest on money loans was morally justified on two grounds: first, that the lender would be deprived during the period of the loan of the opportunity of using the money profitably for his own business purposes; secondly, in order that he might be compensated by those who repaid him for the losses he might suffer from those who did not repay their debts.

Once the morality of charging interest had been accepted, commercial loans became a normal feature of trading; but interest rates rose to very high figures—sometimes as much as 60% per annum. The shortage of capital may have had much to do with this. The Church's earlier view on the immorality of interest in any form was dropped, and what was now condemned as usury was only a rate of interest that was excessive. When, after the Reformation, the State became the sole law-making power in the country, laws were passed to limit rates of interest, and in Britain the maximum rate permitted until early in the 19th century was 5%. These laws were known as the Usury Laws.

They have now been repealed, and the only laws in force concerning rates of interest are those in connexion with loans by licensed moneylenders. By the Money Lenders Act of 1927 any rate of interest over 48% per annum is considered excessive, and contracts at rates above this figure are liable to be set aside by the law courts as 'harsh and unconscionable'. Rates of interest as high as this are not met with in normal business, but arise only on loans from moneylenders against types of security that would not be accepted as safe enough by a banker.

See also LOANS; INTEREST.

V

VALUE AND PRICE. Using the word 'value' in its economic sense, the value of anything is the amount of some other thing that can be obtained in exchange for it. If a hundredweight of coal can be exchanged for 4 pounds of mutton, we might say that the value of a pound of mutton was a quarter of a hundredweight of coal, or the other way round. In the modern world MONEY (q.v.) is the general medium of exchange, and values are more conveniently measured in money. The price of an article is its 'exchange value' in money.

It used to be thought that the value of anything depended solely on what it cost to make. David Ricardo, the British economist, argued in the early 19th century that the comparative values of different articles depended on the 'quantities of labour' that had gone to make them. Thus, if it took 100 man-hours to make article *A*, and 200 man-hours to make article *B*, article *B* would be twice as valuable as article *A*, and one *B* would exchange in the market for two *A*s. Ricardo's theory held the field for quite a time. It was the foundation on which Karl MARX (q.v. Vol. V) built his own theory of value many years later, but by that time an important objection had been raised to Ricardo's theory. If equal amounts of labour had gone to the making of something that was very useful, and of something that was quite useless, would each have the same exchange value, or fetch the same price? Marx got over this difficulty by introducing the idea of 'socially necessary labour'; but this suggested that society—that is, people themselves—had a great deal to say on the question of values and prices.

Towards the end of the 19th century some economists, including W. S. Jevons in England, approached the problem from a different angle. In the main, their views are still held by modern economists. They suggested that the value of anything depends upon what the buyer is prepared to pay for it, and that he will value articles, or 'price' them, according to their scale of usefulness to himself. He might put an equal value upon a hundredweight of coal and 4 pounds of mutton, because each of these quantities of things represented to him an equal amount of usefulness—or 'utility', which is the word that economists have come to use.

Naturally, any individual purchaser may put different values upon the same things at different times or in different places, and even at the same time and in the same place the valuations put upon the same thing by different purchasers may not be the same. Prices are therefore likely to change when demand changes. But prices are just as likely to be influenced by the available supply of the article—by the fact that it is plentiful or scarce. For example, if bad harvests in Canada make wheat scarcer, it is likely that the price of wheat will rise, for in order to get enough of it buyers will have to raise their 'bids' in the market. Goods made of materials of which there is a very limited supply in the world, such as sable fur coats or diamond necklaces, will always, therefore, have a high value. Their actual price at any given time depends mainly on the amount of money people have to spare after buying the necessities of life. Prices are therefore really dependent upon the joint influence of SUPPLY AND DEMAND (q.v.).

VARNISHES, *see* PAINTS AND VARNISHES.

VEGETABLE OILS, *see* OILS, VEGETABLE.

VEGETABLE TRADE, *see* GREENGROCERY.

VENEERS, *see* CABINET-MAKING; PLYWOODS AND VENEERS.

W

WAGES. 1. These are payments made to workers in return for their labour. Wage-rates are usually fixed by direct negotiation between employers' federations and TRADE UNIONS (q.v.). Where this is not satisfactory, wage councils are set up, and the proposed rates are enforced by law. 'Time-rate' and 'piecework' are the two main methods of wage payment, but there are also various bonus or 'incentive' systems that are combinations of the two main methods.

Time-rates are based on the number of hours worked. An ordinary hourly rate of pay is agreed on, and this is increased by a quarter or a half, or is sometimes even doubled, for 'overtime' put in by the worker after normal working hours or at weekends, or on public holidays.

On piecework wages the worker is paid an agreed rate for the quantity of material he produces: for example, a miner may be paid so much per ton of mineral ore dug out and sent to the surface. In most modern industrial processes men work in groups and not singly, and piecework payments are worked out for the group or gang and shared among its members. In COAL-MINING (q.v.), for example, a 'check-weighman' at the pithead weighs the loads of coal sent up by the different gangs.

Most bonus systems of wage payment are based on a 'standard' or minimum performance by the worker; extra payments are made, on a sliding scale, for what is produced above that standard. There are many practical difficulties in working out bonus systems, as the individual performances of the various workers in a group or gang are liable to differ widely from each other.

Wages are affected by many factors, including changes in the supply and demand for different types of labour, trends in productivity and profits, comparisons with levels or trends of incomes in other employment, and changes in prices. There is, moreover, more than one kind of wage rate. In this country wage rates in the principal industries are negotiated or fixed nationally, negotiations generally being initiated by a wage claim from organized workers in the industry. Either weekly or hourly rates of wages are laid down for particular occupations, frequently separately for men, women, and young people. But these nationally-agreed rates usually represent only the minimum amount; in many cases employers are compelled to pay higher rates in order to attract the labour they need, and these are known as local or market rates. The tendency of local or market rates to rise more quickly than national rates is known as 'wage drift'. At one time wage rates used to rise and fall in accordance with the fortunes of the trade or industry concerned. For example, wage cuts in Britain after the First World War particularly affected industries such as coal, engineering, and cotton which suffered from foreign competition. Nowadays, however, it is rare for nationally negotiated wage rates to fall, although this can happen temporarily where wage rates are directly tied to the COST OF LIVING (q.v.).

It is important to distinguish between wages and actual earnings. Under modern conditions most workers' earnings exceed their agreed wage rates as a result of the bonuses, overtime, and other additional payments they earn. Unlike wage rates, earnings are sometimes cut, either because of a recession in the economy as a whole, or because a particular industry or firm is not finding it so easy to sell its goods. In Britain and most other industrial countries, however, the broad tendency has been for both wages and earnings to rise continuously. Frequently, the rise has been faster than the rise in production, and this has led to increases in costs, and in turn, to government attempts to influence wage negotiations. Britain's State intervention has lately taken the form of a voluntary incomes policy, backed by reserve statutory powers.

Some types of payments to workers, mainly to white collar, that is, non-manual, workers, are known as salaries. These are often fixed at an annual figure and paid monthly. Much of what has been said about wages also applies to salaries, although salary earnings often do not differ from salary rates as much as wage earnings differ from wage rates, and salaries are not always negotiated nationally. In recent years there has been a tendency for the number of salaried workers to increase, and the distinction between wage and salary earners is not as sharp as it once was.

2. 'Real' Wages. Changes in 'money wages' and changes in 'real wages' are not always the same thing. 'Money wages' is the term given by economists to the actual pounds, shillings, and pence received. But 'real wages' is the term which indicates how many goods and services those pounds, shillings, and pence will buy. For instance, some workmen may receive 10% more money from their employer in a given year than in the previous year. This means an increase of 10% in their 'money wages'. But if the prices of food, clothes, bus fares, and other necessities have also gone up by 10%, they cannot buy any more than they could the year before. Therefore their 'real wages' are not changed. The welfare of workers depends not on a rise in money wages, but on a rise in real wages. Workers in any particular industry may receive a rise in real wages if that industry increases its productivity, or if the price of the product rises while the general Cost of Living (q.v.) remains stationary; they may then receive a rise in money wages which will mean a rise in real wages as well. For the community as a whole, a rise in real wages can only result from a general increase in productivity in all industries.

See also Trade Unions.

WALLPAPER, *see* Vol. XI: Wallpapers, History of.

WAREHOUSES. Since the earliest days of dock development, warehouses have always been a help to traders. In modern docks some warehouses are built and operated by the dock authority itself. Others are built by the dock authority and leased, more or less permanently, to shipowners and forwarding agents.

In dock areas of extensive acreage, land is often available on which private warehouses may be erected, the constructors paying the dock company a ground rent for the use of the land. All these warehouses are of great commercial service. Goods for export can be sent down to the docks and stored to await a convenient ship. Manufacturers and merchants do not have to build such storage space at their own business headquarters. For import cargoes,

Port of London Authority

A BONDED WAREHOUSE AT LONDON DOCKS

Tea is being weighed so that the dock authority can calculate the storage charge and the customs duty can be assessed

warehouses fulfil a similar purpose: ships can be emptied straight away, reloaded, and dispatched without having to wait a long time until importers are able to come and withdraw their cargoes. Warehouses also assist trade by making possible the sampling of goods. Sampling or inspection orders, or delivery orders for small quantities, may be given to merchants possibly interested in buying the goods, and sampling and inspection can be done in the dock warehouses.

A special kind of warehouse is the bonded warehouse. This is licensed by the Board of CUSTOMS AND EXCISE (q.v. Vol. X) for the storage of imported goods that are subject to Customs duty. Importers of dutiable commodities, such as wines, spirits, and tobacco, may save much expense by storing their goods in a bonded warehouse until they withdraw them in small parcels on payment of duty.

See also Vol. IV: DOCKS.

WATERPROOFING. 1. For countless centuries men of many nations have tried to protect themselves and their possessions either from falling rain or the general dampness of a climate. In particular, their clothes, their living-tents, and their ropes and fishing nets have been in danger of rotting away if they could not be guarded from wet. The skins of beasts have been used as outer garments (*see* CLOTHES, HISTORY OF, Vol. XI); the thickness and natural greasiness of sheep's wool will keep off rain, whether used as a garment or as the covering of a tent. In man's more advanced stages he has used hides and skins without their hair or wool, and has preserved them and made them fairly waterproof by CURRYING (q.v.). The leather jerkin of the Middle Ages was made in this way. But it has been more difficult to keep water out of TEXTILE FIBRES AND FABRICS (q.v.)—woven and knitted materials—and out of ropes and cords.

2. TEXTILES AND FIBRES. There are four ways in which clothes can be made wholly or partly waterproof. (*a*) By making clothes such as raincoats wholly out of sheets of a waterproof plastic material. Many plastic materials such as P.V.C. can be softened by heat, and formed into sheets by squeezing them between heated iron calender rolls. This process, known as 'calendering', was used in the 19th century for rubber materials. Since then, the technique has been greatly improved, and is used on newer plastic materials to produce films of a precise thickness. These are then manufactured into the finished article either by sewing, sticking, or welding the edges together with heat.

(*b*) More substantial garments can be made from fabrics which have been coated with varnish, rubber, or plastic. The earliest use of coated fabric was that of the Egyptians, who coated mummy wrappings with natural gums and resins. More recently, varnishes have been used to coat fabrics to make the oilskins worn at sea. The fabric, which may be cotton or silk, is first treated with a coating of starch. Then an oil varnish (*see* PAINTS AND VARNISHES) is put on in repeated coatings until it is thick enough.

The use of rubber for coating fabrics was known as early as the 16th century. The Spanish colonists settling in South America found that the native Indians used rubber 'latex' (*see* RUBBER MANUFACTURE) for water-proofing their clothes. But for a couple of centuries little could be done with rubber, because the gum became hard soon after it was taken from the tree; when it reached Europe, men did not know how to bring it back again to a fluid state. Many attempts were made to find suitable solvents, that is, spirits which would dissolve the rubber into a liquid solution, and which would then evaporate after the coating was done, leaving only a layer of rubber. At last, in 1819, success was achieved by Charles Macintosh, after whom the macintoshes we wear today are called. He used certain BY-PRODUCTS (q.v.) from coal tar to manufacture a rubber solution which dried to a sticky film when spread on a fabric. He overcame this stickiness by sandwiching the rubber between two layers of fabric.

Like natural rubber, these materials did not resist extremes of heat and cold, and tended to become sticky. But in 1839 the process of 'vulcanization' was discovered, which converts the raw rubber into a much more useful substance (*see* RUBBER MANUFACTURE).

Putting on the rubber, or 'rubberizing', takes place in several stages. Substances such as oil and grease are first removed from the fabric. The rubber is kneaded and mixed with solvent, with the right amounts of sulphur (for vulcanization), colours, and other compounds. This solution is spread over the fabric in a thin even layer. Fresh layers continue to be spread until the right thickness has been built up. After each layer has been put on, the solvent is evaporated by passing the coated fabric over heated rollers. Finally, the fabric is vulcanized or 'cured' by wrapping it tightly around a drum, and baking it in an oven under controlled heat. Some materials are 'cold cured'.

Improved rubbers, known as synthetic rubbers, are used where the rubber-coated fabrics are either in contact with oils and greases, or have to operate at low or high temperatures, or are permanently out of doors. A special use of rubber-coated fabrics is in 'dracones', large flexible bags used for conveying liquids, such as oil, by sea. They are towed by tugs. The outer layer of fabric is coated with a special weather-resistant rubber called 'neoprene', and the inner layer with a special oil-resistant rubber called 'nitrile rubber'. These combinations of different rubbers have other specialised applications, such as in the hoses used for carrying petrol.

The first of the plastic coatings to be used was nitrocellulose, to which castor oil and solvents were added. Fabric coated in this way is called LEATHERCLOTH (q.v.). Similar methods are used to spread layers of PLASTICS (q.v.) such as P.V.C. on fabric. This may be done by using a paste made from powdered P.V.C. and pigments in a plasticiser. The paste is known as a 'plastisol'. After coating, the fabric is heated, and the plasticiser dissolves in the P.V.C. On cooling, the plasticised P.V.C. forms a tough flexible film. Coated fabrics made in this way are widely used for raincoats, furniture, upholstery, and in cars. Another way of applying the plastic to the fabric is to form a sheet of plasticised P.V.C. by squeezing it between heated calender rolls, and then pressing or laminating the hot sheet onto a fabric. Bonded fabrics are made by laminating a thin sheet of plastic foam between two layers of fabric. In a further variation, the sheet of plastic foam is 'calendered' as a hot molten plastic directly onto the fabric by passing the fabric through the calender rolls as well. Another plastic, polyurethane, can be applied to fabrics in the form of hot molten syrup; these are then used to make up garments which must withstand heavy wear.

(*c*) Treating fabrics to fill in the air spaces between the fibres. The method of waterproofing which consists of filling up the 'pores' of a fabric with solid particles, to keep the rain from soaking in, is much used for raincoats or 'showerproof' coats. The particles must be of a substance which will not dissolve in water, and they are

B.P. Chemicals (U.K.) Ltd.

A WEATHERPROOF P.V.C. AIRHOUSE PROVIDES TEMPORARY ACCOMMODATION UNTIL THE TRANSFORMERS ARE COMPLETED

inserted in the fabric by a simple chemical process. The fabric is first soaked in a chemical solution (generally aluminium acetate); then it is dried by heating. During the drying, the chemical changes into two substances: a compound whose solid particles remain in the fabric, and acetic acid which evaporates. Fabrics treated in this way are useful as light-duty waterproofs. They do not resist driving rain very well, and they tend to lose their waterproof property in course of time.

In another waterproofing process, the material is first soaked in a solution of gelatine, glue, or size (all of which are of the same general nature) and then in a solution which will harden it. The second solution makes the gelatine insoluble in water and fixes it inside the structure of the fibre. The gelatine thus makes the fibre able to resist water. Chemicals such as alum, bichromate of potash, or formalin are used for hardening. Tents, sailcoth, awnings, and thick blankets are treated in this way.

Waxes, bitumens, and tars are used to waterproof such things as cordage, ropes, hawsers, fishing lines and nets, and sackings, especially when these things have to be used in water, or exposed to continuous rain, or have to stand in puddles or pools. These materials do not give a waterproof covering as rubber or varnish do to macintoshes and oilskins, but they fill up the spaces in the fibres and thus make them much more difficult to wet. Many ropes and hawsers and cords are now made from plastics such as polyethylene and polypropylene, which are themselves waterproof (*see* ROPE-MAKING).

(*d*) Water-repellent treatments. These consist of dipping the fabric in a solution which deposits a water-repellent coating on the individual fibres without blocking up the air spaces between them. Although this coating can hardly be detected by sight or touch, it has the effect of making water roll up into little drops on the fabric and run off without penetrating it. Today one of the SILICONES (q.v.) is usually used for this. Although not entirely waterproof, fabrics treated in this way have the great advantage of allowing air and water vapour to pass through them so that raincoats, shower-proofed by this process, are much less stuffy and more comfortable to wear than true waterproofs.

See also TEXTILE FIBRES AND FABRICS; RUBBER MANUFACTURE; LEATHER-CLOTH; PLASTICS.

WEALTH, *see* STANDARD OF LIVING.

WEAVING, *see* WOOL WEAVING.

WELFARE, *see* FACTORY ORGANIZATION, Section 4; *see also* Vol. X: INDUSTRIAL WELFARE.

WHALING INDUSTRY, *see* Vol. VI: WHALING.

WHISKY DISTILLING. 1. MATERIALS. Alcoholic drinks are made from starch or sugar found in some natural form. In Scotland barley is used to make whisky, in Japan the wine known as *saké* is made from rice, goats' milk in Arabia gives *koumiss*, grapes in France make wine and brandy, and sugar in the West Indies is used to produce rum.

The making of drinks containing alcohol is a very ancient art. 'Alcohol' is derived from Arabic words for antimony sulphide, which was used by Eastern women in early times to blacken their eyebrows, and it was prepared for them by 'sublimation'. The Arabs regarded sublimation as similar to DISTILLATION (q.v.), as indeed it is, and hence alcohol became so called because, in its preparation, it resembled antimony sulphide. It is not possible to say with any degree of accuracy when alcohol was first produced. We know that alcohol was used as a medicine by the Arabs in the 10th century, and by European monks later in the Middle Ages.

The same principles apply to the making of many kinds of alcoholic drinks. When YEAST (q.v. Vol. II) is allowed to grow in a solution of sugar, the sugar becomes chemically changed to simpler substances. One of these is alcohol. Wine and cider are made in this way by the action of yeast on grape or apple juice. This process is called FERMENTATION (q.v. Vol. II). In many countries not enough fruit is grown to yield juice containing sugar, and another source of alcohol was discovered in very early times. It was found that starch, which forms a large part of cereal grains, could be changed into a fermentable sugar by a substance called diastase, which is present in barley grains which have been allowed to sprout. The first stage in making an alcoholic liquor from barley is to treat the grain so that it begins to sprout, and then dry it. This is known as MALTING (q.v.). The malted barley is then crushed and stirred in warm water, when the change of starch to sugar takes place. Finally yeast is added, and the sugar fermented to alcohol. The liquor obtained in this way, if flavoured with hops, is beer (*see* BEER BREWING).

2. DISTILLING. Liquor of this kind usually contains only a small proportion of alcohol; to make 'spirits', the alcohol is separated from the liquor by DISTILLATION (q.v.). When alcohol is heated, it boils at a much lower temperature than water. If we heat a mixture of alcohol and water, such as one of the liquors made by fermentation, the vapour that comes off when the liquid first begins to boil is very rich in alcohol. By cooling this vapour, we obtain a liquid containing a higher proportion of alcohol than the fermented liquid from which it was made. The more concentrated liquors made in this way are called 'spirits', and include such drinks as whisky and gin. When malt is intended for whisky, it is dried over a fire of PEAT (q.v. Vol. VI) which gives it a special flavour.

Two types of apparatus, called stills, are used for distilling whisky. The original 'pot' still, which resembles a large copper onion in shape, is connected by a 'lyne', or lying arm, from the head of the still to the 'worm', which is a coil of copper pipe which gradually becomes narrower; this coil is surrounded by water to cool it. The still is heated over a fire, and, after a first

Scotch Whisky Assn.

POT STILLS USED FOR THE DISTILLATION OF MALT WHISKY

distillation, the liquor, which is then known as 'crude distillate', is redistilled in a second still of the same type, called the 'spirit-still'. The first and last products of the distillation are discarded; the intermediate portion of the distillate is collected and stored in wooden casks for maturing.

By such a system of double distillation, Pot Still Malt Whisky is produced. It is heavy in character, and carries most of the flavour and bouquet of the ordinary whisky sold in the shops. To lighten it, it is blended with grain whisky, made by fermenting maize with a little malted barley and distilling the liquor in a 'patent' still, invented by Aeneas Coffey over 100 years ago. The features of the patent still process are a continuous instead of intermittent operation, and the extraction of the alcohol from the fermented liquor by means of steam. The grain whisky made in the patent still is much lighter than the heavy malt whisky made in the pot still, with which it is blended.

Scotch whisky is an important item in Britain's export trade, especially as much of it is paid for in American dollars (*see* HARD CURRENCY). The flavour of whisky, like that of wine (*see* WINE TRADE), owes much to local soil and local materials, and attempts to imitate abroad the peculiar aroma and bouquet of Scotch whisky have not been successful.

See also INDUSTRIAL ALCOHOL.
See also Vol. XI: WINES AND SPIRITS.

WHOLESALE TRADING. A wholesaler organizes the supply of goods to shopkeepers who then sell them to the consumers. It is more convenient for a shopkeeper to deal with a few wholesalers than with dozens of manufacturers. Wholesalers who deal in drapery, fashion goods, and haberdashery are often called 'warehousemen'. The amount of stock wholesalers carry varies; in pharmacy wholesalers may deliver orders daily, whereas the wholesale agent in some trades carries little stock, but arranges deliveries direct from the manufacturers.

Wholesalers are a great convenience to the retail shopkeeper. By dealing with them, he can keep a smaller stock of goods in his shop than would otherwise be necessary—a great advantage in the case of commodities that are perishable or likely to lose their quality if kept too long. Also, wholesalers are usually large firms with a good deal of CAPITAL (q.v.), so they can grant extended CREDIT (q.v.) to the shopkeeper, often long enough for him to be able to sell his goods and collect the cash for them before he has to pay for them himself.

Wholesalers are also of service to manufacturers. There is a good deal of competition in most manufacturing trades, and few manufacturers would be content to sit down in their factories and to wait for retail shopkeepers to call upon them: they would probably have to send out travelling REPRESENTATIVES (q.v.) to call on retail shopkeepers and to take their orders. This would mean a series of car or van journeys from most manufacturers to every shop in the country, and much overlapping and waste of transport in distributing goods. Some manufacturers prefer to do their own wholesaling so as to keep in direct touch with retailers. The main reason why most manufacturers avoid doing their own wholesaling is that they specialize in a single limited line of goods, and so the expense of organizing a force of travelling representatives to get orders from retailers is not worth while: travellers' calls are only profitable if they can obtain large orders.

Price policy and methods of trading differ in the various branches of the wholesale trade. Firms dealing in staple products such as iron and steel, building materials, grains, farmers' feeding-stuffs, and so on, usually add on to the producer's price an additional margin or 'mark up' which will cover expenses and leave them a satisfactory profit. Then from time to time they send to their retail customers price-lists, which are amended as manufacturers' prices alter. Warehousemen in the textile trade do the same thing. Wholesalers of branded or proprietary goods, of which cigarettes and tobacco are good examples, used to give the ordinary retail selling-prices in their catalogues, and allow their shopkeeper customers a trade discount. As it is now illegal for manufacturers to fix retail prices, except in special cases, this practice is becoming less common. Most wholesalers allow a quantity discount, which is comparatively low on small orders, but which rises with orders for larger quantities.

See also RETAIL TRADING

WINDOW DRESSING, *see* ADVERTISING AND PUBLICITY.

WINE AND SPIRIT TRADE. 1. The wine trade is of great antiquity. Samian and Faler-

Bodleian Library

MAKING WINE
16th-century engraving

nian wines are mentioned frequently in Greek and Roman classical literature; by the Roman poet Horace, for example. Those countries that have been favoured by nature with the warm, dry, and sunny climate that suits the growing of GRAPES (q.v. Vol. VI) have always produced their own wines, and others not so favoured have relied on importing it. From time immemorial the Mediterranean and adjoining countries have been great producers of wine, and France, Germany, Spain, Portugal, Algeria, Italy, Greece, and some of the Balkan countries are still very important. In more recent years countries much farther afield have become included in the list, and wine is now produced in large quantities in the State of California in the U.S.A., in Chile and Argentina, in Australia, and in the Republic of South Africa.

The earliest records of the importation of wine to Britain are of the 5th century A.D. In the reign of Edward III, owing to a royal decree forbidding the export of coin, Bordeaux merchants ceased to export wine direct to England and as a result an English fleet sailing to Bordeaux was built up, which is held by many to be the origin of the English mercantile marine. During the Anglo-French wars of the 18th century, restrictions and discriminatory taxation were applied to French wines, stimulating the trade in Portuguese and Spanish wines. This policy was reversed in 1860, and the trade in French wines revived. 'Imperial preference' early in the 20th century granted customs relief to wines from the Empire, extending and helping wine growing and selling in Australia and South Africa.

Wine is the product of the fermentation of the grape, but ordinary table grapes do not make good wine. Grapes have to be used from special vines, of which the best known are Riesling, Traminer, Pinot, and Gamay. Grapes are picked when the wine-grower judges they are ripe, usually in September or October, and are then pressed to squeeze out the juice, which is called 'must'. They are very rarely trodden nowadays, but crushed by machines; if the pips and stalks are ground up at the same time, the wine will be inferior.

Red wine is made from black grapes, white wine from white grapes or black grapes whose must has been run off before the skins can stain it. In good years the sugar in the must and the yeast-fungi on the grape skins should be enough to secure proper fermentation in the vats into which it is run; but sometimes sugar and yeast are added. When fermentation is complete the new wine is run out of the vats into casks to mature. It is transferred from cask to cask (racking) to get rid of the lees, and clarified by a process called 'fining'. At the end of 1, 2, or 3 years the wine is judged to be ready and is transferred to bottles, where it continues to mature, lying on its side. If the bottles were stood upright, the corks would dry up, the air would then get in and ruin the wine. Some wines, such as Madeira, port, and sherry, are 'fortified' by the addition of spirits during the process of 'vinification'. This delays their maturing, alters the taste, and makes them stronger. In most countries fortified wines, like sparkling wines, pay a higher rate of duty.

Sparkling wines can be made either naturally or artificially. Those made naturally, by what is called the 'champagne process', are put into bottles while fermentation is still going on. During fermentation carbon dioxide gas is produced; and, if the wine is bottled before fermentation is complete, this gas becomes dissolved in the wine. It is this gas that gives the wine its sparkle. Fermentation after bottling produces an undrinkable sediment, which must be removed before the wine is sold. This is done by placing the bottles cork downwards until the sediment drops down towards the neck. When this process is completed, the neck of the bottle is frozen. The cork is then removed, the frozen ice and sediment are forced out by the pressure of the gas in the bottle, and the wine is quickly recorked. Artificial sparkling wine is made in the same way as mineral water: carbon dioxide gas is introduced mechanically into a bottle of still wine, which is then immediately corked.

In France and Germany the quality of wines

Hennell

A SERIES OF HORIZONTAL WINE PRESSES AT DOMECQ VINEYARDS, JEREZ DE LA FRONTERA, SPAIN

The control panel is on the left. Grape pulp is fed through overhead pipes into the four presses. They rotate and their end walls converge to extract the juice, which filters through a moving grid into tanks below the floor

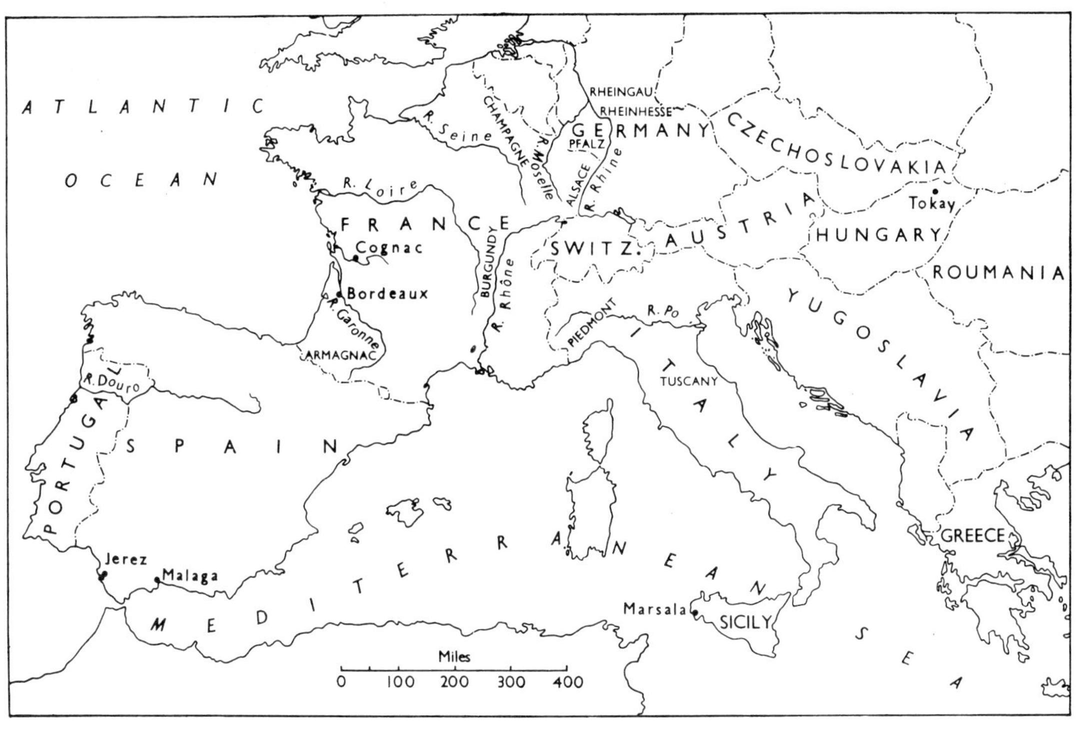

PRINCIPAL WINE-GROWING DISTRICTS OF EUROPE

is safeguarded by strict laws which compel the use of particular vines, and lay down methods of manufacture. Among their most important provisions are those which forbid the use of place names except for wines that come from these strictly defined areas. Thus, a bottle with the label Niersteiner, St. Emilion, or Beaune is bound to contain wine from approved vineyards in the places named, which has been made in the proper manner and has the expected flavour. Similarly, it is illegal in Britain to sell any wine as 'champagne', 'sherry', or 'port' if it does not come from the correct area. Apart from the climate, the soil, and the winegrowers' skill, these regulations are among the chief reasons for the pre-eminence in their particular spheres of French, German, and Portuguese wines. Wines from other countries often annex place names, such as 'Chablis' and 'Moselle', but they do not in fact have the taste of these wines, and are usually inferior. The chief wine-producing areas in France are: Burgundy; the Bordeaux area; the valley of the Rhône; the basin of the Loire river; Alsace; the Champagne area. In Germany: the valley of the river Moselle; the districts beside the river Rhine known as Rheingau, Rheinhesse, and Pfalz or Palatinate; Franconia. In Spain: the area round Jerez, which produces sherry. In Portugal: the upper reaches of the Portuguese section of the Douro river which produces port (*see* Vol. I, p. 374). In Italy: Piedmont and the Po Valley; Tuscany, which produces Chianti. In Hungary: Tokay. Other wines which have secured wide recognition from their place names are Marsala (Sicily), Malaga (South Spain), and Madeira (island of Madeira). Wines were made in Britain during the Middle Ages, mostly for religious purposes; a small amount is made even to-day. So-called 'British wines' are usually made from imported foreign must artificially fermented.

2. Spirits. These are distilled by two methods, pot-still and patent-still. The patent still produces from fermented liquid a continuous stream of colourless, almost neutral spirit to which, in many cases, colour and flavour are added afterwards; it is much cheaper and more productive than pot-still distillation, though the product is comparatively characterless. Gin, vodka, most rum, grain whisky and many liqueurs are produced by this process. The pot-still method, which is the older one, carries over into the final product more of the so-called 'impurities' from the original liquid, giving it more taste and character. The chief spirits so made are the Cognac and Armagnac brandies in France, and malt whisky (*see* WHISKY DISTILLING).

Cognac brandy must be distilled in a carefully defined district around the French town of Cognac, in which the best areas are the Grande and Petite Champagne, which are often blended together as Fine Champagne, a name which causes some natural confusion with the wine. Cognac is however more often sold as one star, two star, or three star, which is supposed to indicate improving quality, though it has in fact no official meaning. Liqueur cognacs are more expensive, sweeter, and have a remarkable taste and bouquet; merchants use various names for them, of which the commonest is V.S.O.P. ('Very Superior Old Pale'). Armagnac brandy comes from the district of that name in south-western France and is more herbal in taste.

3. LIQUEURS. Liqueurs are heavily sweetened and flavoured spirits, served in small glasses after food, and sipped rather than drunk. Their manufacture is commonly described as 'secret', but the secrecy usually extends only to the composition of the flavouring, which is often a fairly complex mixture of herbs, condiments, or rinds. Originally these were frequently supposed to have some medicinal effect, but few doctors would accept this claim nowadays. Among the better known liqueurs, with the predominant taste in each case, are the following: Cointreau (orange peel), Chartreuse (mixed sage-like herbs), Grand Marnier (orange), Benedictine (mixed herbs), Kummel (caraway), cherry brandy (cherries), crème de menthe (mint), Drambuie (whisky), advocaat (eggs).

See also Vol. XI: WINES AND SPIRITS.

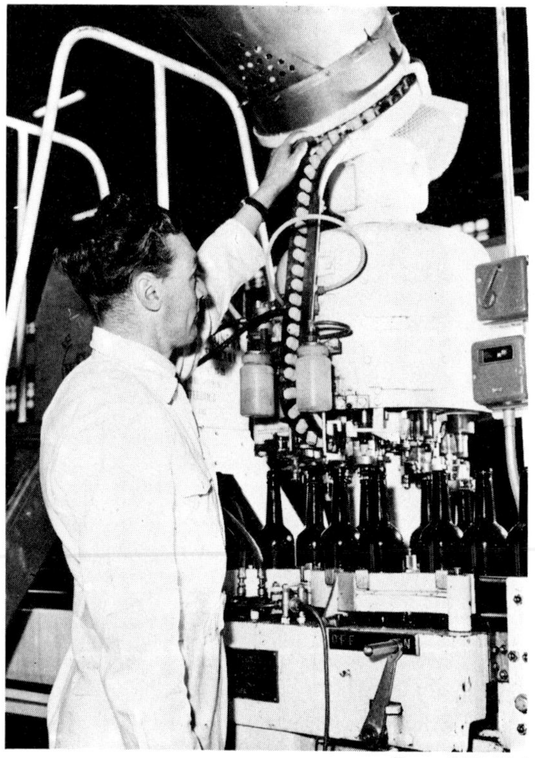

Harveys of Bristol Ltd.

AN AUTOMATIC CORKING MACHINE IN A WINE BOTTLING PLANT

WOOD, *see* TIMBER INDUSTRY; FURNITURE INDUSTRY; PLYWOOD AND VENEERS; WOODWORK, HISTORY OF; HARDWOODS; SOFTWOODS.

See also Vol. VI: TIMBER.

WOOD-PULP. This is the most important material from which paper is made, and a variety of wood-pulp is also used in the manufacture of TEXTILE FIBRES, MAN-MADE and PLASTICS (qq.v.), and for EXPLOSIVES (q.v. Vol. VIII). It also forms part of many of the building boards used in modern building work.

Wood-pulp is made from many different kinds of trees, most of them belonging to the coniferous group—spruce, pine, and balsam fir (*see* TREES, CONIFEROUS, Vol. VI)—which are found in northerly countries, especially in Canada, the U.S.A., Scandinavia, Germany, and Russia. Deciduous trees such as poplar and aspen are also used. Some trees may be 75 years old before they are cut for pulp. The mills in which the logs of wood are made into pulp are usually situated on rivers near the forests, and the logs are floated down the rivers to the mills and into large pools, where they are sorted (*see* LOGGING, Vol. VI). At the mills the logs are cut up into manageable lengths, the bark removed and used as boiler fuel, and the knots taken out.

There are several kinds of wood-pulp, made for different purposes. The simplest form is called 'mechanical wood', and this consists of coarse sawdust ground from the logs, which are held against rough circular grindstones, revolving at a very high speed in water. The wet sawdust, or pulp, is then carried away from the grindstones by the water and passed over screens

Bowaters

LOADING LOGS INTO THE GRINDER FOR PREPARING MECHANICAL PULP

The moving belts on either side press the logs on to the grindstones

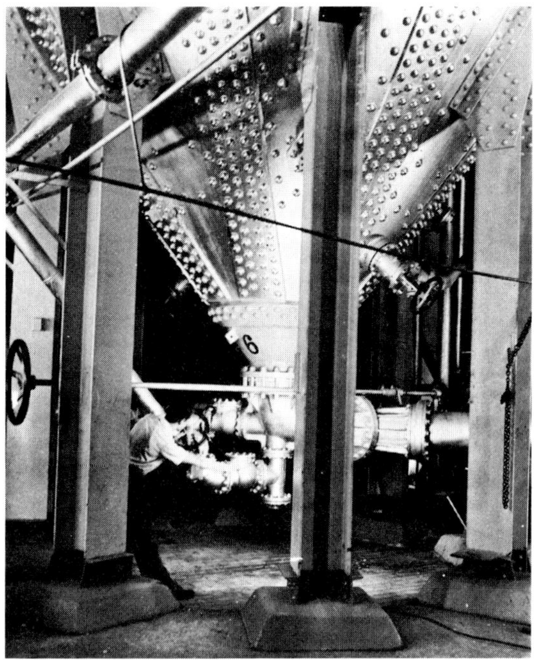

Bowaters

MAKING SULPHITE PULP IN A 'DIGESTER' IN WHICH WOOD CHIPS ARE BOILED WITH CHEMICALS

The pulp is blown out of the valves at the bottom

Bowaters

MECHANICAL PULP BEING THICKENED READY TO BE MADE INTO NEWSPRINT

Bowaters

SULPHITE PULP COMING OFF THE THICKENING MACHINE BEFORE BEING DRIED

which take out any big lumps. The pulp is put through a machine which thickens it by removing excess water, until it is thick enough to hold together, and is then cut into sheets the size of a doormat. If these half-damp sheets have to travel a long way to a paper-mill they are baled together for storage or shipping. Wood-pulp is principally used in the making of NEWSPRINT (q.v.), wallpapers, and other cheap printing-papers which do not have to last a long time; all these papers tend to go yellow and, after a long period of exposure to air, to crumble away. The other pulps made from wood are all called 'chemical pulps', because they are treated with chemicals to remove everything from the wood except the cellulose fibres, which are felted into a pulp from which the paper is made. To make chemical pulp, the logs are more carefully stripped of bark, and the knots more thoroughly removed, than for mechanical pulp. The logs are then taken to a chipping-machine which cuts them up into small, regular-sized chips; these are blown into large vertical digesters, or boilers, where they are boiled with bisulphite of lime or other chemicals to remove any resin, lignin, or other impurities in the wood. These chemical pulps are known as 'sulphite pulp' or 'soda pulp', according to the chemicals used. The different types of pulps are used to produce different types of paper.

If the pulps are required for white papers, they are subsequently bleached by chlorine gas, then treated with caustic soda, and finally bleached with hypochlorite of lime, or other chemicals, to bring them up to a good white colour. Some of these pulps, however, are left in their natural colour, and not bleached. These are generally called 'strong pulps' if treated by the sulphite process, or 'kraft pulps' if treated by the soda or sulphate process.

Chemical pulps, whether bleached or not, are carefully strained to remove lumps and big pieces of badly broken-up fibre. They are then passed on to a machine which works on the same principles as an ordinary paper-machine, and dried either in a vacuum drier or over cylinders, in much the same way as paper is dried (*see* PAPER-MAKING, Section 2). As the pulp comes off the machine it is cut up into sheets, which are made up into bales weighing about four hundredweight each. The pulp is then ready for export.

Chemical pulps are used for a great variety of papers. Strong sulphite pulp forms about 15% of the wood-pulp used in the manufacture of newsprint; it is also used for wrapping-paper, envelope papers, and other strong papers. Bleached sulphite pulp is used for fine writing-papers, typewriting-papers, and (together with esparto grass) for printing-papers and papers for illustrated magazines. Brown kraft pulp is used for strong, brown wrapping-papers, and bleached kraft pulp is also used for a variety of papers, including fine tissues. The pulp mostly used for the manufacture of rayon and plastics, and also for explosives, is the bleached sulphite pulp.

See also PAPER-MAKING; NEWSPRINT.

WOODWORK, HISTORY OF. From earliest times men have turned to wood for making the things they needed in the everyday business of living. There was a plentiful supply of wood in the forests; it was one of the most easily worked materials, being softer than stone or iron; and it was strong and lasting enough for most purposes. Primitive men bound wooden handles on to their flint tools. The first farmers used a sharp piece of hard wood for a plough share, and later attached it to a wooden shaft so that oxen could drag it through the ground. Later, again, they used their simple tools, and also called in the help of fire, to shape rough wheels with axles and to hollow out logs to make boats. Little of this early work remains because wood is far more perishable than stone or iron. But some pieces of woodwork have survived by being buried in dry sand, frozen soil, river mud, or in tombs, and these show that WOOD-CARVING (q.v. Vol. XII) was an art in Siberia as early as 2800 B.C. and that woodwork was a well-developed craft by 1000 B.C. The British Museum has examples of ancient Egyptian doors and furniture which show that many of the joints used to-day for framing woodwork were known at that early date, and that some of the tools still used have an equally distant ancestry. Hardly any specimens of Greek and Roman woodwork remain to us. But they have been written about, and many specimens of Roman tools are exhibited in a number of museums (for example at Reading), which show the originals from which modern saws, chisels, and other tools were derived.

Until the 19th century, all ships were made of wood (*see* SHIPBUILDING INDUSTRY), and wherever wood was easily available it has also been used for house building—at least for smaller houses. Of British woodwork little remains that

J. R. H. Weaver

THE HALL OF WADHAM COLLEGE, OXFORD

The college was built in 1612. The panels of the wainscot and screen are small. The screen and hammerbeam roof are enriched with carving. The trestle tables and benches are contemporary with the hall

is earlier than the 14th century, and what has survived is mainly in churches and cathedrals. In the early Middle Ages, the technique of woodwork, like that of all crafts, was fostered in the monasteries. But as the towns grew, woodworkers set up their own shops and tended to specialize in a single craft. Their trade was organized by their CRAFT GUILDS (q.v.), each craft having its own guild. Many of the names of their trades have survived in common English surnames. The name Wright originally meant someone who made things: cartwrights and wainwrights made carts and wagons, WHEELWRIGHTS (q.v. Vol. VI) made wheels. Coopers specialized in CASK-MAKING (q.v.); bowyers and fletchers made bows and arrows; turners made parts of household furniture.

Most important of all medieval woodworkers were the carpenters. Carpenters were originally cart-makers. The Latin word for cart was *carpentum*, and the man who made it was a *carpentarius*, or carpenter. But by the Middle Ages a carpenter was a man who carried out the structural timber work for houses and, since many houses were half-timbered, carpenters were much in demand (*see* BUILDING INDUSTRY, HISTORY OF). The work included not only the frame but also the roof, floors, and staircase, and the woods they used were mainly oak, elm, and chestnut. The Carpenters' Livery Company of London, founded in 1333, soon became very wealthy, and many master carpenters, like the carpenter in Chaucer's *Canterbury Tales*, were men of considerable substance. Excellent

Crown Copyright

EARLY 16TH-CENTURY CHEST

It is built with a frame and panels, which are decorated with linenfold pattern

Victoria and Albert Museum

medieval carpentry, particularly roofs, survive in many cathedrals and churches, for example in the Angel Roof of Woolpit in Suffolk (*see* Vol. XII, p. 183). Joiners appear later than carpenters and were concerned with furniture, not building. They made those types of furniture whose basic construction was 'jointed', for example, chests and tables; they also made panelling. In the 17th century, with the demand for more elaborate types of furniture, such as cabinets, desks, and book-cases, yet another specialist woodworking craft emerged in Britain—CABINET-MAKING (q.v.). Cabinet-makers made use of INLAY AND MARQUETRY (q.v.) and of the new technique of veneering, introduced from France and Holland and carried out with unfamiliar woods such as walnut and, later, mahogany.

The history of woodwork is the history of the craftsman's mastery of his material. Wood is a splendid ready-made material so long as it is used with some thought for the way it has grown. It is not like metal or plastics which can be worked or moulded into any shape that may be needed. Although modern WOODWORKING MACHINERY (q.v. Vol. VIII) gives more control over the material, even to-day the woodworker is limited, and he cannot do much more than cut the wood into smaller sizes and join bits together. The length and width of his material is in the first place limited by the height and girth of the tree it came from. Another characteristic of wood which the woodworker must take into account is that, as wood 'seasons' or dries out, it shrinks across the grain but remains much the same length. So in order to make a piece of woodwork strong in both length and width, it must be constructed so that the grain runs both ways.

Late medieval craftsmen evolved an ingenious way of getting over this difficulty, known as the 'frame-and-panel' system. A framework was made with pieces of wood fixed together with strong joints. This provided the strength for the whole. The framework was then filled in with panels, which were fitted into deep grooves cut into the inner edges of the frame. These grooves gave room for the panels to shrink without either distorting the shape of the frame or themselves splitting, as would have happened had they been fixed rigidly. This frame-and-panel system remained the basis of woodwork design for several centuries. The width to which the wood panels could be cut was obviously limited

THE GRAND STAIRCASE AT HATFIELD

Built in the early 17th century, it is decorated with a profusion of carved ornament

by the girth of the trees; also, comparatively small panels produced less problem of shrinkage. Thus we find that a feature of early panelling is the small size of the panels. Later, when strong glues came to be used, craftsmen learned to join board together, and the size of the panels increased.

Towards the end of the 19th century, with the introduction of Plywood (q.v.), which shrinks neither in length nor width, new methods of construction became possible. The development of machine tools had led to the emergence of a new craftsman, the woodcutting machinist. With his power-driven saws, planes, and drills he can carry out with speed and accuracy many of the processes of the old hand-tooled carpenter and joiner. Much of the carpenter's work is now done in factories: doors, window frames, and even staircases are now mass-produced, and the carpenter's job is only to fix them in position. His work may be limited to floors and roofs—and not always these. A new task now falls to the carpenter, however, and that is the making of wooden 'form work' or shuttering to serve as moulds for reinforced concrete.

The old-time craftsman with his huge chest of tools who made everything by hand is gone. Many a woodworker to-day can go to his job carrying everything he needs in a small attaché case. A few craftsmen carry on the old tradition, while at the same time making use of some of the machine tools such as a Lathe (q.v. Vol. VIII); and the amateur who learns to love wood and to use his tools well can do much valuable carpentry in his home.

See also Cabinet-making; Furniture Industry; Timber Industry.

See also Vol. VIII: Woodworking Machinery.

See also Vol. XI: Furniture, History of.

WOOL INDUSTRY, MEDIEVAL. 1. England was the great wool-producing country of the Middle Ages, and English wool was looked upon as better than any other. The fact that the Lord Chancellor sits on the Woolsack in the House of Lords is a symbol of England's early dependence on wool for her riches and commercial prosperity.

The wool trade connected England with the Continent. The wool-growing areas of Wiltshire and the Cotswolds were linked up with the cloth-producing region of the Low Countries on the other side of the Channel. English sheep supplied about four-fifths of the money value of all English exports. The Netherlands was by far the most important market in English foreign trade, and its importance led to the setting up of the selling organization called the 'Staple' (*see* Merchants of the Staple), in the interests partly of the merchants' convenience, and partly of royal finance. For it was not only the wool merchants who had a special interest in their business. The Government also had a direct interest in the trade. It was a useful lever in diplomatic negotiations, and produced valuable customs duties which formed a large part of the revenue.

There were many types of English sheep in the Middle Ages, all different from the breeds of today. The best wool came from Shropshire and Herefordshire, especially the famous 'Lemster Ore' of the Leominster district, the Golden Fleece of England. Next in value came the high-priced wool of Lincolnshire and the Cotswolds (*see* Sheep, Vol. VI).

Sheep-farming was in the hands both of large landowners and of small tenant farmers. Many of the monasteries owned large sheep farms, which were the biggest economic units of the Middle Ages. At the time of Domesday Book, Ely Abbey had 13,400 sheep on its estates, spread over six counties. There was a further growth in the size of stock holdings in the 12th

G. C. Mills

FAIRFORD CHURCH, GLOUCESTERSHIRE, BUILT 1490–1500 BY THE CLOTH MERCHANT, JOHN TAME

and 13th centuries, and on the Bishop of Winchester's estate there were about 29,000 sheep in the 13th century. Large-scale production slackened off in the 14th and 15th centuries, and sheep-farming passed into the hands of the tenant farmers. This was the age of the small man, who sold his wool to a middleman dealer.

The story of English sheep farming is buried in a mass of local records, but it is still possible to catch a glimpse from them of the romance of wool production. Shakespeare writes in *The Winter's Tale* of the sheep-shearing feast which always ended the successful sale of the 'clip'. The SHEPHERD (q.v. Vol. VI) was a most important person, and many rules were laid down as to how he should look after his sheep. 'It is a token of the shepherd's kindness if the sheep be not scattered abroad but browse around him in company. Let him provide himself with a barkable dog and lie nightly with his sheep.'

Home-produced wool got into the hands of the merchants in two different ways. The wool that was produced by the big landowners was usually sold direct to an export merchant. The exporter or his agent would ride round to the monasteries or big houses, look at the fleeces as they grew, and contract to buy the clip in advance. The wool of the small man went through a more complicated process of collection. Sometimes agents—wool gatherers—would go around gathering it together. At other times the big landowners would deal with it. Eventually middlemen grew up in the industry, collecting wool and then selling it to exporters for the international markets. As wool production by small farmers grew in relative importance in the 15th century, these middlemen or woolmen became as rich as the export merchants themselves. The greatest of them lived in the Cotswolds, the chief wool centre at this time. The village of Northleach, on the top of the wolds, was a celebrated centre of the trade, as we can still tell from its impressive church and the brasses of its woolmen. Some of the woolmen acknowledged their indebtedness to the sheep for the whole of their riches:

'I praise God and ever shall
It is the sheep hath paid for all.'

Some of the middlemen lived not in the Cotswolds, but in London. They would sometimes buy the wool from the Cotswolds' woolmen and sell it to the clothmakers or exporters. They would buy the wool by samples, and thus a great deal of responsibility fell on to the shoulders of the wool-packer, who was also the valuer of the wool: he had to mark each sample with its place of origin, and to grade it either as good or as middle-quality wool. The welfare of the wool trade depended upon the wool-packers, just as the care of the sheep depended upon the shepherds. The work of the middlemen would have been impossible if it had not been for this careful grading and valuation of the clips.

At first the export of wool was in the hands of foreigners—Italians, Germans, and Flemings. Later (from the 13th century onwards) it was in the hands of the MERCHANTS OF THE STAPLE (q.v.). From 1363 the Staple was centred in Calais, which at that time was in the hands of the British, and was a good gateway to the Low Countries and to the manufacturing districts of France.

The wool was carried by pack-horses from the shearing centres to the ports, divided among several ships to cut down risk of loss, and safely deposited in Calais, where it was examined by representatives of the Staplers. We can build up a clear picture of the organization of the medieval wool industry from a collection of letters and papers which still survives and which belonged to a firm of wool merchants, Cely and Sons. They were London merchants with offices both in London and in Calais. They dealt largely in Cotswold wool, and young Richard Cely, the son who did the buying in London, would ride down frequently from London to Gloucestershire to select Cotswold wool to ship to his brother in Calais. Most of the dealings of the Celys were carried out on CREDIT (q.v.); indeed, this applied to the wool trade as a whole. Wool dealers in the Cotswolds would buy on credit from the sheep farmer; the Celys in London would buy on credit from the dealers; and Dutch and Flemish customers in Calais would buy on credit from the Celys. BILLS OF EXCHANGE (q.v.) would be given for the debts incurred, and an all-round settlement would be made when the Celys collected their money 6 months after they had sold the wool at one of the great fairs in the Low Countries. They would transmit the money back to England—they did not try to buy goods overseas with it—and after that the various other debts would be paid. This highly organized trade shows that the trade of the Middle Ages was not merely a matter of local production. Wool was a truly international industry, and commercial contacts were many and wide.

National Buildings Record

CARVINGS ON A BUTTRESS OF A CHAPEL IN CULLOMPTON CHURCH, DEVON, BUILT IN 1526 BY THOMAS LANE, WOOLSTAPLER

Above, a ship symbolizes the export of wool and below are shears for cropping cloth

2. CLOTH MANUFACTURE. Towards the end of this period, cloth began to take the place of raw wool as England's most important export. Cloth manufacture grew up in certain specialized industrial districts. About half the woollens were made in the West Country: that is, mainly in Gloucestershire, Wiltshire, and Somerset. The best broad-cloth for export was made in Wiltshire. Another branch of the wool industry was in East Anglia. In the Norfolk village of Worstead a new sort of manufacture grew up, which finally took over for itself the name of the village. It used long-fibred wool, and made a smooth and very durable cloth which is now chiefly associated with Yorkshire (*see* WOOL SPINNING, Section 3). At the end of the Middle Ages the West Riding of Yorkshire was beginning to be a rising centre of manufactures, with industry spreading up the dales as far as Kendal in Westmorland.

The organization of the cloth industry differed from place to place. In some places there were small local craftsmen working at home. In other places great 'clothiers', as they were called, put out raw materials to be spun by cottagers, and then collected the finished work. There were many important families—for example those founded by John Tame of Fairford, and Thomas Spring of Lavenham—which prospered by providing raw materials for others to manufacture (*see* DOMESTIC SYSTEM).

Exports of English cloth became of great importance during the 15th century. As early as 1265, English cloths, known as 'Stamford', were being imported into Venice, but it was not until the 15th century that cloth exports began to challenge wool exports in weight and value. In the early 15th century, nearly half the English export trade in cloth was in the hands of foreigners, about a fifth of it being in the hands of the German HANSEATIC LEAGUE (q.v.). Later on in the century the share of cloth exported by the English Company of MERCHANT ADVENTURERS (q.v.) greatly increased; but there was a long struggle between the rival groups, which did not

British Museum

MEDIEVAL WOMEN PREPARING WOOL FOR WEAVING

In the foreground the wool is being combed (right), carded, and spun; at the back the warp is being put into the loom. 14th-century illumination (*Roy. MS. 16 G.v.f.56*)

end in favour of the Adventurers until the early 17th century.

Most of our national economic policy in the Middle Ages was bound up with the wool industry. It far outstripped all other trades in importance. Wool was important first of all as a source of TAXATION (q.v. Vol. X). The wool tax was one of the chief sources of the royal revenue at the end of the 13th century. Many of the struggles between king and merchants revolved round the problem of the tax, and it was not until the middle of the 14th century that a compromise was reached: the king was left in possession of a high subsidy on wool; Parliament was left in control of taxation—a most important privilege; and the wool exporting company, the Merchants of the Staple, was left with what was to all intents and purposes a MONOPOLY (q.v.) of raw wool export.

There were attempts also to work out a national policy to deal not only with wool but also with cloth. As early as 1258, Parliament prohibited the export of raw wool. But the policy of stimulating the native clothing industry had few results at this time, and indeed the industry showed signs of decay in the early 14th century. Edward II made real attempts to revive it, and Edward III offered even greater protection, encouraging many cloth-workers to come to England from overseas; and these brought new life to the industry. Later, Henry VII and Henry VIII did much to encourage the cloth industry and to discourage the export of raw wool; and the most important figures in the English wool industry at the end of the Middle Ages were not the wool dealers but the great clothiers.

History is written in stones as well as in books, and this is particularly true of the wool trade. Some of the most impressive parish churches in England are those of the wool towns, such as Lavenham in Suffolk, Boston in Lincolnshire, and Rotherham in Yorkshire. The south aisle of Cullompton Church in Devon, at the edge of the sheep-rearing country, is decorated with carvings of the instruments used in the wool trade. The church at Cirencester in Gloucestershire has a three-storeyed south porch, in whose upper rooms the CRAFT GUILDS (q.v.) used to hold their meetings. John Tame built a magnificent church at Fairford. Defoe has written that the Cathedral at Salisbury—the town of the famous 'Salisbury Whites'—was believed to rest on a foundation of woolpacks.

Such monuments in stone are testimonials to the wealth of the dealers in wool and the makers of cloth, but they show also that business in the Middle Ages was not entirely a matter of self-advancement.

See also WOOL SPINNING; WOOL WEAVING.
See also Vol. VI: SHEEP.

WOOL INDUSTRY, MODERN. 1. RAW MATERIALS. Two main types of wool are used: merino (or botany), and crossbred. Carpet wool is a coarse or 'low' variety of crossbred. Merino is fine, crossbred is medium; and both are grown mainly for clothing. Nearly 5,500 million lb. of wood are produced in the world every year, and of this about 40% is merino, 36% crossbred, and 24% carpet wool. Australia alone provides over 1,600 million lb.: a large proportion of all the merino wool grown in the world. New Zealand, by contrast, is the largest grower of crossbred wools, while the biggest growers of carpet wools are the U.S.S.R., India, and Pakistan.

The chief properties that make wool so generally useful are strength, durability, and elasticity. Other properties are its low inflammability and its capacity to absorb moisture. A single fibre of wool is as strong as a thread of gold of the same thickness. Wool fibres can be bent repeatedly without breaking—an important property when we consider how often we bend our knees or elbows during the life-time of a wool garment. A wool fibre will return to its original length after being stretched almost double; wool clothing, therefore, crushes less easily than other fabrics, and soon recovers its original shape and appearance. Wool does not easily burn; if it does catch fire it tends merely to smoulder, and then to go out. The capacity of wool to absorb moisture is important to health. Dry wool will absorb water vapour equal to half its own weight; the moisture is absorbed into the actual structure of the fibre, and does not cause the garment to feel wet. While absorbing moisture, the wool fibres generate heat, and the moisture that is absorbed is given off again only very slowly. These properties make wool clothing useful in preventing chills. A good deal of air is also held in the spaces of wool fabrics; this acts as an insulator, and so wool clothing feels warm in cold or damp weather and cool in hot weather.

Chemically, wool is a protein, consisting of carbon 50%, oxygen 22%–25%, nitrogen 16%–17%, hydrogen 7%, and sulphur 3%–4%. Treatment of wool with appropriate chemicals has led to many important developments. Thus, by treatment with chlorine, or with an enzyme or ferment called 'papain'—obtained from the tropical paw-paw tree—the scales covering the wool fibre may be smoothed down, and the wool prevented from matting or 'felting'. Since felting is the main cause of shrinking, unshrinkable socks and other woollens can now be made.

2. Marketing. Each of the three main types of wool can be distinguished from the others by many subtle differences, such as differences in fineness and length of 'staple', or fibres. For accuracy in commercial dealings, these three types are given quality numbers in the trade, on a scale ranging from about 20 to over 100—the finer the wool fibre, the higher the number, and (generally speaking) the dearer the price. In the following table the widths of the fibres are given in microns (1 micron = 0·001 millimetres), because this unit of measurement better emphasizes the differences in their widths.

Wool	*Average width of fibre* (microns)	*Length range* (*inches*)	*Quality number*
Merino	19	0·5– 5	60s–100s (called sixties and hundreds)
Crossbred	28	2·5– 6	36s–58s
Carpet	41	5 –17	22s–34s

The value of raw wool also depends not only on fineness and length of fibre but also on 'yield'—in other words, on the percentage of clean wool remaining after the raw wool has been washed free from grease and dirt. Raw wool may contain from 25% to 70% of natural grease and other impurities, and for this reason its trade name is 'greasy wool' or 'wool in the grease'.

The raw wool is taken from the sheep farms to the nearest big port or other large city, where it is generally sold by Auction (q.v.). As the wool in each bale has been carefully classed at the farm by an expert, the buyers bid for the wool after having inspected samples only. In the old days a bale offered in the auction room did not always match the sample; sometimes it contained not only wool, but also horseshoes, bricks, stones, and sand to make up the weight.

Until recently, a main problem of the wool industry was the great fluctuation in raw wool prices. Supplies are relatively steady, so changes in demand were the chief cause of price changes, which were sometimes spectacular, even over short periods. These changes in demand were due largely to general economic factors, demand naturally being high in good times and low in periods of depression and unemployment. The demand for wool, and therefore its price, were further affected by changes in fashion and public taste. Recently, however, it has become common practice to blend wool with synthetic fibres, and this has considerably helped to stabilize wool prices. In the last 10 years, there has also been a vast increase in the promotion of wool products, and the 'Wool Mark' is now an internationally established sign that a garment is made only from pure wool.

Prices have also altered considerably over

Crown Copyright

WOOL CARDING (LEFT), DRAWING (RIGHT), AND ROVING (BACK) IN 1835

Engraving in the Science Museum, London

longer periods, as a result of changes in the purchasing power of money. As many as 300 British sheep sold in 1762 for as little as £17.

3. PRODUCTION. The wool industry in Britain is organized in several separate and distinct sections, each producing a different kind of wool fabric. (*a*) What is called the woollen industry produces fabrics such as heavy cloths, travelling rugs, and blankets, which are woven from yarns which are soft to the touch, the fibres of which cross each other in a haphazard fashion. They often have a somewhat fuzzy appearance. (*b*) The worsted industry makes smooth cloth, much used for suitings, from selected smoother yarns, the fibres of which lie parallel to one another (*see* WOOL SPINNING, Section 3). (*c*) The knitting industry makes fabrics from one continuous yarn (which may be either woollen or worsted) as distinct from the warp and weft threads from which woven materials are made. (*d*) In the carpet industry the yarns are woven so that they project on one side of a backcloth (*see* CARPET-MAKING). (*e*) In the FELT industry (q.v.) the wool fibres are intermingled at random and compressed into a thick sheet.

All these great branches of the wool industry began as home crafts during the period of the DOMESTIC SYSTEM (q.v.). Under the influence of the inventions of the INDUSTRIAL REVOLUTION (q.v.) they became mechanized and transferred to factories. The factory system now dominates the wool industry of Britain, although there is still a considerable production of homespun and hand-woven materials in the remoter districts.

In the 18th century, when conditions were favourable, a brilliant series of technical inventions transformed British life and British industry. Although these inventions could be applied to both cotton and wool, almost all of them were first taken up for cotton-making. For this industry, based on raw cotton imported from American plantations, was entirely new; and, having no ancient traditions to draw upon, it readily adopted the new machinery. The wool industry, on the other hand, based on long-established methods, was less willing to try new ideas.

The first of the great new inventions was the flying shuttle, which John Kay patented in 1733. This is a small appliance, containing a

Crown Copyright

A MULE SPINNING FACTORY IN 1835

The mule on the right is extended and that on the left is drawn back. Children who had to sweep the floor were in danger from the moving parts. Engraving in the Science Museum, London

bobbin of thread, which moves backwards and forwards in the loom, carrying the thread with it (*see* WOOL WEAVING). The flying shuttle (used first in wool and not in cotton) enabled one person to operate a broad loom, where previously one man had been needed to throw the shuttle from one side of the loom to the other, and another to throw it back again. In 1769 Richard Arkwright improved on earlier ideas and invented the water-frame method of spinning. The water-frame got its name because it was worked by water-power (a water-mill with a wheel turned by the flow of a stream). Its basic idea was to draw out the wool, through sets of rollers, into a strand ready for spinning. Six years later Arkwright invented his 'carding machine' of revolving spiked cylinders, for unravelling the tangles in raw wool (*see* WOOL SPINNING, Section 2).

Other inventors were working on spinning methods at the same time. James Hargreaves had invented his famous spinning-jenny about 1764. This was a wheeled device which enabled one person to spin several threads at once. It was a much lighter apparatus than Arkwright's, did not need power, and could be operated at home; but it was suitable only for soft yarns.

By 1780 Samuel Crompton had designed a machine (the 'mule') which combined the ideas of the water-frame and the jenny, and took the place of both. Woollen yarns are still spun today on an improved form of mule.

In 5 years Edmund Cartwright, a country clergyman, had invented the power-loom, first worked by oxen. Later it was worked by steam, for James Watt had discovered in 1781 how to use a steam-engine to produce circular motion (*see* ENGINES, HISTORY OF, Vol. VIII). Later, Cartwright invented a combing-machine, by which the best fibres are picked out and smoothed to make worsted.

4. LOCALIZATION OF THE INDUSTRY. All these earlier inventions, which reduced for a time the demand for labour, were fiercely opposed by the workers. Trouble began with blows and violent demonstrations, and went on to the burning and smashing of machinery and the LUDDITE riots (q.v.). But the growth of the power-driven machine and of the factory system was inevitable, and in consequence the greater part of the wool industry tended to gather in the West Riding of Yorkshire. There were exceptions, however: knitted goods were made more and more in Nottingham and Leicester; and the industries of the West Country and the Tweed valley, though continuing where they were, reduced their output and began to specialize in high-quality goods only. The East Anglian wool industry, which had given birth to British worsteds, disappeared altogether.

The population of the West Riding more than doubled between 1801 and 1851. A keen competitive spirit was aroused in Yorkshire manufacturers by the vigorous new cotton industry in Lancashire. The Yorkshiremen had the foresight to produce high-quality goods, for which the markets were expanding, instead of the poorer stuffs for which the West Riding had been previously known. Finally, Yorkshiremen were helped by the existence, almost on their doorsteps, of the necessary coal for power, and of the soft water needed for washing and dyeing. To-day, over nine-tenths of the worsted, and two-thirds of the woollen industry of Britain, are still located in the West Riding.

By 1850, as the result of the modern tendency to specialize, Dewsbury, for example, had ten times as many people employed in woollens as in worsteds, whereas Keighley was almost entirely given over to worsted. These differences persisted as time went on. Today such places as Dewsbury, Batley, and Morley are woollen towns; Keighley, Halifax, and Huddersfield are famous for worsteds, the last town also for fine woollens. Bradford—the centre of the British wool trade—is mainly concerned with wool commerce, combing (to make worsted yarns), and manufacturing worsted. With the help of skilled immigrants from eastern and central Europe, Leeds has become one of the most important centres for making up wool cloth into clothing. In general, worsted cloth is made in the west and north, woollen in the east and south of the West Riding. There has been no division into spinning and weaving districts, but rather into woollen and worsted areas.

Fox Photos

AN AUSTRALIAN WOOL AUCTION

The woollen mills are mostly organized on the 'vertical' system: that is, all stages of manufacture, from the raw wool to the finished cloth, are carried out by the same firm. The worsted industry is organized on the 'hotizontal' system, that is, the various stages of manufacture are divided among a number of separate and specialized firms. One firm will convert the raw wool into 'top' by combing out the short fibres; a firm of spinners will convert the top into yarn; another will weave the yarn into cloth; while dyeing and finishing the cloth may be carried out by a fourth firm.

But Yorkshire does not stand alone. The West of England also has an important woollen industry, producing specialities of high quality such as billiard-cloths, blankets, flannels, hunting cloths, serges, and overcoatings. Another important woollen area is the Border country of Scotland, where Galashiels, Selkirk, and Hawick produce tweeds. In the North (from the islands of Harris and Lewis, and from parts of north-east Scotland, as far as Shetland) world-famous tweeds and homespuns are made. Ireland produces Irish tweeds and other special cloths, mostly woollen. Felts are produced at such places as Bury, Denton, Hyde, and Stockport in the north-west of England, and Luton and London in the south. The North Midland centres, which have coal and soft water, produce chiefly knitwear. In this area Leicester, Loughborough, and Nottingham are very important, but there are also mills in Cheshire and Derbyshire. Kidderminster, noted for its carpets, is almost the only survival of the once prosperous wool industries of the Severn Valley. Recently the industry broke new ground in the development areas of North East and North West England.

See also WOOL INDUSTRY, MEDIEVAL; WOOL SPINNING; WOOL WEAVING.

WOOL SPINNING. 1. Raw wool, straight from the sheep's back, is dirty, greasy, lumpy, and matted, and it must go through several processes before it can be woven into fabric. It must be cleaned; opened out, so as to get rid of the lumps as far as possible; its fibres must be smoothed out, formed into a continuous band and drawn out until they form a single thin strand of wool, which is then woollen or worsted yarn. Once made the yarns can be woven or knitted to make the garments and materials familiar to all of us.

Fox Photos

SPINNING WOOL ON A SPINNING-WHEEL

The wheel, which is turned by a foot pedal, turns the spindle on which the wool is wound. This twists the wool as it winds it

The length and fineness of fibres in a single fleece vary in quality, so before the wool passes through any of these processes, an experienced wool-sorter pulls the fleeces apart and divides them into 'lots' according to the fineness and length of the fibres. These lots are called 'matchings'.

To prepare the wool for spinning, it is passed through a series of washings in large washbowls and then it is rinsed and dried. Although scouring removes all the grease and dirt, it does not dislodge vegetable seeds and burrs which may still cling to the fibres of certain tyes of wool. These wools are, therefore, passed through a 'carbonizing' process, in which they are treated with acid, dried in a hot chamber, and then crushed, so that the seeds and burrs crumble to a powder. This is shaken out, and the wools are ready for carding.

Valuable BY-PRODUCTS (q.v.) are obtained from the spent fluids (known as 'liquors') left after the scouring of wool. The most important of these is lanolin, which is used in the manufacture of such diverse things as adhesive plasters, disinfectants, cosmetics, polishes, inks, rust preventatives, veterinary preparations, emulsions, and soaps.

2. CARDING. Wool fibres in the raw state are tangled together, and the loops have to be teased out by tugging at them. This is known as 'carding'. The card, which is the largest machine used in the wool textile industry, consists of a series of revolving cylinders and rollers, covered with thousands of fine wire teeth, over which the mass of wool passes. These open up the wool into a fine veil, which is gathered together at the end of the card into loose bands of wool, called 'slivers'.

In the early days of the industry, carding was done by hand. A handcard is a flat, square, piece of wood with a handle, fitted with fine needles, with the points all sticking out on the same side, rather like a steel-bristled hair brush. If one takes two cards of this kind, one in each hand, and places some wool between them, the cards, when stroked away from each other, gradually smooth out the wool and make it ready for spinning.

The carding process delivers the material as a band, or veil, of wool, almost ready to be spun into yarn.

3. COMBING. There are two basic types of yarn in the wool industry: woollen yarn and worsted yarn. The difference between them is that in woollen yarn the individual fibres are thoroughly intermingled and higgledy piggledy, but in worsted yarn the individual fibres are roughly parallel to each other. As far as the carding process, the two yarns are made in the same way. After carding all the wool fibres are still lying in a rather irregular way, and there are a lot of short, broken fibres mixed up with the long ones. This is the raw material for the woollen spinning process. Before spinning worsted yarn, however, these irregularities must be smoothed out, and the best and longest fibres chosen, all more or less of a standard length. So the bands of wool from the carding-engine are combed in much the same way as one combs one's hair—although, of course, by machinery. This makes all the individual wool fibres lie parallel to one another, while all pieces of broken and short wool, or 'noil', are combed out. The long parallel wool fibres that remain are drawn off in a continuous band which is rolled up into a large ball called the 'top'. This is the raw material for the first stage of the worsted spinning process.

Various kinds of machines, known as 'combs', are used for this. In earlier days hand-combs

British Wool Textile Industry

WOOL SORTING ACCORDING TO LENGTH, FINENESS, ETC. THIS IS THE FIRST PROCESS THE WOOL UNDERGOES

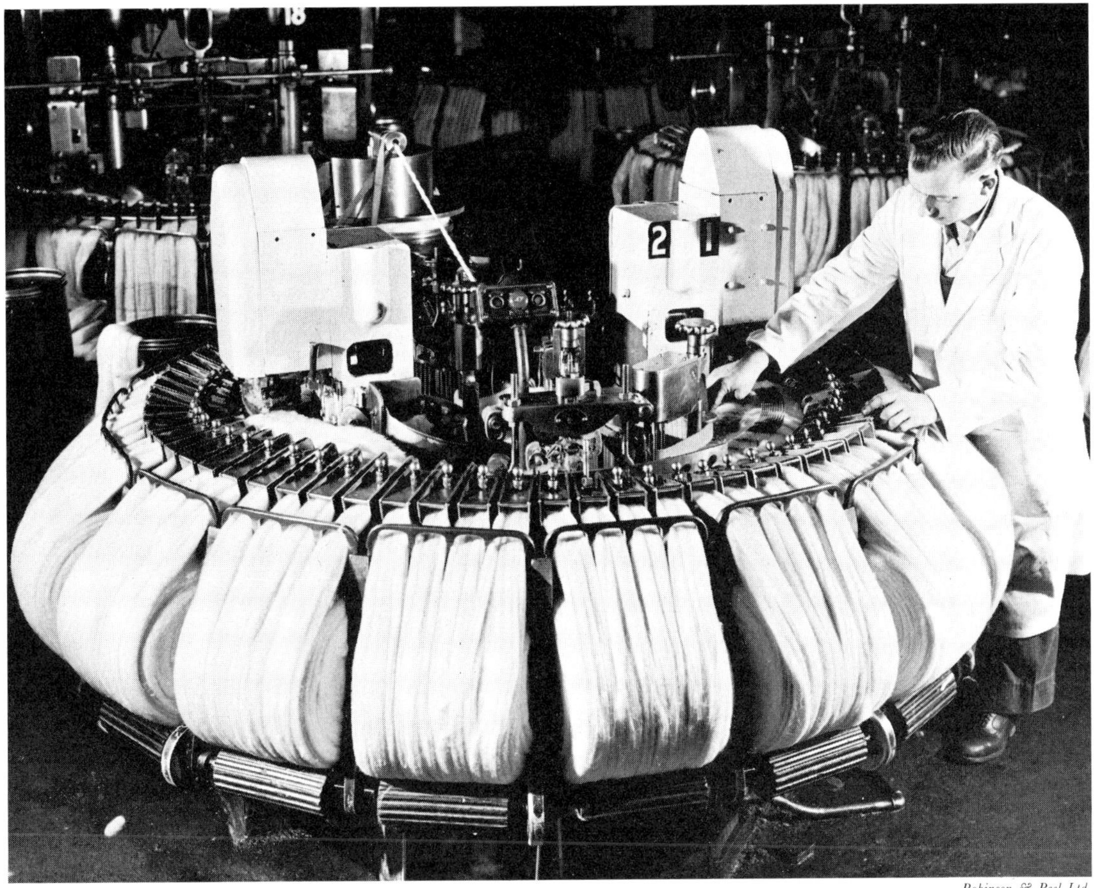

Robinson & Peel Ltd.

A NOBLE COMBING MACHINE USED IN MAKING WORSTED YARN

During this process the comb extracts the short fibres and lays the longer fibres in a parallel formation. This takes place after the grease and vegetable matter have been removed from the wool

shaped rather like a garden rake were used, but they had five or six sets of teeth instead of one. There were two combs: one was fixed to a post and the wool was placed on it, while the other was pulled several times over it. To keep the wool flexible, the combs had to be heated by charcoal stoves called 'comb-pots'. As the fumes of these stoves were poisonous, wool-combing was then an unhealthy occupation.

4. Spinning. This process involves drawing out and twisting the fibres from the early processes, so that they grow slenderer and finally emerge as a single thread of the required fineness. The conversion of the worsted top into yarn involves the several stages of drawing, roving, spinning, and twisting. For woollen yarn, however, slivers of carded fibres need only be drawn out and twisted in a single process.

Our modern power-driven spinning-frames are very complicated improvements on the primitive spinning-wheel. With the early wheel, the thread or ribbon of wool was kept in tension and drawn out to a greater length, while the wheel or spindle gave a twist to it. The modern spinning-frame also draws out the wool into a thin thread, twists it, and winds it on to a bobbin. Machine-spinning has great advantages over the old system of hand-spinning. The amount of stretch, or tension, is arranged mechanically; it is therefore constant and regular, instead of being dependent on the uneven hand of the operator; this makes for a constant size and quality in the yarn being spun. The whole process is now very rapid, and many threads or yarns are spun at one time on the same frame.

The spun yarns differ in their uses. For some

International Wool Secretariat

PHOTOMICROGRAPHS OF WOOLLEN (ABOVE) AND WORSTED YARNS (BELOW)

wool garments, for example, ladies' coats and skirts, the fluffiness and fuzziness of woollen yarn are desirable. On the other hand, worsted yarn is used in manufacturing the even cloths from which men's suits are made, and for these, smoothness is essential. The woven cloths are therefore cropped, to shear off tiny ends of fibres that the worsted spinning process cannot entirely eliminate (*see* WOOL WEAVING). This cropping process also shows up the pattern of the cloths. Worsted yarn was originally made at Worstead in Norfolk, from which it gets its name.

A final stage in spinning is sometimes the manufacture of two-ply, three-ply, and four-ply yarns; such multi-ply yarns are often sold for hand-knitting. These yarns simply go through a second process which twists the required number of single yarns together. A modern spinning-mill has line upon line of quickly revolving spindles, among which the dyed yarns make a gay mixture of colour.

Man-made fibres (*see* TEXTILE FIBRES, MAN-MADE) are often blended with wool in definite proportions to give yarn the characteristics of both substances—warmth and hard wear.

See also COTTON MANUFACTURE; WOOL WEAVING; TEXTILE FIBRES AND FABRICS.

WOOL WEAVING. This is one of the processes that take place after WOOL SPINNING (q.v.).

The simplest kind of woven fabric is made by interlacing threads over and under each other, as in darning. Threads, called the 'warp', are stretched on a frame; other threads, called the 'weft', are darned to and fro across the warp, running over and under alternate threads to make a web.

Weaving is done on a device called a loom. In the simplest looms, the warp is held in crude wooden frames, and the warp threads are lifted by a needle, by sticks, or by loops of cord to allow the weft to be woven in. Such looms are still used by primitive people; but weavers began to make improvements centuries ago to increase speed, and to weave finer cloth with more intricate designs. Looms may vary in size from small ones on which scarves or other narrow fabrics can be woven, to those capable of turning out wide lengths of cloth.

All cloth was woven by hand until the invention of the power-loom, which was introduced at the end of the 18th century, though steam looms became common rather later. Power did not alter the basic principles of weaving; it merely mechanized them and speeded them up. Even after the power-loom was in general use for cloth-production on a large scale, hand-weaving still remained an important craft in most parts of Europe and Asia, but it very nearly died out in Britain. William MORRIS (q.v. Vol. V) tried to revive an interest in hand-crafts in general, including weaving, and there are now quite a number of hand-weavers in Britain. Hand-woven cloth has a quality all its own, with an individuality that is lacking in machine-made fabric, and the weaver can experiment freely in designs and colours. Hand-weaving has this importance in the modern textile factory: a textile designer will often build up a sample of his design on a hand-loom, as this gives him the opportunity of experimenting with texture, weave, and colour,

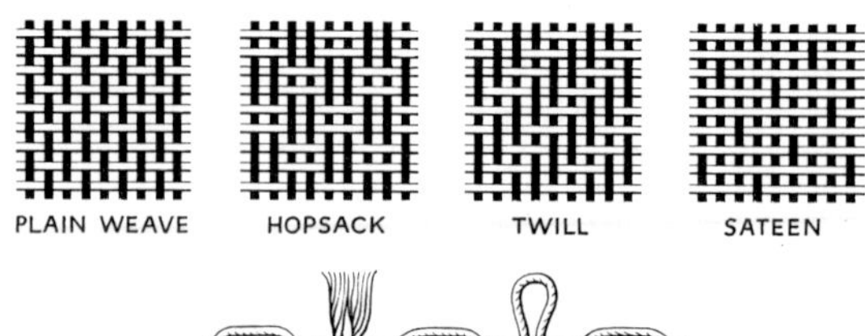

DIAGRAM OF DIFFERENT KINDS OF WEAVE

and then, when the pattern is finally approved, it is woven in bulk on a power-loom.

The machine-weaving process is the same for both woollen and worsted yarns. The design is

Wool (& Allied) Textile Employers' Council

A WARPING MILL

Threads from the creel on the left are wound on to the warping mill at the back in the correct order to produce the woven pattern. They are later wound on to the weaver's beam

first drawn on squared paper, on which it is possible to reproduce each single warp and weft thread, and to show how their intersection and the colour pattern will be arranged.

In a modern factory the yarns that are to form the warp are first wound from the bobbins in a frame or 'creel' on to a warping mill so that the correct colours lie side by side. They are then transferred to the weaver's beam, ready for the weft threads. On most looms, the latter pass alternatively over and under the warp by means of a shuttle containing a bobbin, from which the weft thread gradually unreels. There must be a means of raising some of the warp threads, and depressing others, so as to form a 'shed' or opening through which the shuttle can pass. This is arranged by passing the warp threads through eyelets on wires, called 'healds', fixed in a moveable frame: when the loom is in motion, one set of healds moves up as the other moves down. The shuttle is 'flicked' automatically from side to side through the shed formed by the movement of the healds. As each successive weft thread is passed into the warp, it is automatically pressed hard against its predecessor. As the finished cloth is produced, it is wound on to a roller, and fresh lengths of warp are unwound off another roller. The process is therefore continuous while it lasts, and the lightning motion of the shuttle, and the rise and fall of the healds, combine to give a rhythmical sound.

Today, high-speed weaving machines have begun to replace the shuttle looms, especially for long production runs. Their small pincers grip the end of the weft, carry it through the 'shed', and release it. Looms where the weft is propelled by a jet of water are also being developed.

If a pile fabric is required, the pile threads are

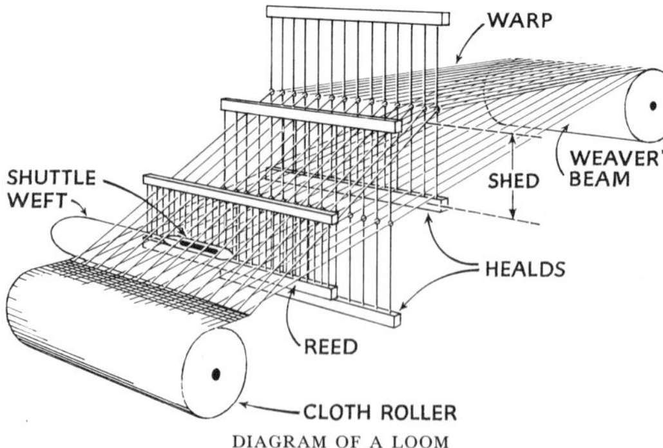

DIAGRAM OF A LOOM

The warp is wound on the weaver's beam at the back of the loom and threaded through the healds and reed on to the cloth roller in front. By pulling down one heald a space or shed is made between the warp threads through which the shuttle containing the weft is passed. By reversing the position of the healds another shed is formed so that the shuttle next passes over the threads which were beneath and under those which were above. The reed is brought forward to press the weft tightly together

looped around flat steel rods that are inserted during manufacture and then withdrawn when the fabric is close-woven and tight. This process leaves a series of projecting loops that will not come loose. If the pile is to be cut, the rods carry a knife-edge, and the cutting is automatic.

It is often said that it is the dyeing and finishing of the cloth that really make it saleable, for it leaves the loom in a very dirty and unattractive condition, and requires much further attention.

It is first thrown over a roller and examined for faults, such as burrs, knots, and missing threads—an inspection called 'perching'. Highly skilled women, in great demand in the trade, sew in by hand any broken or missing threads. These are 'burlers and menders'; their craft is the same as that of 'invisible menders' who can sometimes be seen at work in shop windows.

Norman Wymer

WEAVING ON A HAND-LOOM

The cloth must next be washed or scoured. Worsteds are scoured in soap solution, but woollens usually need only weak soda, as the oil they contain mixes with the soda to form a natural Soap (q.v.). The cloth shrinks during the scouring, and this has to be allowed for in the design and the weaving, as the finished cloth will come out smaller than the design.

If a woollen cloth requires a matted or felted surface (*see* Felt), it is wetted with a soapy solution, and then beaten with wooden stocks in a milling machine. For many cloths, particularly worsted suitings, where smoothness is essential, the protruding fibres are removed in a 'cropping' machine, which has revolving knives like those of a lawn-mover, a vast improvement on the hand shears that were once used. If a fluffy, raised surface is required, as in blankets, the cloth is passed over rollers covered with small, prickly 'teazles', which brush up the surface fibres. This machine is called a 'teazle gig'.

Wool may be dyed at any one of a number of stages in its manufacture. It may be dyed loose, or at various stages of the spinning process, or as finished yarn, or as cloth 'in the piece'. The dyes used depend upon the stage at which dyeing is considered desirable, for dyes differ in their resistance to fading. Wool that is dyed in the loose state—'dyed in the wool'—absorbs the dye well into every separate fibre, but the dye then has to withstand the rigours of all the drastic manufacturing and finishing processes that follow. Only dyes with a high resistance to such treatment can therefore be used when the wool is dyed loose. Wool to be spun into woollen yarn is usually dyed loose; worsted wool is usually dyed after the combing process (*see* Wool Spinning). Fabrics dyed after weaving—dyed 'in the piece'—have to withstand only rather mild finishing processes. Bright, light colours and pastel shades can then be used, most of which would not be 'fast' enough to resist more severe treatment (*see* Dyes).

The use to which cloths will be put has also much influence on the timing and nature of the dyeing. Woollen cloths for women's garments may only have to last until fashion changes, but

Wool (& Allied) Textile Employers' Council

A RANGE OF AUTOMATIC LOOMS

worsted cloths for men's suits and for overcoats have to last during many years of exposure to sun and wet.

In the past much damage has been done to wool clothing by moth larvae. Today, wool can be effectively moth-proofed by a chemical treatment which is not removed by washing, and anti-shrinkage and waterproofing treatments are also available.

After all these processes, the finished cloth is mechanically pressed and folded, and sent to the clothing factory, or direct to the shop.

See also Wool Industry, Modern; Wool Spinning; Cotton Manufacture; Carpet-making; Tapestry.

WORSTED, *see* Wool Spinning, Section 3.

Z

ZINC MINING. Zinc is found in nature in the form of ores that are compounds of zinc (*see* METAL ORES, Vol. III), and most zinc ores are usually found together with those of LEAD (q.v.). The principal commercial zinc ores are zinc blende, which is more or less pure sulphide of zinc, and calamine, consisting mainly of zinc carbonate. Zinc was known and used in ancient times, principally as an ALLOY (q.v. Vol. VIII) with copper to form brass and, in the form of zinc compounds, for use in medicine as ointments. Nowadays zinc ores are mined in the U.S.A., Canada, Australia, Mexico, Russia, Poland, Italy, and (in smaller amounts) in many other parts of the world. Zinc ores are smelted in most industrial countries, including Great Britain. A very important by-product of zinc smelting is sulphuric acid (*see* ACIDS).

The principal industrial use of zinc is in the making of brass. Another important use of metallic zinc is for galvanizing articles made of iron, such as buckets, agricultural fencing-wire, dust-bins, and cattle-troughs, to prevent their rusting (*see* SURFACE TREATMENT, Vol. VIII). Zinc plates are much used in the printing industry (*see* PROCESS REPRODUCTION). Zinc is also often used nowadays instead of tin, in making metal alloys with low melting-points for lining engine BEARINGS (q.v. Vol. VIII). Nickel silver, the material out of which much electro-plated tableware is made, is an alloy of copper, zinc, and nickel. The most important compound of zinc in industry is zinc oxide, or zinc white. This is much used as a pigment in making PAINTS AND VARNISHES (q.v.), and also for medicines and COSMETICS (q.v.). Lithopone, another zinc compound, is used in the manufacture of distempers, paints, and rubber articles.

ZINC SMELTING IN ANCIENT CHINA

The Chinese were among the first to isolate the metal zinc. Sealed pots containing zinc were heated with charcoal. The zinc was driven off as a vapour which solidified on cooling. Woodcut from a Chinese book printed in 1637, reproduced from Li Ch'iao-p'ing's *The Chemical Arts of China* (Journal of Chemical Education)